Video Theories

INTERNATIONAL TEXTS IN CRITICAL MEDIA AESTHETICS

Vol. 14

Volumes in the series:

New Directions in Digital Poetry by C.T. Funkhouser
Cybertext Poetics: The Critical Landscape of New Media Literary Theory by Markku Eskelinen
Creative Enterprise: Contemporary Art between Museum and Marketplace by Martha Buskirk
The Engagement Aesthetic: Experiencing New Media Art through Critique by Francisco J. Ricardo
Software Takes Command by Lev Manovich
3D: History, Theory and Aesthetics of the Transplane Image by Jens Schröter
Projected Art History: Biopics, Celebrity Culture, and the Popularizing of American Art by Doris Berger
When the Machine Made Art: The Troubled History of Computer Art by Grant D. Taylor
The Internet Unconscious: On the Subject of Electronic Literature by Sandy Baldwin
Between Film, Video, and the Digital: Hybrid Moving Images in the Post-Media Age by Jihoon Kim
The Off-Modern by Svetlana Boym
Witness to Phenomenon: Group Zero and the Development of New Media in Postwar European Art by Joseph D. Ketner II
Expanded Internet Art by Ceci Moss

Video Theories

A Transdisciplinary Reader

Edited by
Dieter Daniels and Jan Thoben

BLOOMSBURY ACADEMIC
NEW YORK • LONDON • OXFORD • NEW DELHI • SYDNEY

BLOOMSBURY ACADEMIC
Bloomsbury Publishing Inc
1385 Broadway, New York, NY 10018, USA
50 Bedford Square, London, WC1B 3DP, UK
29 Earlsfort Terrace, Dublin 2, Ireland

BLOOMSBURY, BLOOMSBURY ACADEMIC and the Diana logo are trademarks of Bloomsbury Publishing Plc

First published in the United States of America 2022

Cover design: Jan Thoben, Eleanor Rose
Cover image: "Untitled" (1993) © Dieter Kiessling

Library of Congress Cataloging-in-Publication Data
Names: Daniels, Dieter, editor. | Thoben, Jan, editor.
Title: Video theories : a transdisciplinary reader / edited by Dieter Daniels and Jan Thoben.
Description: New York : Bloomsbury Academic, 2022. | Series: International texts in critical media aesthetics ; vol. 14 | Includes bibliographical references and index.
Identifiers: LCCN 2021040993 (print) | LCCN 2021040994 (ebook) | ISBN 9781501354090 (hardback) | ISBN 9781501354083 (paperback) | ISBN 9781501354106 (epub) | ISBN 9781501354113 (pdf)
Subjects: LCSH: Video recordings. | Digital video. | Video art.
Classification: LCC PN1992.935 .V537 2022 (print) | LCC PN1992.935 (ebook) | DDC 791.4301–dc23
LC record available at https://lccn.loc.gov/2021040993
LC ebook record available at https://lccn.loc.gov/2021040994

ISBN: HB: 978-1-5013-5409-0
PB: 978-1-5013-5408-3
ePDF: 978-1-5013-5411-3
eBook: 978-1-5013-5410-6

Series: International Texts in Critical Media Aesthetics

Typeset by Deanta Global Publishing Services, Chennai, India
Printed and bound in the United States of America

Contents

Figures

Acknowledgments

This publication has been made possible by a fellowship for "Transdisciplinary Video Theory" of the Gutenberg Research College at Johannes Gutenberg University Mainz from 2017 to 2020 as well as the continued support of the Academy of Fine Arts Mainz. Up until the final stages of this publication, the editors have received all manner of help and advice. Our thanks especially go to Dieter Kiessling, Martin Henatsch, and Linda Hentschel from the Academy of Fine Arts Mainz for preparing the fellowship and collaborating on questions on content throughout that time, and to Thomas Hieke and Dominik Bohl from the Gutenberg Research College for their administrative and spiritual support of this project. We also thank Lisa Weber for her organizational help.

For expanding the thematic range of this book, we are grateful to our guest editors, who freely contributed their expertise: Peter Sachs Collopy on "Video and the Self," Barbara Büscher on video and the performing arts, Martha Buskirk on online video, as well as Marc Ries, who has written the introduction on video and film. Thanks also to Thomas Helbig and Andreas Schmiedecker for their invaluable contributions on Jean-Luc Godard and Boris Yukhananov, respectively.

During the realization of this publication, Sandra Naumann helped researching authors and rights holders, Alexandra Hölzer solved questions of copyright, and Frank Holbein was in charge of text processing. Chapter introductions have been translated by Lutz Eitel (Preface, Chapter 1, Chapter 5, Chapter 9), Tessa Smith and Eric Beeson (Chapter 2, Chapter 6), Charlotte Kreutzmüller (Chapter 4, Chapter 7) and Patrick Kremer (Chapter 10, Chapter 11, Chapter 12). A special thanks to Lutz Eitel, who acted as our main copy editor and guide in questions of language.

While researching and working on the chapter introductions, we received important feedback and suggestions from Inke Arns, Heike Behrend, Denise Blickhahn, Ina Blom, Christophe Charles, Nina Czegledy, Anne-Marie Duguet, Kristoffer Gansing, Jung-Yeon Ma, Marc Ries, Camilla Skovbjerg Paldam, Elena Stromberg, Anne Zeitz, and Nils Zurawski.

Andreas Broeckmann remained our dialog partner on central issues during the whole course of the project.

For their help in obtaining authors' rights, we thank Edit Andras, Sean Cubitt, John Ellis, Miguel Flusser, Rudolf Frieling, Ken Hakuta, Wulf Herzogenrath, Anita Jóri, Hiroko Kimura-Myokam, Richard Kriesche, Jens Lutz, Karl McCool, Michael McLuhan, Dorcas Müller, Mike Pepin, Ira Schneider, and Andreas Treske.

—Dieter Daniels, Jan Thoben

Preface

Dieter Daniels and Jan Thoben

Theorizing Video

Video has become a ubiquitous medium. We consume video on demand, we produce and share video-based content online, we connect in video conferences, we discuss video art shown in exhibitions, and we use video as a medium of surveillance and as a medium for teaching and spreading knowledge. Against this backdrop, it seems remarkable that—in contrast to theories of photography, film, and television that have long been canonized in academia—there is no established theory of video either within media studies, visual studies, or art history. The present volume answers this desideratum and offers a survey of approaches to theory building for video as a medium. Reaching across disciplines, it aims to serve as a foundation and an inspiration for further research and teaching. The editors and guest editors have chosen a broad selection of texts, adding commentary and context in detailed chapter introductions. As can be seen in the table of contents, the anthology is structured thematically, while putting a special focus on discursive diversity and a general pluralism of positions. As a result, the book offers the first both comprehensive and critical survey of fifty years of academic and artistic reflection on video.

Contrary to the popular notion of a digital media convergence, the development of video as a medium has been characterized by a constant divergence since the mid-twentieth century. Any attempt to define the term "video" today will have to include decades of changing technology standards and cultural applications—the various technical formats and heterogeneous uses of video have never consolidated but always developed, modified, hybridized, and diversified. This technological and sociotechnical heterogeneity ultimately causes methodological problems, since the subject of video theories can hardly be delimited and thus seems to escape theoretical discourse. As early as 1988, Roy Armes pointed out that "video's very versatility and flexibility as a medium repulses any simple attempt to grasp its 'essence' or 'specificity,' and continual technological development makes it increasingly difficult to pin down any fixed identity."[1] A number of authors referenced in the following sections share this view. Sean Cubitt described the dilemma of theorizing video in his comprehensive 1993 study on the state of video in theory and practice:

> There is no essential form of video, nothing to which one can point as primal source or goal of video activity. . . . There is no video theory in the way that there is a body of knowledge called film theory or, rather differently, television studies. There never will be. Not being really a simple and discrete entity, video prevents

> the prerequisite for a theoretical approach: that is, deciding upon an object about which you wish to know.[2]

To theoretically contain the instability of all the practices and technologies that we subsume under the term "video," we therefore require methodological alternatives to a merely essentialist approach. In 1990, Jacques Derrida, a thinker who gave important impulses for a new understanding of theory formation per se, approached the openness and interminability of the medium and its conception in the form of an internal dialogue:

> — . . . Once again, it seems to me therefore (*mihi videor*) that there is no essential unity among these things that seem to resemble each other or that are assembled together under the name of video.
>
> —But perhaps the video event, among others, reveals precisely the problematic fragility of this distinction between an internal determination and an external determination. That would already be rather disturbing.[3]

Derrida's performative figure of thought suggests that video's "internal" technological and cultural heterogeneity is matched by a corresponding variety of "external" theoretical models. In extension of this thought, Cubitt's skepticism toward a formation of video theory can be seen as part of a larger context of various approaches in the humanities and natural sciences during the second half of the twentieth century to put theory in a historical perspective. Considering the history of theory, analyzing video thus forms a link between single-media analyses (photo, film, television, radio, records, audiotape) and the generalist convergence theories about hybrid media systems (cybernetic and network-based interconnections).

In 1999, Scott McQuire pointed out with reference to Derrida that the keenness to acclaim video as a hybrid medium needs to be measured against the transformations of theoretical discourse over the past decades. This would include post-structuralist, psychoanalytical, (neo-)Marxist, (queer-)feminist, and postcolonial positions that were more interested in hybridity than in purist concepts of identity, in transformations and intersections rather than discrete and stable delimitations. At the same time McQuire insisted: "As much as video offers a new kind of object for theory, it is also *part* of a profound transformation of the social and cultural conditions within which theory is produced."[4] According to Siva Vaidhyanathan, the reciprocity between theory formation and video visuality has further increased due to the "videocracy" that took shape around the mid-2000s. He concludes with the provocative thesis: "Video resists thought, but it doesn't prevent it."[5]

For these reasons, the title of this book uses the plural, "video theories." Thus we take into account the changing basic frameworks for academic theory formation, their historical variability and diachronic diversity. Furthermore, we aim to place video theories within an environment of historically evolving practices between discursive knowledge and medial experience. Cubitt argues in a related vein when he points out that video cannot be analyzed from an objective distance but requires active participation.[6]

A special focus is therefore placed on video art, in which the medium undergoes an aesthetic reflection by means of experimental practices. Jean-Luc Godard modified the Cartesian formula when he said: "Cogito ergo video" (see Chapter 4). Seeing as thinking, or thinking with and through video practice, remains the guiding theme for such considerations. The idea is that video (art) opens theoretical insights that are not preformatted by the medium of verbal discourse. Raymond Bellour elaborates on this idea: "The video image is one of the keenest manifestations of thought, of its jumps and disorderliness. Through thought as image, it gives us an image of thought, vibrant and unstable."[7] There are a number of comparable approaches that aim to bridge the supposedly insurmountable divide between scientific discourse and artistic practice and locate thought in artistic medial processes outside of common verbal discourse. These include W. J. T. Mitchell's concept of "metapictures" or more recent studies such as Dieter Mersch's epistemology of aesthetics. As metapictures (pictures about pictures) in Mitchell's sense, video images address their medial conditions by articulating their own status recursively.[8] Similarly, Edward Small describes experimental video and film productions as their own theoretical mode based in a reflexive examination of the material, perceptual, and ideological aspects of their medium, beyond the written or spoken word.[9] Mersch also points out that the theoretical insights that art might offer must be understood as being performative, since artistic thought not simply expresses itself in the totality of a work but reveals itself as an "act of unlocking or of setting free, of which we can only say that it takes place within aesthetic practices and their use of media and materials."[10] We will see that the different formats of visual and textual reflection on media often enter a symbiotic relationship, think of, for example, Nam June Paik, Bill Viola, Martha Rosler, or Hito Steyerl, who combined their own artistic practice with extensive writings. Sometimes we encounter a dialogue between theory-forming text production and artistic practice, especially in the collected contributions to Chapter 12 of this reader.

Critical writings of practitioners have likewise informed film theory, with prominent examples from Sergei Eisenstein to Maya Deren. Yet while artists' texts on film soon became part of an international discourse, remarkably the majority of theoretical texts on video remained unconnected at the time of their writing—and that largely continues until the present day. Accordingly, we do not see the development of a coherent or even canonical discourse on video, and the diversity of approaches and terminologies has remained difficult to bridge over. It is telling that occasional attempts at naming this theoretical discipline never established themselves. For example, neither the French term "vidéologie," introduced by Alfred Willener, Guy Milliard, and Alex Ganty in 1972, nor Nam June Paik's slightly ironical title "Videology," which he gave to his first collection of texts on the topic in 1973, has gained much currency.[11]

Differentiating its editorial concept from previous video art anthologies, the present reader comprises a broad spectrum of disciplines. Texts on video art play a key role and are present in almost every chapter; however, we believe an integrative, transdisciplinary approach is essential for a wide and in-depth understanding of this multifaceted medium. This approach also allows the editors to open up the perspective of their own discipline for a critical reorientation. Hence, the book's structure deliberately stresses the pluralism of voices from media theory, art theory, philosophy, sociology, cultural studies, psychotherapy, ethnography, anthropology, performance studies, feminist theory, gender studies, social geography, surveillance studies, forensics, and more. In the framework of this reader, the different perspectives of various disciplines can be interconnected in an exemplary fashion, both in editorial contextualizations for each chapter and in several text contributions that already integrate a transdisciplinary viewpoint.[12]

The question of a time frame, of establishing a beginning and different stages for the development of the video era, has remained central mostly to Western-oriented historiographic studies.[13] On the other hand, the narratives offered by hegemonial media structures largely ignore transnational and transcultural aspects as well as the fabrication of subalternity and thus markedly constrict their media historiographies. From a transcultural perspective, we also find that video has caused historically different media turns depending on context. The cultural impact of the introduction of video technology in the United States and Western Europe is very different from the effects in the Eastern Europe,[14] Southern Asia,[15] or Africa,[16] since each context offers different timelines, socio-technological infrastructures, as well as ideological and political circumstances. For this reason, we have decided to abstain from following an overarching linear chronology. For a more pluralistic take on video discourse, this reader aims to relativize the strong focus on US-American academic literature. Translations of texts that have never before appeared in English (from the German, French, Italian, and Russian) as well as contributions from Latin American, Asian, and Eastern-European perspectives increase the range of discursive viewpoints (Figure 0.1).

Technological Incompatibilities and Messy Terminology

The term "video" had a prehistory going back to the 1930s before it established itself in the late 1960s as a noun to designate an autonomous medium.[17] In contrast to cinema and television, where different terms circulate internationally, "video" is used worldwide in almost every language.[18] Yet the variability of video technologies and practices runs counter to the way we naturally use the term today.[19] Accordingly, its multiple applications conflict with a strict, theoretically binding definition of the video medium. For an analysis based in use theory, one would have to account for all possible applications of the term "video." Following Ludwig Wittgenstein's idea that the possible applications of a word configure its meaning without allowing for the extrapolation of a general definition, we are dealing with complex bundles of language games, whose elements do not share a single consistent characteristic. Applications of the word "video" offer a valuable example for this linguistic-philosophical thesis: they cannot be subjected to an authoritative definition but are connected by a network of various characteristics that Wittgenstein termed "family resemblance."[20] This corresponds to Michael Z. Newman's assessment: "As a cultural concept, a medium such as video is a cluster of ideas, historically contingent and located in the relationality of media."[21] Until today, this variability is articulated in numerous words in which "video" as the determinant element does not always carry the same meaning: video art, video clip, video store, video conference, video streaming, video surveillance, video blogging, video tutorial, and so on.

Figure 0.1 Videotapes in different formats at the ZKM Laboratory for Antiquated Video Systems, ZKM | Zentrum für Kunst und Medien Karlsruhe. Photo: Dorcas Müller, © VG Bild-Kunst, Bonn 2020.

Video technology was born from an amalgamation of various media: the monitor was familiar from television, magnetic tape from audiotape and computers, the camera from surveillance and again from television. These were combined at the end of the 1960s for a new, marketable product named "consumer video." The components for recording (camera), storage (videotape), and playback (monitor) remained physically separate for more than twenty years. Only in the 1990s, with the camcorder, were these elements integrated in a single apparatus. Whereas today, the recording, storage, and playback, as well as the editing and distribution of videos, are merely subfunctions of smartphones.[22]

Step by step, video has separated itself from the initial analog data carriers, such as magnetic tape, through digital carrier media such as DVDs, to recording formats, such as mp4 and H.264, that are no longer bound to a physical carrier and have become essential for streaming. As part of this development, video changed from a technologically and aesthetically autonomous medium to a ubiquitous digital application, crossing media-technical formats as well as cultural and industrial contexts. On the internet, video goes viral, and it still has not established a stable dispositive, contrary to cinema: a movie theater rests on the cornerstones of the auditorium, the projection screen, and the entrance ticket, all of which have survived as elements of the cultural and social dispositive despite streaming and digitization.

In the 1950s and the first half of the 1960s, video technology was mainly used in television studios, as stationary machinery invisible to the viewer, operating as production technology to optimize and slowly replace broadcasting based on photochemical film. The role that video played for the television program was not apparent to the viewers at first, as its "time shift" function for more than a decade was overshadowed by the paradigm of the live broadcast. The only exception was offered by the instant replay in sports programs as a video-based "special effect."[23]

Accordingly, the theoretical discourse on video only started when the medium gained broad social impact as video technology became available outside of television studios. A central driving force for theoretical reflection were the portable recorders developed on the basis of magnetic tape technology, which entered the market for affordable prices at the end of the 1960s and thus initiated the socio-technological impact of the medium.[24]

Privatization, miniaturization, and mobilization were the guiding principles for the increasing availability of consumer video technology, initiated by brands such as Sony, Shibaden, National, and Philips. As Ricardo Montaña writes: "These three effects of portable video, namely its ubiquity, individuality, and portability, spread video as an imaging technique used in non-professional contexts, thus transforming anyone carrying a video camera into an *image technician* always ready to produce."[25]

The technical components that make up the video medium are just as heterogeneous as its potential forms of use. There has never been a so-called "killer application" for video, on the contrary: from the beginning manufacturers stressed multiple scenarios of uses for their product. In a folder by Sony from the late 1960s talk is about "unlimited videorecorder applications" for recorders from the CV-2000 series in the areas of business and industry, education, science and medicine, as well as law enforcement.[26]

This wide spectrum of possible applications was mirrored in the variety of content stored on videotape. The most diverse image sources coexisted in the same medium: recordings done with a video camera (in private and public contexts), content from the mass media (TV recordings), or "bootleg" material from gray areas (private copies from movies on tapes bought or rented from a video store). The boom of home video, which started at the end of the 1970s merged heterogeneous image worlds. Image types that had been strictly separated before, now were stored, viewed, maybe deleted, overdubbed, or distributed on the same devices, and potentially on one and the same videotape.[27]

Apart from the application scenarios suggested by the industry, artists and activists developed new forms of using video. Experimental montages in early video art exemplified the fluidity of image classifications that had earlier been established. Then again, portable video for the first time allowed for working on electronic moving images autonomously. This broke up the hegemony of the sender-receiver model inherent to television and suggested far-reaching emancipatory ideas for the self-determined use of media in art, politics, and society.[28] Thus, from the beginning, video served as an instrument of social change and artistic innovation, fulfilling functions that far exceeded the purposes suggested by manufacturers. In turn, marketing strategies of the industry quickly took up these welcome expansions of the market. "Man might conquer disease, stop crime, and save his environment with the help of this little machine," read an advertisement by Sony for the U-matic Recorder from 1974.

After a period of commercial consolidation due to home video in the 1980s, video culture gained new dynamics as digitization led to a more intense interaction between technological development and social relevance. With the introduction of video CDs and DVDs in the early 1990s, storage media was digitized; then in 1996, with the launch of the first DV recorder, the same happened to the recording process. Likewise at the beginning of the 1990s, video streaming grew into a momentous alternative to centralized broadcasting (initially as downloadable video on demand). With bandwidth continually on the rise and ever more effective video codecs, slowly video distribution by physical storage media (such as cassettes or DVDs) was replaced with a streaming-based replication and distribution model starting in the early 2000. Combined with the proliferation of smartphones in the 2010s, digitization has led to an omnipresence of videographic practices. The process of recording and playing videos on a smartphone is everyday and increasingly performed casually and impulsively, something that Marc Ries characterizes with the term "occasionalist image."[29]

Both in the analog and digital ages, video again and again proves to be a medium of incompatibility. No other visual medium has so far seen a comparably quick change of technological standards. Whereas in cinema, the 35mm film remained the standard medium for more than a century, video went through roughly 100 different formats within fifty years.[30] From the magnetic tape reel to ubiquitous digital video streaming on smartphones, the complete set of technological parameters—and with it the complete video dispositive—has fundamentally changed for several times.

It has never been possible to reduce video to a discrete media-technological entity or even a consistent media practice. As mentioned at the start, the incompatibility of technological formats and applications has contributed to a theoretical skepticism regarding a distinct definition of the video medium since the 1980s. The philosopher Jacques Derrida, for example, came to the conclusion that the question of the medium's identity, or the specifics and singularity of video compared to other media, was badly put.[31] Still, we will find that this question has become inscribed in video historiographies, as Ina Blom observes in her substantial investigation *The Autobiography of Video*: "Histories of art and technology have long centered on the ins and outs of medium specificity, the way in which the general material properties of a technical medium determines aesthetic production."[32]

Accordingly, in many of the historical texts introduced in the following chapters, the question of medium specificity, and the characteristics that define video in comparison to other technical media, are raised again and explored in different contexts. Chapter 2 focuses on these questions within the framework of a theoretical discussion of video, especially referring to Rosalind Krauss's concept of a "differential specificity." With this concept, Krauss repudiates the idea of a deterministic medium specificity shaped by Clement Greenberg, where the material properties of a technical medium essentially condition aesthetic production. According to Krauss, Greenberg's very influential position turns reductionist, as it essentially predefines both media characteristics and artistic genre specifics. In her model, Krauss reacts to Greenberg's reduction of the medium to fixed physical-material properties. She regards video as a self-differentiating media system, as a layering of conventions that cannot be reduced to the material characteristics of their technological foundation. Thus she suggests alternative conceptions of media specificity, taking the technology's affordances and different potential forms of usage into account. In the same sense, Ina Blom states: "Video is, above all, a changing assemblage of affordances."[33] Blom describes the video medium not simply as technology but as "a form of agency that encompassed, among other things, electronic and human capacities."[34]

Against this backdrop it is important to see today's accessibility and ubiquity of digital video from a historical perspective, to keep us aware of those passages that have made video what it is now (Figure 0.2).

Field of Discourse and Editorial Concept

As discussed, any attempt to define video as a fixedly self-contained medium necessarily will meet its methodological limits. There is no centralized or institutionalized discourse on video (that would be comparable, e.g., to the magazine *Cahiers du Cinema* leading the discourse in French film theory), and there are no texts or authors one would have to accommodate in every discussion (such as, e.g., Kracauer or Deleuze in film theory). The discursive field is instead characterized by a productive internal pluralism of perspectives and voices. Our reader accounts for this situation by reflecting on diversity and inclusivity. Instead of constructing a canonical approach, we aim to offer a conceptual framework for diverging or even contradictory positions that reflect the constant transformation of video, what it was, what it is, and what it will be.

The editors suggest to address the open field of video discourse through a transdisciplinary approach discernible in the table of contents. The structure of this reader is aimed at a comparative survey of heterogeneous perspectives. In this sense it is important to point out that the texts in this reader cannot be understood as part of an internally connected and institutionally driven formation of discourse as the texts largely remained unconnected at the time of their writing and—in contrast to film-theoretical discourse—were not widely circulated in pertinent publications. This situation prevents a critical analysis of discursive control mechanisms, hegemonial discourse formations, or procedures of inclusion and exclusion in the sense of Michel Foucault.[35] A regulative pattern for our comparatively loose collection of video-theoretical statements is instead offered by the relation of texts to nondiscursive events and processes (such as developments in video technology, sociocultural adoptions of the medium, political regulations, or practices in video art).

Figure 0.2 A selection of books on video used during the making of the present publication. Photo: Stephen Stahn.

Despite these general tendencies, from the 1970s on we find intertextual references with regard to selected topics (such as narcissism, video art, or surveillance), with links to contemporary art or social theories. And yet these did not merge into a coherent video theory. Thus the "absence of a coherent field of video studies," diagnosed by Janna Houwen as recently as 2017,[36] determined the starting point for work on this reader. We aim to start a process that will enable the structuring and interconnecting of video-related theories. As we will exemplarily show in the next section, this first step can offer a methodological basis for future research on the medium.

Since our ambition was to set up a wide area of themes, historical depth, and a topicality connectable to past and future developments, most of the texts were edited to fit the format of this compendium. We have chosen excerpts from books, essays, and papers and often redacted them for this reader—contributions were kept compact to allow for a broad cross-section of video-theoretical texts produced over the last fifty years. This included focusing on specific guiding themes and adding notes on context and terminology, especially for older texts. Where possible, we have involved the authors in this editorial process, and some of them have revised or updated their contributions for this volume.

The reader is structured into four sections:

The first section, *Foundations*, starts with Chapter 1 on the early rudimentary formations of discourse as a direct response to the introduction of video in the 1960s and 1970s. The texts in Chapter 2 address returning questions on the specificity and materiality of video as a medium. Chapter 3 deals with video-related aspects of self-observation and narcissism in the context of psychotherapy on the one hand and artistic practices on the other.

Chapters 4–8 in the second section, *Relations*, explore the manifold intermedial relations between video and film, television, sound, theater/performance, and the internet.

Chapters 9–11 in the third section, *Repercussions*, relate to a complex social and media-cultural range of topics that include video utopias, the role of the amateur, as well as aspects of surveillance and testimony.

Finally, the fourth section, *Dialogues*, addresses the recursive, reflexive relation between video art and its medium in the sense of a self-reflection. Chapter 12 accordingly focuses on the dialogue between theory and artistic practice.

For selected diachronic lines of questioning, we invited guest editors whose areas of expertise further broaden the range of topics: Peter Sachs Collopy on "Video and the Self" (Chapter 3), Barbara Büscher on video and the performing arts (Chapter 7), Martha Buskirk on online video (Chapter 8), and Marc Ries, who contributed an introduction on the interaction between film and video (Chapter 4). Finally, Thomas Helbig has decoded and contextualized the complex source situation of texts by Jean-Luc Godard on the video topic (Chapter 4), and Andreas Schmiedecker has selected and annotated a text by Russian director and theorist Boris Yukhananov (Chapter 12) (Figure 0.3).

The Instantaneous Video Image from a Transdisciplinary Perspective

In some media theories, the discourse is shaped by certain terms, such as "indexicality" in photo theory, the interplay between "apparatus" and "dispositive" in film theory, or "flow" in television theory. In the following discursion, the instantaneity of the video medium will be explored as a comparable guiding term. The instantaneous video image is different from earlier visual media technologies, for example, from ephemeral technical images such as the camera obscura, or from moving technical images that could be stored, such as film.[37] In contrast to photochemically processed images (analog photography and analog film) in video, a storable image can be viewed simultaneously with the initial recording process. It can also be replayed instantly after recording without a time lag (caused, e.g., by the need to process a film).[38] This copresence of the video image in recording and playback probably marks the most

Figure 0.3 Video recorders from the 1960s to the 1980s at the ZKM Laboratory for Antiquated Video Systems, ZKM | Zentrum für Kunst und Medien Karlsruhe. Photo: Franz Wamhoff. Digital montage: Dorcas Müller, © VG Bild-Kunst, Bonn 2020.

decisive shift caused by video technology. Media-theoretically, it marks a relational difference to all other technical image media, and yet there are several video practices in which it does not play any role. Like the video medium itself, the instantaneity of the video image can only be described in relations and differences: it is specific to the medium but does not offer a general, essentialist definition of it. Today, within our digital image worlds, the instantaneity of seeing, showing, and sharing is taken for granted and never questioned.[39] When video was first introduced, on the other hand, this experience of technically mediated instantaneity provoked epiphanies that were central to an understanding of the medium.[40] Several contributors to this reader document this moment.[41] Instantaneity took over different functions in different contexts, for example, in the video surveillance of public spaces, in video conferences, participatory video art installations, the use of live video transmission in theatrical productions, or remote controlling a drone.

With reference to exemplary texts, it is possible to develop a typology of the instantaneous video image. Five of its aspects, each of them a different combination of factors intrinsic to the technology or typical of its use, can help as an orientation. These aspects should not be seen as clearly separable categories but as "soft" distinctions, where numerous combinations and hybrid forms are possible. These hybrid forms of instantaneity were first employed in video art of the 1970s and define the usage of video in social media today.[42]

Live Remote Image (with optional recording)

Objects in front of the camera are made visible in another place in real time. Video adopts this feature from television but puts it to use in different areas outside of the mass media (surveillance, video conferences, remote control, webcams, live video performances, or live video installations). In both a surveillance and art context, this is sometimes subsumed as CCTV (Closed Circuit Television).

Instant Replay (directly after recording)

Immediate availability of a recording cutting through the continual stream of images (often as slow motion). Is used mostly in television, based on video recording technology (e.g. in live sports coverage).[43]

Live Self-Image (with optional recording)

A person in front of the camera and their visual self-representation enter a mediated recursive relationship, where the spectator has to be in front of the camera and in front of the monitor at the same time so that the live remote image can be transformed into a reflexive surface. This is often seen as an electronic mirror function of the medium, or as CCTV in an art context.[44]

Instant Replay Self-Image (recording and subsequent replay)

Persons view their own actions or interactions following a recording of one or more persons. Can be combined with the Live Self-Image (but does not have to be). In a psychological, social, or an artistic context, this is often labeled "feedback."

Live Feedback (with optional recording)

Images produced by recursive signal processes. Multiplication of video images in the form of a "visual echo corridor," or *mise en abyme*.[45] Can be seen as "feedback" in a cybernetic or psychedelic sense. Often combined with bodily interaction, for example, in video art.

The forms of the instantaneous video image can be summarized in a diagram which shows the following relations between technological functions and usage scenarios:

Technological function	Usage and exemplary applications		
Transmission	**Live Remote Image** Immediate transmission, surveillance, videoconferencing, remote control, webcams, closed-circuit television (CCTV)	**Live Self-Image** Electronic mirror function, live video performances or installations, video theater, (video) selfie culture	**Live Feedback** Cybernetic feedback, playful forms of interaction, psychedelic environments combined with live processing and video synthesis
Recording/ Replay	**Instant Replay** Partly in slow motion, live sports coverage, training in sports, dance, and the military	**Instant Replay Self-Image** Time-lagged replay and (group) analysis, psychotherapy, educational group sessions, videotape performance, visual anthropology, participatory video	

Many of the texts in this reader show how different forms of instantaneity gave rise to particular theoretical reflections. The contributions by Paul Ryan and Vilém Flusser in Chapter 1 refer to the primary experience of video described above, regarding both the Live Self-Image and the Instant Replay Self-Image. Starting from a phenomenological description of instantaneity they subsequently derive far-reaching reflexive, social, educational, and finally political potentials of the medium. Ryan describes video as a recursive structure of television, as "TV flipped into itself." Instead of a televisual transmission, according to Ryan video offers a new mode of (self-)perception: "Instant replay offers a living feedback that creates a topology of awareness."[46] Meanwhile, Flusser distinguishes video as a dialogic medium, in contrast to film, and defines the video monitor as a new, interactive form of mirror. Both Ryan and Flusser conclude that video abolishes the hierarchy between actors in front of and behind the camera.[47] Sociologists Alfred Willener, Guy Milliard, and Alex Ganty describe this process as "participant-observation," especially when video is used as a collective Instant Replay Self-Image in group sessions (Chapter 9).[48]

Peter Sachs Collopy explores the facets of Instant Self-Images from a transdisciplinary perspective (introduction to Chapter 3). The contributions on psychotherapy and video art collected in Chapter 3 are linked by the Instant Replay Self-Image, which leads to a (self-)perception process in the reconciliation between recording and replay. As Collopy demonstrates, the term "feedback," borrowed from cybernetics, can take on very different meanings. In psychotherapy, so-called "video feedback" serves as a second stage for the patient's self-analysis by objectivizing their self-perception. Artists such as Paul Ryan, Frank Gillette, Ira Schneider, and Dan Graham, on the other hand, explore experimental combinations of video processes that are "live" or "delayed," which they also label as "feedback."[49] Generally we find that there is no consistent terminology in the literature, beside "feedback"; other terms are used for a variety of phenomena, such as "Instant Replay" and "CCTV." The contributions by Juan Downey and Terence Turner in Chapter 10 show how the Instant Replay Self-Image can support social processes of internal and external representation on the example of video work by and with indigenous communities. Similarly, the joint processes of production and reception, inspection, and evaluation in "participatory video" serve to initiate group processes (introduction to Chapter 10). In both cases, the instantaneity of video proves a factor of identity-establishing social dynamics.

A number of contributions from various chapters discuss an experimental artistic use of the instantaneous image. Several aspects of instantaneity named above come into play, especially the Live Self-Image and the Instant Replay Self-Image. Similar to Ryan and Flusser, Rosalind Krauss refers to the so-called mirror function of video, which she differentiates into three basic dualisms: recording and transmitting, camera and monitor, body and machine (Chapters 1 and 3).[50] Meanwhile, Dan Graham critically revises this mirror function, pointing out two important differences between video and the mirror: the temporality of self-perception and the connection between performers in front of the camera and the audience in front of the monitor (Chapter 3).[51] Graham's approach shows parallels to the use of video in psychotherapy. At the same time it is reminiscent of the video-specific relation between the camera operator and the actors in front of the camera as analyzed by Ryan, Flusser, and Willener et al. Peter Campus likewise points out several factors that differentiate the video self-image from that in a merely optical mirror: the microtemporality of the electronic processes involved and the time-based technology of the image, which is fundamentally different from a mirror even when not recorded (Chapter 12).[52]

Artistic-experimental uses of instantaneity are not confined to the self-image. The "visual echo corridor" produces generative, synthetic images that are also defined as a "feedback" between camera and monitor but do not necessarily imply a self-image. Peter Sachs Collopy points out that these different phenomena of "psychological" or "optical" feedback are designated with the same term in the literature (introduction to Chapter 3). Such forms of feedback without a mirror function are closely connected to the signal-based modulation of the video image in real time (introduction to Chapter 6). The instantaneous image is similarly central to the use of video in a theater or performance context. As Barbara Büscher reveals, performances by, for example, Joan Jonas or stage productions by Bert Neumann combine the liveness of performative actions with video live images (introduction to Chapter 7). A contribution by Nick Kaye expounds the many layerings of "live" and "recorded" that the Wooster Group built their theater work around (Chapter 7).

Like their applications in group processes and in psychotherapy, all these artistic-experimental uses of the instantaneous image are based in "misappropriation" or a creative repurposing of the medium's potentials. Such multifarious applications never were part of the guiding interests the industry followed in developing video technology. They were targeting television stations as their primary market. Corresponding fields of use for the instantaneous video image—aside from self-images, mirror functions, or psychological-dialogical feedback functions—are discussed in the contributions to Chapters 5 and 10. Dylan Mulvin explores the video-based function of "time shifting" for a time-lagged transmission of TV broadcasts and the "instant replay" as a disruption of live television broadcasts, especially in sports programs (Chapter 5).[53] John Thornton Caldwell analyzes the changes in television from the 1970s on that occurred through the use of "live remote" video cameras (Chapter 5). In the varied area of video surveillance (introduction to Chapter 10) the "live remote image" takes on another function: "remote sensing," an instantaneous transmission that becomes a criterion for the real-time indexicality of surveillance cameras (in the simplest case, without recording). Remote-controlled drones offer related functions; their use in military operations are examined by Eyal Weizman, and the performative aspects of webcams are discussed by Wendy Chun (Chapter 10).

We also need to consider video-specific image production in relation to the instantaneous distribution of images in social media. Marc Ries examines how smartphone cameras render the act of photographing or filming "occasional," that is, casual and provisional: video images of violent scenes, for example, connect the bodies of those involved with the lives of all people who perceive the images on the internet (Chapter 4). At the center of Martha Buskirk's thoughts on online video is the interweaving of the production with the practically concurrent consumption of images (introduction to Chapter 8). Two well-known case studies on the instantaneous sharing of videos and their viral distribution and political impact can be found in contributions by Alexandra Juhasz, Siva Vaidhyanathan (Chapter 8), and Kathrin Peters (Chapter 11).

The relevance of the video image's instantaneity can only be gathered from an overview of video-theoretical approaches. It is through the diachronic and interdisciplinary perspectives opened by the source texts in this reader that we can determine instantaneity as the basis of many of the subsequent phenomena, for example, the viral spread of digital photographs and videos on the internet. Our excursion on instantaneity can thus be seen as incentive to explore other desiderata in the medium's theory formation.

The force of such questions is unexpectedly renewed during the editing of this reader by the changed sociopolitical and media-cultural conditions during the Covid-19 pandemic, which spread worldwide in 2020. Especially video conferences and video live streaming, phenomena that so far have received meager theoretical attention, have moved to the center of communication and the cultural exchange of information.[54] While video for a long time was mainly treated as a storage medium, in times of "social distancing" the aspect of real-time transmission gains a new importance. What performative dynamics evolve in a live stream by a musician, actor, or speaker as compared to the infinite resources of comparable video recordings? Do we have a clearer awareness of the profound differences between ephemeral and stored video images again these days? What kind of community can emerge during a video conference? Will the ubiquity of video lead to a new form of copresence and interaction between video agents beyond time zones and territorial borders (e.g., in team meetings from home-based offices for online teaching)?[55] Will video conferences establish themselves as a new medium of authoritarian governmentality (as exemplarily demonstrated by Vladimir Putin)?[56] Such questions surely have no priority over the dramatic recess in matters of health and economy caused by the Covid-19 pandemic. They merely serve as an illustration of the limited temporal horizon of this reader and the interminability of a thematic area that demands an update in the moment it emerges.

Notes

1 Roy Armes, *On Video* (New York: Routledge, 1988), 1; reprinted in Chapter 1 of this volume.
2 Sean Cubitt, *Videography: Video Media as Art and Culture* (New York: Macmillan, 1993), xv–xvi; reprinted in Chapter 2.
3 Jacques Derrida, "Videor," in *Resolutions: Contemporary Video Practices*, ed. Michael Renov and Erika Suderburg, (Minneapolis: University of Minnesota Press, 1996), 73f; reprinted in Chapter 12.
4 Scott McQuire, "Videor: Video Theory," *Globe E-Journal of Contemporary Art* 9 (1999), http://www.artdes.monash.edu.au/globe/issue9/smtxt.html All weblinks were accessed on September 30, 2021.
5 Siva Vaidhyanathan, "The Dangers of Ubiquitous Video," in *Wired*, August 18, 2020, https://www.wired.com/story/dangers-ubiquitous-video-propaganda/; reprinted in Chapter 8.
6 See the contribution by Sean Cubitt in Chapter 2.
7 Raymond Bellour, "Self-Portraits" (1988), in Bellour, *Between-the-Images* (Zürich: JRP|Ringier; Dijon: Les presses du réel, 2012), 319. According to Ina Blom, video technology can change discursive textual thought, "in the sense that video technology operated as a body of knowledge that imposed its parameters at the level of textual reflection, so as to produce a new sort of video thinking or what we might perhaps call a 'videomatic' inscription of thought itself." See Blom, *The Autobiography of Video: The Life and Times of a Memory Technology* (New York: Sternberg Press, 2016), 23; reprinted in Chapter 2.
8 See W. J. T. Mitchell, *Picture Theory: Essays on Verbal and Visual Representation* (Chicago: University of Chicago Press, 1994), 37f.
9 See Edward S. Small, *Direct Theory: Experimental Film/Video as Major Genre* (Carbondale: University of Southern Illinois Press, 1995).
10 Dieter Mersch: *Epistemologien des Ästhetischen* (Zürich: Diaphanes, 2015), 12.
11 Alfred Willener, Guy Milliard, and Alex Ganty, *Vidéo et société virtuelle* (Paris: Tema-Editons, 1972); English translation: *Videology and Utopia: Explorations in a New Medium* (London, Henley, and Boston: Routledge & Kegan Paul, 1976). Nam June Paik: *Videa 'n' Videology 1959–1973*, ed. Judson Rosebush (Syracuse: Everson Museum of Art, 1974). Other ironic coinages by Paik were "Video-Videa-Vidiot-Videology" and "Contemporary American Videory." See Paik, Binghamton Letter, 1972, ibid., n.p.
12 For an example see Rosalind Krauss's contribution to Chapter 3, which integrates art-historical and psychoanalytical considerations.

13 See the chapter "Periodization and Synopsis" in Peter Sachs Collopy, *The Revolution Will Be Videotaped: Making a Technology of Consciousness in the Long 1960s*, PhD (Philadelphia: University of Pennsylvania, 2015), 47–51. Michael Z. Newman distinguishes between three phases: "Video as Television," "Video as Alternative," and "Video as the Moving Image." See Newman, *Video Revolutions: On the History of a Medium* (New York: Columbia University Press, 2014).

14 See the contribution by Marina Gržinić in Chapter 12.

15 See Joshua Neves and Bhaskar Sarkar, eds., *Asian Video Cultures: In the Penumbra of the Global* (Durham and London: Duke University Press, 2017).

16 See the contribution by Brian Larkin and the introduction to Chapter 10.

17 In television technology, the term "video" is used within compound words from the 1930s on, offering a visual equivalent to familiar "audio" processes, as in "video frequency," "video circuit," and "video amplifier." See George Shiers assisted by May Shiers, *Early Television: A Bibliographic Guide to 1940* (London and New York: Garland, 1997). In the press, "video" sometimes serves as an abbreviation for "television," as a counterpart to "radio" (e.g., in the *New York Times*, which after the launch of a regular television program headlined its program announcements "Radio-Video"). See Newman, *Video Revolutions*, 9. After 1949, *Captain Video and His Video Rangers*, the first science-fiction TV series worldwide, contributed to a popularization of the term, although video technology in the narrow sense did not feature in the program. On the futuristic "inventions" of Captain Video see an interview with leading actor Richard Coogan from 1997, https://interviews.televisionacademy.com/shows/captain-video-and-his-video-rangers. Up until the 1960s, video used in art, psychotherapy, or surveillance was often colloquially subsumed under "television" (see the introductions to Chapters 5 and 11). Only with the proliferation of mobile video gear for consumers (see the introduction to Chapter 8) around 1969–70, the noun "video" established itself in everyday language as the term for a distinct medium.

18 International terminology was standardized during the course of the 1970s, except that in France the word "magnétoscope" is still used for a video recorder, whereas the medium itself is called "video" in almost every language.

19 The prehistory of video technology reaches back farther than the beginnings of video terminology. Before recording video on magnetic tape became possible, several processes were tested for the storage of television signals. At Bell Labs in the United States and at Fernseh A.G. in Germany, the intermediate film system was used. In England in the late 1920s, John Logie Baird worked on a "Phonovision" process which recorded television images on discs revolving on a turntable. See Albert Abramson, "Video Recording: 1922 to 1959," in *Video: Apparat/Medium, Kunst, Kultur*, ed. Siegfried Zielinski (Frankfurt am Main: Lang, 1992), 35–40.

20 Ludwig Wittgenstein, *Philosophische Untersuchungen / Philosophical Investigations*, 2nd edition, trans. G. E. M Anscombe (Oxford and Malden, MA: Blackwell, 1997), 32 (§67). For an analysis of Wittgenstein's "family resemblance" in reference to media and image concepts, see especially Mike Sandbothe, "Medien—Kommunikation—Kultur," in *Handbuch der Kulturwissenschaften, Band 2: Grundlagen und Schlüsselbegriffe*, ed. Friedrich Jaeger und Burkhard Liebsch (Stuttgart and Weimar: Metzler, 2004); and W. J. T. Mitchell, "What Is an Image?" *New Literary History: A Journal of Theory and Interpretation*, vol. 15, no. 3 (Spring 1984), 503–537.

21 Newman, *Video Revolutions*, 3. Cf. also Sean Cubitt: "Video works across a plurality of relationships, plundering other media for sources and channels, rarely pursuing

an imagined goal of pure video, video in and of itself." Cubitt, *Videography*, xv; reprinted in Chapter 2.

22 The regulations of the European Commission offer a prime example of the absurdity in trying to determine a classification of video despite the technological variabilities described here. According to the European Classification of Goods, a digital photo camera with more than thirty-minute recording capability has to be classified as a video recorder. This arbitrary regulation increases customs duty for digital photo cameras imported to Europe. See European Commission, "Classification of Goods, Classifying Computers & Software," section "Other Digital Cameras," https://trade.ec.europa.eu/tradehelp/classifying-computers-software.

23 See the introduction to Chapter 5 as well as the contributions by Dylan Mulvin and John Thornton Caldwell in the same chapter.

24 On the commercial launch of portable video technology see the introduction to Chapter 9.

25 Ricardo Cedeño Montaña, *Portable Moving Images: A Media History of Storage Formats* (Berlin: De Gruyter, 2017), 136

26 Each suggested use comes with a short description and a staged photograph of the Sony Recorder in action. For a digitized version of the folder's contents, see https://www.smecc.org/sony_cv_series_video.htm. Still more variable were the possible uses of the portable Sony DVK 2400 recorder, as presented in (Japanese) photographs and extensive (English) descriptions: "At School" (illustrated by sports lessons and organized leisure time), "Industrial Application" (illustrated by the analysis of work practices and the surveillance of safety regulations), "For an Office" (illustrated by staff training for customer support), "For Policemen" (illustrated by traffic surveillance), and "Permanent Record" (illustrated by family festivities). Folder of the Sony Corporation for the combination of their mobile DVK-2400 recorder with the VCK-2400 camera, Sony Video System Illustrated, no date (*c.* 1965).

27 See the introduction to Chapter 10.

28 See the introduction to Chapter 9 and the contribution by Jean-Luc Godard in Chapter 4.

29 See the contribution by Marc Ries in Chapter 4.

30 In detailed diagrams, Ricardo Montaña lists fifty-three analog video formats for the years 1956–94, as well as forty-five digital video formats for the years 1984–2013. Montaña, *Portable Moving Images*, 98f, 168f.

31 Derrida, "Videor," 76.

32 Ina Blom, *The Autobiography of Video: The Life and Times of a Memory Technology* (New York: Sternberg Press, 2016), 29; reprinted in Chapter 2.

33 Ibid., 31.

34 Ibid., 21.

35 Cf. Michel Foucault, "The Order of Discourse" (1970), in *Untying the Text: A Post-Structuralist Reader*, ed. Robert Young (Boston, London, and Henley: Routledge & Kegan Paul, 1981), 51–78.

36 Janna Houwen, *Film and Video Intermediality: The Question of Medium Specificity in Contemporary Moving Images* (New York and London: Bloomsbury, 2017), 12. Houwen's study again shows the disjointedness of video discourse in contrast to the relatively coherent film theory.

37 The instantaneity of the video image is distinguished from earlier forms of ephemeral images (in shadows, mirrors, or camera obscuras) because video, like analog photography and film, produces a technological image based on the

material transformation of light. In contrast to these ephemeral images, the video image can thus be stored and transmitted. Precursors of this special screen-based, electrophysical transformation of the visible can be found in radars and sinus wave displays on electronic measuring devices, although these did not produce images adhering to the paradigm of photography.

38 The possibilities of instant replay had far-reaching effects on film production processes, as pointed out by filmmakers Hollis Frampton and Gabor Bódy (see their contributions in Chapter 4). Frampton tells of the irritation the effect provoked in him when he first encountered video; Bódy names the psychological consequences the function had for the continuation of his filmic work on video.

39 The name of the social media platform Instagram combines two aspects of instantaneity: "instant" (with reference to instant cameras, which also explains the initial Polaroid look of their logo and the square format for images) and "telegram" (with reference to the instantaneous transfer of messages).

40 This experience is specific to a certain generation; today, in the age of smartphones and instant digital (video) selfies, it can only be conveyed by historiographical methods.

41 On these first experiences of video focusing on its instantaneity, see the contributions by Hollis Frampton (Chapter 4) and Andy Warhol (Chapter 12). William Kaizen describes Warhol's reaction during his "unpacking" of the video equipment that Philips provided to him in 1965 (see also the contribution by Dieter Daniels in Chapter 12 for this topic): "For Warhol the 'Oh, wow' of video was the fact that you got a picture immediately, that the moving image was represented in real time and instant replay." William Kaizen, "Live on Tape: Video, Liveness and the Immediate," in *Art and the Moving Image: A Critical Reader* (London: Tate Publishing/Afterall, 2008), 259. Kaizen quotes further artists on the "immediacy" of video (only Paik uses the term "instantaneity"), including Bruce Nauman, Jud Yalkut, Frank Gillette, Lynda Benglis, Dan Graham, and Vito Acconci.

42 Angela Krewani examines the development from early video art to (video) selfies in social media from a genealogical perspective. Angela Krewani, "The Selfie as Feedback: Video, Narcissism, and the Closed-Circuit Video Installation," in *Exploring the Selfie: Historical, Theoretical, and Analytical Approaches to Digital Self-Photography*, ed. Julia Eckel, Jens Ruchatz, and Sabine Wirth (Cham: Palgrave Macmillan, 2018), 95–109.

43 Cf. Dylan Mulvin: "The central feature of magnetic tape is 'instantaneous recording.' Instantaneous recording simply means that recorded content is available for playback as it is recorded." Dylan Wesley Mulvin, *"Human Eye Inadequate": Instant Replay and the Politics of Video*, master thesis (Montreal: McGill University, 2011), 20. Mulvin quotes from the instruction manual of the VR1000 video recorder by Ampex from 1958, where it reads: "During the recording process the tape is moved through the magnetic field at the gap in the record head, and the resultant flux pattern on the tape—created by the ferrous oxide particles being aligned in accordance with the field—is a function of the instantaneous magnitude and direction of the original signal at the moment that the tape leaves the head gap." Ibid.

44 Cf., e.g., Ina Blom: "One of the camera functions that is specific to video and that film cannot replicate; notably, the act of turning the camera on yourself, while simultaneously following your own on-camera action on a monitor in real time." Blom, *The Autobiography of Video*, 34f.

45 Kris Paulsen classifies the "visual echo corridor of feedback" as an archetypal form of the video medium, which frees both camera and screen from their usual iconographical and representational codes (also see the introduction to Chapter 6). Kris Paulsen, "In the Beginning, There Was the Electron," in *X-Tra*, vol. 15, no. 2 (Winter 2013), 58, 61; online at https://www.x-traonline.org/article/in-the-beginning-there-was-the-electron.

46 Paul Ryan, "Videotape: Thinking about a Medium," in *Educators Guide to Media & Methods*, December 1968, 38; reprinted in Chapter 1.

47 Ryan in "Videotape: Thinking about a Medium" (see Chapter 1): "With videotape, the performer and the audience can be one and the same, either simultaneously or sequentially." Flusser in "Mutations in Human Relations" from 1973 to 1974 (see Chapter 1): "The monitor shows all those present as they are seen by the operator. (It is a revolutionary experience to see oneself from behind, and thus to imagine, not only to conceive, the concept of 'being for another.') Tapes may be watched immediately after their registration by those who are registered on it, and thus may serve for immediate dialogical re-use. Therefore those who are present are neither part of the scene (like in photography), nor actors in an event (like in film), but partners of the operator in the same operation. The monitor is a tool for dialogues, it makes 'brothers' of all men within the operation." Without Ryan's and Flusser's social emphasis, John Thornton Caldwell examines the professionalization of the video monitor as an expanded camera viewfinder that allows the director and cameraman to jointly control the image while shooting (Chapter 5).

48 Alfred Willener, Guy Milliard, and Alex Ganty (see Chapter 9): "Furthermore, the observers are also the objects of observation; the researchers are also actors, passing from a participation that is primarily observational to a participant-observation."

49 Slavko Kacunko's extensive study collects the impressive number of video artists who have engaged with different variants and recombinations of the Live Self-Image and the Instant Replay Self-Image with Internal Live Feedback. In all, 1,100 video installations by 650 artists are portrayed in his book and DVD *Closed Circuit Videoinstallationen: Ein Leitfaden zur Geschichte und Theorie der Medienkunst mit Bausteinen eines Künstlerlexikons auf DVD* (Berlin: Logos, 2004). In-depth examinations of video works by Bill Viola, Peter Campus, and Takahiko Iimura can be found in Kacunko's *Culture as Capital* (Berlin: Logos, 2015).

50 Krauss in "Video: The Aesthetics of Narcissism" from 1976 (see Chapter 3): "Unlike the other visual arts, video is capable of recording and transmitting at the same time—producing instant feedback. The body is therefore as it were centered between two machines that are the opening and closing of a parenthesis. The first of these is the camera; the second is the monitor, which re-projects the performer's image with the immediacy of a mirror." "The demand for instant replay in the media—in fact the creation of work that literally does not exist outside of that replay, as is true of conceptual art and its nether side, body art—finds its obvious correlative in an aesthetic mode by which the self is created through the electronic device of feedback."

51 Graham in "Essay on Video, Architecture and Television" from 1979 (see Chapter 3): "The video feedback of 'self'-image, by adding temporality to self-perception, connects 'self'-perception to physiological brain processes. This removes self-perception from the viewing of a detached, static image; video feedback contradicts the mirror model of the perceiving 'self.' Through the use of videotape feedback, the

performer and the audience, the perceiver and his process of perception, are linked, or co-identified."

52 Campus in "Video as a Function of Reality" from 1974 (see Chapter 12): "I have been dealing here with a simultaneous or, more exactly, a nearly simultaneous image. (Nearly simultaneous because there is some time loss but it is of the order of the speed of light, the speed of electrons, or the speed of neural impulses and therefore imperceptible to human consciousness.) In a closed-circuit video situation one is no longer dealing with images of a temporally finite nature. The duration of the image becomes a property of the room." As Wolfgang Ernst has shown in his concept of "time-critical" functions of electronic media, both these factors have relevance beyond the medium of video. Wolfgang Ernst, *Gleichursprünglichkeit: Zeitwesen und Zeitgegebenheit von Medien* (Berlin: Kadmos, 2012).

53 The high investment in the development of video technology during the 1950s was especially motivated by the "time-shifting" function. The medium's instantaneity played a role insofar as time and expenses for transportation and development of film recordings between time zones were eliminated. The possibility of the "instant replay" was more of an instantaneous side benefit.

54 Axel Volmar, Olga Moskatova, and Jan Distelmeyer are preparing a comprehensive publication on "Video Conferencing: Practices, Politics, Aesthetics"; see their call for papers at https://arthist.net/archive/33482.

55 During university closures following the pandemic, students from different time zones simultaneously attended the same online courses, since traveling to one's place of study was no longer possible.

56 While his official place of residence was always Moscow, during the second wave of the Covid-19 pandemic Putin was suspected to attend to government affairs from a property in Sochi on the coast of the Black Sea. For that purpose, two identical offices for video conferences would have been built in Sochi and Moscow. See, e.g., Andrew E. Kramer, "Putin Said to Have Two Identical Offices: One in Moscow, the Other at the Beach," *New York Times*, December 13, 2020, https://www.nytimes.com/2020/12/13/world/europe/putin-russia-office-sochi.html.

Section I

Foundations

1

Formations | Exemplary Discourses

Introduction by Dieter Daniels

Beginnings: Formation of a Theoretical Discourse on Video (1960s–1970s)

As the beginnings of video-related theory formation in the 1960s and 1970s evolved from heterogeneous contexts, contributions in this chapter come from scattered and sometimes remote sources. In hindsight, we can connect the dots between texts, but that would not have been possible at the time of their writing. We now recognize two different discursive genealogies at play: on the one hand, a general media theory still in the making, on the other, art-theoretical discussions on medium specificity that reach back much further. The hybridity and variability of video (described in the introduction to this volume) thus also characterized the origins of the medium's theoretical discourse. Then again, this initial situation positioned video as a predestined intersection where art and media discourses not only met but also influenced and transformed each other. Thus the reflective engagement with the still young video medium can also be seen as the start of a hybrid theory formation, even if intertextual cross-connections rarely developed at the time.

The present chapter will explore this discursive intersection with the help of exemplary contributions by Marshall McLuhan, Paul Ryan, Nam June Paik, Vilém Flusser, and Rosalind Krauss. Their diverse spectrum of methodological approaches at the same time outlines the transdisciplinary environment of this reader. Accordingly, its special focus lies on the complex origins and reception history of the texts, which will be represented in more detail here than in following chapters. Additionally, facsimiles of selected documents visualize the materiality of these historical sources, something that is not usually taken into consideration in an anthology.

It is evident especially from the writings of McLuhan and Flusser that communication and media theories of the 1960s and 1970s proceeded from an analysis and comparison of the specific characteristics of technical media. Theories of photography, film, and television serve as the background for an investigation of video from the perspective of media studies. Precursors of such comparative approaches can be found in debates from the 1920s that pitted film against theater or radio against literature. Further differentiations based on epistemic properties and techno-ontological structures will be taken up in Chapters 4 and 5, where the comparison of video with film and television is elaborated in more detail.

From an art-historical perspective, the autonomy of video art was determined in its distinction from previously established genres or media. Wulf Herzogenrath's list of the "Three Elements of Video" from 1974 exemplarily sums up the criteria: "Because of its electronically produced image, video yields three elements which were simply not available in other media of artistic expression such as painting, photography, theater, and film: 1. Instant control of the picture; 2. Numerous electronic possibilities; 3. Picture playback on monitors."[1] By contrast, when artists explored the electronic image, they were initially less interested in historical classifications of the medium and more in its future potential, as were the first media scholars working on the topic of video. This is paradigmatically shown by a comparison of Marshall McLuhan's theories with the texts and artworks of Nam June Paik and Paul Ryan on television or respectively video as a participative medium. Both Paik and Ryan seized on McLuhan's ideas and at the same time extended and superseded them especially regarding the social potential of video.

Precursors for similar dichotomies of analysis and hypothesis in art discourse include Gotthold Ephraim Lessing's *Laocoön* (1766), a revision of the classical hierarchy of artforms (see introduction to Chapter 2), and Richard Wagner's manifesto on his idea of the *Gesamtkunstwerk*, "The Artwork of the Future" (1849), which ran ahead of his own artistic practice.

At the intersection of art and media discourses, Clement Greenberg's Marxist-inspired writings of the 1930s hold a special place. With reference to modernist painting and literature, Greenberg introduced the term "medium specificity" and diagnosed capitalism as the central cause for a fatal mix of media and materials that led straight into kitsch.[2] The abstract painting of his time was at the center of his art-theoretical writings, and he considered Abstract Expressionism and Post-Painterly Abstraction the most exemplary forms of high culture since both self-reflexively addressed the flatness of painting as a medium. Given this frame of ideas, Greenberg necessarily had to dismiss the intermedial artforms of the 1950s and 1960s, and he did not comment on video art at all. Still his concept of medium specificity had a far-reaching influence on the development of video theory, particularly after being further differentiated in the writings of Rosalind Krauss, which will be discussed in more detail later on.

As early as 1975, David Antin pithily summed up the significance of video as an intersection between discourses of communication and media theories on the one hand and art history, art theory, and artistic as well as activist media practice on the other:

> Two discourses: one, a kind of enthusiastic welcoming prose peppered with fragments of communication theory and McLuhanesque media talk; the other, a rather nervous attempt to locate the "unique properties of the medium." Discourse 1 could be called "cyberscat" and Discourse 2, because it engages the issues that pass for "formalism" in the art world, could be called "the formalist rap."[3]

The following sections will take a closer look at the background and reception histories of some of the positions from this conflicted area.

Marshall McLuhan and Paul Ryan: "Video Is Not Television"

The above quotation from David Antin alludes to Marshall McLuhan's significance as an influential thinker on video art as well as on social, educational, activist, and political utopias from the end of the 1960 to the mid-1970s.[4] And yet we do not find an essential contribution on the video medium in McLuhan's far-ranging text production on remarkably disparate topics. Instead print media, radio, and television are the focus areas for his theses, while film plays only a minor role. Video is mentioned sporadically by McLuhan but never analyzed as an autonomous medium. This paradoxical situation raises two questions: What made McLuhan's thoughts so fascinating that they could serve as a motto for the video practitioners of his time? And why has McLuhan, who was eager to respond to topical issues immediately, never discussed video?

The best contemporary witness for these questions is Paul Ryan, who worked as McLuhan's assistant during the latter's stint as a guest professor at Fordham University in New York from 1967 to 1968 and discovered video for himself during this time.[5] Looking back, Ryan stresses McLuhan's significance within the context of other relevant theoreticians:

> By the time the Portapak became available, Marshall McLuhan's work was being widely read. Other thinkers such as Teilhard de Chardin, Norman O. Brown, Buckminster Fuller, and Herbert Marcuse were also being read, but McLuhan's work was particularly relevant to video. . . . McLuhan's perceptions and language provided an instant framework of understanding both for those interested in processing imagery for the TV screen and for those interested in the social change possibilities of the Portapak.[6]

Even without Ryan's personal access to the man, many of his contemporaries naturally pointed to McLuhan as a source of inspiration for their interest in video. In 1973, for example, Randy Sherman contributed an article from a sociological perspective to the discourse-leading magazine *Radical Software*, in which he wrote: "Our network shared a dream and took on video as tools and toys to activate our survival vision. We came to video via McLuhan, with fantasies of a kinetic carnival."[7]

McLuhan's role as a "guru" for a whole generation of video practitioners appears obvious from such voices. But it is difficult to tell exactly which texts form the basis for his influence. The broader themes set by McLuhan were certainly more relevant than any specific theories: he announced the end of the "Gutenberg Galaxy" defined by the printed page, called electric media an "extension of man," and predicted the upheaval of social and communicative structures by television. McLuhan's thoughts were oriented toward the future and did not shy away from speculative prognoses, challenging practitioners to try them out in practice. His often eclectic mix of ideas thus served as an inspiration for artistic and social experimentation that was likewise media-reflexive and speculative. Additionally, the writings of Gene Youngblood, widely read at the time, made McLuhan's ideas fertile for creative video practice in ample quotations and longer paraphrases.[8]

McLuhan actively promoted the popularization of his ideas, not least by his massive presence in television, radio, and the press. He did not just write about the end of print culture and the return of oral culture in audiovisual media, but, neglecting his academic credibility, he placed himself at the forefront of that development. This helps to explain the erratic and repetitive style of his books: McLuhan speaks and writes not as a taxonomist but as a rhetorician. Michael Shamberg calls McLuhan's style "rapping": "An indigenous electronic morphology is the 'rap.' Rapping is a meandering interplay which renders nothing irrelevant and maximizes feedback options."[9]

The affinity between style and subject is a major factor in McLuhan's mass appeal; his sentences and slogans took on a life of their own in a community of "McLuhanites." Still he hoped to escape canonization by virtue of a massive output: "If I just keep writing with great energy, no McLuhanite will ever be able to digest it all," he said in a 1967 interview.[10] In a sense, McLuhan's media presence made him a precedent for his own theories and he developed media-based formats to carry his ideas. Working with renowned graphic designers, some of his books processed these ideas for a haptic and visual reception. Quentin Fiore's innovative design concept for *The Medium Is the Massage* (1967) even was multimedially expanded into an audio version on LP.[11]

Already before he gained popularity in the mid-1960s, McLuhan conceived of audiovisual formats for his theories, as proven by the draft for "Gutenberg Video" from 1960, an excerpt of which is published for the first time in this reader.[12] The script was written for television as an audiovisual demonstration of the theses he would later flesh out in his book *The Gutenberg Galaxy*. Despite several revisions, the concept was never produced by the TV broadcaster—and at this point we might see McLuhan as a prevented video pioneer on his own account.[13]

Paul Ryan earns the credit for being the first to systematically apply McLuhan's ideas to the video medium both as artist and theorist. Ryan's lifelong dedication to video began at Fordham University, where as McLuhan's assistant he gained access to portable video gear. Since McLuhan's theories often struck him as daring, Ryan started a project to test them experimentally in a medium McLuhan was not dealing with. In 1971, Michael Shamberg reported: "Paul claims that he got into videotape to figure out if McLuhan was right, for if he were then Paul would be able to decode accurately a medium that McLuhan hadn't touched yet."[14] Ryan himself summed up his approach that combined theory and practice (which would be labeled "artistic research" today): "Halfway through that year I was saying to myself, 'This man's rap is either nonsense or it's not. If it's not, it will work with a medium he's never talked about.' I got my hands on some old ½" videotape equipment and began experimenting."[15]

As a result of his experiments, Ryan produced a number of video works (see Chapter 3) as well as the text "Videotape: Thinking about a Medium" from 1968, reprinted in this chapter.[16] While this text received little attention, it was the first to outline central criteria for the medium specificity of video. Two years before a broad discourse on video would start in the pages of *Radical Software*, Ryan's contribution to a pedagogical magazine offered an outlook on the medium's social and educational potential. While McLuhan's theories on television still stuck to the centralist principle of one sender and many receivers, Ryan saw video as a DIY medium through which users could process electronic images themselves.[17] He described the portable videotape recorder as an autonomous cybernetic system and stressed the structural distinction of video as a feedback medium from television as a broadcast medium. The sentence that served as a motto for his text, "VT is not TV" (Video Tape is not Television), emphasized the basic difference between these media.[18]

Nam June Paik and Marshall McLuhan: Electronic Is Not Electric

Nam June Paik's contributions to video theory can be compared to those of Sergei Eisenstein and Dziga Vertov to film theory or John Cage to the theory of electronic audio media: artistic interest in new technologies served as the starting point for reflection on the respective medium in texts that first supported and justified the artist's own practice. Out of practice-based analyses then grew autonomous theories that offered a source of inspiration for following generations of artists.

As Paul Ryan's critique of McLuhan shows, an artist's theory can lead to a revision of academic ideas. Paik referred to McLuhan both in texts and in his artistic work from the mid-1960s on. According to his own evidence, he first heard of McLuhan from John Cage in 1965.[19] Precise dating is important to understand their relation: in 1963, Paik had developed his "Participation TV" in Germany, one year before McLuhan described television as a "cool" medium with a high degree of viewer activation in *Understanding Media*. Paik created his interactive television works independently from McLuhan and they were conceptually ahead of the latter's theories. When McLuhan spoke of the tactility of the television image, he still meant the status quo of the screen raster. Paik, on the other hand, developed some of the first applications for creative interaction with the electronic image. His manipulations of the television picture looked ahead to future developments as real-time synthesis and image modulation replaced the mere consumption of televisual images.

Paik first gained access to video technology in New York in 1965; before that, he had worked with manipulating the circuits of customary secondhand television sets, as presented in 1963 at the *Exposition of Music: Electronic Television* in Wuppertal. By his own admission, it was only later that he hit on the simple idea of distorting the image with a magnet from the outside. A degausser, a magnetic ring for calibrating the television picture, allowed him complex spherical distortions of video images that Paik exhibited at his first US-American solo show, *Electronic Art*, at Galeria Bonino in New York in 1965. Meanwhile Paik had acquainted himself with McLuhan's writings and in the exhibition catalog he lumps McLuhan together with John Cage and Norbert Wiener for an enigmatic formula:[20]

$$\log_a \text{Cage} - \frac{\sqrt[3.5]{\text{McLuhann} = \pm\text{sorry}}}{\text{Norbert Wiener}}$$

This formula can be read as a playful résumé of Paik's theoretical points of reference for his artistic engagement with television and the video image. Two years later the artist elaborated: "McLuhan's famous phrase 'the medium is the message' also existed implicitly in the science of communication since the 1940s. Norbert Wiener wrote that the information, in which a message was sent, plays the same role as the information, in which a message is not sent. It sounds almost Cagean."[21]

This speculative combination of McLuhan, Cage, and Wiener was put into practice in Paik's second solo show at Galeria Bonino in 1968. An interactive video-loop installation titled *McLuhan Caged* treated a television snippet of McLuhan with methods similar to those Cage used on electronic sound (Figure 1.1). Paik later described the setup: "There was an important program about Marshall McLuhan, made by NBC in 1967 or early 1968. . . . I videotaped the program while it was on the air. I put various electromagnets on the set and turned McLuhan right and left. What I wound up with was a McLuhan videotape loop that can be played with around and around."[22] This was a premiere: an interactive video application that could be controlled in real time.[23] The theoretical aspects of the work were just as elaborate as its technical realization: Paik fed a typical McLuhan sentence into the video loop, a variation of what McLuhan

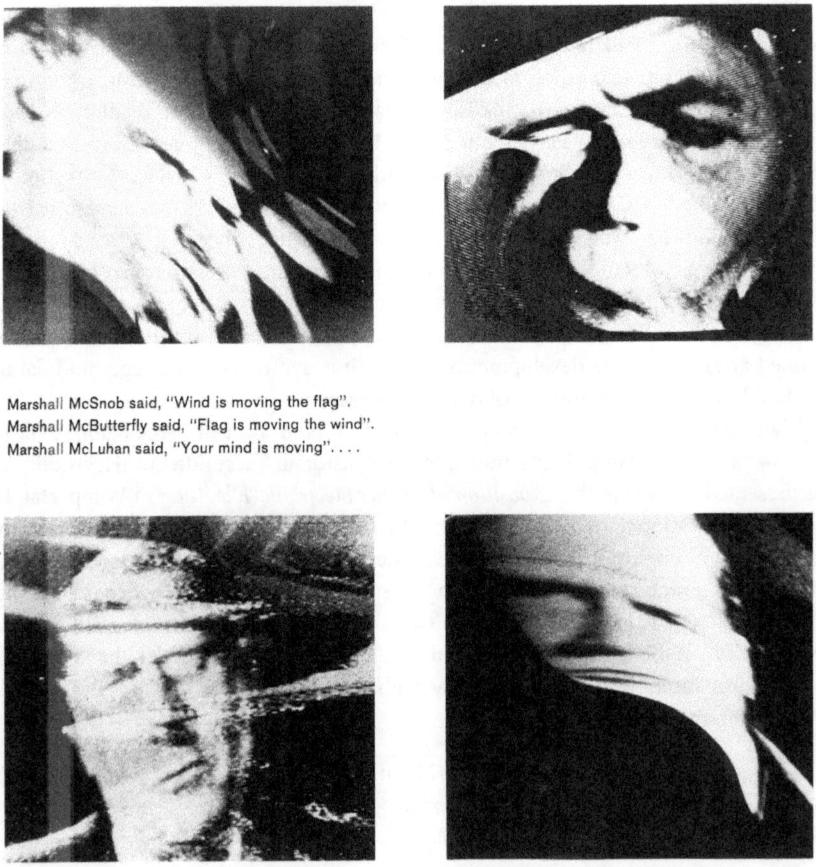
Marshall McSnob said, "Wind is moving the flag".
Marshall McButterfly said, "Flag is moving the wind".
Marshall McLuhan said, "Your mind is moving". . . .

Figure 1.1 Nam June Paik, *McLuhan Caged*, 1967. Facsimile from the exhibition catalog *Nam June Paik: Electronic Art II* (New York: Galeria Bonino, 1968), unpag.

had written in the National Association of Educational Broadcasters (NAEB) Report of 1960: "Movies tend to be the content of TV, and books and novels used to be the content of movies. So every time a new medium arrives, the old medium is the content, and it is highly observable. But the real 'massaging' done by the new medium—it is ignored."[24] Three decades later, Jay David Bolter and Richard Grusin would reengage with such ideas and label them "remediation."[25] Paik had applied a video-technical remediation to McLuhan's sentence, demonstrating how classic linear television could become the content for future interactive and participative capabilities of the electronic image.[26]

Paik recognized and demonstrated the limitations of McLuhan's television theory, which does not take such capabilities into account. In an interview on occasion of his 1968 exhibition he said: "Even McLuhan misuses and mixes up the words 'electric' and 'electronic,' which have as much difference as tonal and atonal. In the electronic trade jargon, we distinguish roughly two sorts of processes: (1) peripheral units . . . (2) central processing units." (We will get back to the far-reaching significance of differentiating between "electric" and "electronic" in the next section.) Paik goes on adding that he will show works with "data processing" in the exhibition for the first time.[27]

While Paik used a conceptual approach to overcome the limitations of McLuhan's centralist understanding of media, Paul Ryan's practice-based revision of McLuhan's theories likewise showed up their shortcomings. These two examples perfectly illustrate the intense interaction between theory and practice in the video field. Again, they position video at the intersection between art and media discourses. Such aspects would return in the work of Vilém Flusser and Fred Forest discussed further below.

Broadcast versus Feedback: McLuhan versus Video

Frank Gillette, video artist and cofounder of the Raindance video collective, compares McLuhan's influence on US-American artists of the 1960s with Sigmund Freud's influence on the origins of Surrealism in the 1920s.[28] Freud, however, found no access to what the Surrealists did with his ideas: "I am not able to clarify for myself what Surrealism is and what it wants. Perhaps I am not destined to understand it, I who am so distant from art," he wrote to André Breton in 1932.[29] Obviously McLuhan kept the same distance from video art that Freud had to Surrealism. In his major texts of the 1960s he did not mention the medium in a single word.[30] This means that perhaps surprisingly McLuhan ignored the social and aesthetic potential of the video medium.[31]

McLuhan's lecture excerpted in this chapter offers a good example for his lack of interest in the aesthetic, technological, and social specifics of video. Invited to the seminal video symposium at the Venice Biennale of 1977 as a keynote speaker, he mentioned video art only in passing. Instead, he devoted a large part of the talk to his controversial theories on the different capacities of the human brain's hemispheres. Elsewhere too McLuhan managed to give the topic of video wide berth. In an eleven-page interview for *Videography* magazine, despite repeated questions regarding video, he merely touched on a failed videophone project by the Bell Telephone Company.[32] As a speaker at a conference on video in Sweden in 1974, he peripherally discussed videocassettes as tools for the distribution of television programs: "The new technology of the portable Video Cassette player (for which programming has yet to be found) offers the means of reducing the single mass audience to many audiences of human scale. Let us say the cancer program has been broadcast to a million people. It could then be rebroadcast to many small publics by the Video Cassette."[33]

In stark contrast to the euphoric embracement of video by artists and activists of the mid-1970s, McLuhan thought that it still needed to find its "programming." This statement is symptomatic of his centralist understanding of media, strictly following the one-to-many principle all the way from printing to television. This brings us back to the fact that McLuhan often spoke of electric instead of electronic media, as Paik has pointed out. Such terminological carelessness reveals a key issue in McLuhan's media genealogy: with his use of the term "electric," he put television and radio broadcasts in a line with other centralized utilities (water, gas, electricity). Thus he was prone to ignore the significance of video at the beginning of the media shift toward personalized electronic media.

By contrast, the video practitioners of the 1960s and 1970s experienced and explored the epochal shift from "broadcasting" to "feedback" in their experimental approaches toward the medium. For Paik, Ryan, and the community around the *Radical Software* magazine, video was significant as the first instantaneous, personalized visual medium. While it shared the surface of the screen with television, it gave access to the world of electronic images for everyone. The personalization of video stands at the beginning of a development whose effects and promises led straight to the YouTube slogan, "broadcast yourself."

McLuhan did attest a tactile, active perception to television. Yet for him this did not include an autonomous creative use of television or video images—the viewer was activated only by perception: "For people long accustomed to the merely visual experience of the typographic and photographic varieties, it would seem to be the synesthesia, or tactual depth of TV experience, that dislocates them from their usual attitudes of passivity and detachment."[34] McLuhan stressed that the mosaic mesh of the electric television picture would have an activating effect regardless of the program shown, on the level of neurological reflexes, so to speak, not as a result of critical reflection: "This change of attitude has nothing to do with programming in any way."[35]

In conclusion, McLuhan's media theory offers a techno-determinist concept that sees artists as merely reacting to media shifts, not creating them. In the trademark rhetoric of *Understanding Media*, McLuhan writes: "It is the poets and painters who react instantly to a new medium like radio or TV. . . . The printed book encouraged artists to reduce all forms of expression as much as possible to the single descriptive and narrative plane of the printed word. The advent of electric media released art from this straitjacket at once, creating the world of Paul Klee, Picasso, Braque, Eisenstein, the Marx Brothers, and James Joyce."[36] Accordingly, McLuhan's television theory proved incompatible with the goals of video activists and artists. While they shared his belief in the transformative powers of the media, contrary to him they saw the possibility of a socially and aesthetically autonomous usurpation of these powers by the users of video technology. Thus McLuhan's role as a "guru" for this community has to be relativized and understood historically. As video activist DeeDee Halleck, who at the time was a professed McLuhanite, retrospectively wrote in 2002:

> If one reads carefully, one sees immediately that in McLuhans's global village the media activity for villagers (and that includes most of us) was seen as passive. When McLuhan talked about media being the extensions of Man (he definitely did not say Persons), for all his cybernetic language, he was talking of media in a Scholastic sense: media as in Gutenberg—media as a way of distributing the Word.[37]

McLuhan's most famous dictum, "the medium is the message," can be understood in opposition to Greenberg's concept of "medium specificity": McLuhan's rigorism follows the dictates of a technical medium, whereas Greenberg's formalism follows the dictates of normative art genres. From the beginning of US-American video theory, the two video-theoretical discourses sketched out above can be traced back to these opposite media concepts following either Greenberg's formalist delimitations or McLuhan's comparativist dissolution of medium specificity.[38] At the same time, the significance of video at the intersection of discourses in the 1970s can be seen to prefigure the relations between media theory and media art today, often characterized by the incompatibility of techno-centric versus art-oriented perspectives.

Vilém Flusser: Video as an "Intersubjective epistemological instrument"

While McLuhan's huge popularity often obstructs a clear understanding of his central ideas, Vilém Flusser's substantial contributions to video theory have met with little recognition so far. This is partly due to the complex history of his texts that have long remained unpublished or were edited only posthumously. Additionally, Flusser lived and worked in São Paulo, Brazil, until 1972, and then later in southern France, outside of the US-American media discourse formative for the 1970s.[39] Even though Flusser wrote many of his texts in several languages in parallel (German, French, and English), his media philosophy found a wider resonance only in the late 1980s, during Flusser's final years, especially in German-speaking countries.

In the early 1970s, Flusser met the French video art pioneer Fred Forest, who kindled his interest in the medium. Between 1973 and 1991, Flusser then wrote several texts on video, most of which have remained unpublished in English to the present day. He developed and revised this theory in different formats, in three languages, and for different occasions. The two texts reprinted in this chapter show the extraordinary variability of his thinking (for details see the editors' note on the texts).

The cooperation between Flusser and Forest also offers a good example of how video functions at the intersection between practice and theory as well as between art and media discourses. With Ryan or Paik, practice and theory merged in a single person; with Flusser and Forest, synergies rose from a dialogic as well as dialectic tension. Often referring to his own experiences, Flusser took on the role of an involved spectator.[40] His personal encounter with video art stimulated a broader theorization of the medium, which he then phenomenologically tied back to his personal experiences. This created a new mode of authorship: Flusser's writings on video mediate between the perspectives of the producer and the spectator, a hybridization that can be seen as video-specific, since in film and television theory the perspectives of production and reception remain largely separated. Flusser's individual experience of the medium initiated the formation of a theory transcending its initial moment and yet always returning to it—sometimes to criticize and even correct Forest's video work. Just as Baudelaire developed his concept of modernity as a new attitude toward perception using the hardly known drawings of Constantin Guys as a starting point, Flusser's text also reaches far beyond Forest's relatively unknown video practice.[41]

According to Flusser, the social relevance of artistic and creative video practice lies in the possibility of using technical tools opposing and expanding their applications envisaged by the industry: in the case of video, the one-sided interests of commercial television. His insistence on intervening in existing communication structures and becoming involved in the "mutations in human relations" would have offered the perfect theoretical toolkit for the American video pioneers of the 1970s, except that for reasons already mentioned Flusser's writings were unknown in the United States at the time.

Flusser's theories on video were closely interwoven with his writings on the phenomenology of television. His experiences with the communicative potential of video led him to a fundamental critique of the centralist one-to-many structure of broadcast TV. In this context, he also criticized McLuhan's concept of a "global village" (misquoted by Flusser as "cosmic village"), since it was still based on hierarchical communication instead of a democratic opening. The structural possibility of changing television into a decentralized, open network today reads like a media-theoretical draft for the internet and the World Wide Web long before they could be technologically implemented: "Phenomenological vision of the TV box shows that it was projected to provide us with a vision of the world outside and to be a means to talk with others. It is being used instead as a tool to manipulate lonely and alienated masses. Can something be done so that it be used more in accordance with its project?"[42] Flusser later expanded his critique of techno-determinism in the manner of McLuhan with his concept of the "Envisioners," described in a chapter of his book *Into the Universe of Technical Images*: "Envisioners are people who try to turn an automatic apparatus against its own condition of being automatic."[43]

Flusser's video-theoretical contributions for the first time combined media-specific, social, political, and art-theoretical approaches to the medium. He elaborated on the dialogic and participative character of video. According to him the potential of the "technoimagination" to have a social impact was founded in the video-specific capability for instantaneous feedback. Here he referred to collaborative group experiences by and with Fred Forest. During the same time in France, Jean-Luc Godard (who remains unmentioned by Flusser) developed similar ideas on video as a sociopolitical medium.[44]

Flusser's approach to video as a self-reflexive medium would be further developed by Yvonne Spielmann, Ina Blom, and Maurizio Lazzarato (see their contributions in Chapter 2). According to Flusser, video allows us to take possession of the world in a new way that he called the medium "intersubjective epistemological instrument" (*instrument épistémologique intersubjectif*) in a text from 1977 written in French.[45] Combining media-specific and epistemological arguments, Flusser differentiated video from film, photography, television, and painting. He continued to stress the medium's epistemic qualities in later writings, for example, in a short text from 1991 on video as a self-reflexive "mirror with a memory," addressed to the coming generation of video artists: "You have to discover that video is a tool for philosophical speculation. This may be technically very primitive, but intellectually and aesthetically it is all but simple."[46] Flusser's accentuation of the philosophical character of video's self-reflexivity thus stands in diametric contrast to Rosalind Krauss's contemporary theory of a genuinely narcissist self-referentiality of the medium, discussed in the following.

Rosalind Krauss: Narcissism as "Video's Real Medium"

Rosalind Krauss's essay "Video: The Aesthetics of Narcissism" from 1976 remains one of the most-quoted texts on video art even today, sparking a continual discourse on the relation between narcissism and video (see Chapter 3).[47] Two factors contributed to the prominence of Krauss's text: she used it to programmatically position herself as a coeditor of the first issue of the magazine *October* (Figure 1.2),[48] and it was reprinted in several important anthologies on video.[49]

The editorial of that first *October* issue cowritten by Krauss announces: "Its major points of focus will be the visual arts, cinema, performance, music; it will consider literature in significant relation to these."[50] With its decidedly interdisciplinary orientation (even though video significantly is not mentioned in the editorial), *October* would have a fundamental impact on the art discourse over the next decade. Krauss's text on narcissism and video is exemplary for this program of a transmedial art and culture criticism.

Her interdisciplinary approach has to be seen against the background of Clement Greenberg's ideas on modernism and his concept of "medium specificity."[51] Without explicitly mentioning Greenberg in her essay, his former student and future critic Krauss undertook a double transformation: on the one hand, she transferred his paradigm of modernist self-reflexivity onto a technical medium; on the other, she expanded a technological feature, which Wulf Herzogenrath two years earlier had simply described as "instant control of the picture," to an encompassing theory of video's immanent narcissism. Her frame of reference included Sigmund Freud's writings on narcissism as well as the mirror stage in Jacques Lacan's psychoanalytic theory.

In contrast to the contemporaneous film theory founded in psychology (which goes unmentioned by Krauss), the constellation between medium and spectator is not described as a dispositive or apparatus. Instead Krauss writes that "video's real medium is a psychological situation," developing the thesis of a narcissism immanent to the medium.[52] This psychologization of video is accompanied by a normative critique of some examples of video art that according to Krauss simply perpetuate contemporary art's reliance on medial self-mirroring instead of questioning it critically: "The demand for instant replay in the media . . . finds its obvious correlative in an aesthetic mode by

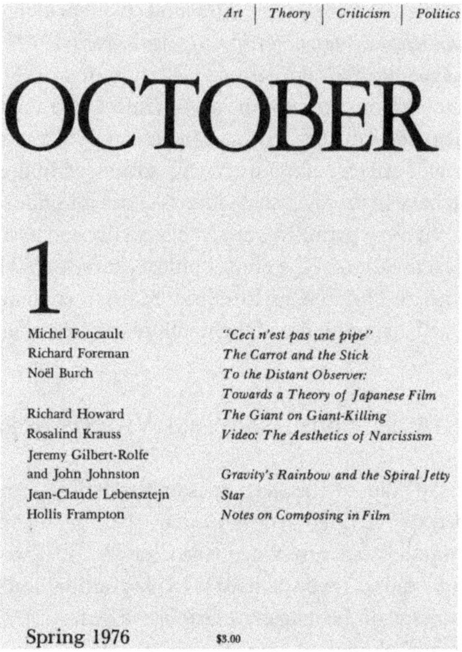

Art | Theory | Criticism | Politics

OCTOBER

1

Michel Foucault	*"Ceci n'est pas une pipe"*
Richard Foreman	*The Carrot and the Stick*
Noël Burch	*To the Distant Observer: Towards a Theory of Japanese Film*
Richard Howard	*The Giant on Giant-Killing*
Rosalind Krauss	*Video: The Aesthetics of Narcissism*
Jeremy Gilbert-Rolfe and John Johnston	*Gravity's Rainbow and the Spiral Jetty*
Jean-Claude Lebensztejn	*Star*
Hollis Frampton	*Notes on Composing in Film*

Spring 1976 $3.00

Figure 1.2 Cover of the first issue of the magazine *October* (Spring 1976), edited by Jeremy Gilbert-Rolfe, Rosalind Krauss, and Annette Michelson.

which the self is created through the electronic device of feedback."[53] Krauss's critique of video's self-referentiality thus places itself within the tradition of the modernist paradigm of reflexiveness in high culture. This is shown in her juxtaposition of "reflection" (video as a narcissist mirror) and "reflexiveness" (painting as a self-reflexive form of art), exemplified by contrasting Vito Acconci's video performances with Jasper Johns paintings.[54]

Numerous other authors have discussed the relation between video and narcissism from media-theoretical and especially art-historical perspectives.[55] Texts by Jean Baudrillard and Mario Perniola from the late 1980s expanded the connection between narcissism and the media toward more general media-theoretical and anthropological questions, without an explicit reference to Krauss.[56] In art theory, Krauss's ideas met with objections. Not naming Krauss but using some of the same examples (Vito Acconci, Joan Jonas), Benjamin H. D. Buchloh in 1985 argued that artists reach a new level of psychological instead of formalist self-reflexivity when using video against the "formalist ban on subject matter and subjectivity (as Greenberg had demanded, it had to be avoided 'like the plague')."[57]

The canonization of Krauss's text went hand in hand with a problematic application of her narcissism theory to later examples of video art without the subtleties of her argument. Ewa Lajer-Burcharth referred to Krauss's "touchstone text of video art theory" and went on to subsume body-related but not necessarily self-referential video pieces of the 1990s under the category of narcissism.[58] Similarly, a number of curatorial projects applied the analogy of video and narcissism to any form of self-images or bodily representations in video.[59] The examination of the self-image function of video, which had been meaningful in a 1970s context, finally lost its media-specific justification, which had been fragile to begin with. Ina Blom summarizes the problematic legacy of this analogy: "This is the contested terrain emerging out of the first attempts to distinguish the specificity of video affordances—fuelled by Krauss's crushing identification of self-monitoring practices in late video art with the late capitalist culture of the self."[60] On the other hand, some of the aspects that Krauss explored could undergo an interesting media-theoretical and art-historical revision with respect to today's self-images in social media. Again, video here can prove its function as an intersection between discourses.

In her later writings, Krauss never explicitly revised the paradigm of video narcissism. Yet when in 1999 she retrospectively held the introduction of video into art accountable as a central factor for the end of the "modernist dream," she also relativized her own attempt to attribute the nonmaterial characteristic of narcissism to the medium itself. She specifically mentioned "the Portapak—a light-weight, cheap video camera and monitor," to which she ascribed the power "to shatter the notion of medium specificity." From here, Krauss derived the new concept of a differential specificity as well as the thesis that art had now entered the era of a "post-medium condition," which would prove consequential for the art theory of recent decades (see the introduction to Chapter 2).[61]

Résumé: Mutual Relationships between Theory and Practice

Despite their originality, Krauss und Flusser continued the two discourses on medium specificity already outlined above: Krauss built on the formalist, art-centered theories of Greenberg, while Flusser made McLuhan's comparativist perspective fertile for video. The examples of Krauss and Flusser also show how authors' predispositions will shape their respective video theories and influence their assessment of the medium. Flusser's communication theory references phenomenology while Krauss refers to models offered by psychoanalysis. Krauss criticizes video art from an art-theoretical perspective while for Flusser the term "art" blocks video's full potential: "Video is a form of perception (a way of knowing). 'Video Art' is a misunderstanding."[62] In contrast to Krauss's theory-based, conceptual method, Flusser's approach is experimental, based on direct experience: "If you want to know what video is you have to handle it."[63] This principle is realized in the practice-based artistic theories of Paik and Ryan.

Apart from the distinction between art-theoretical and media-theoretical perspectives, the texts introduced here define another fundamental difference: the relations between theory and practice that they bring up explicitly or implicitly. The authors either proceed from their own practical work with video (Ryan, Paik), they reflect on their own views of the medium (Flusser, partly also McLuhan), or they take specific applications (e.g., of video art) as an occasion for theory building (Krauss, partly also Flusser). Personal experiences can spark comprehensive theories of the medium (Flusser on video as an epistemological medium). Generalizations on essential characteristics of the medium can emerge from a reflexive critical distance toward video technology (Krauss on the immanent narcissism of video). Concrete individual perception and detached reflective analysis can equally serve as starting points for theories with a claim to general validity.

These examples also reveal another essential question: the relation of video-theoretical approaches to their object, which will be relevant to all contributions in this reader. How do personal experiences with the medium affect theory formation? What effect does individual practice have on the concept of media specificity? These same questions have already been raised in the theories of art, photography, film, and television. In art theory, for example, an objectifying distance has been established as standard in academia. The former knowledge practice of the connoisseurs, who often practiced art themselves and were learning through emulation, was eliminated from academic discourse in this process. A comparable fast-motion change from production to reception theory can be found in the histories of video and film theory, whereas television theory has always been oriented toward reception.[64] A unique characteristic of video lies in the copresence of the reception and production perspectives in the medium, since access to firsthand experience of video technology is not restricted to professionals—as in a film production—but can be had in an everyday context. This becomes especially clear in closed-circuit video experiences as analyzed by Vilém Flusser (for more examples, see Chapter 3). Accordingly, the development of video theory announces the role of the author as an involved spectator, later to become an inevitable ingredient in theories of interactive and internet-based social media.

Notes

1 Wulf Herzogenrath in his contribution to the "Open Circuits" conference in 1974. See Wulf Herzogenrath, "Notes on Video as an Artistic Medium," in *The New Television: A Public/Private Art. Essays, Statements, and Videotapes Based on "Open Circuits: An International Conference on the Future of Television," organized by Fred Barzyk [et al.] for the Museum of Modern Art, New York City*, ed. Douglas Davis, Allison Simmons, and Fred Barzyk (Cambridge, MA: MIT Press, 1977), 88.

2 See especially Greenberg's essays "Avant-Garde and Kitsch" (1939) and "Towards a Newer Laocoon" (1940), which had repercussions for decades (see Chapter 2 for a more detailed discussion).

3 David Antin, "Television: Video's Frightful Parent," *Artforum* 14, no. 4 (December 1975), 36; reprinted in Chapter 5 of this volume.

4 On this point also see Chris Meigh-Andrews, *A History of Video Art* (New York and London: Bloomsbury, 2014), 119–25.

5 Ryan did his alternative service as an assistant to McLuhan. See Peter Sachs Collopy, *The Revolution Will Be Videotaped: Making a Technology of Consciousness in the Long 1960s*, PhD (Philadelphia: University of Pennsylvania, 2015), 152.

6 Paul Ryan, "A Genealogy of Video," *Leonardo* 21, no. 1 (1988), 41.

7 Randy Sherman, "Video Enclosing," *Radical Software* 2, no. 4 (1973), 23.

8 Cf. also Chris Meigh-Andrews, *A History of Video Art*, 122.

9 Michael Shamberg and Raindance Corporation, *Guerrilla Television* (Saint Louis: Holt, Rinehart & Winston, 1971), 24.
10 Gerald Emanuel Stearn, ed., *McLuhan: Hot & Cool, a Primer for the Understanding of & Critical Symposium with a Rebuttal by McLuhan* (New York: The Dial Press, 1967), 300.
11 Marshall McLuhan with graphic artist Quentin Fiore and publicist, producer, and editor Jerome Agel, *The Medium Is the Massage with Marshall McLuhan* (Columbia Records, 1967), produced by John Simon; audio at http://www.ubu.com/sound/mcluhan.html.
12 Marshall McLuhan, "Draft for Gutenberg Video," n.d. [1960], typescript, National Archives of Canada, H. Marshall McLuhan files, MG 31, D 156, vol. 73, file 5; reprinted in the present chapter of this volume.
13 In 1960, the term "video" had different connotations from those that would be developed by end of the decade. McLuhan is referring to the professional VTR equipment in television studios; see the editor's note on McLuhan's "Draft for Gutenberg Video" in this chapter.
14 Shamberg and Raindance Corporation, *Guerrilla Television*, 10.
15 Paul Ryan, *Birth and Death and Cybernation: Cybernetics of the Sacred* (New York: Gordon and Breach, 1973), xii.
16 Paul Ryan, "Videotape: Thinking about a Medium," *Educators Guide to Media & Methods* (December 1968), 36–41.
17 Cf. Paul Ryan's artistic concept *Self-Processing* (1970); reprinted in Chapter 3 of this volume.
18 As far on as 1977, a shortened version of Ryan's statement served as the motto of the video section of Documenta 5, where the signet "VT ≠ TV" warned visitors to expect unusual visual experiences (see Chapter 5).
19 Nam June Paik, "Die Roboter-Opera töten?" (1965), in Paik, *Niederschriften eines Kulturnomaden: Aphorismen, Briefe, Texte*, ed. Edith Decker (Cologne: DuMont, 1992), 111.
20 Diagram in Nam June Paik, *Electronic Art* (New York: Galeria Bonino, 1965).
21 Nam June Paik, Norbert Wiener, and Marshall McLuhan (1967), in Nam June Paik, *We Are in Open Circuits*, ed. John G. Hanhardt, Gregory Zinman, and Edith Decker-Phillips (Cambridge, MA: MIT Press, 2019), 123.
22 Douglas Davis, interview with Nam June Paik, in Douglas Davis, *Art and the Future: A History-Prophecy of the Collaboration between Science, Technology, and Art* (London: Thames & Hudson, 1973), 149.
23 See the contribution by Dieter Daniels in Chapter 12 for the first video-looping device constructed by Paik in 1965, which was more a tool than an interactive piece.
24 Quoted from a contemporary film documentation of *McLuhan Caged*, to be seen as an excerpt in *Nam June Paik: Open Your Eyes*, dir. Maria Anna Tappeiner (Cologne: WDR, 2010).
25 Jay David Bolter and Richard Grusin, *Remediation: Understanding New Media* (Cambridge, MA: MIT Press, 1999). For the debate on Bolter und Grusin's theses see the introduction to Chapter 2.
26 In all probability Paik's *McLuhan Caged* was the first video work to be shown in a big museum exhibition, *The Machine as Seen at the End of the Mechanical Age* at the Museum of Modern Art, New York, 1968. The unsigned description of the work in the catalog reads: "Paik's manipulation of the TV set has the subtle brutality of

judo, which turns someone's own force against himself. It is the frontal attack on the principal modern machine for manipulating men's minds for commercial or ideological reasons." Ibid., 197.

27 Jud Yalkut, "Art and Technology of Nam June Paik," interview, *Arts Magazine* (April 1968), 51.

28 Frank Gillette, "McLuhan and Recent Art History," 1998, http://davidsonsfiles.org/McLuhanandRecentArtHistory.html.

29 Sigmund Freud to André Breton, December 26, 1932, in André Breton, *Communicating Vessels*, trans. Mary Ann Caws and Geoffrey T. Harris (Lincoln: University of Nebraska Press, 1990), 152.

30 Neither in *Understanding Media* (1964), *The Medium Is Massage* (1967), nor *War and Peace in the Global Village* (1968) is there any mention of video. On the other hand, there are fifty-three entries on "television" in *Understanding Media*. McLuhan, *Understanding Media: The Extensions of Man*, critical edition, ed. Terrence Gordon (Corte Madera: Gingko Press, 2003), 602.

31 A problematic exception is the posthumous continuation of McLuhan's ideas nine years after his death in a book edited by Bruce R. Powers. In this allegedly cooperative project between 1976 and 1984, Powers uses McLuhan's name to disseminate theories on "video-related media," including fiber optical cable, computers, and satellites. Marshall McLuhan and Bruce R. Powers, *The Global Village: Transformations in World Life and Media in the 21st Century* (New York and Oxford: Oxford University Press, 1989).

32 Howard Polskin, "Conversation with Marshall McLuhan," *Videography* (October 1977), 30, 57–67.

33 Marshall McLuhan, *Organized Ignorance*, address at Video 74, Sweden, June 5, 1974, typescripts, notes (page 3). National Archives of Canada, H. Marshall McLuhan files, MG 31, D 156, vol. 137, file 41.

34 McLuhan, *Understanding Media*, 445.

35 Ibid., 443.

36 Ibid., 78f.

37 DeeDee Halleck, *Hand-Held Visions: The Impossible Possibilities of Community Media* (New York: Fordham University Press, 2002), 19.

38 In this sense Liz Kim writes: "In video, the technological 'medium' of McLuhan intersected the modernist 'medium' of Greenberg." Kim, "Much Ado about Medium: Greenberg, McLuhan, and the Formalist Problem in Early Video Criticism in New York," *Moving Image Review & Art Journal* 5, nos. 1 & 2 (2016), 47.

39 In 1974, Flusser taught for a few months as a guest professor at the Columbia University, the Fairleigh Dickinson University, and the State University of New York in Buffalo. In the same year, he took part in the conference "Open Circuits: The Future of Television" at the Museum of Modern Art, but then in 1975 moved from the United States to France due to a lack of professional openings.

40 As early as 1973, in his text on Gérald Minkoff's close-circuit video installations, Flusser stressed the significance of his own experiences in interacting with his video self-image for building a theory. Flusser, "Minkoffs Spiegel" (1973), in idem, *Lob der Oberflächlichkeit: Für eine Phänomenologie der Medien* (Mannheim: Bollmann, 1993), 227–32.

41 "France's most famous unknown artist," boasts the blurb for a monograph on Fred Forest written by Michael F. Leruth, https://mitpress.mit.edu/books/fred-forests-u topia.

42 Vilém Flusser, "Toward a Phenomenology of Television," undated, unpublished typescript, www.flusserbrasil.com/arte190.pdf. This text is recommended as a complement to Flusser's contribution on video in the present volume. It was written after he had participated in the conference "Open Circuits: An International Conference on the Future of Television" at the Museum of Modern Art in 1974, developing the thoughts he had delivered at the event and taking works by Nam June Paik, Woody Vasulka, and videos from the US-American underground into consideration. See Flusser, "Two Approaches to the Phenomenon, Television," in *The New Television: A Public/Private Art. Essays, Statements, and Videotapes Based on "Open Circuits: An International Conference on the Future of Television," organized by Fred Barzyk et al. for the Museum of Modern Art, New York City*, ed. Douglas Davis, Allison Simmons, and Fred Barzyk (Cambridge, MA: MIT Press, 1977), 234–47; Vilém Flusser, "Für eine Phänomenologie des Fernsehens," in idem, *Lob der Oberflächlichkeit: Für eine Phänomenologie der Medien* (Mannheim: Bollmann 1995), 180–200.

43 Vilém Flusser, *Into the Universe of Technical Images* (Minneapolis: University of Minnesota Press, 2011), 19.

44 See Jean-Luc Godard's contribution in Chapter 4 of this volume.

45 Vilém Flusser, "L' art sociologique et la vidéo à travers la demarche de Fred Forest," in *Fred Forest: Art sociologique. Vidéo* (Paris: 10 18, Union Générale d'Editions), 409. Here Flusser (like Nam June Paik, Bill Viola, and Maurizio Lazzarato) compares the different temporalities of film and video: "La bande est un miroir qui bouge dans le temps linéaire." Ibid., 104.

46 Vilém Flusser, "Discover European Video," in the catalog to an exhibition of Nam June Paik's students at Kunstakademie Düsseldorf, *Discover European Video* (New York: Anthology Film Archives; Neuss: Kunstraum Neuss, 1990), 6; reprinted in Chapter 3 of this volume.

47 Rosalind Krauss, "Video: The Aesthetics of Narcissism," *October* no. 1 (Spring 1976), ed. Jeremy Gilbert-Rolfe, Rosalind Krauss, and Annette Michelson, vol. 1, 50–64; reprinted in Chapter 3 of this volume.

48 Anne M. Wagner likewise points to the strategic motivation of Krauss's "Video: The Aesthetics of Narcissism": "Her essay remains one of the most stimulating studies of video to date, and whose interest seems to me underscored by its use as her contribution to the inaugural issue of *October*." Wagner, "Performance, Video, and the Rhetoric of Presence," *October* no. 91 (Winter 2000), 68.

49 Reprints of "Video: The Aesthetics of Narcissism" can be found in the following anthologies, among others: Gregory Battcock, ed., *New Artists' Video: A Critical Anthology* (New York: E.P. Dutton, 1978); John G. Hanhardt, *Video Culture: A Critical Investigation* (Rochester, NY: Peregrine Smith Books and Visual Studies Workshop Press, 1987); Tanya Leighton, ed., *Art and the Moving Image: A Critical Reader* (London: Tate Publishing in association with Afterall, 2008); Rosalind Krauss, *Perpetual Inventory* (Cambridge, MA: MIT Press, 2010).

50 The Editors, "About October," *October* no. 1 (Spring 1976), 4.

51 While Krauss does not use the term "medium specificity," she instead speaks of "material factors specific to a particular form," which of course alludes to Clement Greenberg's concept. Krauss, "Video: The Aesthetics of Narcissism," 52. For her direct engagement with Greenberg's ideas, see the introduction to Chapter 2.

52 Ibid., 57. For the context of Krauss's argument, see the reprint of her text in Chapter 3 of this volume.

53 Ibid., 59.

54 Ibid., 56.

55 An overview of reactions to Krauss's narcissism theory can be found in Irene Schubiger, *Selbstdarstellung in der Videokunst: Zwischen Performance und "Self-editing"* (Berlin: Reimer, 2004), 26–30.

56 Jean Baudrillard, "Videowelt und fraktales Subjekt" (1988), in Jean Baudrillard, Hannes Böhringer, Vilém Flusser, Heinz von Foerster, Friedrich Kittler, and Peter Weibel, *Philosophien der neuen Technologien*, ed. Ars Electronica (Berlin: Merve, 1989), 113–31; Mario Pemiola, "Videokulturen als Spiegel," in *Im Netz der Systeme*, ed. Ars Electronica (Berlin: Merve, 1990), 50–74.

57 Benjamin H. D. Buchloh, "From Gadget Video to Agit Video: Some Notes on Four Recent Video Works," *Art Journal* 45, no. 3, issue "Video: The Reflexive Medium" (Autumn 1985), 219.

58 Ewa Lajer-Burcharth, "Real Bodies: Video in the 1990s," *Art History* 20 (June 1997), 186.

59 E.g., the curatorial project *Video Narcissism* at High Line Art, New York, September 28–November 22, 2017; https://www.thehighline.org/art/projects/video-narcissism/.

60 Ina Blom, *The Autobiography of Video: The Life and Times of a Memory Technology* (Berlin: Sternberg Press, 2016), 35. See also Blom's contribution in Chapter 2 of this volume.

61 Rosalind Krauss, *A Voyage on the North Sea: Art in the Age of the Post-Medium Condition* (London: Thames & Hudson, 2000), 30, 24, 32. See also Andreas Broeckmann, "'Postmedia' Discourses: A Working Paper," Version 2, 2014 https://abroeck.in-berlin.de/texts/.

62 Flusser, "Mutations in Human Relations?" typescript (1973–1974), 144.

63 Vilém Flusser, "Das Video erforschen" (1975), in idem., *Lob der Oberflächlichkeit: Für eine Phänomenologie der Medien* (Mannheim: Bollmann, 1995), 234.

64 John Thornton Caldwell examines the implicit theory of television production and offers a detailed critique of television theory's previous orientation toward reception. See Caldwell, *Televisuality: Style, Crisis, and Authority in American Television* (New Brunswick: Rutgers University Press, 1995); excerpted in Chapter 5 of this volume.

Draft for Gutenberg Video (1960): Facsimile

Marshall McLuhan

Editors' note: The origins of Marshall McLuhan's "Draft for Gutenberg Video" are closely connected to his work on the "Report on Project in Understanding New Media" for the National Association of Educational Broadcasters (NAEB), which commissioned him to develop an educational program for "media literacy" in secondary school.[1] In the resulting substantial typescript, written between 1959 and 1960, he laid the cornerstones for his theories on a media genealogy, which he would largely carry over into his book *Understanding Media: The Extensions of Man* (1964).[2] The "Purpose of Project" of the NAEB typescript is "to provide an approach to media and a syllabus for teaching the nature and effects of media in secondary schools. A new tactic was used, namely to consider not so much the constituents nor the 'content' of media, as their *effects*."[3]

In the NAEB Report we see the educational roots of McLuhan's famous dictum, "the medium is the message." He developed a series of charts to visualize his theories on each medium explored in the report (Figure 1.3).[4] The key objective to these diagrams was "to isolate the fact that 'content' of any medium is another medium" and, as McLuhan adds, if his project was successfully doing that, "it would have justified the expense involved many times over."[5] He continues: "In my charts I show as best I can how to spot the message of medium as medium. . . . My entire syllabus proceeds on

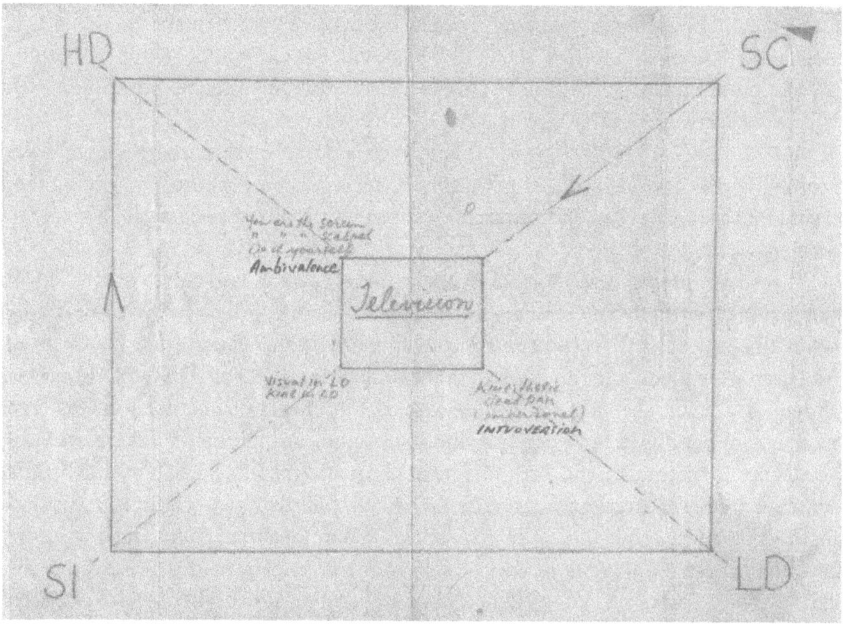

Figure 1.3 Marshall McLuhan's hand-drawn study for the "Television" chart in the NAEB Report, McLuhan Archive, National Archives of Canada.

the principle that Low Definition (LD) is necessary to good teaching. . . . LD works by withholding information. LD media like telephone and television are major educational instruments because they offer inadequate information."[6] Low definition is contrasted by high definition (HD in the charts), and thus McLuhan's famous and often confusing separation between "hot" (high-definition, nonparticipative) versus "cold" (low-definition, participative) media likewise has its origins in this research assignment on the function and effects of media.

In the framework of the NAEB project, these media effects were not merely to be analyzed but also to be tested. In the appendix (Part VII, Exhibits) we find two teleplays to which McLuhan contributed content besides personally appearing in the program. The script titled "The Teenager and the Media" (written by Daryl Duke) combines filmic and language-based scenes with McLuhan impersonating himself, while "The Gutenberg Galaxy: A Voyage between Two Worlds" is the transcript of an eponymous television broadcast of McLuhan in conversation with Harley Parker and Robert Shafer.

The typescript "Draft for Gutenberg Video," an excerpt from which is first published here, was not part of the NAEB Report and most likely never realized as a television broadcast. The McLuhan Archive of the National Archives of Canada holds two drafts for the script, in consecutive states of revision.[7] The second one is titled "Draft for Gutenberg Video" and dated "March 31st/60." In this version, the educational approach of the NAEB project is translated into the scenic form of a film. "Video" is used merely as a technical term mentioned only in the title.[8] Since in 1960 consumer video did not yet exist, McLuhan here refers to the professional VTR facilities of the television studios. Thus "video" is a designated production tool and not the object of an analysis as a medium.

In the NAEB Report, McLuhan provides the following particulars: "March 18–20: Began discussions with Robert Shafer of Wayne, and Lee Dreyfus of Wayne educational TV station, about the possibility of doing a video tape on the Gutenberg era. Subsequent trips were necessary for the rehearsal and shooting of same, as follows: March 31–April 1; May 27–May 28; June 3–June 6."[9] It follows that "Draft for Gutenberg Video," dated March 31, was not realized as a program but served as an experimental preliminary tryout for the scripts (Part VII, Exhibits) subsequently realized as classical TV program formats within the NAEB project.

The scene descriptions for "Gutenberg Video" are relatively abstract and do not contain written-out "Visual–Audio" tracks as the other scripts do. Among other things, excerpts from experimental films by the Canadian director Norman McLaren were planned to be used. In the twenty-seven shots of "Draft for Gutenberg Video," McLuhan sketches out the capacities and effects of historical and current media from handwriting to printing and film, radio, and television in an associative sequence. Structurally, the script is related to McLuhan's later books. His first seminal media-theoretical work, *The Gutenberg Galaxy* from 1962, is comprised of 107 short text sequences ordered associatively rather than following a system.[10] McLuhan's text montage is related to film montage and from this perspective one can see *The Gutenberg Galaxy* as the (later, worked-out) book tying in to the concept of the (unrealized) "Gutenberg Video." In "Draft for Gutenberg Video" McLuhan developed his media theory in a form conceived for the video medium, before two years later it became a book on the end of print culture.

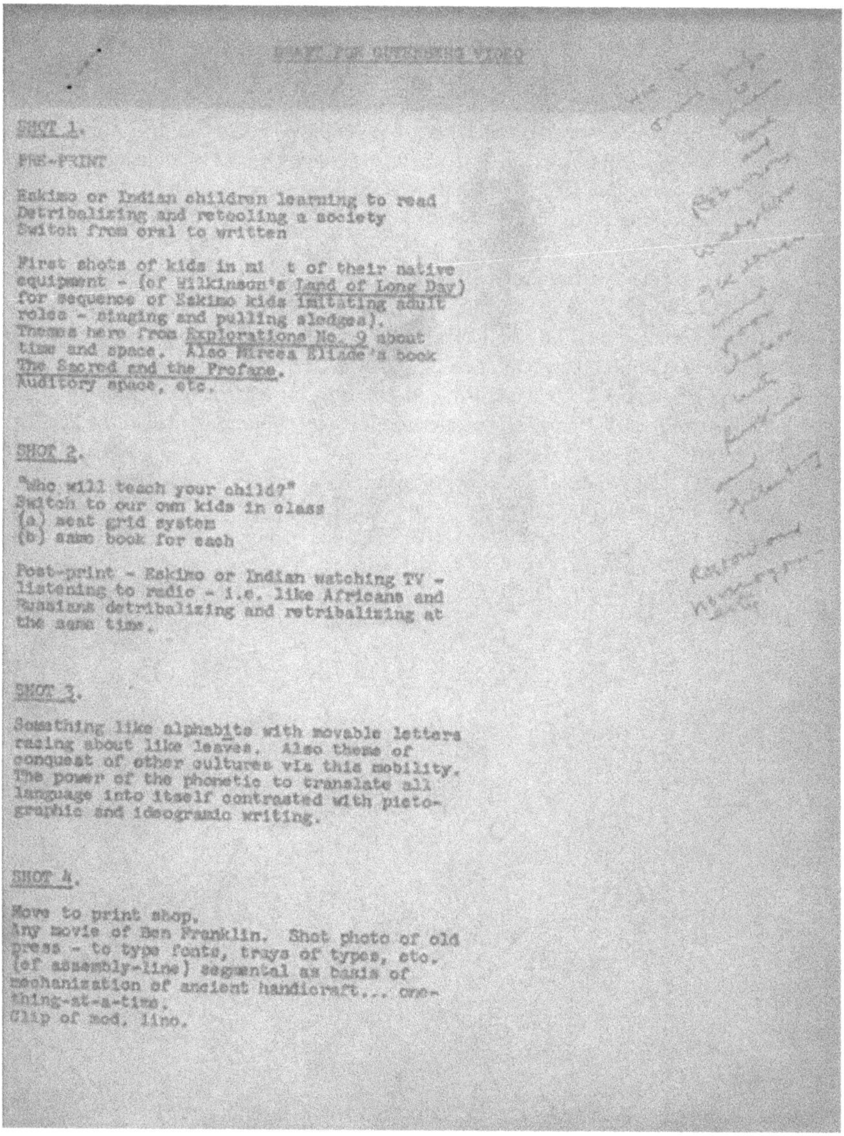

SHOT 1.

PRE-PRINT

Eskimo or Indian children learning to read
Detribalizing and retooling a society
Switch from oral to written

First shots of kids in mi t of their native
equipment - (cf Wilkinson's Land of Long Day)
for sequence of Eskimo kids imitating adult
roles - singing and pulling sledges).
Themes here from Explorations No. 9 about
time and space. Also Mircea Eliade's book
The Sacred and the Profane.
Auditory space, etc.

SHOT 2.

"Who will teach your child?"
Switch to our own kids in class
(a) seat grid system
(b) same book for each

Post-print - Eskimo or Indian watching TV -
listening to radio - i.e. like Africans and
Russians detribalizing and retribalizing at
the same time.

SHOT 3.

Something like alphabits with movable letters
racing about like leaves. Also theme of
conquest of other cultures via this mobility.
The power of the phonetic to translate all
language into itself contrasted with picto-
graphic and ideogramic writing.

SHOT 4.

Move to print shop.
Any movie of Ben Franklin. Shot photo of old
press - to type fonts, trays of types, etc.
(cf assembly-line) segmental as basis of
mechanization of ancient handicraft... one-
thing-at-a-time.
Clip of mod. lino.

Figure 1.4 Marshall McLuhan, "Draft for Gutenberg Video," first page of the typescript, McLuhan Archive, National Archives of Canada.

Notes

1 National Association of Educational Broadcasters, consultant: Marshall McLuhan, "Report on Project in Understanding New Media," typescript, June 30, 1960; online at http://blogs.ubc.ca/nfriesen/files/2014/11/McLuhanRoPiUNM.pdf.

2 See W. Terrence Gordon, "Transforming the Report," in Marshall McLuhan, *Understanding Media: The Extensions of Man*, ed. W. Terrence Gordon (Corte Madera: Ginko Press, 2003), 539–43 and 478.
3 "Purpose of Project 69," NAEB Report, 1.
4 Charts in the NAEB Report: Speech, page 35; Writing, 46; Print, 57; Prints, 65; Press, 78; Photo, 87; Telegraph, 96; Telephone, 105; Phonograph, 112; Film (Movie), 118; Radio, 129; Television, 137.
5 "General Introduction to Charts," NAEB Report, 14.
6 Ibid., 14f.
7 Marshall McLuhan, "Draft for Gutenberg Video," n.d. (1960), typescript; carbon copy typescripts; printed typescripts; notes; charts, National Archives of Canada, H. Marshall McLuhan files, MG 31, D 156, vol. 73, file 5. This is the revised version of the previous, untitled typescript.
8 In the NAEB Report, "videotape" is mentioned only once in passing in the section "NAEB Report: New Media and the New Education," paper presented at the DAVI Convention, Cincinnati (March 1960), v.
9 "Itinerary and Summary of the Activities of the Consultant," NAEB Report, 3.
10 Marshall McLuhan, *The Gutenberg Galaxy. The Making of Typographic Man* (London, 1962).

Biennale Seminar on Video, Venice 1977

Marshall McLuhan

Thank you for your generous welcome and words, senora. Ladies and gentlemen, we have a lot of wonderful things to talk about this afternoon; and most of them are related to the Biennale. One has indicated the scope and development of this enterprise which is in your midst and which uses all these new resources including video and the electronic media. As a student of these media, I would like to say some things about what they have to tell you and some of the things they will do to you by using them.

The nature of any human technology is necessarily the expression of our own bodies. All human technology is an expression of our own physical being, our nervous System, in the case of collective media, an extension of our own central nervous System and these factors are things which present themselves to us as figures against a ground of hidden effects and potential and are in need of a study. [. . .]

But anyway I'm trying to illustrate the principle of figure and ground. The figure is always visible and the ground is always hidden. Now when you come for example to the theme of this conference, videotape, it is a figure: What is the hidden ground that makes it interesting to anybody? I assure you that in North America it holds very little interest for anybody. Here at the Biennale there is a big interest in videotape. Why? What is the hidden ground of videotape that makes it meaningful here at the Biennale right now? Because it is a ground that requires a great deal of study to make any meaning out at all for the North American. [. . .]

Suddenly in the twentieth century, art becomes dominant once more. The study of primitive traditions of life, of anthropology becomes suddenly sympathetic understanding.

What we call an electronic man is a right-hemisphere man. This includes the video world that this Biennale is concerned with. The Biennale world of this institution requires study of what you are interested in. Are you interested in the total ground of human society? Or are you interested in the figure of civilization? [. . .]

Figure-ground is my theme as it were, and when you're dealing with videotape, let me suggest that you are dealing with a form that is highly mythical, that is capable of capturing the mythic structure and patterns of things. It can pick up things so fast that the process itself becomes the pattern that you see. Video recording is mythical in its structure. It is structurally mythical. This is true of any electronic form of knowledge. It apprehends the situation as mythical or total.

And so the Biennale with its new resource of video recording is well on its way to a very successful career of mythological understanding. [. . .]

When TV appeared and film went inside of TV, film became an art form. Cinema was universally and instantly recognized as an art form with the arrival of TV. You can see where I'm heading with videotape. Every object in the environment becomes an art form. It goes inside the new medium of video. So you put the old art inside of video and you have a new art form. Video has become an exciting new toy for the European. It is a new technology. In North America, video is not a toy, it is a major technology for daily work. [. . .]

The great example is perhaps the instant replay which enables sports and athletics to exist simultaneously in two dimensions; in the replay you get the meaning, in the event you get the action. But replay transforms the athletic action into an art form. Many people prefer to see the football game in the video monitor than to watch it in the real outdoor action. When football and cricket or swimming or anything was put on the instant replay, they are transformed from instant cognition into recognition. The instant replay translates your ordinary cognitive experience into an artistic event of recognition, playing it twice, (re-cognition). [. . .]

That brings us back to videotape. The word "happening" was what gave me the clue this morning when I was watching these videotapes: it gave me the clue to the nature of video. Remember the days when happenings were new? A happening is a figure in a ground. Now an event is a figure without a ground. When you pull the ground away, you have an event; when you put the ground in, you have a happening. We can talk about this later. Structurally, a happening is a figure in a ground. Video does this for ordinary objects that can be recorded. And for body language and for anything that you wish to put on that form of communication. It's transformed into a sort of happening, a kind of figure-ground relation is established by video.

Art, great paintings which you see usually in museums or in great collections, have become old hat because the figure-ground relation is dead. But put the same things into video form and they come alive again, new art form. So one of the excitements is to put the daily papers, the advertising world, put popular culture in video form and you have a new experience. The old things are translated into an exciting new art form.

An archive is in a sense a way of transforming ordinary objects of the world into an art form. For I think Malraux in his *Le Musée imaginaire* explained that the museum was a new art form in the eighteenth century. Up to that time there had been no museums, there had only been private collections. And with the coming of the museum, which is an archive, everything was transformed into a new kind of experience. This is happening to us with the video tape recording. One more thing to mention, video has nothing in common with film. It has exactly nothing.

Video is seen by rear projection. The nature of video is this rear projection. And film is all front projection; film is all left hemisphere, and video is all right hemisphere. Two completely opposed ways of looking at the world. The tube comes at you through the screen, whereas film is projected on the screen, when you are watching video or TV you are the screen. You are not the spectator, but you are involved in the action. The fascinating novelty of TV or video experience is that the viewer is involved in the action. Like the instant replay.

Involved with it is right hemisphere and video is a new right hemisphere instrument. The old film world of the microfilm and the old recording mechanisms, completely left hemisphere. Lineal connected, story line, scenario, sound, whereas video tends to use the ordinary environment as a scenario. It does not need any special actors or any special story line. [. . .]

The character in the video action is the environment itself. The whole ground becomes character.

This is pretty complicated, I know. I have spent literally thousands and thousands of hours with my students trying to explain the difference between film and TV. And

I know it is very difficult. I find the hemisphere thing a big help because it makes it much easier to explain the differences that all these years film was using the left hemisphere and TV began to use the right hemisphere. For the first time, videotape is the right hemisphere and therefore ideally suited to record the environment of culture and technology. It is cheap whereas film is expensive. And soft. Well, I have said more than enough. The idea now is to involve the panel here in a discussion of video which they themselves are familiar with. And to hear your questions and thought also. Thank you very much. [. . .]

I tried to explain in my first talk here that television is not visual. It uses the eye as an ear. This is the observation of Tony Schwartz in a book about TV image. He calls this book *The Responsive Chord*. It's a book put out by the Anchor press. He points out and analyses the structure of the TV image, that it is acoustic instruction. It is not an individual point of view. It includes touch and kinetics and sound. The images that we saw this morning on videotape were sculptural, they were dance, they were sound, they were multi-sensuous. The peculiarity of the TV medium is the multi-sensuousness. It includes all of the senses we have. In a single instant. This is not characteristic of print, or of the cinema. And having this strange structure, TV or video naturally encourages the user to explore all sorts of possibilities of this new form. But you ask why it is right hemisphere and I try to say, it is because it is multi-sensuous and not specialist. The left hemisphere is specialist. It creates the specialist sciences and scholarship. It creates the mathematician, the quantifier, the measurer, it makes possible all those forms. But the right hemisphere is not of that kind.

From Marshall McLuhan, "Biennale Seminar on Video, Venice 1977," in *Art, Artist & the Media*, ed. Richard Kriesche (Graz: AVZ books, 1978), unpag. Transcription by Maria Gloria Bicocchi.

Editors' note: In October 1977 McLuhan was the keynote speaker at a seminar on video art organized and curated by Maria Gloria Bicocchi for the ASAC Archivio Storico delle Arti Contemporanee at La Biennale di Venezia. (As the seminar took place between the regular Biennale editions of 1976 and 1978, shortly before the extracurricular "Biennale of Dissent" in 1977, McLuhan's initial remarks address the institution rather than a specific exhibition.) Maria Gloria Bicocchi and her husband Giancarlo had founded art/tapes/22 in Florence, a center for video that in 1972 and 1976 acted as the main setting for the key moments that brought video art to Italy. Bill Viola acted as the center's technical director from 1974 to 1976. In 1976, Maria Gloria and Giancarlo Bicocchi decided to donate the fund consisting of 129 videotapes they had independently produced and distributed to the ASAC.

In two long talks and a discussion with the public at the seminar, McLuhan covered a large field of topics (but said few words about video). A predominant subject is his theory on the cultural differences of the brain hemispheres. He argues: "Now the left hemisphere is being superseded by the right today because underneath the right hemisphere today there is an environment of simultaneous, instantaneous information which is electronic. Electronic information as an environment pushes the right hemisphere up into dominance." For this topic see also: Marshall McLuhan, "The Brain and the Media: The 'Western' Hemisphere," *Journal of Communication*, vol. 28, no. 4 (Fall 1978), 54–60.

Videotape: Thinking about a Medium (1968)

Paul Ryan

[. . .]

Videotaping: Infolding Information

VT is not TV. If anything, it's TV flipped into itself. Television, as the root of the word implies, has to do with transmitting information over distance. Videotape has to do with infolding information. Instant replay offers a living feedback that creates a topology of awareness other than the tic-tac-toe grid.[1] Anthropologist Edmund Carpenter tells a story about two Eskimos who went on solo trips around an island. They were asked independently to draw maps of the island. Their maps were quite good replicas of the island yet they both differed in one significant aspect. Each had camped and hunted near a certain cove and that area on their maps was larger according to the length of time each had stayed there. Videotape creates a kind of Eskimo awareness of time-space. Especially with the half-inch battery operated portables one can sculpt time-space in accord with the contours of experience. Information can be infolded to enrich experience.

Participating in Your Own Audience Participation

With videotape, the performer and the audience can be one and the same, either simultaneously or sequentially. In an actor's class a student did a piece from *Spoon River Anthology* first without the monitor, with me shooting her face from a distance with a 1–10 zoom. Then she did the same piece facing into the monitor so she could see herself while performing. Delighted with both experiences, she said that she felt much more secure facing the monitor than with me at a distance using the camera and no monitor. The distance shooting without monitor left her with no feedback other than the glassy-eyed lens. With her performance extended into the monitor, she was, to use McLuhan's phrase, "participating in her own audience participation." Feedback was immediate and self-supplied. She could use simultaneously her expressive abilities as an actress and the set of responses she had as an ordinary theater-goer. She could take in her own performance. Enter the talented audience. Add to this the dimension of instant replay and a new kind of performer is bound to develop.

This actress's sense of security and confidence with the monitor seems akin to my whole experience with videotape. I am developing a different sense of myself. Very much like the sense of myself I have when I swim lazily. Very much like the Chi sense of myself I have gotten in doing some T'ai Chi Twan. I feel more able to move in my own fullness. And this awareness extends beyond the actual use of tape. Confidence seems almost to be a function of communicating with oneself. [. . .]

Student Liberation by Information

Authority is based on information. Cybernetics and papal pronouncements have made that apparent. Upon introduction of a half-inch system into one school the drama teacher complained: "Students are notoriously their own worst directors. If they start seeing themselves on tape they'll start directing themselves." Her authority as director comes from a tradition she knows and observation of the students' performance in relation to that tradition. With the feedback from videotape the students can take in their own outside, can take in information that increases their control over their performance. The director's role shifts toward that of a consultant, someone who offers perceptions from what is now an alien tradition.

There is a very real sense in which portable VTR is a complete cybernetic system. It is not part of a system like an 8mm camera that needs the drugstore developer; it is not like the TV in your home which is only one terminus of a huge network. Portable VTR is a self-contained system for processing culture—family culture, classroom culture, therapeutic culture. It has input and output and can be operated without experts. It offers a completeness in itself. [. . .]

In the sense that a portable videotape recorder is a complete system in itself, it is structurally different from other VTR equipment. Much like the TV generation which lives in radical cultural discontinuity, claiming they must be father and mother to each other since they in fact have no cultural parents, so this small user equipment is, from a user's point of view, completely new. It is its own baby.

Broadcast television in ten years will reap the fruit of this diversity and decentralization of PVTR in the hands of kids only to the extent that the centralized pattern is not stenciled onto these systems. One factor clearly works in favor of decentralization. The VTR systems of the different manufacturers are incompatible. There are 15 or 16 different formats. Electronic transfer can be made but only on expensive equipment. This will encourage small users to feedback into their own situations rather than feed off it for others. [. . .]

"To Monitor or Not to Monitor"

The videocorder tends to divide process phenomena into those that lend themselves to simultaneous monitoring and those that do not. Putting on makeup, combing hair, shaving, *Spoon River* practice; these lend themselves to simultaneous monitoring. Other things, such as the classroom composition, work better without simultaneous monitoring. The monitor (from *moneo*, warning) acts as a censor and inhibits the experience. In using videotape equipment, it is necessary to understand the process at hand in these terms.

Self-Erasing, Self-Effacing

Once upon a time I had a teacher who considered the eraser to be the worst thing that ever happened to the pencil. He liked things thought out before they were written out.

This defender of the pure pencil was onto something. An eraser creates a different style of thinking. Videotape is erasable. We can redo it if we don't like it. Since videotape, "live" TV is mostly tape, and it's different. Hugh Downs is among the many who defend pure television as the "now" medium.

"Live on tape" means all those tribal things we call living on a magnetic tape that permits detachment *à la* literacy. Adoption agencies now use videotape. The parents see the child on tape first. The "live" child can be considered without the immediacy of his needs present. Sounder judgments can be made. If the child is old enough, the process is also reversed. High level cultural exchange is possible via videotape. Between blacks and whites, for instance. What about a direct exchange by tape between a group of Montessori kids in the U.S. and a group of Suzuki kids in Japan. Live on tape, tribe to tribe, three-year-olds may make the best ambassadors.

Mirror Mirror[2]

The mythology and the use of mirrors deserves serious study by the users of videotape. "Mirror, mirror, up against the wall" . . . the ugly duckling, Narcissus. McLuhan's chapter on the Narcissus myth in *Understanding Media* is extremely important if we are to get beyond the gadget-lover stage with videotape. McLuhan's description of Narcissus applies perfectly to one three-year-old's experience with videotape. She felt compelled to imitate herself on the screen. If we were replaying her singing, she sang; walking down the stairs, she ran up and walked down again. McLuhan, in talking about Narcissus's reflection in the water, wrote: "This extension of himself by mirror numbed his perceptions until he became the servomechanism of his own extended or repeated image . . . He was numb. He had adapted to his extension of himself and become a closed system."[3] As we grow more willing to contemplate "what's happening," this need not be the case with videotape.

From Paul Ryan, "Videotape: Thinking about a Medium," in *Educators Guide to Media & Methods*, December 1968, 37–41.

Editors' note: In one of the earliest theoretical texts on video, Ryan summarizes his experiences with the medium in educational, social, and artistic-experimental contexts. He characterizes the possibilities for participation and interaction offered by video as "infolding information," a concept that will become a guiding theme in his later theoretical and artistic work (see the contribution by Peter Sachs Collopy in Chapter 3 of this reader). In an appendix not reprinted here, Ryan offers practical recommendations for video work alongside a list of suppliers and manufacturers of PVTR (portable videotape equipment).

Notes

1 [Earlier in the text, Ryan characterizes the standard school system: "Classroom space and clock time condemn [the children] to a three-dimensional game of tic-tac-toe, in which experience is blocked out by time schedules and movement from classroom to classroom, a game in which there is very little coherence."]

2 [For a longer discussion of Mc Luhan's chapter on Narcissus in regard to video, also see Ryan's text "Self-Processing" (1970); reprinted in Chapter 3 of the present publication.]

3 Marshall McLuhan, *Understanding Media* (New York: McGraw-Hill, 1964), 68.

Gestures on Videotapes (1973)

Vilém Flusser

This paper is meant as an introduction to the tape which [Fred] Forest and I are trying to make as an experiment to use video to communicate phenomenological vision. What we are trying to do is this: make a tape which shows me gesturing and commenting my gestures. This process involves the following stages: (1) I am proposing a theory of gestures by defining them as specific motions of the body and by distinguishing between various types of gestures. This I do by speaking toward Forest and, behind him, toward those who will watch the tape in the future. (2) I illustrate my theory by performing certain gestures. (3) Forest gestures his camera in a way that mirrors my argument and my gestures, but also comments [on] both and in some way criticizes both. (4) I adjust my gestures to Forest's gestures. (5) The tape which results from our dialogue is to be shown in public. It should show the dialogue as a space-time continuum in which I appear both as an image and as a linguistic discourse, and Forest appears as the structure which orders critically my image and gives my discourse a specific meaning. (6) The public should participate in that dialogue in a form which is left more or less open, but which may take the following directions: (a) the public may discuss the tape, and the discussion may be taped to be shown later to a different public. (b) Some comments by the public on the tape may be included in the tape itself, and the tape thus completed may be shown later to a different public. (c) The tape may become part of a videotheque and be used as a lecture, for instance in schools or museums. But there are other forms of participation by the public which cannot be foreseen and to which the tape should be open.

The purpose of this experiment is this: to learn how to use video for communication of concrete phenomena and theoretical comments on them on an "academic" level. The motivation in this is the hope that video is a medium which may enrich (and even come to substitute) traditional academic media like books, essays, and classroom lectures. That hope is based on the fact that video has certain aspects which other media lack: it is audiovisual, a space-time continuum, it is involved in the phenomenon it shows, it permits immediate projection but does not permit "editing," and it is open to dialogical process. In other words: it synthetizes some aspects of the printed message, some aspects of filmic message, and some aspects of the lecture. This tape means to show how this character of video may be used in the future.

Vilém Flusser, "Gestures on Videotapes. For Fred Forest," 1973, unpublished typescript, no. 2407, Vilém Flusser Archive, Universität der Künste Berlin.

See editors' note after the following text.

Video (1973–1974)

Vilém Flusser

[. . .] (c) *Video*: Compared with photography and film it is a relatively new code, and the apparatus which produces it (camera, reproducer, and monitor) is relatively expensive. Thus a fascination emanates from the video image which has spent itself as far as photography and film are concerned. Habit has not yet made the essence of video invisible by its gray and banalizing cover.

New apparatus is fascinating for two reasons: it is unpredictable and therefore dangerous (like computers and laser beams), and it may be deviated from its original purpose. This second reason contradicts in a way the first one, but in another way it reinforces it: as the uses of a new apparatus are unpredictable, one may discover unsuspected uses in there and thus turn them around ("revolution"): motor cars used for necking are dangerous in a different and revolutionary sense from the danger they represent if used for transportation. In sum: new apparatus is fascinating because it holds both oppressive and liberating virtualities.

The video equipment is an apparatus meant to serve television. It is to pre-register programs to be irradiated, and thus permit previous censorship, and it is to register irradiated programs and thus permit repetitions of broadcasts. Thus it is meant, and widely used, as a support of the TV apparatus. But there are virtualities in video equipment which permit it to be used independently on TV, and against TV, and these virtualities are slowly being discovered. Video is a fascinating apparatus because it holds a promise for revolution.

The video tape is a memory which stores information in a code that is superficially similar to the film code. But the film tape is a series of photographs which were manipulated by an operator to become a movie. A video tape does not permit such a manipulation: it unrolls the way it was registered in the first place. Its time dimension is quite different from filmic time: it is not the result of a manipulation of historical time (of "editing"), but it is a new form of repetition of history (the present is superposed upon the past, which thus becomes background).

There is a curious similarity between video tape and sculpture. Both may be said to have three dimensions: sculpture the well-known dimension of space, and the video the two dimensions of a surface, and a third one in which "depth" is a temporal sequence. Both sculpture and video are codes which somehow "freeze" the flux of time, but each in its own way: in sculpture time freezes to become space (magic), and in video it freezes to become the background of a surface (technoimagination).

There is another, even more curious similarity: the one between video and medieval manuscripts. In medieval parchments two linear texts may be registered, the second one between the lines of the first one. Such palimpsests may provoke a dialectic tension between the two linear texts contained in them. If video tapes are used like palimpsests, the second register will be impressed upon the first one, and the scene first registered will thus he come a sort of shadow of the scene that follows it. If the "same" scene is registered twice, one "on top" of the other register, historical time (which is a concept) becomes an image. And it becomes equally correct to say that on such tapes the past is "presented," or that the present is "perfected."

But though historical time may be rendered an image on video tape, it cannot be manipulated like on film. On the other hand the video tape permits erasions, like a blackboard covered with chalk texts. There are techniques which permit the erasions of a specific layer, if various layers were registered on the same tape. This amounts to an analysis of time stored, a "memory" analysis like psychoanalysis, archaeology, and geology, and it permits layers which were covered up to "emerge." But of course: the analytic disciplines mentioned are conceptual, while the video tape is technoimaginary, and "emergence" is no longer a concept, but the image of a concept.

The operator manipulates the video camera in a way similar to the cameraman, but with this decisive difference: he sees himself in a mirror while operating. Now this mirror, called "monitor," is characteristic of the video tape and quite unlike the reflecting mirror in photographic cameras. It may stand in the center of the scene which is being registered, and the operator sees himself in it not as a reflection, but as he is seen from the point of view he is aiming at. Since he may aim at some other person within the scene, the monitor shows him how he is seen by that other person. And that other person appears itself in the monitor as seen by the operator.

This is a typically dialogical structure: the operator does not manipulate the apparatus in search of his own point of view only (as do photographer and film camera man), but in search of a point of view common to those who are present. Therefore those who are present are neither part of the scene (like in photography), nor actors in an event (like in film), but partners of the operator in the same operation. The monitor is a tool for dialogues, it makes "brothers" of all men within the operation, and it is therefore not surprising (although it may be horrifying) that the present use of monitors is one that makes spies of them in supermarkets and traffic regulations ("big brothers").

The monitor is not a classical mirror. It does not invert the right and the left sides, it is not a "reflection." Those who are not accustomed to monitors are very much upset by this: we are programmed to conceive of "reflection" as being synonymous with "speculation," and to conceive both as inversions. The monitor is a speculation which is not a reflection, it is an image of undialectical opposition for which we have no concept.

The monitor is no classical mirror for a different reason as well: it does not reflect rays which were emitted by the objects mirrored, but it emits cathode rays. This is one of the extremely rare forms of light which do not issue, indirectly, from the sun, and this is a reason why the monitor appears in a fascinating, even hypnotizing, light (in a very literal sense of that term).

Monitors look like TV boxes, and, in fact, most TV boxes may be used as monitors within a video equipment. But if this is done, the functional difference between the two becomes apparent. The TV box works like a window through which images may be seen which were irradiated from beyond the horizon. The monitor works like a mirror of event present (if linked to the camera) and events past (if linked to the tape). The common confusion between monitor and TV box, and between the two functions of the monitor, is a beautiful example of our lack of technoimagination.

But there is an even more fateful confusion. The one between video and film. (The "cinema at home" thing.) There are superficial similarities between the video and filming techniques (travelling, close-up, zooming, and so forth), video cassettes may register movies, and it is possible to buy a film and watch it on television. But these technical and functional similarities cover up a profound structural difference. In film, technoimages are projected against a surface, in video they emanate from a glass lens. This difference may be genetically illustrated thus: "Genealogical tree of the film": cave wall—church wall—framed painting—photograph—film. "Genealogical tree of video": surface of a pond—mirror—telescope—microscope—video. No doubt: the two trees do converge, and both are technoimage codes. But, "essentially," film is an art form (a projection), while video is a form of perception (a way of knowing). "Video art" is a misunderstanding.

This is not meant to quarrel with the obvious fact that "art" is a way of knowing, and perception is always artificial. For with the obvious fact that films may be used for perception ("documentary films") and therefore video tapes as "artistic phenomena" (whatever that may mean). What is meant is that the virtualities hidden within video are being covered up if it is taken to be a kind of film, and that it is necessary to liberate the video from film oppression.

The original purpose of video is to serve television, which means to serve the synchronization between mass media and public opinion. Somewhat later it was discovered that monitors may be used for spying. Thus the purpose of video is to serve the totalitarian state, and this servitude is much more apparent in video than it is in photography and in film, because the apparatus is more recent. This is why any effort to deviate video from its original purpose presupposes that the essential characteristics (the virtualities dormant in it) be discovered.

The "video-artists" are committed to such a deviation. They want to extract monitor and tape from their apparatus context, they want to tear them from the hands of totalitarian operators, and they want to use them against "mass culture" and for "counter culture." But they cannot succeed unless they become aware of its essence: that it renders historical time imaginable, that it permits memory analysis, that it speculates without reflecting, but, most of all, that it permits dialogical communication in a revolutionary sense of that term.

The monitor shows all those present as they are seen by the operator. (It is a revolutionary experience to see oneself from behind, and thus to imagine, not only to conceive, the concept of "being for another.") Tapes may be watched immediately after their registration by those who are registered on it, and thus may serve for immediate dialogical re-use. Articulations during the dialogue may be "withdrawn" (erased from the tape) and, like on musical records, an ever more perfect dialogue can be aimed at. And there are several other dialogical virtualities in video which may be suspected. Many more are certainly not yet discovered.

Now if "dialogue" and "politics" are understood to be closely related, video technoimagination holds the virtuality of a new level of political consciousness. Some parallels may be discovered on different levels. There are the Chinese scrolls which contain commentaries and thus form dialogues which synchronize widely separated epochs, there are the omnipresent graffiti, there are the "chains of good and bad luck," and so forth. Still: video is a radically new dialogical tool, one that may, if used appropriately, inject technoimagination into politics and thus permit "democracy" on the level of technoimagination.

The dangers dormant in video are just as great as are the hopes for liberation. Video permits a new experience of time, a new type of speculation, a new experience of existence in view of the "other," a new political awareness. But all these virtualities will not prevent video to become a powerful tool of totalitarian massification, unless we succeed in becoming conscious of the level of technoimagination hidden in it.

From Vilém Flusser, "Some Technoimages Deciphered: a) Photographs b) Films c) Video d) TV Box e) Cinema," in *Mutations in Human Relations?*, 1973–1974, unpublished typescript, no. 1712, Vilém Flusser Archive, Universität der Künste Berlin, 142–145.

Editors' note: The two texts by Vilém Flusser reprinted in this chapter are excerpts from his scattered writings on the topic of video, which result from a long and complex gestation process with four different text versions:

1973. The beginning is marked by Flusser's appearance in Fred Forest's collaborative video project *Les Gestes du Professeur* (1973). In the video, Flusser freely deliberates on his theory of gestures in French, offering a gestural interpretation at the same time (see Figure 1.5). He reacts in dialogue to Forest and the video camera facing him, as well as to the estimated duration of the videotape regulating the length of his speech. While he speaks without notes in the video, Flusser additionally wrote a short, reflective introductory text in three languages (typescripts in German, English, and French: "Gesten auf Videobaendern," "Gestures on Videotapes," "Gestes sur Bandes Video," Flusser Archive, nos. 2385, 2407, 2424; first published from the English version here). These typescripts explain the dialogical collaboration between media philosopher and video artist, between theory and practice. Additionally, they offer three suggestions for screening situations including audience feedback.

1973–4. The English text reprinted here is taken from the chapter "Some Technoimages Deciphered: a) Photographs b) Films c) Video d) TV Box e) Cinema" in Flusser's typescript of the book *Mutations in Human Relations?* It was written during 1973–4 again in three languages but remained unpublished at the time. Only after the author's death did the German typescript appear under the title "Umbruch der menschlichen Beziehungen" as part of the anthology *Kommunikologie* along with other essays (Mannheim: Bollmann, 1996; see pp. 196–200 for our excerpt). The English version from the Flusser Archive is published here for the first time and varies from the German in many passages; it goes into additional detail and generally is structured and worded more clearly. Along with the sequence of numbers in the Flusser Archive (no. 1687 for the German version, no. 1712 for the English), this suggests that it was written at a later date. As Stefan Bollmann has pointed out, Flusser regularly translated his own texts after some time with extensive revisions; see Bollmann in Vilém Flusser, *Lob der Oberflächlichkeit: Für eine Phänomenologie der Medien* (Bensheim and Düsseldorf: Bollmann, 1995), 333.

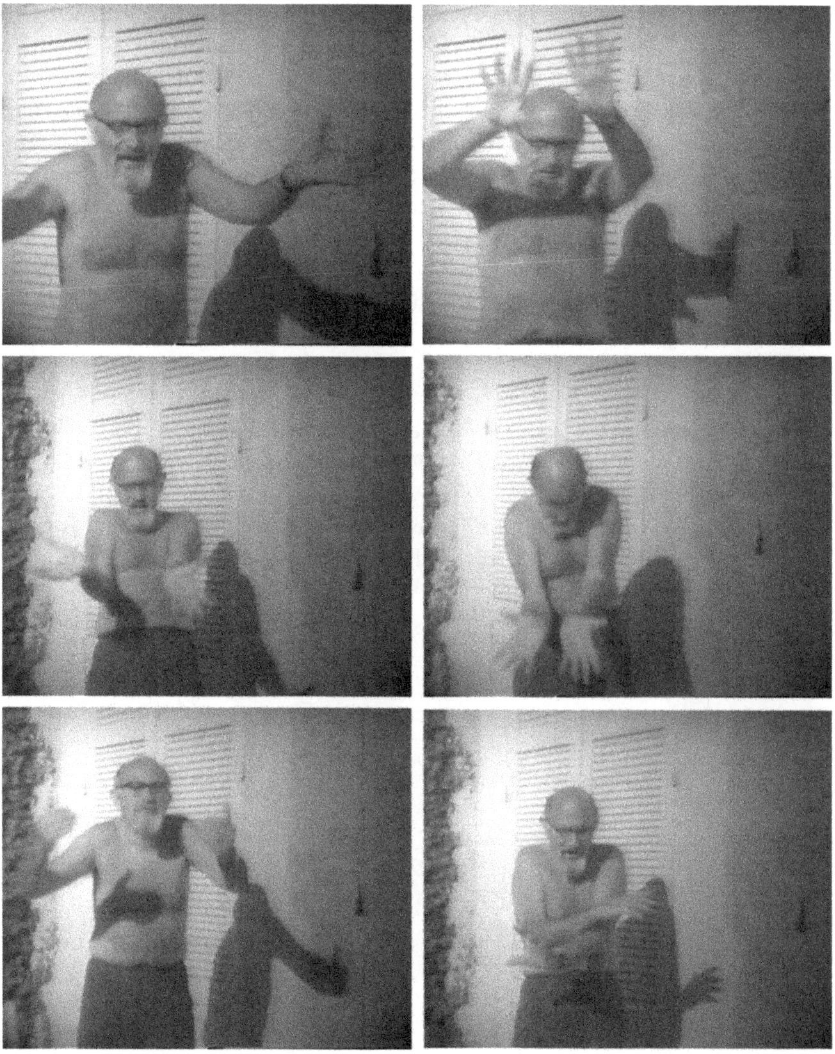

Figure 1.5 Vilém Flusser in the video *Les Gestes du Professeur* by Fred Forest, 1973. © VG Bild-Kunst, Bonn 2020.

1977. Fred Forest invited Flusser to write a comprehensive contribution to his publication for the prominent 1018 pocket book series by French publisher Union Générale d'Editions. During the six chapters on video in the context of "sociological art," Flusser refers to their collaborative video project from 1973 and gives a comprehensive overview of Forest's use of video. In chapter IV, Flusser picks up on his earlier theses on the medium from 1973 to 1974, again complementing and modifying them. Finally, he readdresses the work of Fred Forest from the perspective of these theoretical foundations and offers a radical, in-depth critique of the artist's videos. Vilém Flusser, "L' art sociologique et la vidéo à travers la demarche de Fred Forest," in Fred Forest, *Art sociologique. Vidéo* (Paris: 10 18, Union Générale d'Editions), 402–19.

1991. Flusser's book on the phenomenology of gestures, published with the author's collaboration while he was still alive, contains a short chapter, "Die Geste des Video," in which he readdresses and condenses his earlier theses on video, now again (as in 1973–4) as a "cleaned-up" theoretical text without any reference to Fred Forest and the origin of his thoughts in their collaborative video experiment of 1973. Vilém Flusser, *Gesten: Versuch einer Phänomenologie* (Bensheim and Düsseldorf: Bollmann), 1991, English translation by Flusser himself later published as *Gestures* (Minneapolis: University of Minnesota Press, 2014).

Additional short texts on video by Flusser: "Minkoffs Spiegel" (1973), in Vilém Flusser, *Lob der Oberflächlichkeit: Für eine Phänomenologie der Medien* (Mannheim: Bollmann, 1995), 227–32. "Das Video erforschen" (1975), in ibid., 233–5. "Der Libanon und das Video" (1982–3), in ibid., 222–6. "Discover European Video," in *Discover European Video* (New York: Anthology Film Archives; Neuss: Verein der Freunde und Förderer des Kunstraum Neuss, 1990), 6f.; reprinted in Chapter 3 of this volume.

2

Medium Specificity and Hybridity: The Materiality of the Electronic Image

Introduction by Jan Thoben

The search for a medium specificity of video, which started right after the medium was introduced, is still an object of theoretical reflection today. Generally the specificity of video was bound up with its differentiation from other media, particularly in the context of comparative approaches explored the relationship of video to adjacent media such as film and television as early as the 1960s.[1] In the digital realm, however, these formerly distinct media appear to converge. Convergence theories and theories of medium specificity are therefore to be understood as antagonistic concepts: while convergence refers to the leveling of medial differences through the removal of formerly distinct medial configurations, medium specificity implies the continual (re) construction of differences.

The concept of medium specificity has been discussed from various theoretical positions. Most well-known are the art-historical arguments of Clement Greenberg and Rosalind Krauss. They can be seen as belonging to a theoretical-historical perspective referring back to eighteenth-century debates within Western theories of art. These debates were shaped by attempts to develop a comprehensive system of the arts and to systematize the various forms of artistic expression under theoretical viewpoints. The discussion was less about which art form could lay claim to primacy from an aesthetic perspective and emerge from the *paragone* discourse carried on since the Renaissance to assume a peak hierarchical position. Instead the significance of the aesthetic discourse of the eighteenth century lay in a systematical differentiation between the individual art forms and their various capabilities of imitation (Latin: *mimesis*).[2] The most important historical reference point in this discussion is Gotthold Ephraim Lessing's 1766 text *Laocoön: An Essay on the Limits of Painting and Poetry*.[3] Lessing occupies himself with the relationship between visual art and poetry. He criticizes Horace's doctrine of *ut pictura poesis*, according to which painting and poetry were identical in their aesthetic effects.[4] Lessing uses as examples the various renderings of the Laocoön myth, in the form of the Laocoön Group sculpture, preserved today as a marble copy in the Vatican Museum, on the one hand, and Virgil's *Aeneid* epic, on the other.[5] In the comparative observation of visual art and poetry, Lessing argues that the interdependency of the arts must be uncoupled from the question of hierarchies of art forms. According to him the central criterion for the essential determination of each of the arts—which stand on an equal footing next to each other in their differing potentialities—lies in their material qualities.[6]

Thus, Lessing develops a media-aesthetic perspective, so to speak, according to which "the material limits of art confine all its imitations."[7] The arts' specific modes of representation "are altogether derived from the peculiar conditions" of an art form "and its necessary limits."[8] He goes on to differentiate between synchronic forms of articulation (sculpture, painting) and diachronic modes of artistic expression (literature, theater, music).

With his essays "Avant-Garde and Kitsch" (1939) and "Towards a Newer Laocoön" (1940), Clement Greenberg draws on Lessing's thesis for the purposes of his own theorizing. Taking up Lessing's argument that each art form is shaped by material limits and requirements, Greenberg introduces the concept of the artistic medium as providing the respective normative frame of reference for a given artistic practice:

> Each art had to determine, through its own operations and works, the effects exclusive to itself. . . . It quickly emerged that the unique and proper area of competence of each art coincided with all that was unique in the nature of its medium. . . . Thus would each art be rendered "pure," and in its "purity" find the guarantee of its standards of quality as well as of its independence.[9]

Greenberg understood medium specificity not merely as a self-critical interrogation of the respective material conditions of a given art form. He furthermore called for a kind of media purism that would, in the sense of an aesthetic standard, guarantee a purity of artistic forms of articulation to be derived from their material substrate.[10] The fact that artists continued to discover new ways of using and repurposing media, however, was hardly compatible with Greenberg's idea of the essential, supratemporal properties of media.[11] Accordingly, he vehemently distanced himself from intermediality in the arts, that is, the media interactions, combinatorial practices, and transformations that characterized the work of his contemporaries (John Cage, Robert Rauschenberg, Fluxus, etc.).[12]

Unsurprisingly, Greenberg was criticized for his essentialist theoretical position. Objections also came from within the circle of his students and were directed primarily at the ahistorical character of his concept of medium specificity. From within the Greenberg circle, Michael Fried, for one, voiced his opinion on the problem of essentialism as follows:

> Modernism in the arts involved a process of *reduction* . . . until in the end one arrived at a kind of timeless, irreducible core (in painting, flatness and the delimitation of flatness). The implication of this account was that such a core had been the essence of painting all along, a view that seemed to me ahistorical.[13]

Rosalind Krauss, another former student of Greenberg, primarily found the teleological orientation of his modernist media specificity to be problematic: "The pattern of modernism is thought to be teleological: a relentless one-way drive toward the logical reduction of a given medium to its essence, each stage of this reduction outmoding and supplanting its predecessor."[14] Krauss began to distance herself from Greenberg's position in 1999 with her analysis of media as mutable and differential structures.[15] Her criticism was very influential, as she did not merely problematize Greenberg's reductionism but at the same time presented an expanded theoretical viewpoint. According to Krauss, medium specificity is to be thought of as a variable set of conventions or rules. While these conventions are indeed to be derived from the physical-material properties of the medium in use, they are not reducible to these: "The specificity of mediums, even modernist ones, must be understood as differential, self-differing, and thus as a layering of conventions never simply collapsed into the physicality of their support."[16] Krauss thus made a firm distinction between the physical materiality of the medium and the multiplicity of potential courses of action that could be derived from it. She further explored the concept of the "technical support" in two essays published in *October* in 2009 and 2011.[17] Here she adopted a central concept of Stanley Cavell's that described the relationship between technical materiality and media practice as a serial system: "Cavell's use of the term *automatism* to suggest the idea of a medium as a support for practice . . . sees the relation between a given 'automatism' and the form its development would take as necessarily serial in nature, each member of the series being a new instance of the medium itself."[18]

Unlike Greenberg, Krauss expressly does not support the view that supposedly essential properties already prefigure the manner and mode of a given media practice. In her view, the materiality of a medium remains open to reconfigurations and repurposings.[19] Krauss's conception of medium therefore encompasses the entirety of the "technical support" together with the regulatory system of conventions and affordances that it implies.

Central to Krauss's concept of medium specificity is the fact that it is articulated via a reflexive gesture with which the works refer back to their own medium. This reflexive gesture integrates the artistic works into a post-Greenbergian modernist canon: "Contemporary artists . . . wrest from that support a new set of aesthetic conventions to which their works can then reflexively gesture, should they want to join those works to the canon of modernism."[20]

Approaches toward the continuation of this debate outside of Greenberg's circle and in reference to technical visual media can be found in the commentaries of Erika Balsom and Ina Blom. Balsom begins by underlining the significance of the reflexive gesture for Krauss's concept of medium specificity. Reflexivity, according to Balsom, aims for the reconstruction of an aesthetic autonomy that seals the work of art off from mass-cultural commodification. She sees the concept of medium specificity as a commitment to an enduring modernism, albeit one with an inherent problematic tendency toward formalism. On the other hand, she acknowledges that differential specificity and the self-interrogation of the medium (in Krauss's sense) no longer aim for the kind of transparent, ahistorical self-identity once attributed to Greenberg's modernist conception of media.[21] For Balsom, it is crucially important to point out the historical variability of medium specificities.[22]

In a similar reading of Krauss's arguments, Ina Blom points to the difference between modernist "self-referentiality" and "recursivity." While, in Blom's view, "the concept of self-reference is often misread as solipsism, the concept of recursion places emphasis on the fact that reflexive attention to the properties of an artistic medium does not reproduce this medium as self-identical."[23] Rather, Blom sees medium-specific recursion as an instantiation of the medium that is different in each individual case.[24] She therefore makes the case for updating the modernist analysis of medium specificity as a means of counteracting the erasure of critical differences in today's information economy.

The question of medium specificity as outlined by Krauss—that is, as a question about the relationality (manifested differentially in each individual instance) between technical supports and concrete modes of media (re)use—thereby also touches on the debate, increasingly under discussion since the 1960s, as to whether technology is to be understood as something that shapes society or whether technologies are themselves shaped by society. Marshall McLuhan and Raymond Williams are two important theorists often called upon to serve as representatives of each end of this spectrum. Williams accuses McLuhan of reducing the effects of the social use of technology to simple technological determinism. The decisive factor in this accusation was above all McLuhan's view that the effects of media use are not connected to societal concepts but rather have an effect upon society in the form of a change or a shift in patterns of perception. "The effects of technology do not occur at the level of opinion or concepts but alter the sense ratios or patterns of perception steadily and without resistance" is an argument that appears in many variations throughout McLuhan's writings.[25] In contrast to this technological determinism, Williams's position can be ascribed to a social constructivism that primarily understands the effects of media technologies as sociocultural constructs, that is, through the way in which they are utilized by society. Here, the question of media specificities that Williams recognizes and emphasizes in McLuhan's position seems to point to an overriding relevance and common interest: "Much of the initial appeal of McLuhan's work was his apparent attention to the specificity of the media: the differences in quality between speech, print, radio, television, and so on."[26] Since then, a moderate form of determinism has often been advocated for in media ecology and sociology that draws on actor-network theory and affordance theories for its analysis of media usage. These theories offer action-theoretical concepts for describing the relationality between technical objects, affordances, and functional context. As such, the question of the medium specificity of technical visual media is also relevant to them.

Taking into account the heterogeneous usages of video and television, Rosalind Krauss sketched out the limits of medium specificity in her 1999 text *A Voyage on the North Sea*:

> Television and video seem Hydra-headed, existing in endlessly diverse forms, spaces and temporalities for which no single instance seems to provide formal unity for the whole. For, even if video had a distinct technical support—its own apparatus, so to speak—it occupied a kind of discursive chaos, a heterogeneity of activities that could not be theorized as coherent or conceived of as having something like an essence or unifying core. . . . It proclaimed the end of medium-specificity.[27]

According to Krauss, the various media-technical uses of video are too heterogeneous to be reduced to a set of technical properties. With the rise of video, then, a situation appeared on the horizon that would persist into the digital present, one that Krauss terms the "post-medium condition" and introduces as an antithesis to medium specificity. The "post-medium condition" addresses the crisis, triggered by the intermedial contexts of electronic technologies, of a modernist conception of media based on medial differentiation.[28] As such, two terms derived from differing theoretical positions—"media convergence" (media theory) and "post-medium condition" (art theory)—are related to one another.[29]

In the early 2000s, the discussion surrounding convergence and medium specificity reignited against the backdrop of ubiquitous digitization. Asking himself to what degree medium specificity can still be meaningfully discussed in the age of digitization, Lev Manovich, for instance, takes the following position:

> In fact, regardless of how often we repeat in public that the modernist notion of medium specificity ("every medium should develop its own unique language") is obsolete, we do expect computer narratives to showcase new aesthetic possibilities that did not exist before digital computers. In short, we want them to be new-media specific.[30]

In further arguments, Stephen Maras and David Sutton point to the fact that the concept of medium specificity also plays a role in regard to digital media. They subject the seminal 1999 study *Remediation: Understanding Media* by Jay David Bolter and Richard Grusin to a critical reading. In their book, Bolter and Grusin develop the concept of remediation, drawing on McLuhan's ideas, according to which new, emerging media consistently represent and refashion older, preceding, established media formats. Bolter and Grusin fundamentally understand new media as hybrids that stand in a constant dialectical relationship to established analog media and draw on them as resources:

> What is new about digital media lies in their particular strategies for remediating television, film, photography, and painting. Repurposing as remediation is both what is "unique to digital worlds" and what denies the possibility of that uniqueness.[31]

Maras and Sutton correctly point out that remediation is being invoked here as a unique characteristic of digital media, which ultimately, contrary to the intended argumentation, connotes a specificity of digital media.[32] Ostensibly, Bolter and Grusin are aware of this connection when they emphasize, very much in the spirit of Rosalind Krauss, that the phenomenon of remediation does not have to do with an essential property but rather a currently predominant convention or affordance of digital visual media:

> In arguing that all mediation is remediation, we do not mean that remediation is the irreducible essence of either digital media or mediation generally, but rather

> that at our historical moment, remediation is the predominant convention at work in establishing the identity of new digital media.[33]

In this context—albeit without referencing Krauss—Maras and Sutton argue against undertaking an analysis of hybrid digitality and its phenomena of remediation and convergence without renewed critical recourse to the concept of medium specificity.[34] This medium-specific perspective can help identify how even hybrid digital media establish specific forms of mediality.[35] Media should be observed in a historicizing manner, comparing between established and emergent forms, and in the context of intermedial connections rather than in isolation from one another.

Accordingly, questions of medium specificity were taken up once more in connection with the concept of intermediality, itself under discussion since the 1990s and 2000s. With reference to the positions of Manovich and Krauss, Jens Schröter suggests that the concept of the artistic medium in particular is increasingly difficult to define. The cause for this, according to Schröter, is the artistic use of electronic media such as (digital) video, on the one hand, and the rising prevalence since the 1960s of installation-based art forms that have broken with the notion of a medium-specific justification of modernism, on the other.[36] In his analysis of the political dimension of the concept of intermediality, Schröter refers principally to Krauss's concept of the post-medium condition (outlined above), as Krauss, too, brings a political dimension to bear upon this idea: "Art *essentially* finds itself complicit with a globalization of the image in the service of capital."[37] Art is therefore faced with the task of freeing itself from the mass-media use of the electronic image within a ubiquitous culture of the multimedia spectacle.[38] Drawing on Walter Benjamin, Krauss takes the view that this distancing is to be achieved primarily through the artistic appropriation of obsolete media that have come to the end of their careers as commercial technologies. Obsolete media thus avoid the risk of being reintegrated into the capitalist culture industry and put to use in the service of its spectacular effects.[39] In her discussion of Rosalind Krauss's hypotheses, Erika Balsom expounds upon the dialectic relationship between obsolescence and media convergence in the era of techno-capitalism in somewhat more detail:

> One can, for example, identify moving image work that embraces the antispectacular, cultivating an interest in the obsolete and discarded forms that constitute the dialectical other of capitalism's focus on the incessant production of novelty. . . . Though they might seem to be diametrically opposed to spectacular culture, they in fact agitate from within it by mining its detritus.[40]

According to Balsom, the artistic appropriation of obsolete technologies does not necessarily correspond to a modernist-autonomous reinvention of the medium in Krauss's sense. Obsolete technologies are often intentionally staged as objects of aesthetic contemplation in order to indicate the history of a particular media usage.[41] In the course of his contributions to the theory of intermediality, Jens Schröter correctly states that the identity of media is not simply a given but can only be arrived at by means of deliberate, differential demarcations and intermedial references: "The definition of the 'specific character' of a medium requires the differential demarcation from other media."[42] Erika Balsom even develops the argument that it is precisely historical situations marked by convergence and hybridization that produce media-specific strategies.[43] Janna Houwen also makes reference to this continual interaction between hybridization and specificity in her examination of the relationship between film and video. She draws attention once again to the position advocated by Krauss and Blom on the historical variability of media specificities, while similarly taking up the theoretical approach of remediation: "The arrival of video not only changed the specificity of film by taking some of its genres. The video-specific characteristic of instant broadcast very much altered the way in which film was specified."[44]

At this point, it can be stated that the concept of differential specificity as developed by Krauss represents an important point of reference for the video-theoretical text contributions that make up this chapter. Medium specificity can be understood as an incomplete, complex differentiation of medial affordances that are subject to historical variability and are articulated artistically in the form of recursive structures. The question of medium specificity forms a constant in the discourse on an independent video aesthetic that remains significant today—one that goes beyond classic modernist reductionism and is compatible with contemporary concepts of material agency as well as dispositive and action theories.

Electromagnetic Signal Transformation: The Materiality of Video Flow (Yvonne Spielmann, Maurizio Lazzarato, Wolfgang Ernst)

Like Rosalind Krauss, Yvonne Spielmann differentiates in her contribution to this volume between technology and medium. Within video as artistic medium, says Spielmann, specific methods and forms of expression can be recognized that, while derived from their particular technology, are not reducible to it.

Having initially worked on questions of intermediality, Spielmann offers a comprehensive video-theoretical contribution from an art and media-studies perspective in her 2005 monograph *Video: The Reflexive Medium*.[45] In this book, she first and foremost investigates the aesthetic repertoire of video as a medium and in so doing incorporates—similarly to Maurizio Lazzarato—the aspiration for the development of a comprehensive theory of video. Her initial thesis states that video technology, with its specific possibilities for image synthesis and manipulation, invites artists to develop a distinct medium-reflexive video aesthetic. Spielmann differentiates here between two fundamental medium-aesthetic qualities, or basic categories, of video: audiovisuality (transformativity) and reflexivity (processuality).[46] She regards the artistic positions discussed in her book (particularly those of Vito Acconci, Ulrike Rosenbach, Nam June Paik, the Vasulkas, Peter Campus, and Robert Cahen) as "deployments specific to media, which establish video as a reflexive audiovisual medium."[47] In her contribution to this volume, Spielmann sketches out the evolution of a medium specificity as the development of the technology into a medium. Medium specificity is thus not a given set of qualities for Spielmann but rather the result of process-related—and, in this case, artistically reflexive—engagements with a technology. It is only when a specificity of expressive possibilities has developed within the framework of artistic practice that video becomes a medium that, to Spielmann, can be differentiated from others.

Spielmann pays particular attention on the one hand to the use of video processing tools, such as keyers and synthesizers, and on the other to characteristic signal processes such as closed-circuit feedback, raster manipulation, and electromagnetic modulations, which can reveal the flow of the video signal, influence it, or change it. Spielmann's assessment, like that of other authors included in this volume, such as Mauricio Lazzarato or Bill Viola, is that in video we are dealing with an open, unstable, and incoherent form of technical image that is subject to constant transformation. In the context of a media comparison to cinema (projection) and television (transmission), Spielmann analyzes, like Anne-Marie Duguet, the *video dispositive*—but unlike Duguet, Spielmann opts for the concept of the "apparatus" as influenced by Jean-Louis Baudry. While cinema and television determine the orders of seeing in the public space of the movie theater or the private space of the domestic living room, no comparably systemized regime of the gaze exists in video, as its apparatus-based structure is too modular and incoherent. Theories of convergence, which seek solely to present video as an intermediate form on the way from film to digital, are accordingly unsuited to take into account the historic specificity of forms of expression developed on video. One reason for the hasty classification of video by an all-too-linear media historiography, Spielmann concludes, is that there has thus far been no video theory comparable to film theory that could provide the orientation necessary for this debate.[48]

While the sociologist and philosopher Maurizio Lazzarato is known for his studies on the relationship between labor, economy, and society, he has also worked on cinema, video, and new technologies of image production. He has made a pivotal contribution to video theory with his wide-ranging study of time perception in the post-Fordist era, significantly entitled *Videophilosophy*. In this study, written as an analysis of information economy in the context of immaterial labor, Lazzarato dedicates himself to a comprehensive theoretical consideration of the electronic image. Building on Henri Bergson's analysis of the temporality of the moving image, and with particular reference to relevant artist's texts by Nam June Paik and Bill Viola, Lazzarato turns his focus to the "time-matter" of the video image—that is to say, the fluctuating electromagnetic image signal.[49]

Here, Lazzarato explicitly differentiates between the signifying flow of images on video, as alluded to by Fredric Jameson and Raymond Williams, and the asignifying flow of the electrons underpinning the technical signal. Lazzarato begins by focusing on the constitution of the video signals and the way in which an image emerges from the signal. As for many other authors, Lazzarato's point of departure is the difference between the video image and the film image: the video image is not an issue of a mechanically animated stationary photogram, as in the case of film, but rather "an image in continuous formation painted by an electronic brush."[50] Because of the progressive line scannings, the analog-electronic image should be thought of as a frame of points and lines comparable to a weaving pattern, the difference being that the video flow ultimately weaves itself on into infinity.[51] With reference to theses of Bill Viola and Nam June Paik, Lazzarato discusses the time-character of the electronic image. Whereas film unspools photograms, merely switching on a video camera reveals the signal itself to be time-matter. As the modulation of an electronic signal flow, video maintains a more direct relationship to the vibration of light than film does. Lazzarato's argument is supported from the technical perspective insofar as, on video, the color spectrum is modulated as chrominance onto a subcarrier and must thus continually be temporally coded and updated as a vibration.[52] Lazzarato recognizes in the video medium a reproduction of the relationship between perception and material in Henri Bergson's sense. Bergson conceives of perception as a material process, initially as pure perception—to which Lazzarato refers a number of times. As Bergson emphasizes, "pure perception" is to be understood as a theoretical hypothesis, for it would be a quasi-mechanical process of perception without affectivity or cognitive performance.[53] The continual current of vibrations that reach the human sensorium in the process of perception, says Lazzarato, displays a structural similarity to the technical signal flow of video. In both cases, an actual image must first be extracted through selection and contraction of asignifying flows. As signifying images are synthesized out of the flow of "pure perception" through the labor of intellectual synthesis, video processing may be understood, according to Lazzarato, as a corresponding kind of synthesis. Video montage simulates intellectual labor—and from this perspective it is not the moving image (as the etymological roots of *video* suggest) but rather time that becomes the intrinsic concept of the medium.

From the position of media archaeology, Wolfgang Ernst poses the question of a specific videocity. This addresses a specific quality and technical mode of being and operation of video, intended as a conceptually analogous construction to the word "electricity." The particularity of Wolfgang Ernst's media-archaeological approach is that it is directed not at cultural semantics but rather at the "non-discursive level of medial praxis in its epistemological consequences, faithful to an information theory that does not interpret communication hermeneutically, but calculates it mathematically."[54] Working from this perspective, Ernst, in the tradition of Friedrich Kittler, conceives of media as artifacts—that is to say, as apparative materiality—that must be explicated on the level of their signaling operations. As a point of departure for his argument, Ernst—like Lazzarato and Jameson—looks to the characterization of video as flow, as an image stream that constantly undermines the authority of the narrative.

To get to the bottom of the electronic image's texture, Ernst calls particular attention to the aesthetic of disruption in video as a medium. It is through static and interference that video first reveals its time-based nature. In his book *Sonic Time Machines*, Ernst devotes a section to the sonic nature of the electronic image.[55] Referring to Marshall McLuhan's concept of acoustic space, he points out that the reception of an analog-electronic image does not have quite the same character as a distant visual representation but comes much closer to a quasi-"acoustic," or, more specifically, sonic experience of resonance.[56] In this sense, it is also necessary to analyze the time-sensitive video image in its sonic aspects, once again revealing its difference to the purely optical film image.[57] While the time-basedness of the electronic image is in fact subliminal and runs below the perceptional threshold, it nevertheless reveals itself, says Ernst, when the pause button is pressed as a video plays. In that state, artifacts destabilize the video image, thereby indicating the continual execution of line-scanning and revealing the temporality of the video image, as it were. Unlike Raymond Bellour, who also develops his theoretical consideration of video by means of the still image—and in so doing calls attention to the particular passages of the photographic that live on in electronic image media as the freeze frame—Wolfgang Ernst limits himself to the material specifics of the electronic still image. He furthermore characterizes video, like Bellour, as an "in-between medium" in the history of audiovisual media—albeit here, too, from a strict technological perspective. As a digital-analog hybrid medium, he says, video stands between the television and the computer in that it is based upon analog signals but is nevertheless also digitally addressable via the timecode generated by synchronization signals.[58] From a media-archaeological standpoint, it is in the universal machine, the computer—one that does not operatively differentiate between image, sound, and text, and thus levels medial differences—that specific videocity necessarily meets its end.

Intermediate Spaces: The Video Dispositive (Anne-Marie Duguet, Raymond Bellour, Siegfried Zielinski)

As a theorist and curator, Anne-Marie Duguet began to delve into the role of technology in art quite early. Her first video book, *Vidéo, la mémoire au poing*, appeared in 1981.[59] With her 1988 essay "Dispositifs," Duguet made a seminal contribution on the dispositive structure of the video medium—one that, up to this point, has only been available in French and as such has not yet received the consideration it deserves within the English-language debate.[60] Duguet understands her concept of the dispositive to be at once a continuation of and differentiation from apparatus theories, particularly as they influenced French cinema studies in the 1970s (with specific reference here to Jean-Louis Baudry). While the apparatus theorists analyzed cinema as an ideological agent that acts upon passive spectators, the spectators in Duguet's model of the dispositive are incorporated explicitly as an active component. In this way, Duguet also turns against traditional media-theoretical standpoints that create a dichotomy, with communication systems on the one side and society on the other.

Duguet conceives of the spectators of videos not as purely visual, disembodied subjects but rather as embodied spectators who, especially in installation settings, may no longer be understood as fixed and passive.[61] On the other hand, Duguet points to the enmeshment of technical actors, institutional frameworks, and the singular-subjective experience of perception. Understood as such, the dispositive is fundamentally subject to a scenographic order: that is to say, the way in which spectators are implied—which may be different from case to case—plays a role not only in the framework of a video installation but even in the viewing of a videotape. Each time a video is played, the configuration of the medial staging must be considered anew. Duguet's feminist theoretical position concerns itself first and foremost with a representation-critical interrogation of the intersections between the medial and physical apparatus, the image-body and the body-image, the dispositive and the subject capable of action.[62]

Raymond Bellour is one of the few authors to bridge the gap between the great tradition of French film criticism and video.[63] He developed an interest in video art through engagement with the works of his friend, the video artist Thierry Kuntzel. A comprehensive theoretical consideration of video as medium, primarily in the context of a relational configuration of technical image media, is to be found in Bellour's work since the late 1980s—especially in the essays "Video Utopia" (1986), "Self-Portraits" (1988), "Double Helix" (1990), and "Between-the-Images" (1990). Summaries of a number of these texts can be found, along with other essays, in the essay collection *Between-the-Images*, published in English in 2012 as a revised edition of the original 1990 French text.

The term *between-the-images* primarily addresses the intermediary space between individual images. Bellour describes this "in-between" topologically as a virtual passage-space, a point of intersection between image-media, in both the mental and physical sense.[64] According to Bellour, this passage is primarily evident in video. Video, he claims, can be thought of as a medium that dissolves the boundaries of photography and film at once, as it integrates both the static and the moving images. In this sense, video is the medium of liminal passages through and transitions between images. Bellour analyzes the form of this image transition via the example of the still image or the frozen moving image: here, a passage of the photographic emerges in the context of moving-image media that begs a reconsideration of the dichotomy of standstill and movement. For Bellour, it is thus no accident that the freeze frame and other forms of the photographic that increasingly found their way into the cinema of the 1960s coincide with the image processing nascent in video.

Bellour conceives of video as embodiment of the capacity for the passage through images as such. The medium materializes the power of divergence on the level of the image's technical construction. With all of its possibilities for the integration and processing of images of other technical media, video appears as a potentiality with an inexhaustible reservoir of image mutations at the ready—one that, looking toward digital media, becomes a floodgate, a "go-between."[65] Bellour sees this transformational strength of video as being particularly realized in artistic explorations. Like Fredric Jameson, he describes the video medium as a spectrum, reaching from experimental video art on one end to the commercial application of video in television production on the other. Video should therefore only be thought of in its interplay with other media, that is to say, in its reciprocal connections not only to other image-media, such as film or television, but also to music.[66] This notion is integral to Bellour's approach, as video is never understood as a solitary entity but rather as a genuinely intermedial configuration.

In providing a deep temporal dimension to current media practices, Siegfried Zielinski also regards video - its technological structure as well as its socio-economical dispositive – as a "transitional medium."[67] Early on, Zielinski put emphasis on video as a recording technology. His seminal historiography of the video recorder from 1986 provided an extensive survey on the topic.[68] The saturation of households with video recorders in the 1980s, its effect on the distribution of media content and its entanglement with the economics of television also serves as a point of departure for his analysis of what he calls a "new audiovisual discourse" in *Audiovisions: Cinema and Television as Entr'actes in History*, first published in German in 1989.[69]

His essay "Video Intimus" (2010) revisits video theoretical considerations and begins by analyzing the differences between the economical dispositives of cinema and video. In cinema, none of the equipment affording the film experience in a material sense is owned by the audience. While cinema's semi-public space is rented to the temporary community of those who have purchased a ticket, television began to reform this institutionalized ownership structure. Eventually, with the advent of the video recorder, the technology as well as the broadcast products became available to those who recorded them. Zielinski regards this as a paradigm shift, since audiovisual production now moved into the private realm and allowed to preserve pieces of life-time-events. Video art has reflected on this as well by deliberately exhibiting lived-through time events. As Zielinski observes, video slowly liberated itself from the hegemonic structures of mass broadcasting towards a dispositive of intimacy and privacy.

Hybridity and Plurality (Fredric Jameson, Sean Cubitt)

In the course of his engagement with questions of aesthetics, American literary critic Fredric Jameson became a leading voice of the new Marxist theoretical discourse within cultural studies in the 1980s and 1990s. Alongside his work's focal point in literature, Jameson has attended to contemporary developments in film, architecture, and, last not but least, video. Given Jameson's background, it should come as no surprise that the protocols of modernist-influenced discourse on medium specificity sketched out in many of this chapter's texts are nowhere to be found in his theoretical engagement with video. For Jameson, who is more than acquainted with Roland Barthes's theories of intertextuality, as well as the writings of Raymond Williams and Jean Baudrillard, video represents, as it were, the exemplary medium of the postmodern. In his view, the flickering medium of video art reflects the characteristics of a late-capitalist consumer society that has fully turned away from categories such as authenticity, originality, and attention, as the cultural sphere of the everyday has quite simply been saturated with images. Along with it, the concept of aesthetic autonomy has been gradually hollowed out. It is significant that, with her theory of differential medium specificity, Rosalind Krauss turned explicitly against Jameson's universalistic thesis.[70]

In his seminal work *Postmodernism, or, the Cultural Logic of Late Capitalism*, Jameson dedicates a chapter especially to video. Here he invokes Raymond Williams's description of television as "a situation of total flow . . . streaming before us all day long without interruption."[71] To Jameson, this image stream of television and video consequently turns into surface phenomena whose objectifiable, memorable forms are revoked, implying a structural exclusion of memory. Where critical distance shaped the reception of political modern cinema, video is in contrast a depersonalized "total-flow" experience that characterizes itself far more through immersion into the flood of images. Jameson understands video as textual structure or a stream of signs that stands in opposition to objectifiable semantic content and thus subverts traditional models of interpretation.[72] He sees the free flow of signifiers in the video medium as a prototypical example of his general thesis of the postmodern end of grand narratives.[73]

Based on the postmodern positing he sketches out, Jameson discounts not only the possibility of a canon of video art but fundamentally the concept of the author in the video medium: "There are no video masterpieces, there can never be a video canon, even an auteur theory of video . . . becomes very problematic indeed."[74]

Looking at the reception of video art, by 1988 Jameson had already developed the controversial thesis that an analysis of the content of "video texts" was fundamentally wrong: "Only the most misguided museum visitor would look for art in the content of the video images themselves."[75] Jameson seeks here to head off any analytic isolation of a singular video piece that would transform it into an autonomous work and ascribe to it the characteristics of an older modernist aesthetic.

With two extensive studies of video, Sean Cubitt dedicated himself in the early 1990s to the increasingly broad appeal of video culture.[76] Like Jameson, Bellour, and others, Cubitt pointed to the intrinsic relationship between video and broadcast television but also called attention to the fact that this was but one of the many relations in which video found itself.[77] In video, he saw an alternative to the TV-broadcast principle (one to many) and the centralization of the means of production and public consensus on medial content via the use of home video. On the other hand, contemporary video culture increasingly distinguished itself in relation to cinema as an individual culture, as video subverted the social event of the communal visit to the cinema.[78]

Because of its complex structure, Cubitt describes video as a semiautonomous medium that is to be considered as neither completely dependent on nor totally independent from other forms of communication. In this regard, he aligns himself quite closely with Raymond Bellour's description of video as a genuinely intermedial configuration. Cubitt accordingly turns against an essentialist consideration of the medium and emphasizes: "There is no essential form of video, nothing to which one can point as the primal source or goal of video activity."[79] In so doing, Cubitt builds upon Roy Armes's observation that, on the basis of the continual changes in video technology, it is increasingly difficult to reduce the medium to specific, fixable qualities.[80] He proposes to avoid referring to video in the singular entirely and instead uses the plural "video media." He eventually comes to the oft-cited judgment on the impossibility of a theory of video, as there is no clearly delimitable object that can be brought into focus.[81] However, Cubitt's skepticism of theory does not fundamentally refer to the theoretical interrogation of video but far more to the idea of a discipline of video theory analogous to film theory or television studies. Writings on video never lead to a distinct discipline, Cubitt says, but should instead be understood as a strand of cultural studies or media studies. At the same time, video should always be analyzed in close relation to art.

Video as Memory Technology (Ina Blom)

In her wide-ranging study *Autobiography of Video*, Ina Blom introduces a research approach that brings together media art historiography and media archaeology. According to Blom, autobiography and video are related in two respects: first, video as a technology in service of techno-cultural self-representation of social subjects stands as a signal-based corollary to the first-person narrative shaped by corresponding literary formats. On the other hand, Blom's central concern is in tracing an autobiography of the medium itself—beyond the supposed subserviences or alliances between video and social subjects. Discontinuities and differences regarding the localization of media technologies and human actors should thus be brought to the forefront.[82] Proceeding from numerous artistic assessments (also discussed by Yvonne Spielmann in her book on video) that grant the medium of video a co-creativity or capacity to act, Blom inquires about the consequence of this agency that is ascribed to the medium and the interrelated performative capability for critical action. Her focus lies on the fundamental relationship between memory technologies (such as video) and a social ontology, as well as associated questions about the relations between art, technology, and social memory. These problems are to be elucidated through material traces (video recordings), discourses, as well as both hardware and software. Blom's approach does not therefore proceed from the poetic powers of artists and artworks but conversely from the efficacy of the video medium as a memory technology that itself makes use of artistic frameworks, their personnel, and their skills as an experimentation with its own capacity for remembering.[83] Understood as such, the autobiography of video is not a history (of the invention) of developments in video technologies and their appropriation into art but rather a depiction of processes or operations of technical individuation and connectivity.

Notes

1 See Chapter 5 for the relationship between film and television.

2 Charles Batteux's 1746 treatise *The Fine Arts Reduced to a Single Principle* may serve as an example here. See Charles Batteux, *Les beaux-arts réduits à un même principe*, ed. Jean-Rémy Mantion, Collection Théorie et critique à l'âge classique, vol. 2 (Paris: Aux Amateurs de Livres, 1989). Cf. Noël Carroll, *Theorizing the Moving Image* (Cambridge: Cambridge University Press, 1996), 7.

3 Gotthold Ephraim Lessing, *Laocoön: An Essay on the Limits of Painting and Poetry*, trans. E. C. Beasley (London: Longman, Brown, Green, and Longmans, 1853).

4 This formula was subsequently misinterpreted to assign one art form a higher rank than the other.

5 With this text, Lessing emerged as an antagonist of Johann Joachim Winckelmann and his *Thoughts on the Imitation of Greek Works in Painting and Sculpture* of 1756. Using the various adaptations of the Laocoön myth in sculpture and poetry as an example, Winckelmann argued for the visual arts' predominance over poetry. While the Roman poet Virgil has the Trojan priest Laocoön scream horribly in his fight to the death with the snake in order to lend expression to his suffering, in Greek sculpture (according to Winckelmann), this misery is sublimated in that the tormented priest is displayed in noble simplicity and quiet grandeur, thereby demonstrating his spiritual transcendence even in the throes of death.

6 See also the afterword ("Nachwort") in Gotthold Ephraim Lessing, *Laokoon oder Über die Grenzen der Malerei und Poesie* (Stuttgart: Reclam, 1998), 219f.

7 Lessing, *Laocoön*, 16.

8 Ibid., 21.

9 Clement Greenberg, "Modernist Painting," in *Clement Greenberg: The Collected Essays and Criticism. Vol. 4: Modernism with a Vengeance, 1957–1969*, ed. John O'Brian (Chicago and London: University of Chicago Press, 1993), 86.
10 Greenberg, "Modernist Painting," 97.
11 Carroll, *Theorizing the Moving Image*, 32.
12 "What's ominous is that the decline of taste now, for the first time, threatens to overtake art itself. I see 'intermedia' and the permissiveness that goes with it as symptom of this. . . . Good art can come from anywhere, but it hasn't yet come from intermedia or anything like it." Clement Greenberg, "Intermedia," *Arts Magazine* 56, no. 2 (1981), 93.
13 Michael Fried, "Theories of Art after Minimalism and Pop," in *Discussions in Contemporary Culture*, ed. Hal Foster (Seattle: Bay Press, 1987), 57.
14 Rosalind Krauss, *Under Blue Cup* (Cambridge, MA: MIT Press, 2011), 203.
15 Rosalind Krauss, *A Voyage on the North Sea: Art in the Age of the Post-Medium Condition* (New York: Thames and Hudson, 1999).
16 Krauss, *Voyage on the North Sea*, 53.
17 Rosalind Krauss, "Two Moments from the Post-Medium Condition," *October* 116 (2006), 55–62.
18 Krauss, *Voyage on the North Sea*, 59.
19 Krauss, *Under Blue Cup*, 18 et seq.
20 Rosalind Krauss, "Two Moments from the Post-Medium Condition," 56.
21 Erika Balsom, *Exhibiting Cinema in Contemporary Art* (Amsterdam: Amsterdam University Press, 2013), 92f. See also Balsom's contribution to this volume in Chapter 12.
22 Balsom, *Exhibiting Cinema*, 74.
23 Ina Blom, "Inhabiting the Technosphere: Art and Technology beyond Technical Invention," in *Contemporary Art: 1989 to the Present*, ed. Alexander Dumbadze and Suzanne Hudson (Chichester: Wiley-Blackwell, 2013), 150.
24 Ibid.
25 Marshall McLuhan, *Understanding Media: The Extensions of Man* (Cambridge, MA: MIT Press, 1994), 18.
26 Raymond Williams, *Television: Technology and Cultural Form* (London: Routledge, 1974), 130.
27 Krauss, *Voyage on the North Sea*, 31f.
28 In light of Krauss's concept of the post-medium condition, Christian Spies subjects the medium of video to a differentiated analysis: Christian Spies, "Video: In between Its Medium and Post-Medium Condition," in *Affekte: Analysen ästhetisch-medialer Prozesse*, ed. Antje Krause-Wahl, Heike Oehlschlägel, and Serjoscha Wiemer (Bielefeld: transcript, 2006), 99–115.
29 Erika Balsom speaks here of "twin phenomena." See Balsom, *Exhibiting Cinema*, 73.
30 Lev Manovich, *The Language of New Media* (Cambridge, MA: MIT Press, 2001), 237.
31 Jay David Bolter and Richard Grusin, *Remediation: Understanding New Media* (Cambridge, MA: MIT Press, 2000), 50.
32 Steven Maras and David Sutton, "Medium Specificity Re-visited," *Convergence: The International Journal of Research into New Media Technologies* 6 (June 2000), 107.
33 Bolter and Grusin, *Remediation*, 54.
34 Even if there are certain commonalities between this and the argumentation of Rosalind Krauss, her theoretical position does not play a role for Maras and Sutton. Their reflections on the emergence of medium specificity are based to a significant

extent on Deleuze and Guattari's theoretical concept of media assemblage. Cf. Maras and Sutton, "Medium Specificity Re-visited," 101 et seq.

35 Maras and Sutton, "Medium Specificity Re-visited," 109.

36 Jens Schröter, "The Politics of Intermediality," *Acta Universitatis Sapientiae: Film and Media Studies* 2 (2010), 109f.

37 Krauss, *Voyage on the North Sea*, 56.

38 Accordingly, "Art in the Age of the Post-Medium Condition" is the subtitle of her book, *A Voyage on the North Sea*.

39 Krauss, *Voyage on the North Sea*, 41.

40 Balsom, *Exhibiting Cinema*, 62.

41 Ibid., 94f. The video installations of Joep van Liefland offer a prime example of this.

42 Jens Schröter, "Discourses and Models of Intermediality," *CLCWeb: Comparative Literature and Culture* 13, no. 3 (2011), https://doi.org/10.7771/1481-4374.1790.

43 Balsom, *Exhibiting Cinema*, 74.

44 Janna Houwen, *Film and Video Intermediality: The Question of Medium Specificity in Contemporary Moving Images* (New York: Bloomsbury Academic, 2017), 55.

45 Yvonne Spielmann, *Video: Das reflexive Medium* (Frankfurt am Main: Suhrkamp, 2005). English edition: *Video: The Reflexive Medium*, trans. Anja Welle and Stan Jones (Cambridge, MA: MIT Press, 2008).

46 Spielmann, *Video: The Reflexive Medium*, 137. On the audiovisuality of video, cf. Chapter 6 in the present volume.

47 Ibid. Though Spielmann refers in her book almost exclusively to examples from the visual arts, she connects her analysis to the aspiration to elaborate a general media specificity of video that is not limited to the artistic context.

48 "When the understanding of media-specificity is not at the core of discussing video, the conversation can become purely academic. This occurs mainly in debates on the convergence of various technical media tools that have no body of video theory comparable to film theory to provide the necessary orientation." Yvonne Spielmann, "Video: From Technology to Medium," *Art Journal* 65, no. 3 (Fall 2006), 62; reprinted in this chapter.

49 Maurizio Lazzarato, "Video, Flows, and Real Time," in *Videophilosophy: The Perception of Time in Post-Fordism*, ed. and trans. Jay Hetrick (New York: Columbia University Press, 2019), 81; reprinted in this chapter.

50 Lazzarato, "Video, Flows, and Real Time," 83.

51 See also the dialogical collaboration between Angela Melitopoulos and Maurizio Lazzarato, "Digital Montage and Weaving: An Ecology of the Brain for Machine Subjectivities," in *Stuff It: The Video Essay in the Digital Age*, ed. Ursula Biemann (Vienna: Springer, 2003), 117–25. Melitopoulos also references Lazzarato's theories numerous times in her video works, while Lazzarato's texts lean extensively on assertions made by Melitopoulos. This is, then, a dialogue between theory and practice as laid out in Chapter 12 of the present volume.

52 Color and brightness signals on video may accordingly be depicted oscillographically.

53 Cf. Henri Bergson, *Matter and Memory*, trans. N. Margaret Paul and W. Scott Palmer (New York: MacMillan, 1912).

54 Wolfgang Ernst, "Medientheorie als Medienarchäologie: Einsichten im technischen Vollzug," https://www.musikundmedien.hu-berlin.de/de/medienwissenschaft/medientheorien/Schriften-zur-medienarchaeologie/notizbuch/pdfs/med-definition-notiz.pdf.

55 Wolfgang Ernst, *Sonic Time Machines: Explicit Sound, Sirenic Voices, and Implicit Sonicity* (Amsterdam: Amsterdam University Press, 2016), 27 et seq. The concept of the sonic is intended to demarcate a difference from the anthropocentrically determined notion of sound.

56 Edmund Carpenter and Marshall McLuhan, "Acoustic Space" (1960), in *Explorations in Communication: An Anthology*, ed. Edmund Carpenter and Marshall McLuhan (Boston: Beacon Press, 1960), 65–70. On sound and video, see Chapter 6 of this reader.

57 On film and video, see Chapter 4 of this reader.

58 Timecode display for analog tapes was established in the 1980s and had become standard by the introduction of full-digital formats. For more on timecode standards, see Marcus Weise and Diana Weynand, *How Video Works: From Analog to High Definition*, 2nd ed. (Burlington, MA: Focal Press, 2013).

59 Anne-Marie Duguet, *Vidéo, la mémoire au poing* (Paris: Hachette, 1981). This book also contains the essay "La vidéo des femmes," reprinted in Chapter 9 as "Women's Video."

60 Anne-Marie Duguet, "Dispositifs," *Communications* 48, Vidéo (1988), 221–42; reprinted in the present chapter.

61 Duguet, "Dispositifs," 228.

62 Cf. Sigrid Adorf, *Operation Video: Eine Technik des Nahsehens und ihr spezifisches Subjekt. Die Videokünstlerin der 1970er Jahre* (Bielefeld: transcript, 2008), 13. For more on the contextualization of video's technical history and the sociopolitical emancipatory movements of the 1970s, see the introduction to Chapter 9.

63 Jean-Paul Fargier and Philippe Dubois represent comparable French theoretical positions. Cf. Arnaud Widendaële, "La vidéo au regard du cinéma : Pour une archéologie des 'idées de vidéo' dans la presse cinématographique française (1959–1995)," dissertation (Lille: Université Lille Nord de France, 2016), http://www.sudoc.fr/199814015.

64 Raymond Bellour, *Between-the-Images*, trans. Allyn Hardyck (Zürich and Dijon: JRP/Ringier with Les presses du réel, 2012), 17; reprinted in the present chapter.

65 Ibid.

66 Ibid. See also Raymond Bellour, "An Interview with Bill Viola," *October* 34 (Autumn 1985), 91–119 (in particular p. 92).

67 Siegfried Zielinski, "Video Intimus," in *Record—Again! 40yearsofvideoart.de, Part 2*, ed. Peter Weibel and Christoph Blase (Ostfildern: Hatje Cantz, 2010), 388; reprinted in this chapter.

68 Zielinski, *Zur Geschichte des Videorecorders* (Berlin: Spiess, 1986). C.f. the diagram in chapter 5 of this volume.

69 Siegfried Zielinski, *Audiovisions: Cinema and Television as Entr'actes in History*, trans. Gloria Custance (Amsterdam: Amsterdam University Press, 1999), 219–272.

70 Krauss, *Voyage on the North Sea*, 57. Here, the beginnings of a hitherto uncommon intertextual reference in video discourse start to emerge.

71 Fredric Jameson, "Reading without Interpretation: Post-Modernism and the Video-Text," in *The Linguistics of Writing: Arguments between Language and Literature*, ed. Nigel Fabb, Derek Attridge, Alan Durant, and Colin MacCabe (Manchester: Manchester University Press, 1987), 202.

72 Jameson, "Reading without Interpretation," 219. Cf. also Jameson's extended analysis of the experimental music video "AlienNATION" (1979) by Edward Rankus, John

Manning, and Barbara Latham in *Postmodernism, or, the Cultural Logic of Late Capitalism* (Durham, NC: Duke University Press, 1991), 79–92.

73 "We are left with that pure and random play of signifiers that we call postmodernism, which no longer produces monumental works of the modernist type but ceaselessly reshuffles the fragments of preexistent texts, the building blocks of older cultural and social production, in some new and heightened bricolage." Fredric Jameson, "Video: Surrealism without the Unconscious," in *Postmodernism, or, the Cultural Logic of Late Capitalism*, 67–96.

74 Jameson, "Reading without Interpretation," 208f.

75 Fredric Jameson, *Utopia Post Utopia: Configurations of Nature and Culture in Recent Sculpture and Photography* (Boston: Institute of Contemporary Art, 1988), 18. On the critical discussion of Jameson's hypotheses on video art, see in particular Nicholas Zurbrugg, "Jameson's Complaint: Video-Art and the Intertextual 'Time-Wall,'" *Screen* 32, no. 1 (Spring 1991), 16–34.

76 Sean Cubitt, *Videography: Video Media as Art and Culture* (London: Palgrave Macmillan, 1993) and Sean Cubitt, *Timeshift: On Video Culture* (London: Routledge, 1991).

77 Cf. the entire Section II, "Relations," in this volume.

78 Cf. Cubitt, *Timeshift*, 8 et seq.

79 Cubitt, *Videography*, 2.

80 Roy Armes, *On Video* (London: Routledge, 1988), 1; reprinted in Chapter 4 of the present volume.

81 Cubitt, *Videography*, XV–XVI: "There is no video theory in the way that there is a body of knowledge called film theory or, rather differently, television studies. There never will be. Not being really a simple and discrete entity, video prevents the prerequisite for a theoretical approach: that is, deciding upon an object about which you wish to know." See also the introduction to this volume.

82 Ina Blom, *The Autobiography of Video: The Life and Times of a Memory Technology* (New York: Sternberg Press, 2016), 31–3.

83 "I will attempt to trace the effectuating powers of a memory technology—analog video—that used artistic frameworks and art-related materials, personnel, and skills as part of an exploration of its own capacity for memory." Blom, *Autobiography of Video*, 16.

Video: From Technology to Medium (2006)

Yvonne Spielmann

Technologies of the Electronic Medium

In this article I propose to discuss video in two ways. First, I will examine video as an electronic technology of signal processing and transmission that shares these properties with other electronic media, notably television. Second, I understand video as a medium in its own right that—like any other medium—develops step by step from the emergence of a novel technology and through the articulation of a specific media language and semiotic system to successfully establish an aesthetic vocabulary, in this case specific to the videographic capacities of electronic signal processing. Once such a media-specific set of means of expression is achieved, video becomes a medium that can be distinguished from other, already existing media. The development from technology to medium also demonstrates that video has some features of analogue recording in common with film and shares processes of both signal-encoded information and transmission with television, but it also incorporates programmable functions in image processors that closely connect to digital programming in computers. I wish to focus on the matter of specificity from two angles: the first is the development from technology to medium, the second is the position of video in the context of analogue and digital media forms and the conceptual linkage among video, analogue processors, and digital computers.[1] [. . .]

To start with, we need to acknowledge that the introduction of a new technology interrelates in many ways with surrounding media and involves dynamic processes that shape the emergence of a new medium. As André Gaudreault and Philippe Marion explain: "When a medium appears, an intelligible media culture already exists. When a medium comes into the world, it must also come to grips with preestablished codes (genres, institutions, other media, etc.)."[2] What differentiates video from other media technologies lies in the expression of electronic signal processing, for example, in closed-circuit video feedback, delayed line processing, and other electromagnetic manipulations of the electronic flow of the video signal. These modulations of the signal lines take place inside the machine or are effected by a series of tools and may also occur through the exchange of video and audio signals. The flexible and transformative characteristics of video are highlighted by the specific possibility that the visible form of an image can arise from different machines in the electronic setting: from cameras, from monitors and screens, and in various effects devices such as synthesizers, keyers, and analogue computers. Video processing means that real-time visual effects can be directly presented within an external monitor (they do not need to be fixed on magnetic tape) or can arise in the integrated screen of a processor that shows the scanning of the video signals in horizontal lines.

This technical setting defines the open structure of video. The ability to process the electronic signal and the interchangeability of the audio and video signals manifest the transformative qualities of video. These are the technical conditions for the realization of video as a medium that employs specific forms of presentation that emerge directly from electronic signal processing.

To say that video is an electronic medium means that its emergence requires electronic signal transfer. Video signals are in constant motion. They are generated within the camera and can circulate inside the system of recording and transmission (the closed circuit). It is possible to modulate video signals through processors and keyers and to display the signal aurally, visually, or both simultaneously (you can "hear" what you "see" and vice versa). Conventional film comprises separate visual and audio elements, physically positioned next to each other on the material film strip. In the electronic medium, however, signals are output interchangeably as audio or video and can be fed back as video input, and so forth. This specific audiovisual capacity of video is expressed when signals generated by an audio synthesizer are transformed into visual signals, so that audio signals steer the appearance of video forms, and contrarily when information encoded in the video signal is displayed visually and aurally at the same time. Because of this generic interchangeability of audio and video in both directions, it is appropriate to call video the first *audiovisual medium*.[3]

The immediacy of video, the simultaneity of recording and playing, differs from photochemical media, like photography and film, even though video similarly has the optical mechanism of recording at its disposal. But the optical recording of light impulses is not the only way to produce video. Different from external input, the waveforms in a video signal can be created by oscillators in the machines. In fact, there are multiple ways to input a signal aside from the recording process (for example, the signal output of one device can be used as the input to another); more important, video can be realized through signal processes that are generated inside the devices and run through the machines without any recording process at all. I emphasize these basic characteristics of video in order to demonstrate that there is no determinant place and also no fixed order required to generate, transmit, and represent electronic imagery.

Video's Position in the Media System

[. . .] Video-specific images differ from those produced in the electronic transmission of television. In conventional television, the goal is to stabilize signal processes and avoid the visibility of scanning lines that create a televisual impression of flow. Stabilization is necessary to achieve a recognizable image of the "world"—a representation of something that has been recorded. The constant flow of signals in electronic imagery takes stable form to represent the televisual image only when the video information that is written in lines (scan lines) from left to right and top to bottom (like writing on a page in Western culture) is adjusted according to the standardized broadcast formats of PAL (the common European standard) and NTSC (North America and Japan). So this standard form of stabilized "frames" adheres to the semiotic convention of Western culture.[4] The form as such gets disrupted and manipulated in all possible ways by video artists who experiment with the conventional technology. Among these practitioners have been Paik, Steina and Woody Vasulka, Dan Sandin, and Gary Hill, to name only a few prominent ones.

Video's immediacy and potential for processing generate a concept of the image that is different from other time-based media, namely photography and film. The status of the image changes in video: it is electronically recorded, transferred to another device, and finally transmitted to a monitor. In fact, it can be properly described as image only if we keep in mind that the electronic image is a constantly moving flow of signals. Due to its unstable and incoherent characteristics, it is more precise to emphasize the transformative capacities of the video image, anchored in signal processes that differ from the spatial-temporal unity of a "tableau" or "frame" image. So video is best understood as "transformation image," that is, because of the line-signal process, video produces an image that is constantly undergoing transformation. In film and photography, the individual frame or a sequence of frames embodies the media-specific characteristics; in video, the passages between frames and frame positions are central. Moreover, these passages between images and half-images (since video images consist of half-images that are interlaced) can be constantly modulated, which allows video-still imaging, forward and reverse movements, and figurations that are reversible and can be endlessly repeated in feedback. The flexible, unstable, incoherent, and nonfixed forms of the video image I will refer to as *imagery*.

Video also differs from television and film due to the function of the apparatus specific to each medium. While television and film both maintain their specifically fixed setting of temporal-spatial relationships between the projection (film) or transmission (television) and the positioning of the viewer in the public space of the cinema or the private space of the living room, video differs in that it has no coherent apparatus structure. It has not developed a systematic model of viewing comparable to the orders of seeing in cinematography, which borrows its apparatus structure of the appearance of distance from Renaissance perspective. In contrast to this system of perspectival construction, video appears in modular presentations wherever the machines can be plugged together, so there is no systematic relationship between the placement of the apparatus and the medium's temporal-spatial model of addressing the viewer. Video's open apparatus structure includes the multiple possibilities for the audiovisual exchange of electronic waveforms.

Due to its open apparatus—the processing and transformative characteristics of the electronic image—video, despite its status as an analogue medium, shares significant features of the digital. Both the electronic and the digital media forms of video have the potential to produce imagery in any direction and dimension in an open structure. In video, these operations result in the flexible and unstable appearance of electronic media images through changes of scale and the layering of image fields. [. . .]

In the late 1960s, video pioneers like the Vasulkas, Hill, and Paik started to work with such tools as synthesizers, keyers, and image processors to manipulate, modulate, and control the flow of electronic signals and their waveforms in ways that deliberately departed from the coherent image and the usual televisual appearance of the electronic form, in which the video signal is "forced" to maintain a coherent form.[5] The structural openness of the electronic image determined its maneuverability and technically connected video to digital processing. This development at the same time departed from the cinematic form of the frame. Video effects such as closed-circuit feedback and delay transgressed and dissolved the concept of a coherent image, just as programming with digital computers would do. [. . .]

Does Difference Matter?

[. . .] Video has entered a larger arena of media production and as a result is represented in many media applications, such as video-film, video installations, and video clips on Web sites; once video was successfully established as a proper medium, it then converged into mixed-media forms. And due to the wide range of interrelationships and the increase in technical development, in the end there is no need to distinguish video and film. This perspective overlooks historical factors that are responsible for the specificity of the medium and for the dynamics within the media system where interrelationships with other media are not stable but shifting. Because of its flexible, nonfixed, and unstable structure, video is an easy tool to adapt to all different kinds of media. Therefore it cannot employ much specificity at all. And because it cannot have many features of its own, it does not constitute a real medium, but rather holds the position of an intermediary state, somewhere on the continuum between analogue and digital computers. The observation that video apparently is a multipurpose instrument would then be understood as an indication that historically it has spread into a variety of media practices and arts but has not created its own cultural forum. This view misunderstands the directions of media development and reverses the history of the use of video, reducing its status as a medium back to the level of a technology.

A closer look reveals a second way to understand the medium. Because video was aesthetically different from film and television and despite its poor image quality and limited applications, video was welcomed by experimental practitioners of performance, Happenings, and Fluxus events, who were looking for new means of expression to transgress the vocabularies and territories of established institutions. Video was clearly seen as a new medium and not as an applicable technology. The waveforms of the electronic image, particularly feedback, and the immediacy of presentation were expressive means of an emerging video culture. As Woody Vasulka put it, "Video feedback is a dynamic flow of imagery created by the camera looking at its own monitor. It was often (and still is) the first phenomenon that seduced users of video by its sheer beauty . . . The acknowledged master of feedback was Skip Sweeney, organizer of the first video festivals and founder of Video Free America in San Francisco. To Sweeney feedback was 'a religion—a wave to ride.'"[6]

The critique that video is not a proper medium was also put forward in the early days of video. It was precisely because of the characteristics of video relating to the constant transformation of the waveform that filmmakers in the 1970s [. . .] found the medium unacceptable. In addition, the small-scale, black-and-white image had very low resolution and lacked depth of field. The rejection of video at first meant it would be neither accepted at film festivals nor discussed in relation to art. Later, in the 1980s, filmmakers started working with video equipment for economic reasons, but most were interested only in shooting in conventional feature film format on video and not in producing for the medium. Furthermore, video for a long period was not acceptable to the art market: it did not enter collections and museums, and it was considered too poor-quality, fragile, and difficult to preserve. In this cultural environment, video developed in the experimental fields of art where there was strong concern with live art and the ephemeral. In addition video played an important role for political groups that had no media expertise but were dissatisfied with media coverage in institutionalized television. Many of these independent television groups, however, later moved into the television system.

Some technicians, engineers, and computer pioneers engaged in the new technology and collaborated with the early experimental video artists to explore the aesthetic forms of abstract video. Artists and engineers worked together to build new devices that were not available on the market, generally for manipulation of the electronic image through feedback, delay, and layering: most prominently the Paik-Abe Synthesizer (used by Paik) and the Rutt/Etra-Scan Processor (used by the Vasulkas and Hill). Interestingly, such modulation and distortion effects were also applied to the existing televisual image. Paik especially was interested in defamiliarizing the television frame, while the Vasulkas sought to create video imagery from scratch, from signals, and Hill explored similarities between the electronic and other language systems.

Because of the diversity of these activities and their focus on the immediacy of the live medium, video until recently was not prone to institutionalization, by comparison with the work in cinemas and museums. Even today, when there is a growing concern with the preservation of video art in archives and collections, video represents a much smaller section than film. From this media-historical perspective, I would like to strengthen the argument that difference does matter: only on the grounds of media difference will it be possible to discuss specificity and determine the basic characteristics of video. As early experimentation with feedback demonstrates, specificity lies in the abstractness of transforming waveforms, which results from the susceptibility of electronic signals to processing. So both of the modes of understanding video discussed above are subject to critique, because they lack an appreciation of the dynamic development of video based on the specific nature of the medium. First, there is lack of concern with the articulation of an electronic vocabulary developed in interrelation with existing aesthetic forms. Second, a narrow perspective on the introduction of video technology fails to differentiate between applications that are specific (like feedback) and those nonspecific to video (e.g., the use of video for documentation).

When the understanding of media-specificity is not at the core of discussing video, the conversation can become purely academic. This occurs mainly in debates on the convergence of various technical media tools that have no body of video theory comparable to film theory to provide the necessary orientation. [. . .]

Although the matter of media-specificity needs more attention in the video debates, nevertheless the recent adaptations of video techniques and aesthetics in multimedia installations and the implementations of video sequences in virtual and interactive media arts produce the side effect of finally helping video works enter museums and collections. One prerequisite of this move toward video, however, seems to be the categorization of the electronic as an "old" medium, something that has outlived its own era and has turned into an interesting tool for aesthetic productions in newer, more contemporary media. Again, the overriding concern is with video technology, not with media-specificity. [. . .]

Another challenge arises when the larger media development seems to incorporate all media differences and notions of specificity under the umbrella of the digital. When film, video, and computer imagery are conflated technically, the distinctions among them cease to be a topic of interest in critical debates. A consideration of media-specificity in video seemingly becomes rather anachronistic. Following the logic of the digital as a universal medium, a new paradigm of sameness and loss of differentiation inevitably evolves, including a rather ahistorical understanding of the historically separate development of film, video, and computers; they are no longer seen as distinct. [. . .]

Two aspects of the argument that video has become obsolete—because technological difference does not matter in the digital and because video was a technology, never a fully developed medium—converge in a new direction when we look at the sudden increase in video works since the 1990s. A close examination suggests that the artists newly involved in video regard it as an old technology and do not work with its media-specific language. The use of video in contemporary media arts is not necessarily driven by exploration and further development of video as an electronic form. Instead, the artists draw on video techniques in film (interactive cinema installations), in multiple-screen installations (mainly of narrative sequences), and in virtual-reality settings (which use video applications to convey the sense of movement).

The point I want to stress is that such contemporary "video installations" are less concerned with video than with other media forms: for instance, with painting in Bill Viola's recent works, with film and cinematic movement in Douglas Gordon's video-films, and with photography and film in Fiona Tan's work, to give examples of the variety. Evidently, in the context of new media, the older medium of video has become a means and a technique in the service of interactive installations in which video sequences are implemented to expand and enrich the "new" medium. For example, video and virtual-reality techniques are brought together in the new form of augmented reality. Clearly, when we discuss such elements of interactive and multimedia installations, we do not recognize video per se. [. . .]

The Electronic Medium

The emergence of a medium usually occurs through dynamic and interrelated processes and not in breaks and ruptures that would draw divisions in media history of the "before" and "after" kind (in painting, film, video, digital media, and so on). This suggests that both integration and differentiation come into play in the consideration of video as an electronic medium: "Various criteria interact when we paint the portrait of a medium or design its identity card: its relationship to an institution, its semiotic configurations, its means of transmission and the technological possibilities of this means, the ways it is disseminated, the communicative and relational devices that are put in place or induced, etc."[7]

To the extent that video departs from the frame-bound imagery that is essential to photography and film and transgresses the standardized format of the televisual image, an electronic language is put into place. The possibilities of electronic manipulation mean that the scale, form, directions, and dimensions of an image are all variable elements. [. . .]

In a comparative examination of media forms, the predisposition of the electronic to processing and the interchangeability of its audio and video streams together characterize the technical conditions that ground the realization of the aesthetic forms specific to video. Once these specific presentational forms were established, video developed into a medium. This brief history of the audiovisual medium of video also demonstrates that the articulation of an electronic language must be discussed in the context of a larger dynamic development from technology to medium. The first steps, however, toward the articulation of a media language distinct from preexisting media reflect the struggles of each medium to realize its singularity and specificity.

From Yvonne Spielmann, "Video: From Technology to Medium," *Art Journal* 65, no. 3 (Fall 2006), 55–70.

Notes

1 See also Yvonne Spielmann, *Video: Das reflexive Medium* (Frankfurt am Main: Suhrkamp, 2005). An edition in English, *Video: The Reflexive Medium*, is forthcoming from MIT Press, 2007 [actually published in 2008].

2 André Gaudreault and Philippe Marion, "The Cinema as a Model for the Genealogy of Media," *Convergence* 8, no. 4 (2002), 12. This is a special issue on intermedia, edited by Jürgen Heinrich and the present author.

3 It is important to note that the use of terminology in this area is not coherent and mostly not very precise. To characterize video as audiovisual for the most part merges a technical and an aesthetic definition. Strictly speaking, "audio" and "video" refer to the status of the signal, whereas "aural" and "visual" would characterize the aesthetic processes (of using or working with audio and video signals) and would be used to describe the media properties of video in relationship to other media that also have aural and visual forms of presentation.

4 These formal parameters of television are deliberately set and not specific to the technology because if the signal flow were not adjusted to build the standard format it would just run horizontally in time. Some readers will remember the white line of the horizontal running signal visible on early monitors that were not functioning properly (according to the broadcast norm).

5 See Yvonne Spielmann, "Video and Computer: The Aesthetics of Steina and Woody Vasulka," 2003, available online at www.fondation-langlois.org/media/activites/vasulka/Spielmann_EN.pdf.

6 Woody Vasulka, "Video Feedback with Audio Input Modulation and CVI Data Camera," in *Eigenwelt der Apparate-Welt: Pioneers of Electronic Art*, ed. David Dunn, Woody Vasulka, and Steina Vasulka (Linz: Ars Electronica, 1992), 148.

7 Gaudreault and Marion, "The Cinema as a Model for the Genealogy of Media," 15.

Video, Flows, and Real Time (1996)

Maurizio Lazzarato

3.1 Recording (or Habit)

3.1.1

If cinema has revealed that the world is a flow of images and that the world of images is in continuous variation, video technology initiates a further deterritorialization of these flows. It reveals not only the movements, the infinite variation of images, but also the time-matter of which these images are made: electromagnetic waves. Video technology is a machinic assemblage that establishes a relationship between asignifying flows (waves) and signifying flows (images). It is the first technical means of image production that corresponds to the generalized decoding of flows.[1] Photography is already a technology that crystallizes time, since the image it creates is connected to the camera's shutter speed and its capacity to retain time. Photography seizes a becoming by fixing it. Cinema, by unrolling the photogram, gives the illusion of movement, according to Henri Bergson's definition.[2] But only video technology manages to capture movement—not simply the movement through space, but the pure vibrations of light.

> In video, movement is light. It is movements, before anything else, that make up the structure of the video image. It is much more in the structure of the image than in the movement itself, that is, in the image that traverses space. Video is directly associated with light since it is a technological transformation-codification. Movement is produced by the electronic structure of the image: its grains, its lines, its frame. In objects there are movements, there are frequencies, there are atoms, there is energy. Video makes possible the perception of these energetic objects and thus the discovery of a different reality.[3]

The genetic element of cinema is still the photogram—at the technological level of image creation, since montage will introduce another genetic element, a temporal element—while in video it is time.[4] Cinema technology, from this point of view, corresponds to a moment of transition toward a generalized decoding of flows: its technology is an assemblage of photographic impressions—chemical imprints of light upon a support—and flows, the scrolling of the photogram. The automatic production of the image is not yet the product of any electronic flow, it does not yet extract from the infinite variation of asignifying figures, and it does not yet plunge into image-matter. Video technology is a good metaphor for the relationship between matter, as Bergson understands it, and the perception of the body. The video image is not a stationary photogram set in motion by a mechanical assemblage, but an image in continuous formation painted by an electronic brush. It gets its movement directly from the undulation of matter. In fact, it is this very undulation. Video technology is a modulation of flows, and its image is nothing but a relation of flows. It is contraction-dilation of time-matter.[5] And this image of raw perception comes before memory (montage), not as an icon, but as a frame of points and lines. Thus video does not present images but simply shows the weaving of lines. The difference between weaving and video is that video keeps weaving and reweaving to infinity, according to new motifs.

This process of synthesis is even present, albeit in a disguised way, in Marshall McLuhan's work. The video image projects about three million pixels per second to the viewer, who can only retain a few dozen at a time, with which he will construct an image. Every video image is a mosaic of clear and less clear pixels, and it forces us in each moment to synthesize the elements of this mosaic in an intense participation of all the senses.

3.1.2

In this regard, the Bergsonian characteristics of video, as well as its specific relation to cinema, had already been defined by video artists in the 1960s. The cinema camera is still too close to the illusion of perception as the impression of an object on a support, whereas it is sufficient to simply connect a video camera in order to see images. "You don't need a recorder to have video. You turn it on, and the circuits are all activated—it's humming, it's going . . . it's all connected—a living, dynamic system, an energy field."[6] We are plunged into pure vibrations, into the circulation of time-matter. The decision to record consists in turning on the recorder, not the camera. "The camera is always on, there is always an image. This duration, this always-there, can be said to be real time."[7] When one makes a video, one plugs into and interferes with the continuous process of universal variation that exists prior to any intention of working with it; one installs oneself in the flow. This duration can be called "real time," a duration that cinema does not know. Television has rendered visible the characteristic of video in which the proliferation of images is infinite. With television, the world has always been made up of images. It is therefore no longer necessary to represent or create images. As the artists tell us, we are "working with images" not "creating images."[8]

3.1.3

In order to understand the specific differences between the technological assemblages of cinema and video, further analysis is necessary. A rapprochement between cinema and Bergson's interpretation of it has already been brilliantly conducted by Gilles Deleuze. In fact, it is thanks to his work that my reflection on this topic was able to assume consistency. Deleuze makes a very original and relevant comparison between the concept of pure perception and the fact that cinema returns the world to us as a world of images. Starting from these insights, I would like to illustrate not only how video technology returns the world to us as image but also that it reproduces the relationship between perception and memory, as theorized by Bergson. In this regard, I compare the way that Nam June Paik discusses the production of color by video technology with Bergson's analysis of the apparatus of color perception in consciousness.

We have defined pure perception as an image, but it must be remembered it is the image in itself, the image that is not seen by any eye. It would be more accurate to speak about the flow of light or even, as Bergson suggests, to make this concept perceptible, through an image, to our consciousness of pure, infinite vibrations. The image itself is already a synthesis, a fixation of pure perception. It is a selection and contraction of pure vibrations, performed according to the needs of action. "The truth is that this independent image is a late and artificial product of the mind."[9] To use a beautiful Bergsonian metaphor, the image in perception, like a video image, emerges from visual dust.

Video allows us to go beyond the image, to access something of the dimension of pure perception: flows of light, matter-flows. It can venture to places that our consciousness cannot, accessing and working on something like Bergsonian pure perception. According to Deleuze, pure perception exists for us only in principle. It is therefore an abstraction, since it is inseparable from a filter through which things emerge. "A great screen has to be placed in between them. Like a formless elastic membrane, an electromagnetic field . . . it makes something issue from chaos . . . From a physical point of view, chaos would be a universal giddiness, the sum of all possible perceptions being infinitesimal or infinitely minute; but the screen would extract differentials that could be integrated in ordered perceptions."[10] According to Deleuze, there are an infinity of filters or superimposed screens, from our senses to the ultimate filter beyond which there would be pure perception or chaos. The electromagnetic screen of video is a filter that is closer to pure perception than the filter of our senses.

The difficulty in thinking pure perception lies in the fact that we must abandon the homogeneous categories of space and time with which we are accustomed to think and see. If we abandon these categories—which correspond to the schemas of our power to act and to the conditions of our faculty of understanding, but not to the qualities of things—we enter into another dimension, that of perception-matter. A world of extensive and intensive forces, a mixture of extended and unextended, of quality and quantity.

Bergson's work functions like one of Paik's synthesizers; that is, with the capacity to reconstruct a continuity between beings similar to the unity of human and nature, which offers a new conception of matter and a new power of metamorphosis and creation. The definition of pure perception as a dimension beyond our categories of space and time—constituted by a mixture of extended and unextended, quality and quantity—seems, at first glance, difficult to understand. But new technologies and science allow us to see something of this world.

3.1.4

According to Bergson, our concrete perception is the instantaneous contraction of infinite vibrations; a synthesis of the flow of pure vibrations of perception-matter. What is a sensation or an image? It is the operation of contracting trillions of vibrations on a receptive surface, trillions of little shocks. The image is therefore a contraction of flows. "The qualitative heterogeneity of our successive perceptions of the universe results from the fact that each, in itself, extends over a certain depth of duration and that memory condenses in each an enormous multiplicity of vibrations which appear to us all at once, although they are successive."[11] Perception, as either image or sensation, is located, according to Bergson, at the confluence of consciousness and matter. It condenses, within a duration that is proper to us and that characterizes our consciousness, immense periods that Bergson defines as the "duration of things" themselves. We instantaneously condense an extremely long history that occurs in the outside world.

Let us take the example of red light, which has the longest wavelength and whose vibrations are therefore the least frequent. In an instant, it undergoes four hundred trillion successive vibrations. What we perceive as red light is a division and contraction of duration according to the capacity of contraction-relaxation in our own duration, which is not defined by physiology but by the power of action. Bergson often says that perception ceases at the point where our capacity to act does. Under these conditions, perception is a relation of time, of duration. By utilizing one's category of understanding, time, the duration of pure perception, is confused with space and the duration of human action. The role of the body and mind is, in different ways, to connect the successive moments of the duration of things in a time and space in which one can act; that is, to contract the duration of things into a human duration. "May we not conceive, for instance, that the irreducibility of two perceived colors is due mainly to the narrow duration into which are contracted the billions of vibrations which they execute in one of our moments? If we could stretch out this duration, that is to say, live it at a slower rhythm, should we not, as the rhythm slowed down, see these colors pale and lengthen into successive impressions, still colored, no doubt, but nearer and nearer to coincidence with pure vibrations?"[12]

Bergson calculates that in order to see the duration "in itself" of an instant of the color red, given the rhythm of our consciousness, it would take 250 centuries. Memory therefore performs a contraction of pure duration, which is capable of storing an infinite number of phenomena, into a human duration that divides and solidifies it. This division is done spatially. Indeed, Bergson asserts that our inability to conceive of perception as a relationship between temporalities is due to our habit of relating all movements to space. Our perception always inhabits a homogeneous space within the indefinite multiplicity of matter. But we must instead consider the movements in time. As we shall see, this is exactly what video technology does. From this perspective, video is more veracious than the natural perception whose disappearance we mourn.

3.1.5

Now we can fully understand Nam June Paik's mysterious affirmation that video is time. According to him, the technological assemblage of video imitates the relationship between the different temporalities of which Bergson speaks. How does video produce color? By modulating, in a specific manner, the flow of matter through a technology that deals with the becoming of this flow. The video machine functions exactly like the human brain, translating a movement that is imperceptible to our categories of space and time into another movement that is perceptible. The pure perception of video, its matter-energy, is constituted by electromagnetic waves that are the pure vibrations from which images are constructed. Color is an electromagnetic wave made up of specific vibrations that are contracted by the video machine into a duration suitable to humans. But in this case, it is technology that functions like a mind or subject in order to reduce the duration of pure perception into a human duration. It is the technological assemblage that organizes the relationship between flows. Just listen to Paik:

> Since televisual space does not exist, all spatial information has to be translated into lines and points without thickness. Therefore the signal can be transmitted wirelessly, on a single channel. They also had to put all the colors on that line. To do this, they invented a sort of social contract. A wave, known as the chromatic carrier, is 3.5 millionths of a second long. Although they are already very small, these waves are again divided into many phases, for example, seven phases representing the colors of the rainbow. The first seventh of this wave is called "blue," the next seventh is called "yellow," the next "orange," and so on. This circuit opens and closes very quickly—21 million times per second—passing through the colors in order. As in nature, it is the very, very rapid temporal succession that produces color in television. It's a social contract. When you make a movie, nature colors the film strip through the lens. But in television, there is no direct relationship between reality and images, only code-systems. *We therefore enter the temporal dimension.*[13]

The video image is a contraction-modulation of flows of light. This relation is not determined in the machine by the memory, but by a technological apparatus. Video perception is closer to the apparatus described by Bergson than to the physiology of the eye. In fact, it is a technology that contracts perception-matter, movement-matter, wave-matter, and infinite vibrations within a human duration. Color is restored to our perception through a technological treatment of duration and time. Natural perception is ultimately a particular transformation of the asignifying fluxes that, through the intervention of the memory and the brain, are rendered perceptible. Video technology imitates this relationship between flows and consciousness. We also find hints of Bergsonian metaphysics in the relationship that Bill Viola defines between human perception and the perception of the video camera. Here the transition from pure perception, with its vibrations and frequencies, to the image defined as a "division in time" highlights the specific differences and limits of human perception.

> The video image is a standing wave pattern of electrical energy, a vibrating system composed of specific frequencies as one would expect to find in any resonating object. As has been described many times, the image we see on the surface of the cathode ray tube is the trace of a single moving focused point of light from a stream of electrons striking the screen from behind, causing its phosphor coated surface to glow. In video, a still image does not exist, in fact at any given moment a complete image does not exist at all. The fabric of all video images, moving or still, is the activated constantly sweeping electron beam—the steady stream of electrical impulses coming from the camera or video recorder driving it. The divisions into lines and frames are solely divisions in time, the opening and closing of temporal windows that demarcate periods of activity within the flowing stream of electrons.

> Thus, the video image is a living dynamic energy field, a vibration appearing solid only because it exceeds our ability to discern such fine slices of time.[14]

3.2 Montage: Processing (or Memory)

3.2.1

As I have just described, shooting with video can be related, by analogy, to the sensory-motor function of the human body described by Bergson. Indeed, the technological apparatus of video only transforms one movement into another, even if the possibilities of contraction-relaxation are much more numerous than those of the body. They operate solely on the plane of the present. However, image processing techniques make possible the reproduction of the "free" labor of memory.[15] Just as raw perception is reworked by the activity of synthesis in intellectual labor, video recording and editing allows for the infinite production of images. Technology increases the power of intellectual labor, but it is only with video that the first step is taken to endow the machine with a memory that resonates with the actual object and thus reproduces the circuit between the actual image and memory. Image processing technologies are syntheses of flows that introduce a degree of freedom into the treatment of durations through shooting. On the one hand, video renders the world of pure perception, with all its virtualities and actualities, accessible to humans, and on the other hand, the contraction and relaxation of time-matter finds in editing technology almost infinite possibilities of creation. That is, the relationship between durations—human duration and other durations in the universe—reveals assemblages that allow us to go beyond human forms of experience and representation.

For Nam June Paik, only image processing allows for the introduction of true memory into video. For him, the video camera is simply an "input-time" and "output-time" apparatus that is inserted into flows (waves) of light, an apparatus without freedom that reproduces contractions and relaxations in the form of habit. If we limit ourselves to the apparatus of the camera, we remain within the present; that is, within the simple contraction-relaxation of time-matter and perception-matter. But in order to contract and relax the time of memory, technologies of image processing should be implemented.

> However in our real life—say, live life—the relationship of input-time and output-time is much more complex—e.g., in some extreme situations or in dreams our whole life can be experienced as a flashback compressed into a split second (the survivors from air crashes or ski accidents tell of it often) . . . or, as in the example of Proust, one can brood over a brief childhood experience practically all of one's life in the isolation of a cork-lined room. That means, certain input-time can be extended or compressed in output-time at will . . . and this metamorphosis (not only in quantity, but also in quality) is the very function of our brain which is, in computer terms, the central processing unit itself. The painstaking process of editing is nothing but the simulation of this brain function.[16]

More precisely, we could say, with Bergson, that video montage simulates memory and intellectual labor rather than "material syntheses." The movements of extension and compression that Paik mentions operate with the crystallized duration of the video camera. Once again, the difference between video and film montage is remarkable.

Viola defines the transition from video to simulation and digital technologies as the development of the relationship between perception and memory, since the video recorder is already a simulation of intellectual labor, even if only in a crude form. "After the first video camera, with its recorder, gave us an eye connected to a coarse form of nonselective memory, we are now in the next stage of evolution: the era of artificial perception and intelligence."[17] By claiming that simulation technologies progressively reduce the crudeness of the work of memory as they develop, Viola allows us to retrace the machinic phyla of different technologies in a new way.

3.2.2

If cinema reaches the end of its development in the time-image—solely through aesthetic procedures—in which the mind makes of all motor movements of bodies a direct experience of past time, as far as video is concerned, this experience is inscribed in its very technological operation. The essential concept for video is time and not movement. It is time that is intrinsic to video and not vision, as implied by the etymological root of *video.* The essential capital of video resides, as Viola suggests, not in "chronological time but in a movement that is contained within thought, a topology of time that has become accessible."[18] As we have just seen, this happens in three different ways: the contraction of time-matter, the synthesis of the past, and the conservation and accumulation of time in order to intervene into time in the making. This capacity to intervene into time, *to retain time in order to intervene into the durations of the world* and act upon the present in the making—is the "live" quality of video.

"While Plato said that art imitates nature, video imitates time," according to one of Paik's formulations. Video is the first technology that imitates the various functions and syntheses of time. Video technology is not a temporal technology simply because it modulates time-matter, but also because it always works on a duration. That is, unlike the technology of cinema, it exists, strictly speaking, only immediately, in the event. In cinema, time is by definition a delayed time—in which we can represent time and its syntheses—while electronic and digital systems exist in the real time of the production of social time, its overflowing and continuous renewal. The only people who have taught us anything about this technology—artists—never compare it, or otherwise only negatively, with cinema, precisely because they work in real time. "From an existential-technological point of view, we are close to the telephone and the radar screen, which require that we respond, otherwise communication is not only interrupted, but it has not even begun."[19] It cannot be emphasized enough that the real time of video technology is completely different from the real time of television. The technological machine is often confused with the apparatus of power. Television is an apparatus of power, which is constituted precisely as the denial and diversion of the ontological consistency inherent to video: real time, time in the making, time that passes and splits. This time, it must be stressed, is the indeterminate time of creation, choice, and event. [. . .]

From Maurizio Lazzarato, "Video, Flows, and Real Time," chapter 3 of *Videophilosophy: The Perception of Time in Post-Fordism*, ed. and trans. Jay Hetrick (New York: Columbia University Press, 2019), 81–94; originally published as *Videofilosofia: La percezione del tempo nel postfordismo* (Rome: Manifestolibri, 1996).

Notes

1 It is noteworthy that Bergson, limiting himself to a critique of the illusion of movement, did not grasp the force of the crystallization of time that was already active in cinema: "For the first time in the history of the arts, in the history of culture, man found the means *to take an impression of time.* And simultaneously the possibility of reproducing that time on screen as often as he wanted, to repeat it and go back to it. He acquired a matrix of *real time.* Once seen and recorded, time could now be preserved in metal boxes over a long period (theoretically forever)." Andrei Tarkovski, *Sculpting in Time: Reflections on the Cinema*, trans. Kitty Hunter-Blair (Austin: University of Texas Press), 62. But it is only with video that this "matrix of real time" finds an adequate technological assemblage.

2 Angela Melitopoulos, "Video, temps et mémoire," interview by Maurizio Lazzarato, *Chimeras* 27 (Winter 1996), 95.

3 Despite the claim made by Bergson, who compared human perception to the illusion of movement created by the cinematograph, in montage movement is not given to images through the projection apparatus. The cinematograph, according to Bergson, takes snapshots of reality (the photogram) and then reconstructs motion by adding a mechanical movement to the images. What Bergson did not see is that montage is the element that distributes a past and a future in film, the real emergence of time.

4 "In video, unlike cinema, it is not the succession of shots that creates movement, but the movement of light itself . . . I do not work with the succession of shots, but with light . . . If I fail, it is because I have lapsed into cinematographic schemes. When I started working with video, I noticed that movement is not about simply moving something in space . . . I only discovered this with video, before that I did not think about it . . . By slowing down the video image, by dilating and stretching it, I saw that movement did not decrease but that, on the contrary, it might accelerate since the grains moved differently. In cinema, slow motion is a slower succession of shots, but this has nothing to do with video." Melitopoulos, "Video, temps et memoire," 96.

5 Raymond Bellour, "An Interview with Bill Viola," *October* 34 (Autumn 1985), 100.

6 Ibid.

7 Ibid.

8 Henri Bergson, *Matter and Memory*, trans. Nancy Margaret Paul and W. Scott Palmer (New York: Zone, 1991), 165.

9 Gilles Deleuze, *The Fold*, trans. Tom Conley (Minneapolis: University of Minnesota Press, 1993), 77.

10 Bergson, *Matter and Memory*, 70.

11 Ibid., 203.

12 Nam June Paik, *Du cheval à Christo et autres écrits* (Paris: Lebeer Hossman, 1993), 110.

13 Bill Viola, "The Sound of One Line Scanning," in *Reasons for Knocking at an Empty House*, ed. Robert Violette (Cambridge, MA: MIT Press, 1995), 158.

14 The labor of the body and brain is automatic; memory has no freedom, since it is completely occupied by the realization of an action. Memory contracts and expands time, but it is a habit that is repeated. Memory cannot begin to produce images freely and becomes intellectual labor only when it has succeeded in extricating itself from the necessity of the finalized action. It can then introduce indeterminacy, the unpredictable, into the process of perception. In the same way, the video recorder and more sophisticated techniques of image processing enable greater freedom in the contraction-relaxation of flows.

15 Nam June Paik, "Input-Time and Output-Time," in *Video Art: An Anthology*, ed. Beryl Korot and Ira Schneider (New York: Harcourt Brace, 1977), 98. [. . .]

16 Bill Viola, *Video* (Paris: Seuil/Communications, 1988), 72.

17 Ibid., 74.

18 Paik, *Du cheval à Christo et autres écrits*, 145.

Is There a Specific Videocity? (2002)

Wolfgang Ernst

Maybe the luminosity of the screen is all there is to it—if so, video is inseparably connected to the television medium. Because the mobility of the video camera alone cannot be responsible for the specific quality of video (rather, it is dramaturgically borrowed from film, the aesthetics of Nouvelle Vague and Direct Cinema up to the current Dogma movement using portable cameras, 8 or 16 mm, and above all synchronized sound that allows even unexpected noises to be heard)—an aesthetics that makes the recorder become a part of the body, an artificial limb, an extension of senses in the sense of Marshall McLuhan, culminating in camcorders the size of the palm of your hand.

Rather, it is the flashing and fading, the temporality (to the death) of the electronic image consisting of image points, where with considerable technological effort a point of light continually has to be refreshed to stand still—unlike the photographic film still, which is a static, stable image, even while it becomes a moving image in sequence. So does the specific quality of the video image go back to its double time-based character: at the electro-technical, microphysical level on the one hand, and through the coupling with the recorder as peripheral equipment on the other? Is the concept of video depending on the camera, the image/screen, or the video recorder and player? And do these parts merge into a unity in the camcorder?

In his *Teletheory*, Gregory Ulmer discusses the paradigm shift from an oral culture to literacy, and on to an electronic culture, introducing the idea of "videocity" in analogy to the term "literacy."[1] At the same time, videocity offers a conceptual analogy to electricity—not just superficially but by an inherent logic. For electricity is the prerequisite of video as an operation (flow in the sense of Deleuze/Guattari) and as an image. And this is what sets the stylistic videocity apart from documentary film, which still strives for a coherent visual argument in the flow of images: reality video is politically resistant, permanently "recombinant," an associative image flow that continually undermines the authority of the narrative and therefore (*sit venia verbo*) is a postmodern medium.

Is Video an Original Memory Medium?

Here I take as a starting point a fossil of media archaeology, which I found on first entering my office as a visiting professor at Bochum University when I curiously opened the doors of the compartment under the monitor. There were no readable scanning lines anymore, only an undated operating manual, the paper archives so to speak, of the apparatus called BK 3000 COLOR. The decisive contribution of the new video medium for understanding film was not the camera, but the recording system, the VCR. It made the cuts visible, as did the Video-Cassette-Recorder by Grundig:

> With this set you can record and play back color as well as black-and-white TV programs anytime. The timer and the integrated receiver enable you to record programs even when you are not at home or while watching a different program.

Here we can see the uncoupling of *memoria* and space; the *loci memoriae* become metaphorical, i.e. transferable. Television images are endowed with memory by syn- and diachronic time-axis-manipulation; the tape can be erased and re-recorded anytime, "as familiar from tape recorders." It's the electromemoriallogic of the palimpsest (erasing as overwriting): with any recording one automatically erases. Old recordings can be erased without recording any new content: "Push the record button and pull out the recorder's aerial cable. Now you are recording only static (so-called 'grain')." Erasing is therefore not nothing, but an inverted signal-to-noise ratio.

When images become writable in figures, then one is approaching the digitization of the image itself (e.g. by a video scanner that converts the video signal into a digital one, to be able to process it with computer software). Analog video is restricted to a merely external attribution of time. The coupling of image and number first occurred in the unreal pre-digital time code external to the memory media; the counter served to find particular places on the tape—in contrast to the immediate time code within the images, where any element of the image itself can be addressed discretely. The time of the memory function is that of time made to stand still. "Stills" in time-based media, however, produce interferences.

Aesthetics of Interference

Only the noise, the interference, reveals the time-based character of the video image in contrast to the film image. This is never more obvious than in the moment of activating the pause button while playing a video: the video image does not stand still—unlike the film still it is an image that has to be permanently refreshed in order to become visible to the human eye. It is not a photograph, but a time-image—the self of video. Maybe videocity is only disclosed in the moment of (image) interference. Noise is a specific quality of the video image—not an exceptional occurrence but a basic rule:

> Musically speaking, the physics of a broadcast is a type of drone. The video image perpetually repeats itself without rest at the same set of frequencies. This new common condition of the drone represents a significant shift in our culturally derived thought patterns. (Bill Viola)[2]

// parallel to the mathematical theory of information, which does not proceed from texts and their interpretation, but from the signal-to-noise-ratio of all acts of communication.

In her video productions, Angela Melitopoulos has repeatedly made acoustical and optical noise/interference the subject of her reflections.[3] Memory here is no longer derived from a personally experienced trauma, but is formed in a constructivist way—in the same way that video in fact re-produces, regenerates an image as a light-event again and again, instead of simply projecting a fixed prefabricated image like film does. In that, the video image is akin to the neurological process of memorizing and remembering. Noise is the essence of videocity, the simultaneous "drone" of the electronic image. In the technical sense, interferences do not occur as irritations on the screen, but are the nature of transmission itself.

Film versus Video

In a precise media-archaeological sense, Siegfried Zielinski has described the explicitly "cultural-technical" consequences of video technology.

> In the interaction of work and remaining time, the video recorder has to be interpreted as a cultural technique that helps compensate the deficits produced by the industrialized and technicalized routines of our everyday lives.[4]

For a long time, that did not apply to television as a live-media, whose function was to give out signals. Video as surveillance or as media art, on the other hand, offers interpretations through the interrelations between visible reality and its storage. When video is only used to transport electronically generated pictures, then the video tape is not the original. Exactly this question can prove a dilemma for the aesthetics of video (art), something the jury of the 10th International Videofestival Bochum experienced in May 2000. Before the award ceremony, the jury tried to comment on that fact that some videos obviously tended toward the feature film—which left the jury with the difficulty whether to regard video simply as a medium for recording, producing, and projecting, or in its specific, unmistakable media aesthetic. Is video a new way of making movies, or rather TV? Is it possible to find an aesthetical borderline between video and other visual media on the basis of formal technological characteristics? Videocity often is profiled in comparison to film:

> The fundamental aspect of cinema, the montage (and articulation in time), was interpreted by the fundamental aspect of early television, the live (an articulation in space), in a key piece of equipment in the studio, the video switcher. This was the central creative device for organizing what was to finally be seen by the viewer at home. The basic elements of cinematic language were hard-wired into its design. A simple switch button represented Eisenstein's paramount montage, the cut, and with a switch on each camera cuts could be made to any point of view desired. Griffith's fade to black became a gradual reduction in signal voltage with a variable potentiometer . . . Thus, without the ability to record, a simulation of cinematic edited time was constructed by a live electronic instrument. (Bill Viola)[5]

However, technical overhaul of video by digital technology did not really give time to producers, still mainly influenced by film images, to adopt or even develop a genuine video aesthetic. As in other new media, the aesthetic got stuck in experimental attempts by an avant-garde that treated the medium as test case and accident. Does the aesthetic core of videocity lie in the differential interference with the television picture's attempted iconic sleekness? With his legendary *Exposition of Music: Electronic Television* at Galerie Parnaß, Wuppertal, from March 11 to 20 in 1963, Nam June Paik aesthetically discovered the interference of the picture by magnetic modulation of the wave images as "participative" television.

The figures of the television image are exposed as a function of technological rastering. That Paik himself is still speaking of television again suggests the difficulty of distinguishing between video and television, "a difficulty that lies in the fact that electronic video technology is the basis for both. Consequently, by the terms 'television' and 'video' we do not really mean their content or any electronic aspects, but a communication structure."[6]

It follows that the interference is experienced "not as a misfortune but as an aesthetic stroke of luck,"[7] in the same sense that is manifested in an early videotape by Bill Viola from 1973, fittingly titled *Information*. Video here modulates the (electronic) current itself, it is happening in actual real time, not just modulating the stored version of a recording as in film. This principle of processing electric power, which ultimately culminates in digital computers, is manifested in the notion of the switch, the relay.

In contrast to the definition of media art, which is no longer attached to a specific object, video art is still distinguished by its technology. Only when the media specificity of video had been discovered—instead of simply imitating film—videocity emerged as an independent aesthetic. Artists such as Nam June Paik pursued a proper media archaeology, a surgical operation in the medium itself:

> It wasn't until the late 1960s that this emulation of cinema was broken, when artists began poking beneath the surface to uncover the basic characteristics of the medium and release the unique visual potentials of the electronic image. (Bill Viola)[8]

The initial fascination with the techno-proprieties of video—the "scandalon of the medium" (Irmela Schneider)—increasingly vanished in favor of (mostly narrative) content, once more proving the law that media archaeology ends where content—as a distraction from the medium as defined by Boris Groys's idea of the submedial—begins.

Memory on Demand?

The traditional development of image storing and transmission methods ended with photography and film technology; then the broadcasting media started a new episteme, based on the currents of electricity. In between there is the magnetic tape of video, a carrier combining all advantages of film with the speed of electronic systems. Bill Viola emphasizes the acoustic rather than cinematographic origins of video, which—before recorders—had its roots in live television shows:

> All video has its roots in the live. This vibrational acoustic character of video as a virtual image is the essence of its "liveness." Technologically, video has evolved out of sound (the electromagnetic) and its close association with cinema is misleading since film and its grandparent the photographic process are members of a completely different branch of the genealogical tree (the mechanical/chemical). The video camera, being an electronic transducer of physical energy into electrical impulses, bears a closer original relation to the microphone than it does to the film camera.[9]

This means disconnecting video aesthetics from its discursive as well as practical coupling to the recorder, including the fact that for the spectator the "live" quality is not authorized by the technological device: "With the introduction of magnetic recording in 1958/59, the viewer is no longer in a position to judge whether the program he watches is live or recorded."[10] This information can only be gathered from without the picture—a chronologically distorted variant of the idea of an original, a mixture of the traditional time layers between (a)live and tape-recorded. Conversely, when video cameras were placed onboard a missile during the Gulf War, there was a coincidence of event, transmission, and reception; the difference between the act (*res gestae*) and its narration (*historia rerum gestarum*), known since antiquity, now implodes.

In machine-based vision, the perception of time and space, formerly a feature of living beings, has become a technically organized process. Video as a dispositive opens this range of possibilities, as an in-between medium, existing as an analog-digital hybrid: still running analog (on a reel) as hardware, but with its time code digitally addressable, allowing non-linear editing by cutting and pasting complete chronological structures.

Video is an "in-between medium" in the history of audiovisual media because it is located right between television and the computer. Video still means a delay of time and is genuinely time-based. This delay approaches zero as soon as physical time is being replaced with the logical time of the computer.

The material of the images is "neither body nor writing, neither experience nor 'meaning,' it is simply 'information.'"[11] And if satellites no longer send out video signals but streams of data that only become images through an imaging process, we have reached the limits of videocity—the difference between pixels and the imaging methods of computer visualization.

In the future, the differentiation between video image, sound, text, and computer will disappear and they will exist as a multimedia confluence on the universal platform of the digital. If "video" has a future in this digital space, it will be as a phantom existence, as an anachronistic name. What in times of the BK 3000 Color by Grundig was still called the video cassette recorder, will disappear with the cassette. When the chip replaces earlier storage media, recording, processing, and storing—the three components in a technological definition of media—converge in one material form of existence, the closed integrated circuit.

In a time when digital storage becomes cheaper and cheaper and TV programs can be downloaded faster than we are able to watch them (which means faster than real time), video seems to be literally superfluous for streaming data. The question of videocity reappears when the classical analog video system is challenged by digital video, another format of the same medium. Such moments sensitize people for historical retrospection, re-visions of video.

Wolfgang Ernst, "Gibt es eine spezifische Videozität? / Is There a Specific Videocity?" in the program book for the 12th International Bochumer Videofestival, Bochum 2002, 106–114; English translation edited for the present publication.

Notes

1 Gregory Ulmer, *Teletheory: Grammatology in the Age of Video* (New York: Routledge, 1989), 5.
2 Bill Viola, "The Sound of One Line Scanning" (1986), in *Sound by Artists*, ed. Dan Lander and Micah Lexier (Ontario and Alberta: Art Metropole and Walter Phillips Gallery, 1990), 46.
3 Cf. Angela Melitopoulos, "Timescapes," in *Lab. Jahrbuch 1996/97 für Künste und Apparate* (Cologne: Kunsthochschule für Medien, 1997), 173–83.
4 Siegfried Zielinski, *Zur Geschichte des Videorecorders* (Berlin: Spiess, 1986), 330.
5 Viola, "The Sound of One Line Scanning," 45.
6 Wulf Herzogenrath, "Videokunst: Ein neues Medium—aber kein neuer Stil," in Herzogenrath, ed., *Videokunst in Deutschland 1963–1982* (Stuttgart: Hatje, 1983), 13.
7 Wulf Herzogenrath, "Der Fernseher als Objekt: Videokunst und Videoskulptur in vier Jahrzehnten," in *TV-Kultur: Das Fernsehen in der Kunst seit 1879*, ed. Wulf Herzogenrath, Thomas W. Gaehtgens, Sven Thomas, and Peter Hoenisch (Dresden: Verlag der Kunst, 1997), 113.
8 Viola, "The Sound of One Line Scanning," 45.
9 Ibid., 44.
10 Knut Hickethier, "Fernsehen, Modernisierung und kultureller Wandel," in *Fernsehperspektiven: Aspekte zeitgenössischer Medienkultur*, ed. Sabine Flach and Michael Grisko (Munich: KoPäd, 2000), 32.
11 Georg Seeßlen, "Wirklicher als wirklich," *Die Zeit*, August 23, 2001, 33.

Video as Dispositif (1988)

Anne-Marie Duguet

The days of a "staunch defense" of video are over: no more seeking the essence of the medium, based on basic technical considerations; no more pointless battles over the definition of a necessarily vague field. Today it is more important to identify a few fundamental problematics that have prompted artists to use the medium. Their interest cannot be simply explained by technical developments, nor industrial strategies, nor the effects of fashion. It is no longer a question of the nature of video but rather of its contribution to the infinitely pluralist art of the past two decades. This calls for a look back at the context of its emergence, addressing the way in which video has participated in critical and self-reflexive investigations into the status of art and representation. It is undoubtedly through experimentation with respect to its *dispositif* that video has contributed most keenly to the development of new concepts of the contemporary work of art.[1] In many video installations that foreground representation itself, theatricality turns out to be a central category, simultaneously a critical principle and a mode of existence for the work.

Video emerged in an artistic context radically removed from the modernism promoted by Clement Greenberg.[2] The formalism associated with "specificity" (each art should employ only its own specific means) and with a work's independence from all external context (rejection of illusionism, narrative elements, and so on) was a concern alien to the development of 1950s happenings, followed by Pop art, new dance and performance arts, minimal art, etc. [. . .] Video was part of almost all those trends, whether labeled conceptual art, performance art, body art, land art . . . It crashed every party, joined every school. Whether a record of a performance (although right away the tool imposed its own givens, and the recording implicated the work itself), or the only tangible manifestation of some conceptual proposition, or one of many components in a multimedia piece, video has become the key medium of new artworks.

Its position is nevertheless paradoxical. Right from the start video was impure, being involved with dance, music, and the visual arts. And breaking down various barriers was precisely a key aspect of the art of that time. However, having freshly arrived on the art scene, video has been enjoined by several still-tenacious defenders of modernism to prove its specificity and establish its self-definition. While a few productions apparently explore purely formal issues based on specific technical features such as live recording, the most fertile works undertake a critical examination of broader scope. They invoke contexts and allusions, they play out multiple hybrids and confrontations that largely extend beyond the "territorial" boundaries of each art, thereby questioning the boundaries of art itself. [. . .]

Devising systems [*dispositifs*] for the recording/production/perception of images and sound has therefore become an essential paradigm of video work. The point is not to produce just another image, as conceptual artist Douglas Huebler has put it with respect to artworks, but to demonstrate the process of image production, revealing modes of perception through new explorations.

Crucial here is the concept of the *dispositif* as simultaneously machine and machination (in the Greeks sense of *mechane*), seeking to produce specific effects. This "arrangement of the parts of a mechanism" is firstly a generative operation that structures tangible experience, in an original way every time. More than a simple technical organization, the *dispositif* brings different figurative or expressive proceedings into play, mobilizes institutional situations as perceptual processes. While the *dispositif* is necessarily theatrical in nature, it is not the sole way to explore the representational system. Certain visual mechanisms or special modes of beholder participation can also be explored in videotapes themselves.

Many works have experimented with the cinematic *dispositif*, using multiple screens, employing various projection surfaces (bodies, mirrors, moving objects, etc.), and inventing new ways to record pictures.[3] However, on one hand technical considerations—such as the limited duration of a reel of film (which calls for looping methods) and the darkness required for film projection—limit the ways in which this approach can be modulated. And on the other hand, cinema relies on strongly established norms, such as frontal projection on a large screen in a dark room where the spectator is "immobilized" in a seat between screen and projector. This fiction-generating machine tolerates only tiny variations.

In fact, the cinematic *dispositif* is defined by the demands of a process of identification, by a kind of beholder perception related to narrative. That is the standpoint from which the movies have been the object of theoretical analysis by the likes of Christian Metz, Thierry Kuntzel, and Jean-Louis Baudry.[4] Only experimental cinema—"literal" and "non-narrative"—is conducive to a more direct interrogation of that whole procedure.

Thus several artists unconcerned with the constraints of conventional narrative took an immediate interest in video as a tool of representation. This electronic *dispositif* offered them great freedom in organizing its constituent components (the autonomy of camera and monitor, an image-object that could be placed—or displaced—anywhere, etc.) as well as a wider range of screening possibilities (not only movie-like video projectors, but also monitors whose image is not dependent on ambient light levels). There is not just *one* way to watch television. It was this very flexibility—the variety of configurations open to video—that spurred artists to use it. One parameter is nevertheless crucial in explaining why video has essentially adopted a metacritical role: the possibility of immediate confrontation between the production and reception of an image, via live recording. Thus the *dispositif* can serve simultaneously as the concept of the work and the tool of a propaedeutic. A certain category of video installations thus functions as an analysis of the foundations of dominant representation since the Renaissance, based on the perspective model and perpetuated through the design and settings of various moving-image cameras today. Video carries out this meticulous reexamination not specifically of the movies, nor painting, nor photography, but on the primal *dispositifs*, whether legendary or not, from Plato's cave to Brunelleschi's perspective panel, Leonardo's window, and Dürer's frame, and from the camera obscura to modern surveillance systems. Video, the most recent means of reproduction, thereby replays an entire history of representation.

It functions primarily through staging. Video sets up a theater of viewing/envisioning by dramatizing the *dispositif* itself, envisaging it through various roles.

Theatrical mimesis is deployed in its heuristic function. A simulacrum tests the model, revealing what is not apparent, producing intelligibility based on a principle similar to the "structuralist activity" of the 1960s as defined by Roland Barthes.[5]

If installations are the favored method of this analysis, that is because they can "exhibit" the very process of producing an image, because they elaborate their fiction in real space. Like the objects of minimal art, the image is placed in a situation making it just one term in a relationship that jointly involves the optical and electronic equipment (a light source, a camera, and a monitor or video projector), the surrounding space or specific framework, and the body of the beholder caught on camera or simply involved in perceiving the *dispositif*.

This approach entails isolating and deploying the basic components of representation in space, in order to reorganize and reposition them in new configurations. It carries out fundamental *dissociations* of the *costruzione legittima*—that is, of the construction of viewpoint and vanishing point, the picture plane (wall, screen, etc.), the central compositional point, and so on. It unpacks them, shifts them around, and creates specific gaps. In so doing, it recaptures the scene from an angle effaced by the image, reestablishing its three-dimensionality and creating a penetrable, practicable space where new relationships can play out. Space normally condensed into the moment of the surface is here dilated for observation, is subjected to a kind of slow motion—in order to see better, see differently, see how to see. Installations have created a video "eye lag," to paraphrase Duchamp's comment on his *Large Glass*.[6] Since they simultaneously display the images resulting from this new approach, they combine and contrast two spaces of fiction, one of which—that of the image—in turn attempts to *recover* the surrounding space in its two-dimensionality, to adjust the gaps, to close the loop.

The electronic machine produces these transformations through at least three essential operations:

- by testing space with time, submitting it to the effects of live recording and the subtleties of a slight time-lag or "fake live," thus of the past or future anterior, converting the vanishing point into time, and making perspectives "relative";
- by contrasting virtual, immaterial, electronic space to reference spaces such as architectural frameworks or constructions;
- by turning the beholder's body into a privileged tool of exploration, that is to say into the revealer of the *dispositif*. It is the beholder who activates the system and will outwit its riddle.

The models on which Western representation was founded are thus displayed and warped via various procedures and figures mainly structured around sets of oppositions between seeing vs. seen, interior vs. exterior, private vs. public, presence vs. absence, present vs. past, two dimensions vs. three, and so on.

Those models are revealed firstly by plays on absence, dissociation, and expectation: the deprivation, instability, or multiplication of the image, partial recovery or distortion of that image, etc. The image is no longer presented according to the usual perceptual settings, but must henceforth be earned, desired. And if such desire can be produced outside of narrative fiction, that is because the scopic drive is fueled by the very image of the beholder, because the constantly replayed image holds out the promise of the beholder's own image, exhibited to other eyes, made guilt-free and legitimate by the artistic context. Rosalind Krauss, invoking the closure of the video recording system by feedback and the self-regarding process it institutes, viewed narcissism as a defining quality of video itself.[7] Without totally adopting Krauss's generalization, which heavily "psychologizes" the medium, yet recognizing the importance of that phenomenon in a great number of works, narcissistic investment will here be viewed rather as a key engine that drives the *dispositif*, a generator of energy permitting experimentation on a work whose stakes include the discovery of its own rules.

When hybridized, these models can also be subject to processes of "miscognition," for example when Brunelleschi's perspective panel is grafted onto a camera obscura. In such works, rendering visible the components of visibility entails shifting from one system to another, yielding surprising combinations.

Interconnections, conflations, reversals, doublings, and transgressions are effected through several preferential channels/operators, namely the body, architecture, image, and time. [. . .]

From Anne-Marie Duguet, "Dispositifs," in *Communications* no. 48 (1988), "Vidéo" issue, 221–242; translated for the present publication by Deke Dusinberre.

Notes

1 [Translator's note: The word *dispositif* in French has multiple connotations, ranging from very abstract ("system") to very concrete ("mechanism") via a combination of the two ("installation"). In English the word is used in the sense of Michel Foucault, who defined *dispositif* as "a thoroughly heterogeneous ensemble consisting of discourses, institutions, architectural forms, regulatory decisions, laws, administrative measures, scientific statements, philosophical, moral and philanthropic propositions—in short, the said as much as the unsaid. Such are the elements of the [*dispositif*]. The [*dispositif*] itself is the system of relations that can be established between these elements." From *Power/Knowledge: Selected Interviews*, ed. Colin Gordon (New York: Pantheon, 1980), 194, where *dispostif* was translated with "apparatus."]

2 Clement Greenberg, "Modernist Painting," in *Modern Art and Modernism*, ed. Francis Frascina and Charles Harrison (London: Harper & Row, 1982). See notably: "What had to be exhibited and made explicit was that which was unique and irreducible not only in art in general, but also in each particular art. Each art had to determine, through the operations peculiar to itself, the effects peculiar and exclusive to itself" (p. 5); "The task of self-criticism became to eliminate from the effects of each art any and every effect that might conceivably be borrowed from or by the medium of any other art. Thereby each art would be rendered 'pure' and in its 'purity' find the guarantee of its standard of quality as well as of its independence" (p. 6).

3 See Dominique Noguez, *Éloge du cinéma expérimental* (Paris: Musée National d'Art Moderne/Centre Georges-Pompidou, 1979), especially chapter 10, "Le cinéma prend le large," and Dominique Noguez, *Une renaissance du cinéma: Le cinéma a underground américain* (Paris: Klincksieck, 1985), especially chapter 28, "Le cinéma littéral."

4 See *Communications* 23 (1975), special issue on "Psychanalyse et Cinéma," notably Christian Metz, "Le film de fiction et son spectateur"; Jean-Louis Baudry, "Le dispositif"; and Thierry Kuntzel, "Le travail du film, 2."

5 Roland Barthes, "L'activité structuraliste," in *Essais critiques* (Paris: Éd. du Seuil, 1964), 213–20.

6 [Translator's note: Duchamp punned on the title of his *Grand Verre* (Large Glass) by referring to it as a *retard en verre*, homophonically evoking, all at once, "glass lag," "backward delay," "delay toward," etc.]

7 Rosalind Krauss, "Video: The Aesthetics of Narcissism," in *New Artists Video*, ed. Gregory Battcock (New York: Dutton, 1978), 43–64.

Between-the-Images (1990)

Raymond Bellour

You are in darkness. On the small rectangle of the editing table, imagery goes by. Slightly clenched on the control, your hand feels the image. It feels, it knows, it thinks it can control the image. Yes, but for what image? In the name of what image? There were times when the hand forgot, when the image appeared almost of its own accord. A force. A frame. A gaze. Fixity made unbearable. Eyes dilated, mouth on the edge of something that is no longer even fully imaginable, a face has fallen and takes you in its fall. Perhaps you still remember that you are Joan Fontaine in *Suspicion* (1941)—Lina—in this editing room, with a declared goal. Or else nothing. In the time it takes to lower your head and bring your face toward this hole of light, your face that is both too present and absent there, there is a moment of weakness. Fear, to put it simply. Being captured this way within the borderless circle of this ghostly close-up, without origin or destination. As you learn over time, such is the first side of the experience. Its point of anchorage, as well as its flip side in the quite sensible activity, really, of taking your time before the image, stealing its time from it, time that is then sold off for knowledge, research, thirst for ideas. But you also know that there is a second side to the experience. While probably less pure—nothing is more implacable than the cold recognition of the motionless body[1]—the ordeal is no less violent; and in a way it is only the inner lining, the layer beneath the false bottom of the first. You follow Joan Fontaine again, in this story where she has no first name because another woman, a dead woman, has, practically as a preliminary, ingested its substance: *Rebecca* (1940). Hitchcock again. The heroine returns to the Manderley estate in flames. Almost sharing her point of view, we enter Rebecca's room where Mrs Danvers, the housekeeper who set the blaze, stands: a stiff, terrifying figure in the jumble of collapsing beams. It may be that if you paused the image, you would not recognize her, that Mrs Danvers's black silhouette, licked by long white flames, would be nothing but a universe of pure forms. In short, you are for a moment, which could last a lifetime, facing an invented, disfigured image, whose strength comes from its source—a drama—only to offer a forgotten quintessence, a latent energy of lines and spots, of strokes and points, something like an outline (*trame*) extracted from the action underway, but which constitutes its strength.

Why return once again to the experience of the freeze-frame, the induced stillness that obviously just evokes all the others, those that really stop, all the exhibited moments, the flagrant interruptions—not to mention the metamorphoses of the images associated with them? Why? Let us look at the question from two different angles. Why did Serge Daney, one fine day in June 1982, find it necessary to publish in *Libération* eight still frames from *North by Northwest* (1959), taken from the 3,426 images of the scene where Cary Grant and Eva Marie Saint kiss, thereby offering a mirage to the hurried readers of his newspaper, in order to celebrate with them the re-release of a great classic? He comments on this mirage by twice dividing the (English) title to make us see what we only glimpse in this scene where the kiss, the moment that lasts while remaining a moment, obviously represents both bliss and death (thus the harsh beauty of the French title, *La mort aux trousses*[2]). So there is the North toward which the film (let us say the Hollywood film) goes; and there is the Northwest, the direction taken by "the real film, the one you hallucinate, that nurtures your most undaunted dreams," this film then split between the North, where the film as such is headed, and the West, the orientation of "this unknown flesh of the film": the still frames.[3] Second angle: why did Robert Frank write that he would really like to make a film (his "real film"?), which would combine his (private) life and his work, a "photo- film," in order to "work out a dialogue between the movement of the camera and the freezing of the still image, between the present and the past, inside and outside, front and back"?[4] The remarkable thing here has to do with the three last "betweens." They affect the time, the body-soul and the position of the body-gaze, which all find themselves associated with the force that could produce them, or that could at least attest to their visibility: the time between the still and the moving image.

In this way, critical gaze and creative desire come together in a shared gesture which, by encompassing the elliptical space between photograph and still frame, has become one of the chosen gestures of the image's conscience—of its destiny as well as its survival. The VCR has now made it available to everyone, in the same way that television and the film world that accompanies it have ceaselessly trivialized the tormented research (while simultaneously fueling it) through which real filmmakers have attempted to determine their identity.

If the freeze-frame, or the stilled image—what could also be called a snapshot of the film, a pose or pause of the image expressing the capturing power of immobility—if this experience is so strong, it is obviously because it touches upon *l'arrêt de mort*, the finality of death: its vanishing point and in a sense the whole of the real (we all know that the dead become wax figures, a fragment of immobility). But we must grasp what is conjugated in Blanchot's exemplary title,[5] serving as the thread to his narrative: the ruling that pronounces death is also the halt that manages to hold it at bay,[6] turn it around and give it back to life, for a lifetime yet to be determined, and the story endures, in order to replace death with the rapturous force of enigma in its fullness, where there would otherwise be nothing but decay, as if in a *fort und da* of a new kind.

Sauve qui peut (la vie)[7]: rarely has a title been so well chosen. For Godard, returning to cinema after a break devoted to experimentation, it is a matter of noticing that the freeze-frame and the breakdown of movement have become in a way internal to the life of film, and therefore to life itself, and that this means saving them together. This also involves the invention of a new image, which detaches itself (partly, but enough to distinguish itself) from its photographic transparency in order to be open to other matters, to usher in a new physicality. In short, an image that, through disfiguration, becomes open to refiguration. What I have called the second side of the experience. Stretching things a little to express their most active truth, we could say that there is no passage between mobile and immobile (therefore involving the analogy of movement) that does not suppose a formal mutation of the image (therefore of the analogy in its most photographic sense).

It is no accident that the development of the freeze-frame, and of all the forms of "the photographic" that invaded cinema at the beginning of the 1960s, coincided with the transformations that have intensified since then as a result of developments in electronic image processing. One word encompasses this transformation—*video*, a word open on its two sides: television and video art. An improbable word; and it is still not fully understood to what extent it leads the arts of mechanical reproduction that preceded it—photography and cinema—into an unprecedented situation, via the opening of a realm where the question of reproduction is overwhelmed by the as yet barely glimpsed possibilities of the computed image. That is to say a potentiality that is itself unaware of the mutation that the timeless human capacity to create images—and more specifically to define them as art—will discover deep within itself.

This book will not go into such a debate. At least not directly. It has come into being—little by little—from a need to understand what happened to cinema when at some point it became impossible for it to extract itself from the pressure of two forces: one that seemed to rise up from within itself, and another that was modifying it through its collusion (direct or indirect) with video. The difficulty comes from the fact that video art, as external to cinema as it is, cannot be grasped without referring to what it affects—cinema as well as the other arts (plastic arts, music), in short everything it comes from and to which it endlessly returns, to forge itself an identity that eludes it. To be honest, the strength of video art—an art that does exist (it is just 25 years old), and that already has a set of works and masterworks (even if this is still too often overlooked)—the great strength of video has been, is, will be to have opened *passageways*. Video is above all a go-between. Passageways (for my purposes) to the two great levels of experience I have mentioned: between mobile and immobile, between the photographic analogy and that which transforms it. Passageways, corollaries, that traverse without exactly encompassing these "universals" of the image: thus, between *photography*, *cinema*, *video*, a multiplicity of superimpositions, of highly unpredictable configurations, is produced. Finally, passageways, because everything (or almost) is seen on television (or defines itself by putting up a resistance to it). The very nature of a medium capable of incorporating and transforming all the others, connected with the special knack the resulting products have of appearing, at every moment, inside a box that is both intimate and global, has profoundly transformed (this has become obvious to all) our sense of the creation as well as the apprehension of images.

Between-the-images is thus (virtually speaking) the space for all of these passageways. A many-sided place, physically and mentally. Both very visible and secretly immersed in the artworks remodeling the interiors of our bodies in order to prescribe new positions, it functions between images, in the very general and still particular sense of the term. Floating between two still frames and between two screens, between two layers of matter and between two speeds, it is hard to ascribe: it is variation and dispersion incarnate. This is how images now come to us: within the space where we must decide which of them are real images. That is to say a reality of the world, as virtual and abstract as it may be, reality of an image-as-possible-world.

Between-the-images is that space still new enough to be treated as an enigma, and already established enough to have limits. It is not my concern here to write its history (as with all mixtures, that would be hard to envision). Nor is it a matter of coming up with a theory, in the sense of specific concepts that between-the-images evokes and that would constitute the conditions for discussing it. For me, the question has mainly been to try and put into words an experience, such as it has constituted itself little by little, that started when it became clear that we have entered, via video and all its consequences, a new time of the image.

As will be seen, two names come up repeatedly in these pages: Thierry Kuntzel and Jean-Luc Godard. This is because they have had emblematic careers. The first, who came from the world of film theory and was in fact one of its initiators in France, has since become one of the most assured video artists of his generation; and it looks as though this shift that came about via video continues to fuel the same interest through other means. The second, who started out in criticism, later inventing the cinema we all know, was the first filmmaker to seize on video (and television) as fully as he did. He thus made us realize that if something was coming to an end in cinema and with cinema, it was because he was at home between-the-images like no one else, leading cinema (what else could it be called?) toward what was newest within it. Taking all the images along with him, and more as well.

The intent of all this is to help define a twofold movement without which the reality between-the-images would be hard to conceive. The first movement has for some time now led both cinema, and thinking on cinema, toward painting—as though the violence inherent to video (with regard to representation in general) had made the question inevitable (once more), requiring it to be asked more critically of cinema as a whole (and of course of video art, which draws much from painting). The second movement brought the image (cinema and video, and one via the other, but also photography) closer to literature and to language. Literature, for the positions of enunciation, the nature of the creative gesture, the indeterminacy of the works, their reflexive capabilities. Language, in the sense where words are now, more and more, at one with the image (instead of just getting mixed in with it, as was the case with silent film, which had foreseen this tendency). This is the exemplary strength behind Godard's *Puissance de la parole* (1988, and his *Histoire(s) du cinéma*, 1988–1998) for which all his previous work served as preparation. [. . .]

Finally, concerning the three terms that constitute *Between-the-Images*—photography, cinema, video—I will say this: Photography (only considered in passing as an art form here) appears most of all as both the smallest decomposable unit of the image subjected to *défilement* (in other words as a still frame) and as the emblem of a planetary dispersion of the image that causes it to be, everywhere and always, this fragment of irreducible iconicity connected to every life. It therefore gains ever more significance as the circulation of images grows and accelerates, tirelessly representing the motionless index of this movement. This is what can also be gleaned from the reverie of Robert Frank.[8] In contrast, however, video, mostly considered as an art in itself, must be understood from the point of view of what, in my view, it represents historically above all: a passageway and a system of transformations of images interpenetrating each other. There are the images that preceded it—painting, photography, and cinema; there are those that it produced itself; lastly, there are those that it has brought into being, "the new images," of which it is an integral part and for which it is already a sort of prehistory. Finally, between photography and video, there is film, this already somewhat old art all the more shaped by photography—which almost returns it to a stage before itself—as video has now captured it, projecting it into a hereafter where it is hard to know what will become of it. It can also choose to keep up what it believes it still inherently is, if only because it has been that way for so long. But even so, hollowed out from within, surrounded by the new forces that irrigate it, it is clear to see that it never stops transforming itself.

From Raymond Bellour, "Between-the-Images," in *Between-the-Images*, trans. Allyn Hardyck (Zürich: JRP|Ringier; Dijon: Les presses du réel, 2012), shortened version of the introduction to the collection, slightly modified by the author; French original in *L'entre-images: Photo, cinéma, vidéo* (Paris: Les Editions de La Difference, 1990).

Notes

1 See Maurice Blanchot, "La resemblance cadavérique," in *L'espace littéraire* (Paris: Gallimard, 1955), 346 ["The Cadaverous Resemblance," trans. Ann Smock, in *The Space of Literature* (Lincoln: University of Nebraska Press, 1982, 257].
2 Which could be translated as "Death on His Tail" or "Tracked by Death" [translator's note].
3 Serge Daney, *Ciné Journal* (Paris: Cahiers du cinemá, 1986), 115f.
4 Robert Frank, "I'd Like to Make a Film. . .," preface to *Robert Frank* (London: Thames and Hudson, 1985).
5 Maurice Blanchot, *L'arrêt de mort* (Paris: Gallimard, 1984) [*Death Sentence*, trans. Lydia Davis (Barrytown, NY: Station Hill, 1978)].
6 "Arrêt" may mean "ruling" as well as "stop." The conventional translation of this phrase is "death sentence," but Blanchot plays with the word-for-word sense: "the stopping of death" [translator's note].
7 This could be translated as "Save (your life) if you can"—the film was released in English-speaking countries under the titles *Every Man for Himself* (US) and *Slow Motion* (UK), 1980 [translator's note].
8 "In my film—and because of the very way they float in the current of my normal life—my photographs will become pauses in its flux, breaths of fresh air, windows on another time, on other places." Frank, "I'd like to make another film. . ."

Video Intimus (2010)

Siegfried Zielinski

The Last Analogy before the Digital

Video has become a colorful word. Often this malapropism of the Latin for "I see" is simply used as a synonym for temporal images that appear on a monitor or are projected electronically. A video can be the recording of a feature film, a rock music video clip, a piece of electronic documentation embedded in a Keynote or PowerPoint presentation. But video has also become the term for artworks, quasi-filmic single-channel pieces, or components of more complex installations, sold to collectors—usually no longer as cassettes or even reels but on digital video discs, called DVDs.

The present study treats video as a concrete technological system of things. The aim was to be exact on the history of both the technology and culture. This system of things has become a specific topic by focusing on its central artifact, namely, the apparatus which allows the electromagnetic recording of sound images: the video recorder.

At the beginning of the twenty-first century, young media activists know this artifact merely from hearsay. They see it as a technological monster from the distant media past. They no longer work with electromagnetic tape. The media bottleneck through which they must pass all they have to say and show is the computer. They record with small digital cameras, feed all the footage into fast-performing power packages, and edit the material themselves, digitally of course, with easily acquirable industrial software, which may be called Final Cut, with a PRO added to its name to suggest that the machine itself will handle everything necessary for a finished video. As a young media artist recently told me, they have simply skipped over the biographical experience of video as a media technology with its own materiality, a special case of applying an electromagnetic set-up.

Video Intimus[1]

Video evolved from a divide in the history of audiovisual media. The technological medium, designed to record temporal images and sounds in close to real-time, emerged from amidst the traditional mass media, such as cinema and television on the one hand, and the advancement of telematic networks on the other. In several respects video must be regarded as a transitional medium. From a semiotic perspective, it oscillates between the iconic images present in photography or cinematography, and the simulations of the visible generated from algorithms. Being conveyed by electromagnetic script, the information imprinted on tape is almost impossible to trace and barely made visible through the use of oscilloscopes, for example. In this sense, video symbolizes the final analog era before the arrival of the digital format. In the course of the digital age, the medium's original hardware configuration came to be dismantled as video signals deserted the electromagnetically coated tapes on reels, or cassettes, or laser-written optoelectronic discs, to settle in on hard drives amidst software and text packages stored on SGIs, PCs, and Macs. The only constant being that the appliances previously used to perform data on video tapes, videocassettes, CD-ROMs, and DVDs have essentially remained unchanged: namely monitors and electronic projection devices.

Economically, the divide is characterized by video paving the way for a new era that saw the acquisition of all the equipment and accessories required for the production, distribution, and consumption of technical sound and image worlds transferred into the private realm. In contrast, at the cinema none of the equipment comprising the film experience in a material sense is owned by the audience. The projectors and theaters are property of the cinema operators; the film copies—soon to be playback files—belong to the distributors; while the stars, directors, manufacturing equipment, and musical compositions are owned by the producers and agents. By purchasing a ticket, the cinema-goer merely acquires the right to use—for the duration of the screening—the dark space in which the effects and imaginations are organized. Thus he rents objectified time as film time in a semi-public space, constituted by the temporary community of those who have paid. It was through television that ownership structures began to be reformed. As regards different screening versions in the public space, be it in department stores or hospitals, television rooms, or news cinemas, the organizers were still the privileged owners. However, when the first small-scale personal receivers were built and sold around the time of German fascism and in the postwar era, viewing and listening audiences also got hold of the artifact required for consumption. Most people were already familiar with radio, a privileged few also with narrow-gauge film. The broadcasting stations principally retained the power of disposition over programs, movies, shows, newscasts, not least over the resources required to manufacture broadcast material. They were exclusively owned by public or private institutions, which had acquired the relevant state broadcasting licenses for the distribution of TV programs.

With the arrival of the video tape recorder, the products that had already been broadcast became available to those who recorded them; these could now be modified and manipulated. The possibility of connecting an electronic camera to the recording device soon moved audiovisual production into the private realm completely. As tape formats became more convenient, distribution was able to piggyback on the magazine or book trade, and different implementation strategies could be explored. Audiovisual products, such as art magazines or films, could be rented or purchased. Anyone in possession of players or monitors would organize their own video screenings at home, independently and privately. This was a crucially important step for the arts: the ability to reproduce visible and audible events using technical artifacts gave artists the autonomy to dispose of their art as they saw fit, beyond the industry and its development labs, independently of the typically male-dominated domains of mass cultural production. Studio enterprises and technical reproductions or experiments could now be merged into one.

Only the area of distribution continued to remain tied to the power structures of the broadcasting companies. The Internet managed to overcome this final constraint in the sense that audiovisual processes were now subject to "blanket privatization," as it were. The cultural pessimists' hue and cry about some splintered egos displaying their dodgy self-portrayals on YouTube and MySpace can certainly be regarded as absurd from the perspective of media genealogy. Right from the beginning, video activists and movement groups from the realms of art and politics joined forces in their claim that the new medium should not be limited to a privileged political and artistic elite, but that indeed it should be open to anyone wishing to contribute. Peculiarly, now that this technological utopia has actually arrived—and mainly advanced the industry—we are surprised to discover that many people have, in fact, nothing to show but pictures of themselves. Quite odd indeed, considering that abandoning the author function in exchange for the delirium of making commonplace arbitrary statements should be deemed a natural consequence. As early as 1928, the same tendencies were observed by Bertolt Brecht in regard to the radio. However, this did not prevent media activists worldwide from uniting in their attempt to seize broadcasting channels with their respective views of the world.

In the history of civilization, video as a cultural technique emerged between the two poles in the pursuit to form relationships between the individual and society as a whole (in groups or companies, locations, regions, countries, states, and other communities). Within the traditions of civil society, free markets and mass democracy, political and commercial publicity emerged as the most precious good, which was to be further enhanced and protected by giving all communicating parties an equal voice. Representative of the other pole was the kind of intimacy which has been ascribed a tyrannical quality by Richard Sennett—the private, the isolated, the separated. As alpha and omega, separation became the focal point in Guy Debord's *Society of the Spectacle*.

Technologically speaking, video has been derived from the phylum of broadcasting (the generic term for television and radio), of telephony and visual monitoring technology by radar. It was designed as a subsystem of telecommunication able to transfer large volumes of data (temporal images and sounds), as an audiovisual time machine used to bridge the differences between time zones on single continents and to record fleeting events almost instantly. Video was slow to liberate itself from its destiny as a hegemonic media system after a gradual process of roughly ten years following its introduction to the world of media as a technological innovation. For decades, the activities not only of political groups but also of artists were dictated by this hegemony. However, developing a critical stance toward its media parents, as it were, namely television as the powerful mother medium and, to a lesser extent, the war in the role of the father, constitutes one of the most significant and permanent artistic statements in the history of video art, ranging from the early Fluxus movement happenings designed by artists such as Wolf Vostell or Nam June Paik to Gary Hill or Antoni Muntadas to Klaus vom Bruch. "It is the consumer who is consumed . . . You are the product of TV"—Richard Serra's 1973 video tape *Television Delivers People* was exclusively composed of artificially constructed mnemonic sentences and phrases like these.[2]

When on October 4, 1965, Paik used a transportable video system from Sony, quite likely a TCV 2010,[3] to film the pope's visit to St. Patrick's Cathedral in New York out of a moving taxi, it was not his intention to have the sequence broadcast on TV to a widely scattered, anonymous audience. Rather, he soon after showed the unedited tape at the Au Go Go, a trendy café in Bleecker Street in Greenwich Village to an intimate audience comprising friends, artists, writers, musicians, and people he knew. It embraced the kind of publicity that appeared adequate, both from an artistic and a political perspective.

Compiled from the preface to the new edition of Siegfried Zielinski, *Zur Geschichte des Videorecorders* (Potsdam: Polzer Media Group, 2010), 11; and Siegfried Zielinski "Video Intimus," in *Record—Again! 40yearsofvideoart.de, Part 2*, ed. Peter Weibel and Christoph Blase (Ostfildern: Hatje Cantz, 2010), 388–92.

Notes

1 Latin, "I see the familiar friend."
2 An unabridged contemporary version can be found in the reader *Video Art*, ed. Ira Schneider and Beryl Korot (New York: Harcourt Brace Jovanovich, 1976).
3 "The first Sony half inch 2010 series (I think it is VC 2010) was also often so called [Portapak] for the same reason. Compared to the Ampex studio *geraete* . . . also this Sony was sometimes called Mickey Mouse, because it was so small, like a toy, and often broke down. Needless to say, for the first day shooting (indeed on October 4th) I had to borrow a *zerhacker* (dc-ac converter)." Paik, quoted from a personal interview with the author in 1984.

Surrealism without the Unconscious (1991)

Fredric Jameson

It has often been said that every age is dominated by a privileged form, or genre, which seems by its structure the fittest to express its secret truths; or perhaps, if you prefer a more contemporary way of thinking about it, which seems to offer the richest symptom of what Sartre would have called the "objective neurosis" of that particular time and place. Today, however, I think we would no longer look for such characteristic or symptomatic objects in the world and the language of forms or genres. Capitalism, and the modern age, is a period in which, with the extinction of the sacred and the "spiritual," the deep underlying materiality of all things has finally risen dripping and convulsive into the light of day; and it is clear that culture itself is one of those things whose fundamental materiality is now for us not merely evident but quite inescapable. This has, however, also been a historical lesson: it is because culture has become material that we are now in a position to understand that it always was material, or materialistic, in its structures and functions. We postcontemporary people have a word for that discovery—a word that has tended to displace the older language of genres and forms—and this is, of course, the word medium, and in particular its plural, media, a word which now conjoins three relatively distinct signals: that of an artistic mode or specific form of aesthetic production, that of a specific technology, generally organized around a central apparatus or machine; and that, finally, of a social institution. These three areas of meaning do not define a medium, or the media, but designate the distinct dimensions that must be addressed in order for such a definition to be completed or constructed. [. . .]

It is because we have had to learn that culture today is a matter of media that we have finally begun to get it through our heads that culture was always that, and that the older forms and genres, or indeed the older spiritual exercises and meditations, thoughts and expressions, were also in their very different ways media products. The intervention of the machine, the mechanization of culture, and the mediation of culture by the Consciousness Industry are now everywhere the case, and perhaps it might be interesting to explore the possibility that they were always the case throughout human history, and within even the radical difference of older, precapitalist modes of production. [. . .]

For some seventy years the cleverest prophets have warned us regularly that the dominant art form of the twentieth century was not literature at all—nor even painting or theater or the symphony—but rather the one new and historically unique art invented in the contemporary period, namely film; that is to say, the first distinctively mediatic art form. What is strange about this prognosis—whose unassailable validity has with time become a commonplace—is that it should have had so little practical effect. Indeed, literature, sometimes intelligently and opportunistically absorbing the techniques of film back into its own substance, remained throughout the modern period the ideologically dominant paradigm of the aesthetic and continued to hold open a space in which the richest varieties of innovation were pursued. [. . .]

What this account suggests is that however helpful the declaration of the priority of film over literature in jolting us out of print culture and/or logocentrism, it remained an essentially modernist formulation, locked in a set of cultural values and categories which are in full postmodernism demonstrably antiquated and "historical." That film has today become postmodernist, or at least that certain films have, is obvious enough; but so have some forms of literary production. The argument turned, however, on the priority of these forms, that is, their capacity to serve as some supreme and privileged, symptomatic, index of the zeitgeist; to stand, using a more contemporary language, as the cultural dominant of a new social and economic conjuncture; to stand—now finally putting the most philosophically adequate face on the matter—as the richest allegorical and hermeneutic vehicles for some new description of the system itself. Film and literature no longer do that, although I will not belabor the largely circumstantial evidence of the increasing dependency of each on materials, forms, technology, and even thematics borrowed from the other art or medium I have in mind as the most likely candidate for cultural hegemony today.

The identity of that candidate is certainly no secret: it is clearly video, in its twin manifestations as commercial television and experimental video, or "video art." This is not a proposition one proves; rather, one seeks, as I will in the remainder of this chapter, to demonstrate the interest of presupposing it, and in particular the variety of new consequences that flow from assigning some new and more central priority to video processes.

One very significant feature of this presupposition must, however, be underscored at the outset, for it logically involves the radical and virtually a priori differentiation of film theory from whatever is to be proposed in the nature of a theory or even a description of video itself. The very richness of film theory today makes this decision and this warning unavoidable. If the experience of the movie screen and its mesmerizing images is distinct, and fundamentally different, from the experience of the television monitor—something that might be scientifically inferred by technical differences in their respective modes of encoding visual information but which could also be phenomenologically argued—then the very maturity and sophistication of film conceptualities will necessarily obscure the originality of its cousin, whose specific features demand to be reconstructed afresh and empty-handed, without imported and extrapolated categories. A parable can indeed be adduced here to support this methodological decision: discussing the hesitation Central European Jewish writers faced between writing in German and writing in Yiddish, Kafka once observed that these languages were too close to each other for any satisfactory translation from one into the other to be possible. Something like this, then, is what one would want to affirm about the relationship of the language of film theory to that of video theory, if indeed anything like this last exists in the first place.

Doubts on that score have frequently been raised, nowhere more dramatically than at an ambitious conference on the subject sponsored by The Kitchen in October 1980, at which a long line of dignitaries trooped to the podium only to complain that they couldn't understand why they had been invited, since they had no particular thoughts about television (which some of them admitted they watched), many then adding, as in afterthought, that only one halfway viable concept "produced" about television occurred to them, and that was Raymond Williams's idea of "whole flow."[1]

Perhaps these two remarks go together more intimately than we imagine: the blockage of fresh thinking before this solid little window against which we strike our heads being not unrelated to precisely that whole or total flow we observe through it.

For it seems plausible that in a situation of total flow, the contents of the screen streaming before us all day long without interruption (or where the interruptions—called commercials—are less intermissions than they are fleeting opportunities to visit the bathroom or throw a sandwich together), what used to be called "critical distance" seems to have become obsolete. Turning the television set off has little in common either with the intermission of a play or an opera or with the grand finale of a feature film, when the lights slowly come back on and memory begins its mysterious work. Indeed, if anything like critical distance is still possible in film, it is surely bound up with memory itself. But memory seems to play no role in television, commercial or otherwise (or, I am tempted to say, in postmodernism generally): nothing here haunts the mind or leaves its afterimages in the manner of the great moments of film (which do not necessarily happen, of course, in the "great" films). A description of the structural exclusion of memory, then, and of critical distance, might well lead on into the impossible, namely, a theory of video itself—how the thing blocks its own theorization becoming a theory in its own right.

My experience, however, is that you can't manage to think about things simply by deciding to, and that the mind's deeper currents often need to be surprised by indirection, sometimes, indeed, by treachery and ruse, as when you steer away from a goal in order to reach it more directly or look away from an object to register it more exactly. In that sense, thinking anything adequate about commercial television may well involve ignoring it and thinking about something else; in this instance, experimental video (or alternatively, that new form or genre called MTV, which I cannot deal with here). [. . .] Released from all conventional constraints, experimental video allows us to witness the full range of possibilities and potentialities of the medium in a way which illuminates its various more restricted uses, the latter being subsets and special cases of the former.

Even this approach to television via experimental video, however, needs to be estranged and displaced if the language of formal innovation and enlarged possibility leads us to expect a flowering and a multiplicity of new forms and visual languages: they exist, of course, and to a degree so bewildering in the short history of video art (sometimes dated from Nam June Paik's first experiments in 1963) that one is tempted to wonder whether any description or theory could ever encompass their variety. I have found it enlightening to come at this issue from a different direction, however, by raising the question of boredom as an aesthetic response and a phenomenological problem. [. . .]

It is nevertheless clear that experimental video, whether we date it from the work of the ancestor Paik in the early 1960s or from the very floodtide of this new art which sets in in the mid-1970s, is rigorously coterminous with postmodernism itself as a historical period.

The machine on both sides, then; the machine as subject and object, alike and indifferently: the machine of the photographic apparatus peering across like a gun barrel at the subject, whose body is clamped into its mechanical correlative in some apparatus of registration/reception. The helpless spectators of video time are then as immobilized and mechanically integrated and neutralized as the older photographic subjects, who became, for a time, part of the technology of the medium. [. . .] I have the feeling that mechanical depersonalization (or decentering of the subject) goes even further in the new medium, where the auteurs themselves are dissolved along with the spectator [. . .].

At any rate, [. . .] what one would want to affirm is that experimental video is not fictive in this sense, does not project fictive time, and does not work with fiction or fictions (although it may well work with narrative structures). This initial distinction then makes other ones possible, as well as interesting new problems. Film, for example, would clearly seem to approach this status of the nonfictive in its documentary form; but I suspect for various reasons that most documentary film (and documentary video) still projects a kind of residual fictionality—a kind of documentary constructed time—at the very heart of its aesthetic ideology and its sequential rhythms and effects. Meanwhile, alongside the nonfictional processes of experimental video, at least one form of video clearly does aspire to fictionality of a filmic type, and that is commercial television, whose specificities, whether one deplores or celebrates them, are also perhaps best approached by way of a description of experimental video. To characterize television series, dramas and the like, in other words, in terms of the imitation by this medium of other arts and media (most notably filmic narrative) probably dooms one to miss the most interesting feature of their production situation: namely, how, out of the rigorously nonfictive languages of video, commercial television manages to produce the simulacrum of fictive time.

[. . .] Yet the involvement of the machine in all this allows us now perhaps to escape phenomenology and the rhetoric of consciousness and experience, and to confront this seemingly subjective temporality in a new and materialist way, a way which constitutes a new kind of materialism as well, one not of matter but of machinery. It is as though, rephrasing our initial discussion of the retroactive effect of new genres, the emergence of the machine itself (so central to Marx's organization of *Capital*) deconcealed in some unexpected way the produced materiality of human life and time. [. . .]

I have tried to suggest that video is unique—and in that sense historically privileged or symptomatic—because it is the only art or medium in which this ultimate seam between space and time is the very locus of the form, and also because its machinery uniquely dominates and depersonalizes subject and object alike, transforming the former into a quasi-material registering apparatus for the machine time of the latter and of the video image or "total flow." If we are willing to entertain the hypothesis that capitalism can be periodized by the quantum leaps or technological mutations by which it responds to its deepest systemic crises, then it may become a little clearer why and how video—so closely related to the dominant computer and information technology of the late, or third, stage of capitalism—has a powerful claim for being the art form par excellence of late capitalism. [. . .]

It is, of course, no accident that today, in full postmodernism, the older language of the "work"—the work of art, the masterwork—has everywhere largely been displaced by the rather different language of the "text," of texts and textuality—a language from which the achievement of organic or monumental form is strategically excluded. Everything can now be a text in that sense (daily life, the body, political representations), while objects that were formerly "works" can now be reread as immense ensembles or systems of texts of various kinds, superimposed on each other by way of the various intertextualities, successions of fragments, or, yet again, sheer process (henceforth called textual production or textualization). The autonomous work of art thereby—along with the old autonomous subject or ego—seems to have vanished, to have been volatilized.

Nowhere is this more materially demonstrable than with the "texts" of experimental video—a situation which, however, now confronts the analyst with some new and unusual problems characteristic in one way or another of all the postmodernisms, but even more acute here. If the old modernizing and monumental forms—the Book of the World, the "magic mountains" of the architectural modernisms, the central mythic opera cycle of a Bayreuth, the Museum itself as the center of all the possibilities of painting—if such totalizing ensembles are no longer the fundamental organizing frames for analysis and interpretation; if, in other words, there are no more masterpieces, let alone their canon, no more "great" books (and if even the concept of good books has become problematic)—if we find ourselves confronted henceforth with "texts," that is, with the ephemeral, with disposable works that wish to fold back immediately into the accumulating detritus of historical time—then it becomes difficult and even contradictory to organize an analysis and an interpretation around any single one of these fragments in flight. To select—even as an "example"—a single videotext, and to discuss it in isolation, is fatally to regenerate the illusion of the masterpiece or the canonical text and to reify the experience of total flow from which it was momentarily extracted. Video viewing indeed involves immersion in the total flow of the thing itself, preferably a kind of random succession of three or four hours of tapes at regular intervals. Indeed, video is in this sense (and owing to the commercialization of public television and cable) an urban phenomenon demanding video banks or museums in your neighborhood which can thus be visited with something of the institutional habits and relaxed informality with which we used to visit the theater or the opera house (or even the movie palace). What is quite out of the question is to look at a single "video work" all by itself; in that sense, one would want to say, there are no video masterpieces, there can never be a video canon, and even an auteur theory of video (where signatures are still evidently present) becomes very problematical indeed. The "interesting" text now has to stand out of an undifferentiated and random flow of other texts. Something like a Heisenberg principle of video analysis thereby emerges: analysts and readers are shackled to the examination of specific and individual texts, one after the other; or, if you prefer, they are condemned to a kind of linear *Darstellung* in which they have to talk about individual texts one at a time. But this very form of perception and criticism at once interferes with the reality of the thing perceived and intercepts it in mid-lightstream, distorting all the findings beyond recognition. The discussion, the indispensable preliminary selection and isolation, of a single "text" then automatically transforms it back into a "work," turns the anonymous videomaker[2] back into a named artist or auteur, and opens the way for the return of all those features of an older modernist aesthetic which it was in the revolutionary nature of the newer medium to have precisely effaced and dispelled. [. . .]

Once upon a time at the dawn of capitalism and middle-class society, there emerged something called the sign, which seemed to entertain unproblematical relations with its referent. This initial heyday of the sign—the moment of literal or referential language or of the unproblematic claims of so-called scientific discourse—came into being because of the corrosive dissolution of older forms of magical language by a force which I will call that of reification, a force whose logic is one of ruthless separation and disjunction, of specialization and rationalization, of a Taylorizing division of labor in all realms. Unfortunately, that force—which brought traditional reference into being—continued unremittingly, being the very logic of capital itself. Thus this first moment of decoding or of realism cannot long endure; by a dialectical reversal it then itself in turn becomes the object of the corrosive force of reification, which enters the realm of language to disjoin the sign from the referent. Such a disjunction does not completely abolish the referent, or the objective world, or reality, which still continue to entertain a feeble existence on the horizon like a shrunken star or red dwarf. But its great distance from the sign now allows the latter to enter a moment of autonomy, of a relatively free-floating Utopian existence, as over against its former objects. This autonomy of culture, this semiautonomy of language, is the moment of modernism, and of a realm of the aesthetic which redoubles the world without being altogether of it, thereby winning a certain negative or critical power, but also a certain otherworldly futility. Yet the force of reification, which was responsible for this new moment, does not stop there either: in another stage, heightened, a kind of reversal of quantity into quality, reification penetrates the sign itself and disjoins the signifier from the signified. Now reference and reality disappear altogether, and even meaning—the signified—is problematized. We are left with that pure and random play of signifiers that we call postmodernism, which no longer produces monumental works of the modernist type but ceaselessly reshuffles the fragments of preexistent texts, the building blocks of older cultural and social production, in some new and heightened bricolage: metabooks which cannibalize other books, metatexts which collate bits of other texts—such is the logic of postmodernism in general, which finds one of its strongest and most original, authentic forms in the new art of experimental video.

From the chapter "Video: Surrealism without the Unconscious," in Fredric Jameson, *Postmodernism or, The Cultural Logic of Late Capitalism* (Durham, N.C.: Duke University Press, 1991), 67–96.

Notes

1 Raymond Williams, *Television* (New York: Schocken Books, 1975), 92.
2 I mean here essentially the *good* anonymity of handicraft work of the medieval kind, as opposed to the supreme demiurgic subjectivity or "genius" of the modern Master.

Video Media (1993)

Sean Cubitt

Why video *media*? Video, after all, is a familiar enough medium in its own right. We know, or feel we know, what it is: a recording medium using magnetic tape to distribute synchronized sound and image. But then, the word "video" is also used to distinguish between types of camera: film cameras using the more traditional photochemical strip, and video cameras using electronics, either tubes or now, more frequently, silicon chips, to convert light and sound into electrical impulses. Filmmakers, long used to video viewfinders, now often turn to video editing, transferring filmed images to magnetic recording media in post-production. Or, even more recently, they are turning to laser disc transfers, allowing greater speed in finding, comparing, and selecting alternative versions of a shot. Magnetic and laser media share a base in digital technology. Film is an analog medium, providing with every frame an imitation of whatever was before the lens when the aperture was opened. But digital media, instead of storing representations (little photographs), store their visual and audio information as blips of electricity, little "on" and "off" signals, little ones and zeros. You can look at a piece of film against the light and see what is recorded, but you can't with magnetic tape, or magnetic or laser discs. [. . .]

I often find myself using the analogy of the guitar and the piano. Film is like the guitar: you select your note with your left hand as well as sounding it with your right. But the piano player doesn't select the note in the way a guitarist or violinist does, or sound it the same way: her hands never actually touch the string that vibrates. It's not that there is any less skill involved, or that equally wonderful music cannot be made on each instrument; it is simply that they are different, albeit related. Video is like the piano: it is at that slightly greater distance from the physical world when you actually try to "play" it. The analogy won't bear much extension: the point is that video doesn't need a camera as it has many sources from which it can derive its visual and auditory effects: from MIDI interfaces, touchscreens, light-pencils, alphanumeric keyboards, libraries of text, sound and image stored as tape, disc, laser and magnetic media, computer programs, and, of course, from all the traditional media. Video media are plural, then, in terms of their origination, the places in which they are produced. [. . .]

Video is, then, at the heart of the increasingly interlinked webs of previously separate media. I don't want to make any imperial claims for the medium, however; quite the opposite. No matter how a magazine is produced, we consume it more or less in the same way. A film using laser effects, film effects, or computer effects is still a film if we consume it in the cinema. Certainly, there are nuances in such texts that will evoke specific responses. Peter Greenaway's *Prospero's Books* (1991) feels different from his *The Cook, The Thief, His Wife, and Her Lover* of the previous year, though both had their premier as theatrical movies and shared some stylistic and thematic tendencies. *Terminator 2* (1991) has more in common with the pioneering optical wizardry of Méliès than it has with thermal imaging of uninsulated housing. But all of these cultural forms share, potentially if not actually, another existence as electronic information prepared for display on a video screen or projector. At the heart of this argument is a feeling that video is neither an autonomous medium, free of all links with other forms of communication, nor entirely dependent on any one of them.

It's for this reason that discussions of video need to be prefaced with a caveat against essentialism. There is no essential form of video, nothing to which one can point as the primal source or goal of video activity. It isn't intrinsically good or bad and, as Roy Armes argues, "continual technological development makes it increasingly difficult to pin down a fixed identity."[1] At the same time, it is important to note that video cannot be narrowed down to a subset of television, either in practice or theoretically. There is a special relationship between video and broadcast television, one that accounts for the majority of video practice today: video cameras, video editing, video viewing. But that is only one of the relationships into which video enters and, though statistically important, it does not exhaust (and should not be allowed to exhaust) its potentialities, potentialities which are, precisely, the relationships into which it enters.

The phrase "video media" is chosen specifically to disrupt such a centering of video as single, uniquely this or that, essentially something. By using the plural form, I want to indicate that video works across a plurality of relationships, plundering other media for sources and channels, rarely pursuing an imagined goal of pure video, video in and of itself. Such a beast, I believe, could not exist. Video, a core element of the multimedia devices and networks into which, increasingly, people in industrial societies are connected, is nevertheless only a part of that world, a single aspect. If, as seems possible, we are to be invited to purchase home office and entertainment machines which will combine the functions currently shared between the computer, the TV, the hi-fi, and various domestic and financial technologies—telephony, banking, security, thermostats, shopping, and perhaps newsprint, letter post, facsimile, photocopying, and who knows what else—if so, the video monitor will play an even more central role in social life. This multimedia environment is, in more dispersed form, characteristic of our period of history.

In general, my book eschews futurology. Guessing the shape of the future from present trends is fraught with perils. Instead, I want to engage with the state of play now, at the time of writing and in the immediate past. Video media are currently changing the way we interact, perhaps less profoundly than some commentators would have us believe, but nonetheless in significant ways. Whether that will continue, we have no way of knowing. There seems little reason to doubt the medium-term continuance of technological development, or the widening of the gap in levels of access to it between industrialized and developing nations. Nonetheless, decisions are being made today which will affect the eventual shape of the media technologies we can expect to see in that medium-term future, decisions which at present are being made entirely on military and commercial grounds. [. . .]

There is no video theory in the way that there is a body of knowledge called film theory or, rather differently, television studies. There never will be. Not being really a simple and discrete entity, video prevents the prerequisite for a theoretical approach:

that is, deciding upon an object about which you wish to know. Yet there is a field in which a variety of intersecting activities gather around the video apparatus: the field of culture. The word culture, too, has its complex histories and conflicting definitions, largely because it is itself complex and contradictory. Thought of culturally, video is both a symptom of the societies in which it has emerged and is being used, and a tool in their further development. Materialist philosophy insists that culture, like the societies in which it is inextricably suffused, is at once a product, a site, and a source of struggle. Whether we think of that struggle as one over power, truth, meaning, wealth, or some other great abstraction, the words culture and struggle are inseparable. What we have gained, what we wish to see happen, we must fight for. So the attempt to understand what video does cannot be a passive, distanced, or objective gaze from the sidelines: it must be an active participant in the wider cultural struggle, just as video practice is. Writing about video is writing about some small areas of this wider domain, a strand of cultural studies or media studies rather than an autonomous discipline of its own.

At the same time, video practice offers important challenges to media theory. Like culture as an object of study, video demands a holistic approach, investigating all the determinations focused upon and opportunities latent within a given situation. Like culture, video requires a historical understanding in order to clarify its present functioning. And because it operates in so many domains of social life, it needs to be addressed using all the techniques at our disposal. It was argued above that video is not reliant upon the camera for its images (or the microphone for its sounds). Video is thus freed of its dependence upon the real world which the camera must record, even though the camera is a tool in the hands of an operator, whose ideological formation constrains the breadth and style of images captured. With video, we no longer need to restrict ourselves to issues of representation, in practice or in theory: much video work is simply uninterested in representing the world as it is or might be. That representational job is only one of its functions. In video media, the moving and the still image attain the kind of autonomy from the demands of the everyday world which was attained in Europe by painting at the end of the nineteenth century, and by music with the rise of the symphony at the time of Haydn and Beethoven. Yet the histories of the arts should alert us to the pitfalls of autonomy, the dangers and responsibilities that emerge along with a new freedom. Considered as a medium or family of media, video needs to be understood in close relation to the development of art.

From the chapter "Introduction: Video Media" in Sean Cubitt, *Videography: Video Media as Art and Culture* (New York: Macmillan, 1993), xi–xviii.

Note

1 Roy Armes, *On Video* (London: Routledge, 1988), 1.

Toward an Autobiography of Video (2016)

Ina Blom

[. . .] Since the revival of historical avant-garde strategies in the 1960s, the creation or manipulation of social situations or contexts has generally been seen as a prominent feature of contemporary art. The rapid development of new media technologies has been a key factor in this development, since such technologies do not just provide new forms of visual expression but also new modes of production, distribution, and public presence; in short, new social surfaces. Hence art's increasingly reflexive approach to the social—as seen in the context of early video art, where the feedback mechanisms of closed-circuit television became a general model for artworks orchestrating social feedback situations.

Yet, the standard assignment of agency does not really account for the fact that art's social reflexivity also at times opens onto the more fundamental question of social ontology. The concept of the social comes under pressure and becomes an object of thinking and experimentation. My book argues that such efforts to rethink the social are an effect of dramatic changes in social memory due to the increasing impact of so-called real-time technologies. Today, the archive is in motion; a culture and technology of storage, preservation, and classification are transformed by constant updating and transfer functions, as well as live interaction and communication.[1] Faced with this technical mobilization of memory, the discourses of memory containment seem increasingly inadequate. If we subscribe to the Durkheimian idea that society *is* memory, significant changes in the available technologies of memory must necessarily also affect the definition of the social itself—including the sociality of recent art forms or practices. Analog video appears to have been a site where such changes in social memory/social ontology were registered. If anything, the video memory crisis outlined by [Bill] Viola indicates this.[2] Yet, even if memory has been a recurring topic in analyses of video art, the more fundamental relation between memory technologies and social ontology has not been a guiding theme in histories of the subject. Efforts to see video's historical implication in this development may have been obstructed by the social ontology underpinning most accounts of performative artworks, since one still tends to posit a default boundary between artistic productions and a larger surround labeled the social and in which art as such can only "intervene." However, once you attempt a wider interrogation of the relations between art, technology, and social memory, an art-centered privileging of one standardized boundary—between art and the social—simply seems to presuppose what in fact needs to be explained.

To move beyond this impasse, I want to propose an experimental opening: a change in the art-historical attribution of agency. Rather than using the performative powers of artists or artworks as a point of departure, I will attempt to trace the effectuating powers of a memory technology—analog video—that *used* artistic frameworks and art-related materials, personnel, and skills as part of an exploration of its own capacity for memory. I will pay attention to the way in which analog video forged associations or alliances with other objects, perceptual systems, and subjectivities so as to expand or propagate the time-critical operations that are among its key features. The concept of time-criticality is above all associated with the media-archeological work of Wolfgang Ernst, in which the classic distinction between humanist and mathematical-technical approaches to new media is replaced by a distinction between macrotemporal and microtemporal practices and perspectives.[3] Microtemporal events define video. Consider, for instance, the PAL standard for a video frame, which consists of 625 lines scanned by an electron beam. What the human eye perceives as a stable, if moving, image is actually the activity of 25 frames or 15,625 lines being scanned *each second*. In this context, terms like "lines" and "frames" are deceptive, since they only indicate the opening and closing of time windows. They are purely differential indicators that serve to remind us about the noncontinuity or periodicity of the flow of electrons. Similarly, the "image points" often referred to in discussions of video images are only ideal entities. Measured in nanoseconds, and by means of interval arithmetics, they are points in time rather than in space, indicating the limits of an interval rather than numbers.[4] Media archeology is thus an approach to the materiality of the media that places emphasis on such nonhuman temporalities of processes, flows, or signals—in particular, the miniature dimensions of the time-axis manipulations that Friedrich Kittler saw as a key feature of modern media technologies in general.[5] Once time-axis manipulation is no longer just a mechanical feature, as in the sound-reversing phonograph of Thomas Alva Edison, but an effect of signal processing, the notion of static objects of memory is replaced by an understanding of memory as temporal events, defined by a dynamics of difference and repetition.

From such a perspective, the technical powers of video cannot simply be defined in terms of standardized operating systems or machine hardware that remain more or less hidden under a familiar cultural layer based on theatrical, literary, journalistic, visual, and actionist modes of narration, presentation, and intervention. Their particular performance in concrete contexts or situations becomes more important; that is, the way in which their operational logic creates connections between different levels of expression and processuality, which must be understood both as new memory-events and as the constitution of new social links.[6] To the extent that there may be analogies between such microtemporal contractions and neuronal processing, video memory may even be seen as a form of thought/action whose ramifications extend beyond the framework of machine memory in the more limited sense of the term.

Briefly stated: works of art, understood as monuments that persist over time and that both influence and are influenced by the always ongoing construction of the present, are key instances of what Maurice Halbwachs called "collective memory."[7] Yet, under the media-technological revolutions of the twentieth century, the representational and monumental functions of painting and sculpture were radically weakened, and the work of art itself (as well as any notion of its social "function") seemed to exist only in a state of perpetual crisis or negativity. However, by actively foregrounding the *technicity* of memory—i.e., the technical conditions under which the past is conserved in the present—video presents us with a definition of memory that does not *locate* memory in this or that monument, representation, or practice. Memory is quite simply a force of retention at work in all perception and sensation, carrying past materials across the temporal divide that installs itself even in the articulation of the syllables of a single word. Time, here, is essentially understood *as* a delay "that prevents that everything be given at once."[8] The force of memory is not given by the social institutions that Halbwachs saw as the frameworks of collective remembering; on the contrary, they depend on such forces to function. Languages, institutions, rituals, artworks, and habits obviously play a major role in connecting the collective past with the present—the question is only what explanatory power these frameworks actually have. For without memory's ability to produce delays between sensations, and to pull them together in new composites of time and sensation, institutions, languages, and rituals would simply be dead forms. They only persist as living practices to the extent that they are continuously animated by the temporalizing technicity of memory, its events of association.[9] By installing this technical concept of memory at the heart of neo-avant-garde art practices, video emerges as an actant that bypasses the modern identification of art with negativity and crisis, instead opening onto a new realm of social invention.

The agency of video, in this technocentric account, has a limited lifespan. It begins around the time when television producers could for the first time choose to record their transmissions on videotape and ends when analog video is made obsolete by the digital platforms that reduce the difference between film and video to a question of rhetorical (as opposed to technical) formatting. If video was designed to store televisual time, just as cinema stored past time or real durations, the analogy did not hold since video is a signal-based technology that facilitates constant, live modulation of time. The fact that early television was generally seen to be live even when it was, very patently, a transmission of recorded material, attests to this fact, as do the philosophical discourses that see video as the paradigm of time-production. The most distinct voice here is that of Maurizio Lazzarato, who draws on Bergson's nonpsychological account of memory to theorize the political and economic powers of contemporary time technologies, from electronic video to digital networks. In this context, video is not understood as an image technology based on optical principles but as a machine whose ability to contract and distribute temporal materials in an unfolding present resembles (in a rudimentary way) the working of human memory. This analysis is grounded in a Bergsonian ontology in which perception is the constitutive element of the material world itself. Here, the human brain is essentially an interface that creates its own cuts and delays in the flow of unmodulated perceptions, translating one speed or movement into another for the purposes of bodily action. Hence, memory is simply a microtemporal delay between action and reaction, as well as a force that expands on the moment of indeterminacy within this delay. The real-time operations of video—made ever more sophisticated with devices that allow you to manipulate the signaletic flow in numerous ways—foreground video as an analogous type of interface, a specific machinic organizer of a relation between a world of chaotic uncoded luminance patterns and frequencies neatly arranged as signals. Video even seems to replicate Bergson's distinction between habit and conscious memory. On the one hand, the speedy electronic operations recall the automated memories of sensory motor reactions that move too fast for our conscious registration, and, on the other hand, the real-time manipulation of recorded material evokes the creation of conscious memories or images.[10]

As is clear, video is judged solely on its capacity to act, and the mode of memory it articulates is based on the genuinely creative or indeterminate elements within its contractions of time. If video and other time technologies are key to contemporary social organization, the material reality of Halbwachs's social frameworks is not limited to what can be felt and represented—it is also made up of the differentiating forces at work in all memory. For this reason, society and its institutions cannot simply be posited objects for study, but must be explained in terms of the events that constantly produce them. This bond between the technicity of memory and social ontology may be traced back to Gabriel Tarde's nineteenth-century sociology of imitation and differentiation. As Lazzarato puts it, Tarde made memory the constitutive element of the social or economic quantity and understood it as a production of time and of difference. Time here is not a measure, as in the work of Marx, but a constitutive force, and the social is not a thing to be represented, as in the work Durkheim.[11] Hence, the task of the sociologist is to work alongside this radically dynamized concept of time and memory; that is, to follow the emerging associations of all sorts of agencies or powers of effectuation. [. . .]

The autobiography of video is therefore not a history of the development of video technologies and their uses in the world of art; rather, it is an account of acts of technical connectivity, with emphasis on the fact that such action is always the result of multiple actors or forces working on each other. But this also means that the term "video" in this book has a particular and perhaps unusual inflection. Video is not simply "a" technology but the name for a form of agency that encompassed, among other things, electronic and human capacities, and that brought about certain new realities in the realm of postwar art.

I am using the past tense here. In contrast to what the title of the book may suggest, the autobiography of video does not write itself in the present text. Video's autobiography is not a literary genre, and it does not have a human narrator. I neither can nor will speak for video, or reconstruct its dynamics through a quasi-fictional strategy. For the autobiographical operations of video—video's acts of technical individuation—took place decades ago and left plenty of material traces that can still be accessed today: video productions and texts, hardware and software. My task has rather been that of the archeologist who tries to reassemble these traces from the point of view of certain contemporary concerns with the relation between memory, technology, and the social. There are reasons why these traces affect us, and why I felt that this book about video should be written—among the many other books one could write on the subject. The most I can hope for is that this approach has some relation to Simondon's all-important point that the individuation of beings cannot be understood, except through the individuation of the knowledge of the subject. We cannot know individuation in the common sense of the phrase, we can only individuate.[12] In this sense—and in this sense only—the autobiography of video could perhaps still be said to be at work in the present text. [. . .]

And so it is a matter of returning to the technical performances of early video once more. Or, more precisely, to those sites where a range of affordances available under the term video—signaletic and electromagnetic processes; scanning and synchronization; the audiovisual character of the signal; transmission and modulation without recording; instant playback, real-time, and closed-circuit operationality; time-coding and time-base correction, and a bewildering variety of tape formats—forge new associational events. The specificity and diversity of such events become important once one recalls the wholly incidental nature of what was for decades the monolithic institution of television. In the 1920s and '30s, televisual technologies offered a vast range of possibilities, including facsimile systems for texts and images, visual newswire, and videophone systems. It was only through a distinct industry decision that television became a theatrical and cinema-like medium, which soon made all the other options seem like failures.[13] [. . .]

On a concrete level, the autobiography of video produced a variety of articulations that were expressed through analog videotape works or closed-circuit cameras and monitor setups, which may or may not include recording or signal manipulation by means of video synthesizers. They included the organization of bodies, technologies, institutions, and natural sites. But they could also be discursive, in the sense that video technology operated as a body of knowledge that imposed its parameters at the level of textual reflection, so as to produce a new sort of video thinking or what we might perhaps call a "videomatic" inscription of thought itself. [. . .]

Histories of art and technology have long centered on the ins and outs of medium specificity, the way in which the general material properties of a technical medium determines aesthetic production. Tracing video individuation changes such perspectives, since research is not premised on the idea of a finished technical individual and stable set of properties. Video is, above all, a changing assemblage of affordances. And this is why the first part of its autobiography [. . .] is found in an artistic context in which video, as habitually understood, was not yet a fully realized or generally accessible technology. A particular prehension of video emerged in a form of postwar painterly abstraction that was obsessed with forces rather than with form, and that increasingly revolved around the ontological and social aspects of the modulation of light and time. In other words, painting acted as an instance of video becoming. And (thanks to the efforts of Aldo Tambellini and Otto Piene) toward the end of the 1960s these painterly strategies migrated to a German television context where studio audiences, normally taking in polite communications on war and conflict, were reformatted as a pulsating, hallucinatory electronic collective, acting out scenarios of violent political affect. Had video been steeped in tradition, it might be said to have had a history before it had a history—but it was not. It was vested in (self-)invention and practiced autobiography, which is a different thing.

From the introductory chapter of Ina Blom, *The Autobiography of Video: The Life and Times of a Memory Technology* (New York: Sternberg Press, 2016), 12–30; excerpted and adapted for the present publication by the author.

Notes

1 Wolfgang Ernst, *Das Gesetz des Gedächtnisses: Medien und Archive am Ende des 20. Jahrhunderts* (Berlin: Kulturverlag Kadmos, 2007).
2 Bill Viola, *Reasons for Knocking at an Empty House: Writings 1973–1994* (Cambridge, MA: MIT Press, 2002), 197.

3 Jussi Parikka, "Operative Media Archaeology: Wolfgang Ernst's Materialist Media Diagrammatics," *Theory, Culture & Society* 28, no. 5 (2011), 55.
4 Wolfgang Ernst, *Gleichursprünglichkeit: Zeitwesen und Zeitgegebenheit technischer Medien* (Berlin: Kulturverlag Kadmos, 2012), 210.
5 Parikka, "Operative Media Archaeology," 58f.
6 In *Media Ecology: Materialist Energies in Art and Technoculture* (Cambridge, MA: MIT Press, 2005), Matthew Fuller describes a number of different media scenarios based on such connectivity across material levels.
7 Maurice Halbwachs, *On Collective Memory*, ed. and trans. Lewis A. Coser (Chicago: The University of Chicago Press), 1992.
8 Maurizio Lazzarato, "Machines to Crystallize Time," *Theory, Culture & Society* 24, no. 6 (2007), 94.
9 Maurizio Lazzarato, *Puissances de l'invention: La Psychologie économique de Gabriel Tarde contre l'économie politique* (Paris: Les empêcheurs de penser en rond, 2002), 216–23.
10 Lazzarato, "Machines to Crystallize Time," 2007.
11 Lazzarato, *Puissances de l'invention*, 246.
12 Gilbert Simondon, "The Genesis of the Individual," trans. Mark Cohen and Sanford Kwinter, in *Incorporations*, ed. Jonathan Crary and Sanford Kwinter (New York: Zone Books, 1992), 317.
13 John T. Caldwell, "Modes of Production: The Televisual Apparatus," in idem, *Televisuality: Style, Crisis, and Authority in American Television* (New Brunswick, NJ: Rutgers University Press, 1995), 73.

3

Video and the Self: Closed Circuit | Feedback | Narcissism

Introduction by Peter Sachs Collopy (Guest Editor)

The relationship between video and the self has been one of the central concerns of video theory. Prominent artists such as Vito Acconci, Dan Graham, Joan Jonas, and Bruce Nauman have organized their artistic practice around mediated self-observation, either using video to document and complicate their own expressions of self or building installations with which viewers can see and experience themselves in new ways. Such self-portraiture is the subject of the most widely cited essay in this volume, Rosalind Krauss's 1976 "Video: The Aesthetics of Narcissism," and of several essays responding to it.

Even before videotape became an artistic medium in 1965, though, video, self-observation, and narcissism were already the subjects of a theoretical literature produced by psychiatrists and psychologists. If patients saw how disordered they appeared to others, some psychotherapists suggested, they might be motivated to change. Other clinicians rewatched sessions with patients so that either could pause the video to discuss emotions or experiences which they hadn't articulated, essentially putting themselves back into a moment in the conversation. Some of the most prominent artists and theorists working with video were directly influenced by this video therapy tradition.

Video Therapy

Video therapists followed in the footsteps of predecessors who had adopted photography as a therapeutic intervention. In the 1850s, English psychiatrist Hugh Welch Diamond claimed that some patients improved after they had examined and discussed his photographs of them and other patients.[1] A century later, Boston State Hospital psychiatrist Floyd Cornelison and psychologist Jean Arsenian used Polaroid instant photographs and moving image film to reinvent this technique, which they termed "self-confrontation." They also gave it an explicitly psychoanalytic interpretation which was widely cited by video therapists:

> Since self-confrontation focuses perception upon an external image of self, this may bring a psychotic individual into better contact with the realistic self. In psychoanalytic formulation, psychosis is a withdrawal of libido from the world of external objects. The photograph of self may be a means of redirecting libido outward. Whether it is surprising, reassuring, or shocking, the image does present a familiar object. It is almost a part of self upon which cathexes have reverted, yet the image is external to the person, and thus is a part of reality to which others can respond, as well as the patient. It is an object that potentially has safe investment value, and the experience it generates may initiate further libidinal investments toward the outside world.[2]

Seeing oneself, argued Cornelison and Arsenian, was an opportunity for patients to invest emotional energy in an inviting external object—their own image—and thus begin to cure themselves of the narcissism, or investment in the self, underlying their mental illness.

Cornelison and Arsenian's research, suggested Columbia University psychiatrist Milton Berger, was a "historical breakthrough and stimulus to other workers to use photographs, motion pictures, or videotape for self-image confrontation with patients."[3]

Psychiatry and other fields of medicine were among the first disciplines to employ videotape: Ampex demonstrated educational videotapes of surgery in a 1958 meeting of the American Medical Association, only two years after they began manufacturing the first videotape recorders for television broadcasting.[4] Psychotherapists first used videotape as a pedagogical technology, watching tapes of practice sessions with their students. Soon, some watched these tapes with patients as well.

Among the first to do so were University of Mississippi psychiatrists Floy Jack Moore, Eugene Chernell, and Maxwell West, who in 1963 videotaped conversations with eighty patients admitted to their neuropsychiatric unit. Citing Cornelison and Arsenian to explain their results, they found that the mental health of patients who viewed tapes of their own sessions improved more substantially and that they were discharged more rapidly than those in a control group.[5]

Moore and his colleagues introduced to video therapy both the methods and the rhetoric of scientific objectivity. They opened and closed the article in which they reported their results with a phrase from Robert Burns's 1786 poem "To a Louse" that would become a commonplace in the writing of video therapists:

> O wad some Pow'r the giftie gie us
> To see oursels as others see us![6]

Video, suggested the researchers, would provide patients with knowledge based on shared rather than idiosyncratic observation, the sort of awareness which historian of science Lorraine Daston has termed aperspectival objectivity.[7] This objective knowledge of self would motivate patients to change.

Video therapy could also be a more meditative exploration of self. In "Some Aspects of the Significance to Psychoanalysis of the Exposure of a Patient to the Televised Audiovisual Reproduction of His Activities," Lawrence Kubie recounts an experiment in which a subject—apparently himself, based on the biographical details he provides—conversed with his own live video image.[8] Kubie, a prominent American neurophysiologist and psychoanalyst, served as president of the New York Psychoanalytic Institute, editor in chief of the *Journal of Nervous and Mental Disease*, and professor at Yale University and the University of Maryland.[9] According to "Some Aspects," when Kubie watched himself on a monitor, he experienced a deep awareness of his family's roles in forming his personality. With this technique, Kubie suggests, a patient can "speak to himself" and develop self-understanding without the external influence of a psychotherapist.

Feedback

To describe this process of taking in one's own output, Kubie borrowed the word "feedback" from cybernetics, a new science which he had a hand in founding. Although the idea of feedback had a long history in the engineering of control systems, mathematician Norbert Wiener, in collaboration with physiologists Arturo Rosenblueth and Walter Cannon, began to apply it in the human sciences of physiology and neurology for the first time in 1942.[10] In the 1940s and early 1950s, Kubie and these men were among those who met in the Macy Conferences to build the discipline of cybernetics on the premise that similar systems of circular causality and flows of information could be found in minds, machines, organisms, societies, and ecologies.[11]

The art and technology movement of the 1960s, in which video art was incubated, was one of the communities in which the ideas and rhetoric of cybernetics circulated. Video artists were so enthusiastic about feedback that they applied the term to two distinct phenomena: One was the psychological feedback of seeing oneself on a video monitor, which formally involved a flow of information from a human body to a camera to a monitor and back to the person. The other was the optical feedback produced by pointing a camera at its own monitor, which formally involved a flow of information only from monitor to camera and back and which was often used to produce a kaleidoscopic or psychedelic effect by artists such as Eric Siegel, Nam June Paik, and Skip Sweeney.

Both these forms of feedback produced circular causality. They differed, though, in the role of the human, who was integrated into three-party psychological feedback but peripheral to two-party optical feedback, which indeed was attractive in part because the chaotic and emergent visual effects it produced seemed to defy control by the person actually holding and moving the camera.

Infolding

When video art and video therapy encountered each other, then, they both spoke the language of cybernetics. In 1968 Paul Ryan was a former Catholic monk serving as a research assistant to media theorist Marshall McLuhan. McLuhan was fond of quoting Ezra Pound to the effect that "artists are the antennae of the race," so when Ryan met painter Frank Gillette in 1968, he loaned him McLuhan's video recorders.[12] Gillette was shooting a documentary in New York's East Village when he in turn met Adelphi University philosopher-sociologist Victor Gioscia working at a drop-in drug treatment center there.[13] Gioscia had first been introduced to video feedback—"turned on, as usual, by a hip student"—in the Queens College video studio in 1962.[14] Together, the painter and the philosopher "experimented," in Gillette's words, "with the effects of videotape on kids with bad trips—15 to 19 year olds—burnt-out acid cases—let them use the cameras on me, themselves, as a means of expression."[15]

Ryan also collaborated with Gioscia. In one experiment, the two men imitated each other's videotaped movements in order to understand each other better. "When I woke up the next morning," recalled Ryan, "I felt like I was wearing his body."[16]

In 1969, New York's Howard Wise Gallery mounted the pioneering exhibition *TV as a Creative Medium*. Gillette and psychologist-turned-filmmaker Ira Schneider exhibited *Wipe Cycle* (Figure 3.1), an array of nine television monitors playing what Gillette referred to as "live and delayed feedback." They cut between live images of the viewers, images from several seconds before, broadcast television, and pretaped footage of cows, the earth from space, and the exhibit itself being constructed. "The general reaction," said Schneider, "seems to have been a somewhat objectifying experience, and also a somewhat integrating experience in terms of one's place in the Universe."[17]

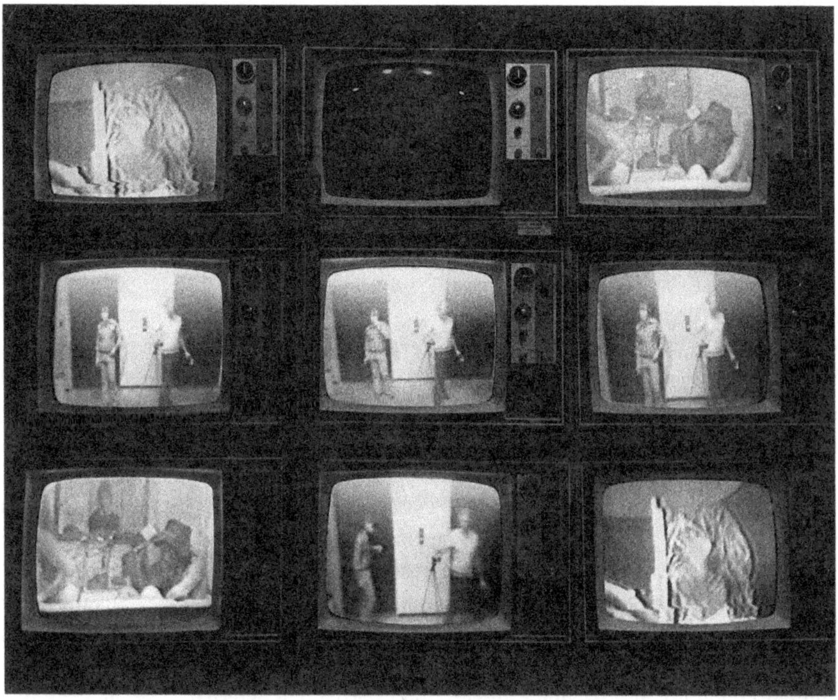

Figure 3.1 Frank Gillette and Ira Schneider, *Wipe Cycle*, 1969. Photo: Allen Frank.

With such installations, artists grasped for experiences of mind as shared rather than individual. "Videotaping with friends is like having a collective consciousness," wrote Michael Shamberg, who participated in the video collective Raindance along with Gillette, Schneider, and Ryan.[18] The ideal end of such experimentation was a kind of cybernetic panpsychism, a universal experience of a single mind shared through information circuits of community, society, and ecology. This was the phenomenon which McLuhan and art theorist Gene Youngblood—both inspired by French paleontologist and Jesuit priest Pierre Teilhard de Chardin's idea of the *noosphere*, an evolving global consciousness—respectively called the "global village" and the "videosphere."[19]

Ryan's essay "Self-Processing," published in the second issue of Raindance's magazine *Radical Software*, traverses the range of relationships between video and the self.[20] The essay begins with Ryan's own contribution to *TV as a Creative Medium*, a translation of self-confrontation to the medium of video installation entitled *Everyman's Moebius Strip*.[21] When an individual entered a curtained booth, they found a video camera, a blank monitor, and an audio recording prompting participation, a cybernetic confessional. After two minutes of this guidance, an attendant played a videotape of the viewer back for them.[22]

In the remainder of the essay, Ryan draws on the theories of his mentors McLuhan and anthropologist-therapist Gregory Bateson—another participant in the Macy Conferences who Ryan and Gillette met through Gioscia—to suggest some ways in which one could use video to develop an awareness of the interconnectedness of being, rather than a narcissistic "zooming in on 'self.'" As in his earlier "Videotape: Thinking about a Medium," Ryan marks a continuity between self-observation and communal awareness by using the term "infolding," which Teilhard had coined to refer to humanity evolving into a single mind, to also describe the individual experience of watching oneself on tape.[23]

In his later essays, Ryan built on the triadic "calculus of intention" of neurophysiologist Warren McCulloch—yet another Macy participant—to develop new topologies which modeled interpersonal and interspecies relationships.[24] Ryan also applied these abstruse theories by founding a "utopian video community," Earthscore, which would "decode the ecology and feed it back to a local community over cable TV." Although it never grew beyond three members, over three years in the 1970s Earthscore "produced shelves of videotape interpretations of natural and built environments . . . as well as 45 hours of triadic tape (tape of people interacting in three-person combinations)."[25]

Paul Ryan's influence is perhaps most evident in the work of American conceptual artist and curator Dan Graham, who has cited Ryan as a source of his interests in both video and topology and has described him as "one of the great video philosophers and pioneers."[26] In "Two Consciousness Projection(s)," Graham analyzes one of his first video works, which used the medium to embody the abstract psychoanalytic theory of projection.[27] In his "Essay on Video, Architecture, and Television," Graham describes how manipulating one's experience of time with a brief video delay allows a viewer to compare intention and behavior, integrating internal and external selves as Ryan had described through the metaphor of a Möbius strip.[28]

The Gendered Aesthetics of Narcissism, Subjectivity, and Performance

The discourse around video and the self was already a rich one when American art theorist Rosalind Krauss published her influential "Video: The Aesthetics of Narcissism" in the debut issue of art criticism journal *October*, which she cofounded in 1976. Focusing not on video therapists or the countercultural communities around *Radical Software* but on artists working at the intersection of video and performance, Krauss argued that "video's real medium" was not the material apparatus of video but "a psychological situation" in which artists engaged with their own selves as mediated by it. Though she too drew on psychoanalysis, Krauss presented an interpretation of video diametrically (or perhaps dialectically) opposed to those of psychotherapists; where Cornelison, Arsenian, and others suggested that self-confrontation could draw a narcissistic patient out into engagement with the outside world, Krauss concluded instead that it typically led artists "to withdraw attention from an external object—an Other—and invest it in the Self." Far from a formalist exploration of the unique affordances of new technology, argued Krauss, video art was—with a few exceptions—a concession to neoliberalism's demand that artists market themselves as brands.[29]

In "Video Art, the Imaginary and the *Parole Vide*," British composer and video artist Stuart Marshall also critiqued video art for its narcissism. He related the two forms of video feedback to each other, describing a process through which artists first pointed cameras at their own monitors and then inserted their own bodies into the feedback loop. This self-observation, suggested Marshall, recapitulates the encounter with one's mirror image as an infant, an encounter which, according to French psychoanalyst Jacques Lacan, precipitates the formation of the ego, an identification with an image which is both self and other. Marshall rejected not only self-oriented video art but also video therapy for fostering "an indulgent video narcissism."[30] He also acknowledged elsewhere, though, that "within the women's movement . . . such work gathers a political insistence, . . . drawing the viewer into a bracketed structure of viewing which then collapses problematically with the introduction of facts of sexual difference."[31]

In the decades since, most artists and theorists who have engaged with the relationship between video and subjectivity have done so from this feminist perspective. "Although Krauss used the term 'narcissism' pejoratively," wrote artist and art historian Ann-Sargent Wooster, "this so-called narcissism had a positive aspect. Video allowed women artists to put themselves in the picture for the first time because they became the producers of their own images."[32]

American artist and critic Micki McGee's "Narcissism, Feminism, and Video Art: Some Solutions to a Problem in Representation" was an early response to Krauss and Marshall. Feminist video artists, argued McGee, had developed several methods for including their own bodies and experiences in their work in order to represent part of the experience of women as a class, rather than succumbing to narcissism.[33]

McGee paid particular attention to the 1977 video *Vital Statistics of a Citizen, Simply Observed*, in which American artist Martha Rosler also used video, and her body, in a feminist critique of objectification. Rosler made herself an object of scientific measurement and judgment in order to critique the imposition of aperspectival objectivity, the coercion of women to "see herself as others see her," to which video therapy had contributed a decade earlier.[34]

The video *Vertical Roll* (1972), in which American sculptor and performance artist Joan Jonas performed around the scrolling horizontal bar created by a maladjusted video monitor, tapping a spoon to produce an industrial rhythm, has also been a recurring subject of debate about narcissism in video. Despite its status as self-portraiture, Krauss saw *Vertical Roll* as an exception to the dominance of narcissism in video art. She interpreted the work formally, analyzing the effects of the bar on a viewer's perception of time and space, and as a metaphor for the materiality of the video apparatus itself.[35] McGee, in contrast, perceived *Vertical Roll* as essentially narcissistic, writing that it "reproduces the characteristics of narcissism unintentionally, neither critiquing the cultural sources of the condition nor investigating its prevalence among women."[36]

More recently, scholars have disagreed with both and interpreted *Vertical Roll* as a feminist work. "What Krauss's analysis fails to recognize in Joan Jonas's piece is the specific manner in which it theorizes how the 'personal becomes political,'" writes media scholar Krista Geneviève Lynes in *Prismatic Media, Transnational Circuits*, a study of how feminist experimental media refract multiplicities of identity into emancipatory unities. To Lynes, *Vertical Roll* is "not only a rich exploration of the mediating function of video's closed circuit, but also of the process of subject constitution, especially for women."[37] Jonas "disrupted the pleasure of viewing . . . aggressively," writes art historian Jayne Wark, turning her body and the apparatus of video into a single disorienting experience and challenging the routine objectification of women.[38] Revisiting several of the works Krauss examined, art historian and critic Anne M. Wagner evaluates them as interactions between artist and spectator rather than solo exercises. "Their self-absorption (what Krauss called narcissism)," she writes, "is conjoined with an especially aggressive—we can rightly say coercive—posture toward the viewer, by which a new awareness and mode of vision might be urged. (Perhaps an artist needs narcissism to get aggression across.)" Such art demanded a new form of spectatorship, concludes Wagner, in which viewers need "to see actively, to see critically, to see suspiciously. To see themselves doubled, maybe duped, by the artist who is the object of their gaze. . . . To see that art's summoning of selfhood is compromised by what we might call a 'media effect.'"[39]

A Mirror with a Memory

This new, skeptical spectatorship is no longer so new. That our expressions of self are performative and intentional has become a commonplace in art and criticism. And yet, although mediated self-observation no longer plays a central role in either video art or video therapy (a term which now usually refers to remote counseling using internet video), it remains culturally present.

Many of the video experiments discussed in this chapter involved simultaneously observing an image of oneself on a monitor and recording it on tape. This "copresence of recording and representation," a phenomenon which Angela Krewani terms "isochronism," now distinguishes the smartphone selfie from other modes of portraiture. "The complex relationship between self and image" constructed by both video and the selfie is, Krewani concludes, "divergent from photography and . . . from television as well."[40]

Czech-born philosopher Vilém Flusser had this dynamic in mind when he described video as "a mirror with a memory." Video, he argued, was therefore uniquely suited to philosophical visualization, to "render visible our most abstract concepts, and thus deliver us from alienated speculations."[41] From this perspective, the medium was not (or not only) a cultivator of narcissism or objectivity but a tool for thinking about them—and many other things—deeply and intensively.

Danish media scholar Tobias Raun examines how transgender vloggers use simultaneous self-observation and recording to construct identities and new presentations of self, rendering visible the abstraction of gender identity. Watching oneself on screen has continuities, writes Raun, with memoir and film depictions of trans people recognizing their transitioning or transitioned selves in literal mirrors. But internet video also displays the same image to distant others, and being seen can foster "self-validation" and "healthy narcissism," as Carson, one of Raun's research subjects, suggests. "It is the image," Raun writes, "that allows the self to love the self."[42]

Following Flusser, each work of video art discussed in this chapter can be read as a work of philosophy, as can each experiment in video therapy. It is only fitting, though,

Figure 3.2 Nam June Paik, performance with *TV Buddha* at Projekt 74, Kölnischer Kunstverein, Cologne 1974. Photo: Joschik Kerstin, © Archiv Herzogenrath.

to end this introduction with a video installation which is particularly assertive about its embodiment of a philosophy of the self, so much so that philosopher Tae-seung Lim writes that it "expresses 'visualized ideology.'"[43] *TV Buddha* (1974; Figure 3.2), by Korean-born artist Nam June Paik, presents an ancient Buddha statue meditating not on a blank wall, as was traditional, but on his own video image.[44] "The meditating Buddha image," writes Walter Smith, "represents *nirvana*, or enlightenment. . . . And so, the Buddha contemplating himself is contemplating, or absorbed within, his own *nirvana*."[45] For the rest of us, then, is Burns's "giftie" one of self-knowledge, self-realization, narcissism, shared subjectivity, or a new path to enlightenment?

Notes

1 Sander L. Gilman, ed., *The Face of Madness: Hugh W. Diamond and the Origin of Psychiatric Photography* (New York: Brunner/Mazel, 1976); Adrienne Burrows and Iwan Schumacher, *Portraits of the Insane: The Case of Dr. Diamond* (London: Quartet, 1990); Sharrona Pearl, *About Faces: Physiognomy in Nineteenth-Century Britain* (Cambridge, MA: Harvard University Press, 2010), 148–85.

2 Floyd S. Cornelison, Jr. and Jean Arsenian, "A Study of the Response of Psychotic Patients to Photographic Self-Image Experience," *Psychiatric Quarterly* 34, no. 1 (1960), 7.

3 Milton M. Berger, "Confrontation through Videotape," in *Videotape Techniques in Psychiatric Training and Treatment*, ed. Milton M. Berger (New York: Brunner/Mazel, 1970), 19.

4 *Annual Report to the Shareholders and Employees of Ampex Corporation for the Fiscal Year Ended April 30, 1958* (Redwood City, CA: Ampex, 1958), 26.

5 Floy Jack Moore, Eugene Chernell, and Maxwell J. West, "Television as a Therapeutic Tool," *Archives of General Psychiatry* 12, no. 2 (1965), 217–20.

6 Robert Burns, "To a Louse, On Seeing One on a Lady's Bonnet at Church," st. 8.

7 Lorraine Daston, "Objectivity and the Escape from Perspective," *Social Studies of Science* 22 (1992), 599.

8 Lawrence S. Kubie, "Some Aspects of the Significance to Psychoanalysis of the Exposure of a Patient to the Televised Audiovisual Reproduction of His Activities," *Journal of Nervous and Mental Disease* 148, no. 4 (1969), 301–9, reprinted in this chapter; Nellie L. Thompson, "Introduction to Lawrence S. Kubie's 'The Drive to Become Both Sexes' (1974)," *Psychoanalytic Quarterly* 80, no. 2 (2011), 357.

9 Edward Glover, "In Honor of Lawrence Kubie," *Journal of Nervous and Mental Disease* 149, no. 1 (1969), 5f, 10.

10 David A. Mindell, *Between Human and Machine: Feedback, Control, and Computing before Cybernetics* (Baltimore: Johns Hopkins University Press, 2002), 282.

11 Steve Joshua Heims, *The Cybernetics Group* (Cambridge, MA: MIT Press, 1991); Ronald R. Kline, *The Cybernetics Moment; Or Why We Call Our Age the Information Age* (Baltimore: Johns Hopkins University Press, 2015).

12 Paul Ryan, interview by Felicity D. Scott and Mark Wasiuta, "Cybernetic Guerrilla Warfare Revisited: From Klein Worms to Relational Circuits," *Grey Room* 44 (2011), 117.

13 Davidson Gigliotti, "A Brief History of RainDance" (2003), Radical Software, http://radicalsoftware.org/e/history.html.
14 Vic Gioscia, "Notes on Videotherapy," *Radical Software* 2, no. 4 (1973), 1.
15 Frank Gillette and Ira Schneider, interview by Jud Yalkut, *East Village Other*, July 30, 1969.
16 Paul Ryan, *Birth and Death and Cybernation: Cybernetics of the Sacred* (New York: Gordon and Breach, 1973), 39.
17 Gillette and Schneider, interview by Yalkut.
18 Michael Shamberg and Raindance Corporation, *Guerrilla Television* (New York: Holt, Rinehart and Winston, 1971), ix, section II, 49, 52.
19 Pierre Teilhard de Chardin, *The Phenomenon of Man*, trans. Bernard Wall (1959; New York: Harper Torchbooks, 1965), 182; Marshall McLuhan, *The Gutenberg Galaxy: The Making of Typographic Man* (1962; New York: Signet, 1969), 43; Gene Youngblood, *Expanded Cinema* (New York: Dutton, 1970), 78.
20 Paul Ryan, "Self-Processing," *Radical Software* 1, no. 2 (1970), 15; reprinted in this chapter.
21 Stephanie Harrington, "TV: Awaiting a Genius," *Village Voice*, May 29, 1969.
22 Paul Ryan, interview by Willoughby Sharp, "Paul Ryan: Video Pioneer," *Video 81* 2, no. 1 (1981), 14; Peter Sachs Collopy, "*Ego Me Absolvo*: Catholicism as Prototype in Paul Ryan's Experimental Video," *Archée*, July 2016, http://archee.qc.ca/ar.php?page=article&no=517.
23 Paul Ryan, "Videotape: Thinking about a Medium," *Educators Guide to Media & Methods*, December 1968, 38; reprinted in Chapter 1.
24 Paul Ryan, "Cybernetic Guerrilla Warfare," *Radical Software* 1, no. 3 (1971), 1f.
25 Paul Ryan, "Video Journey through Utopia," *Afterimage* 27, no. 3 (November/December 1999), 10; Ryan, interview by Sharp, 14.
26 Dan Graham, interview by Eric de Bruyn, in Dan Graham, *Two-Way Mirror Power: Selected Writings by Dan Graham on His Art*, ed. Alexander Alberro (Cambridge, MA: MIT Press, 1999), 114.
27 Dan Graham, "Two Consciousness Projection(s)," in *Video/Television/Architecture: Writings on Video and Video Works, 1970–1978*, ed. Benjamin H. D. Buchloh (Halifax: Press of the Nova Scotia College of Art and Design, 1979), 4; reprinted in this chapter.
28 Dan Graham, "Essay on Video, Architecture, and Television," in *Video/Television/Architecture*, 62–76; reprinted in this chapter.
29 Rosalind Krauss, "Video: The Aesthetics of Narcissism," *October* no. 1 (1976), 50–64; reprinted in this volume.
30 Stuart Marshall, "Video Art, the Imaginary and the *Parole Vide*," *Studio International* 191, no. 981 (1976), 243–7; reprinted in this chapter.
31 Stuart Marshall, "Video: Technology and Practice," *Screen* 20 (1979), 115.
32 Ann-Sargent Wooster, "The Way We Were," in *The First Generation: Women and Video, 1970–75* (New York: Independent Curators, 1993), 33.
33 Micki McGee, "Narcissism, Feminism, and Video Art: Some Solutions to a Problem in Representation," *Heresies* 3, no. 4 (1981), 88–91; reprinted in this chapter.
34 Martha Rosler, *Vital Statistics of a Citizen, Simply Obtained*, video, 1977; Catherine de Zegher, ed., *Martha Rosler: Positions in the Life World* (Birmingham and Vienna: Ikon Gallery and Generali Foundation, 1999), 208–15; reprinted in this chapter.
35 Krauss, "Video," 60–1.
36 McGee, "Narcissism, Feminism, and Video Art," 89–90.

37 Krista Geneviève Lynes, *Prismatic Media, Transnational Circuits: Feminism in a Globalized Present* (New York: Palgrave MacMillan, 2012), 10; reprinted in this volume.
38 Jayne Wark, *Radical Gestures: Feminism and Performance Art in North America* (Montreal: McGill-Queen's University Press, 2006), 189.
39 Anne M. Wagner, "Performance, Video, and the Rhetoric of Presence," *October* 91 (2000), 79f.
40 Angela Krewani, "The Selfie as Feedback: Video, Narcissism, and the Closed-Circuit Video Installation," in *Exploring the Selfie: Historical, Theoretical, and Analytical Approaches to Digital Self-Photography*, ed. Julia Eckel, Jens Ruchatz, and Sabine Wirth (Cham: Palgrave Macmillan, 2018), 95f.
41 Vilém Flusser, "Discover European Video: For a Catalog of an Exhibition," *Discover European Video* (New York: Anthology Film Archives, 1990), 6f; reprinted in this chapter.
42 Tobias Raun, *Out Online: Trans Self-Representation and Community Building on YouTube* (Abington: Routledge, 2016), 111; reprinted in this chapter.
43 Tae-seung Lim, "Moving Meditation: Paik Nam June's *TV Buddha* and Its Zen Buddhist Aesthetic Meaning," *Dao* 18 (2019), 105.
44 Edith Decker-Phillips, *Paik Video*, trans. Karin Koppensteiner, Marie-Genviève Iselin, and George Quasha (Barrytown, NY: Barrytown, 1998), 75.
45 Walter Smith, "Nam June Paik's *TV Buddha* as Buddhist Art," *Religion and the Arts* 4, no. 3 (2000), 361.

Some Aspects of the Significance to Psychoanalysis of the Exposure of a Patient to the Televised Audiovisual Reproduction of His Activities (1969)

Lawrence S. Kubie

An experienced psychoanalyst, well on in years, had twice subjected himself to personal analyses. The first was at the beginning of his training; the second analysis came after 20 years of intensive experience as a practicing analyst. Twenty years later still, he volunteered to be the skeptical subject of the following experiment:

He sat in front of a one-way screen in a partially air- and sound-conditioned room with moderate illumination, before a TV camera and a monitoring television screen. When the camera was turned on he could see his own image and hear his own voice. He had not been asked to do anything; but he soon found himself doing spontaneously essentially what he had always asked his analytic patients to do: i.e., he allowed his thoughts to run freely while putting them into audible words without attempting to guide or screen them. Also within a short time he found himself watching his own TV image and attending to his own taped voice. Any initial awareness of the electronic gadgetry dropped into the background and disappeared, as did all awareness that there was someone listening in and watching him through a one-way mirror.

His associations ranged freely over many topics, widely spread in time and space. They took off from residues of recent experiences: e.g., sadness at the recent death of a friend, and rueful chuckles at some of the incongruities of life even on sad occasions. Gradually, however, they focused on reverberating impressions from his own image. He saw it. It was familiar and real. It was himself. Yet at the same time it was unfamiliar; or rather it seemed to have several layers of familiarity and of unfamiliarity. He felt rather than saw faces behind his own face, presences behind the image of his own presence; and he felt rather than heard voices behind his own voice. Yet there was nothing uncanny or eerie about any of this. It was rather as a dreamer sees himself in a dream; or as though he sensed layers of earlier identifications reaching back over years through brother, sister, father, to a succession of mother surrogates, who had in reality entered his life after the death of his mother when he was very young. This visualization of preconscious feelings and fantasies about his own image was interwoven with a vivid sense of the close presence of these predecessors. He found this a moving experience quite unlike any which he had ever had in response to photographs, or to his image in a mirror, or to biographical reconstructions during his two formal analyses. All of this was both illuminating and charged with mixed emotions. [. . .]

The vivid awareness of this mixture of positive and hostile attachments and identifications made the subject realize more clearly than ever before that he was a personality with a dimension in time which derived from the lives of those others who had been formative early influences in his life and with whom he had identified to such an extent that even the way he laughed carried imprints from these family predecessors. The shape of his face was not his own alone: nor the jutting jaw, or the tightness of the lips and smile, or the furrowed brow. These represented a complex legacy from others, among them the young father, widowered early, hurt and angry, as well as the inexperienced young aunt who had dealt with her own insecurities by inflicting quite cruel and uniquely harsh punishments on her young charges. Nothing that had ever been said to him by anyone had brought home to him both the hostile and the loving elements in these relationships as vividly [as] he felt, saw, and heard them now while looking at himself and listening to his own words on TV. He also saw and heard how these old familiars were condensed into one being, one face, one voice: to wit, his own. He felt deeply how these streams had come together to produce him. Intellectually he had known much of this before; but it had never before had the intensity of illuminating feelings with which he now experienced it before the visual and auditory image on TV. [. . .]

The Impact of the Visual Image and Another's Spoken Words

[. . .] Even when we talk out loud to ourselves, under ordinary circumstances our words seem to be coming from someone else, to be reaching us from the non-I world. Even words of self-praise or of self-blame feel akin to the experience of being appraised by someone else: all words, whether our own or those of someone else, carry hidden echoes of the value judgments of others who have used words to and at us, i.e., those vocal parents who first judged us, praising (which can also mean condescending), scolding and disapproving, educating and training. [. . .]

Such considerations as these led me to seek some form of communication which would enable a patient to *speak to himself* with relatively little contamination by those impressions which are inevitably carried over from others in the non-I world. If a method could be developed by which my own image could speak to me in my own voice, words, intonations, gestures, expressions, and mimicry, would this not introduce into analytic communications a new dimension, i.e., communications with a true image of oneself on all of one's chronological layers? It is precisely this which we seem to achieve when our own image speaks to us from a TV screen. No one can predict the effects of this. Certainly one would not expect it to supplant verbal communications and interpretations made by a therapist. But it might well supplement these, adding to them a contrasting form of description and interpretation for controlled comparisons. [. . .]

Perhaps if one could have had an opportunity to perceive one's moving, talking image on a TV screen [. . .], and to link this image to the sound of one's own private and solitary ruminations and free associations, such a combination might have made the controlling identifications so vivid and so haunting that it would have become impossible to bury or deny or distort them. [. . .]

When I see and hear myself in action, I must deal with my own perceptions and not with my responses to someone else, except insofar as my self-image contains unconscious components in which the past, present, and future, the near and the far, the I and non-I have merged.

From Lawrence S. Kubie, "Some Aspects of the Significance to Psychoanalysis of the Exposure of a Patient to the Televised Audiovisual Reproduction of His Activities," in *Journal of Nervous and Mental Disease* 148, no. 4 (1969), 301–9; and in *Studies in Self-Cognition: Techniques of Videotape Self-Observation in the Behavioral Sciences*, ed. Robert H. Geertsma and James B. Mackie (Baltimore: Williams & Wilkins, 1969), 301–9.

Self-Processing (1970)

Paul Ryan

Your inside is out when your outside is in
Your outside is in when your inside is out
So come on, come on
Come on, it's such a joy
Come on, it's such a joy
Come on, let's make it easy
Come on, let's make it easy
Make it easy, make it easy
Everybody's got something to hide
Except for me and my monkey

—Lennon and McCartney[1]

A moebius strip is a one-sided surface that is made by taking a long rectangle of paper, giving it a half twist, and then joining its ends. Any two points on the strip can be connected by starting at one point and tracing a line to the other without crossing over a boundary or lifting a pencil.

The moebius strip provides a model for dealing with the power videotape gives us to take in our own outside. With film, we are taking in the edited experience of others. What follows is a composition for video to be edited, directed, acted, and viewed by you in privacy. Feel free to bend, fold, and mutilate as you wish. It is not designed to peel your own skins off until you find some fiction called the true you. Rather it is designed so that you might get a taste of processing yourself through tape, so that you might begin to play and replay with yourself. Hopefully it will suggest ideas for your own compositions.

Your strip.

Your trip.

Technically, this is the way it works.

Using an audio tape recorder, record the following series of cues, pausing after each instruction for as long as you would want to follow it out.

Set yourself up in front of the video camera for a head and shoulders shot.

Have the monitor off.

Roll the tape.

Follow/don't follow the cues.

Relax and breathe deeply, just relax and breathe deeply
Loosen up your face by yawning
stretching your neck
working your jaw

Now, explore your face with your fingertips
Touch the favorite part of your face

Close your eyes and think of someone you love
Remember a happy moment with them
With eyes open give facial responses to the following people
Joe Nameth
Don Rickels
Spiro Agnew
Your Mother
Huey Newton
You
For the next twenty seconds do what you want
Now let your face be sad
Turn your back to the camera
Now face the camera
take a bow
replay

> As long as we adopt the Narcissus attitude of regarding the extensions of our own bodies as really out there and really independent of us, we will meet all technological challenges with the same sort of banana-skin pirouette and collapse.
>
> —McLuhan, *Understanding Media*[2]

McLuhan understands all extensions of man as inducing a corresponding numbness and closure. Narcissus's image in the pool is the kind of self-amputation brought on by irritating pressures. To counter the irritant of amputation, his image in the pool produces a numbness in Narcissus which makes it impossible for him to recognize his extended self.

This mechanism is at work with people seeing themselves on tape. The most telling instance I know of is a replay I did for a three-year-old girl in a family setting. She felt compelled to imitate what she saw herself doing on the screen: if her taped self was singing, she sang; if dancing, she danced. In one section of the tape she was walking downstairs—upon seeing this section of the tape she ran up the stairs and walked down again. This three-year-old seemed to be using real-time mirror ground rules to deal with her videotape experience. It seemed she was playing a mirror part for her video image—the part the mirror would ordinarily play for her. In doing so she became a numb servomechanism of her extended self. The next time I brought the camera around she ran. She refused to become spellbound by her tape-extended self. By contract I hear a children's sensitivity leader once brag that he had seem so much of himself on tape that he was desensitized to it.

The moebius video strip is a tactic for avoiding both servomechanistic closure and desensitizing in using videotape. Tape can be a tender way of getting in touch with oneself. In privacy, with full control over the process, one can learn to accept the extension out there on tape as part of self. There is the possibility of taking the extending back in and reprocessing over and again on one's personal time warp.

There will be tape, there will be time,
To prepare a face to meet the faces that you meet.

It may be wise to invite a good friend to watch some of the replay with you. Yet avoid inhibiting word labels on what you're doing. The moebius tape strip is a tactic for infolding information unto a fullness. "Exuberance is Beauty." "The cistern contains, the fountain overflows."[3] To overflow one need be infolding. The process of infolding cannot be frozen in words. Let go the formulation and take another trip round the moebius strip.

Videotape is the "some power" that is answer to the prayer of Burns people which they instinctively quote when talking about tape.

O wad some Pow'r the giftie gie us
To see oursels as others see us!
It wad frae monie a blunder free us
An' foolish notion:
What airs in dress an' gait wad lea'e us,
And ev'n Devotion![4]
"It would from many a blunder free us."
It would enlarge our ability to self-correct.
It would extend us in a cybernetic way.

With video we know the difference between how we intend to come across and how we actually do come across. What we put out, what is taken by the tape, is an imitation of our intended image, it is our monkey. A video system enables us to get the monkey off our backs where we can't see him, out onto the tape where we can see him. That is the precise way in which we've been making a monkey of ourselves. The monkey has been able to get away with his business because he operates on the other side of the inside/outside barrier. The moebius tape strip snips the barrier between inside/outside. It offers us one continuous (sur)face with nothing to hide. We have the option of taking in our monkey and teaching him his business or letting him go on with his.

Taking in your own outside with video means more than just tripping around the moebius strip in private. One can pass through the barrier of the skin—pass through the pseudo-self to explore the entirety of one's cybernet—i.e., the nexus of information processes one is part of. You can listen to the Beatles too much. You can turn a moebius strip composition into a merry go round of ego-tripping on a single loop. In fact, we live in multiple loops. Moebius composition can touch on these loops; Agnew–mother–Huey Newton. But to confine ourselves to this use of video is to confine a cybertool to closet drama.

Cybernetics . . . "recognizes that the 'self' as ordinarily understood is only a small part of a much larger trial-and-error system which does the thinking, acting, and deciding. This system includes all the informational pathways which are relevant at any given moment to any given decision. The 'self' is a false reification of an improperly delimited part of this much larger field of interlocking processes."[5]

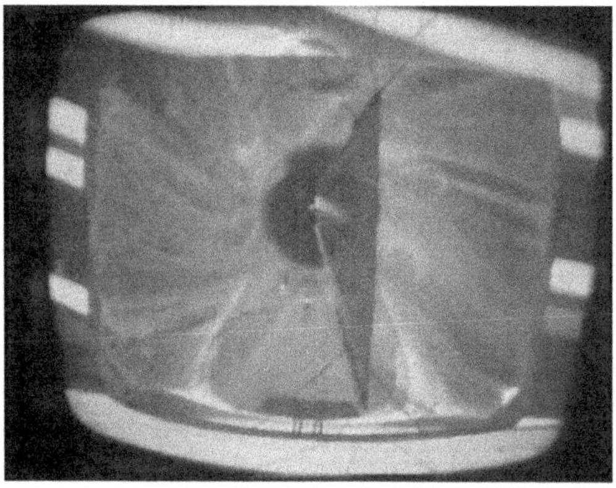

Figure 3.3 Paul Ryan, *Everyman's Moebius Strip*, still frame from Jud Yalkut, *Television as a Creative Medium*, 1969, 16 mm film, 6 min. Courtesy of Electronic Arts Intermix (EAI), New York.

The cybernetic extension of ourselves possible with videotape does not mean a reinforcement of the ordinarily understood "self." Total touch with one's cybernet precludes the capitalism of identity at the expense of understanding processes that the West has habitually engaged in. One's resume is not one's reality. Master Charge does not make you master of anything but involves you in an expensive economy of credit information processed by computer, your checking account, TV ads, long lines in banks and busy telephones. The Master Charge card exploits the illusion of unilateral control over life the West has suffered with. "I am the Captain of My Soul; I am the Master of My Fate." We have yet to understand that there is no master self. They are now putting photos on charge cards when they should be mapping the credit system the card involves you in. Video users are prone to the same illusion. *It is easy to be zooming in on "self" to the exclusion of environmental or social systems.*

Doing feedback for others one comes to realize the necessity of taping and replaying context. I had the opportunity to do a kind of video meditation on the house of two friends while they were away. The replay served to deepen their sensitivity to their everyday surroundings (Figure 3.3).

From Paul Ryan, "Self-Processing;" in *Radical Software* 1, no. 2 (1970), 15.

Notes

1 [The Beatles, "Everybody's Got Something to Hide Except Me and My Monkey," by John Lennon and Paul McCartney, on *The Beatles*, Apple, 1968.]

2 [Marshall McLuhan, *Understanding Media: The Extensions of Man* (1964; Cambridge, MA: MIT Press, 1994), 68.]

3 [William Blake, *The Marriage of Heaven and Hell* (London, 1790), plates 10 and 8.]

4 [Robert Burns, "To a Louse, On Seeing One on a Lady's Bonnet at Church," st. 8.]

5 [Gregory Bateson, "The Cybernetics of 'Self': A Theory of Alcoholism," in *Steps to an Ecology of Mind* (1972; Berkeley: University of California Press, 2000), 331.]

Two Consciousness Projection(s) (1972)

Dan Graham

The woman focuses consciousness only on a television-monitor-image of herself and must immediately verbalize (as accurately as possible) the content of her consciousness. The man focuses consciousness only outside himself on the woman, observing her objectively through the camera connected to the monitor. He also verbalizes his perceptions. The man's and the woman's self-contained conscious, unconscious, or fantasized intention—*consciousness*—is projected. The audience sees on the video screen what the man and woman "objectively" are seeing at the same time they hear the two performers' interior views.[1] Because of each of the performer's different time-process of perception, verbalization, and perception-response to the other's verbalization, there is an overlap of consciousness (of the projections of each upon the other). Each one's verbal impression, in turn, affects the other's perception: the man's projection on the periphery of the woman's affects her consciousness or behavior. A field is created in which audience and performers place reciprocal controls on the other. The audience's reaction to the man's responses (his projection of the woman) may function for him as a "superego," inhibiting or subtly influencing the course of his behavior or consciousness of the situation. Likewise, the man's responses on the periphery of the woman's consciousness interfere with her self-consciousness so that her behavioral responses,

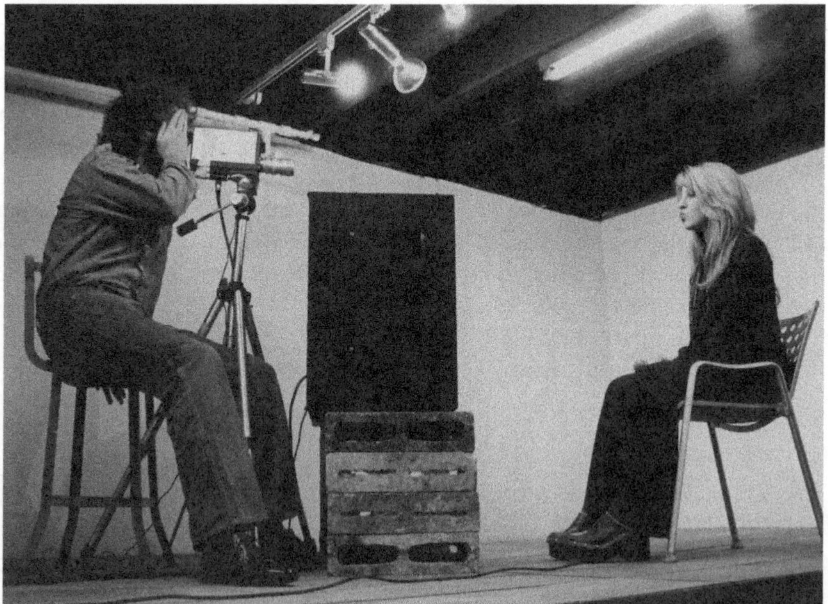

Figure 3.4 Dan Graham, *Two Consciousness Projection(s)*, 1972, performance at Lisson Gallery, London 1972. © Dan Graham, courtesy of Lisson Gallery.

including those of self-perception, may be "subconsciously" affected. Each of the three elements functions mutually as a feedback-device governing behavior—a "superego," or "subconscious" to the consciousness, and response of the others.

An abstractly presupposed psychological[2] (or social[3]) model is physically observable by the audience. The specific results of the piece vary according to the context in which it is performed, with changing historical circumstances, locale, or use of different social classes of audience or actors (Figure 3.4).

Dan Graham, "Two Consciousness Projection(s)" (1972), in Dan Graham, *Video/Television/Architecture: Writings on Video and Video Works, 1970–1978*, ed. Benjamin H. D. Buchloh (Halifax: Press of the Nova Scotia College of Art and Design, 1979), 4.

Notes

1 While an audience might initially assume that the woman was being "made into an object," it becomes apparent that her position is more powerful than the man's, as her subject and her object are not separated (separable). Whereas, the more the man (to himself) strives to be objective, that much more does he appear unconsciously subjective to any observer from the outside (the audience).

2 The Freudian axiom that one person is always projecting himself or herself into his or her observation of a second person.

3 Imposed behavioral ("psychological") differentiations between men and women.

Essay on Video, Architecture, and Television (1979)

Dan Graham

Mirrors and "Self"

Mirrors are metaphors for the Western concept of the "self." In his theory of the "mirror phase," Jacques Lacan has posited that a developing child first discovers his "self" by a mirror-like identification with the image of an other. When the mother holds the child up to a mirror, the child views his body-image reflected in the mirror as an objectified and complete form, at a time when it is subjectively experienced as incomplete and uncoordinated. The child identifies itself with an image of an other, or an image which is outside its body sensations, but, in terms of social reality, must be taken to be its identity.

Video Feedback

The video feedback of "self"-image, by adding temporality to self-perception, connects "self"-perception to physiological brain processes; this removes self-perception from the viewing of a detached, static image; video feedback contradicts the mirror model of the perceiving "self." Through the use of video-tape feedback, the performer and the audience, the perceiver and his process of perception, are linked, or co-identified. Psychological premises of "privacy" (as against publicness) which would be derived from the mirror-model, depend on an assumed split between observed behavior and supposedly unobservable, interior *intention*. However, if a perceiver views his behavior on a five to eight second delay[1] via videotape (so that his responses are part of and influencing his perception), "private" mental intention and external behavior are experienced as one. The difference between intention and actual behavior is fed back on the monitor and immediately influences the observer's future intentions and behavior. By linking perception of exterior behavior and its interior, mental perception, an observer's "self," like a topological moebius strip, can be apparently without "inside" or "outside." Video feedback time is the immediate present, without relation to past and hypothetical future states—a continuous topological or feedback loop forward or backward between just-past or immediate future. Instead of self-perception being a series of fixed "perspectives" for a detached ego, observing past actions with the intent of location "objective truth" about its essence, video feedback encloses the perceiver in what appears to be (only) what is subjectively present. While the mirror alienates the "self," video encloses the "self" within its perception of its own functioning, giving a person the feeling of a perceptible control over his responses through the feedback mechanism.

From Dan Graham, *Video/Television/Architecture: Writings on Video and Video Works, 1970–1978*, ed. Benjamin H. D. Buchloh (Halifax: Press of the Nova Scotia College of Art and Design, 1979), 62–76.

Note

1 Five to eight seconds is the limit of "short-term" memory, or memory which is part of and influences a person's (present) perception.

Video: The Aesthetics of Narcissism (1976)

Rosalind Krauss

It was a commonplace of criticism in the 1960s that a strict application of symmetry allowed a painter "to point to the center of the canvas" and, in so doing, to invoke the internal structure of the picture-object. Thus "pointing to the center" was made to serve as one of the many blocks in that intricately constructed arch by which the criticism of the last decade sought to connect art to ethics through the "aesthetics of acknowledgment." But what does it mean to point to the center of a TV screen?

In a way that is surely conditioned by the attitudes of Pop Art, artists' video is largely involved in parodying the critical terms of abstraction. Thus when Vito Acconci makes a videotape called *Centers* (1971), what he does is literalize the critical notion of "pointing" by filming himself pointing to the center of a television monitor, a gesture he sustains for the 20-minute running time of the work. The parodistic quality of Acconci's gesture, with its obvious debt to Duchampian irony, is clearly intended to disrupt and dispense with an entire critical tradition. It is meant to render nonsensical a critical engagement with the formal properties of a work, or indeed, a genre of works—such as "video." The kind of criticism *Centers* attacks is obviously one that takes seriously the formal qualities of a work, or tries to assay the particular logic of a given medium. And yet, by its very *mis-en-scène*, *Centers* typifies the structural characteristics of the video medium. For *Centers* was made by Acconci's using the video monitor as a mirror. As we look at the artist sighting along his outstretched arm and forefinger toward the center of the screen we are watching, what we see is a sustained tautology: a line of sight that begins at Acconci's plane of vision and ends at the eyes of his projected double. In that image of self-regard is configured a narcissism so endemic to works of video that I find myself wanting to generalize it as the condition of the entire genre. Yet, what would it mean to say, "The medium of video is narcissism?"

For one thing, that remark tends to open up a rift between the nature of video and that of the other visual arts. Because that statement describes a psychological rather than a physical condition; and while we are accustomed to thinking of psychological states as the possible subject of works of art, we do not think of psychology as constituting their medium. Rather, the medium of painting, sculpture or film has much more to do with the objective, material factors specific to a particular form: pigment-bearing surfaces; matter extended through space; light projected through a moving strip of celluloid. That is, the notion of a medium contains the concept of an object-state, separate from the artist's own being, through which his intentions must pass.

Video depends—in order for anything to be experienced at all—on a set of physical mechanisms. So perhaps it would be easiest to say that this apparatus—both at its present and future levels of technology—comprises the television medium, and leave it at that. Yet with the subject of video, the ease of defining it in terms of its machinery does not seem to coincide with accuracy; and my own experience of video keeps urging me toward the psychological model.

Everyday speech contains an example of the word "medium" used in a psychological sense; the uncommon terrain for that common-enough usage is the world of parapsychology: telepathy, extra-sensory-perception, and communication with an after-life, for which people with certain kinds of psychic powers are understood to be Mediums. Whether or not we give credence to the fact of mediumistic experience, we understand the referents for the language that describes it. We know, for instance, that configured within the parapsychological sense of the word 'medium' is the image of a human receiver (and sender) of communications arising from an invisible source. Further, this term contains the notion that the human conduit exists in a particular relation to the message, which is one of temporal concurrence. Thus, when Freud lectures on the phenomenon of telepathic dreams, he tells his audience that the fact insisted upon by reports of such matters is that the dreams occur at the *same time* as the actual (but invariably distant) event.

Now these are the two features of the everyday use of "medium" that are suggestive for a discussion of video: the simultaneous reception and projection of an image; and the human psyche used as a conduit. Because most of the work produced over the very short span of video art's existence has used the human body as its central instrument. In the case of work on tape this has most often been the body of the artist-practitioner. In the case of video installations, it has usually been the body of the responding viewer. And no matter whose body has been selected for the occasion, there is a further condition which is always present. Unlike the other visual arts, video is capable of recording and transmitting at the same time—producing instant feedback. The body is therefore as it were centered between two machines that are the opening and closing of a parenthesis. The first of these is the camera; the second is the monitor, which re-projects the performer's image with the immediacy of a mirror. [. . .]

It is at this point that one might want to go back to the proposition with which this argument began, and raise a particular objection. Even if it is agreed, one might ask, that the medium of video art is the psychological condition of the self split and doubled by the mirror-reflection of synchronous feedback, how does that entail a "rift" between video and the other arts? Isn't it rather a case of video's using a new technique to achieve continuity with the modernist intentions of the rest of the visual media? Specifically, isn't the mirror-reflection a variant on the reflexive mode in which contemporary painting, sculpture and film have successively entrenched themselves? Implicit in this question is the idea that autoreflection and reflexiveness refer to the same thing—that both are cases of consciousness doubling back upon itself in order to perform and portray a separation between forms of art and their contents, between the procedures of thought and their objects. In its simplest form this question would be the following: Aside from their divergent technologies, what is the difference, really, between Vito Acconci's *Centers* and Jasper John's *American Flag*?

Answer: The difference is total. Reflection, when it is a case of mirroring, is a move toward an external symmetry; while reflexiveness is a strategy to achieve a radical asymmetry, from within. In his *American Flag*, Johns uses the synonymy between an image (the flag) and its ground (the limits of the picture surface) to unbalance the relationship between the terms "picture" and "painting." By forcing us to see the actual wall on which the canvas hangs as the background for the pictorial object as-a-whole,

Johns drives a wedge between two types of figure/ground relationships: the one that is internal to the image; and the one that works from without to define this object as Painting. The figure/ground of a flat, bounded surface hung against a wall is isolated as a primary, categorical condition, within which the terms of the process of painting are given. The category "Painting" is established as an object (or a text) whose subject becomes this particular painting—*American Flag*. The flag is thus both the object of the picture, and the subject of a more general object (Painting) to which *American Flag* can reflexively point. Reflexiveness is precisely this fracture into two categorically different entities which can elucidate one another insofar as their separateness is maintained.

Mirror-reflection, on the other hand, implies the vanquishing of separateness. Its inherent movement is toward fusion. The self and its reflected image are of course literally separate. But the agency of reflection is a mode of appropriation, of illusionistically erasing the difference between subject and object. Facing mirrors on opposite walls squeeze out the real space between them. When we look at *Centers* we see Acconci sighting along his arm to the center of the screen we are watching. But latent in this setup is the monitor that he is, himself, looking at. There is no way for us to see *Centers* without reading that sustained connection between the artist and his double. So for us as for Acconci, video is a process which allows these two terms to fuse.

One could say that if the reflexiveness of modernist art is a *dédoublement* or doubling back in order to locate the object (and thus the objective conditions of one's experience), the mirror-reflection of absolute feedback is a process of bracketing out the object. This is why it seems inappropriate to speak of a physical medium in relation to video. For the object (the electronic equipment and its capabilities) has become merely an appurtenance. And instead, video's real medium is a psychological situation, the very terms of which are to withdraw attention from an external object—an Other—and invest it in the Self. Therefore, it is not just any psychological condition one is speaking of. Rather it is the condition of someone who has, in Freud's words, "abandoned the investment of objects with libido and transformed object-libido into ego-libido." And that is the specific condition of narcissism.

By making this connection, then, one can recast the opposition between the reflective and reflexive, into the terms of the psychoanalytic project. Because it is there, too, in the drama of the couched subject, that the narcissistic re-projection of a frozen self is pitted against the analytic (or reflexive) mode. One finds a particularly useful description of that struggle in the writing of Jacques Lacan. [. . .]

If psychoanalysis understands that the patient is engaged in a recovery of his being in terms of its real history, modernism has understood that the artist locates his own expressiveness through a discovery of the objective conditions of his medium and their history. That is, the very possibilities of finding his subjectivity necessitate that the artist recognize the material and historical independence of an external object (or medium).

In distinction to this, the feedback coil of video seems to be the instrument of a double repression: for through it consciousness of temporality and of separation between subject and object are simultaneously submerged. The result of this submergence is, for the maker and the viewer of most video-art, a kind of weightless fall through the suspended space of narcissism.

There are, of course, a complex set of answers to the question of why video has attracted a growing set of practitioners and collectors. These answers would involve an analysis of everything from the problem of narcissism within the wider context of our culture, to the specific inner workings of the present art-market. Although I would like to postpone that analysis for a future essay, I do wish to make one connection here. And that is between the institution of a self formed by video feedback and the real situation that exists in the artworld from which the makers of video come. In the last fifteen years that world has been deeply and disastrously affected by its relation to mass media. That an artist's work be published, reproduced, and disseminated through the media has become, for the generation that has matured in the course of the last decade, virtually the only means of verifying its existence as art. The demand for instant replay in the media—in fact the creation of work that literally does not exist outside of that replay, as is true of conceptual art and its nether side, body art—finds its obvious correlative in an aesthetic mode by which the self is created through the electronic device of feedback.

There exist, however, three phenomena within the corpus of video art which run counter to what I have been saying so far. Or at least are somewhat tangential to it. They are: 1) tapes that exploit the medium in order to criticize it from within; 2) tapes that represent a physical assault on the video mechanism in order to break out of its psychological hold; and 3) installation forms of video which use the medium as a subspecies of painting or sculpture. The first is represented by Richard Serra's *Boomerang*. The second can be exemplified by Joan Jonas's *Vertical Roll*. And the third is limited to certain of the installation works of Bruce Nauman and Peter Campus, particularly Campus's two companion pieces *mem* and *dor*. [. . .]

Vertical Roll is another case where time has been forced to enter the video situation, and where that time is understood as a propulsion toward an end. In this work access to a sense of time has come from fouling the stability of the projected image by desynchronizing the frequencies of the signals on camera and monitor. The rhythmic roll of the image, as the bottom of its frame scans upward to hit the top of the screen, causes a sense of decomposition that seems to work against the grain of those 525 lines of which the video picture is made. Because one recognizes it as intended, the vertical roll appears as the agency of a will that runs counter to an electronically stabilized condition. Through the effect of its constant wiping away of the image, one has a sense of a reflexive relation to the video grid and the ground or support for what happens to the image. [. . .]

The monitor, as an instrument, seems to be winding into itself a ribbon of experience, like a fishing line being taken up upon a reel, or like magnetic tape being wound upon a spool. The motion of continuous dissolve becomes, then, a metaphor for the physical reality not only of the scanlines of the video raster, but of the physical reality of the tape deck, whose reels objectify a finite amount of time.

Earlier, I described the paradigm situation of video as a body centered between the parenthesis of camera and monitor. Due to *Vertical Roll*'s visual reference through the monitor's action to the physical reality of the tape, one side of this parenthesis is made more active than the other. The monitor side of the double bracket becomes a reel through which one feels prefigured the imminence of a goal or terminus for the motion. That end is reached when Jonas, who has been performing the actions recorded on the tape, from within the coils of the camera/monitor circuit, breaks through the parenthetical closure of the feedback situation to face the camera directly—without the agency of the monitor's rolling image. [. . .]

From Rosalind Krauss, "Video: The Aesthetics of Narcissism," *October* no. 1 (Spring 1976), 50–64.

Video Art, the Imaginary and the *Parole Vide* (1976)

Stuart Marshall

> *"The relations between this* Homo psychologicus *and the machines he uses are very striking, and this is especially so in the case of the motor car. We get the impression that his relationship to this machine is so very intimate that it is almost as if the two were actually conjoined—its mechanical defects and breakdowns often parallel his neurotic symptoms. Its emotional significance for him comes from the fact that is exteriorizes the protective shell of his ego."*
>
> —Jacques Lacan[1]

It is surprising that although video was hailed in quasi-cybernetic eulogy as the most important new medium to be appropriated by artists, it has suddenly found itself with few places to go. If video art is in a state of malaise (which I tend to think it is), it is for a variety of reasons. The problem of accessibility has to be a central one for artists, galleries, gallery alternatives, and the art audience alike. [. . .]

The situation is undoubtedly complex, involving the economics of the art world, the politics of television, and the paucity of theory, but also affecting the work of artists themselves. Their discourse becomes more solipsistic as the predicted video distribution channels fail to materialize, and certain galleries with the money and the inclination to provide viewing-rooms and taping facilities monopolize more of the action. [. . .]

My intention is not to establish quite who is to blame if the video artist ends up talking to him/herself, but rather to point to the effects that such repression can have when applied to a medium with a decidedly solipsistic pull of its own. If the artist does not literally end up in a situation of monologue, the technology itself can function as a barricade, a kind of externalized ego, hiding the artist's alienation by providing situations in which the audience members can become engrossed in their own alienation, as objects of their own consciousness.

[. . .] With a lack of references, history, or shared objectives, it is predictable that artists begin from the deceptively benign artist/video equipment confrontation, not only in an attempt to discover what they can do with the medium but also to discover just what the medium does to them. This elementary configuration consists of a video camera connected to a video recorder, which is in turn connected to a video monitor providing the live camera view. The possibility of feedback suggests itself immediately: the camera views the monitor and a regression of monitors appears within the monitor. Tautology has been a mainstay of video art, and although reflexivity has characterized much of the art of the sixties and seventies, nowhere has it appeared as frequently as in video. In a sense this image is a metaphor of any theory capable of examining its own axioms (semiotics, mathematics, psychoanalysis, etc.), and it is in this way that video artists have become theorists, often attempting an analysis of video codes as a central aspect of works themselves. The medium becomes the subject matter of the work, the process of structuring and manipulating the image being dictated by artists' intuitions about the plays between illusion and reality that the medium most readily (truthfully) supports.

If the elementary artist/video equipment confrontation results in the medium acting as its own object, the most obvious redeployment takes the form of the medium acting as a feedback system enabling the artist to become an object of his/her own consciousness. Here the artist confronts both equipment and image of the self, and it is at this point that the curiosity of the artist about the medium becomes diverted into a curiosity about the self. The artist's theory of video has therefore frequently developed into an examination of the notions of consciousness and selfhood, an area readily associable with psychoanalytic theory. From the viewpoint of this theory, the work suffers from being at the same time the discourse of the medium and discourse about the medium. This is not necessarily to criticize the works as artworks but rather as theoretical bases. The confusion of logical typing or metalevels that this work displays gives rise to a neuroticism in the works as theory, in that the theory serves to disavow (as a mode of defense) aspects of the artworks. The constant lure of the discourse of the medium will be the central concern of this article. It poses problems for artists and theorists alike. [. . .]

Lacan first presented the "mirror phase" and the Imaginary order as a psychoanalytic "stage." [. . .] Lacan proposes a dramatic event which takes place between the ages of six and 18 months in the form of a primary identification with the image of the self. He describes a situation in which the child in a state of dependency (lack of motor coordination) and incomplete neurophysiological development (the result of what Lacan terms "a specific prematurity of birth") perceives itself as a gestalt in a mirror, as a harmonic and unified image of an anticipated maturity. The ego is consequently precipitated as an imaginary construct, as a misconstruction, alienating the subject in his/her own image. The oscillation inherent in this situation (the self is always another, the other is always the self) snares the subject in a constant search for a lost self (the anterior state of asubjectivity).[2] [Psychoanalyst Jean] Laplanche and [philosopher Jean-Bertrand] Pontalis in *The Language of Psycho-Analysis* suggest that the Imaginary involves a "sort of coalescence of the signifier with the signified."[3]

It seems fairly apparent that much video art is entrenched in the Imaginary, not only in the everyday sense of fantasy but also in the Lacanian sense of dualisms, oppositions, anguished searches for self-realization and nostalgia for a lost self. [. . .]

Video's possibility of instant playback, in comparison with the long delays of film processing, has been remarked upon repeatedly by artists as being an important factor in their work, and it would not seem too extreme to describe this quality of image translation and representation as having the "insidious capturing effect" (captation) described by Lacan as appropriate to the mirror phase. This specular identification with the image of the self is, of course, very different from the child's first confrontation with its image in the mirror, as it is that experience which inaugurates an awareness of selfhood, the precipitation of the *je*, from a state of undifferentiated asubjectivity.[4] Later confrontations between egos and alter egos constitute a secondary identification, a ritual-like repetitive re-miscognition serving to affirm the notions of selfhood arising after the mirror phase.

The video system is a very new and different mirror, not only presenting a non-reversed image but also allowing for an observation of the self which is not spatially or temporally fixed, all the more effectively promoting the reification of the self. Video's power as a mirror lies in this novelty, and many of the works of Dan Graham and Peter Campus have consisted of simple installations exploring these aspects of the video mirror. The suggestion that these aspects of video can be used to achieve a hitherto impossible subjectivity, a therapeutic heightened self-awareness, is as suspicious as ego psychology. These explorations usually lead to an indulgent video narcissism and a chasing of the subject of the Cogito. [. . .]

From Stuart Marshall, "Video Art, the Imaginary and the *Parole Vide*," in *Studio International* 191, no. 981 (1976), 243–7.

Notes

1 Jacques Lacan, "Some Reflections on the Ego," *International Journal of Psychoanalysis* 34 (1953), 11–17.
2 [Jacques Lacan, "The Mirror-Phase as Formative of the Function of the I," *New Left Review* 51 (1968), 71–7.]
3 [Jean Laplanche and Jean-Bertrand Pontalis, *The Language of Psycho-Analysis*, trans. Donald Nicholson-Smith (London: Hogarth, 1973), 210.]
4 Lacan, "Mirror-Phase."

Vital Statistics of a Citizen, Simply Obtained (1977)

Martha Rosler

FEMALE VOICEOVER (matter-of-factly):

This is a work about perception. [. . .] It is about the perception of self. It's about the meaning of truth. *(short pause)* The *definition* of fact. [. . .]

This is a work about being done to. This is a work about learning how to think. [. . .]

This is a work about coercion. Coercion can be quick, and brutal. That is the worst crime. Coercion can also extend over the whole of life. That is the ordinary, the usual crime. Bureaucratic crime can be brutal or merely devastating. We need not make a choice. Sartre says, "Evil demands only the systematic substitution of the abstract for the concrete." That is, it demands only the de-realization of the fully human status of the people on whom you carry out your ideas and plans. *(pause)*

Statistics.

For an institution to be evil it need not be run by Hitler. As Stephen Kurtz has observed, it need only be run by heartless people, sometimes called intellectuals or scientists. In the name of responsibility, native peoples have been colonized and enslaved, the lives of women, children, workers, and subject peoples regulated in every degree, "for their own good."

This is a work about the tyranny of expectation. [. . .]

I needn't remind you about scrutiny, about the scientific study of human beings. Visions of the self, about the excruciating look at the self from outside, as though it were a thing divorced from the inner self. How one learns to manufacture oneself as a product. How one learns to see oneself as a being in a state of culture, as opposed to a being in a state of nature. How to measure oneself by the degree of artifice: The remanufacture of the look of the external self to simulate an idealized version of the natural. How anxiety is built into these looks. How ambiguity, ambivalence, uncertainty are meant to accompany every attempt to see ourselves—to see herself—as others see her.

This is a work about how to think about yourself. It is a work about how *she* is forced to think about *her*self. How she learns to scrutinize herself, to see herself as a map, a terrain, a product constantly recreating itself inch by inch, groomed, manufactured, programmed, reprogrammed, controlled, a servomechanism in which one learns to utilize every possible method of feedback, to reassert control.

Read from a work on cybernetic servomechanisms, read from a work on self-abuse, read from a list of items for the trousseau, a list of gifts for the wedding guests to choose from, read from a list of dos and don'ts, read from a list of glamorous makeovers, read from a list of what men do and what women do, read from a list of girls' toys and of boys' toys. Read from a list of average incomes of men and of women. Read from a book of resignations and defeats.

Read from a manual on revolutionary society. [. . .]

Figure 3.5 Martha Rosler, *Vital Statistics of a Citizen, Simply Obtained*, 1977, video, color, 39:20 min. Courtesy of Martha Rosler and Electronic Arts Intermix (EAI), New York.

Her mind learns to think of her body as something different from her self. It learns to think, perhaps without awareness, of her body as having parts. These parts are to be judged. The self has already learned to attach value to itself, to see itself as a whole entity with an external vision. She sees herself from outside with the anxious eyes of the judged who holds within her mind the critical standards of the ones who judge. She knows the boundaries of her body. She does not know the boundaries of her self. She's been carefully trained in a mechanical narcissism that it is a sign of madness or deviance to be without. Her body grows accustomed to certain proscribed poses, certain characteristic gestures, certain constraints and pressures of clothing. [. . .] (Figure 3.5).

This text combines elements of Rosler's script and her actual voiceover performance: Martha Rosler, *Vital Statistics of a Citizen, Simply Obtained*, video, 1977; script reprinted in *Martha Rosler: Positions in the Life World*, ed. Catherine de Zegher (Birmingham: Ikon Gallery; Vienna: Generali Foundation, 1999), 208–15.

Narcissism, Feminism, and Video Art: Some Solutions to a Problem in Representation (1981)

Micki McGee

Feminist art has often received the disparaging label "narcissistic" from audiences unaccustomed to seeing female subjectivity in the arts. And video has been described as an inherently narcissistic medium.[1] So when a feminist artist works in video, it would seem she increases her chances of producing work which will be read as narcissistic. But a narcissistic representation, whether it results from audience predisposition or is produced in the technology of the medium, is incompatible with a feminist aesthetic.

Early feminist art, particularly as it developed on the West Coast, began with a consideration of women's personal experience.[2] Work took the form of autobiography, exploration of self, and affirmation of female experience. [. . .] Feminists viewing autobiographical work could readily locate an individual woman's experience within an emerging analysis of women's oppression. For this audience, feminist art was not narcissistic but profoundly political.

But for any audience unfamiliar with feminist ideology, making the connection between individual women's experiences and a larger social context was often a frustrating task. The therapeutic working through of personal experiences (particularly common in performance art) was inaccessible to many audiences, who were ill-equipped to recognize the political significance of women's stories. For these audiences, the inaccessibility of the work recalled the insular quality of the narcissist. They saw the artist as wrapped up in herself, much as the narcissist is trapped in her/himself. [. . .]

Specifics of feminine narcissism are at odds with feminist representation. Feminine narcissism results from a basic mechanism of women's oppression: the emphasis placed on women's appearance.[3] Patriarchal cultures demand narcissism of women and simultaneously disparage women for their self-obsession. As Simone de Beauvoir has written, "conditions lead woman, more than man, to turn toward herself and devote her love to herself."[4] What are these conditions? Economic and social relations which require women to gain access to power (albeit cosmetic power) via men make a preoccupation with the self nothing less than a survival tactic for women. For a woman to relinquish her narcissism, to stop presenting herself as an object of delectation, is to abandon the privileges allotted to her.

An art which reproduces narcissism, and a hierarchical artworld which requires self-aggrandizement, aligns itself with the social relations of domination required in a corporate structure. Literature on mass media suggests that the narcissist is the ideal personality in a consumer economy, since s/he will participate in endless consumption when confronted with advertising which appeals to the enhancement of self.[5] A narcissistic art implies a tacit acceptance of the self-obsession so crucial to the maintenance of an expansive economic system.

There are unique characteristics of video art which predispose it to narcissistic uses. Critics Rosalind Krauss and Stuart Marshall have commented on the narcissistic character of video produced by both men and women. They locate the source of narcissism in video in the apparatus of video production, which has certain structural similarities to a mirror. When an artist sets up a simple closed circuit of camera monitor, s/he performs for her/himself in a non-reversing mirror. [. . .]

Tapes by Lynda Benglis (*Collage*, *Now*, *On Screen*, and *Document*), Hermine Freed (*Two Faces*), and Joan Jonas (*Duet*, *Left Side/Right Side*, and *Vertical Roll*) have all been discussed as examples of the aesthetics of narcissism.[6] [. . .] In these "self-portraits" the artists bracket all but the objects of their immediate concern—themselves. Such bracketing out of the world is analogous to the narcissist's withdrawal into her/himself. However, it would be a mistake to believe, as Marshall asserts, that these works carry a "political insistence" because their makers are women.[7] Simply representing the condition of narcissism does not constitute a critique of the condition or of the social relations which produce self-obsession. Such representation reifies the process of narcissism. [. . .]

Joan Jonas's images of herself exploring the video medium exemplify the problem of the inadvertent reified representation of narcissism. *Vertical Roll* is a series of images taped off of a monitor in which the vertical hold has been adjusted to establish a steady vertical motion of passing frames. The image and sound of Jonas tapping a spoon set up one rhythm; the steady jumping of the image, another. The image, the sound, and the flickering of the screen move in and out of phase. The sound of the tapping of the spoon continues with a variety of vertically rolling images—Jonas moving her feed back and forth, wearing a mask, walking and running in place, turning her hand palm up, palm down. Her motion and the camera movement are subordinate to the steady motion created within the electronics of the monitor. One has the sense of being trapped by the technology: while trying to invest the image with some status of reality, one is constantly confronted with the reality of electronic mediation. Jonas and her image are insulated, bracketed between the camera and the monitor, much as the narcissist is trapped between the self and the image of self. And the spectator's frustrated attempts to disavow the presence of the monitor echo the narcissist's futile desire to be simultaneously the subject and the object of her/his own love.[8] Jonas's unintentional enactment of narcissism in *Vertical Roll* is an aside: secondary to her concern with rhythm, form, and the technology of the medium. [. . .] Jonas's and Benglis's early video reproduces the characteristics of narcissism unintentionally, neither critiquing the cultural sources of the condition nor investigating its prevalence among women.

How do feminist artists, committed to producing politically engaged artworks, confront the narcissism encouraged by the artworld, prompted by the video apparatus, and attributed to feminist art? Several strategies are employed. Working in a documentary mode or devising a narrative using actors are two direct ways of avoiding a narcissistic representation. The simplest means is to turn the camera onto the world, rather than pointing it at oneself. In the more problematic case of a feminist dealing with autobiographical material or the perception of self, turning the camera on oneself is not only appropriate, but necessary. How do feminists avoid the representational problem of narcissism in tapes about personal experiences and in work where they're the "stars"? Considering the work of Martha Rosler, Marge Dean, Nancy Angelo, and Candace Compton offers some answers to this question.

Martha Rosler's *Vital Statistics of a Citizen, Simply Obtained* addresses the issue of the perception of the self, but her theoretical stance in relation to the subject forestalls a narcissistic reading of the tape. In real-time footage Rosler is systematically undressed and measured by two white-coated technicians. Three female assistants appear, each employing a noisemaker (a bell, a kazoo) to indicate whether her measurements are above average, average, or below average. After this seemingly interminable procedure ends, Rosler is led away by the women, who assist her in dressing, alternately, in a white gown and a black evening dress. The two sequences of Rosler being dressed are intercut, creating a virgin/whore montage and concluding the real-time footage. Throughout this first act Rosler presents her analysis through the voiceover, discussing dehumanization through testing and measurement and scientific "truth" as a means of social control. [. . .]

One could argue that Rosler's nude appearance in *Vital Statistics* necessitates a narcissistic reading of the work. Such a stance fails to consider the distancing Rosler develops by placing herself relatively far away from a fixed camera. No closeups or cuts are used to titillate the audience or to break the tedium of the measuring procedure. There are no slow plans up a calf to a thigh, no cuts to parted lips. She interrupts the voyeuristic pleasure attributed to traditional narrative film and television devices by producing the image of a clinical, bureaucratic stripping, rather than a seductive burlesque.[9]

Although Rosler's theoretical stance and camera location distance the audience from her image, the work raises an issue that has plagued women's body art. Lucy Lippard notes:

> Men can use beautiful, sexy women as neutral objects or surfaces, but when women use their own faces or bodies they are immediately accused of narcissism. There is an element of exhibitionism in all body art, perhaps a legitimate result of the choice between exploiting oneself or someone else. Yet the degree to which narcissism informs the work varies immensely. Because women are considered sex objects, it is taken for granted that any woman who presents her nude body in public is doing so because she thinks she is beautiful. She is a narcissist, and Acconci, with his less romantic image and pimply back, is an artist.[10]

The narcissist and the exhibitionist share an enslavement to the attention of others. But Rosler appears not as the exhibitionist, the image to be admired, but as the anonymous statistic of a totally administrated environment. Her role as anonymous subject, combined with her analysis of the self-scrutiny requisite to "femininity" and the use of de-eroticized camera, work to preclude a narcissistic reading of *Vital Statistics*. [. . .]

From Micki McGee, "Narcissism, Feminism, and Video Art: Some Solutions to a Problem in Representation," in *Heresies* 3, no. 4 (1981), 88–91.

Notes

1 Stuart Marshall, "Video Art, the Imaginary and the *Parole Vide*," in *New Artists' Video*, ed. Gregory Battock (New York: Dutton, 1978), 103–20, reprinted in the present chapter of this volume; Stuart Marshall, "Video: Technology and Practice,"

Screen 20 (1979), 109–19; Rosalind Krauss, "Video: The Aesthetics of Narcissism," *October* 1 (Spring 1976), 50–64, reprinted in the present chapter of this volume.

2 Martha Rosler, "The Private and the Public: Feminist Art in California," *Artforum* (September 1977), 66–74.

3 Sandra Lee Bartky, "Feminine Narcissism," presented at "*The Second Sex* Thirty Years Later," New York University, September 27–29, 1979.

4 Simone de Beauvoir, *The Second Sex* (1959; New York: Vintage, 1974), 699.

5 Joel Kovel, "Narcissism and the Family," *Telos* 44 (1980), 93.

6 Krauss, "Video"; Marshall, "Video Art, the Imaginary and the *Parole Vide*"; Marshall, "Video."

7 Marshall, "Video," 115 [quoted in the chapter introduction].

8 John Riddler, "The Regime of the Video State," *LAICA Journal* (February 1980), 42–4.

9 Laura Mulvey, "Visual Pleasure and Narrative Cinema," *Screen* 16, no. 3 (1975), 8–18.

10 Lucy Lippard, "The Pains and Pleasures of Rebirth: European and American Women's Body Art," in *From the Center: Feminist Essays on Women's Art* (New York: Dutton, 1976), 125.

Discover European Video: For a Catalog of an Exhibition (1990)

Vilém Flusser

The title is appropriate: first we invent, and then we discover what we have invented. Who could have guessed all the virtualities inherent in (for instance) the letters of the alphabet, when linear writing was invented? And who would dare to affirm that we have already discovered everything one can do with a computer? But with video, the need to discover its latent potentialities is especially urgent. The reason why this is so is a curious one: it does not look at all like the thing it is, and this is why it is misleading. It looks like an electromagnetic film camera, and thus it misleads people to make films with it. In fact, however, it is a mirror with a memory attached to it. And people are slow to discover this.

The mirror is, of course, [. . .] used for reflections and speculations. If you look into a mirror, your glance is thrown back at you. You may say that your glance (and therefore your thought) is turned around like a glove by the mirror. Now this inversion of vision and thought has been developed and refined in the course of history, and ever since the ancient Greeks it is called "philosophy" (at least within the Occidental tradition). But something curious has happened: as philosophical discipline became ever more refined, and as it gave birth to the sciences, the original mirror was abandoned, and the term "speculation" acquired a metaphorical meaning. People forget that they are looking into an imaginary mirror while reflecting about themselves and the world. The consequence is that philosophical and scientific reflections and speculations have become unimaginable. Something must be done about this, unless we admit that we can no longer imagine our own concepts, which is a form of alienation.

To remedy this, video has been invented. It is a new sort of mirror. If you look into its "monitor," your glance and thought is still thrown back at you, but this time the two sides "left and right" are not inverted. This is very surprising: we are so accustomed to mirror inversion that we are disoriented by a mirror which does not do so. But the monitor is an active mirror: when you look into it, you see yourself and your surroundings from the point of view of the video camera (the Big Brother). Not only do you see in the mirror the way other people see you, but you may see yourself from your back side. And this is not all to that miraculous invention: the monitor has a memory (a tape), and you may see yourself in it as you were five minutes ago. And since the memory may be manipulated, you might even see yourself in the mirror as you never were, but as others imagined you to be.

Now what has just been said is technically very primitive, and anybody who can afford a video equipment can do it. But does he do it? To do so, you have to discover that video is a tool for philosophical speculation. This may be technically very primitive, but intellectually and aesthetically it is all but simple. It is both intellectually and aesthetically much easier to handle the video camera to do technically complex films with it. And this, of course, prevents people to discover what video may do in the future: render visible our most abstract concepts, and thus deliver us from alienated speculations.

But the matter is less simple. People might handle the video camera with a view to producing a film-like tape, and the very essence of the video (its being an electromagnetic mirror equipped with a memory) might impose on them the motion of philosophical speculation. They may think of themselves that they are "artists" (whatever that term may mean), and in fact they may be philosophizing. In spite of themselves (or only half-conscious of themselves) they may be discovering what video is about (and what philosophy is about). This is why exhibitions like the one introduced by this catalog are useful: to permit viewers (receivers of video information) to see for themselves to what extent the producers have discovered what they are doing.

You might object that such is not the job of viewers, but of critics. You might believe that it is the critics who view the tapes, who judge them, and who exhibit them for the public to admire the depth of their judgment. But you will be mistaken. The critics are even less capable of discovering video (be it European or whatever) than are the artists, because they are just as much prisoners of the "film prejudice" as the artists are, and they lack the concrete experience with the video apparatus. It is the viewers of the exhibition who are in the "phenomenological" position (one that is relatively unprejudiced) to see for themselves, and to show to the video manipulators, how video may come to be the mirror of man, of society, and of the world. Not like a photograph or a film, but more like a visual philosophical treatise.

The exhibition here introduced is called *Discover European Video*. Those who have chosen that title might not have intended this, but the title suggests that the exhibition is meant for those who want to discover what Europeans have found out about the hidden possibilities within the video apparatus. And it is in order to provoke precisely such an attitude in the viewers of the exhibition that this article is written.

Vilém Flusser, "Discover European Video: For a Catalog of an Exhibition," in *Discover European Video* (New York: Anthology Film Archives, 1990), 6f.

Prismatic Media, Transnational Circuits (2012)

Krista Geneviève Lynes

[. . .] One of the most widely cited considerations of the medium of video, Rosalind Krauss's "The Aesthetics of Narcissism," specifically forecloses the medium's potential to engage the social subject, in gender but also engendered in the experience of race, class, and sexuality. Although Krauss is not a feminist scholar—and thus does not have as her aim the embeddedness of video in technologies of gender—she nevertheless resolves too quickly the vacillation of the female subject inside social and discursive determinations, and, in [film theorist Teresa] de Lauretis's terms, "outside and excessive to them."[1] Krauss makes an opposition between the narcissistic quality of "reflection" (often characterized as "mirror-reflection") in video works such as Lynda Benglis's *Now* (1973) and the more successful (in her view) forms of "reflexivity" in works such as Joan Jonas's *Vertical Roll* (1972). She argues, "Reflection, when it is a case of mirroring, is a move toward an external symmetry; while reflexivity is a strategy to achieve a radical asymmetry, from within."[2] Whereas reflection "vanquishes separateness"—moving toward a fusion of subject and object and an "erasing of differences"—reflexivity in modernist art involves a "doubling back in order to locate the object (and thus the objective conditions of one's experience)."[3] The success of video art, for Krauss, lies in its capacity to express the objective conditions of the medium and its history, and thus to locate video's radical aesthetics within its self-referring character, and therefore, its autonomy. In fact, rather than a mirror-reflection, what Krauss celebrates is the mirror through which the work refers to itself, its traditions, and media, and calls this process a *dédoublement* or doubling back in order to locate the object (and thus the objective conditions of one's experience).[4] The reflexive analysis of the medium's capacity to mediate (to ensnare the subject in a closed circuit) is joined in Krauss's argument by reflexivity on the distinction between lived subjectivity and fantasy projections, in other words between the phenomenological experience of the lived body and the ideal ego.

The trouble with Krauss's analysis for feminist criticism is the absence of a consideration of the manner in which video is also a social technology, embedded in institutionalized discourses, critical practices and forms of experience. What Krauss's analysis fails to recognize in Joan Jonas's piece is the specific manner in which it theorizes how the "personal becomes political" (i.e., the ways in which "the political becomes the personal by way of its subjective effects");[5] and further, Krauss's account does not attend to the fact that what Jonas might be articulating may be grounded in the simultaneity of video's closed circuit, surely, but also the subjective and social contradictions of the category "woman."

Left out of Krauss's analysis, therefore, are the significant and generative contradictions within media that take up questions of embodiment, representation, and sexual difference. De Lauretis argues that feminism's epistemological potential resides in its conceiving of the social subject and relations of subjectivity to sociality in gender, "though not by sexual difference alone, but rather across languages and cultural representations; a subject en-gendered in the experiencing of race and class, as well as sexual relations; a subject, therefore, not unified but rather multiple, and not so much divided as contradicted."[6] This is true also of feminist media, and of its representation of the processes by which subjects are en-gendered in the interaction of individuals with the outer world. The reflexivity of Joan Jonas's *Vertical Roll*—the distortion of the recorded image to produce a vertical roll, the consistent crashing and skipping of the figure of the female body and the shattering sound of a metal object banging repetitively—entails not only a rich exploration of the mediating function of video's closed circuit, but also of the process of subject constitution, especially for women, through a constant renegotiation of external pressures, social and semiotic structures and internal resistances.

The subject of Jonas's work is displaced, both inside and outside the determinations of semiotic structures and social reality, occupying what de Lauretis calls an "eccentric point of view."[7] This eccentricity (literally a displacement from the center) provides an account of subjectivity at odds with itself. More than this however, it provides an account of subject positions that do not so much fail to achieve identification (Jonas's failure to match up with the figure of the female nude, for instance), but whose excesses provide a resistance to identification, outside ideological structures of power/knowledge, as a personal and political practice.

Jonas's experiments with frequency modulation expose a foundational paradox surrounding the subject of feminism: namely, that when feminism first posed the question "Who or what is a woman?" it discovered, in de Lauretis's terms, the "non-being of woman" and the paradox of a being that is "at once captive and absent in discourse, constantly spoken of but of itself inaudible or inexpressible, displayed as spectacle and still unrepresented or unrepresentable, invisible yet constituted as the object and the guarantee of vision."[8] For de Lauretis, a historically conscious and self-conscious feminist theory cannot dispense with this paradox, with the inconsistency or internal contradiction that the question of the subject of feminism reveals.[9] [. . .]

From Krista Geneviève Lynes, *Prismatic Media, Transnational Circuits: Feminism in a Globalized Present* (New York: Palgrave MacMillan, 2012), 9–11.

Notes

1 Teresa de Lauretis, "Eccentric Subjects," in *Figures of Resistance: Essays in Feminist Theory* (Urbana: University of Illinois Press, 2007), 152.
2 Rosalind Krauss, "Video: The Aesthetics of Narcissism," *October* no. 1 (Spring 1976), 56; reprinted in the present chapter.
3 Ibid., 56f.
4 Ibid., 57.
5 De Lauretis, "Eccentric Subjects," 152.
6 Teresa de Lauretis, "The Technology of Gender," in *Technologies of Gender: Essays on Theory, Film and Fiction* (Bloomington: Indiana University Press, 1987), 2.
7 De Lauretis, "Eccentric Subjects," 175.
8 Ibid., 151.
9 Ibid.

Screen Births: Trans Vlogs as a Transformative Media for Self-Representation (2016)

Tobias Raun

The Mirror as a Well-Established Trope of Trans Representation

Without that mirroring that this camera gives you, I am not sure it's really possible to transition fully.

—Carson, September 19, 2010

[. . .] [For many transgender people] the vlog as a medium becomes a multifaceted mirror, enabling self-creation and self-labeling, while also establishing contact and interaction with like-minded others who can encourage and support one's (transitioned) self-recognition. YouTube as a platform becomes a site for identification, for trying out and assuming various identities and for seeing one's own experiences and thoughts reflected in others.

The metaphor of the mirror is, like rebirth, an established trope within the genre of written trans autobiographies. [. . .]

The written autobiography includes mirror scenes in order to highlight transsexuality as a plot, wherein transition enables the trans subject to move from disidentification to full identification with the mirror image.

Likewise, "mirror scenes" are also extremely common within mainstream visual representation of transsexuals. For instance, in the beginning of *Transamerica* (Tucker 2005), Bree gets dressed and throws one last look at herself in the mirror, slightly disappointed, before walking out the door; this occurs several times in *Boys Don't Cry* (Peirce 1999), as Brandon dresses up and tries out his masculinity in front of the mirror. [. . .]

Mirroring as Healthy Narcissism

The mirror plays a different and much more complex role in the trans vlogs. First, the vlog acts as a mirror in a very literal way, as recording and uploading a video using a webcam enables one to look at one's own reflection. [. . .]

The mirror function invites the vlogger to assume the shape of a desired identity/representation by assuming and evaluating oneself as an attractive image and trying out different "styles of the flesh,"[1] poses, and appearances. Charlotte makes several very short vlogs using the medium as a moving-image mirror to capture her appearance with a certain kind of makeup or clothing, or when posing in a certain way. She continuously acts and poses as if she were standing (alone) in front of a mirror, self-reflexively adjusting her hair, clothing, facial expression, and bodily gestures. [. . .] She seems highly preoccupied with exploring and monitoring her own appearance, continuously commenting on it while obviously looking at herself in the mirror reflection. She looks like "a mess," she states, while adjusting her hair (August 19, 2007), or she decides "to get a little funky with my makeup tonight . . . a little more dramatic than usual to see how I look" (September 8, 2007). Charlotte and Carson's styles of vlogging bear some striking similarities, as they both seem to explicitly flirt with the camera. Their flirtatious interaction is constituted by their self-aware poses in their closeups, their smiles, and the way in which they speak softly into the camera, all of which establish them as attractive images. [. . .] Charlotte and Carson offer themselves to the camera, opening the circuit of desire and highlighting the ways in which gender identity is contingent on relations with others. Charlotte and Carson's highly self-aware mirroring spectacles raise several questions: Who is placed as the addressed others behind the mirror? Who are they posing for—and who is watching whom? It seems partly the act of posing that the medium of the vlog allows them to experiment with—simultaneously assuming an image and watching themselves do it. One might say that the flirtatious and seductive interaction with the camera is connected to a (re)discovery of oneself as an attractive image. In that sense, the trans vlogs (like all vlogs) have elements of narcissism, not in a pathologizing manner but through introspection and visual self-absorption.[2] In the narcissistic scenario, it is the image that allows the self to love the self; yet in narcissism, the image is the self, and an other is both presupposed and excluded.[3] I understand the vlogs as narcissistic in the sense that they are attempts to connect with one's visual self and to self-reflect and see oneself traveling through the gaze of the other.

As I reflect on the narcissistic mirroring in Charlotte's and Carson's vlogs, I am reminded of my interview with Carson. Discussing his motivations for vlogging, he explained it as "a kind of self-validation" and "a sort of healthy narcissism," as "the camera acts as a mirror to the world." [. . .]

The vlog as a medium with mirroring qualities can enable both an individual act of self-validation and a social act of recognition and encouragement. Recording oneself on camera signifies a need for social acknowledgement or recognition. The activity seems both to lift these trans vloggers out of life and into representation (as being an image is to be someone) and to make them more real (legitimate and authentic in their trans identity). However, the vlogs are not just private mirror scenes but also public broadcasts that Carson and Charlotte, in particular, are well aware that others are watching. This aspect seems to be an integral part of the narcissism, as the vloggers install and confirm themselves as an attractive "image" or identity not just by watching themselves act as such, but also by knowing that others are watching too. It might not be the actual interaction or response to their attractiveness that enforces their gender identity, but simply the knowledge that an infinite number of abstracted strangers are watching. The camera—or maybe even themselves as images—becomes that mirroring and/or significant other with whom they flirtatiously interact.

Connecting with Others through Mirroring

[. . .] Carson notes that trans people often feel very alone and alienated, which makes YouTube very important. [. . .]

One can recognize oneself in others, and this can diminish feelings of solitude and alienation and reassure the viewer that there are others "out there" like them. Vlogging becomes a way to not "transition in a vacuum," as Carson notes, highlighting the interactive or interrelational dimension of the mirroring effect of the vlogs. What Carson seems to suggest is the importance of feedback, and of having one's own image reflected back in various and supportive ways:

> Because I think there is a part of going through transition that is adolescent and you do need to have other people out there holding a mirror up to you and saying, year, you look great and you're doing okay, you're changing and we love you even if your parents don't. [laughing while saying the last part] (September 9, 2010)

The mirroring effect emphasized in this quote activates a Lacanian specular dynamic, outlined in his theory of the mirror stage.[4] [. . .] Identity formation is not something that takes place (solely) inside the subject but, according to Lacan, is closely connected to visuality (taking on or assuming an image) and interaction with others. What is determinative is not (just) how we see or would like to see ourselves, but how we are perceived by the cultural gaze. As psychoanalytic film theorist Kaja Silverman states in her development of a psychoanalytic politics of visual representation via, among others, Lacan:

> All of this suggests that we cannot simply "choose" how we are seen. Nor can we in any simple way conjure a new screen into place. We can struggle at a collective level to transform the existing one. Alternately, we can try at an individual level to substitute another image for the one through which we are conventionally seen, or to deform or resemanticize the normative image.[5]

As suggested by Carson, the vlog can be an important transitioning device through which the ego is constituted by and as a projection of a surface, and the viewers act as stand-ins for the mother (or parents), offering supportive confirmation of the (gender) identity of the vlogger. However, as Lacan also emphasizes, the infant recognizes himself or herself in the image of the being whose physical capacity outstrips their own. The mirror image seems more complete and coherent than the child actually experiences or sees oneself to be. In that sense, the mirroring vlog can be considered a medium through which one can master one's identity, trying out and incorporating the ideal reflection of the ego. [. . .]

The vlog acts as an extended motion picture mirror with certain affordances, the ability to reflect on how one looks/appears in the present moment while also archiving the image for comparison later, and the ability to use the medium as a testing ground for trying out and adjusting one's appearance and enabling specular interaction. [. . .]

From Tobias Raun, *Out Online: Trans Self-Representation and Community Building on YouTube* (Abingdon: Routledge, 2016), 108–16.

Notes

1 Judith Butler, *Gender Trouble: Feminism and the Subversion of Identity* (New York: Routledge, 1990), 177.
2 Zizi A. Papacharissi, *A Private Sphere: Democracy in a Digital Age* (Cambridge: Polity, 2010), 145.
3 Amelia Jones, *Body Art/Performing the Subject* (Minneapolis: University of Minnesota Press, 1998), 180.
4 Film theory has been highly influenced by Lacan's theory of the mirror phase, grounded in the alienation of visuality from the body. The mirror phase theory of subjectivity is based on the child's awareness of self and being through being seen from the outside, suggesting a fundamentally alienated selfhood that is visually constructed. See Laura U. Marks, *The Skin of the Film: International Cinema, Embodiment, and the Senses* (Durham, NC: Duke University Press, 2000), 150.
5 Kaja Silverman, *The Threshold of the Visible World* (New York: Routledge, 1996), 19.

Section II

Relations

4

Video | Film

Introduction by Marc Ries

Today, the digital image, the second variant of video following its initial analog, electronic existence, seems to be entirely definitive, even within the technical framework of cinema. Nonetheless, the relevance of the perceptual difference between the film image and the video image, in both technical and aesthetic-material respects, remains to be addressed. As does the significance of their current convergence in the broader context of their historically fluctuating relations. The texts presented in this chapter intend to describe the diversity of approaches to, and outcomes of, film and video in the light of their diverging characters.

Film is *there*. A solid body of images, produced by collaborative efforts in the areas of creation and design and presented to the world as a mostly storytelling unit, formerly in designated locations only (i.e., movie theaters) but now also in the smaller format of telecommunication devices. Film perceived in this mode of its existence is received as a work, as a self-contained, objective artifact and in the commodified form of a pictorial product, even if it costs nothing.

Video, in contrast, is *gone/there*.[1] Video, this particular picture and sound, is a multitude of signals, is a "signal image" that moves itself away from and toward things and bodies but, within this flow, can take on many different stable intermediate forms. Video is only conditionally available yet has many subcomponents of all modes of existence at its disposal, feeds narratives but is not one itself, has an only porous commodity form, yet is economically and politically viable. Video is the positive foil of Nietzsche's god, who "saw with eyes that saw everything; he saw man's depths and ultimate grounds, all his concealed disgrace and ugliness. . . . He crawled into my dirtiest nooks. This most curious, over-obtrusive one."[2] Or, to echo Jonas Mekas, "film is an art, but video is a god."[3]

This chapter will first consider the interrelations between film and video before outlining the relationship between image and reality in the context of cinema, television, and video, beyond the formal parameters of each. In the third section, the cinematic modes of video usage as considered in the texts in this chapter will be described and explored.

Phenomenology of a Relationship

1. Video in Film

What interest do movies show in video? To what end is the other image incorporated into filmic narratives? Cinema has considered video subsequent to television and has constructed a meta-image to mold the social nexus of video technology into a narrative, for example, of a false TV regime duping populations with devilish ideological details.[4] There are, at first glance, four broad intermedial modes of relationship between film and video. In each of them, video is marked as the other, the image that is alien to cinema, that enters from beyond cinema's bounds. Yet at the same time, cinema has found video to be a useful foil against which it can show its own subjectivity in higher definition.[5]

Video as news. The discrete filmic narrative, self-sufficient in its completeness, can be perforated by the reality of broadcast television images—image flows from the outside world that penetrate homes, living rooms, and narratives, and influence the course of events.[6] The *hors-champs*—the out-of-field—brings in a different dispositive from that of cinema. This beyond is a "more radical elsewhere," another entity, with which cinema forms a close partnership in order to generate additional epistemic and narrative value.[7] A news program broadcasts images containing information that propels the filmic narrative; TV verifies fictional events by citing an imagined reality. These images come from an outside world; they construct a paradoxical confirmation of film's *as if*—paradoxical because it cannot be realized by means of film technology—and promote narrative forces. The images thus simulated, or produced by duplicating the co-reality generated by the TV channels' regime, are a resource for filmic storytelling.[8] At the same time, they stimulate reflection by the viewer on the media difference; they breed a reflexivity that exposes both image types to scrutiny.[9]

Video as a celebration of self. In a second mode of relationship, the video image is used to celebrate a (filmic) individuation within the narrative logic. In Luis García Berlanga's film *Tamaño natural* (Spain 1974), the character Michel makes a life-sized, mail-order, female doll his live-in lover. He gives her seven different names, dresses her in different outfits, and films their interaction with his own Portapak equipment. After filming, Michel and the doll sit on the sofa together and watch the videos of their shared happiness. It is a happiness that could be described in the words of Hollis Frampton: "The gratification was so intense and immediate."[10] Here, again, video is a medium for verifying and validating an individual life script. While the film itself assumes an observer role, the pictures within the picture document the character's unusual actions. In this way, Michel and the doll are not only playing to the camera but also creating their own biographical picture-world through video. The viewer gets the uneasy feeling that these images, in contrast to the body of filmic images, are not entirely theirs, do not address them. The secondary images, the film-alien, individuated video images, which are instantaneously integrated into the character's lifeworld, celebrate the self—even if this self is "only" an actor with a doll. Social media have long since vindicated this form of video celebration.

Video as scene-of-the-crime and surveillance device. Filmmakers were quick to develop an interest in surveillance scenarios and to imagine systems of monitoring that soon became part of everyday life.[11] What fascinates cinema about video is no doubt its potential—as an alternative dispositive—to convey the reality of a disorder, a deviation, a flaw. Speaking without the mediation of director or script, in the rough, objectivized form of *video brut*—in mostly black-and-white, blurred, or oddly framed images—video allows cinema to tap into new associative resources. Michel eventually uses his Portapak to monitor his lover and, as a result, catches her cheating on him.[12] Today, images recorded by surveillance cameras are frequently used to convey evidence of delinquency both in movies and series.

Video as new flesh. Cinema uses the electromagnetic properties of television and video to generate occult, demiurgic, dystopian qualities, or fictions. The meta-images created in this way throw transmedia light on the ontology of the images, both retrospectively and constructively. The forces that are thus attributed to the other medium, meanwhile, provide affirmation of cinema's *as-if* creationism.[13]

2. Becoming Film: Video as Film

Cinema has adopted video as a viable image act, which has proven useful for storytelling due to its contingent relation with reality. The fragmentariness peculiar to video images, their function of capturing and securing evidence, their semiotic surplus, their association with the nonvisible and the excluded, was initially used by filmmakers and video activists to add a kind of proto-political value to their own aesthetic through video films. Jean-Luc Godard's video essays of the 1970s, *Six fois deux* and *France tout détour deux enfants*, for example, though made for television, employ cinematic concepts of organizing the subcomponents, condensing them into a semantically—theoretically and narratively—coherent form, which operates asynchronously to television grammar.[14] They are one expression of a tendency to promote film's heretical development, allowing excursions into video activism or left-wing video ethnography.

Digitization has caused the film-becoming of video to diversify. Cinema has shed parts of its system of production. Video images are appropriated as found footage material, as mechanically produced, automatized, or affected videos by unknown videomakers. Focus is placed on montage and off-screen text, giving rise to new film aesthetics and new narrative forms. The image as news, as a testimony, as the trace of an occurrence has gained autonomy, has detached itself from conventional models to follow its own intrinsic value, has become a hyper-naturalist fiction or an irrefutable statement of fact. In Daniel Myrick and Eduardo Sánchez's *Blair Witch Project* (USA, 1999), we still see a 16-mm camera and a video camera competing to create a hyperrealism; *Faceless* (Austria/UK, 2007) by Manu Luksch is comprised exclusively of recordings from London surveillance cameras combined with a suggestive, narrative voice-over spoken by Tilda Swinton; *Silvered Water, Syria Self-Portrait* (Syria/France, 2014) by Ossama Mohammed and Simav Bedirxan presents a film collage consisting of video fragments and cellphone footage of the collapsing Syrian city of Homs, clandestinely filmed and collated from video platforms.[15]

3. Becoming Video: Film as Video

Digital video—as a *recording medium* and *support material*, as a *postproduction technology* and as a *medium of distribution*—has risen to become the universal medium for moving pictures. But this takeover occurred without causing any structural changes to the cinema system. Tried and tested film languages and aesthetics have adopted the technology on their own terms. Likewise, the means of distribution have merely been extended. Films are now also made available for transmission beyond the territorial cinema screening via Internet platforms. These film videos are scaled-down entities that have merely adapted their presentation format—their dimensions—to a different technology. The intrinsic constitution of the film, its inherent logic, based on a coherent, predetermined, conditional body of images, is still asserted in the reshaping and reformatting undertaken by video and, before that, television.[16]

Model Reality/Co-Reality/Corporeality

Film in cinema and as a mass medium pursues the generation of a *model reality*, a *model world*. Although the model is constituted of elements of the here-world, the narrative, aesthetic act of generation asserts its own intrinsic right and interprets the here-world in different ways. The concept of film is always removed from our concept of reality; the two are simply different. Even if a film purports to show a realistic portrayal of a certain context, its inherent logic nevertheless alludes to a model without which the film could not exist. The model is formed essentially via principles of selecting and condensing. In and through the scenes, the film formulates its *model proposition*. The plot focuses on fragments that enable the story or account to be coherently encapsulated and direct the viewer to an (anticipated) understanding, whether it is shared or not. Of course, many films also operate with ambiguity and mystification. But that, too, is only possible in the context of a preformulated model. The narrative and actors operate within the model.

While cinema generates model realities, television, as a social technology, produces a co-reality: a second reality that correlates with social reality, *just like* real life. The TV reality of news, specials, shows, and documentaries engages in a constant exchange with the viewer's social and natural reality. Although the pictures shown, similarly to those of film, are only fragments, they are congruent with these outer realities due to the space/time regime of the medium. The "performers" do not act according to a script but appear as themselves. Television promotes standardized views that are therefore easily translatable to the viewer's personal world of experience.

By its inherent logic, video, in contrast, creates a *corporeality*: images that produce *themselves*, directly via the body. This occurs in various modes, which correspond with the diversity of objects filmed, and are minutely true to the various respective corporeal relationships between the body and image. The film/video discrepancy caused by corporeality can perhaps be best described thus: While death is a common theme in narrative films, not a single actor dies. But people die in videos. Recently, for example, the death of George Floyd was captured on video and so witnessed across the world.[17] Video is a kind of social index, a sensor for the contemporary state of the body.

Film remains in the fictional *as-if* mode. The dying shown on television takes place under the mediating censorship of a moral and political authority and on the terms of the co-reality contract negotiated with the viewer. The reverse, of course, is also true: birth and becoming can also be seen in videos.

Corporeal videos negotiate the reality of a body, a machine, a street, an individual—manifested in its actions, changes, transformations. These video images are produced without script, actors, or studios. Video is essentially a form of tracking. If the photographic image is the impression of an indexical relationship, overlaid with symbolic codes, video is often pure indexical recording; that is, an unfiltered documentation of the body's existential relationship with the camera, its environment, the video material. This is best observed in video technologies that work completely independently of human interaction, such as the various surveillance systems, medical image recording, and video-supported coaching. Here, any aesthetic and/or symbolic configuration is kept to an absolute minimum or integrated into functional key conventions, patterns, or standardizations (the monitoring perspective, the medical perspective). A crucial aspect is that the relationship between the body and the camera is immediate—that is, undisturbed by any scenic considerations. These videos are inextricably linked with their referent and assume the kind of relationship logic that Barthes has described for the photographic image.[18] However, unlike Barthes's concept of photography, the video image inhabits a temporality of *past contemporaneity*, an insistent present that fans out in divergent "peaks of present."[19] The corporeal is always an event, an event time, which resists historical segmentation and forms a "direct time-image." Nowadays, smartphone-integrated cameras most commonly invite the reflex-like handling that produces visual corporealities in the highly pluralized present day.[20]

Modes of Art and Modes of Usage

The dawn of portable, mobile video technology in the late 1960s was explicitly welcomed in various (sub)cultural spaces, since it marked the arrival of a picture with a new identity, which promised to "remedy" the cultural and industrial indoctrination effected by television's regime and testified to the existence of a productive force seeking social change.[21]

The arrival of video was tantamount to the symbolic dispossession of the institutional mass media. Screenwriters, artists, and political activists in this early phase seized upon the technology's viability for application to social realities. The possibilities for democratic use of the camera and recorder, the low costs, the straightforward and fast availability of results, the equality of sound and image ensured by the electronic resolution, facilitating the productive distortion of images through the video synthesizer, the immediate appearance of the image on the display, the porosity of the material, the new indifference to authorship—all this tallied with a will to create pictures independently of scripts and studios but through actual encounters, collisions in public spaces, situations and coincidences, and social contradictions. Video images became "image acts" (Horst Bredekamp),[22] penetrating social life beyond representation and the politics of affects. That, at least, was the ideal envisaged by both the political and artistic avant-garde of the day.[23]

In the four texts by film/video artists presented here, the enthusiasm and belief in unlimited possibilities of those early days can still be sensed. They evoke a counter-institutional force, buoyed by the discovery of an instrument requiring no political or economic regulation between the tool—the camera, the recorder—and the user; the producer and his or her images are "free." The medium and its egalitarian means of production were crucially associated with the desire to change the television system, to participatively design "better"" television, and so have a positive impact on society. For this reason, the terms "video" and "television" are often used synonymously in the texts below; an element of technological and aesthetic indecision lingers.[24] Video's ascendancy in this early period was still uncertain.

The texts focus on the differences between film and video. Film, as all other arts, is "prepared," "predetermined," "conditional," says Douglas Davis.[25] The film paradigm follows its own laws of recording, montage, narrative. It operates within an industrial system, engaged in the manufacture of pop-cultural products, by which an intention to overwhelm the viewer is always implied: it is a "larger-than-life existence." Yet these films do not belong to the audience; they are hired, so to speak, for the duration of the viewing. Nobody cares that they belong to corporations. Video, in contrast, is a product which is open to appropriation from the outset, which communicates with its users on an equal footing. Video, having possession of the hardware, is detached from all state-subsidized and, to some extent, private-enterprise production systems; anyone can make and control the disposal of their own pictures.[26] The recorded pictures are instantaneously visible and mobile, that is, independent of location (not tied to a base, like television). They react to the occasion from which they arise and show themselves to this situation without any interval.

Video was initially perceived as a performative medium. Nam June Paik's manipulations of the monitor formed the primal scene. Tetsuo Kogawa defines the interactivity inscribed in the image and its dispositive, and the agency attributed to the user in the context of his or her relationship with the medium, as the access potentiality of video.[27] Video initializes a plethora of accesses, hits, and links during the user's exchange with the camera, pictures, and alternative distribution networks. This state is amplified, in turn, by the broadcastability of video images. Video's digitization, its connection to computers and consequently to the internet, has emphatically underlined this access quality.

Video elicits a broader examination of the images; it becomes an analytic medium. It opens the film images, TV images, "operational images" (Harun Farocki) thus made available to an investigation of their medial, political, and economic contexts and potentialities. It generates self-reflexive chains of sound and images, which, like Godard's video essay *Histoire(s) du Cinéma*, work toward a historiography of cinema. Film images transmitted as video images become discursive elements, forming visual argumentations. Farocki has conceived a truly didactic approach to film, by which the viewer is invited to share the "analyst's"—that is, the editor's—workplace, assessing images that commentate other images—images that slide into and over one another in "unlimited semiosis" (Charles Sanders Peirce). In Farocki's self-portrait

Schnittstelle (1995), the viewer is drawn into a "positively pedagogic screening of the production of an electronically 'mixed' (and not mechanically 'edited') picture (resembling) an exemplary test set-up."[28] Many of Harun Farocki's "instructional" films center on comparisons between two pictures at the video editing desk. "The lowest plural dizzyingly generated infinity," says Farocki, describing his first experience of an Andy Warhol split screen.[29] With this analytical turn, a *third actor* alongside the film and the viewer is integrated in the field of view: the author or analyst of the images. Video is seen here as an empowering technological ritual that makes visible—as an active party—the otherwise excluded third party to a film production.

In his essay "Quereinfluss/Weiche Montage" Farocki makes direct reference to Godard:

> My point of departure was that when editing a film you only see one picture, but when editing video you see two: the one you already mounted and a preview of the next. In 1975, when Godard released *Numéro deux*, a 35mm film that (mostly) shows two video monitors, I was sure that this was a first portrayal of the new experience of video editing, comparing two pictures. What do these two pictures have in common? What can one picture have in common with another?[30]

For Gábor Bódy, the "genetic" relationship between image and sound, achieved via electronic physics, is a key stimulus for working with pictures, as a consequence of which the computer has become the universal medium for filmmaking, "which grants the artist an ornamental freedom of image-organization."[31]

According to Hollis Frampton, video produces a *generic eroticism*, evident in the *mandalas of feedback*—the specific image variations—that video technology deploys in order to supply alternating perspectives on its fields of interest.[32] The search for the right, true image has been abandoned in favor of a comparison, a juxtaposition, a multiplication of the possibilities that an image has for mobilizing portions of truth. Although the video synthesizer has no practical relevance for many cinematographers, this "monster of possibilities" nonetheless plays a role as a concept within their own work.[33]

A crucial decision for enabling video to be a tool for "wild" recordings of specific realities was to shift power from the eye to the hand. Video demotes the interplay between vision and thought and lets images emerge by coincidence; images arise from situations and occasions, which do not submit to any optic-rational controls.[34]

Godard has explicitly praised the work of the hands in various contexts. In *Six fois deux*, he is seen speaking to a farmer in a field, asking him to recall the manual gestures he performs in a day—in comparison to those of a factory worker. At first, the farmer is a little embarrassed, but then he proceeds to eloquently describe his daily routine with his hands. The camera simply records the manual conversation at hand height, nothing more. It does not film from an analytical or trained perspective but is an integral part of the choreography, recreating occasions in the image without visual supremacy. The video camera, Godard says, shifts "the eye from its usual place to the hand."[35] In the video essay *Histoire(s) du Cinéma*, we see a still from the Fritz Lang movie *M*, at the point where an underworld agent draws an M on his hand, to print on the murderer's coat as a sign for everyone to read. As part of the video image this still holds an inscription: "Seul la main qui efface peut écrire / Only the hand that erases can write." In Godard's last video essay to date, *Livre d'image*, the words are spoken: "La vraie condition de l'homme, c'est de penser avec ses mains" (Man's true condition is to think with his hands).

In the second phase, following the introduction of the digitized video image and the appearance on the market of the corresponding cameras in the late 1990s, the video image became a universal haptic image. Thanks, above all, to miniaturized video technology integrated in smartphones, videomaking has become an activity *à part*, performed without any specific aesthetic intentions. Quickly recording everything that matters—whom or what—by and with the body is *de rigeur* today. Image processing programs on PCs and apps on smartphones meanwhile facilitate the continued creative/manipulative use of video. And cinema engages in the film-becoming of the infinitely growing video archives and video populations.

Film Theory and Video

In the 1970s, semiology/semiotics-informed methods of image analysis in film theory exposed the "linguistic," semiotic mechanisms embedded in the microstructure of the body of film. These cannot be simply transposed to video's "anti-body," as Kogawa has stressed: "To the extent that semiotics considers video a capsule of image-signs, it must restrict its work to the signification system. To deal with the 'outside' or to look beyond the image-sign system is illegitimate."[36] Due to the medium's high *access* performance, attempts at formulating a theory focusing exclusively on the structures of meaning within the image have not been fruitful. Neither have the narratological, audience-oriented concepts of neo-formalist film analysis, which gained ground internationally soon afterward, proved conducive to exploring the less coherent, nonnarrative, contingent image planes of video. It is understandable, then, that Roy Armes rejects the idea of advancing video studies from film studies as a dead end in his book *On Video* (1988). Considering video in the broader context of all audiovisual technologies of the nineteenth and twentieth centuries, Armes proposes, would facilitate an escape from the "self-sufficiency" of orthodox film theory. Indeed, he makes a start in *On Video* by conceiving an inherent logic of the video aesthetic from its historical and social contexts.[37]

In the second volume of his philosophy of cinema, *Cinema 2: The Time-Image*, published in 1985, Gilles Deleuze indicates a need to extend the film image toward the "audio-visual image"; the audiovisual then becomes part of the complex, proliferating differentiations of the time-image; it creates "two 'heautonomous' images, one visual and one sound, with a fault, an interstice, an irrational cut between them."[38] Deleuze conveys the impression at various points—for example, by the comment that "the visual image becomes archeological, stratigraphic, and tectonic"—that he sees elements in postwar film that are directly translatable to video (Syberberg, Straub & Huillet, Duras . . .). Because this kind of image "is *read* at the same time as it is seen. . . . To read is to relink instead of link; it is to turn, and turn round, instead of to follow on the right side:

a new Analytic of the image."[39] This then gives rise to the kind of new "mental automats and psychic automats"[40] that also enlivened Gene Youngblood's *videosphere*. In a letter to film critic Serge Daney, Deleuze argues that "cinema ought to stop 'being cinematic,' stop playacting, and set up specific relationships with video, with electronic and digital images, in order to develop a new form of resistance and combat the televisual function of surveillance and control." To fight the controlling powers, the point is "whether one could develop an art of control that would be a kind of new form of resistance."[41] And with this speculation, Deleuze in a sense revives the early days of video actionism!

Notes

1 In reference to the "fort/da" formula Sigmund Freud describes in *Beyond the Pleasure Principle*. Freud's observation has considerable relevance for interpreting communications media usage: something is taken from me, is absent, but I can retrieve it, and bring it back to my present situation. Rather than an act of substitution, this game is one of self-empowerment. Video can make things that seemed unavailable or lost, such as the individual body, individual expression, and so on, become visible and available again. See Sigmund Freud, "Jenseits des Lustprinzips," in *Gesammelte Werke*, vol. XIII (Frankfurt am Main: S. Fischer, 1999), 11f.

2 Friedrich Nietzsche, "The Ugliest Man," in *Thus Spoke Zarathustra*, trans. Walter Kaufmann (Harmondsworth: Penguin, 1978), 266. Video is a *positive* foil because it survives the human individual and not vice versa!

3 Jonas Mekas quoted by Hollis Frampton, "The Withering Away of the State of the Art," in *The New Television: A Public/Private Art*, ed. Douglas Davis and Allison Simmons (Cambridge, MA: MIT Press, 1977), 24; reprinted in this chapter.

4 Satires of the media and especially the television industry recur regularly throughout film history. Examples include Frederico Fellini, *Ginger and Fred* (Italy 1985) and Gus van Sant, *To Die For* (USA 1995).

5 For a precise historical analysis of the questions addressed in this chapter, see Jonathan Rosenkrantz in *Videographic Cinema: An Archaeology of Electronic Images and Imaginaries* (London and New York: Bloomsbury, 2020).

6 I am referring here specifically to television news but the same could apply to smartphones and their input into video news in films.

7 On the relative and absolute out of field, see Gilles Deleuze, *Cinema 1: The Movement Image* (Minneapolis: University of Minnesota Press, 1986), 12f.

8 An especially eloquent incorporation of television can be seen in Fritz Lang's *While the City Sleeps* (USA, 1956). Here a TV journalist, both reporter and newsreader, uses his TV show to directly address a murderer who—in a parallel shot/countershot—is watching the broadcast in his living room.

9 But it is not only news that emanates from media devices; the TV set also serves as an index of certain bourgeois lifeworlds: when children sit on the couch and watch cartoons, they are *elsewhere*, while the filmic adults deal with serious matters in the here and now.

10 "The gratification was so intense and immediate that I felt confused. I thought I might be turning into a barbarian . . . or maybe even a musician." This is how Hollis

Frampton described his first experience of video. See Frampton, "The Withering Away of the State of the Art," 167; reprinted in this chapter.

11 See, e.g., Andrea Arnold, *Read Road* (UK, 2006). For more examples, see Dietmar Kammerer, *Bilder der Überwachung* (Frankfurt am Main: Suhrkamp, 2008), esp. "Verbrecher im Kino und vor der Kamera," 273–84; also Nicole Falkenhayner, *Media, Surveillance and Affect: Narrating Feeling-States* (London: Routledge, 2018), esp. chapter 3, "Being Captured: Tools of Surveillance as Tools of Fictional Becoming."

12 *Peeping Tom* by Michael Powell (GB 1960) can be regarded as an example *avant la lettre* of a portrayal of a "disorder" for which the video dispositive proved a suitable instrument, as it did for the porn industry later. In John Glenn's *James Bond: Octopussy* (UK/USA, 1983) video is used by the antihero for sexist closed-circuit surveillance purposes.

13 See, e.g., Tobe Hooper, *Poltergeist* (Canada/USA, 1982); David Cronenberg, *Videodrome* (USA, 1983); Kathryn Bigelow, *Strange Days* (USA, 1995).

14 See Thomas Helbig's essay in this chapter, "Video in the Work of Jean-Luc Godard."

15 On the latter, see Marc Ries, "Penultimate Pictures / Vorletzte Bilder," in *Film und Gesellschaft denken mit Siegfried Kracauer*, ed. Bernhard Groß and Drehli Robnik (Vienna and Berlin: Turia + Kant, 2018), 132–43; reprinted in this chapter.

16 From the point of view of reception aesthetics, however, there is likely a sense of differentiation in picture perception. See, e.g., Tetsuo Kogawa, "Video: The Access Medium," in *Resolutions: Contemporary Video Practices*, ed. Michael Renov and Erika Suderburg (Minneapolis: University of Minnesota Press, 1996), 51–9; reprinted in this chapter. Digital home cinema not only constitutes a different atmospheric dispositive but also gives rise to greater contingency in terms of control over the films, allowing pauses, rewinding, switching back and forth between channels, etc. The viewer also has a different physical relationship to the scaled-down picture; by a converse logic to the cinematic experience, the viewers' bodies are now larger than the often radically miniaturized pictures on their iPads or smartphones.

17 *The New York Times*, "How George Floyd Was Killed in Police Custody/Visual Investigations," June 1, 2020, https://www.youtube.com/watch?v=vksEJR9EPQ8&bpctr=1595486157: "The Times has reconstructed the death of George Floyd on May 25. Security footage, witness videos, and official documents show how a series of actions by officers turned fatal. (This video contains scenes of graphic violence.)" This is also an example of the transmedia use of video, appearing on the websites of print media.

18 See Roland Barthes, *Camera Lucida* (New York: Hill and Wang, 1981).

19 This is not the place to go into temporality in video in depth. For more on this concept, see, e.g., Maurizio Lazzarato, *Videophilosophy: The Perception of Time in Post-Fordism*, ed. and trans. Jay Hetrick (New York: Columbia University Press, 2019), 81–94. One could also transpose Gilles Deleuze's argumentation of the "simultaneity of peaks of present" in chapter 5 of *Cinema 2: The Time Image* (Minneapolis: University of Minnesota Press, 1989), to the contemporaneity doctrine of the video image.

20 One example of a contemporary metamorphotic phenomenon of video culture is the "transitions" on TikTok.

21 See the activist editions of *Radical Software*, especially the first edition of spring 1970, online at https://www.radicalsoftware.org/e/volume1nr1.html.

22 See Horst Bredekamp, *Image Acts: A Systematic Approach to Visual Agency*, trans. Elizabeth Clegg (Berlin: De Gruyter, 2017).

23 On the social and utopian potential of video, see the introduction to Chapter 9.
24 See, e.g., Gene Youngblood in the first edition of *Radical Software*: "Television is one of the most revolutionary tools in the entire spectrum of technoanarchy. Television, like the computer, is a sleeping giant. But those who are beginning to use it in revolutionary new ways are very much awake." On distinctions within the terminology, see the introduction to Chapter 5.
25 See the text by Douglas Davis, "Filmgoing/Videogoing: Making Distinctions," *The American Film Institute Reports: "The Movie Going Experience,"* 4, no. 2 (May 1973); reprinted in this chapter.
26 On home video, see the introduction to Chapter 10. This innovation is now threatened by online video on demand, insofar as the "hardware" is divided between the users and the servers, i.e., the memory for distribution is again in the hands of private-enterprise production systems.
27 See Kogawa, "Video: The Access Media," reprinted in this chapter.
28 Christa Blümlinger, *Kino aus zweiter Hand: Zur Ästhetik materieller Aneignung im Film und in der Medienkunst* (Berlin: Vorwerk, 2009), 239.
29 See "Quereinfluss/Weiche Montage" (2002), online at https://newfilmkritik.de/archiv/2002-06/quereinflussweiche-montage/. The exhibition *Kino wie noch nie / Cinema Like Never Before* (Generali Foundation, Vienna 2006), mounted by Antje Ehmann and Harun Farocki, continued this analysis in the exhibition context. Curiously, all the works operate with film images but show them as video images; the list of works merely records the presentation of "cinema-historical archetypes," for instance, as "5 videos, b/w and color, sound." The media switch goes uncommented.
30 Ibid.
31 See the essay by Gábor Bódy, "Video and Film," in *State of Images: The Media Pioneers Zbigniew Rybczynski and Gabor Body*, ed. Siegfried Zielinski and Peter Weibel (Nuremberg: Verlag für Moderne Kunst, 2011), 80–4; reprinted in this chapter.
32 See Frampton, "The Withering Away of the State of the Art"; reprinted in this chapter.
33 See *Vision*, the magazine of the Television Laboratory at WNET/Thirteen, August 1973. The abovementioned text by Douglas Davis was also published in this issue of the magazine.
34 See, e.g., Ries, "Penultimate Pictures / Vorletzte Bilder"; reprinted in this chapter.
35 See the survey by Thomas Helbig, "Video in the Work of Jean-Luc Godard," in this chapter. Another interesting aspect here is Godard's wish for a small 35mm camera and his conversation with the developer Jean-Pierre Beauviala in "Genèse d'une camera: Première épisode, Deuxième episode," in *Jean-Luc Godard par Jean-Luc Godard* (Paris: Éditions de l'Étoile/Cahiers du cinéma, 1985), 519–57.
36 See Kogawa, "Video: The Access Medium," 2; reprinted in this chapter.
37 See the preface by Roy Armes to *On Video* (New York: Routledge, 1988); reprinted in this chapter.
38 Deleuze, *Cinema 2: The Time-Image*, 251.
39 Ibid., 245. Deleuze uses the term "heautonomy" in the sense of self-legislation—the visual and the sonic each follow their own laws.
40 Ibid., conclusion to chapter 10.
41 Gilles Deleuze, "Letter to Serge Daney: Optimism, Pessimism, and Travel," in *Negotiations 1972–1990*, trans. Martin Joughlin (New York: Columbia University Press, 1995), 75f.

Filmgoing/Videogoing: Making Distinctions (1973)

Douglas Davis

Thinking about the differences between video and film—which is nothing less than thinking about the essences of each—must begin in the experience of seeing. What we see depends on how we see, and where, and when. There is the experience of going out to see a film, an experience that begins early in our lives, with the approach of the theater marquee, the press of the crowds, the seat found in the darkness, and then the huge, overpowering screen, larger than any imaginable life, images as big as a child imagines a building to be. Later the act of perception takes place in a dwindled space, brought on by reaching adulthood, and by the change in taste. The screen may be smaller, the noises around us less exuberant, but still we have gone to this space, gone out to sit in the dark before large moving images. We go "out" to see a painting or a drawing, too, to a public place, to a museum or a gallery, or a cathedral. Since the nineteenth century, however, since the growth of an audience that could purchase works of art and hang them in private spaces (instead of an audience limited to princes and cathedrals), we have seen [in] these museums or galleries works intended for small, private spaces, for city apartments and suburban homes. We see them even in the public museum in environments grown increasingly intimate; we focus in upon these images in light directed so as to draw us further inside them; we focus, stand, and then move on, noiselessly, from one work to another, in control of our own time. The scale of man to image is equalized, particularly in this century, when the epic or public painting has only lately begun to appear again. And then there is the experience of seeing video.

Think about this act, this totality of perception. It falls somewhere between the experiences I have just described, between film and painting. A small screen, lit from within, its moving images paradoxically built, as E. H. Gombrich points out, on the physical limitation in our vision: our eyes cannot keep up with the luminous dot that sweeps continually across the inner face of that tube. We do not go out to see video. We turn it on without any sense of occasion; often, indeed, we turn it on unconsciously and leave it there, the images moving across the screen, the sounds emerging from their tiny speakers without our knowing. The focusing, as in painting and drawing and sculpture, is inward, onto something. (While watching a film, the eye looks up and out; the mind is drawn helplessly away from itself, into a larger-than-life existence.) We give video our attention, not the reverse; even in moments of absorption the screen is left without compunction, for a drink, a phone call, an errand. There is no one around me, usually, that I do not know. Often I am alone before the screen, as I might choose to be alone before a painting. Yet there is a felt link to some larger consensus. The viewer is alone but he knows, subconsciously, that he is part of an audience, whose remaining members he can neither see nor hear.

The video experience is not, I am trying to suggest, a simple experience. It has affinities with film, painting, and theater, but there are as many contradictions. Even the experience we know, difficult enough to understand, is changing. Television screens are growing larger; audiences are becoming lonelier, more individuated, thanks to cable television, half-inch videotape, and videocassettes, all of which provide specialized programming choices. Our attitude toward the screen—of which this essay is a part—is becoming more self-conscious. Even so, it is clear that video's affinity with other media, and particularly with film, is conditional. *How* we see it, physically and psychically, is the major condition. Film performers, seen on the street, carry an aura; they can overpower us, in real life. Video performers remind their public when seen in the street—of next-door neighbors; we reach out to shake their hands instinctively.

If I seem to be describing a medium that is less iconic in its nature than film, remember that I am doing so from a basis in perception. If we are going to capture video as a medium for high, difficult, and intense art, we will only do so by utilizing it for its own sake. Artist, critic, and public must act on the certain basis of how video is seen. The painter does not need to think this issue through; he knows (without knowing) the perceptual system into which his work will fit. So does the filmmaker. From the earliest age he is engaged in that perceptual system. We are all moviegoers first, even those of us who weaned on video. For television has not yet been defined. From its inception, it has been controlled by men and women forced to pay for its existence by reaching an impossibly wide audience. We have not seen video yet. Television until now has been made by sensibilities conditioned in popular fiction, film, and theater. I cannot think of a completely equivalent case in the history of the arts. It is the case of an enormously rich and potential medium coming to birth in the hands of people forbidden (by economics) to discover its essence.

This is precisely why artists untrained in either television, film, or the theater are beginning to show us more about video than we have yet dreamt of. This awakening has nothing to do with the technology of half-inch videotape except insofar as its appearance made personal investigations possible, as the arrival of the easel painting (as distinct from the frieze or the fresco) made another art accessible. It has to do with thinking afresh, looking at video as if for the first time. I cannot stress too much the necessity of this freshness. When I talk to students about video I always begin by asking them what "television" is (because I don't know myself) and we always conclude, at the end of this session, that we aren't sure of very much. The more I work in it, the less I know. Nam June Paik once told me that he always discovers more in his work when he sees it broadcast than he put into it. I do not claim that all artists are like this. James Rosenquist once refused to work in experimental video because the screen wasn't large enough. "Come back when it is at least three feet by five feet," he said. He brought the conditions of painting to bear on what he saw, as a filmmaker might, who fills up the tiny screen with epic-sized images. There is nothing more intriguing to me than the size—and the variety of the size—of the video screen. I once telecast on cable in New York City a color tape (*Studies in Color Videotape II*) that focuses upon a moving red light image at the very end. Depending on the size, shape, and nature of the receiving set, the viewers see many different lights, in some case highly luminous, multicolored images. The reactions depended upon the condition of the set, which is a condition of the medium to be faced and used, not denied.

Let me return again to where and how we see video, to catch it there in a very special moment. Alone once more, in the home, not formally seated, or surrounded by large numbers of people. In that moment, we can also be connected to the uncertainty of real life. Film is always prepared for us, its time telescoped by the making hand. In the theater we inhabit the same time in which the players perform, but we know that the next step, and the step after that, has been predetermined by the playwright. What we have come to call "live" video links with "life" in a highly concentrated form; when we are watching "live" phenomena on the screen we participate in a subtle existentialism. Often it is so subtle that it nears boredom. Yet we stay, participating. The endless moon walk, the endless convention, the endless (in another way) *American Family*. In all these cases, the "live" dimension kept its audience there, before the small screen, alone, at home, waiting, because it knows that anything may happen next, as in life. I mention *An American Family* deliberately; though edited, it made less attempt to structure and pace narrative events than any popular television series yet. Often, long stretches of meaningless, boring conversation were allowed to play out, unstructured. "Live" time approached life time. For this reason and because we knew the Family was "real," we stayed, waiting, aware that something unpredictably "live" might occur next.

Video is not life, of course, any more than any art is. Unlike the other arts, though, it approaches the pace and unpredictability of life, and is seen in a perceptual system grounded in the home and the self. I do not know how we moviegoers are going to understand this, thoroughly, but we must. The link between the formal occasion that is film and the private occasion that is video must be both recognized and forgotten. There will be no video art until we approach this medium as if it had not existed before.

Douglas Davis, "Filmgoing/Videogoing: Making Distinctions," in *The American Film Institute Report: The Movie Going Experience* 4, no. 2 (May 1973), 51f.

Video in the Work of Jean-Luc Godard: Interviews and Statements (1969–2001)

Jean-Luc Godard (Compiled and Introduced by Thomas Helbig)

Jean-Luc Godard's early engagement with video coincided with a time of strong antagonisms. The fact that such a prominent director and protagonist of the Nouvelle Vague was not only interested in video but at times even stopped working with film raised eyebrows. While some reacted to this decision with disappointment, others took it as an encouragement. In Godard's approach, video is discussed from the outset within the parameters of "theoretical work," which is bound to lead to an experimentally changed practice from where to "correct" the theory.[1] Technical aspects merge with social and political ones (*bruit social*), theoretical aspects with practical ones. By pointing out that the etymology of the term "video" derives from seeing (*video*), Godard also lends plausibility to the idea that this technique is particularly suitable for "searching and researching."[2] "Cogito ergo video," he states in a text insert in his video essay *Histoire(s) du cinéma* (1988–1998), thus also positing a theorem that is precisely no longer formulated on the basis of texts. Not least for this reason, there exists no integral text in which Godard develops a consistent video theory. Besides the ideas resulting directly from his film and video practice, there are however a number of statements to be found in which Godard, in different contexts, reflects on working with video.

During the filming of *La Chinoise* (1967), Godard already considered using this technology, which was still inaccessible to him at the time. In line with the circumstances then, video technology was considered from its inception as an instrument of (self-)criticism in the context leading up to the May protests. The first practical attempts were made in 1968 as part of the video magazine *Vidéo 5*, which was distributed by François Maspero through his Paris bookstore and to which Alain Jacquier and Chris Marker contributed.[3] However, it was not until the early 1970s that Godard was able to harness the technology for his own purposes. With considerable financial commitment, he and Anne-Marie Miéville, his partner in life and work, set up the video laboratory Sonimage[4]—first in 1973/74 in Grenoble, then in 1977 in Rolle, Switzerland—with the aim of enabling him to work freely and independently in the manner of an "(artist) craftsman."[5] While *Ici et ailleurs* (1970–1974) was still based on 16 mm film material that was transferred to video and then edited, for *Numéro deux* (1975) he used video from the outset; the subsequent transfer to 35 mm was merely made for the purpose of distribution to movie theaters. With the experimental twelve-part TV series *Six fois deux [sur et sous la communication]* (1976) and *France tour détour deux enfants* (1979), Godard and Miéville finally dispensed with film distribution altogether and outlined new ways, in both form and content, to establish television as a discursive medium. Their work with video does not rely on the logic of either/or but rather on a productive expansion in which the boundaries between cinema and television, film and video, and author and producer are blurred. "Video," Godard mused retrospectively, "taught me to see film and to rethink the work with film differently."[6] It is therefore hardly surprising that he considers his four-and-a-half-hour video essay *Histoire(s) du cinéma*, in which not only images from the history of film but also 35 mm film strips are repeatedly appearing in the video image, to be "the product of thirty years of video."[7] The recently completed video essay *The Image Book* (2018) also continues this discussion, which thanks to the offensive inclusion of digital formats now operates at the interface of the post-cinematographic.

A description of the technical and aesthetic reorientation in Godard's oeuvre inaugurated by his work with video would be incomplete if one failed to emphasize the collaborative character that began already with the founding of the film collective Dziga Vertov Group (1968–71) and was ultimately reinforced by the use of video. For example, Godard worked for a while with Jean-Pierre Beauviala, who developed a miniature-sized video camera (Paluche) in early 1975.[8] Besides intense collaborations, especially with Miéville,[9] but also with Jean-Pierre Gorin, Gérard Martin, William Lubtchansky, Gérard Teissèdre, Dominique Chapuis, Philippe Rony, Pierre Binggeli, Caroline Champetier, and for some time now with Fabrice Aragno, his work with video was from the very beginning marked by the search for mediating and collaborative formats. Among other things, he held a series of film lectures ("Introduction to a True History of Cinema and Television") in Montreal in 1978,[10] directed a film and video workshop in Rotterdam in 1980/81, and together with Miéville tried to set up a video and television company in Mozambique in a project named *Naissance (de l'image) d'une nation* (1978).[11] His no less ambitious concept for the establishment of a Centre de recherches cinéma et vidéo (Center for Film and Video Research, Palais de Tokyo, Paris 1990), which was supposed to collaborate with the French national film school Fémis and the Centre national du cinéma (CNC) on the major project that eventually became known under the title *Histoire(s) du cinéma*, also remained unrealized.[12]

Jean-Luc Godard on Video

The following compilation brings together a series of fragments documenting more than half a century of Godard's work with video.[13] Not only the candidness of the comparisons Godard uses to relate video to music and painting is surprising, but also the matter-of-factness with which he links video technology to the early days of cinema (Méliès, Lumière, and Chaplin) on the one hand, and to the expanded cinema of his day (Warhol) on the other.

1. Paracinema

I try to remember how one day I happened to buy a Sony. It must have been in 1968/69, around the time when the first black-and-white recording devices came onto the market. As a filmmaker, I was very interested in this technology and especially in how it could be changed, because changing it is almost . . . a moral issue.[14] (1976)

When *La Chinoise* [1967] was being made, I'd seen a camera and video recorder in Philips's window, and said to myself that the discussion in the room between the Maoists could be filmed on video by them and they could then make their autocritiques, as the fashion then was. We went to see Philips, it was a bit like getting into the defense ministry at the time . . . remember it was thirty years ago. But video is, in real-estate parlance, an adjacent wing of cinema. It's paracinema that can be used, in a way, to do what cinema couldn't do without loss of quality—that's it really—and more cheaply too . . .[15] (2000)

Video, in Latin, means roughly "I see"; technically, it refers to a contact or signal that is required to produce an electronic image—in much the same way as one could say of film that it is a photoelectrical effect or something like that. I prefer to use the terms "film" and "television." They denote two different aspects, two media; the first is chemical-photographic and is a technical invention that is about 120 years old, the second is electronic and has existed practically since World War II.[16] (1976)

I still remember that already ten years ago [1968] there were people who preferred to work with a small video system simply because it gave them the possibility to record for an hour, and who two or three years later started working with a portable device. It was just easier for interviews or filming demonstrations, even if it meant reverting to black-and-white, which incidentally was very interesting. They were able to produce images they could not have produced as cheaply, as good and as fast with 16 mm. And they didn't try to hook up with a large distribution system but preferred instead to make their images immediately accessible to a small public, for example at a meeting.[17] (1976)

2. Popular Cinema

The professional filmmaker must be turned into an amateur again.[18] (1969)

[. . .] "family" films are the real popular cinema, and at the same time, they are making the Kodak company happy. This business with images relies on man's fundamental need to have an image of himself—it is not by chance that Lumière began by filming *Baby's Lunch*—one image at a time in movement: cinema, television, and frozen. Hence the permanent success of still photography, which caters to this conservative instinct to freeze the moment. Besides, it is from the desire for this image to be immediate that the inventions of the Polaroid and the video recorder were born; we should not forget that all these developments were initiated by amateurs, in the sense that they are a response to popular demands.[19] (1973)

So let's start from there. Instead of starting from professional cinema, let's start from amateur cinema, which is in a way even more professional than the former. But let's do it differently. *Numéro deux*, for example, is an amateur film, it's a family film. Except that it isn't shown in the place where it is, where it should be.[20] (1975)

I think what's really going to help is the "video recorder for amateurs" that is supposed to come out now. There is already one by Sony, in Germany there will be one by Grundig that is supposed to be cheaper than Sony's. This will help a lot because you can make films faster, at a lesser cost, you can erase them and then make others. There is no processing, no censorship. They can be carried along immediately and filming will be made easier. There's no more hassle, no thousands of actors, no big things. It will change little by little. You will be able to do a news program with it,[21] everyone for themselves, that's the most important point.[22] (1969)

The interesting thing about video is not so much that you can check the image immediately after recording it; more important is the process of searching and researching the image you produce in this way.[23] (1976)

People should write scripts on video [. . .].[24] (1978)

3. Social Noise

Perhaps the most interesting thing with video is that you can grab the camera easily. But if you can grab it more easily, maybe you can put it down more easily and think about it better. [. . .] To communicate what? What kind of information? We can't speak of information *per se*, in heaven. [. . .] This is cybernetics. You have very few ways of working with video in other than movie terms, and you have to know that movie terms are determined by TV terms, by the relationship of millions of TV sets. There was an American scientist, [Claude E.] Shannon,[25] who put down general ideas about information thirty years ago. He said there is a transmitter and a channel and then another transmitter and then a receiver. In the channel, the cable for instance, is where the noise is. What we are aware of is the noise. For us as moviemakers the noise is not merely something technical, it's something social.[26] (1972)

So I started thinking, not about the viewer, but about the fact that viewers exist. [. . .] Sometimes television and video have helped me think about this in a material way simply because the fact of having a monitor, a television screen at the end of the line—video gives you the entire production line, meaning that it lets you think of yourself as a producer [. . .]. Meaning you see the entire production line that you don't see in cinema: the camera, the lab, the movie theater. Because in video you see the image right away, meaning that you think yourself as one of the first viewers.[27] (1978)

4. Thinking in Video

The interest of video consists first and foremost in that it allows me to reinject all the images I want: it allows for all kinds of transpositions and manipulations.[28] And, most of all, it allows me to think in images and not in texts.[29] (1975)

You have only two images to work with in editing; it's like having only two motifs in music, and the possibilities of creating a relationship between two images are infinite. The big difference is that if you shoot the three stone lions of Eisenstein in video, it can be an entire Warhol movie.[30] (1997)

[. . .] and sometimes you have to reedit in order to better prepare and change some things. I noticed that [Gustav] Mahler did that, sometimes he reworked his scores after playing a work once.[31] (1985)

You would have to provide proof. Unfortunately, film criticism doesn't really use video. [. . .] How can you prove that it's good? Not an easy task. Even in seminars, that is not really done. It should be done in class, using video.[32] (2000–2001)

5. Home Videos

[*Numéro deux* was] shot on video to prove that you can make feature films at an affordable price and in line with all the characteristics of professional film. We could very well have shot it in 16 mm, but we did it on video because this medium makes it possible to consider human relationships from another angle. The image, thanks to video, becomes less tyrannical. [. . .] But beyond that, video makes you want to express yourself fully, while film stifles creation insofar as the artistic product is programmed and distributed in advance. Here, we are free, we invent our own means of dissemination.[33] (1975)

The work relationships were gentler and less aggressive. As they were less aggressive, the others no longer sensed a technical hierarchy, they felt a bit like they were creating. It made them want to dabble too . . .[34] (1975)

Video taught me to see film and to rethink the work with film differently. With video you go back to simpler elements. In particular to having sound and image together.[35] For film people they are separate. [. . .] I've noticed that people in film and in video were not ready to work together, they didn't want to. It's a bit like classical music and rock, it doesn't go together, so you shouldn't force things. Now, maybe with [François] Musy and [Jean-Bernard] Menoud, we want to start again from sound, with more sophisticated equipment, also having our own camera and being able to do everything ourselves except the lab. It's the old idea by [Charlie] Chaplin and [Marcel] Pagnol.[36] (1985)

6. Transitions between Video, Painting and Music

Video is closer to painting or to music. You work with your hands like a musician with an instrument, and you play it. In moviemaking, you can't say that the camera is an instrument you play through; it's something different.[37] (1997)

Histoire(s) [*du cinéma*] was cinema. Technically it was textbook stuff, very simple things. Of the forty possibilities in the list I used one or two, mostly overprinting to help retain the original cinema image, while if I'd tried to do the same thing with film I'd have had to use reverse negative copies and that causes a loss of quality; above all you can alter the image easily with video, while with film all variation has to be preplanned. [. . .] The overprints, all that comes from cinema, they were tricks Méliès used . . .[38] (2000)

In video [superimposition is] elementary. The two images mix like two sounds, like music. It was a lot of fun to do, and the superimposition correspond with the metaphor of one idea taking the place of another.[39] (2000–2001)

Illustrations

With Sonimage, the video company they established in Grenoble, Godard/Miéville were trying to gain control over the entire production chain of film work:

> With the help of [Jean-Pierre] Rassam and [Nicolas] Seydoux, I set up a small company in Grenoble called Sonimage that allows me to work like an artisan.

> We make small programs here. We have invested 2 million francs worth of video material, a camera, a recording and mixing desk [. . .]. By working like this, I discovered there were other techniques [. . .] that could be used with little expense, without opposing them to cinema but in order to conjoin them.[40] (1975)

Numéro deux shows Godard at the editing desk of his video "factory," surrounded by an early IVC video system, while a woman's voice coming from the left monitor underlines the importance of taking control of the means of production yourself: "But letting others tell your story is a crime. Especially when you don't get paid for it. You go to the cinema. You buy a ticket. In exchange, you sell your role as producer. Turn on the TV and you're an accomplice" (Figure 4.1).

In *Six fois deux*, Godard/Miéville use the "videopen," or "telestrator," an electronic writing device that allows one to add writing or graphic notations onto the screen:

> Paint or draw. It's like in television or in video; there are instruments which let you draw on screen. These could be improved. Or writing could again play a role and not just be a trace . . .[41] (1978)

Video technology moreover makes it possible to intervene directly in the image and its aesthetic. In an experimental split-screen process,[42] Godard/Miéville combine two different camera positions on the surface of one and the same image. The silent dialogue of two people turns into a dialogue of overlapping images and writings:

> For example, it will be interesting to shoot certain movies with a VCR not only from a financial standpoint but for grammatical and aesthetic reasons. For a face-off, for example, shot with two cameras, in a different way than the shot/counter-shot

Figure 4.1 Jean-Luc Godard, *Numéro deux*, 1975, 35 mm film and video, color, 88 min.

> relationship, in other words question/answer, you will have to think about the dialogue and you will realize that you can no longer write it in the same way. Through the sheer fact that it makes you ask yourself questions, this technique will make the approach more complex at the same time as it will free it, clarify it.[43] (1973) (Figure 4.2)

As its name suggests, *Naissance (de l'image) d'une nation*, Godard/Miéville's attempt to establish a video and television society in Mozambique in 1978, hoped to frame the political history of the young republic not only in the context of film history (*Birth of a Nation*, Griffith, 1915), but also as part of a media history of the electronic image. "Not a just image, but just an image," writes Godard in *Histoire (s) du cinéma* onto the material of the failed project, acknowledging that the one-time emancipatory dream of achieving media independence in conjunction with political independence has left behind nothing more than an image.

> Profit from the audio-visual situation of the country to study television before it exists, before it inundates [. . .] the entire social and geographic Mozambican corpus. Study the image, the desire for images (the wish to remember, the wish to show this memory, to make a mark on it). [. . .] Study the production of these desires for images and their distribution via the airwaves (oh sirens!) or cables. Study, for once, production, before distribution comes into the mix. Study the programs before making a grid out of them, behind which the spectators will be plonked, who will no longer know that that they are behind the television set and not in front of it as they believe.[44] (1979) (Figure 4.3)

Figure 4.2 Jean-Luc Godard and Anne-Marie Miéville, *Six fois deux / Sur et sous la communication, Part 5A: Nous trois*, 1976, video, b/w and color, 52 min.

Figure 4.3 Jean-Luc Godard, "La premiére / image / ce n'est pas une image juste / [c'est] juste und image," *Histoire(s) du cinéma, Part 1B: Une histoire seule*, 1988–98, video, color, 42 min.

Figure 4.4 Jean-Luc Godard, *Histoire(s) du cinéma, Part 1B: Une histoire seule*, 1988–98, video, color, 42 min.

According to Alexandre Astruc (see his manifesto *camera-pen*, 1948), if Descartes had lived in the film era, he would have shot his *Discourse on Method* with a 16 mm camera. "Cogito ergo video," writes Godard, suggesting that such a discourse could be seen and reflected on much better in the video medium. This also implies rethinking the language of technology or the forms of its use:

> As if by chance, in video, the left-hand reel is called the "slave" and the right-hand one the "master."[45] (1988)
>
> Why did the frame become square, why are lenses round? It's a lot to think about.[46] (1978) (Figure 4.4).

Translated for the present publication by Boris Patrick Kremer.

Notes

1 Jean-Luc Godard, "Die Kunst der Massen ist eine Idee der Kapitalisten," *Film* 7, no. 4 (1969), 24. On the practice of a theory developed through film, see Volker Pantenburg, *Farocki/Godard: Film as Theory* (Amsterdam: Amsterdam University Press, 2015).

2 Jean-Luc Godard, "Die Video-Technik im Dienste der Film-Produktion und der Kommunikation," *Filmkritik* 22, no. 7 (1978), 365.

3 See Michael Witt, *Jean-Luc Godard, Cinema Historian* (Bloomington: Indiana University Press, 2013), 51; Michael Witt, "On and Under Communication," in *A Companion to Jean-Luc Godard*, ed. Tom Conley and T. Jefferson Kline (Chichester: Wiley-Blackwell, 2014), 324.

4 Jean-Luc Godard, "L'important c'est les producteurs," interview by Monique Annaud, *Le Film français*, March 14, 1975, 13. See also Anne-Marie Duguet, *Vidéo, la mémoire au poing* (Paris: Hachette, 1981), 160–3.

5 Godard, "L'important c'est les producteurs," 13. See Thomas Helbig, "Speaking with Godard: Wilfried Reichart about German-French Film and Television History," *Sabzian*, July 25, 2018, https://www.sabzian.be/article/speaking-with-godard.

6 Jean-Luc Godard, "L'art à partir de la vie," interview by Alain Bergala, March 12, 1985, in *Jean-Luc Godard par Jean-Luc Godard, Vol. 1, 1950–1984*, ed. Alain Bergala (Paris: Éditions de l'Étoile, 1998), 24.

7 Jean-Luc Godard and Youssef Ishaghpour, *Cinema: The Archaeology of Film and the Memory of a Century*, trans. John Howe (Oxford: Berg Publishers, 2005), 35.

8 "One saw an image that came from the hand" and the camera "shifted the eye from its familiar place into the hand," writes Godard in anticipation of the idea of the Paluche as an "extension of the hand" that Raymond Bellour developed in relation to Thierry Kuntzel. Godard, "Video-Technik," 361. See also Raymond Bellour, "Thierry Kuntzel and the Return of Writing," in *Between-the-Images* (Zürich: JRP Ringier, 2012), 30–62.

9 For further insight into the different stages of their collaboration, see Jerry White, *Two Bicycles: The Work of Jean-Luc Godard and Anne-Marie Miéville* (Waterloo, ON: Wilfried Laurier University Press, 2013).

10 The version of the lectures that was initially published in French in 1980 is now available in a thoroughly revised version that has been translated into English. Jean-Luc Godard, *Introduction to a True History of Cinema and Television*, ed. Timothy Barnard (Montreal: Caboose, 2014).

11 The project is the subject of a special issue of *Cahiers du cinéma* (no. 300) edited by Godard in 1979. See Daniel Fairfax, "Birth (of the Image) of a Nation: Jean-Luc

Godard in Mozambique," *Acta Universitatis Sapentiae*, Film and Media Studies series 3 (2010), 55–67, http://www.acta.sapientia.ro/acta-film/C3/film3-4.pdf; and White, *Two Bicycles*, 49–53.

12 Witt, *Cinema Historian*, 43.

13 The statements include sources that are only available in German and that have been translated into English for this contribution.

14 Godard, "Video-Technik," 359.

15 Godard and Ishaghpour, *Cinema*, 36. Godard makes similar statements in an interview with Colin MacCabe in 1979; see Colin MacCabe, Mick Eaton, and Laura Mulvey, *Godard: Images, Sounds, Politics* (Bloomington: Macmillan, 1980), 133.

16 Godard, "Video-Technik," 359.

17 Godard, "Video-Technik," 367.

18 Godard, "Kunst der Massen," 24.

19 Jean-Luc Godard, "Juin 1973: Jean-Luc Godard fait le point," interview by Philippe Durand, in David Faroult, *Godard. Inventions d'un cinéma politique* (Paris: Les Prairies ordinaires, 2018), 538. Elsewhere, Godard describes how video amateurs soon felt the need to "work creatively, that is, selectively." Initially, however, companies such as Sony and Shibaden had not intended this kind of use, "but as more and more people wanted to 'cut,' they eventually had to deal with it and drive this development. It was always the amateurs who forced them to do something, and it was the same with 16 mm: it's always the researchers and the amateurs." Godard, "Video-Technik," 367.

20 Jean-Luc Godard, "Penser la maison en termes d'usine," in *Jean-Luc Godard par Jean-Luc Godard*, 380.

21 This intention was also noted by Gene Youngblood: "The potentials are so impressive that Jean-Luc Godard, possibly in a moment of passion, once vowed to abandon his feature-film career to make 'instant newsreels' via portable videotape equipment." Youngblood, *Expanded Cinema* (New York: P. Dutton & Co., 1970), 264.

22 Godard, "Kunst der Massen," 24.

23 Godard, "Video-Technik," 365.

24 Godard, *Introduction*, 41. Besides the three video sketches *Scénario de "Sauve qui peut (la vie)"* (1979), *Passion, le travail et l'amour: Introduction à un scénario* (1982) and *Petites notes à propos du film "Je vous salue, Marie"* (1983), Godard also created a video reflection in retrospect with *Scénario du film "Passion"* (1982). See Philippe Dubois, "'Video thinks what cinema creates': Notes on Jean-Luc Godard's Work in Video and Television," in *Jean-Luc Godard: Son + Image, 1974–1991*, ed. Raymond Bellour and Mary Lea Bandy (New York: Museum of Modern Art, 1992), 169–85.

25 On Godard's reference to Claude E. Shannon and its consequences for his work with video, see Witt, "On and Under Communication," 322–5.

26 Jean-Luc Godard and Jean-Pierre Gorin, *Angle and Reality: Godard and Gorin in America* (1972), interview by Robert Phillip Kolker, in *Jean-Luc Godard: Interviews*, ed. David Sterritt (Jackson: University Press of Mississippi, 1998), 65–6.

27 Godard, *Introduction*, 198.

28 Caroline Champetier, who worked as Godard's cinematographer on several film projects from the late 1980s onward, offers a similar description: "Because the video medium enables him to question the image, to slow down, to accelerate, all these things that he does extraordinarily. [. . .] Video likes flatness and frontal lights, not sculpturalness. We had a digital imaging technician who checked with us on an

oscilloscope and a vectorscope the possible poses." Interview by Thierry Jousse, *Cahiers du cinéma*, supplement *Godard, 30 ans depuis* 437 (November 1990), 56.

29 Godard, "L'important c'est les producteurs," 13.

30 Jonathan Rosenbaum and Jean-Luc Godard, "Trailer for Godard's *Histoire(s) du cinéma*," in Jean-Luc Godard, *Histoire(s) du cinéma (Complete Soundtrack)*, ed. Manfred Eicher, trans. John Howe, ECM New Series (Munich: ECM Records, 1999), vol. 4, 168. Because video editing "is usually done while sitting in front of two monitors," explains Harun Farocki in reference to *Numéro deux*, the editor "becomes accustomed to thinking of two images at the same time." With the concept of "soft montage," Farocki developed an approach that was directly related to this idea. Kaja Silverman and Harun Farocki, *Speaking about Godard* (New York: NYU Press, 1998), 142.

31 Godard, "L'art à partir de la vie," 24.

32 Jean-Luc Godard, *Future(s) of Film: Three Interviews 2000/01*, trans. John O'Toole (Bern: Gachnang & Springer, 2002), 24f.

33 Jean-Luc Godard, "Les aventures de Kodak et de Polaroïd," interview by Hervé Delilia and Roger Dosse, *Politique Hebdo* 189 (September 18–24, 1975), 28.

34 Godard, "Penser la maison en termes d'usine," 380f.

35 This programmatic idea also explains why Godard and Miéville chose the name "Sonimage" for their joint video work.

36 Godard, "L'art à partir de la vie," 24.

37 Godard and Rosenbaum, "Trailer," 168.

38 Godard and Ishaghpour, *Cinema*, 33.

39 Godard, *Future(s) of Film*, 26.

40 Godard, "L'important c'est les producteurs," 13.

41 Godard, *Introduction*, 138.

42 This effect had previously been employed by Peter Campus in *Three Transitions* (1973, 4:53 min, video, color).

43 Godard, "Godard fait le point," 541.

44 Godard, "Le dernier rêve d'un producteur," *Cahiers du cinéma* 300 (May 1979), 73. English translation quoted from Fairfax, *Birth*, 60.

45 Godard, *Histoire(s) du cinéma*, vol. 1, 73.

46 Godard, *Introduction*, 22.

The Withering Away of the State of the Art (1974)

Hollis Frampton

[. . .] First of all, then, what delights and miseries do film and video share? Both the film frame and the complementary paired fields of video are, of course, metaphorical descendants of the Newtonian infinitesimal, so that both are doomed, as from a kind of Original Sin, to the irony of mapping relativistic perceptions upon an atavistic fiction of classical mechanics long since repudiated, along with the simian paradoxes of Zeno that prefigure the calculus, by the sciences. Still more comically, film and video share similar paleontologies: that of film yields racehorses, and that of video, wrestlers. But within the compressed moment that constitutes their mutual Historical Period, we may say that film and video art have in common:

1. A need.

It belongs to the artists who make the art, this need, and it is a need to make images, apparently moving, within what both film and video understand to be a highly plastic temporality. Notably absent is the need, formerly its normal congener, to mark surfaces. Painters still have that need, along with some others, and we may suppose that is why they are painters.

2. A thermodynamic level.

The procedures of most of the arts amount to heat engines; film and video first entrain energy higher up in the entropic scale. Photons impress upon the random delirium of silver halide crystals in the film emulsion an illusion of order; electrons warp the ordered video raster, determinate as a crystal lattice, into an illusion of delirium.

3. An ecstatic and wearisome trouble.

I refer to the synesthetic problem of the place and use of sound in the visual arts. We may take the course of grand opera as a summary of the catastrophes awaiting fools and angels alike in this aesthetic quagmire. It is a commonplace that lip sync sound sank film art for decades. A few film artists, at least in their doppelgänger roles as theoreticians, penetrated some way into the nature of the problem, both before and after Al Jolson uttered those famous *last* words: "You ain't heard nothin' yet!" But I freely admit that film has not, on the whole, advanced very far in that montage for two senses that seems to imply a dialectical mutuality between the dual inhabitants of the human cranium . . . granting, certainly, that we have abandoned the bourgeois assumption that purported surface verisimilitude is Art's Truest Note.

Ten years ago, filmmakers in New York used to say that you could tell a California film with your eyes shut, because there was invariably a sound track, and that sound track invariably consisted of sitar music. Times have changed, but the problem has not, and most video artists seem still to be living in that moment. The unexamined assumption, that there *must* be sound, now yields, typically, the exotic whines and warbles of an audio synthesizer. I am not myself innocent in this respect, so it is scarcely to be assumed that I abjure audio synthesizers, which bear to the symphony orchestra somewhat the sort of relation that a turret lathe bears to a stone axe. Quite simply, though, most of the video sound I have heard bears, at best, a decorative or indexical relation to its coeval image, and at worst (and more often) obscures it.

At least one major filmmaker has, for twenty years, directed against the use of any sound a reasonable rhetoric that has increased in stridency as the muteness of his work has grown more eloquent; the same man has, of course, sinned often against his own doctrine, as we all must if we are to honor the good animal within us. But again, and yet again, this chimerical problem of sound rises up to strike us down in our tracks, film and video artist alike, and we cannot forever solve it by annihilating it. Sooner or later, we must embrace the monster, and dance with it.

4. Finally, film and video share, it now seems, an ambition I have heard stated in various idioms, with varying degrees of urgency. It first appears whole, to my knowledge, in a text of Eisenstein dating to 1932, at a time when a similarly utopian project, involving the dissolution of the boundaries between subject and object, *Finnegans Wake*, was in progress. That ambition is nothing less than the mimesis, incarnation, bodying forth of the movement of human consciousness itself.

Now that we have seen how film and video art are similar, how are they like things other than each other?

I think it is clear that the most obvious antecedents of cinematic enterprise, at least in its beginnings, are to be found in painting, an art which, justly losing faith in itself as a technology of illusion, had gradually relinquished its hold on a three-dimensional space that cinema seized once more, for itself, on its first try. The Lumière brothers' passenger train, sailing into the sensorium straight out of the vanishing point of perspective, punctures the frontal picture-plane against which painting had gradually flattened itself during nearly a century. Early accounts of the situation tell us that the image had power to move the audience—clean out of the theater—and "instruction" be damned. The video image assumes the frontality that painting has since had continual difficulty in maintaining.

On the other hand, it would seem that video, like music, is not only articulated and expended in time (as film is), but indeed that its whole substance may be referred to in terms of temporality, rhythm, frequency. The video raster itself would seem a kind of metric stencil, *ostinato*, heartbeat. As such, like music, it is susceptible of being quantified, and thus expressed completely in a linear notation. In fact, it is quite commonly so expressed. I do not refer to anything like a musical "score," of course. The notation of video is called tape, and it is perfectly adequate. The film strip of cinema is not a notation, but a physical object which we are encouraged to misinterpret under special circumstances. Video has, and needs, no such artifact.

Finally: how do film and video art differ, in fundamental ways that define the qualities of both?

We might examine first the frame, that is, the dimensionless boundary, that separates both sorts of image from the Everything Else in which that image is a hole.

The film frame is a rectangle, rather anonymous in its proportions, that has been fiddled with recently in the interest of publicizing, so far as I can see, nothing much more interesting than the notion of an unbroken and boundless horizon. The wide screen glorifies, it would seem, frontiers long gone: the landscapes of the American prairies and the Soviet steppes; it is accommodating to the human body only when that body is lying in state. Eisenstein once proposed that the frame be condensed into a "dynamic" square, which is as close to a circle as a rectangle can get, but his arguments failed to prosper.

In any event, cinema inherits its rectangle from Renaissance easel paintings, which tend to behave like the windows in post-and-lintel architecture. The video frame is not a rectangle. It is a degenerate amoeboid shape passing for a rectangle to accommodate the cheap programming of late night movies. The first video image I ever saw, on a little cathode ray tube at the top of a four-foot mastaba, was circular. At least I think I believe that's what I remember I saw.

Things find their true shapes most readily as they look at themselves. Film, looking at itself, as the total machine that is cinema, rephotographs and reprojects its own image, simply reiterates to unmodified infinity its radiant rectangle, asserting with perfect redundancy its edge, or perimeter, which has become for us inhabitants of film culture an icon of the boundary between the known and the unknown, the seen and the unseen, what is present and possible to consciousness and what is absolutely elsewhere and . . . unimaginable.

But let video contemplate itself, and it produces, under endless guises, not identical avatars of its two-dimensional "container," but rather exquisitely *specific* variations upon its own most typical content. I mean the mandalas of feedback, in whose graphically diagrammed illusion of alternating thrust and withdrawal, most often spiraling ambiguously like a pun of Duchamp, video confirms, finally, a generic eroticism. That eroticism belongs to the photographic cinema as well, through the virtually tactile and kinesthetic illusion of surface and space afforded by an image whose structure seems as fine as that of "nature"; video, encoding the universe on 525 lines precisely, like George Washington's face reduced to a dot-and-dash semaphore on the dollar bill, resorts to other tactics.

And as the feedback mandala confirms the covert circularity, the *centripetal* nature, of the video image, it offers also an obscure suggestion. If the spiral implies a copulative interaction between the image and the seeing mind, it also may become, when love is gone (through that systematic withdrawal of nourishment for the affections that is "television"), a navel—the mortal scar of eroticism past—and thus an *omphalos*, a center, a sucking and spitting vortex into which the whole household is drawn, and within which it is consumed.

If I seem to be verging on superstition, please recall that the images we make are part of our minds; they are living organisms, that carry on our mental lives for us, darkly, whether we pay them any mind or not.

Nonetheless, if video and film ultimately unite in an erotic impulse, a thrust away from *thanatos* and toward life, they diverge in many particulars. For instance:

1. We filmmakers have heard that hysterical video artists say: "We will bury you." In one instance—and it is a very important one—I agree entirely. That instance is the mode we call animation. I have always felt animation, in its assertion of objecthood over illusion, to be an art separate from film, using the photographic cinema as a tool, as cinema uses the means of still photography (24 times every second) as a tool. Film and video typically extend their making processes within a temporality that bears some discoverable likeness to real time; and that simply is not true of the animated film.

But I suspect that video will soon afford, if it does not already, the means of fulfilling, in something "like" real time, every serious ambition animation retains. And that, of course, would mean a wonderful saving of time, out of the only life we may reasonably expect to enjoy.

2. For the working artist, film is object as well as illusion. The ribbon of acetate is material, in a way that is particularly susceptible of manipulations akin to those of sculpture. It may be cut and welded, and painted upon, and subjected to every kind of addition and attrition that doesn't too seriously impair its mechanical qualities. Upon that single fact of film's materiality, an edifice has been erected, that of montage, from which all film art measures its aesthetic distances.

In short, film builds upon the straight cut, and the direct collision of images, of "shots," extending a perceptual domain whose most noticeable trait we might call *successiveness*. (In this respect, film resembles history.) But video does not seem to take kindly to the cut. Rather, those inconclusions of video art during which I have come closest to moments of real discovery and *peripeteia* seem most often to exhibit a tropism toward a kind (or many kinds) of metamorphic *simultaneity*. (In this respect, video resembles Ovidian myth.)

So that it strikes me that video art, which must find its own Muse or else struggle under the tyranny of film, as film did for so long under the tyrannies of drama and prose fiction, might best build its strategies of articulation upon an elasticized notion of what I might call—for serious lack of a better term—the lap dissolve.

Here the two arts of film and video separate most distinctly from one another. Film art, supremely at home in deep spaces both visual and aural, has need of intricate invention to depart from the "frontal plane" of temporality—an aspect purporting to be neither imperfective nor perfective, but Absolute. Conversely, video, immanently graphic, polemically anti-illusionist, comes to spatiotemporal equilibrium through a dissolution, a fluidification, of all the segments of that temporal unity we call Eternity, into an uncooked version of Once Upon A Time.

Hence the mythification of the seven o'clock news, and the grand suggestion that the denizens of the talk shows are about to be transformed into persons: one feels, almost, Daphne's thighs encased in laurel bark. Hence also . . . distantly . . . television's deadly charm. Is it a cobra, or is it a mongoose?

3. Sigmund Freud, in *Civilization and Its Discontents*, suggests that civilization depends upon the delay of gratification. I might caricature this to mean that, by denying myself one hundred million lollypops, I'll end up with a steam yacht . . . and go on to envision a perfect civilization entirely devoid of gratification. But every filmmaker must perforce believe in part of this cartoon, since filmmaking involves long delays, during which the work more than once disappears into the dark night of the mind and the laboratory. I remember, on the other hand, the first time I ever used video. I made a piece, a half-hour long, in one continuous take. Then I rewound the notation, and saw my work right away. That was three years ago, and to tell the truth some part of my puritanical filmmaker's nature remains appalled to this day. The gratification was so intense and immediate that I felt confused. I thought I might be turning into a barbarian . . . or maybe even a musician.

4. The photographic cinema must be "driven," as synthesizer folk say, from the outside. But video can generate its own forms, internally, like DNA. It is the difference

between lost-wax casting and making a baby. The most important consequence of this is that video (again, like music) is susceptible of two approaches: the deliberative and the improvisational. Certain video artists have rationalized the synthesis of their images into closed fields of elements and operations, *raga* and *tala*. It is mildly paradoxical that this work, which seems to me, with respect to the density of its making activity, to correspond to the work of Méliès in film, need produce no record whatsoever, and may suffer itself to remain ephemeral, while the Lumières of video, the improvisational purists of the Portapak, are bound absolutely to the making of tape notations. (I do not doubt that the exterior *experience* of work of either sort may be fully replete.)

5. There is something to be said about video color. One might speak of its disembodied character, its "spirituality," were one inclined. That the spirituality in question is as vulgar as that of the painting from which (I conjecture) it took its bearings, is not surprising. The decade of the sixties saw—or rather, mostly did not see—the early development of the video synthesizer contemporaneously with the hardening of a posture, within painting, that aspired to founding a chasm between color and substance. The photographic cinema, viewing its unstable dye-stuffs as modulators of primal Light, mostly stayed at home and tended to its temporal knitting during a crucial period in chromatic thought.

For those who take note of such things, it will eventually become clear that video won out: were it not for the confusing matter of scale (video, after all, is "furniture," and has the protruding status of an object within living space; whereas public painting has gradually assimilated itself to the "heroic" scale of public cinema) video images should rightly have replaced a good deal of painting.

6. If the motion we attribute to the film image is an illusion, nevertheless the serial still frames of cinema are discretely apprehensible entities that may be held in the hand and examined at our leisure. When these frames are projected, they are uniformly interleaved with equal intervals of total darkness, which afford us intermittent moments to think about what we have just seen.

Conversely, the video field is continuous, incessantly growing and decaying before our eyes. Strictly speaking, there is no instant of time during which the video image may properly be said to "exist." Rather, a little like Bishop Berkeley's imaginary tree—falling forever in a real forest—each video frame represents a brief summation within the eye of the beholder. [. . .]

From Hollis Frampton, "The Withering Away of the State of the Art," in *The New Television: A Public/Private Art*, ed. Douglas Davis and Allison Simmons (Cambridge, MA: MIT Press, 1977), 24–37. The text was written for, and delivered at, the conference "Open Circuits: The Future of Television," held January 23–25, 1974, at the Museum of Modern Art in New York.

Video and Film (1987)

Gábor Bódy

I am a film director, though in ten years I may be called a video director. Let's just say that I am a cinematographer—an image-writer who tries to pursue image-writing as a profession. I could say that, for me, video promises to fulfill all those possibilities that we have considered applicable to film for decades: cinematography or filmmaking is actually a language capable of transmitting thoughts in all kinds of ways.

It is worth examining why it was precisely video that fulfilled these expectations. The notion of film as language is as old as filmmaking itself, or at least dates to the earliest decades of film. Since the 1960s, generations of film directors have grown up with the motto that "the camera is our fountain pen" or "the camera is our pencil." In fact though, film production continues to be a very expensive enterprise, a costly, industrial undertaking whose costs somehow must be recuperated; it must at least make efforts in this direction. As a result, despite all experimentation with the genre, it remains bound to the inflexible forms of production that typify the feature-length movie. This fact contains the assumption that masses of people—tens or hundreds of thousands, perhaps even millions—will see what you have made, at a given time and a predetermined place. As long as film (or cinematography) remains in the movie house, it will never truly break free of this framework, nor is there any need for it to do so. Even so, the '60s and '70s have produced generations who are coming to realize that film is capable of much more, expressing a greatly more flexible range of subjects. The movies have given rise to a process that is anti-movie, but whose existence depends on the genre in which it is compelled to remain. I might even call this process the progressive crisis of a paradoxical development cycle. I have no doubt that video will bring the ultimate breakthrough liberating film from these constraints. It is video that creates the conditions for us to use this language freely in the creative sphere of production and of distribution. This might even mean using it in an extremely restricted sphere, for a tiny audience or perhaps even for a family, or for the videographer alone.

Video's other advantage, as a form of distribution, is that it liberates the product from limitations of time and space. It makes our work accessible to the individual, enabling viewing wherever there is a player and a videocassette. So the technology is more or less available to make cinematography truly cinemato*graphy*, or written speech, a language that expresses itself through movement and image. The question is, through what genres and along what paths it can develop.

I would like to briefly summarize the differences between video and film. The treatment of time is a significant one. Video makes it easy to create shifts in time (immediately, on higher-end equipment) such as slow motion.

It is very significant that, being an electronic instrument, video can be directly connected to other electronic systems. Picture and sound can be coordinated with electronic sound systems and synthesizers, all managed together by computer. This is the realization of an idea that was conceived by the film avant-gardists in the days of the Bauhaus, an extension of the light-organ from the realm of pure abstraction to the most broadly distributed formats. Naturally, this is not achievable within the realm of simple everyday video; it requires complex studio systems. There, editing is fed into the computer, which grants the artist an ornamental freedom of image-organization. One interesting difference between video and film is their entirely divergent treatment of space. This is probably partly because of the size of the image, and partly owing to its manner of transmission or projection. The video image is always in one plane and thus is more picture-like, while film generally has a more spatial effect. There are aspects particular to each, despite the fact that I regard video as the completion (real or possible) of cinematographic culture as a whole.

What are the differences? One fundamental distinction arises from what we might call the "mirror-effect." Video works like an electronic mirror: you see the image instantly. This has far-reaching perspectival and psychological consequences for those working in the medium. It is completely different from working on a strip of film that you get back from the lab weeks later. There, you are working blind and the results are never one hundred percent certain. But video is instant. This mirror effect is the basis for a number of technical tricks. The word "trick" strikes people as suspicious; they think of pulling a rabbit out of a hat. In fact these are not tricks, but imaging mechanisms, like multiplying images via the echo effect.

So, when watching a film, you imagine yourself in a space in which the characters and objects move, while the video image is much more like an oleograph. Clearly the size of the image has something to do with this, but there is also something in the way it is replayed. Video is personal: it is you-are-there. It avoids the story-element of the movie, which we experience within that space. With a video image, we always experience personally and immediately what is on-screen, and at the same time everything is much more symbolic. Part of the reason may be that video images come to the viewer from behind a surface and meet him frontally from beyond the screen, the image plane, while the film image is projected from behind and above the viewers' heads. This is an interesting paradox that is active even in art videos. [. . .]

I would like to add two thoughts. First, it is truly astonishing to consider television and how much visual material people take in on a daily basis without their lives being changed by it. It is astonishing that we watch various news stories every day and then continue our lives exactly the same way. Yet it remains likely that people do not become immoral, or pathological; what changes is partly their strategy of self-protection and partly their manner of understanding. McLuhan is still somehow correct. Television news is a closed system, an abstract, absolute mass of image information, music, and commentators, all of which we process in a simultaneous, intuitive fashion. Our relationship to it is like being on the street, where we do not take on the emotional state of a passerby, though we may see it in his face. So it is undoubtedly simultaneity that gives possibilities of expression to those working in video.

To return to my starting point, there are great differences between film and video. I see the significance of video in the help it gives to cinematographic, language-like thought, continuing the changes introduced by film, alongside which it has taken its place.

I would summarize by saying that these changes reinforce a consciousness of signifiers that, given the right distribution, will find its way to its public. It predestines us to look at things through a tapestry of signifiers. It is ultimately possible that this semiotic consciousness is what video can accomplish better than film, which must necessarily remain entertaining and narrative-based, accomplishing any intellectual work only in the background.

From Gábor Bódy, "Video and Film," in *State of Images: The Media Pioneers Zbigniew Rybczyński and Gábor Bódy*, ed. Siegfried Zielinski and Peter Weibel (Nuremberg: Verlag für Moderne Kunst, 2011), 80–4. Hungarian Original in *Videó alfa* (Budapest: Selyemgombolyító, 1987).

The text is reprinted here in full, except for a lengthy, unsourced quote from Marshall McLuhan on his theory of the brain hemispheres, according to which the left hemisphere of linearity and logic is now overtaken by the intuitive right hemisphere, as we live in an electronic age characterized by simultaneity—not least due to video technology. While Bódy introduces the theory as "part bluff, yet genuinely exciting," it does not pertain to his own thoughts.

On Video (1988)

Roy Armes

The argument of this text is that the understanding of video demands that it be seen within the whole spectrum of nineteenth- and twentieth-century audio, visual, and audiovisual media, including radio and photography, the gramophone, and the tape recorder. Video's very versatility and flexibility as a medium repulse any simple attempt to grasp its "essence" or "specificity," and continual technological development makes it increasingly difficult to pin down a fixed identity: video in the 1980s is a very different proposition from video in the 1960s, when the first portable black-and-white reel-to-reel systems were introduced.

Video is at one level merely a neutral recording device, with little more evident scope for creativity than a xerox copying machine. It can record and reproduce perfectly the systems developed within the film industry and the broadcasting institutions to depict reality and to create meaningful combinations of sounds and images. In its most prevalent form as a commodity—the video tapes universally available for hire or purchase—has clear similarities to the gramophone record and cassette and, as music videos have become more popular, closer links have been established with the record industry. At the same time, video's method of electromagnetic recording and its spread of often seemingly contradictory social applications echo those of sound tape. Moreover, as we shall see, most of the key issues relating to video are already anticipated in the nineteenth-century developments of still photography. Seen in a void video is a puzzling phenomenon, but viewed in relation to these other diverse media video's full range and potential become apparent.

One of the reasons for writing this book is to contest the tendency to see video as no more than a latter-day descendant of film and television. I myself came to the study of video after twenty years or more spent on critical and historical consideration of cinema. My initial difficulties in coming to terms with the new medium stemmed largely, I now believe, from attempting to define it in ways more appropriate to film—a view I held in common with many of my colleagues in the 1970s. There is now a very large body of valuable writing on many aspects of cinema, its history and economics, its technology and systems for creating meaning. The 1970s saw a resurgence of theoretical consideration of cinema—stemming particularly from the magazine *Screen*—and this work has shaped the perceptions of a whole new generation of students of film. But at least three aspects of this theoretical work make its direct application to video hazardous.

Firstly, the social definition of cinema as a new form of theatrical entertainment is very different from that of the other new media. The particular role of the feature film led 1970s theorists to stress the storytelling function of cinema, to ignore the diversity of filmic approaches, and to see film and narrative as inseparable. As early as the mid-1960s Christian Metz was describing the fictional feature film as "the king's highway of filmic expression," while all the nonnarrative genres—such as the documentary and the technical or educational film—were to be regarded as "marginal provinces, border regions, so to speak."[1] While I for one would not wish to contest the centrality of the fictional feature film in any consideration of cinema as an institution, seeing film *exclusively* in terms of feature films has had certain regrettable consequences, especially a refusal to give any theoretical consideration to documentary. Even greater distortions have arisen when the attempt has been made to apply categories derived from this narrative-based theorization of film either to the broadcast institution of television (where fiction, documentary, news, and entertainment have equal status) or to the recording medium of video (for which no one, to my knowledge, has ever proclaimed the centrality of narrative).

A second difficulty in applying to video the insights of film theory lies in the particular literary flavor of this theoretical work. It is a body of knowledge remarkable for its self-sufficiency. Over the years it has proved itself indifferent to contributions which might be derived from production activity, sociological study, film history, and the kind of formal analysis undertaken as a matter of routine in the study of art or music. In particular it refuses to see films as social texts, fully understandable only in relation to wider economic, social, and cultural contexts. As Dudley Andrew notes, it derives its impact almost exclusively from the application to film of metaphors drawn from other disciplines.[2]

It is the nature of these metaphors which causes the third problem in relation to video. All the successive metaphors which have dominated conceptualizations of film theory—the framed image, the window, the mirror—are purely visual.[3] They point to a tendency in virtually all 1970s film theory not merely to privilege the visual over the aural, but to concentrate exclusive attention on it—to deal only with the camera when considering the history of technology,[4] or to offer schemes of analysis of the image track while ignoring totally the parallel sound track.[5]

Television study, on the other hand, lacks virtually any coherent body of theoretical insights.[6] As long ago as 1970, in the introduction to his study of *The Effects of Television*, James Halloran gave his characterization of the three principal contending positions in the debate about television: those of the academic elitist—who "may not even possess a set," the practical media man—who "is usually ready to defend or idealize the operation of the medium," and the social scientist—"a curious if cautious creature who is not known for his involvement or commitment."[7] Succeeding years have seen little real dialogue between representatives of these positions, and there is little explicit interconnection between the work which has been undertaken on television institutions and studies dealing with the television audience or with specific television genres. With the sole exception of John Ellis's book, *Visible Fictions* (1982), we lack any study of television's operation which invites meaningful comparisons with cinema, and there is hardly as much as an article which allows us to begin the task of relating the dominant audio-visual systems of film and television to video.

Roy Armes, "Introduction: The Need for a New Perspective," in *On Video* (New York: Routledge, 1988), 1–4.

Notes

1 Christian Metz, *Film Language*, trans. Michael Taylor (New York: Oxford University Press, 1974), 94.
2 Dudley Andrew, *Concepts in Film Theory* (New York: Oxford University Press, 1984), 9.
3 Ibid., 12.
4 Jean-Louis Comolli, "Technique and Ideology: Camera Perspective, Depth of Field (Part I)," *Film Reader* 2 (1977), 128–40, and "Technique and Ideology: Camera Perspective, Depth of Field (Parts III and IV)," in *Narrative, Apparatus, Ideology*, ed. Philip Rosen (New York: Columbia University Press, 1986), 421–43.
5 Metz, *Film Language*, 108–76.
6 John Caughie, "Television Criticism: 'A Discourse in Search of an Object,'" *Screen* 25, 4–5 (1984), 109–20.
7 James Halloran, ed., *The Effects of Television* (London: Panther, 1970), 10–11.

Video: The Access Medium (1996)

Tetsuo Kogawa

Film and Video

Video has not yet achieved independence from the cinema. Aware of its indebtedness, video has remained eager to receive its inheritance. But it is necessary to understand video's difference, to theorize the conditions of its specificity. Now that today's video technology achieves as high a definition as film, the video theater will gradually take over the movie theater. This does not, however, mean that the cinema will cease to exist. Video can be a new type of movie. The material differences of video and film are not the most crucial points for differentiation. After all, cinema itself has undergone many technological changes. The arc lamp is no longer the source of light; film is no longer simply celluloid; recent films rely more and more on computer-generated images. At the same time, nothing has changed for the audience of the video theater. The audience faces a screen in a dark space, watching it until the end of the show. No one "fast-forwards" or "rewinds" the sequences, nor do they "pause" motion. This renunciation of access to the control of the image on the part of the audience guarantees video's status as identical to the cinema. As long as this renunciation remains in place, the cinema is what it has been.

However, this renunciation of access is not inherent but historical. In transition, every medium is used and understood through the extended (time-tested) conventional standards, but sometimes new possibilities are revealed. The early stage of video art revealed its radical possibilities most explicitly: it was inseparably accompanied by bodily performance actions. In 1963 when Nam June Paik showed his *Exposition of Music—Electronic Television*, the earliest video artwork at Galerie Parnass in Wuppertal, he created artistic video images through improvisation, manipulating, as he did, the electronic conditions of used television sets. It was a one-time event that could not be recycled in the future.

Starting in the late sixties, public broadcasting stations in the United States such as WGBH (Boston), KQED (San Francisco), and WNET (New York) began programming artists' video. These circumstances should have encouraged the interactive and performative aspects of video.[1] The problem is that video art has not always developed its full potentialities. Ironically, the retreat from video's radical possibilities began with the advance of electronic technology. The recorded package took the shape of the videocassette, powerfully boosting video art into a new self-understanding.

This was the inception of video art as a "work of art," a commodity to be bought and sold with the "live" process of creation separated from the video itself. Video has increasingly become an object of representation to be enjoyed without direct reference to the "nascent" process. The industrial pursuit of ever-higher image definition—as well as ever-greater compactness of the package—steadily compounds this separation. Despite these circumstances, performance actions cannot be dispensed with entirely:

viewers handle the TV set when they change the channel or volume; they operate the VCR by fast-forwarding, pausing, and even recording. Furthermore, they watch not only the screen but also the horizon surrounding it. The interactive aspect of performance actions cannot be ignored in an analysis of video. Indeed, video's performative dimension constitutes its defining difference from cinema.

Video holds the technological potential to realize direct sensory systems beyond the flat screen (e.g., the hologram). However, when video images are packaged, a "screen" is structurally introduced. The packaged video screens out the very chain of events that initiates the entire process of showing and watching. Given its hermetic nature, the packaged video offers a mere window onto performative events, one that is technologically reified as monitor and projector. Thus, video becomes cinema.

Semiotics and Video Art

Film theory has been applied to video art, but this is possible only as long as the aspect of performance in video is ignored. In fact, the semiotics of Christian Metz and others was fairly successful in articulating film and video images. However, it had to enter a cul-de-sac.[2] To the extent that semiotics considers video a capsule of image-signs, it must restrict its work to the signification system. To deal with the "outside" or to look beyond the image-sign system is illegitimate. Consequently, semiotics was unable to carry out any social critique, such as that of Siegfried Kracauer's *From Caligari to Hitler*, which succeeds in providing both formal analysis and social criticism of the filmic images of Germany's Weimar cinema.[3]

Semiotics had to tacitly assume that when it gave up the "outside," it would be attended to by sociology or anthropology or psychology. The "slick" analysis by semiotics and the "vulgar" approaches of the human sciences (which deal with images as a social, cultural, or mental index) are complementary. It is not accidental that in spite of Ferdinand de Saussure's proposition that semiotics is "a science that studies the life of signs within society" while "linguistics is only a part of the general science of semiology," his followers never succeeded in overcoming the "either/or" of linguistics/sociology as separate disciplines with distinct fields of analysis.[4] The difficulty of Saussurian semiotics has something to do with the fact that its basic model of language comes from the printed word, which is considered a capsule of "living" language. To the extent that the world is closed off, linguists and then semioticians must limit their working field to the bounds of the signifier and must maintain an indeterminate attitude toward the signified (with the referent existing entirely outside the domain of semiotic interest). In fact, Saussurian semiotics assumes that "the bond between the signifier and signified is arbitrary."[5] Consequently, this idealist theory comes into its own through analyzing abstract rather than socially-oriented images.[6]

This may explain why semiotics and video art have found themselves in close association. Video art shies away from messages. The more "artistic" it tends to be, the less message-oriented it becomes. This implies that conventional communication theory has inflated the centrality of the message; it considers the media as nothing more than a vehicle for messages. However, the message is not a mere bullet shot from the media machine. As Felix Guattari wrote, the nature of media is "transversal." So, radical media must belong to the "schizo-analyse" of the schizophrenic who "is floundering in a world in which relationships of signs, or productions of signification, far outstrip our individual madnesses and neuroses."[7] To the degree that semiotics cannot operate at this transversal level, it screens out the image's performative side.

However, every image—packaged or not—transcends itself and forms various horizons of the "signified," "content," the "social," the "transcendental," and so on. It is quite natural that when Gilles Deleuze wrote *Cinema 1* he had to deconstruct the sign itself, starting not from Saussure but from Charles S. Peirce who established a systematic classification of images and signs without using the linguistic model.[8] [. . .]

From Tetsuo Kogawa, "Video: The Access Medium," in *Resolutions: Contemporary Video Practices*, ed. Michael Renov and Erika Suderberg (Minneapolis: University of Minnesota Press, 1996), 51–60.

Notes

1 On the historical relationship between video art and broadcasting, see: Kathy Rae Huffman, "Video Art: What's TV Got to Do with It?" in *Illuminating Video*, ed. Doug Hall and Sally Jo Fiffer (Seattle: Bay Press, 1990), 81–90.

2 In order to evade this, Christian Metz reinforces his semiotics by phenomenology, writing, on one occasion, that every semiotics is an extension of phenomenology. See Christian Metz, "Semiotics and Phenomenology," in *Esse Semiotikku* (Essais sémiotiques), trans. Keiko Higuchi (Tokyo: Keiso-shobo, 1977), 184–7.

3 Siegfried Kracauer, *From Caligari to Hitler: A Psychological History of the German Film* (Princeton, NJ: Princeton University Press, 1947).

4 Ferdinand de Saussure, *Course in General Linguistics*, trans. Wade Baskin (New York: McGraw-Hill, 1959), 16.

5 Ibid., 67.

6 Mikhail Bakhtin already revealed the limitations of semiotics within the literary field. "Semiotics deals primarily with the transmission of ready-made communication using a ready-made code. But in live speech, strictly speaking, communication is first created in the process of transmission, and there is, in essence, no code." See Mikhail Bakhtin, "From Notes Made in 1970–71," in idem, *Speech Genres and Other Late Essays*, ed. Caryl Emerson and Michael Holquist, trans. Vern W. McGee (Austin: University of Texas Press, 1986), 147.

7 Félix Guattari, *Molecular Revolution: Psychiatry and Politics*, trans. Rosemary Sheed (New York: Penguin, 1984), 172.

8 Gilles Deleuze, *Cinema 1: The Movement-Image*, trans. Hugh Tomlinson and Barbara Habberjam (Minneapolis: University of Minnesota, 1986), 69.

Interface (1995)

Harun Farocki

I can hardly write a word these days if there isn't an image on the screen at the same time. Actually: on both screens. This is a work station, an editing station, for the reworking of images and sounds. The control desk, the player, the recorder. The thing is . . . that there are two images seen at the same time—one image in relation to the other. [. . .]

When working with film instead of video, you have to make an actual cut in the image or sound strip. As opposed to video editing, where you simply copy from one tape to the next, making an imaginary cut and not a real one. While working at the film editing table, I keep the tip of my finger on the running image or sound reel to feel the cut or the glue before I see it or hear it. This is a gesture indicating "fine perception" or "sensitivity." The hand had almost no contact with the object, but perceived it nonetheless. When working with video, I don't touch the tape, I only push buttons. Another activity for the fingertips.

Here we have the gesture of counting money, which is probably done like this because we need the subtlety on the fingertips to count money with the necessary precision. With a bill it becomes particularly clear how little essence and appearance coincide.

This editing station has two screens, to see whether two images fit well together which are to appear in sequence in a film. Does this image go with that one? Does this image offer itself to that one? Does this image close itself off from that one? We can grasp this duality by suggesting that one image comments on the other. To date only words, or sometimes music, comment on images. Here images comment on images. [. . .] (Figure 4.5).

Transcript of English subtitles from *Schnittstelle*, 1995, video, color, 23 min., directed, written, and narrated by Harun Farocki, produced by Musée Moderne d'art de Villeneuve d'Ascq and Harun Farocki Filmproduktion, Berlin.

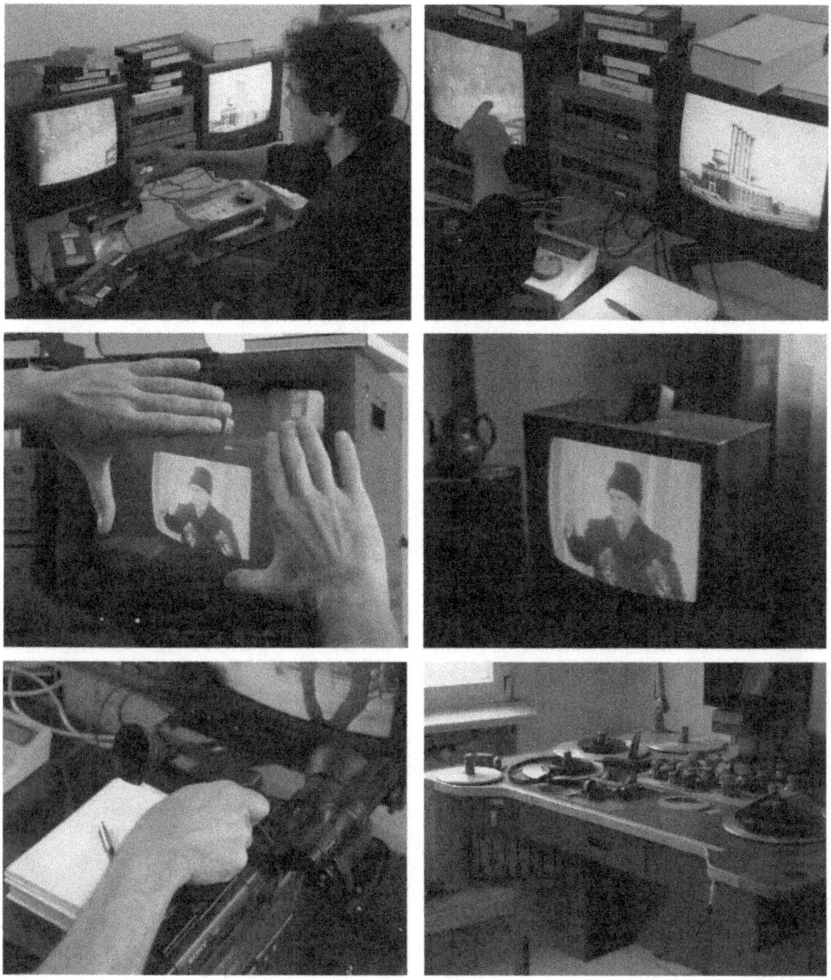

Figure 4.5 Harun Farocki, *Interface / Schnittstelle*, 1995, video, color, 23 min.

Figure 4.5 *Continued*

Penultimate Pictures (2018)

Marc Ries

[. . .] In Siegfried Kracauer's last work, *History: The Last Things Before the Last*, the author draws significant parallels between historiography and the technique of photographing, or filming. In the fourth chapter of the book, Kracauer remarks on the historian's duty to "extinguish his self," to practice self-discipline when confronting the overwhelming fund of material; to perform an "act of self-emptying,"[1] since it is only by being "a stranger to the world evoked by the sources" that "the historian can commune with the material of his concern" and the facts become "products of a reduced self."[2] "It is only in this state of self-effacement, or homelessness," Kracauer insists, only by waiting and letting himself drift along, and taking in, "with all his senses strained," the various messages that reach him, that the historian can gain a perception and an appreciation of the findings and the historical realities embodied in them.[3] The reward for performing this quasi-existential exorcise is an expansion of the self, which consequently facilitates the appropriation, classification, and evaluation of materials, to the point of forming "truths of the highest generality," or "historical ideas."[4] Self-effacement causes self-expansion, is the conclusion to be drawn.

I would like to pursue the analogy between cinema and history-writing further and consider the principle of self-emptying from the position of contemporary visual techniques, and in this way heuristically replace the historian with the apparatus, or audience. I am referring here to the use of integrated cameras, to interconnected picture archives and picture populations, to a new understanding of found footage. These visual techniques are sui generis "emptied"; by their technical parameters and mode of handling, they embody the waiting, the "active passivity" (Kracauer), or indifference, upon which their image-generation processes are predicated. The occasionally practiced act of opening the lens, of activating a software, lets an enormous wealth of visual data flood on to the *waiting* carrier material and become pictures, and chains of pictures. Their flowing references are then condensed into an *indifferentia specifica*; images that are meaningful on many levels but do not typify any distinctions, do not generalize, but possibly articulate a specific *medial idea* about their subject, or at least offer themselves for concrete, local self-extension by viewing via online media.[5] I will explore this below.

The following reflections will follow a film, the film *Silvered Water, Syria Self-Portrait* (France 2014) by Ossama Mohammed and Simav Bedirxan, one of a series of comparable films primarily produced in the context of the war in Syria, which seek to ally the small pictures taken with cellphone cameras with the large format of cinema and seek—and find—a resonance that makes for extraordinary viewing.

The Film

The film *Silvered Water, Syria Self-Portrait* shows a montage of video clips, arranged in phases of varying intensity, some placed on YouTube by anonymous residents of the collapsing Syrian city Homs, some secretly filmed by Bedirxan, which attest to an unusual directness. With a subtle, perhaps suggestive arrangement—the montage—of the individual fragments (which could be criticized as "tendentious"), and its musical score, coupled with self-reflective, lyrical, correspondence-like texts by Ossama Mohammed and Simav Bedirxan, it forms a kind of filmic lament. I am not interested here in the dramaturgical, aestheticizing postproduction of the material but only in the charge pressed in and through the found footage, by a destroyed city and its inhabitants. This charge prompts inquiry into the source of the singular expressive force of this new filmic form, which permits the existential movements of the amateur filmmakers, the nonproprietary, abbreviated, and provisional pictures of moving people and things in front of the camera, to be linked with the montage-film aesthetic. The question raised is whether films which are—largely—built on material filmed in this way, that is, material *automatically* inscribed with an *indifferentia specifica* both before and after recording, which does not follow any normative aesthetic and so in a sense embodies "penultimate pictures" *in statu nascendi* ("last pictures" will be considered below), have the capacity to expand on and conclude research in their own context and produce new "open wholenesses" (Deleuze). Or whether, more modestly, they can elicit "pity with the dead."[6] Below, then, I will start by considering the tools that produce these pictures.

Phenomenology of Image Creation

The cellphone-integrated camera, which may be highly sophisticated, is no longer an isolated object, an entity of its own, no fetish. It is part of a *different wholeness*, of a smartphone, for instance, a tablet, or computer—all cybernetic universal devices with partly identical, partly diverging modes of use. Camera usage, the act, occurs in passing; it is evident in a para-instrumental mode of creating images. *Para-cameras*. As the camera is just one of the device's many functions, one of the many possibilities for using a smartphone, for example, its operation is no longer designed to be specialized and individualized. Diminished, with its authority reduced, its secondariness one of several secondarinesses, photographing and filming with this camera becomes a random, casual activity; it takes place in a context that is only vaguely intentional. There is, then, no longer a photographic-filmic act as such. Rather, the photographing or filming becomes *occasional*; it does not involve any preparatory selection or aesthetic intention. It is impulsive, interjacent, tentative.[7] It becomes commonplace, incidental, contingent, trivial. We film in the same way as telephoning, writing text messages, using apps, surfing the Internet.

Conducting such *diminished* photography and filming, we participate in a peculiar way in the life around us. In the vibrations of the physical world, of people, things, temporal spaces, nonsignificant light waves, and the significant visual surfaces that they update. Maurizio Lazzarato asserts that the video image draws its movement from the vibration of matter, that it consists of this vibration. To him, the electronic image "imitates" the relationship between streams of matter and streams of consciousness in such a way that the transmitted picture can be seen to intervene in the duration of the world, i.e. the capacity to impact on the present as it occurs.[8]

Digital filming becomes a routine that does not require the distinction of specific gestures, or specific knowledge, but takes place just like that, peripherally. It is highly unnormalized, is not premised upon any submission to technology or aesthetic standards; it wants and allows—obviously and directly—the real to appear before the camera. In this way, it has given rise to a "naturalization" of photographing and filming. Recording is no longer a controlled, "techno-rational" act, guided by the eye and analytic considerations, and therefore by the "subject," but is rather a psychosomatic process arising from the movements, the attractions and repulsions affecting the body itself. It is, then, a kind of *direct video*, with images that can no longer be regarded as point-of-view shots but rather as point-of-flesh shots. The fact of filming has become a matter of the corporeal, muscular body; it is part of its movements; part of the accelerations, shocks, jolts it endures. Yet in turning away from the pressure of the situation, it is *nevertheless* filming, back-to-the-front filming, making *something* appear precisely in turning away, making *something* experience a filmic equivalent through the body's self-recording. To borrow from Gilles Deleuze, by filming things precisely where they pressurize and threaten me, I "grasp the 'virtual action' that they have on me, and simultaneously the 'possible action' that I have on them, in order to associate me with them or to avoid them, by diminishing or increasing the distance."[9] The fragments constituting this video, the videos from the contexts that *Silvered Water* accesses, are mined from the situationally dependent fragmentation of the body at times when it is *under pressure*. Hence one can no longer say, "I film what I see," but "my body films, depending on what compels it to react, to act." Filming becomes a struggle in which the body engages, and at the same time is an expression of its curiosity, as of its alerted attention. Filming becomes a kind of *counter-pressure*. Seen in this light, the "secondness" noted by Charles Sanders Peirce in the relationship between signs and objects, based on indexicality, can also be attributed to the relationship between the digital matrix and object-reality—in the pragmatic respect that the power relations impacting on the body are directly and existentially repeated in the (re)actions of the smartphone's secondary camera and its picture production. Isabelle Graw's remarks on the predominance of indexical signs in painting, which to her manifest the incorporation of the artist's lifetime in the picture,[10] could be applied to the pictures recorded by the filming observers of Homs, incorporating their lifetimes.

Seen in this light, the videos are inevitably part of the lives of their makers; their perception follows the dictates of their action. They are, so to speak, "involved pictures." They are the moving expression of situations in which the individual finds him- or herself, in which he or she is called on to act or react. The pictures are, then, documents not so much of the filmmaker's *observations* than of the filmmaker's *actions* in these situations. The videos are therefore inscribed with a certain agency. How they perceive what they witness is determined by their actions. An initial perception-image is not followed—in reaction—by an action-image.[11] First there is an image in direct relation to a non-filmic act, such as that of running away from danger. It is not until the second stage that the image is perceived, that the action becomes a "picture."[12] The millions of videos posted on YouTube—without the intermediate stage of postproduction—are the multiple expressions of subjectless perspectivity, contingent situations, unspecific actions, overwhelming events. So, Kracauer's remark also holds true for the picture fragments of *Silvered Water*: "Subjectivity at its most intensive transcends itself."[13]

They are *penultimate pictures* as they were recorded shortly before perception became an impossibility. They can only be followed by *last pictures*, either because their "author" no longer has the facilities to film or because he or she dies while recording. Rabih Mroué exhibited such last pictures at *dOCUMENTA (13)* (Kassel 2012). His *The Pixelated Revolution* shows, among other things, video fragments of men who are about to shoot—to shoot dead—someone who is filming them with their cellphone.[14]

Forward-to-the-World

The specific properties of video make it a visual form that does not initially need, or depend upon, projection. It continues to exist immediately after recording as part of the camera dispositive; the premise of its perception can be likened to the reverse of the face that records life in front of the camera. The video camera's control image, identical with what we see on the cellphone's display as the camera's work, is the same as what appears after the images' transmission to monitors. For these images are transmitted, not projected. The smartphone images are transmitted on to computer monitors or television screens, mostly via social networks. Yet they always remain these small, modest pictures within the framing of the interface.

Within this production logic, the mode of existence of these videos is only factual in a first part. Moreover, they have a quasi-ontological obligation to "go public." Transferred, uploaded on to digital video platforms, they instantaneously communicate. Participation in the life of those who produced them then becomes participation in the life of all those who perceive them in the worldwide web. These platforms are archives, living spaces for picture populations, extraordinary sources, then, in which sense and nonsense cohabit. Audiovisual traces of people who have not been asked or authorized to testify to their existence. An unapologetic ensemble of prosaic impressions of an invisible and silent reality; a nation of video objects.

The pictures are not under anyone's direct control. Rather, they are freely available via their publication in Internet forums as a resource, a kind of sui generis found footage, for any number of uses and appropriations. This peculiar quality of free, non-proprietary, always provisional, never conclusive thingness enables the pictures to be used in completely new ways. The productive, random use of the fragments—the "shorts" and "ultra-shorts," in various adaptation and appropriation processes, from the pure addition and collaging of image files to their manipulation and distortion—enables new forms of expression, new formations of meaning, new associations to be made.

Assembled to appear as an "entire" body of film, temporally expanded to correspond with the cinema format, the video fragments are transformed for projection. Mostly produced in cooperation with TV companies, they eventually arrive—via festivals—in cinemas, are projected as "feature films," made visible, perceptible. And in cinema, projection becomes a "sleight of technology" that lends the "hidden interior of physicality" an "external existence."[15] Continuing this nice thought of

Heide Schlüpmann's, in the case of cellphone pictures becoming cinema, the sleight appears not to be one that gives "dreamed life" (the imagination) an existence but one by which these now projected images allow the recorded—endured, suffered or simply experienced—life to exist *elsewhere*; they generate a communion, promising figurations of solidarity—in a sense, the added value of cinema.

The uniqueness of this practice of raising fragments to a new wholeness is that it causes perception to occur twice, so to speak. In the cinema, or retrieved to television screens and computer monitors, viewing is guided, for one, by the expectation of a "grand form" that, in the case of *Silvered Water*, with its musical score, letters, and in parts strongly narrative montage, is indeed fulfilled. On the other hand, the countless fragments still stand alone, for themselves. Their isolated, always singular existence asserts an autonomy that prompts a different understanding of "wholeness," perhaps that which Lévi-Strauss described as a "discontinuous set."[16] It is good that many unknown people have recorded the anomy of the city of Homs as they experienced it firsthand, that their clips were distributed and circulated, placed in the quasi-unregulated space known as Social Media. It is good that Ossama Mohammed made a collection of these pictures, arranged them, created neighborhoods, designed continuities. By viewing, I acquiesce in the order of visibility thus generated, but what I see is "shaped times," shaped by the individual fragments, and not or only partly their mise-en-scène.[17] [. . .]

From Marc Ries, "Vorletzte Bilder," in *Film und Gesellschaft denken mit Siegfried Kracauer*, ed. Bernhard Groß, Vrääth Öhner, and Drehli Robnik (Vienna and Berlin: Turia + Kant, 2018), 132–143. Translated for the present publication by Charlotte Kreutzmüller.

Notes

1 Siegfried Kracauer, *History: The Last Things before the Last (1969)* (Princeton: Markus Wiener Publishers, 1995), 82, 89.

2 Ibid., 84, 89.

3 Ibid., 84 ff.

4 Ibid., 102.

5 All visual media technologies invoke this "negative-productive" quality of unconditional availability. But digital technologies most closely approximate the research-context asceticism described above insofar as their operation does not involve adhering to any special technical or aesthetic criteria that would influence the intention to record. They are simply there, registering and recording, comparable to John Locke's "white paper, void of all characters, without any ideas." John Locke, An Essay Concerning Human Understanding (1689), chap. "Of Ideas in General, and their Original," sec. 2.

6 Kracauer, *History: The Last Things before the Last*, 136.

7 I regard the "occasionalist image" in the same context as post-Cartesian philosophy that rejects the notion of primary causes and unambiguous causal relations between body and mind and speaks instead of relative occasional causes, and of the mind/

image as material and the body as a tool that creates forms situationally. In my view, this relates directly to the image/body relation negotiated in this text. On the subject in general, see the entry "Occasionalism" in the *Internet Encyclopedia of Philosophy* (Jordan, undated). In a recent publication, Graham Harman has attributed occasionalist thought to Bruno Latour. See Harman, "A New Occasionalism?" in *Reset Modernity!*, ed. Bruno Latour and Peter Weibel (Cambridge, MA: MIT Press, 2016), 129–38.

8 Maurizio Lazzarato, *Videophilosophy: The Perception of Time in Post-Fordism* (New York: Columbia University Press, 2019).

9 Gilles Deleuze, *Cinema 1: The Movement Image (1986)* (Minneapolis: University of Minnesota Press, 2003), 64–5.

10 "Vorherrschaft indexikalischer Zeichen in der Malerei." Isabelle Graw, "Das Versprechen der Malerei: Anmerkungen zu Medienunspezifik, Indexikalität und Wert," in Isabelle Graw and Peter Geimer, *Über Malerei: Eine Diskussion* (Berlin: August, 2012), 27ff.

11 After Gilles Deleuze's typology in *Cinema 1: The Movement Image*.

12 In agreement with Bergson, Lazzarato generalizes this case: "Perception is a function of action; therefore the limits of perception are the limits of action. This methodology enables us to depsychologize and denaturalize the problem of perception." Lazzarato, Videophilosophy, 69.

13 Kracauer, *History: The Last Things before the Last*, 103.

14 See Fawz Kabra, "Rabih Mroué and the Pixelated Revolution," *ibraaz*, June 29, 2012, http://www.ibraaz.org/news/21.

15 In German: "List einer Technik" and "das Verborgene unserer Physis [. . .] zu äußerem Dasein." Heide Schlüpmann, *Ungeheure Einbildungskraft: Die dunkle Moralität des Kinos* (Frankfurt am Main and Basel: Stroemfeld, 2007), 221f.

16 Claude Lévi-Strauss, *The Savage Mind* (Chicago: University of Chicago Press, 1966), 259. See Kracauer on Lévi-Strauss, *History: The Last Things before the Last*, 145.

17 See Kracauer on George Kubler, ibid., 144.

5

Video | Television

Introduction by Dieter Daniels

Terminology: Video—A Medium without a Name of Its Own?

Originally, the term "video" did not describe a separate medium but a partial characteristic of television. As Michael Z. Newman writes in his terminological study of video history: "When television was new, the term 'video' distinguished it from 'radio,' a similar sounding word, out of which television grew as a commercial medium of broadcasting."[1] From the mid-1950s on, "video" was also used in the context of professional TV productions, as a discreet term for a broadcast produced on videotape.[2] Yet only when video recorders for private use started proliferating around 1969–70 did "video" become a household word.

Early academic texts subsumed video as part of television without assigning a name to it. One of the first scientific studies on video, presenting the medium's use in psychiatry in 1965, was titled "Television as a Therapeutic Tool."[3] This specialist discourse on the use of video for the self-observation of patients in psychiatric therapy anteceded the widespread distribution of consumer video and thus can serve as an indicator of the very gradual emancipation of video terminology from television in the second half of the 1960s[4] (see the introduction to Chapter 3 by Peter Sachs Collopy).

In texts on the visual arts, the electronic image was again generally identified with television up until 1969–70. In 1969, an issue of *Art in America* concerned with the "confluence of media" in modern art ran an essay largely discussing recent video art under the title "TV—The Next Medium."[5] Likewise, the first two large-scale survey exhibitions of video art in the United States carried television in their titles: *TV as a Creative Medium* (Howard Wise Gallery, New York, 1969) and *Vision and Television* (Rose Art Museum, Waltham, Massachusetts, 1970). In his introduction to the exhibition catalog for *Vision and Television*, Russell Connor mentions the term "video art" in passing, which marks its first appearance in print.[6] Another distinctive example for the transition toward a specific video terminology is Gene Youngblood's book *Expanded Cinema* from 1970. Corresponding to the multimedial expansion of cinema propagated in the book, Youngblood introduces a future form of participatory global television under the term "videosphere."[7] In the same year that Youngblood's book was published, the Victor Company of Japan launched a portable television set called Videosphere that is still considered a design icon today.[8] While its futurist shape recalls the helmet of an astronaut, it is merely a standard receiving unit without video technology. This use of "videosphere" as a catchword illustrates how metaphorically charged the medium appeared, both for avant-garde art and the language of advertising, without contributing to a clarification of terms.

A sharper terminological distinction between the specifics of video and television was developed by Paul Ryan in a text from 1969, which carried the graphically prominent subtitle "VT is not TV" (see excerpts reprinted in Chapter 1). Eight years later, the same juxtaposition announced the entry to the video section of Documenta 5 in Kassel: "VT ≠ TV" (Video Tape is not Television).[9] Even if visitors to big art exhibitions in the meantime had become accustomed to video technology, the experimental approach of video art was still conveyed in contrast to the more familiar idea of television.

Technology: Video–TV Interdependencies

Various aspects motivated the development of video technology, among them the use in surveillance as early as the 1950s (see the introduction to Chapter 11), in military training and sports, as well as the production and distribution of television programs.[10] And yet video has often been understood strictly as a successor to the television medium for different reasons, including the historical genesis of the technology growing out of the production apparatus of television broadcasters, as well as the fact that the technological basis of the video image, the scanning lines and image ratio, were taken over from television. Accordingly, in 1975 David Antin reminded his fellow video utopians of television as a "frightful parent." If we accept Antin's metaphor, video is the rebellious child—and in the following we will see how this child caused a variety of repercussions for the development of its parental home.

Firstly, beginning in the 1970s, concepts for the liberation of television from its economic and political constraints were devised at the intersection of video art and video activism, as witnessed by word coinages such as "Guerilla Television" (Michael Shamberg, 1971) and "TVTV" (Top Value Television, 1972). Nam June Paik expanded his practice toward the idea of "participation television," and he designed projects to overcome the national boundaries of television (*Global Groove*, 1970–3). In 1974, this future-oriented claim to changing the institution of television by alternatives and interventions based in video culminated with the conference "Open Circuits: An International Conference on the Future of Television" at the Museum of Modern Art, New York.[11]

On the other hand, video technology successively changed programming, production methods, and the aesthetics of the TV system. From the introduction of video technology in the mid-1950s to the digital video effects of the 1990s, a complex and varied interplay between video and television evolved, as documented in this chapter from the perspective of television theory in contributions by Dylan Mulvin, John Thornton Caldwell, and John Ellis. Accordingly, the chapter offers an interdisciplinary survey where video art and television theory interlock to show to what extent television was retroactively changed by video technology. These counterinfluences involved both TV production and viewing habits, so video changed the relation between transmitter and receiver from both sides. This will become more clear when we look at the "time shift" function of video.

"Time Shift" and "Instant Replay": Video Technology for the Production and Distribution of Television

In the first decades of television, programs were either broadcast live with electronic studio cameras or preproduced on film and then electronically scanned for transmission.[12] There were no electronic storage media for the electronic image. "TV was born with no memory," Ricardo Cedeño Montaña sums up this state of affairs.[13] In the United States and Japan, the biggest market for video recording on magnetic tape was due to its use in television stations.[14] In the United States the focus of interest lay on bridging the time zones of the North American subcontinent.[15] Programs that were produced and transmitted live in the first time zone were recorded on video and broadcast successively in the other three zones from the East to the West coast each hour at the same local time. As a "time machine" (Siegfried Zielinski) for daily, time-lagged broadcasting, the video medium remained quasi-invisible, a means to keep up the illusion of liveness without disturbance.[16] The repercussions of video on the television medium in this context mainly lay in trimmed-down production processes and the time economics of program planning.[17]

To audiences, the interplay between video and television first became visible when recordings on magnetic tape allowed for the effect of the "instant replay." In the United States, this way of repeating the action within live events was especially used in the coverage of NFL games starting in 1963.[18] In Japan, the favorite subject for such video-specific interventions into the linear television timeline was Sumo wrestling, where bouts sometimes last mere seconds.[19] Although this shift in the live paradigm of television was technologically and formally incisive, it has met with a relatively meager theoretical response. In a few lectures and an interview, Marshall McLuhan engaged in brilliant but erratic remarks on "replay mentality—a demand to have it all now to look at, again."[20] The epistemological significance of the instant replay, which reaches far beyond sports broadcasts, has first been explored by Dylan Mulvin: "As a technique of truth determination, replay helps form an epistemological architecture constituted in and through the circulation of broadcasting texts as pieces of evidence."[21]

"Live" versus "Time Shift": The Reception of Television on Home Video

In the 1980s, the "time shift" function switched sides: from an "invisible" technology for broadcasters it became, once consumer home video had entered the market, a new mode of watching television. Private recordings of programs allowed viewing them independent of schedule, which led to a profound change in television habits, a phenomenon that has been studied extensively[22] (see the diagram by Siegfried Zielinski in Figure 5.1 as well as Lucas Hilderbrand's contribution in Chapter 10). In this regard

Schematic comparison

Traditional television reception	Television reception via video recorder
(i) On the level of the program as a whole	
The program is experienced as an externally controlled flow	The program is experienced as an accumulation of set pieces
with fixed determination of the temporal sequence	whose temporal sequence can be manipulated/determined by the user
and continuous regularity.	or organized in discontinuous fashion.
Reception is a regionally, nationally, or globally collective experience	Reception occurs on a solitary or individualized basis
and has a centralizing character.	and has a decentralizing character.
Live broadcasts synchronize event time, time, and life-time.	Reception time, event time, and broadcast broadcast-time are always asynchronous.
Television and radio have an aura of immediacy.	Video recorders foreground the character of technological mediation.
The program is ephemeral.	The program is always available
(ii) On the level of the individual program sequence	
The sequence of segments is fixed (linear).	The sequence of segments can be arranged arbitrarily.
Interruption of the reception always communicative gaps.	Sequences may be stopped at any entails point without perceptual gaps in the reception.
The filmic rhythm is predetermined.	The filmic rhythm can be altered even to a stand-still.
The message of images cannot be controlled after the fact.	The message of images can be controlled at any point.
The temporal extent (viewing time) of individual segments as well as the entire sequence is fixed.	The temporal extent (viewing time) of individual segments as well as the entire sequence can be extended or stretched.

Figure 5.1 Diagram comparing traditional television reception against the additional use of a video recorder. From Siegfried Zielinski, "Audiovisuelle Zeitmaschine: Schlussthesen zur Kulturtechnik des Videorecorders," in *Zur Geschichte des Videorecorders* (Berlin: Wissenschaftsverlag, 1986), 325. English translation: "The Audiovisual Time Machine: Concluding Theses on the Cultural Technique of the Video Recorder," in *Variations on Media Thinking* (Minneapolis: University of Minnesota Press, 2019).

video also had a reciprocal effect on television, as producers feared a loss of income resulting from viewers skipping the advertisements in their recordings of broadcasts.[23] Meanwhile, the big movie studios carried on a lawsuit against private TV recordings of big-screen motion pictures for eight years.[24] Advertisements by Sony wrapped the new enlarged consumer supply in pseudo-revolutionary rhetoric with their slogan: "You should control TV, it should not control you."[25] Since this development could not be stopped, broadcasters reacted by adapting their program planning to more individualized viewing habits.

With home video, broadcast television lost control over the private screen. The sale and rent of videocassettes augmented the available choice of programs, especially for segments that were not usually seen on TV. This included pornography, horror, and splatter movies, genres that provoked a video-specific form of perception: the particular study of specific scenes that could be repeated.[26] This practice of an individualized reading of home videos can be compared to the video-based technology of the "instant replay" in sports broadcasts, which likewise allows a slowed-down, intensified study of single sequences.

With the advent of home video, the "television box" became a "terminal" with heterogeneous media channels whose contents could partly be decided or even produced by the viewer. Home video combined content from previously separated spheres: content that was autonomous (video camera), commercial (bought or rented tapes), or "public" (TV recordings). Television's claim to authority depends on its perception as not only a collective, truthful, simultaneous but also controlled and even censored medium. In contrast, the contents of home video were individualized, heterogeneous, potentially uncensored, and uncontrolled.

"Ideology of Liveness" (Jane Feuer) and "Metaphysics of Presence" (Sean Cubitt)

The new everyday practice of viewing television at one's own time sharpened the eye for a critical view on the conventions and constructs behind live television's pretensions to authenticity. In 1983, Jane Feuer diagnosed an "ideology of liveness" on part of the broadcasters, which for programming and finally for political reasons was kept up despite comprehensive video intervention into the live broadcast.[27] Among other things, Feuer refers to the paradoxical expression "live on tape," common in television practice, and the technology of the "instant replay." Her analysis rests on video recordings of broadcasts of the 1980 Olympics recorded by the author herself.[28] In 1988, Sean Cubitt analyzed the "metaphysics of presence" of live television compared to private video recordings: "Videotapes don't talk back. If television's characteristic mode of address is the invitation to dialogue (the ubiquitous 'we' of presenterspeak, the 'Thank you for inviting us into your home tonight'), it is so only because of the metaphysics of presence. Time-shifting alters the viewer relation to the shifters: obviously to the referent of 'tonight,' but also to the complementary particles 'we,' 'us,' 'you,' 'your.'"[29] Cubitt adds: "It is only in the light of video that I have been able to make my propositions about television, by reference back through the new technology to see how the old has been altered."[30] Both Feuer and Cubitt point out that the use of home video changes our idea of television. They reference Walter Benjamin to determine that a video recording will destroy the "aura" of live television.[31] In fact, the aura appears lost from both sides: due to the "invisible" use of video on part of the broadcasters (Feuer) and the time-shifted TV of home video on part of the receivers (Cubitt).

"Transparency Lost" (Umberto Eco)

Up to the 1970s, television was described as a relatively stable dispositive. Then, in the 1980s, we see a fundamental change in the aesthetics, economics, and politics of television. Home video presented only one aspect of this upheaval, which was analyzed by Umberto Eco in his relatively obscure text "TV: La trasparenza perduta" from 1983.[32] Two decades earlier, in his discussion of the *Open Work*, Eco had still seen live television as a space opening up new aesthetic possibilities (*Opera aperta*, 1962). With the end of "Paleo-TV," this window to the world, "open" in two different senses, closes due to the loss of transparency that Eco finds in "Neo-TV," whose visual surface mainly focuses all attention on the medium itself.[33] Besides an equally precise and entertaining analysis of the new formats and their strategies of viewer retention, Eco also specifies three central outside factors for the break from Paleo- to Neo-TV: the introduction of private television channels in Europe, the remote control, and the home video recorder.

The texts by Umberto Eco and Jane Feuer do not belong to video theory in a narrow sense, but they clarify the ways in which economic, political, social, and technological factors interact in the relation between television and video. The "ideology of liveness" examined by Feuer had already been "fake" even before it was further deconstructed by the autonomous television time via home video. Paleo-TV's aura of authenticity dissolved into the visual surface of Neo-TV—later categorized as "videographic" by John Ellis. Again we see the double retroactive effect video had on the reception and production of television.

"MTV Is TV Most Televisual" (John Fiske, E. Ann Kaplan, Will Straw)

According to Eco, the "lost transparency" of Neo-TV was linked to an expansion of broadcasting hours late into the night. Both factors were epitomized by the MTV channel. Its schema of cyclical repetition of video clips for twenty-four hours every day of the week, taken over from pop music radio, contradicted Paleo-TV's central paradigms of currentness and authenticity. The formally inventive, sometimes media-reflective stylings of the clips have often been discussed as the symptom of a specific video aesthetics, even if they were still shot on film stock throughout the 1980s.[34] Referring to theories of postmodernism, the clips were interpreted as a semantic shift ending the referentiality of television by authors such as Fredric Jameson, John Fiske, and E. Ann Kaplan.[35]

The launch of MTV in 1981 evidenced a radical new format in the economics of television. For MTV, video clips constituted both television content and advertisement for the respective pop songs. While up to then the separation of television economics and the message of television had been kept at least superficially apart, with MTV it was completely eroded: television time finally became pure advertising time without any editorial framing. This is why MTV can be understood primarily as a transformation of television and less as an evolution of the video medium. As John Fiske wrote in 1986: "MTV is TV most televisual. The segmented medium, a mosaic of fragments: no sense but sensation."[36] And E. Ann Kaplan understood the round-the-clock operation of MTV as "the extremes of what is inherent in the televisual apparatus."[37]

Furthermore, the music videos themselves were both advertising and product in a highly paradoxical yet efficient manner: they advertised a record on sale but could themselves be purchased on videocassettes.[38] "The fact that you could also buy these videotape-objects at music and record stores underscored the artifactual nature of the video. As video, television was being conceptualized differently," John Thornton Caldwell diagnosed this development.[39]

Shaped by the music industry, video clip aesthetics triggered a phase of innovation in the visual design of television programs. The clips took elements from the traditions of experimental film and video art and transferred them into the televisual mainstream. Even news programs, talk shows, and sports reports adopted the quick edits and digital effects that define the term "videographic" used by John Ellis and also John Thornton Caldwell. Thus MTV, and more generally music videos, can be seen as a Janus-faced phenomenon at the intersection of avant-garde traditions and neoliberal media innovations.

MTV's twenty-four-hour programming became the model for a television program structure aiming for permanence. Gradually, nonstop broadcasting became the standard for television channels. Behind the scenes, video technology played a decisive role for broadcasters. Permanent operation was like a side effect of the video-technological automation introduced to reduce labor costs. In this sense, we again find a retroactive effect on the reception and production of television caused by video: the aesthetics of television were changed by video clips, the temporality of television reception was decoupled from real time, and on the production side video technology soon ended live television's sign off of for the night.

In retrospect, MTV's 24/7 programming could be seen as a precursor of the permanent availability of online videos. Yet on the internet the perception of music videos is radically different: a search on YouTube or comparable online platforms provides several results for almost any piece of music. "Here, the artistically ambitious video clip finds itself lost amidst the static photographs, images of spinning vinyl records, or footage of ephemeral live performances that accompany so much of the music that YouTube makes available," Will Straw writes.[40] Additionally, countless fan-made visuals, mash-ups, and memes can make it hard to hit upon the "official" music video. Thus a music video today can be seen less as part of a singular artwork but as one of many options for the visualization of a given piece.[41]

For that reason, Will Straw sees the music video as a "minor cultural form."[42] He compares the theoretical discourse in times of MTV with that in times of YouTube:

"In the first wave of writing on the video clip, its form was often seen as caught between those of cinema and television. [. . .] At the same time, in the non-stop streams of clips unfolding on networks like MTV, one found the most fully realized confirmation of Raymond Williams's definition of television as 'flow.'"[43] Besides, Straw observes that television has again become a medium of highly attentive reception as TV series can now be watched on demand: "On television, the constant flow between different genres of programming has given way to a seriality in which viewers spend hours within worlds marked by narrative and stylistic continuity. In this new context, the video clip seems disagreeably brief and incomplete."[44] He draws the conclusion: "The intermediality of the video clip is less and less a function of its relationships to cinema and television. It is now a particular arrangement of elements within a wide variety of long and short forms, and within a broader explosion of (audio) visual culture."[45]

These tendencies are reinforced by the success of the music video app TikTok, whose users mime and dance to tracks sometimes offered by TikTok itself. Other users answer with their own performances to the same music and such "challenges" boost the popularity of the original musicians whose sounds are used in these most effectively viral short videos. In 2020, the relatively simple lip sync performance by Bella Poarch, who was widely unknown up unto that moment, to a song by rapper Millie B. from 2016 became the first video on the internet to gather more than 40 million likes. Meanwhile the sounds of "Laxed (Siren Beat)" by an equally unknown seventeen-year-old New Zealander calling himself Jawsh 685 were used in more than 55 million TikTok videos in 2020. This dynamic is controlled by the TikTok algorithm and works without a "product" or an "author" in the proper sense. Likes constitute a new currency to replace audience ratings or the number of views, which—in contrast to YouTube—TikTok does not count. The music industry reacts to the phenomenon by integrating scenes into new videos designed for viral distribution via the app.

Rating versus Clicking: Broadcast Television versus On-Demand Video

The 1980s debate on video killing the aura of live TV might appear as nostalgic in the age of on-demand video and online television libraries as the thought of 24/7 MTV programming. Still in retrospect it becomes clear that the interaction between television and video paved the way for today's developments: media formats are no longer categorically divided between "broadcast" and "storage." YouTube's early slogan "broadcast yourself" implicitly included this promise of a synthesis of individual media production and mass-media reception. But since audience numbers for online video and on-demand streaming now rival those of television, the same models of monetization that we know from television economics become effective, marginalizing the individual moment of self-expression and self-exhibition.

When simultaneous broadcasts for an uncertain number of viewers transitioned to distribution by video streaming, the methods of measuring audience numbers also changed. Like in radio before, audience ratings for television programs were quantified by elaborate measuring procedures and statistical calculations, with the purpose of quantizing monetization for the advertising clients of a station by audience numbers. Principally this kind of broadcast "for everyone" (Lenin) is a medium without a back channel, and ratings can be measured not in the control room of the sender but only among a number of dispersed receivers. Providers of online and on-demand video, on the other hand, can exactly measure the number of clicks and the length of viewing; analysis and control of viewer habits are implemented in the digital dialogue offered by the media.

In contrast, the era of home video, based on cassettes and DVDs, largely avoided measurability and the control or censorship of its contents. Seen from today, analog home video was a moment of transition, when the central agencies of the production and distribution of moving images no longer or not yet knew what audiences really wanted to see, and from which sources they received their content. Today, the death of video stores and the termination of production of video equipment for physical storage media are symptoms of the end of an era in which a private culture of video opened up a partially autonomous parallel world to centralized distribution via television or the internet.[46]

A Particular Case: Video for Archiving and Analyzing Television

In the context of video theory, the use of video for archiving television and for the scientific, social, and artistic re-vision of television content is an interesting particularity. Without video recording, the ephemeral character of broadcasts renders live television an ahistorical medium.[47] This is true both for the audience and for broadcasters themselves, whose archives initially comprised only preproduced features on film stock but no current reportage. At first, video technology was not aimed to archive and possibly repeat programs, but to lower costs, since magnetic tape, in contrast to film stock, allowed for repeated dubbings. A first initiative to archive live broadcasts as historical evidence was launched from outside the TV system and was looked upon critically by broadcasters themselves.

In 1968 the Vanderbilt Television News Archive began "to record and collect the nightly network news for political, historical, and scholarly analysis."[48] This led to a conflict with the CBS network over the legitimacy of such recordings, which lasted for three years and in the end was decided not legally but politically. It resulted in a first law on the "Fair Use" of copyright and the establishment of the American Television and Radio Archive by the Library of Congress. As Lucas Hilderbrand writes: "Not only did video recording introduce a new relationship to television news, giving it a controversial new status as an object of study during a period of cultural conflicts, but this new relationship also raised critical issues of politics, preservation, and the rights of access."[49]

Even after the legalization of recordings for libraries and public archives, television remained a medium without private, educational, or artistic access to its materials.

It was only autonomous video recording that allowed a self-determined inspection and potential reuse of ephemeral broadcasts. Recordings would serve very different purposes: strictly private collections of favorite programs for rewatching; collective screenings in groups that shared social, political, or thematic interests; scientific analysis of a program's structure and format; or artistic appropriation and deconstruction of television via video montage.

As we have seen, home video was crucial to the television studies of Jane Feuer and Sean Cubitt in the 1980s. Earlier examples from the 1970s prove that even before the advent of home video, academics were interested in analyzing television with the help of video. In Germany the "invention of media sciences" was closely connected to the acquisition of video recorders by institutions, and examples of TV programs could be studied in seminars on television offered at Hamburg University (1969) or the Technische Universität Berlin (1971 by Friedrich Knilli).[50]

At the same time, sociologists Alfred Willener, Guy Milliard, and Alex Ganty in Switzerland worked with screenings and discussions of broadcasts in thematically interested groups, recording these discussions and then viewing them again with the group. According to the authors, the "video milieu" completely transformed the "TV milieu" (Figure 5.2): "The medium of mass communication is metamorphosed into a medium of group communication."[51] Later, US-American artist Dara Birnbaum described the goal of her video works edited from TV materials starting in 1978: "To slow down the 'technological speed' of television and arrest moments of TV-time for the viewer, which would allow for examination and questioning."[52] In film studies, too, video became the basis for a selective viewing of movie history from the 1970s on. Jean-Luc Godard made the video-based access to movie history artistically explicit in his *Histoire(s) du cinéma* from the late 1980s onward (see the text by Thomas Helbig in Chapter 4).

Despite the heterogeneity of these examples, they share a crucial common factor: by means of video, television became a material that could be treated in discourse,

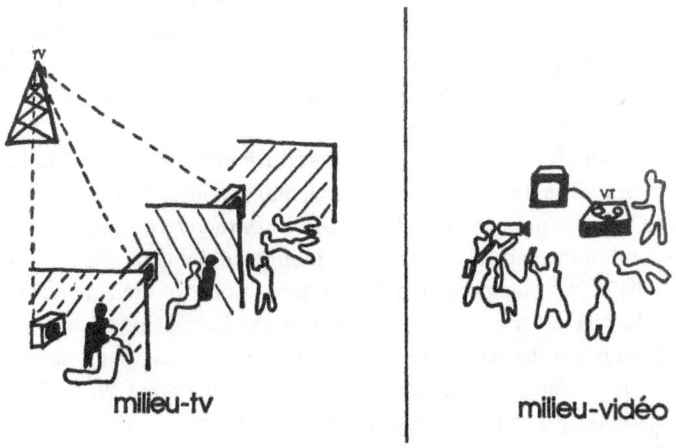

Figure 5.2 "Milieu TV / Mileu Vidéo." Diagram from Alfred Willener, Guy Milliard, and Alex Ganty, *Vidéo et société virtuelle* (Paris: Tema-Editons, 1972), 103.

used in education, manipulated aesthetically and sometimes affectively. Video changed the perception of television both through its "time shift" and "space shift" functions: instead of a widespread, simultaneous reception of programs, video integrated television into an autonomous communicative and social space. Today, this historical characteristic of video allowing a privileged access to television is rendered anachronistic by the common expectation of permanent online access to any content anywhere and anytime. In Rodney Graham's photo piece *Media Studies '77* (2016)—a carefully staged diptych portraying a lecturer and his shrine-like trolley that carries a television screen and video recorder—we find that this characteristic of an irrevocable past has in return become the subject of an artwork that ironically offers a glance back at the old power structures.

The texts in this chapter open up a dialogue between perspectives of television theory that are analyzing the changes in television caused by video technology and contributions by artists who use video to offer alternatives to, or analyses of, the status quo of television. The interplay between developments in television and video sketched out above will be documented in selected contributions from both scholars and artists to offer an interdisciplinary overview that should be understood as a continuing intermedial process.

Nam June Paik and Dara Birnbaum

Nam June Paik and Dara Birnbaum exemplarily offer two opposite approaches to television in video art: artistic intervention in the medium versus artistic analysis of the medium. They also embody different relations between theory and practice: Paik drafts his texts as an outline of future practice, while Birnbaum reflects and comments on her works of the past.

With "Global Groove and Video Common Market" (1970), Paik first suggested internationalizing television, which was still bound to regional and national borders in the 1970s, by exchanging TV programs on video tapes as a medium for world peace and understanding. This text built the theoretical foundation for his video piece *Global Groove*, realized in 1973. It begins with the words: "This is a glimpse of a video landscape of tomorrow when you will be able to switch on any TV station on the earth and TV guides will be as fat as the Manhattan telephone book." Paik's video montage simulates global zapping, offering us a model of the future. The elaborate video effects were realized during a residency at WNET-TV studios, and the station premiered *Global Groove* on January 30, 1974. While the 1970 text was accompanied by a diagram forecasting further developments up to 1980 for the "new political system—Video Common Market—non satellite," Paik updated his artistic approach to satellite TV during the 1980s. This culminated in the transcontinental live broadcast *Wrap around the World*, which reached an audience of 50 million in over ten countries as a contribution to the 1988 Summer Olympics in Seoul.

With "Talking Back to the Media" (1985), Dara Birnbaum took stock of the conceptual underpinnings of the video works she had realized to explore typologies of imagery and gender roles in television between 1978 and 1982. In conceptual-analytical montages, these works combine fragments of TV programs very familiar to contemporary viewers, with an eye to "reconstructing conventions of television."[53] In contrast to Paik, Birnbaum has always kept a reflective distance from television. This also characterizes the different production conditions: while Paik realized *Global Groove* in 1973 as a guest artist invited by a TV studio, Birnbaum describes how in 1978 she had to illegally procure material from the sitcom *Laverne & Shirley*, since home video for private recording still wasn't available at that date. In contrast to the use of found footage in experimental film, Birnbaum does not aim to unsettle with images of the unknown, instead using methods of de-montage and re-montage to sharpen the viewer's gaze on the overly familiar. Along with video artists such as Klaus vom Bruch and General Idea, she can be seen as one of the precursors of 1980s Appropriation Art.[54]

David Antin (and Rosalind Krauss)

David Antin's text "Television: Video's Frightful Parent" from 1975 moves at the intersection of video art and television theory, occupying a special place both at the time of its writing and in this chapter. For the most part, 1970s video art avoided any engagement with television—Nam June Paik and Dara Birnbaum were the exceptions to the rule. Antin's concern was to tie back the discourse on video art to the technological and economic origins of the medium within the television system. Methodically, he developed a hybrid argument from a mix of media and art theories, characterizing the media specifity of video as well as its interdependencies with television.

Antin's contribution can be seen as a fundamental text of the 1970s on a level with the "Aesthetics of Narcissism" by Rosalind Krauss.[55] Both were published in influential art magazines (in *Artforum* and *October*, respectively), and both are still copiously quoted from and referred to in anthologies today. While Krauss is interested in video as a medium for self-projection from within an art discourse, leaving aside works that concern themselves with television as a mass medium, Antin's complementary approach is to examine the structures of this mass medium from an art-theoretical perspective. He incisively dissects the commercial framework of US-American broadcasters and describes in what ways and why economic conditions also have molded TV aesthetics: in the United States, television took over the separation into "two time signatures" for programming and advertising from commercial radio. The time economics of television thus were based on "the social and economic nature of the industry itself" and not on the technological or phenomenological foundations of the apparatus. According to Antin, the asymmetry between transmitter and receiver was not a technological necessity but a hierarchy enforced by economical pressures.

Against this background, Antin analyzes the different time structures of television (where the "commodity" of time is commercially allotted according to the "money metric") and video art (which follows "inherent time," whose slowness is often perceived as "boring"). Comparable thoughts on the time economics of video could later be found in the 1980s in the writings of Fredric Jameson and more in-depth in the 1990s by Maurizio Lazzarato, although these authors do not include any comparisons with television.

Dylan Mulvin, John Thornton Caldwell, and John Ellis

These three contributions from a background in television theory analyze the repercussions that video technology had on television with reference to three significant moments of change: Dylan Mulvin studies the introduction of video as a "time shift" medium in the 1950s; John Thornton Caldwell analyzes the persistence of the live-remote broadcast as a reason why video only very belatedly replaced film in news broadcasts in the 1980s; while John Ellis examines the consequences of digital video effects on television imagery from the 1990s on.

The texts by Caldwell and Ellis engage with each other; they are both excerpts of a much larger, often controversial debate. Following his idea of "televisuality," Caldwell criticizes the "glance theory" of distracted TV viewers that Ellis has formulated based on Raymond Williams's concept of the "flow." Instead, Caldwell diagnoses a development toward more conscious and selective television viewing habits, not least due to the availability of video recordings: "The videophile—an impossibility according to Ellis—by the 1990s is actually a very informed and motivated viewer."[56] This purposeful and repeated reception of television programs on video can even surpass the intensity of the movie theater experience.

Ellis, on the other hand, borrows the term "videographic" from Caldwell but treats the subject more narrowly and precisely. He does not agree that "as Caldwell tends to argue, [. . .] the increased production values and degree of overt visual stylization of much television fiction brings it closer to the cinema experience."[57] Instead, he stresses the different consequences that digital imaging had for both media: the simulation of a photographical reality in digital films and the videographic ordering of images that succeeded the text-based classification of realities in television. In the excerpt reprinted here, Ellis stresses that videographic television fully suits the "glance-like mode of attention" put forward in his earlier texts on television. At the same time, he opposes the thesis of a postmodern disintegration of the referentiality of television especially through video clips, as argued by John Fiske, E. Ann Kaplan, or Fredric Jameson. Instead Ellis posits a function of videographics that carries, or at least claims to carry, meaning, especially in news reports on wars and other crises: "The graphics seek to contain the disorder of the world, but fail to do so adequately."[58]

At this point, the methodological differences between television theory and video theory come into play: in television theory, the focus generally lies on reception, while video theory is concerned with the intersections between production, reception, and distribution. While in television theory, the viewer has a passive role, video theory is interested in the interdependencies between viewing and the viewer's actions. Contributions to this reader by Vilém Flusser (Chapter 1), Alexandra Juhasz (Chapter 8), Sean Cubitt, and Lucas Hilderbrand (Chapter 10) each in their different way explore this type of the "involved spectator" as a characteristic of video theory. Even home video users are seen as active figures whose consumer behavior is self-determined; the only analogy for this in the television camp would be semiautonomous reception while channel surfing. In summary, we find that television theory understands itself as a survey of the status quo, while video theory can implicitly or explicitly describe new possibilities for actions, including those of the recipient. Here the texts by Dylan

Mulvin, John Thornton Caldwell, and John Ellis illustrate how the interplay between television and video also influences developments in television theory by putting a clearer focus on the connection between production and reception.

Additionally, television theory adds another twist to the question of video theory's referentiality (discussed in the introduction to Chapter 1). For a long time it appeared self-evident that the practice of television production did not depend on theory, and that the theory did not speak to the producer but to the recipient of television. Contrary to this, Caldwell's project offers a comprehensive critique of academic "high theory" and a discussion of the implicit knowledge behind television practice. According to the author, the advanced technology of video processing contains theoretically relevant premises, and parallel to text-based "high theory" there is an implicit theory immanent to the technology: "At a basic level, each model of video equipment theorizes, since its design supposes a specific kind of video task."[59] This approach can be compared to positions in early video theory that were based on experience and practice (see the contributions by Nam June Paik and Vilém Flusser in Chapter 1 and Michael Shamberg in Chapter 10). Caldwell goes a step further: to him video theory appears conceivable even outside of texts.

Notes

1 Michael Z. Newman, *Video Revolutions: On the History of a Medium* (New York: Columbia University Press, 2014), 7. Newman includes a reference to the earliest occurrence of the word in the 1937 Oxford English Dictionary where the definition of "Video" reads, "the sight channel of television, as opposed to audio." Ibid., 9. For the beginnings of video terminology also see the introduction to the present volume.

2 Marshall McLuhan, e.g., used the term "video" in the title of a television script: "Draft for Gutenberg Video" (1960); reprinted in Chapter 1 of this volume.

3 Floy Jack Moore, Eugene Chernell, and Maxwell J. West, "Television as a Therapeutic Tool," *Archives of General Psychiatry* 12, no. 2 (1965), 217–20. In psychiatric practice, relatively expensive semi-professional devices were used, mostly 1-inch reel-to-reel machines launched by Ampex in 1965.

4 See the combination of the terms "television" and "videotape" in Harry A. Wilmer, "Television: Technical and Artistic Aspects of Videotape in Psychiatric Teaching," *Journal of Nervous and Mental Disease* 144, no. 3 (1967).

5 John S. Margolies, "TV—The Next Medium," *Art in America* 57, no. 5 (September/October 1969), 48–55.

6 Russell Connor, "Foreword," in *Vision and Television* (Waltham, MA: Rose Art Museum, Brandis University, 1970).

7 "I have found the term 'videosphere' valuable as a conceptual tool to indicate the vast scope and influence of television on a global scale in many simultaneous fields of sense-extension." Gene Youngblood, *Expanded Cinema* (New York: P. Dutton & Co., Inc., 1970), 260. While Youngblood announced a book on his notion of the videosphere (ibid., 3), this never was published. See also Gene Youngblood, "Hardware: The Videosphere," *Radical Software* 1, no. 1 (Spring 1970), 1.

8 JVC Videosphere Model 3241UK, portable television receiver, 1970.

9 Paul Ryan, "Videotape: Thinking about a Medium," in *Educators Guide to Media & Methods* (December 1968), 36–41; reprinted in Chapter 1.

10 For usage in military training and sports see Dylan Mulvin, "Game Time: A History of the Managerial Authority of the Instant Replay," in *The NFL: Critical and Cultural Perspectives*, ed. Thomas Oates and Zack Furness (Philadelphia: Temple University Press, 2014).

11 See *The New Television: A Public/Private Art. Essays, Statements, and Videotapes Based on "Open Circuits: An International Conference on the Future of Television,"* ed. Douglas Davis, Allison Simmons, and Fred Barzyk (New York: Museum of Modern Art; Cambridge, MA: MIT Press, 1977). Most contributions in this book discuss video; only a few are primarily about television.

12 Current news reports for television broadcast were mainly shot on film stock up to the 1980s. On the reasons for the belated introduction of "portable video" to television productions, see the text by John Thornton Caldwell in this chapter.

13 Ricardo Cedeño Montaña, *Portable Moving Images: A Media History of Storage Formats* (Berlin: De Gruyter, 2017), 112.

14 Another impulse for these costly developments was a project tender by the US Air Force in 1951. Albert Abramson, "Video Recording: 1922 to 1959," in *Video: Apparat/Medium, Kunst, Kultur*, ed. Siegfried Zielinski (Frankfurt am Main: Lang, 1992), 41.

15 The first commercially available recorder was introduced by Ampex in 1956. The company estimated to sell thirty items over four years but demand was much larger: within those four years, Ampex sold 600 devices for $75,000 each, two-thirds of them to the three big US-American television broadcasters. Eugene Marlow and Eugene Secunda, *Shifting Time and Space: The Story of Videotape* (New York: Praeger, 1991), 16.

16 See Siegfried Zielinski, "Audiovisuelle Zeitmaschine: Schlussthesen zur Kulturtechnik des Videorecorders," in idem, *Zur Geschichte des Videorecorders* (Berlin: Wissenschaftsverlag, 1986), 315–31. English translation: "The Audiovisual Time Machine: Concluding Theses on the Cultural Technique of the Video Recorder," in Zielinski, *Variations on Media Thinking* (Minneapolis: University of Minnesota Press, 2019).

17 Before video recorders became available, broadcasters used the kinescope process to record the television program on film, quickly develop it, and send the reels by airplane to a TV station in the next time zone. See Dylan Mulvin, *Human Eye Inadequate: Instant Replay and the Politics of Video*, master thesis (Montreal: Department of Art History and Communication Studies, McGill University, 2011), 24; as well as Montaña, *Portable Moving Images*, 112.

18 See Mulvin, "Game Time," 40–59.

19 Peter Sachs Collopy, *The Revolution Will Be Videotaped: Making a Technology of Consciousness in the Long 1960s*, PhD (Philadelphia: University of Pennsylvania, 2015), 80.

20 Howard Polskin, "Conversation with Marshall McLuhan," *Videography* (October 1977), 65. Ibid, 58: "The replay is not cognition but recognition." Cf. Marshall McLuhan, "Biennale Seminar on Video, Venice 1977," in *Art, Artist & the Media*, ed. Richard Kriesche (Graz: AVZ books, 1978), n.p. (excerpt reprinted in Chapter 1 of this volume): "The instant replay translates your ordinary cognitive experience into an artistic event of recognition, playing it twice (re-cognition)."

21 Mulvin, "Game Time," 41
22 See Marlow and Secunda, *Shifting Time and Space*, 39–54, 78, and 139
23 The A. C. Nielsen Report from 1984 found that 36 percent of viewers would omit advertisements when recording broadcasts, and 49 percent would fast forward on viewing them. Marlow and Secunda, *Shifting Time and Space*, 47.
24 In 1976, the Hollywood studios of Disney and Universal brought litigation against Sony, as they saw the possibility of recording their TV shows on Betamax home video as copyright infringement. Only in 1984 did the Supreme Court decide that private home recording was legal. See Lucas Hilderbrand, "The Betamax Decision," in idem, *Inherent Vice: Bootleg Histories of Videotape and Copyright* (Durham, NC: Duke University Press, 2009), 89–101.
25 Illustrated in Marlow and Secunda, *Shifting Time and Space*, 124.
26 For an exploration of this idea see Tobias Haupts, *Die Videothek: Zur Geschichte und medialen Praxis einer kulturellen Institution* (Bielefeld: transcript, 2014), 300–9; excerpts reprinted in Chapter 10 of this volume. Haupts here elaborates on thoughts already outlined by Siegfried Zielinski.
27 Jane Feuer, "The Concept of Live TV: Ontology as Ideology," in *Regarding Television: Critical Approaches. An Anthology*, ed. E. Ann Kaplan (Los Angeles: American Film Institute, University Publications of America, 1983), 14 and 16. A theory of liveness in television that is expanded to include techno-ontological aspects is presented by Wolfgang Ernst, "Between Real Time and Memory on Demand: Reflections on/of Television," *South Atlantic Quarterly* 101, no. 3 (July 2002).
28 Feuer, "The Concept of Live TV," 16.
29 Sean Cubitt, "Time Shift: Reflections on Video Viewing," *Screen* 29, no. 2 (March 1, 1988), 78.
30 Ibid., 80f.
31 Feuer, The Concept of Live TV," 15; Cubitt, "Time Shift," 78f.
32 Umberto Eco, "TV: Transparency Lost," in *TeleGen: Kunst und Fernsehen / TeleGen. Art and Television*, ed. Dieter Daniels and Stephan Berg (Bonn: Kunstmuseum Bonn; Liechtenstein: Kunstmuseum Liechtenstein; Munich: Hirmer, 2015), 194–216. Originally published as "TV: La trasparenza perduta," in idem, *Sette anni di desiderio. Cronache 1977–1983* (Milan: Bompiani), 163–79.
33 Even if Eco's text has not been widely regarded, the two terms coined by him, "Paleo-TV" and "Neo-TV," have a lasting significance in television theory. See Francesco Casetti and Roger Odin, "De la paléo- à la néotelevision: Approche sémio-pragmatique," *Communications* 51 (1990).
34 See the text by John Thornton Caldwell reprinted in this chapter.
35 See, e.g., Fredric Jameson, *Postmodernism or, The Cultural Logic of Late Capitalism* (Durham, NC: Duke University Press, 1991), esp. 79–92, where he offers an extended analysis using the example of the experimental music video *AlienNATION* (1979) by Edward Rankus, John Manning, and Barbara Latham. Other excerpts of Jameson's text concerning video are reprinted in Chapter 2 of this volume.
36 John Fiske, "MTV: Post-Structural, Post-Modern," *Journal of Communication Inquiry* 10, no. 1 (1986), 77.
37 E. Ann Kaplan, *Rocking around the Clock: Music Television, Postmodernism, and Consumer Culture* (New York: Methuen, 1987), 4.
38 The most successful sales video is *Michael Jackson's Thriller*. Only three months after publications, 300,000 video tapes (VHS and Betamax) were sold for $29.98 each. See

Russel Sanjek, *American Popular Music Business in the 20th Century: The First Four Hundred Years. Volume III: From 1900 to 1984* (New York: Oxford University Press, 1988), 647. In all, 9,500,000 videos (DVDs and tapes) supposedly sold until 2013. See Phil Hebblethwaite, "How Michael Jackson's 'Thriller' Changed Music Videos for Ever," *The Guardian*, November 11, 2013, online at https://www.theguardian.com/music/2013/nov/21/michael-jackson-thriller-changed-music-videos.

39 John Thornton Caldwell, *Televisuality: Style, Crisis, and Authority in American Television* (Rutgers University Press: New Brunswick, 1995), 270; excerpt reprinted in this chapter.

40 Will Straw, "Music Video in Its Contexts: 30 Years Later," *Volume!* 14, no. 2 (2018), 1; https://journals.openedition.org/volume/5696.

41 Robert Sakrowski has explored this phenomenon on his CuratingYouTube platform, where he allows users to navigate several videos accompanying the same piece of music. See Robert Sakrowski, *Skrillex Variationen* (2013), presented at the CTM Festival exhibition and the Sonar Festival in 2013; https://archive2013-2020.ctm-festival.de/archive/all-artists/a-e/curatingyoutubenet

42 Straw, "Music Video in Its Contexts," 1.

43 Ibid., 5.

44 Ibid.

45 Ibid.

46 Funai Electric, the last producer of VHS recorders, stopped production in 2016. In the same year, Apple took the last MacBook with an inbuilt DVD drive off the market.

47 Cf. Wolfgang Ernst, "Between Real Time and Memory on Demand: Reflections on/of Television," in *South Atlantic Quarterly* 101, no. 3 (July 2002).

48 Hilderbrand, *Inherent Vice*, xvii.

49 Ibid.

50 See Knut Hickethier, *Medienkultur und Medienwissenschaft: Das Hamburger Modell. Vorgeschichte, Entstehung, Konzept* (Hamburg: Zentrum für Medien und Medienkultur, 2001), 10, as well as Joachim Paech, "Die Erfindung der Medienwissenschaft," in *Was waren Medien?*, ed. Claus Pias (Berlin and Zürich: Diaphanes, 2011), 4.

51 Alfred Willener, Guy Milliard, and Alex Ganty, *Videology and Utopia: Explorations in a New Medium* (London, Henley, and Boston: Routledge & Kegan Paul, 1976), 53; first published as *Vidéo et société virtuelle* (Paris: Tema-Editons, 1972), 103.

52 Dara Birnbaum, *Rough Edits: Popular Image Video Works, 1977–1980* (Halifax: Press of the Nova Scotia College of Art and Design, 1987), 13.

53 Birnbaum, *Rough Edits*, 13.

54 Birnbaum's function as a role model for 1980s art can also be gathered from the fact that the title of the exhibition and publication *Talking Back to the Media* by Time Based Arts in Amsterdam 1985 was taken from her contribution.

55 Rosalind Krauss, "Video: The Aesthetic of Narcissism," *October* no. 1 (Spring 1976), 50–64. See also Chapters 1, 2, and 3 for the debate following Krauss's essay.

56 Caldwell, *Televisuality*, 26. Other excerpts of the book reprinted in this chapter.

57 John Ellis, *Seeing Things: Television in the Age of Uncertainty* (London and New York: I. B. Tauris Publishers, 2002), 99. Other excerpts of the book reprinted in this chapter.

58 Ibid., 98.

59 Caldwell, *Televisuality*, 154.

The Politics of Timeshifting (2011)

Dylan Mulvin

"The politics of timeshifting," refers to the appearance of practical magnetic video recording and the technical, commercial, and aesthetic reconfigurations that accompanied its widespread adoption. Though videotape entered the American market as a practical solution to the well-established challenge of transcontinental broadcasting, the earliest video recorders were already imagined to offer a potentially radical reorganization of television, including greater control over the labor, production schedules, and repeat broadcasting of programming, and a higher fidelity to the original broadcast material. Moreover, within a decade of its introduction, the politics of timeshifting had been transposed from the large-scale, bureaucratic concerns of broadcast timing, to the microscale analysis of movement and space in the form of the "instant replay."

My history begins with the initial attempt to synchronize television time with "clock time."[1] In the 1950s, broadcast time was divided for purposes of television standardization as the commercial pressures of television management pushed the broadcast networks toward more localized experiences of time, so that the uniform, national audience was in fact a series of smaller, subdivided audiences.[2] Just as national borders constrain the flow of information because of conflicts between rights holders, American TV networks had long attempted to maintain programming continuity across time zones to make the sale of audiences to advertisers predictable and commensurable. Thus, the networks divided their broadcast territory into time blocks, used to delay broadcasts and to deliver roughly equivalent viewership percentages.[3] This form of timeshifting was sanctioned by the exigencies of capitalism—exigencies that always compromised any notion that television was a fundamentally "live" medium before it was a timeshifted one.

In mobilizing videotape technologies, networks and electronics manufacturers appealed to a particularly postwar, capitalist logic of efficient distribution—prerecord a surplus of content and distribute as needed—which was a proxy solution to a number of economic, aesthetic, and social challenges associated with the centralized process of transcontinental broadcasting. The alignment of an apparent need for efficiently distributed, higher quality TV recordings, aligned with the ideological view that American television networks were crucial to maintaining national unity.[4]

In future decades, the VCR, PVR, and other forms of personally timeshifting television content—so that it fit with one's own rhythms and tempos of labor and leisure time—were met with fierce pushback from American networks, and often supported by state regulations on the appropriate uses of personal recording. Such attempts to limit the timeshifting of content are an act, by property holders, to maintain what Slack and Wise call *social space*, "the production of social relations over time,"[5] including, in this case, the social relations compelled by predictable and commodifiable exposure to advertising. Timeshifting the flow of television programming threatened the social contingency of infrastructural space by threatening the consistent flow of commodities.

In other words, the personal video recorder did not compromise the "liveness" of television alone; liveness was always already a fantasy, and compromised by the imperatives of creating demographically similar—and commercially interchangeable—audiences across time zones. *It was less important to have live programming than it was to have a live audience.* From the beginning, timeshifting mutated the flow of programming as a principally commercial activity. [. . .]

There are many genealogies of videotape, including kinescope recording, stop-motion photography, and magnetic audiotape. The latter is the most prominent in the commercial and engineering historiography, and long before videotape debuted there had been widespread interest in adapting the techniques of magnetic audio recording for use in video.[6] In the standard story the Ampex Corporation, having developed German Magnetophon technology into the first commercially practical audiotape recorders,[7] finally adapted these same principles to develop the first broadcast-quality television videotape recorder.[8] The central affordance of magnetic tape recording over its alternatives (film, wax, shellac, and vinyl) is "instantaneous recording," which makes recorded content available for playback *as it is recorded.* This affordance comes from the concentration of recording and playback functions in a single set of mechanisms. There were enormous commercial implications of this concentration of mechanism, as the temporal shift of instantaneity closed the gap between the time a program was performed and when it was ready for broadcast and rebroadcast. This signaled a significant acceleration in the production of television commodities. Beyond commodification, however, the temporal dynamics of instantaneous recording provoked aesthetic, economic, and social consequences across television industries, and seeped into the corners of public life.

One of the longest lasting and most conspicuous artifacts of videotape's timeshifting potential is the "instant replay"—the immediate reuse of video content meant for close analysis. Here, I focus on instant replay as an example of operational aesthetics[9] where the otherwise invisible fact that a program is recorded becomes visible, and transforms a practice of (micro) timeshifting as an experience of aesthetic appreciation and, eventually, empirical scrutiny. Though the instant replay is strongly associated with sports broadcasting, a prototypical form of the replay was present from videotape's earliest days and the first subject of video recording, and replay, was the television industry itself. Videotape was introduced by Ampex at the National Association of Radio and Television Broadcasters convention in 1956. In the engineering and corporate mythology, the demonstration of the VRX-1000 was revelatory. One of the attendees of the demonstration describes in vivid detail the uncanny moment of recognition that followed the appearance of a replay:

> Well, the first thing we knew, after a brief introduction from Bill, we were looking at pictures of ourselves on the monitors not only taken just seconds before, but of a quality that was hard to realize was actually electronically duplicated and not "live." It took a few seconds before we realized the significance of what we had seen, and then, for all the world like a football crowd cheering Doak Walker or Bobby Layne trotting off the field after the winning touchdown, the entire audience rose to its feet and applauded spontaneously.[10]

This quote handily foreshadows the central place sports replays would later come to occupy in the thematization of video recording, and also echoes other moments of uncanny recognition that are a standard feature of media history.[11] When a replay interrupts the linear time of television broadcast, the stuttering flow of television exposes the cracks in the (apparent) liveness of the television signal, and reveals the structure of an always timeshifted medium. When, a year after this demonstration, during President Eisenhower's second inauguration the networks replayed his oath of office, it supposedly startled at-home viewers who felt a similar uncanniness in response to a video signal that was both *live* and *not-live*.[12]

Despite or in spite of the uncanniness of the replay, Ampex vastly underestimated the demand for video recorders and, relative to their eventual success, invested little in developing the technology. Ampex had anticipated sales of around two dozen machines over the first four years but by 1960 had sold 550 machines to networks, individual stations, and private firms interested in the possibility of instantaneous recording.[13] Within a decade, video recorders and replay were adapted to a wide and diverse set of applications from law enforcement and psychiatric care to industrial training, personal development, and every facet of television production.[14] The question is, then: Was Ampex merely poor at judging the "desire" for a magnetic tape recorder, or, did the VRX-1000 and subsequent recorders manufacture a demand for video-based practices?

Perhaps one reason for Ampex's own skepticism was the fact that early video recording was an expensive and finicky practice. Not only were the machines prohibitively expensive for small outfits, they were equipped with several sets of temperamental vacuum tubes necessary to attain the precision required for broadcast-quality video. Early machines were also highly idiosyncratic and videotapes were machine-dependent. With early machines, each recorder had slight variations in how it guided the magnetic tape and recordings could only be played back on the same machine on which they were recorded: "If a show had to be held for a long time . . . CBS stored the heads with the tapes and hoped for the best."[15] Use of the medium as a long-term storage technology was far off but this machine-tape symbiosis may have helped foreclose the archival potential of videotape. Early recording for playback was thus a machine-localized practice, a fact that vanished during broadcast, when the infrastructure of recording and playback were camouflaged. [. . .]

Thus, the politics of timeshifting conditioned television from the top down, as the ability to easily timeshift programming altered the economics and logistics of TV production; they also mutated the aesthetics and experience of television from the bottom up, as the instant replay became a ubiquitous aspect of the television viewing experience, even while broadcasters continued to efface the use of tape in the maintenance of the illusion of liveness. Liveness was a hallmark of the nationally united audience.[16] Liveness as an ideology depends also on the constant "flow" of programming,[17] and on the perception that "the text issues from an endless supply that is sourceless, natural, inexhaustible, and coextensive with psychological reality itself."[18] But videotape animated a paradox of television, where the illusion of a coherent, live experience was regularly interrupted by the technological apparatus, and the stuttering of the televisual timeline.

Videotape's instant-access temporality fit with the corporate striving for accelerated and centralized television production in the conjuncture of the 1950s. By the early 1960s, circumstances would change, and the mediation of the video recorder would appear on television as an aesthetic trope for the representation of time and action in the form of the instant replay. Eventually, instant playback became a codified, standardized, and preferred technique of observation, evidence production, and judgment.

From the chapter "The Politics of Timeshifting" in Dylan Wesley Mulvin, "Human Eye Inadequate": Instant Replay and the Politics of Video, master thesis (Montreal: McGill University, 2011); excerpted and adapted for the present publication by the author.

Notes

1 Eugene Marlow and Eugene Secunda, *Shifting Time and Space: The Story of Videotape* (New York: Praeger, 1991).
2 Jonathan Sterne, "Television under Construction: American Television and the Problem of Distribution, 1926–1962," *Media, Culture & Society* 21, no. 4 (1999).
3 William Lafferty, "'A New Era in TV Programming' Becomes 'Business as Usual': Videotape Technology, Local Stations, and Network Power, 1957–1961," *Quarterly Review of Film and Video* 16, no. 3 (1997).
4 Ibid., 4.
5 Jennifer Daryl Slack and J. Macgregor Wise, *Culture + Technology: A Primer* (New York: Peter Lang, 2005), 136.
6 Lucas Hilderbrand, via Roy Armes, argues that videotape's specificity as a medium is more closely aligned with the history of audio than that of cinema or photography. See Hilderbrand, *Inherent Vice: Bootleg Histories of Videotape and Copyright* (Durham: Duke University Press, 2009); Roy Armes, *On Video* (London and New York: Routledge, 1988); Frederick M. Remley, "The Challenge of Recording Video," in *Magnetic Recording: The First 100 Years*, ed. Eric D. Daniel, C. Denis Mee, and Mark H. Clark (New York: IEEE Press, 1999).
7 Beverley R. Gooch, "Building on the Magnetophon," in *Magnetic Recording: The First 100 Years*, 82–9. By 1950, Ampex was the number-one producer of audio recorders.
8 Remley, "The Challenge of Recording Video."
9 Operational aesthetics, as Neil Harris describes it, refers to "a delight in observing process and examining for literal truth." Neil Harris, *Humbug: The Art of P.T. Barnum* (Boston: Little, Brown, 1973), 79.
10 Attendee, quoted in Jeff Martin, "The Dawn of Tape: Transmission Device as Preservation Medium," *Moving Image* 5, no. 1 (2005), 53.
11 Jeffrey Sconce, *Haunted Media: Electronic Presence from Telegraphy to Television* (Durham, NC: Duke University Press, 2000).
12 Laurence Laurent, "Viewers Startled by Tape's Quick Repeat," *The Washington Post*, January 22, 1957.
13 Lafferty, "'A New Era in TV Programming' Becomes 'Business as Usual.'"

14 See Dylan Mulvin, “Game Time: A History of the Managerial Authority of the Instant Replay,” in *The NFL: Critical and Cultural Perspectives*, ed. Thomas P. Oates and Zack Furness (Philadelphia: Temple University Press, 2014), 40–59.
15 Martin, “The Dawn of Tape,” 56.
16 Jane Feuer, “The Concept of Live Television: Ontology as Ideology,” in *Regarding Television: Critical Approaches*, ed. E. Ann Kaplan (Frederick, MD: University Publications of America, 1983).
17 Here I mean the second of the three senses of “flow” elucidated by Williams: “Flow of this second kind, however, is centrally important in our experience of television, since it shows, over a sufficient range, the process of relative unification, in a flow, of otherwise diverse or at best loosely related items.” Raymond Williams, *Television: Technology and Cultural Form* (New York: Schocken Books, 1974), 97.
18 Beverle Houston, “Viewing Television: The Metapsychology of Endless Consumption,” *Quarterly Review of Film Studies* 9, no. 3 (1984), 184.

Global Groove and Video Common Market (1970)

Nam June Paik

The Treaty of Rome (1957) was preceded for a decade by vocal exhortations of prophetic statesmen like Robert Schuman, Jean Monnet, or Hallstein, and tedious, painstaking, and prolonged negotiations by the economists of six European countries. Many times the process was termed hopeless, utopian or academic. But the result, the European Common Market, a long dreamed of free trade zone, surpassed even the most wild imaginings in terms of growth and prosperity. England's trouble is a well-known fact.

Videoland on this spaceship Earth resembles the divided state of European countries before 1957. Many TV stations around the world are hoarding videotapes totaling thousands of hours and asking impossibly high prices or compliance with complicated procedures to obtain some commodity for which they have almost no prospect of selling. Or Videoland, a so-called communications media, is so discommunicative with each other that practically no one knows what to buy, to import, or export. Should video culture stay as divided, nationalistic, and protectionistic as the block economy of the Thirties, which amplified the depression, instigated Fascism and helped promote World War II?

World peace and survival of earth is Public Interest Number I and, needless to say, Public Interest Number I must be Interest Number I of Public Television. What we need now is a champion of free trade, who will form a Video Common Market modeled after the European Common Market in its spirit and procedure; this would strip the hieratic monism of TV culture and promote the free flow of video information through an inexpensive barter system or convenient free market.

McLuhan's premature high hope for the Global Village via TV is based on an obscure book, *The Bias of Communication*, by H. A. Innis (1951), which traced the origin of nationalism to the invention of movable type. But, ironically, today's video culture is far more nationalistic than print media. You simply cannot escape Camus or Sartre in a bookstore. But do you remember seeing a production of French TV recently? Is it conceivable that the wonderful people who delivered a line of genius from Molière to Godard become suddenly petrified in front of silver flick? David Atwood, a director at WGBH, reports a contrary thing. TV cameras are following so busily the latest spots of violence that kids, who receive most of their education from TV, think that such noble countries as Switzerland and Norway are chunks of real estate lying somewhere in the Milky Way or, at best, beyond Madagascar. How can we teach about peace while blocking out one of the few existing examples from the screen? Most Asian faces we encounter on the American TV screen are either miserable refugees, wretched prisoners, or hated dictators. But most middle-class Asians are seeing essentially the same kind of clean-cut entertainment shows on their home screens as most American Nielsen families. Did this vast information gap contribute to the recent tragedies in Vietnam? Weren't those simple-minded GIs in Song My prejudiced, even in the slightest degree, by the All-American TV screen of the Mid-West before landing in Saigon, which necessarily has all of the miseries of a war-torn country? If yes, those accused GIs are also victims of monistic TV networks to a certain extent. Don Luce, a former director of the International Voluntary Service in Vietnam with a ten year service record, notes: "American failures in Vietnam have been essentially failures in communication and understanding."[1] And how about Russian TV? They might not be that bad if they ran such bourgeois soap operas as *The Forsythe Saga*, and I am curious how their Huntley-Brinkley-vich talk the pravda (truth) every evening. Understandably, negotiations for the Video Common Market will be as tiresome and frustrating as those for the European Common Market. But its huge reward will be not only philosophical. Faster rotation of capital is also a supreme requirement for cost-efficiency in a cultural economy. A new paper money created by the International Monetary Fund to check the gold outflow, indicated by the Special Drawing Right or SDR, would serve as a model for the proposed Video Common Market. I suggested this in my Stony Brook report, in February 1968, before SDR was approved.

The American Public Television System is, by its nature, destined to be a vanguard for this movement. A persistent and protracted effort should be initiated by WGBH. It is radical in the sense that it attacks the radix, or root, of conventionalism, beyond the success or failure of the individual program or weekly series.

Jazz was the first tie between Blacks and Whites. Mozart was the first tie between Europeans and Asians. Beethoven was the last tie between Germans and Americans during World War II. Currently rock music is the only channel between young and old. But the power of music as a nonverbal communications medium has been wasted as much as were the vast resources under the ocean. Therefore, if we could assemble a weekly television festival comprised of music and dance from every nation and disseminate it freely via the proposed Video Common Market to the world, its effects on education and entertainment would be phenomenal. Peace can be as exciting as a John Wayne war movie. The tired slogan of "world peace" will again become fresh and marketable.

Back in 1938 Buckminster Fuller defined the word "ecology" as follows: ". . . that very word 'economics' springs etymologically from 'ecology' meaning the body of knowledge developed out of the house. We stress not housing but essentiality of comprehensive research and design . . . The question is survival, and the answer, which is unit, lies in the progressive sum-totaling of man's evolving knowledge. Individual survival is identifiable with the whole as extension or extinction."[2]

On the last Earth Day, ecology was treated as a temporary face-lifting or local anesthesia. Ecology is not "politics" but a devoutful Weltanschauung, which believes in world design, global recyclization, the shift of our attitude from "you OR me" to "you AND me," as Mr. Fuller, the guru of the whole movement, never ceases to emphasize. Global Groove and Video Common Market treat the root of pollution much more than one more conventional documentary on a lake.

Let me finish this essay in a digital way:

The *New York Times* spends about 70% of her important pages on international coverage.

The *New York Daily News* spends about 7% for the equivalent.

NET's average is closer to the *Daily News* than to the *Times*.

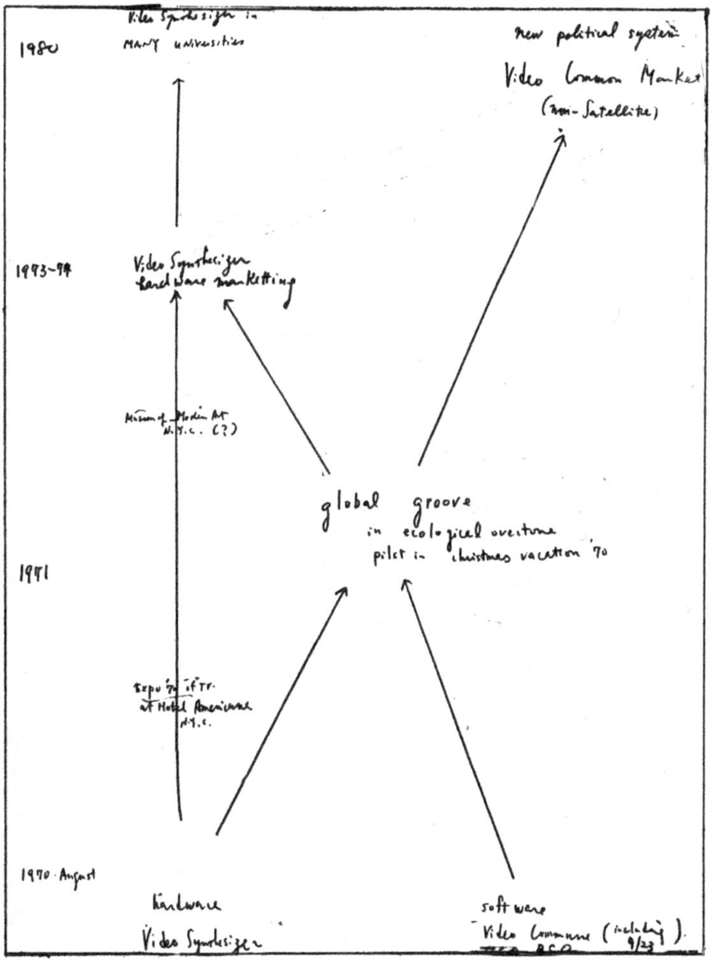

Figure 5.3 Nam June Paik, diagram on the future development of video 1970–80, accompanying his text "Global Groove and Video Common Market," 1970.

Nam June Paik, "Global Groove and Video Common Market," written February 1970, printed in *The WNET-TV Lab New* 2, 1973; reprinted from *Videa 'n' Videology: Nam June Paik 1959–1973*, ed. Judson Rosebush (Syracuse: Verson Museum of Art, 1974), unpag.

Notes

1 Quoted in the *Saturday Review* from *Vietnam: Unheard Voice*, Cornell University Press (authors note, i.e. *Viet Nam: The Unheard Voices*, ed. Don Luce and John G. Sommer (Ithaca: Cornell University Press, 1969).

2 Buckminster Fuller, *Nine Chains to the Moon* (1938; repr. New York: Anchor Books, 1971), 14, xi.

Television: Video's Frightful Parent (1975)

David Antin

Video Art. The name is equivocal. A good name. It leaves open all the questions and asks them anyway. Is this an art form, a new genre? An anthology of valued activity conducted in a particular arena defined by display on a cathode ray tube? The kind of video made by a special class of people—artists—whose works are exhibited primarily in what is called "the art world"—Artist's Video? And if so, is this a class apart? Artists have been making video pieces for scarcely ten years, if we disregard Nam June Paik's 1963 kamikaze TV modifications, and video has been a fact of gallery life for barely five years. Yet we've already had group exhibitions, panels, symposia, magazine issues devoted to this phenomenon, for the very good reason that more and more artists are using video, and some of the best work being done in the art world is being done with video. Which is why a discourse has already arisen to greet it.

Actually two discourses: one, a kind of enthusiastic welcoming prose peppered with fragments of communication theory and McLuhanesque media talk; the other, a rather nervous attempt to locate the "unique properties of the medium." Discourse 1 could be called "cyberscat" and Discourse 2, because it engages the issues that pass for "formalism" in the art world, could be called "the formalist rap." Though there is no necessary relation between them, the two discourses occasionally occur together as they do in the talk of Frank Gillette, which offers a convenient sample:

> 1) The emergence of relations between the culture you're in and the parameters that allow you expression are fed back through a technology. It's the state of the art technology within a particular culture that gives shape to ideas.
>
> 2) What I'm consciously involved in is devising a way that is structurally intrinsic to television. For example, what makes it *not* film? Part of it is that you look *in*to the source of light, with film you look *with* the source of light. In television the source of light and the source of information are one.[1]

It is not quite clear what "high-class" technology has to do with the rather pleasantly shabby technical state of contemporary video art; nor what is the significance to human beings of the light source in two adjacent representational media, though statements of this type are characteristic, and similar quotes could be multiplied endlessly. And if these concerns seem somewhat gratuitous or insufficient regarding the work at hand, they often share a kind of aptness of detail, even though it is rarely clear what the detail explains of the larger pattern of activity in which these artists are involved. In fact what seems most typical of both types of discourse is a certain anxiety that may be seen most clearly in a recent piece by Hollis Frampton:

> Moreover it is doubly important that we try to say what video is at present because we posit for it a privileged future. Since the birth of video art from the Jovian backside (I dare not say brow) of the Other Thing called television, I for one have

> felt a more and more pressing need for precise definitions of what film art *is*, since I extend to film, as well, the hope of a privileged future.[2]

It would be so much more convenient to develop the refined discussion of the possible differences between film and video, if we could only forget the Other Thing—television. Yet commercial television, which controls the technology and shares the essential conditions of production and viewing of everything seen on the video monitor screen, has also provided almost all the background viewing experience of the video audience and even of the video artists. So, no matter how different from television the works of individual video artists may be, the television experience dominates the phenomenology of viewing and haunts video exhibitions the way the experience of movies haunts all film. Many video artists are aware of this, and their work reflects stances taken in relation to television, only the most obvious of which manifest themselves directly in quotes, allusion, celebration, parody and protest. [. . .]

Nevertheless, it is unwise to despise an enemy, especially a more powerful, older enemy, who happens also to be your frightful parent. So it is with television that we have to begin to consider video, because if anything has defined the formal and technical properties of the video medium, it is the television industry. [. . .]

For television also there is a special-use domain—educational, industrial, and now artistic—where the relation between the camera and receiver may be more or less equalized, but this is because transmission is not an issue and the distribution of the images is severely restricted. The economic fact remains: transmission is more expensive than reception. This ensures a power hierarchy: transmission dominates reception. And it follows from this asymmetry of power relations that the taker-transmitter dominates whatever communication takes place. [. . .]

Now while this asymmetry is not inherent in the technology, it has become so normative for the medium that it forms the all-pervasive and invisible background of all video. This may not be so dramatically manifested in most artwork video, but that's because most artworks have very equivocal relations to the notion of communication and are, like industry, producer-dominated.[3] Yet it has a formidable effect on all attempts at interactive video, which operates primarily in reaction to this norm. In this sense, the social structure of the medium is a matrix that defines the formal properties of the medium—since it limits the possibilities of a video communication genre—and these limits then become the target against which any number of artists have aimed their works.

What else could Ira Schneider have had in mind about the 1969 piece *Wipe-Cycle* he devised with Frank Gillette:

> The most important thing was the notion of information presentation, and the notion of the integration of the audience into the information. One sees oneself exiting from the elevator. If one stands there for eight seconds, one sees oneself entering the gallery from the elevator again. Now at the same time one is apt to be seeing oneself standing there watching *Wipe-Cycle*. You can watch yourself live watching yourself eight seconds ago, watching yourself 16 seconds ago, *eventually feeling free enough to interact with this matrix, realizing one's own potential as an actor* [my italics].[4]

What is attempted is the conversion (liberation) of an audience (receiver) into an actor (transmitter), which Schneider and Gillette must have hoped to accomplish by neutralizing as much as possible the acts of "taking" and electronic transmission. If they failed to accomplish this, they were hardly alone in their failure, which seems to have been the fate of just about every interactive artwork employing significantly technological means. Apparently, the social and economic distribution of technological resources in this culture has a nearly determining effect on the semiotics of technological resources.

More concretely, an expensive video camera and transmission system switched on and ready for use don't lose their peculiar prestigious properties just because an artist may make them available under special circumstances to an otherwise passive public. In fact, this kind of interactive video situation almost invariably begins by intimidating an unprepared audience, which has already been indoctrinated about the amount of preparedness (professionalism) the video camera deserves, regardless of the trivial nature of television professionalism, which is not measured by competence (as in the elegant relation of ends to means) but by the amount of money notably expended on this preparation.

Yet while the most fundamental property of television is its social organization, this is manifested more clearly in its money metric, which applies to every aspect of the medium, determining the tempo of its representations and the style of the performances, as well as the visual syntax of its editing. The money metric has also played a determining role in neutralizing what is usually considered the most markedly distinctive feature of the medium: the capacity for instantaneous transmission. [. . .]

The industry wishes or feels obligated to maintain the illusion of immediacy, which it defines rather precisely as "the feeling that what one sees on the TV screen is living and actual reality, at that very moment taking place."[5] The perfection of videotape made possible the careful manipulation and selective presentation of desirable "errors" and "minor crises" as marks of spontaneity, which became as equivocal in their implications as the drips and blots of third-generation Abstract Expressionists. It's not that you couldn't see the Los Angeles police department's tactical assault squad in real time, in full living color, in your own living room, leveling a small section of the city in search of three or four suspected criminals, but that what you would see couldn't be certainly discriminated from a carefully edited videotape screened three hours later. So television provides video with a tradition not of falseness, which would be a kind of guarantee of at least a certain negative reliability, but of a profoundly menacing equivocation and mannerism, determining a species of unlikeliness.

At first glance artists' video seems to be defined by the total absence of any of the features that define television. But this apparent lack of relation is in fact a very definite and predictable inverse relation. If we temporarily ignore the subfamily of installation pieces, which are actually quite diverse among themselves, but nevertheless constitute a single genre, the most striking contrast between video pieces and television is in relation to time. It may not be quite hip to say so without qualification, but it is a commonplace to describe artists' videotapes as "boring" or "long," even when one feels that this in no way invalidates or dishonors the tapes in question (viz. Bruce Boice's comment that Lynda Benglis's video is "boring, interesting and funny,"[6] or Richard

Serra's own videotape *Prisoner's Dilemma*, where one character advises another that he may have to spend two hours in the basement of the Castelli Gallery, which is "twice as long as the average boring videotape").

This perceived quality of being boring or long has little to do with the actual length of the tapes, it has much more to do with the attitude of just about all the artists using video. John Baldessari has a tape called *Some Words I Mispronounce*. He turns to a blackboard and writes:

1. poor	4. Beelzebub
2. cask	5. bough
3. bade	6. sword

As soon as he completes the "d" of "sword" the tape is over. Running time is under a minute. It feels amazingly short. But it is longer than most commercials.

Robert Morris's *Exchange*, a series of verbal meditations on exchanges of information, collaborations, and interferences with a woman, accompanied by a variety of images taped and retaped from other tapes and photographs for the most part as indefinite and suggestive as the discourse, goes on till it arrives at a single distinct and comic story of not getting to see Donatello's *Gattamelata*, after which the tape trails off in a more or less leisurely fashion. Running time: 43 minutes. Television has many programs that are much longer. The two artists' tapes are very different. Baldessari's is a routine, explicitly defined from the outset and carried out deadpan to its swift conclusion. *Exchange* is a typical member of what is by now a well-defined genre of artist narrative, essentially an extended voice-over in a carefully framed literary style that seeks its end intuitively in the exhaustion of its mild narrative energy. But they both have the same attitude toward time: the work ends whenever its intention is accomplished. The time is inherent time, the time required for the task at hand. The work is "boring," as Les Levine remarked, "if you demand that it be something else. If you demand that it be itself then it is not boring."[7] Which is not to say that the videotapes are inevitably interesting.[8] Whether they are interesting or not is largely a matter of judging the value of the task at hand, and this could hardly be the issue for people who can look with equanimity at what hangs on the wall in the most distinguished galleries. For whatever we think of the videotapes of Morris, or Sonnier, or Serra, they are certainly not inferior to whatever else they put in the gallery. Levine is right. Videotapes are boring if you demand that they be something else. But they're not judged boring by comparison with paintings or sculpture, they're judged boring in comparison with television, which for the last 20 years has set the standard of video time.

But the time standard of television is based firmly on the social and economic nature of the industry itself and has nothing whatever to do with the absolute technical and phenomenological possibilities of visual representation by cathode ray tube. For television, time has an absolute existence independent of any imagery that may or may not be transmitted over its well-defended airwaves and cables. It is television's only solid, a tangible commodity that is precisely divisible into further and further subdivisible homogeneous units, the smallest quantum of which is measured by the smallest segment that could be purchased by a potential advertiser. This is itself defined by the minimum particle required to isolate a salable product from a variable number of equivalent choices. The smallest salable piece turns out to be the ten-second spot, and all television is assembled from it.

But the social conventions of television dictate a code of behavior according to which the transmitter must assume two apparently different roles in transmission. In one he must appear to address the viewer on the station's behalf as entertainer; in the other on the sponsor's behalf as salesman. The rules of the game, which are legally codified, prescribe a sharp demarcation between the roles, and the industry makes a great show of marking off the boundaries between its two types of performances—the programs and the commercials.

At their extremes of hard-sell and soft-show, one might suppose that the stylistic features of the two roles would be sufficient to distinguish them, but the extremes are rare, the social function of the roles not so distinct, and the stylistic features seldom provide sufficient separation. Since the industry's most tangible presentation is metrically divisible time, the industry seems to mark the separation emphatically by assigning the two roles different time signatures. The commercial is built on a scale of the minute out of multiple 10-second units. It comes in four common sizes—10, 30, 60, and 120 seconds—of which the 30-second slot is by far the commonest. The program is built on the scale of the hour out of truncated and hinged 15-minute units that are also commonly assembled in four sizes—15, 30, 60, and 120 minutes—of which the half-hour program is the commonest, though the hour length is usual for important programs, two hours quite frequent for specials and feature films, and 15 minutes not entirely a rarity for commentary.

Television inherited the split roles and the two time signatures from radio, as well as the habit of alternating them in regularly recurrent intervals, creating the arbitrary-appearing, mechanical segmentation of both media's presentations. But television carried this mechanical segmentation to a new extreme and presented it in such a novel way, through a special combination of its own peculiar technology and production conventions, that television time, in spite of structural similarity with radio time, has an entirely different appearance from it, bearing the relationship to radio time that an electronically driven, digital counter does to a spring-driven, hand-wound alarm clock. [. . .]

Because of the television industry's special aesthetic of time and the electronics industry's primary adaptation of the technology to the needs and desires of television, the appearance of an art-world video had to wait for the electronics industry to attempt to expand the market for its technology into special institutional and consumer domains. The basic tool kit of artists' video is the Portapak with its small, mobile camera and one-half-inch black and white videotape recorder that can accommodate nothing larger than 30-minute tapes. Put together with a small monitor and perhaps an additional microphone, the whole operation costs something in the vicinity of $2,000—a bit less than a cheap car and a bit more than a good stereo system.

This is the fundamental unit, but it allows no editing whatever. The most minimal editing—edge to edge assembling of tapes into units larger than 30 minutes— requires access to at least another videotape recorder with a built-in editing facility, which means at least the investment of another $1,200. This is a primitive editing capacity, but increases the unit cost by 50 percent to about $3,000.

Yet precision editing and smoothness are still out of the question. Unlike film, where editing is a scissors and paste job anyone can do with very little equipment, and where you can sit in a small room and shave pieces of film down to the half frame with no great difficulty, video pictures have to be edited electronically by assembling image sequences from some source or sources in the desired order on the tape of a second machine. The images are electronically marked off from each other by an electronic signal recurring (in the U.S.) 60 times a second. If you want to place one sequence of images right after another that you've already recorded onto the second tape, you have to join the front edge of the first new frame to the final edge of the other, which means that motors of both machines have to be synchronized to the sixtieth of a second and that there must be a way of reading off each frame edge to assure that the two recorded sequences are in phase with each other. Half-inch equipment is not designed to do this, and the alignment of frame edge with frame edge is a matter of accident.

Alignment of a particular frame edge with a particular frame edge is out of the question. If the frame edges don't come together the tape is marked by a characteristic momentary breakup or instability of the image. You may or may not mind this, but it's the distinctive mark of this type of editing. Since this is absolutely unlike television editing, it carries its special mark of "homemade" or "cheap" or "unfinicky" or "direct" or "honest." But the dominance of television esthetics over anything seen on a TV screen makes this rather casual punctuation mark very emphatic and loaded with either positive or negative value. An installation with synchronized, multiple cameras, with capabilities for switching through cutting, fading, and dissolving, and some few special effects like black and white reversal will cost somewhere in the $10,000 range, provided you stick to black and white and half-inch equipment. This is only a minor increase in editing control and a cost increase of one order of magnitude. If you want reliably smooth edits that will allow you to join predictably an edge to an edge, without specifying which edge, you will need access to an installation whose cost begins at around $100,000.[99]

One major art gallery has a reduced form of such a facility that permits this sort of editing, which costs about half that. Again we have an increase of control that is nearly minimal and a cost increase of another order of magnitude. Some artists have solved this problem by obtaining occasional access to institutions possessing this kind of installation, but usually this takes complete editing control out of the hands of most artists. There are also ways of adapting the one-inch system to precisionist frame-for-frame capacity, but that requires the investment of several thousand dollars more. A rule of thumb might specify that each increase in editing capacity represents an order of magnitude increase in cost.

Color is still another special problem. Though it is beset by difficulties, technical and economic, and though much color video is nearly senseless (viz. Sonnier's pointless color work), it is by now television's common form and has certain normative marks associated with it. To use black and white is a marked move, regardless of what the mark may be construed to mean. So, many artists will seek color for mere neutrality. But it comes at a price. There are bargain-basement color systems, wonderfully cheesy in appearance, but the most common system is the three-quarter-inch cassette ensemble, which together with camera, videotape recorder, and monitor goes at about $10,000. If the Portapak is the Volkswagen, this is the Porsche of individual artists' video. For editing control, the system of escalation in color runs parallel to black and white. The model of ultimate refinement and control is the television industry's two-inch system, and since that's what you see in action in any motel over the TV set, interesting or not, everyone takes it for the state of the art.

These conditions may not seem promising, but artists are as good at surviving as cockroaches, and they've developed three basic strategies for action. They can take the lack of technical refinements as a given and explore the theater of poverty. They can beg, borrow, or steal access to technical wealth and explore the ambiguous role of the poor relation, the unwelcome guest, the court jester, the sycophant, or the spy. This isn't a common solution. The studios don't make their facilities available so readily. But it includes works done by Allan Kaprow, Peter Campus, Les Levine, Nam June Paik, and numerous others. Artists can also raid the technology as a set of found objects or instruments with phenomenological implications in installation pieces. There are numerous examples from the work of Peter Campus, Dan Graham, Nam June Paik, Frank Gillette, etc.

To a great extent the significance of all types of video art derives from its stance with respect to some aspect of television, which is itself profoundly related to the present state of our culture. In this way video art embarks on a curiously mediated but serious critique of the culture. And this reference to television, and through it to the culture, is not dependent on whether or not the artist sees the work in relation to television. The relation between television and video is created by the shared technologies and conditions of viewing, in the same way the relation of movies to underground film is created by the shared conditions of cinema. Nevertheless, an artist may exploit the relation very knowingly and may choose any aspect of the relation for attack. [. . .]

What the artists constantly reevoke and engage is television's fundamental equivocation and mannerism, which may really be the distinctive feature of the medium. But they may do this from diametrically opposed angles, either by parodying the television system and providing some amazing bubble, or by offering to demonstrate how, with virtually no resources, they can do all the worthwhile things that television should do or could do in principle and has never yet done and never will do. [. . .]

From David Antin, "Television: Video's Frightful Parent," *Artforum* 14, no. 4 (December 1975), 36–45. The text was announced as "Part I," but a "Part II" never followed.

Notes

1 Frank Gillette, *Video: Process and Meta-Process* (Syracuse, NY: Everson Museum of Art, 1973), 21.

2 Hollis Frampton, "The Withering Away of the State of Art," *Artforum* 13, no. 4 (December 1974), 50.

3 Art is “producer-dominated” in much the same way that American industry is “producer-dominated,” in that it is not “consumer responsive.” There is an ensemble of “art people,” including a number of critics and dealers, who form each of the diverse “scenes” of the art world, of which there are a fair number. Each of these “scenes” produces art as a series of individual offerings the way a biological species produces novel individuals from its single gene pool out of the various interactions of its members. The kind of communication these “producers” have with whatever “public” they reach is essentially Darwinian, like the “communication” of a species with nature whose only communicative act is to extinguish those individuals who are not minimally fitted to survive in its niches.

4 Jud Yalkut, “TV as a Creative Medium at the Howard Wise Gallery,” *Arts Magazine*, September 1967, 21.

5 Edward Stasheff and Rudy Bretz, *The Television Program: Its Writing, Direction, and Production* (New York: A. A. Wyn, 1951), 8.

6 Bruce Boice, “Lynda Benglis at Paula Cooper Gallery,” *Artforum* 11, no. 9 (May 1973), 83.

7 Les Levine, “Excerpts from a Tape: ‘Artistic,’” *Art-Rite. Video* 7 (Autumn 1974), 27.

8 I understand the terms “interesting” and “uninteresting” to have no more psychological sense than a mathematician does who judges a theorem “interesting” when it reverberates significantly throughout the system or systems it applies to and “uninteresting” when its reverberation is trivial. On the other hand, I understand the term “boring” to have essentially a psychological significance and to refer to those presentations which are judged to have too few or too poorly marked features for the mind in its normal career to attend to, and “boredom” to refer to that sense of frustration felt when the effort of attending goes unrewarded. Certain advocates of ’60s art considered “boredom” a valuable transition state between two states of attention, an initial state in which the mind attended to what it expected but was not present, and a second state in which the mind attended to what was in fact there. Work which achieved this transition would have been considered “boring,” but hardly “uninteresting.”

9 These figures are necessarily approximate and depend on variations in marketing and the fluctuation of the dollar. At present there is a new three-quarter-inch facility capable of giving a clean frame-to-frame edit with an indeterminacy of about a third of a second that is going for about $25,000.

Talking Back to the Media (1985)

Dara Birnbaum

The use of television imagery began in my work with the first exhibition at Artists Space, NY, in 1977. That work was composed of 25 photographic images taken from prime-time TV and a super-8 film loop. However, it was at an exhibition at The Kitchen, NY, in 1978, that I first decided to use this "medium on itself," making a firm commitment not to translate the imagery into a different form or material. This became the approach for those works which followed (1978–1982); works which had in common the basic intentions of revealing the relationships existent within the medium of video/television and defining the industry of television as the root of video art independent of the traditional arts into this medium. In the 1960s and 1970s video largely had been developed as the extended vocabulary of painting, sculpture, and performance—completing its task through a necessary denial of the very origin and nature of video itself, TV. By the mid-seventies, I believed that by giving this medium back its institutional and historical base, new forms of artistic expression could be developed.

Much of the video work completed from 1978 to 1982 attempts to slow down the "technological speed" attributed to this medium; thus "arresting" moments of TV-time for the viewer. For it is the speed at which issues are absorbed and consumed by the medium of video/television, without examination and without self-questioning, which at present still remains astonishing. Earlier works mark direct reference to this "speed," as in *Technology/Transformation: Wonder Woman* (1978; Figure 5.4), when psychological needs are visually expressed as physical transformation—in a burst of blinding light. Or, as in the work *Kojak/Wang* (1980), where the needs of a young fugitive immediately trigger in Kojak a cool, nonhesitant response:

> *"No! No! . . . Listen, I did wrong . . . I'll take the blame for that. Just don't ask me to give you this name . . ."*
> *"I'm asking."*

The earlier works are all composed of TV-fragments; structured on the reconstructed conventions of television. I see them as new "ready mades" for the late twentieth century—composed of dislocated visuals and altered syntax; images cut from their original narrative flow and countered with additional musical text. It was my desire that the viewer be caught in a limbo of alternation where she/he would be able to plunge headlong into the very *experience* of TV.

There is a cohesive effort throughout these works to establish the possibilities of manipulating a medium already known to be highly manipulative. I had wanted to establish, and set as a representative model (before the onslaught of media by-products for the home), the ability to explore the possibilities of a two-way system of communication—a "talking back" to the media.

Figure 5.4 Dara Birnbaum, *Technology/Transformation: Wonder Woman*, 1978, video, color, 5:50 min. Courtesy of Electronic Arts Intermix (EAI), New York.

The growing network of video distribution in the 1970s made working with and within this medium all the more tempting; a new map with points of "access" to a public previously uncharted within our designation of "art audience." A new parameter emerged: could this new accessibility allow for a critical stance and new perspectives which challenge the dominant form? By 1985, the growing distribution of "software," matched with a growing industry of consumer hardware, changed the accessibility of "media imagery" for the public. In order for me to produce my first videowork, *(A) Drift of Politics (comprised of TV imagery from the popular show, Laverne & Shirley)* (1978), its appropriated material had to be obtained by "having friends of the inside." Source material was gathered late at night in commercial studios through friends, or through sympathetic producers of local cable TV. Whereas in 1985, all it might take to gather "off-air" imagery, for works similar in nature, would be a simple phone call to a friend with a home video recorder (VCR). If that person is not out, running to their local video distribution store to rent yet another overnight video-movie (for as little as $1.95), they will most likely record the program for you. In addition, alternative spaces to view the "software" of the new technology were spreading in all directions—from the home arena of large-screen projection to video game arcades and new societies of rock clubs to other large-crowd "spectacles," such as baseball and other sports. In 1978 it had been nearly impossible for me to have direct access to television's imagery; in 1985 it is nearly impossible for me not to have that access.

I view my last two years of production as being initiated and carried through much in the same way as the earlier "appropriated works" of 1978–1982. The gathered footage (now from life and not television) is, as with the earlier material, subjected to minute examination—opening its composition and revealing its hidden agendas. Editing is still a highly refined process revealing the subtlest gestures—whether they be from the opening shot of a nearly-forgotten star in *Hollywood Squares (Kiss The Girls: Make Them Cry*, 1979), or a teenager in the streets of NYC (*Damnation of Faust: Evocation*, 1983). For endemic in both "characters" are the forms of restraint and near suffocation imposed through this current technological society; pressures which force a person to find the means of openly declaring, through communicated gestures, their own identity. These "looks," produced in part by mass media, require us to maintain the ability to scrutinize those projected and communicated images surrounding us. This necessity furthers itself everyday in a world which is bound by its technology—seemingly rational yet simultaneously giving rise to its irrational underside. For me, all the works completed from 1978 to 1985 are "altered states" causing the viewer to reexamine those "looks" which on the surface seem so banal that even the supernatural transformation of a secretary into a "wonder woman" is reduced to a burst of blinding light and a turn of the body—a child's play of rhythmical devices inserted within the morose belligerence of the fodder that is our average daily television diet. I consider it to be our responsibility to become increasingly aware of alternative perspectives which can be achieved through our use of media—and to consciously find the ability for expression of the "individual voice"—whether it be dissension, affirmation, or neutrality (rather than a deletion of the issues and numbness, due to the constant "bombardment," which this medium can all too easily maintain.) In the 1970s it seemed best to approach this task by directly appropriating imagery from the mass media—imagery which had made itself unavailable for redirected use within the public's domain while still being allowed to issue itself at that public. In the 1980s, I feel that it is a better strategy to openly reengage the issue of possible new forms of representation, image, and meaning through our own use of the tools and by-products of the industry. We could approach these tools as possible "folk instruments," creating works which would allow new issues to surface and engaging in a practice which could reveal new "views and values"—while created through a dominant language and form.

From Dara Birnbaum, *Talking Back to the Media* (Amsterdam: Stichting Amsterdam, 1985), 46–9.

[Portable Video] (1995)

John Thornton Caldwell

Live-Remote and Videotaped Interventions

Tape is everywhere, and everyone seems conscious of its presence. For all those who thought that television was defined by the flow, think again. Increasingly, television has come to be associated more with something you can hold, push into an appliance, and physically move around with a controller. With the widespread dissemination of the tape and the VCR, the very status of the television and its image has been altered. Not only has the conceptual frame through which we view television changed, but the relationship between the public and private spheres that characterized television vis à vis the world in the past has been altered. [. . .] First, in what ways does television's current flaunting of videotape as a material object relate to a simultaneous historical trend evident since the early 1980s, that is, to television's increasing penchant for stylistic excess? Second, in what ways does this stylistic exhibitionism, centered around videotape, change the idealized terms of the viewer-television relationship? Television, since 1980, has hailed the viewer differently, and its technological mode of production is partly to blame. Participation is as much on the minds of broadcasters as it is on the minds of academics and oppositional producers. Given this, how can viewers engage television's participatory fantasies in constructive or subversive ways?

Three Generations of the Revolution

[. . .] For guerrilla video activists and video artists in the 1960s, tape was the means by which a movement of individuals could wrest control of the dominant media or at least sabotage its mindless workings with alternative imagery. Finally [being] able to control the means of production also meant changing the terms of the relationship between the mass and the personal. [. . .]

Yet a persuasive enough model for the use of tape had not been developed effectively enough to insure that video's *portable* forms would be adopted by broadcasters in the late 1960s. In short, although the scientific competence and working prototypes were available during that time, no persuasive or dominant intellectual paradigm existed in broadcasting to force the widespread use or adoption of small-format portable tape.

Unless half-inch alternative tapes were particularly sensational, broadcasters simply refused to air them or to emulate their methods.[1] The conceptual framing paradigm necessary for historical change was not in place. Broadcasters typically rejected small-format tapes on the basis of two recurrent myths: they were either not technically up to broadcast standards, or they were not in the public interest. Both claims were clearly problematic and somewhat duplicitous.[2] The tapes, for example, could be electronically modified and enhanced for broadcast, and many tapes had clear public and social motivations. As arbiters of fairness, however, broadcasters acted according to their own definition of the public good. They also simultaneously upheld what David Bordwell, Kristin Thompson, and Janet Staiger consider to be one of the three explanations for technological and stylistic change in classical Hollywood: the industry's "adherence to standards of quality."[3] Such an ideal is also a business strategy that grows out of a broader ideology of progress. Standards of technical quality then, according to these theorists, also function to maximize corporate profits.

Why was this new technology, the model of portable videotape, not enthusiastically embraced by the industry? Television economists describe those various forces that affect and encourage the adoption of new technologies as externalities. Positive externalities include such forces as increasing economies of scale, the timing of introduction, and the number of users.[4] At this point in history, there was really no financial incentive for television to shift to the new technology. [. . .] Half-inch videotape was not rejected simply because the broadcasters were conservative capitalists, although that designation may indeed have been accurate. Rather, there was simply no positive externality in place to encourage the kind of portability that came with tape. Film was proving more than adequate for news, and television had settled on a very viable alternative to portable tape, the live hookup. [. . .]

Mechanized Extensions of the Camera Eye

[. . .] Portable videotape was not just a discovery or invention—it was a different way of making and conceptualizing television. It was also an institutional threat in that it undercut the kinds of commitments that the industry had already made—commitments to expensive pedestal cameras, to microwave technologies, satellite hookups, and to a highly specialized labor system that worked as a clear extension of the studio, not as an alternative to it. Videotape's nemesis during its first two failed generations was the live, multicamera remote. The remote was a production mode that gave the audience the liveness that historians claim was at the center of broadcasting from the start. Remotes also seemed able to transform even mundane events coverage into memorable spectacles. The remote mode came replete with a wide range of multiple visual perspectives, an array of keyed graphics and image-text combinations, and—unlike portable tape—*immediate editorial interpretations*. Better yet, the remote's overwhelming technology brought to situations and events a highly visible and physical presence that simultaneously allowed broadcasters to cover the event and perform in it. [. . .]

Television legitimized and promoted itself with remotes in a number of important ways. First, the pedestal, tripod, or vehicle-mounted cameras became literal extensions of a central studio, roving but disembodied eyes of the producers. This was Michel Foucault's "panopticon" in its finest form.[5] The multicamera configuration, with microwave or cable hookups for simultaneous feeds, kept the editorial power to select and sequence imagery in the hands of a very few. [. . .]

The choice and dominance of the remote over tape in the 1970s exemplifies what Bordwell, Thompson, and Staiger describe as "trended change."[6] Unlike portable tape, the remote was not a threat to the broadcaster's status quo. The live remote allowed television significant continuities, rather than discontinuities. Production style, management structure, and labor all could remain essentially the same. Broadcasters also underscored their own legitimacy and technological prowess by emphasizing the remote. No matter how infinite and spread-out the eyes of the remote paradigm may have seemed, television used the mode to centralize power and reduce diversity. [. . .]

Cultural Capital as a Supervening Necessity

While this notion of the live remote as trended change explains how portable tape remained underutilized in broadcast television through the 1970s, it does not account for why the remote paradigm eventually gave way to the portable tape paradigm in the 1980s. The current preoccupation with videotape cannot be tied to one single cause. A range of factors, economic, technological, and conceptual, have converged to make tape a favored mode of production and reception in recent years. Not the least of these factors was the growth of what sociologist Pierre Bourdieu would describe as "cultural capital"—an aesthetic and experiential knowledge of the looks and possibilities of the television image.[7] Tape became an apt symbol for two driving factors in what academics have termed postmodernism: consumption and cultural distinction.

Tape teaches consumption. By 1986 more dollars were made by feature film producers through video and television than through theatrical exhibition. More often than not people experience film only as video. Tape is what one typically watches when one watches "film." Furthermore, starting in 1980, CNN and others began teaching audiences about the endless possibilities of tape. Disasters like the space shuttle Challenger explosion were played like endless möbius strips. Such tapes were perpetually redefined when broadcasters encrusted the footage with graphic subtitles, boxes, dates, names. The same thing happened with other newsworthy disasters. The home video shot by tourists during the San Francisco earthquake in 1989, and George Holliday Rodney King beating footage in 1991, both lived extensive global lives as tape-based news events. Broadcasters even cloned populist production organizations like CNN's Newshounds, which were really thinly veiled bottom line, national surveillance projects that made semiofficial networks out of camcorder-toting citizens. The camcorder became the inexpensive farm system for cost-conscious major league broadcasters.

The music video genre was also instrumental in preparing the conceptual ground for a new kind of audience consciousness and format. It did so in two ways. From the start, the jukebox approach of sequencing videos on MTV did much to characterize the genre as a collection of individual units or objects. First, the fact that you could also buy these videotape-objects at music and record stores underscored the artifactual nature of the video. As video, television was being conceptualized differently. Second, videotaped footage became an almost obligatory element in the collage style that came to be known as music video. Even though such works were invariably shot on film, this footage announced itself as video—by its scan lines, pixels, and/or electronic artifacts. The self-reflexivity of most music videos also taught the viewer-fan the role that video played in the production process. The apparatus that produced tape was frequently the content of the video. Music videos, therefore, were simultaneously: 1) primers of production method, 2) products of videotape, and 3) consumer operations that caused and dispersed ancillary videotape forms. Everyone could do it, or so some ads suggested. Radio stations in Los Angeles ran promotional campaigns asking fans to submit their own music video interpretations of hit songs, that is, their own independent home-video productions, in order to win tickets to concerts during which the winning videos would be played.[8] Consumers were now, apparently, well aware of videotape as a production element. Videotape was something that they could both consume and produce. [. . .]

The "Successful" Video Revolution

[. . .] Although the very idea of picking up a camera and VCR as a weapon has always played a part in alternative media, mass market television, at least in the home video genre, does not ostensibly resist such interventions. Instead, it appropriates resistant modes by adopting and overdetermining those same activities. In this case the audience and the private home are highly articulated, codified, and interactive parts of the program. ABC encourages and rewards the consumer revolution. Even as the higher and more cinematic televisual modes stroke niche individualism, the earlier primetime home video shows resurrect television's historic domestic ideology in order to overhaul and sedate the oppositional potential implicit in decentralized portability. By doing this, the producers suggest that they are somehow on the outside even as they quietly structure and secure for themselves a position of insider privilege. [. . .]

In the first video revolution, television controlled the definition of portable tape by avoiding it. By investing in an alternative paradigm, the live remote, television ignored both the era of digital sound an HDTV, on the other hand, the dominant industry *immediately* announces and defines for the audience the logical uses for its new technologies, through stylish teaching and handholding operations on and off primetime. The supervening necessity and logic for a technology now come prepackaged with the technology.

Complicating matters further still is the fact that the very question of radicality has been transformed into a marketing strategy. Oppositionality is here but a shifting sign, whose connection to actual social practice or audience power is clearly arbitrary. Modes of viewing are not simply things that technology does to us or causes. Nor does television change when new alternatives are available. Rather, television seems to change, but only on its own terms. *The question of audience can no longer be isolated from the issue of television's industrial base, since television now creates and sanctions specific rituals for viewers, ones inextricably tied to new video production and home entertainment technologies.* In the case of portable video in the 1980s, there were both aesthetic and economic benefits to showcasing videotaped footage. On one level, the process embraced and hailed the new audience as active and free-thinking, even as it reduced practical politics and oppositional activity to mere semiotics, to questions of style and lifestyle.

From the chapter "Televisual Audience" in John Thornton Caldwell, *Televisuality: Style, Crisis, and Authority in American Television* (New Brunswick, NJ: Rutgers University Press, 1995), 262–83.

Notes

1 When independent tapes offered private looks at sensational or inaccessible figures the networks *would* find a way to air the tapes. A half-inch tape on radical Abbie Hoffman, for example, was aired by CBS news.
2 The development of the first generation of time-base correctors allowed engineers to correct the skew and timing errors caused by imperfections in small format half-inch videotape recorders. These TBCs essentially squared up the blanked ends of each scanning line in the frame in order for taped footage to meet FCC requirements.
3 David Bordwell et al., *Classical Hollywood Cinema* (New York: Columbia University Press, 1985), 251–60.
4 Bruce Owen and Steven Wildman, *Video Economics* (Cambridge, MA: Harvard University Press, 1992), 266–75.
5 Michel Foucault, *Discipline and Punish* (New York: Vintage, 1979).
6 Bordwell, *Classical Hollywood Cinema*, 247f.
7 Pierre Bourdieu, *Distinction: A Social Critique of the Judgement of Taste* (Cambridge, MA: Harvard University Press, 1984).
8 KROQ, a Los Angeles area radio station, ran this campaign for fan participation in U2's national tour, fall 1992.

[The Videographic] (2002)

John Ellis

[. . .] In the 1980s, television found a crucial new ally in its evolution as a forum for working through current concerns and contemporary meanings. It adapted the new technologies of digital image manipulation to the task. These allowed television to take advantage of the flat quality of its images, rather than to be hampered by it. Digital image technologies allow television to treat its images as pictures that can be manipulated in an electronic space, rather than as photographic images which reduplicate three-dimensional spaces. Television viewers are now familiar with images that spin towards them from, as it were, the back of the television screen, with titles and logos that appear to be emerging out of the screen. This is the small change of digital image manipulation, the ability to take television pictures and move them around within an artificial depth that can be conjured from the screen itself.

In this, television's use of the technology contrasts strongly with that of the cinema. Cinema uses digital image technologies to simulate realities and extend the range of its illusionism. The film industry has gleefully morphed characters ever since *Terminator 2*, and created entirely non-existent moving creatures in Jurassic Park, as well as adding the technologies to the existing arsenals of special effects to create ever more thrilling and convincing scenes of jeopardy. In filmmaking, the technologies of digital image manipulation and computer-generated effects are usually used in combination with other processes, like animatronics. The creators of these hybrid "special effects" have become stars in their own right, and "how they did it" has become one of the marketing pitches of mega-budget films. In cinema, these technologies are used for essentially illusionistic purposes. Nothing, apart from the passage of time and the expectations of audiences, separates them from Melìès's men on the moon or Frederic March's metamorphosis from Dr Jekyll to Mr Hyde in Rouben Mamoulian's film of 1932. Cinema remains a photographic medium, dedicated to the construction and reproduction of three-dimensional space upon a screen. Television has scarcely ventured down this track since the days when blue-screen shooting allowed the marriage of people in a studio with background footage from the image banks of the world. Instead, as John Caldwell has persuasively argued, it has taken its images in a different direction. Television uses images as the raw material for a process of work, transmuting, combining, changing, and layering them in a way that can only be described as graphic. While cinema remains triumphantly photographic, television has found itself as a graphic medium.

Digital image technologies have, since their popularization in the industry at the beginning of the 1980s, treated the television image as a transmutable object. The pace of technological change has been fast, but the take-up of the techniques and their acceptance by audiences have been faster. For television had always harbored graphics in its everyday routines: television was a medium of writing as well as picture, far more than cinema. From the beginnings of television, it was felt necessary to identify speakers in order to place their utterances in a social context of class, power, and knowledge. Chest captions gave names and social status, telling us that we were seeing and hearing the representatives of organizations or people speaking in their private capacity. The use of superimposed captions is such a long-established and unobtrusive television technique that it is hardly ever remarked upon in critical studies. Similarly, the limited vocabulary of the live mixing desk provides forms of dissolve between camera signals that could, if desired, be very prolonged indeed. So captions and image mixing, along with the use of graphics in advertising, all established fertile ground for audience acceptance of digital image manipulation. We are now used to ghostly slow-motion effects worked upon video footage that were out of reach until the beginning of the 1990s. We see step motion and think nothing of it. We take morphing in our stride when we see it on title sequences. We expect logos and cleverly formatted program captions on even the cheapest of studio-based talk shows. We see images that mold themselves to the shape of a human face or body and do not bother to ask how much computing power went into making this possible. The change has been unnoticed and pervasive, as though it were already expected. [. . .]

This curious effect of electronic image combination became more pronounced as designers, editors, producers, directors, and technicians began to explore the possibilities of combining transparent layers of video images. Once limited by the number of tape sources that could be input at any one time, the layering of images has taken on a new complexity since digital storage allowed a large number of images to be held simultaneously. Now multiple layers of imagery can be laid on top of each other in transparent layers, so that the furthest away can be seen through the nearer layers. Again, this does not necessarily create the impression of a three-dimensional space in which these images are "hung," like the receding planes of a Disney animation of the 1940s (when this was literally the technique that was used). Instead, the effect is more conceptual than illusionistic. As Caldwell points out perceptively, "transparent layering suggests a hierarchy of image levels relative to the distance the image components are to the viewer: deep layers seem farther; shallow ones seem closer. The tactic, then, creates a sense of depth less from illusionism than from aerial proximity and atmosphere."[11] The key term here is "hierarchy." The images gain in importance the closer they are to the viewer. In the classic title sequence use of the layering effect, actions take place in the background layers, while in the foreground we see the close-up, emoting faces of the principal performers, whose names are superimposed in a custom-designed graphic style. The person and the emotion are the key elements, the ones we have come to experience. The situations are their trigger. Title sequences are just one example of the effect of layering images. News providers invested heavily in the new real-time digital image manipulation technologies in the mid-1980s, and news changed as a result of using their possibilities. The effects quickly spread out into other studio-based programs and thence into factual programs in general. The documentary form, as usual, tended to refuse the new techniques as a way of proving the authenticity of its images. [. . .]

The distinguishing feature of the modern news editor, the state-of-the-art factual program-maker and the successful magazine program editor is their willingness to use such techniques, and their ability to render them unobtrusive. It is now easy to display simultaneous events together so that their concurrent, yet separate, nature is emphasized. Cause can be piled up on effect. Images can summarize a complex situation into an elegant sequence of graphicized images and writing. Whole situations can be encapsulated into maps, diagrams, punning graphics, and borrowed emblems. Graphic television offers its fragments of images as in some way typical. The frozen image of a refugee is treated to make a high-contrast background to a list of bullet points on the news; slow-motion bleached-out images of holidaymakers provide a background for specific images on the program menu of a travel show. These are summarizing images, encapsulating experiences or ideas for a grazing audience. [. . .]

Graphics are used to summarize, and assemble within one frame or within a short sequence, providing layers of information in one frame, compressing material into a single but fractured space. They are designed to attract attention and to provide an instant overview. They seem to suit a glance-like mode of attention which is all that television can assume of its audiences.

Graphic television is therefore the visual counterpart of the largely verbal explanations that jostle for attention as television processes the raw data of reality. Many would (and do) argue that this makes TV somehow inherently "post-modernist," that it simply treats everything as a picture that can be stuck any old how in the album that is the postmodern world: an album that has no end, no index, no structure, no overall meaning and value. But the videographic consists of a constant placing of images in ever new relations. Equivalences are produced by putting two images of the same size in one frame; a sense of hierarchy by placing two of different sizes in one frame. The layering of images implies, depending on its specific use, spatial relationships, a hierarchy, or a relationship based on time. The videographic is not a post-modern soup of meaning. It is a crucial part of television's constant, even neurotic, attempt to place, classify, relate, give a semblance of order and generic meaning to the images that TV generates from the world and from itself. Graphics are another form of editing, of creating relations between material-in-images. This is the very opposite of a post-modern aesthetic, as it aches with the desire to create meaning and to measure one form of understanding against another. Rather the videographic is a working over, placing, and processing of the witnessed fragments of the real. It is part of an explicit process of speculation, labeling, classification, reclassification, filing, placing, and defining. It treats the televisual image as a manipulable object rather than as a picture of something. Through digital image manipulation, television has come of age as a visual medium. No longer tied to its mimetic base, it uses this base—the process of witness—as a springboard for ambitious yet routine graphic recombinations of meanings and frameworks of understanding. A crucial part of television's working through is undertaken in a purely visual way. Central to the creation of a new television environment, where working through has replaced the definitive statement, is the electronic recasting of the television image itself.

From the chapter "Working Through and the Videographic" in John Ellis, *Seeing Things: Television in the Age of Uncertainty* (London and New York: I. B. Tauris Publishers, 2002), 91–101.

Note

1 John T. Caldwell, *Televisuality: Style, Crisis, and Authority in American Television* (Piscataway, NJ: Rutgers University Press, 1995), 148.

6

Video | Sound and Synthesis

Introduction by Jan Thoben

Like sound film, video synchronizes and stores images and sounds. In contrast to the chemical-optical film image, however, the electronic image can be transmitted instantaneously and generates in this capacity a simultaneity of transmission and reception. Previously, electric transmission of this nature was limited to acoustic media, namely telephone and radio. Indeed, as described in the following, video is fundamentally related to sound. As Wolfgang Ernst underlines in his book *Sonic Time Machines*, an immanent connection to sound already exists on the level of the video image's electronic signal: "Different from the cinematographic image, the classical electronic TV image is closer to sound. . . . The auditive is thus *immanent* to the electronic image."[1] This chapter will examine this auditory aspect of the electronic image in greater detail.

The Temporal Constitution of the Video Image: Line Scanning and Signal

Friedrich Kittler described the basic functions of technical media as a triad of transmission, storage, and processing.[2] Transmission and storage, that is, recording and playback, are known to be functions of the video camera and the video recorder. However, strictly speaking, video already exists without these peripheral devices and can be sufficiently described at the level of electronic signal processing. Video images—as laid out in Chapter 2—should not be understood as two-dimensional surfaces, like the stationary photograms of analog film, but rather as being continually scanned, line by line. This line-scanning process takes place successively over a discrete period of time, making video a time-critical medium.[3]

Whereas in the case of film time evokes virtual movements by means of the succession of single still images, with video the image itself is already virtual and temporally constituted. Even a still video image is thus always also a moving image: "The basic illusion of film is motion. The basic illusion of video is stillness."[4] While the photographic film frame also exists independently of the film projector, the existence of the video image relies on the electron currents in the circuits. The scanning and information processing of images, first conceived by Paul Nipkow in 1883, allows two-dimensional surfaces to be transformed into one-dimensional time signals and transmitted electronically via cable, antenna, or satellite receivers.[5]

Complex signal processing is thus the basic requirement for every image flickering on the video screen. Television and video images owe their existence to the technological process of line scanning, in which coordinated synchronization signals scan and construct the image line by line. The analog cathode ray tube achieves this by guiding a point of light at great speed, line by line, across the screen, bombarding the phosphorous-coated surface with electrons. The electron beam leaves the phosphorous atoms in a higher state of quantum-physical excitement and, during the change in and out of this state, they emit light—known in technical terms as fluorescence and phosphorescence.[6] Once the cathode ray has scanned a line and, on its way, caused the corresponding points of the screen to glow, the emission of electrons is briefly interrupted by a horizontal synchronization signal and reset back to the beginning of the next line. At the end of an image scanned in this way, the vertical synchronization signal sets the ray back to its starting position and the scanning process for the next image begins. To reduce flickering at the lowest possible signal bandwidth, television engineers developed interlacing, in which the video image is composed out of odd and even fields (see Figure 6.1 and the illustrations to Barbara Buckner's text in Figure 6.8).

For the television standards developed in Germany (PAL), France (Secam), and the United States (NTSC), different refresh rates were chosen and adapted to the respective network frequencies of the countries' alternating current grids.[7] Nipkow was already confronted with the synchronization problem of image transmission, in that he wanted to run television senders and receivers via synchronous motors fed by one and the same AC network. In modern television studios, the role of a central timer is taken up by a master sync generator to which all video devices are connected (in a process known as generator locking or genlock), for example, while mixing different video sources. This technically necessary connection to a timer syncing up the machinery in video studios illustrates even more clearly the radical time dependence of the electronic image. In this respect, the analog video image can be specified in terms of

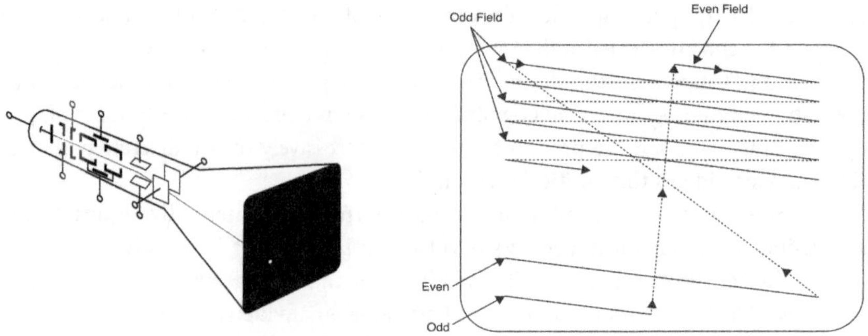

Figure 6.1 Cathode ray tube and interlaced line scanning.

frequencies. A few of the characteristic time dimensions for analog video are presented in the following table:

	PAL	NTSC
Refresh rate/frame rate (full videoframe = two interlaced fields)	25 Hz	30/1001 Hz (29.97 Hz)[8]
Field rate	50 Hz	59.94 Hz
Line rate (vertical resolution)	15625 Hz (625 scanlines × 25 frames)	15734 Hz (525 scanlines × 30/1001 Hz frames)

The following graphic depicts the voltage characteristics of a scanline using the example of a simple black-and-white composite video waveform. The first negative pulse of the signal represents the synchronization signal, which is responsible for resetting the cathode ray at the beginning of each scan line (retracing). This is followed by the so-called back porch, which attenuates transients that occur because of the rapid horizontal retrace (Figure 6.2).

As an example of the contents of a single scanline, the graphic depicts a four-part grayscale (with the voltage levels climbing in accordance with the increasing luminance of the picture), meaning four vertical bars would be visible. Depending on the standard, a video image is composed of 525 (NTSC) or 625 (PAL) such scanlines. Video, as a processual, cybernetic image machine with its precisely synchronized time sequences, subverts the temporal resolution of human perception to create an image impression. Brice Howard, director of the National Center for Experiments in Television (NCET) in San Francisco, summed up this time-critical logic of the video medium in his programmatic 1972 essay *Video Space* as follows:

> The material of the medium is an electron. Its mass is 1/1835th the mass of a hydrogen atom. Though it moves so swiftly it cannot be perceived by the eyes of

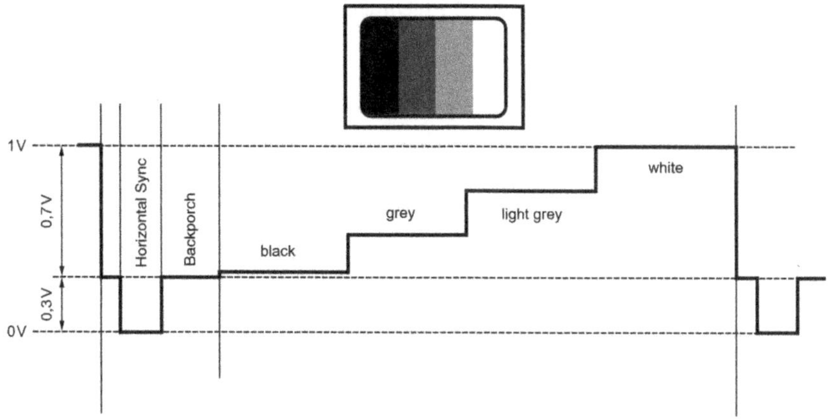

Figure 6.2 Composite video waveform.

> man, it is finite. Its effects can be studied upon the surface graphs of oscilloscopes. And these effects are seen as sine curves and wave forms. Synchronization, amplitude, amplification, and modulation are what electronic circuitry is mainly about. It's also about storage and delay. But mostly, it's all about time.[9]

The inertia of visual perception alone makes this process appear as a coherent image in two dimensions. As such, human perception is just as constituent to these image processes as the mechanical signal processing itself. The temporality of the electronic signal proceeds subliminally here, below the threshold of perception, while images appear above this threshold, as Hollis Frampton emphasizes: "Strictly speaking, there is no instant of time during which the video image may properly be said to 'exist.' . . . [E]ach video frame represents a brief summation within the eye of the beholder."[10]

As became clear in Chapter 2 by way of Lazzarato's video-theoretical considerations and with reference to Bergson's theory of perception, the video image proves itself a kind of instantaneous simulated image.[11] It transmits movement already fragmented in time and thus undermines the concept of the mimetic image carrier. Video reaches the human eye not as a two-dimensional image but as a continuous signal flow. This flow does not convey images but rather visual processes. The temporality of these processes forms, according to Lazzarato, a structural analogy to the time-based synthetic functions of visual perception as Bergson analyzed them. This image—cut up into lines and continuously assembled anew by unceasing line scanning, perpetually written and overwritten on the monitor—forms the processual paradigm of electronic image cultures. Accordingly, in her lecture from 1978 reprinted in this chapter, Barbara Buckner speaks of the "built-in cyclic nature" of the electronic image.[12]

It becomes clear against this backdrop that the very existence of the video image fundamentally rests on the medial function of continuous processing. This immanent processing of the video image is antecedent to the artistic process, as Bill Viola stresses. He calls attention to the fact that, unlike filmmakers, video artists are not necessarily dependent on visual recordings but can rather reach straight for the electronic material in activated circuits: "You don't need a recorder to have video. You turn it on, and the circuits are all activated—it's humming, it's going. . . . It gave me a sense that the electronic signal was a material that could be worked with."[13] Similarly, Stephen Beck characterizes his work with the video synthesizer less as image making than as a physical manipulation of already existing material: "For me the direct video synthesizer functions not as something artificial, as the term 'synthetic' has come to connote, but as a compositional device which 'sculpts' electronic current in the hands of an artisan."[14]

Video as Audiovisual Medium

The sculptural or compositional interaction with the electronic video signal described above stands in methodological proximity to the artistic practice of electronic sound mixing and editing. Viola thus recommends:

> Now I always advise my students to take a class in electronic music, because a lot of video technology was predated by electronic music technology. . . . When electronic energies finally became concrete for me, like sounds are to a composer, I really began to learn. . . . Soon I made what was for me an easy switch over to video. I never thought about it in terms of images so much as electronic processes, a signal.[15]

Viola also asserts that the video camera is less comparable to the still camera or film camera than it is to the microphone.[16] His text *The Sound of One-Line Scanning* includes a comprehensive reflection specifically on these relationships. The decisive point for Viola is that video can be understood as an oscillation system: "The video image is a standing wave pattern of electrical energy, a vibrating system composed of specific frequencies as one would expect to find in any resonating object. . . . Musically speaking, the physics of a broadcast is a type of drone."[17]

Media scholar Yvonne Spielmann also calls attention to the specific audiovisuality of the video medium. For example, signals generated by an audio synthesizer can be displayed on a video screen and, conversely, video signals in certain frequency ranges can be made audible via amplifiers and loudspeakers: "Because of this general interchangeability of audio and video in both directions, it is appropriate to call video the first *audiovisual medium*."[18] In the artistic context, she claims, it finds expression as the signal-based reciprocity of hearing and seeing. Among the video artists who reflect on video as an explicitly audiovisual medium, Nam June Paik, Gary Hill, and Steina Vasulka are particularly notable.

The preparation of sound-modulated cathode ray tubes provided Paik with a means of exploring indeterminist models of image creation: "To determine electronic movement is a contradiction in itself," he wrote in a 1963 text accompanying his *Exposition of Music*. Guiding his early television experiments was the notion "that an electronic image which is to be created productively (not reproductively) has to be defined in a way as non-deterministic."[19] Paik understood video as a consistent further development and reinvention of indeterministic procedures already tested in experimental music: "In most indeterminate music, the composer gives the possibility for the indeterminacy or the freedom to the interpreter, but not to the audience," Paik wrote. "I wanted to let the audience . . . act and play by itself. So I have resigned the performance of music. I expose the music."[20] One of the many artistic solutions Paik used to put his programmatic declaration of intent into practice is *Participation TV* (1963–6). Here, microphone signals modulate sinusoidal control voltages that deflect the cathode ray in the monitor tube. Acoustic processes write themselves, as it were, into the video image. The audio signal is situated in the electronic image like a parasite that dynamically distorts and modulates the picture plane. While enabling a reflexivity of the medium, this parasitic and uncontrolled audiovisuality is nevertheless experienced as an aesthetic serendipity.

In his 1964 *Afterlude to the Exposition of Experimental Television*, Paik commented on the increasing parameterization of musical material by the Cologne School of electronic music. He considered compositional control that was extended to the smallest technically manageable musical structures to be a fetishization of the Platonic-Hegelian idea. According to Paik, this approach conceptualizes technology instrumentally as the *telos* of compositional vision. With his experimental television, on the other hand, he arrived at results that were in no way foreseeable. This then led him to the laconic remark that his "experimental TV is not always interesting but not always uninteresting."[21]

The musical variability of the video image accordingly was the principal idea for Paik's conception of a video synthesizer in 1969 (Figure 6.6). A black-and-white video image was to be transmitted onto eight monitors, manipulated at various levels both electronically and optically, and—with the help of eight cameras, a keyboard-controlled video switcher, and a color encoder—synthesized into a color video image. Following this principle, Paik's video synthesizer, later realized in cooperation with electronics engineer Shuya Abe, represented a combination of colorizer and scan manipulator. In the tradition of the color organ, Paik developed the idea of controlling video using a Hammond organ or a Moog synthesizer.

From 1970 to 1978, Steina Vasulka developed *Violin Power* (Figure 6.3), a video work in which the trained violinist used her musical instrument for image manipulation. Recorded by a microphone, the sound of the violin was fed into a frequency shifter, scan processor and a multikeyer, which in turn interfered with the instantaneous self-image of the artist, at whose performance the camera was pointed. In varying the narcissistic model of the self-image, Vasulka destabilized the medium's mirror function musically liquefying the video image, thus provoking a "dissolution of the identity through sound waves," as Jean Gagnon aptly commented.[22]

Gary Hill thematized the video-specific transformativity between image and sound in his 1979 work *Soundings*.[23] Video circuits by Dave Jones, which at the time of *Soundings*' conception were still in part prototypes that the two had soldered themselves, subjected the video signal to various modulations, controlled in turn by Serge audio modules.[24] Hill then used the technique of the voice-over to make a reflexive gesture: "My voice is heard 'processed' by each action, reciting a particular passage that, reflexively, refers to the specific material/action being carried out."[25] The inscription of the voice-over into the video image in *Soundings* also found its conceptual correspondence on the level of the image content, as the camera image of a loudspeaker transmitting Hill's voice was modulated and also manipulated by the hand of the artist. In *Soundings*, Hill thus staged analogies to the vibrating movement of the electronic image on different levels: as acoustic tactility of the loudspeaker membrane, as performative modulation effect of the synthesizer, and finally as linguistic gesture, very much in keeping with his notion of speech as a correlate of an electronic linguistics.[26]

Video Synthesis and Image Processing

As becomes apparent in the examples of Paik, Vasulka, and Hill, the technical development and artistic exploration of the video medium often went hand in hand, particularly in the 1960s and 1970s. Often engineers, circuit builders, and developers such as Shuya Abe, Bill Etra, or Dave Jones worked side by side with artists in a synergetic collaboration

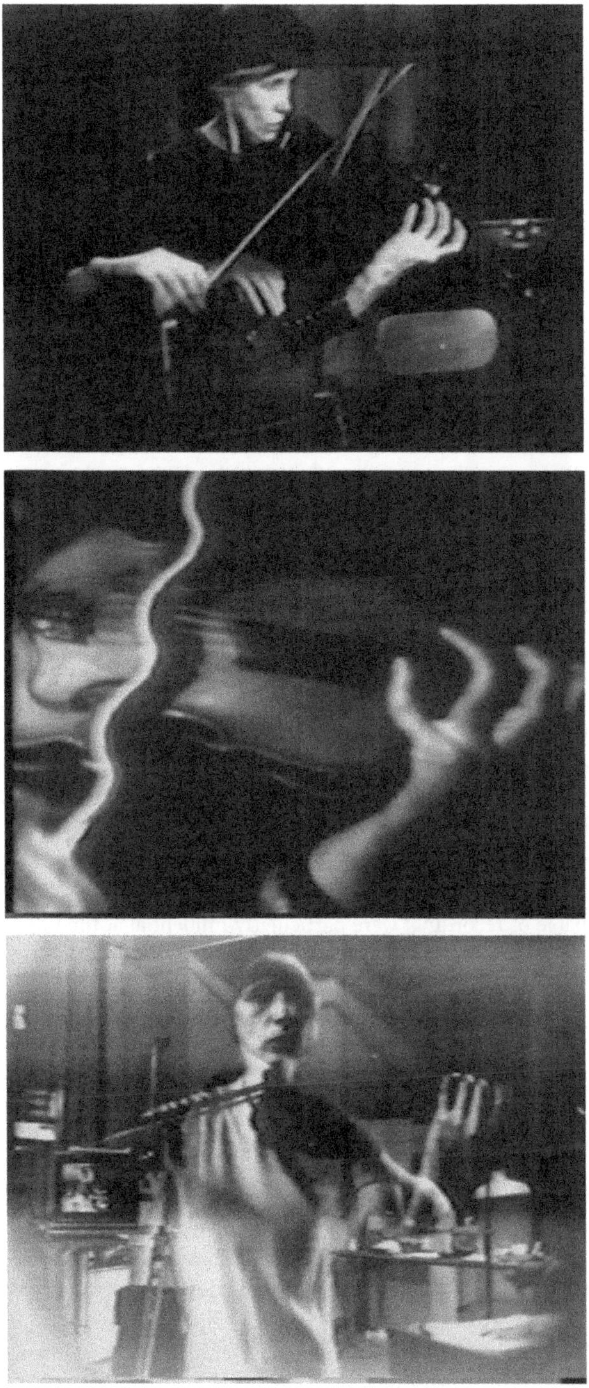

Figure 6.3 Steina Vasulka, *Violin Power*, 1978, video, black and white, 9:53 min. Courtesy of Electronic Arts Intermix (EAI), New York.

bridging art and engineering. The synthesis and processing of video signals allowed above all for emancipation from the representative image: "To free video artists from the confines of the real camera-recorded world, it is necessary to develop instruments which generate a television compatible signal from raw electronics. A synthesizer is the paint and palette of the video artist."[27] Video processing thus implies a number of fundamental approaches, to which the following will seek to provide a cursory introduction.

Feedback

Video feedback is, precisely speaking, not a synthesis but nevertheless a generative process.[28] It can either be created with the help of a live image via video camera or completely camera-free by way of connecting video circuits.[29] Video feedback generally occurs through the coupling of a camera's recording signal with the monitor's output signal. The cybernetic feedback loop of a video camera pointed at a monitor produces the "feedback tunnel" or "echo corridor" of visual feedback that has become emblematic of the 1960s, in which the electronic image appears to repeat itself as a centripetal cascade (see Figure 6.4). This effect is similar to that of the *mise en abyme* created by two mirrors facing one another. In contrast to the stationary mirror image, however, video feedback not only appears as spatial repetitions but rather as layered time. Each change in the image thus tumbles down the echo corridor with a tiny but perceptible time delay. Bill Gwinn moreover points to specific connections between the direction of the scanlines and the angle between camera and screen: "Changing the relationship between the camera and the monitor will alter the feedback. A camera standing upright will give a spiral pattern; when the camera is tilted slightly, a circle occurs; a camera placed at a 90° angle produces a rectangular shape."[30] Zooming in or changing the depth of focus also destabilizes the feedback corridor and produces centripetal and repetitively pulsing structures.

Eric Siegel's feedback video works, which he presented at the 1969 exhibit *TV as a Creative Medium* in the Howard Wise Gallery at a point when his video synthesizer was still incapable of recording, were particularly influential at the time. Following the exhibition, Siegel produced the video *Einstine* using video feedback in psychedelic colors, in which a portrait of Albert Einstein dissipates into a kaleidoscopic spatiotemporal play of lights.[31] "Something extraordinary happened when we saw that flaming face of Einstein at the end of the corridor," writes Woody Vasulka, "something finally free of film."[32]

Switching, Mixing, Keying, Colorizing

Switching describes the most basic process in working with video signals. It involves the simple switching on, switching off, and toggling of a video signal. As a video signal entails a complex temporal fabric, however, switching processes that are carried out at a higher frequency than within half the frame rate manifest themselves as scanning artifacts that lead to cascading images.[33]

Mixing describes the phenomenon of image blending. The instantaneous mixing of two or more video signals leads to additive image overlays that, particularly in the case of camera images, depend on the exact synchronization of video frames.

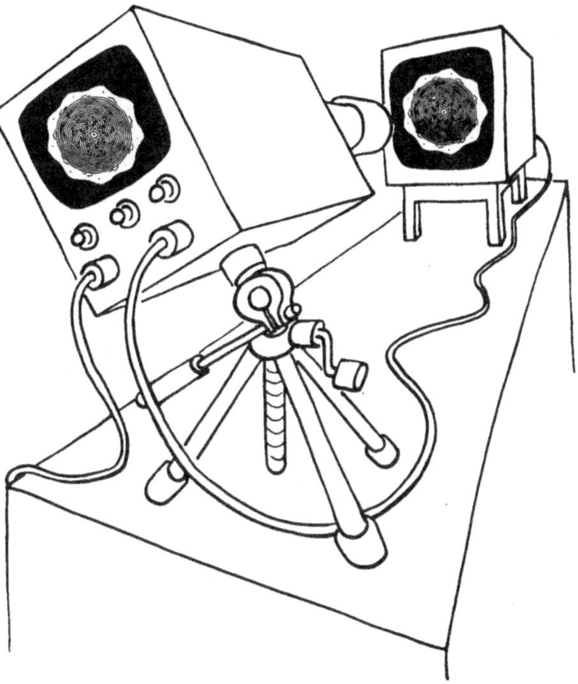

Figure 6.4 Single video feedback: information flows counter-clockwise through the electronic and optical pathways. From James P. Crutchfield, "Space-Time Dynamics in Video Feedback," *Physika* 10D (1984), 230.

Keying may be understood as the switching process within a single line of image.[34] Depending on the given voltage in a video image, the choice is made to switch to a signal from another source. These switching processes can theoretically be undertaken for each individual pixel. Keying allows for specific parts of a video image to be "keyed" into parts of another video image (well known in the studio world as green screen technology). George Brown's Multikeyer, for instance, which was built in the early 1970s, already controlled the switching processes digitally.[35]

Colorizing is based on RGB video encoders that channel different signal curves as red, green, and blue components. The Paik-Abe Video Synthesizer, for example, multiplied black-and-white camera signals and merged them back together via the different color channels. Colorizing video again implies a basic difference to color film technology, as Barbara Buckner underlines:

> Unlike film, color and light in video are disengaged from their objects, because they are added and subtracted independently from the initial image. Color may fly from one object to another; it may pass from foreground to background, electronically flown out of reach of gravity or attachment. Color added to an image is not the naturalistic color of a color camera—it is artificially created internally by changing the phase relationships between the three primary colors of light—red, green, and blue.[36]

Vector Synthesis and Scan Processing

Vector synthesis or *direct synthesis* describes an analog video process in which the cathode ray is directly deflected to create a two-dimensional image, similar to an oscilloscope. This vector scanning is independent from a video raster with its line-scanning raster. Crucial for vector synthesis is the principle of orthogonal superposition of two oscillations. One waveform each is plotted on the x-axis and the other on the y-axis; together they span the image area. Directly synthesized video images have in common that they are subject to the laws of general oscillation theory and thus similar in character to older types of oscillograms.[37] Bill Hearn's *Vidium* (1970) is one of the best-known direct video synthesizers that generates synthetic images according to this principle and is controlled by audio signals.

Scan processing or *raster manipulation*, on the other hand, describes modulation techniques for the line structure of a video image. Distortions of the video raster are achieved with external signals that are fed to the monitor tube's deflector coil, thereby modulating the cathode ray's line scanning. Nam June Paik's Wobbulator is based on this principle. In scan processing, external modulation signals are added to the horizontal and vertical synchronization signals. These signals may come from audio oscillators or, as in the cases of Nam June Paik's *Kuba TV* (1963) or Steina Vasulka's *Violin Power* (1969–78), from a tape recording or musical instrument. In 1972, Steve Rutt and Bill Etra developed a scan processor that inspired Steina and Woody Vasulka to experiment extensively. The Rutt/Etra Scan Processor essentially built on the Wobbulator, with a number of crucial changes: "We DC coupled everything which had been AC coupled. That was the main thing. Without that you couldn't get positional movement, you could only get waveform distortion. You couldn't actually take something and slowly flip it upside down."[38] The positional movement described by Etra is a unique quality of the scan processor that allows a video image to modulate itself by means of the image's brightness values deflecting the horizontal scanlines vertically and thus lifting up the image at corresponding areas, causing a sculptural impression to emerge. Yvonne Spielmann speaks aptly about how with this scan processor "an absolute 'image' arises in the electronic medium, as it is a question of a reflexive progression making video's generic nature as process visible."[39]

In summary, it must be emphasized that the generative video technologies described above emerged largely from outside established broadcasting stations, that is to say, out of a dynamic DIY-community of artists and electronics developers. Interest in analog video circuits today lives on in the context of media-archaeological methods and the development of modular synthesizers.[40]

Digital Video and Algorithmic Audiovisuality

While Viola's notion of the standing wave pattern captures the buzzing line-scanned image of the cathode ray tube, digital video corresponds rather to Vilém Flusser's "particle universe."[41] As RAM memory in computers have become powerful enough to store entire video frames, images are broken up into pixels and data packages and then addressed in a targeted manner. Digital graphics processors suspend the analog video flow by means of discrete algorithmic control. The circular modulations that once brought analog video so close to sound are, in the digital realm, taken over by clocked algorithms. They operate in integrated microchips, which have long since ceased to correspond with the model of open circuits. Digital calculation no longer obeys the image-based order of surfaces and lines, as in the aforementioned example of vector synthesis. The video scanline disintegrates into fully calculable particles of information. Against this backdrop, Paik's notion of the indeterminism of electronic movement proves itself an analog concept through and through, as digital electronics today are subject to strict algorithmic calculation. The specific physical characteristics and confines of audiovisual transformation provided an important level of reflection for the artistic examinations of the 1960s and 1970s that allowed these artists to explore the affordances and the media materiality of analog video. Under digital conditions, however, audiovisual transformation is just one of many possibilities of data mapping. Digital transformation is entirely determined by arbitrary medial mappings (text, image, sound) on the basis of a unifying code. In digital video, there no longer is any physical-material interface between image and sound—rather, audiovisuality is emulated. In this way, all analog media, with their specific technical possibilities for transformation, can be represented by means of digital dispositives, though this emulation is calculated and thus free of analog contingencies and indeterminacies.[42] The structural equivalence of analog electronic signals to sensory perception described above is not a given in the digital realm.[43]

The computing of information, according to Flusser, is no longer concerned with physical things like electrons, but rather with bits (of information). The cathode ray tube's standing waveform, constructed via accelerating high-voltage transformers, disintegrates through digitization into an inertia-free dot matrix: "What remains are particles without dimension that can be neither grasped nor represented nor understood. They are inaccessible to hands, eyes, or fingers. But they can be calculated."[44] Computation takes the place of electromagnetic modulation, and thus "all cultural phenomena started to replace the linear structure of sliding with the staccato structure of programmed combinations; . . . to adopt a cybernetic structure such as that programmed into apparatuses."[45] In this sense, Flusser is less concerned with a "sounding image" but much more with music as an explanatory model for technical images and "telematic" communication. Flusser regards digital images, like music, as "pure" entities, freed from semantic dimensions.[46] He contends:

> The technical image [is] the first instance of music becoming an image and an image becoming music. There are, in fact, contemporary devices that automatically translate image into sound and sound into images (electronic mixers), but this is exactly what is not meant here. In a sounding image, the image does not mix with music; rather both are raised to a new level.[47]

Flusser is formulating his utopia of the abstract, musicalized use of images in a "telematic society" here in 1985. For him, it is only through computation that the image becomes music. Although the abstract calculation that music represents in Flusser's system has little to do anymore with the concrete hum of the analog video signal, it is nevertheless noteworthy that explanatory models for (digital) video continue to be found in the musical realm. The artistic experiments of the 1960s and 1970s in particular paved the way for such a perspective on video.

Notes

1 Wolfgang Ernst, *Sonic Time Machines: Explicit Sound, Sirenic Voices, and Implicit Sonicity* (Amsterdam: Amsterdam University Press, 2016), 28.
2 Cf. Hartmut Winkler, *Prozessieren* (Munich: Fink, 2015). While the term "processing" is usually associated more with digital data processing, in this context it is intended to explicitly address the electronic signal processing of video technology.
3 Cf. on the concept of time-critical media Axel Volmar, *Zeitkritische Medien* (Berlin: Kadmos, 2009); and Wolfgang Ernst, "A Close Reading of the Electronic 'Time Image,'" in *Chronopoetics: The Temporal Being and Operativity of Technological Media* (London: Rowman & Littlefield, 2016).
4 Sherry Miller Hocking, "The Grammar of Electronic Image Processing," in *The Emergence of Video Processing Tools*, ed. Kathy High, Mona Jimenez, and Sherry Miller Hocking (Chicago: Intellect Books, 2014), vol. 2, 443. Cf. also Peter Berz, "Bitmapped Graphics," in Volmar, *Zeitkritische Medien*, 144.
5 Paul Nipkow's principle of electromechanical image scanning based on a perforated disc in 1885 and Karl Ferdinand Braun's cathode ray tube developed in 1897 set the stage for the further developments of electronic image transmission by Manfred von Ardenne, John Logie Baird, and Vladimir Zworykin up to television and video as we know it today.
6 Cf. Peter Berz, "Bitmapped Graphics," 144.
7 In Europe, the alternating current oscillates at 50 Hz, in North America at 60 Hz. Accordingly, a frame rate of 25 Hz (with two interlaced fields of 50 Hz each) has become established for Europe and of around 30 Hz (two fields of 60 Hz each) in the United States, Japan, and Mexico (NTSC).
8 When color was added to the system, the field rate was shifted slightly downward by 0.1 percent to approximately 59.94 Hz to eliminate stationary dot patterns in the difference frequency between the sound and color carriers.
9 Brice Howard, *Videospace*, The National Center for Experiments in Television, San Francisco 1972, 25. NCET was operated in 1967–75 by Brice Howard as part of the San Francisco-based public television station, KQED TV. Howard saw this facility as an experimental research laboratory for video art.
10 Hollis Frampton, "The Withering Away of the State of the Art," in *The New Television: A Public/Private Art*, ed. Douglas Davis and Allison Simmons (Cambridge, MA: MIT Press, 1977), 24–37, 34; reprinted in Chapter 4.
11 Cf. Christina Vagt "Zeitkritische Bilder. Bergsons Bildphilosophie zwischen Topologie und Fernsehen," in Axel Volmar, *Zeitkritische Medien*, 105–25.
12 Barbara Buckner, *Light and Darkness in the Electronic Landscape: Some Aspects of the Video Image*, unpublished typescript, February 1978, 2.
13 Bill Viola in Raymond Bellour, "An Interview with Bill Viola," *October*34 (Autumn 1985), 100.
14 Stephen Beck, "Videographics: Reflections on the Art of Video," in *Video Art: An Anthology*, ed. Beryl Korot und Ira Schneider (New York: Harcourt Brace Jovanovich, 1976), 20.

15 Bellour, "An Interview with Bill Viola," 92f.
16 Ibid., 100: "It's more related to sound than to film or photography because it's exactly the same as the microphone/speaker relationship. We have a microphone here and all of a sudden your voice is coming out across the room, it's all connected—a living, dynamic system, an energy field. There are no frozen, discrete moments." In a similar way, Marshall McLuhan had compared television with radio: "The medium of television has many characteristics which have been unheeded. Mostly it is seen under the aspect of movie form. The TV camera does not have a shutter, does not take pictures. It picks up, as radio picks up . . . its environment, handles it, scans it—and the effect of the TV image is iconic in the sense that it shapes things by contours rather than by little snapshots." Marshall McLuhan, *The Future of Man in the Electric Age*, interview by Frank Kermode, BBC 1965; video and transcript online at the *Marshall McLuhan Speaks Special Collection*, http://www.marshallmcluhanspeaks.com/interview/1965-the-future-of-man-in-the-electric-age/.
17 Bill Viola, "The Sound of One Line Scanning," in *Sound by Artists*, ed. Dan Lander and Micah Lexier (Banff: Walter Phillips Gallery; Toronto: Art Metropole, 1990), 43 and 46; reprinted in this chapter.
18 Yvonne Spielmann, "Video: From Technology to Medium," *Art Journal* 65, no. 3 (Fall 2006), 56; excerpts of this text reprinted in the present chapter.
19 Nam June Paik, "About the Exposition of Music (1963)," in *We Are in Open Circuits: Writing by Nam June Paik*, ed. John G. Hanhardt, Gregory Zinman, and Edith Decker-Philips (Cambridge, MA: MIT Press, 2019), 91.
20 Ibid, 92.
21 Nam June Paik, "Afterlude to the Exposition of Experimental Television," *Fluxus cc fiVe ThReE* (Fluxus Newspaper #4), 1964, n.p., reprinted in *Videa 'n' Videology 1959–1973*, ed. Judson Rosebush (Syracuse, NY: Everson Museum of Art., 1974), n.p., also reprinted in Paik, *We Are in Open Circuits*, 94.
22 Jean Gagnon, "A Demo Tape on How to Play Video on a Violin," in *The Emergence of Video Processing Tools*, 314.
23 A transcript of the voice-over in Hill's video is reprinted in the present chapter.
24 Email from Gary Hill to the author, June 11, 2020.
25 Gary Hill, "Soundings," in George Quasha and Charles Stein, *An Art of Limina: Gary Hill's Works and Writings* (Barcelona: Ediciones Polígrafa, 2009), 592.
26 Cf. Gary Hill's text in Chapter 12.
27 Tom De Witt, "The Video Synthesizer," in David Dunn, Woody Vasulka, and Steina Vasulka, *Eigenwelt der Apparatewelt: Pioneers of Electronic Art* (Linz: Oberösterreichisches Landesmuseum Francisco Carolinum, 1992), 165.
28 For the different meanings of the term "video feedback" (psychological, social, technical), see Chapter 3, which focuses on technical-generative feedback.
29 For example, in Bill Viola's video work *Information* from 1973, which is based on internal feedback.
30 Bill Gwin, "Video Feedback: How to Make It; An Artist's Comments on Its Use; A Systems Approach," typescript, p. 2; online at http://www.experimentaltvcenter.org/sites/default/files/history/pdf/gwinvideofeedback_397.pdf.
31 Eric Siegel, "Eric Siegel's Statement" (2001), *Electronic Arts Intermix*, last modified June 12, 2008, http://eai.org/user_files/supporting_documents/statement.pdf, 1.
32 Woody Vasulka, "Eric Siegel EVS Electronic Video Synthesizer," in *Eigenwelt der Apparatewelt*, 116.
33 Cf. Miller Hocking, *The Grammar of Image Processing Tools*, 450.

34 Ibid., 454.

35 Ibid.

36 Barbara Buckner, *Light and Darkness in the Electronic Landscape: Some Aspects of the Video Image*, unpublished manuscript (February 1978), 14; reprinted in the present chapter.

37 In 1815, the mathematician Nathaniel Bowditch first described functions of perpendicular superposition of harmonic pendulum oscillation. As a result of this discovery, a wide variety of mechanical instruments were constructed to generate such Bowditch curves, including numerous so-called harmonographs and Charles Wheatstone's Kaleidophone (1827) for direct observation of visible vibration patterns of sounding metal rods. The curves eventually became known as Lissajous figures because Jules Antoine Lissajous studied them in 1857–8 as part of acoustic experiments on the vibrational behavior of solids. The invention of electronic imaging methods in 1897 by Karl Ferdinand Braun allowed for the observation of electromagnetic signals.

38 Steve Rutt, "Rutt/Etra Scan Processor," in *Eigenwelt der Apparatewelt*, 138.

39 Yvonne Spielmann, *Video: The Reflexive Medium* (Cambridge, MA: MIT Press, 2008), 103.

40 Cf. the discussions in the *muff wiggler* online forum, https://www.muffwiggler.com/, and the video tools by LZX industries, https://lzxindustries.net/. See also Derek Holzer, *Vector Synthesis: A Media-Archaeological Investigation into Sound-Modulated Light*, master thesis (Helsinki: Aalto University, 2019).

41 Vilém Flusser, *Into the Universe of Technical Images*, trans. Nancy Ann Roth (Minneapolis: University of Minnesota Press, 2011), 17.

42 The fact that digital media have their own, not primarily audiovisual, materialities is unaffected by this.

43 Cf. Wolfgang Ernst, "The Temporal Gap: On Asymmetries within the So-Called 'Audiovisual' Regime (in Sensory Perception and in Technical Media," in *Habitus in Habitat III. Synaesthesia and Kinaesthetics*, ed. Joerg Fingerhut, Sabine Flach, and Jan Söffner (Berlin: Peter Lang, 2011), 225–40.

44 Flusser, *Into the Universe of Technical Images*, 10.

45 Vilém Flusser, *Towards a Philosophy of Photography* (London: Reaktion Books, 2000), 71. For Flusser, this development of programmed cybernetic techno-images already began with the invention of photography.

46 "Technical images are pure art in the same sense that music alone once was." Flusser, *Into the Universe of Technical Images*, 165. Certainly Flusser's concept of music is not unproblematic. Here, however, it shall be presented merely as an explanatory model of the technical image.

47 Ibid.

The Sound of One Line Scanning (1986/1990)

Bill Viola

[. . .] "In the beginning was the Word . . ." provokes one to ask, where was the image? But like the Biblical creation myth, Indian religion (for example Yoga and Tantra) and later Asian religions (for example Buddhism) also describe the origin of the world in sound, with the original creative potency still accessible to the individual in the forms of sacred speech and chanting (sympathetic vibrations). This idea of the origin of images in sound is mirrored in the invention and development of communication technology. In the age of the electronic image, it is easy to forget that the earliest electrical communication systems were designed to carry the word. For example, Edison initially tried to market the phonograph to the business community as an automated replacement for the stenographer in the office. If speech is the genesis of the media body electric—the telegraph and the subsequent systems of the telephone, radio, and television—then acoustics (or general wave theory) is the basic structural principle of its many manifestations.

The video image is a standing wave pattern of electrical energy, a vibrating system composed of specific frequencies as one would expect to find in any resonating object. As has been described many times, the image we see on the surface of the cathode ray tube is the trace of a single moving focused point of light from a stream of electrons hitting the screen from behind, causing its phosphor-coated surface to glow. In video, a still image does not exist. The fabric of all video images, moving or still, is the activated, constantly sweeping electron beam—the steady stream of electrical impulses coming from the camera or video recorder. The divisions into lines and frames are solely divisions in time, the opening and closing of temporal windows that demarcate periods of activity within the flowing stream of electrons. Thus, the video image is a living dynamic energy field, a vibration appearing solid only because it exceeds our ability to discern such fine slices of time.

All video has its roots in the live. The vibrational acoustic character of video as a virtual image is the essence of its "liveness." Technologically, video has evolved out of sound (the electromagnetic) and its close association with cinema is misleading since film and its grandparent, the photographic process, are members of a completely different branch of the genealogical tree (the mechanical/chemical). The video camera, as an electronic transducer of physical energy into electrical impulses, bears a closer original relation to the microphone than to the film camera.

The original television studio was a hybrid of radio, theater, and cinema. Its images existed in the present tense. Its construction was based on the radio studio with the isolated control room behind glass, "on air" signs and cameras placed out on the floor to pick up the action. The structure of the elements in the studio can also be viewed as the physical embodiment of the aesthetics of cinema, an ingenious solution of the "limitation" of having to exist live. Multiple cameras, usually three (representing film's classic long, medium, and close-up shots), view the action from their individual points of view. Unlike cinema, where activity within a given scene must give illusion of simultaneity and sequential time flow, with the action often shot out of order, video represents a point of view that is literally shifted around the space in the present tense, parallel to the action. The illusion which video had to work very hard to create was one of recorded time, doing so only where necessary by using different parts of the studio in combination with lighting effects. Direct translations of a sister art form of present-tense time, the theater, were used to format early television dramas and many of the burlesque-like variety shows. They were almost always performed in the theatrical setting of the live audience, who functioned as surrogate home viewers until later replaced by laugh track and applause machine.

The fundamental aspect of cinema, the montage (an articulation in time), was interpreted by the fundamental aspect of early television, the live (an articulation in space), in a key piece of equipment in the studio, the video switcher. This was the central creative device for organizing what was finally to be seen by the viewer at home. The basic elements of cinematic language were hard-wired into its design. A simple switch button represented Eisenstein's paramount montage, the cut, and with a switch on each camera, cuts could be made to any point of view desired. Griffith's fade to black became a gradual reduction in signal voltage with a variable potentiometer. Wipes and split screens were translated by engineers into circuit designs to electronically interfere with and offset the regular voltages in the signal flow, the most symmetrical stationary wipe patterns being harmonic overtones of the fundamental frequencies of the basic video signal. Thus, without the ability to record, a simulation of cinematic edited time was constructed by a live electronic instrument.

It wasn't until the late 1960s that this emulation of the cinema was broken, when artists began poking beneath the surface to uncover the basic characteristics of the medium and release the unique visual potentials of the electronic image, now taken for granted with a yawn, and oftentimes a grimace, as standard TV fare. The video switcher was redesigned into the first video synthesizer. Its principles were acoustic and musical, a further evolution of the early electronic music systems like the Moog. The videotape recorder was the last link in the chain to be developed, coming a good decade after the arrival of television and only fully integrated into video's image processing system with the introduction of the time-based corrector in the early 1970s. With the seamless incorporation of recorded material into the image stream and the advancements of electronic editing, a need arose to specifically identify remote feeds as "live." Not only did video begin to look and act like cinema, but it began to look and act like everything else—fashion, conversation, politics, visual art, and music. [. . .]

Musically speaking, the physics of a broadcast is a type of drone. The video image perpetually repeats itself without rest at the same set of frequencies. This new common condition of the drone represents a significant shift in our culturally derived thought patterns. It can be evidenced by contrasting another drone-based system, traditional Indian music, with our own European classical music.

Western music builds things up, piling notes on top of notes, forms on top of forms, in the way one would construct a building, until at last the piece is complete. It is additive: its base is silence, all musical sounds proceed from this point. Indian music, on the other hand, begins from sound. It is subtractive. All the notes and possible notes to be played are present before the main musicians even start playing, stated by the presence and function of the tambura. A tambura is a drone instrument, usually of four or five strings, that, due to the particular construction of its bridge, amplifies the overtone or harmonic series of the individual notes in each tuned string. It is most distinctly heard at the start and end of the performance, but is continually present throughout. The series of overtones describes the scale of the music to be played. Therefore, when the primary musicians play, they are considered to be pulling notes out of an already ongoing sound field, the drone.

This music structure reflects the Hindu philosophical concept of the origin of all the things in sound, represented by the essential vibration Om, which is believed to be always present, without beginning or end, everywhere in the universe, generating all forms of the phenomenal world. In the music, there is great emphasis on tuning, while the philosophers speak of "tuning the individual" as a means to contact and replenish these fundamental energies. The idea of a sound field that is always present shifts the emphasis away from the objects of perception to the field on which the perception is occurring; a nonspecific viewpoint.

As a drone, video's significant aspect is that its electronic images exist everywhere at once, the receiver is free to pull the signal out of the line at any given point along its path or any location out in the broadcast field. Children have been known to pick up radio signals in their dental braces, a contemporary manifestation of "speaking in tongues." The "space" of broadcast recalls the acoustic space of the Gothic cathedral, where all sounds, no matter how near, far or loud, appear to be originating at the same distant place. They seem detached from the immediate scene, floating somewhere where the point of view has become the entire space. In technology, the current shift from analog's sequential waves to digital's recombinant codes further accelerates the diffusion of the point of view. Like the transformation of matter, there is a movement from the tangibility of the solid and liquid states into the gaseous. There is less coherency, previously solid barriers become porous, and the perspective is that of the whole space, the point of view of the air.

Within several weeks of launching its satellite, Brazil established communicating links to all corners of the country and mapped every square mile of one of the largest unchartered territories left on the planet, the Amazon basin. One can now, theoretically, make a phone call relaying one's position from anywhere in the jungle and even see *Dynasty* if a TV set and generator are on hand. A system is already in place in the U.S. for new cars where the vehicle's position and direction are relayed to a navigational satellite and pinpoints its location and displays an electronic map on a dashboard screen. On the map every street in the country is selectable in varying scales down to a few square blocks, with all the individual street names noted. It is now impossible to get lost—a disturbingly boring thought, not to mention a paranoid one.

In the late twentieth century, the Unknown, the "other side of the mountain," so central to structure of our thoughts, has ceased to exist in geographic spatial terms. By the early 1980s the entire surface of the earth had been satellite-mapped down to a resolution of thirty feet or more. This "Known" of everything creates some bizarre new models of consciousness, like the military's computer navigation system where there is no direct sensory link to the outside world. Here, a jet rocket can travel at high velocities hugging the landscape while relying solely on information of the precise terrain and features ahead stored in the on-board computer memory; data gathered again from satellite remote sensing. Memory replaces sensory experience; a Proustian nightmare. [. . .]

As the telegraph and subsequent "wireless" communication technologies were provoked by a response to the separation of individuals over the vast spaces of the New World, so thought transference and "seeing at a distance" for the Aborigines are a manifestation of the vastness and stillness of the Australian desert. Desert solitude is an early form of visionary technology. It figures strongly in the history of religion. Individuals have used it to hear the voices of the past and future, to become "prophets," to receive images, or for Native Americans to host "vision quests." It seems that when all the clutter and noise of everyday life is reduced to such brutal minimalism, the usual control valves are released and images well up from within. The boundary between the software of the private interior and the hardware of the exterior landscape is blurred; their forms intermingle and converse.

Evidence of synesthesia, the crossover between and interchangeability of the senses, has been reported in individuals since the earliest civilizations. It has been particularly evocative for artists who have dreamed of the unification of the senses, and there are many examples in recent art history, ranging from the Russian composer Scriabin's chromatic piano, which played colors from a keyboard, to the nausea of the *son et lumiere* shows of public tourism. Visual artists have often described hearing music or sounds when they work, as composers have mentioned perceiving their music in imagistic form. [. . .]

Synesthesia is the natural inclination of the structure of contemporary media. The material that produces music from a stereo sound system, transmits the voice over the telephone, and materializes the image on a television set is, at the base level, the same. With the further implementation of digital codes to bring personal chequing, buying gas, cooking with the microwave and other functions into this same domain, there will be an even more extensive common linguistic root. Efforts with artificial technology have made it necessary to distinguish between synesthesia as an artistic theory and practice, and synesthesia as a genuine subjective ability or involuntary condition for certain individuals. There is a natural propensity in all of us to relate sound and image. The beauty of these experiences is in their fluid language of personal imagination and in their ties to mood and moment. As long as their individual subjective nature is understood, that is, that they can never become conventional, we will be spared the tedium of the dogma and proprietary theorizing of the practitioners, from the visual musicians to the music videoists. [. . .]

When the first technologies of image and sound codified the functioning of the human senses into a surrogate artificial form, a tremendous and unpredictable understanding was gained of the operations of human perception. Similarly, as the implementation of the computer becomes an embodiment of mind, the new links to the "mind stuff" of digital data processing will certainly provide even more potent translation possibilities beyond basic sensory inputs. Although it is tempting to ponder a possible synesthetic "putting back together" of science's discrete perceptual and cognitive compartments inspired by these electronic free and fluid interchanges of our ways of seeing, what seems to be emerging at the moment is the amnesia and anesthesia of a vast cluttered and confused landscape of image fragments, the semiotician's field day of delights. [. . .]

Today, our self-created media systems offer us creative potentials previously only available to individuals with special powers. The synesthetic possibilities in the sensory and conceptual domains are inspirational, but instead, as victims of "sane" communicators with equally "sane" imaginations, we are becoming like Luria's mnemonist—overwhelmed and incapacitated by rootless images and amplified voices. It is the village "seer" we sense the absence of, not the formal structures of efficient information management systems and professional communicators.

Artists, poets, composers, and scientists who have heard the voices know they are not mad—their work testifies to this fact. However, severe mental breakdown can be a type of occupational hazard for persons working at the boundary of commonly accepted consensus reality, a space culturally fabricated by the perceptual conventions imposed by the structuring devices of language, customary behavior, and forgotten histories.

From Bill Viola, "The Sound of One Line Scanning," first published in the catalog for the National Video Festival (Los Angeles: The American Film Institute, 1986); reprinted here from the augmented version in *Sound by Artists*, ed. Dan Lander and Micah Lexier (Toronto: Art Metropole; Alberta: Walter Phillips Gallery, 1990), 39–54. Final, newly revised version in Viola, *Reasons for Knocking at an Empty House: Writings 1973–1994*, ed. Robert Violette (Cambridge, MA: MIT Press, 1995).

Afterlude to the Exposition of Experimental Television (1964): Facsimile

Nam June Paik

"All the News That's Fit to Print"

LATE CITY EDITION

fLuxus cc fiVe ThReE

FINANCIAL
OFFERINGS TO BUYERS
PAGE 4

ROBERT WATTS: PAGE 2
NEWSPAPER EVENT

Section 2

afterlude to the EXPOSITION of EXPERIMENTAL TELEVISION 1963, March. Ga'-rie Parnass. nam june PAIK.

(1)

My experimental TV is

not always interesting

but

not always uninteresting

like nature, which is beautiful,

not bècause it changes beautifully,

but simply because it changes.

The core of the beauty of nature is, that, the limitless QUANTITY of nature disarmed the category of QUALITY, which is used unconsciously mixed and confused with double meanings.

1) character
2) value.

In my experimental TV, the words "QUALITY" means only the CHARACTER, but not the VALUE.

A is different from B,
but not that
A is better than B.

Sometimes I need red apple
Sometimes I need red lips.

(2)))

2 My experimental TV is the first ART (?), in which the "perfect crime" is possible.................... I had put just a diode into opposite direction, and got a "waving" negative Television. If my epigons do the same trick, the result will be completely the same (unlike Webern and Webern-epigons).............. that is.............

My TV is <u>NOT</u> the expression of my personality, but merely

a "<u>PHYSICAL MUSIC</u>"

optical and semantical event, in Nineteen-sixties. The beauty of distorted Kennedy is different from the beau..y of football hero, or not always pretty but always stupid female announcer.

b) <u>Second dimension of variability.</u>
13 sets suffered 13 sorts of variation in their VIDEO-HORIZONTAL-VERTICAL units. I am proud to be able to say that all 13 sets actually changed their inner circuits. No Two sets had the same kind of technical operation. Not one is the simple blur, which occurs, when you turn the vertical and horizontal control-button at home. I enjoyed very much the study of electronics, which I began in 1961, and some life-danger, I met while working with 15 Kilo-Volts. I had the luck to meet nice collaborators: HIDEO UCHIDA (president of UCHIDA Radio Research institute), a genial avantgarde electronican, who discovered the principle of Transistor 2 years earlier than the Americans, and SHUYA ABE, allmighty poli-technican, who knows that the science is more a beauty than the logic. UCHIDA is now trying to prove the telepathy and prophesy electromagnetically.

c) As the third dimension of variability, the waves from various generators, tape-recorders and radios are fed to various points to give different rhythms to each other. This rather old-typed beauty, which is not essentially combined with High Frequency Technique, was easier to understand to the normal audience, maybe because it had some humanistic aspects.

d) There are as many sorts of TV circuits, as French cheese-sorts. F.I. some old models of 1952 do certain kind of variation, which new *models with automatic frequency control cannot* do.

e) Many mystics are interested to spring out from ONE-ROW-TIME, ONE-WAY-TIME, in order to

GRASP the Eternity.

aa) To stop at the consummated or steril Zero-point is a classical method to grasp the eternity.

I AM ALWAYS, WHAT I AM NOT and
I AM ALWAYS NOT, WHAT I AM.

This uncessant EX-TASIS (to go out of oneself) is the "NORMAL" character in the normal situation of our consciousness. The word "Ecstasy" (ex=tasis) is used here, almost as an antonym to the first case (xx). In xx) our consciousness is UNIFIED with itself. It has synthesized the dualism of our consciousness. But in zz), this dualism, or the dialectic evolution of our esprit is kept precious as the proof of our freedom,...

))) 6 (((

The aa) (to stop at the consummated or steril zero=point to grasp the eternity ....) and the xx), (the ecstasy, in the sense of" mental transport or rapture from the contemplation of divine things") is the same thing.
But the bb) (the perception of parallel flows of many independent movements simultaneously) and the zz) (the ecstasy in the sense of Sartre,,, that is, the perpetual proceeding of our consciousness in the normal state,,,) seems to be completely different. But there are important common things between these two (bb) and zz)).
Both bb) and zz) don't know the terminal station, conclusion, stopped absolute moment, consummation, ascension. In other words, they are relative, relative, suspending, plain and common, movable, variable, hanging in mid-air,,

NOT VERY SATISFIED,
BUT NOT VERY UNSATISFIED..........
like my experimental TV, which is
NOT ALWAYS INTERESTING,
BUT NOT ALWAYS UNINTERESTING..............

--- 7 ---

Now let me talk about Zen, although I avoid it usually, not to become the salesman of "OUR" culture like Daisetsu Suzuki, bacause the cultural patriotism is more harmful than the political patriotism, because the former is the disguised one, and especially the self-propaganda of Zen (the doctrine of the self-abandonment) must be the stupid suicide of Zen.

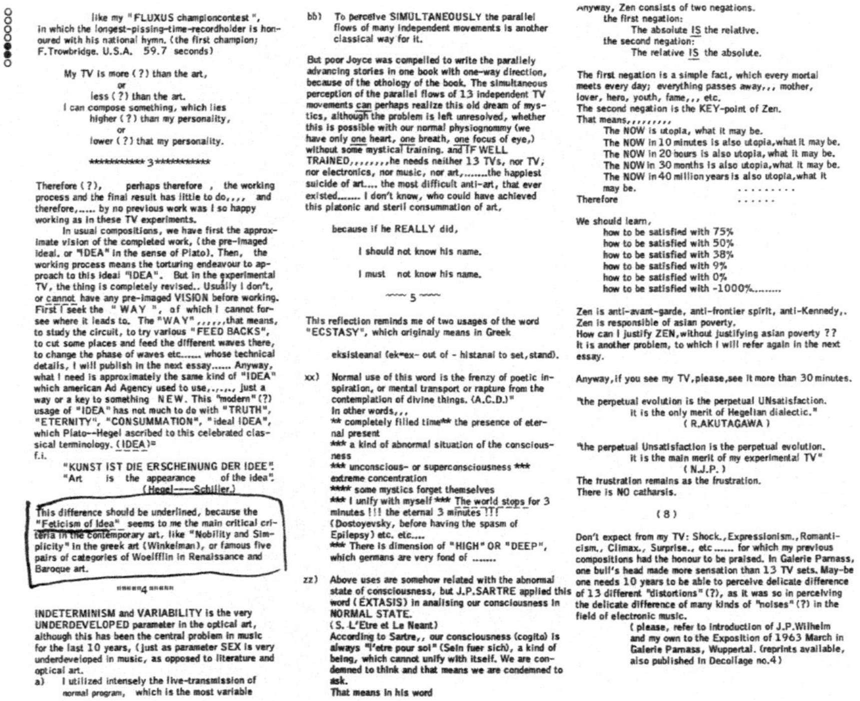

like my "FLUXUS championcontest",
in which the longest-pissing-time-recordholder is honoured with his national hymn. (the first champion; F.Trowbridge. U.S.A. 59.7 seconds)

My TV is more (?) than the art,
or
less (?) than the art.
I can compose something, which lies
higher (?) than my personality,
or
lower (?) that my personality.

************ 3 ************

Therefore (?), perhaps therefore , the working process and the final result has little to do,,,, and therefore,..... by no previous work was I so happy working as in these TV experiments.

In usual compositions, we have first the approximate vision of the completed work, (the pre-imaged ideal. or "IDEA" in the sense of Plato). Then, the working process means the torturing endeavour to approach to this ideal "IDEA". But in the experimental TV, the thing is completely revised.. Usually I don't, or cannot have any pre-imaged VISION before working. First I seek the " WAY ", of which I cannot forsee where it leads to. The "WAY",,,,,,that means, to study the circuit, to try various "FEED BACKS", to cut some places and feed the different waves there, to change the phase of waves etc...... whose technical details, I will publish in the next essay...... Anyway, what I need is approximately the same kind of "IDEA" which american Ad Agency used to use,.,.,., just a way or a key to something NEW. This "modern" (?) usage of "IDEA" has not much to do with "TRUTH", "ETERNITY", "CONSUMMATION", "ideal IDEA", which Plato--Hegel ascribed to this celebrated classical terminology. (IDEA)=
f.i.

"KUNST IST DIE ERSCHEINUNG DER IDEE".
"Art is the appearance of the idea".
(Hegel----Schiller.)

This difference should be underlined, because the "Feticism of Idea" seems to me the main critical criteria in the contemporary art, like "Nobility and Simplicity" in the greek art (Winkelman), or famous five pairs of categories of Woelfflin in Renaissance and Baroque art.

"""""4"""""

INDETERMINISM and VARIABILITY is the very UNDERDEVELOPED parameter in the optical art, although this has been the central problem in music for the last 10 years, (just as parameter SEX is very underdeveloped in music, as opposed to literature and optical art.

a) I utilized intensely the live-transmission of normal program, which is the most variable

bb) To perceive SIMULTANEOUSLY the parallel flows of many independent movements is another classical way for it.

But poor Joyce was compelled to write the parallely advancing stories in one book with one-way direction, because of the othology of the book. The simultaneous perception of the parallel flows of 13 independent TV movements can perhaps realize this old dream of mystics, although the problem is left unresolved, whether this is possible with our normal physiognommy (we have only one heart, one breath, one focus of eye,) without some mystical training. and IF WELL TRAINED,,,,,,,,he needs neither 13 TVs, nor TV, nor electronics, nor music, nor art,........the happiest suicide of art.... the most difficult anti-art, that ever existed........ I don't know, who could have achieved this platonic and steril consummation of art,

because if he REALLY did,

I should not know his name.

I must not know his name.

~~~ 5 ~~~

This reflection reminds me of two usages of the word "ECSTASY", which originaly means in Greek

eksisteanai (ek=ex- out of - histanai to set, stand).

xx) Normal use of this word is the frenzy of poetic inspiration, or mental transport or rapture from the contemplation of divine things. (A.C.D.)"
In other words,,,
** completely filled time** the presence of eternal present
*** a kind of abnormal situation of the consciousness
*** unconscious- or superconsciousness ***
extreme concentration
**** some mystics forget themselves
*** I unify with myself *** The world stops for 3 minutes !!! the eternal 3 minutes !!!
(Dostoyevsky, before having the spasm of Epilepsy) etc. etc....
*** There is dimension of "HIGH" OR "DEEP", which germans are very fond of ....

zz) Above uses are somehow related with the abnormal state of consciousness, but J.P.SARTRE applied this word (EXTASIS) in analising our consciousness in NORMAL STATE.
(S. L'Etre et Le Neant)
According to Sartre,, our consciousness (cogito) is always "l'etre pour soi" (Sein fuer sich), a kind of being, which cannot unify with itself. We are condemned to think and that means we are condemned to ask.
That means in his word

Anyway, Zen consists of two negations.
the first negation:
The absolute IS the relative.
the second negation:
The relative IS the absolute.

The first negation is a simple fact, which every mortal meets every day; everything passes away,,, mother, lover, hero, youth, fame,,, etc.
The second negation is the KEY-point of Zen.
That means,,,,,,,,,
The NOW is utopia, what it may be.
The NOW in 10 minutes is also utopia, what it may be.
The NOW in 20 hours is also utopia, what it may be.
The NOW in 30 months is also utopia, what it may be.
The NOW in 40 million years is also utopia, what it may be. ....
Therefore ......

We should learn,
how to be satisfied with 75%
how to be satisfied with 50%
how to be satisfied with 38%
how to be satisfied with 9%
how to be satisfied with 0%
how to be satisfied with -1000%........

Zen is anti-avant-garde, anti-frontier spirit, anti-Kennedy,.
Zen is responsible of asian poverty.
How can I justify ZEN, without justifying asian poverty ??
It is another problem, to which I will refer again in the next essay.

Anyway, if you see my TV, please, see it more than 30 minutes.

"the perpetual evolution is the perpetual UNsatisfaction.
it is the only merit of Hegelian dialectic."
(R.AKUTAGAWA)

"the perpetual Unsatisfaction is the perpetual evolution.
it is the main merit of my experimental TV"
(N.J.P.)
The frustration remains as the frustration.
There is NO catharsis.

(8)

Don't expect from my TV: Shock., Expressionism., Romanticism., Climax., Surprise., etc ...... for which my previous compositions had the honour to be praised. In Galerie Parnass, one bull's head made more sensation than 13 TV sets. May-be one needs 10 years to be able to perceive delicate difference of 13 different "distortions" (?), as it was so in perceiving the delicate difference of many kinds of "noises" (?) in the field of electronic music.

(please, refer to introduction of J.P.Wilhelm and my own to the Exposition of 1963 March in Galerie Parnass, Wuppertal. (reprints available, also published in Decollage no.4)

Figure 6.5 Facsimile of Nam June Paik, "Afterlude to the Exposition of Experimental Television," in *FLuxus cc fiVe ThReE* (Fluxus newspaper #4), ed. George Brecht and George Maciunas, June 1964; reprinted in *Videa 'n' Videology: Nam June Paik 1959–1973*, ed. Judson Rosebush (Syracuse, NY: Everson Museum of Art), unpag.
~~~

Versatile Color TV Synthesizer (1969)

Nam June Paik

This will enable us to shape the TV screen canvas

as precisely	as Leonardo
as freely	as Picasso
as colorfully	as Renoir
as profoundly	as Mondrian
as violently	as Pollock and
as lyrically	as Jasper Johns.

In the long-range future, such a versatile color synthesizer will become a standard equipment like today's Hammond organ or Moog synthesizer in the musical field, but even in the immediate future it will find wide application.

1) TV-tranquilizer, which is at the same time an avant-garde art work in its own right. As *Time* magazine quoted me with emphasis, the tranquilizing "groovy" TV will be an important function of future TV, like today's mood music at WPAT or WOR-FM.
2) Enormous enrichment of background scenery of music programs or talkshows, combined with sharp reduction in the production cost is especially effective for young generation's rock programs. Traditional psychedelic light show cannot compete with electronic color synthesizer, as much as Ferrari racing car cannot catch even a good old DC-4.
3) This will provide valuable experiments for EVR,[1] which would be aimed for more sophisticated or educational layer of consumer. E.g., what kind of visual material will accompany the vast repertoire of classical and pop music? People will quickly be tired of von Karajan's turtle neck or Beatles' long hair. The study of this problem cannot be started too soon, and it might end up by producing a new fertile genre, called "electronic opera."

Nam June Paik, "Versatile Color TV Synthesizer" (1969), in *Videa 'n' Videology: Nam June Paik 1959–1973*, ed. Judson Rosebush (Syracuse, NY: Everson Museum of Art), unpag.

Note

1 [See the facsimile of Nam June Paik's leaflet "Electronic Video Recorder" (1965), in *Videa 'n' Videology: Nam June Paik 1959–1973*, ed. Judson Rosebush (Syracuse: Everson Museum of Art, 1974), unpag.; reprinted in Chapter 12 of the present volume.]

Video-Synthesizer (1969): Fascimile

Nam June Paik

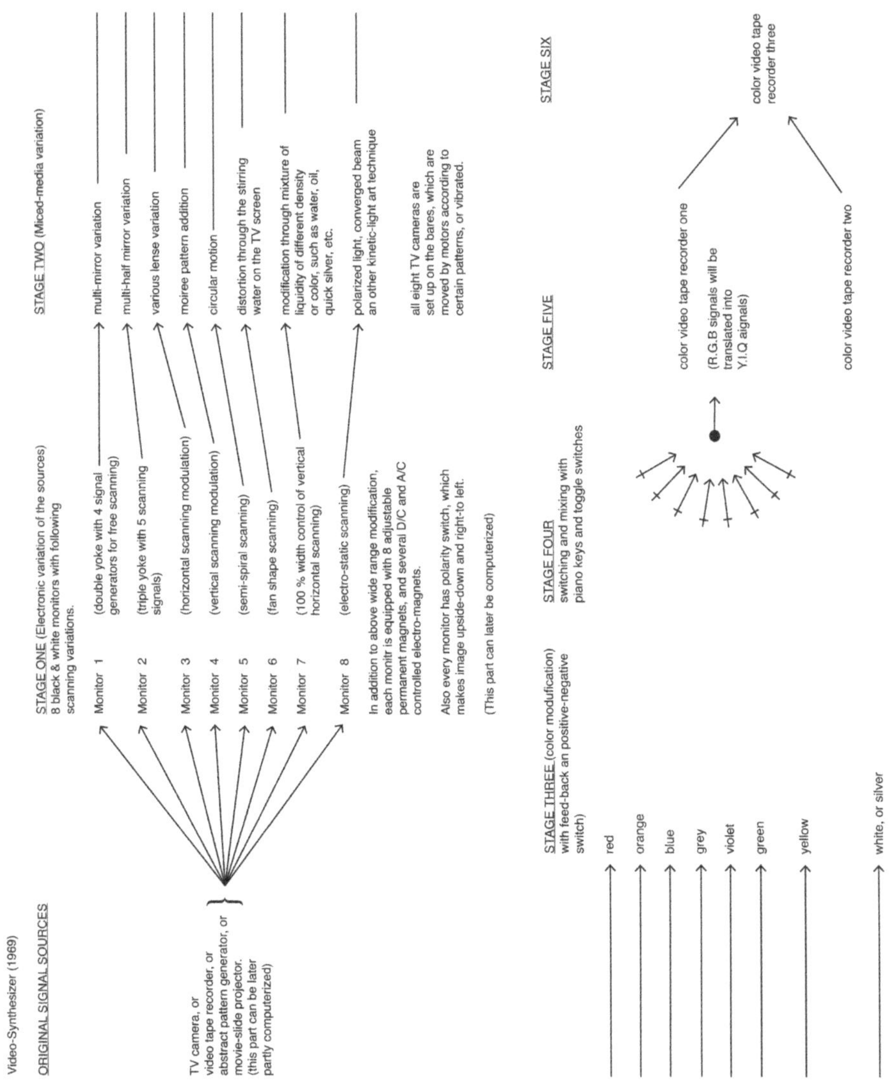

Figure 6.6 Nam June Paik, Diagram "Video-Synthesizer" (1969) in *Videa 'n' Videology: Nam June Paik 1959–1973*, ed. Judson Rosebush (Syracuse, NY: Everson Museum of Art), unpag.

Soundings (1979)

Gary Hill

Transcription of Spoken Text [Part Two of Seven-Part-Video]:

sounding the image
imaging a sound
locating the sound of my voice
imaging my voice
pushing my voice through the object
setting my voice to the image
to the sound
sounding the image
imaging the sound
touching my voice
encoding the object
touching the object
decoding my voice
fingering the threshold
surfing the space
following the edge
circuitous spiral inverting the polarities
investigating both beginnings and both ends
around an extended period of time
the time of my voice
the space of determination
tangent with my finger
my voice my finger
two nodes tuning the meaning of an action
sounding the image
imaging the sound
my skin its skin forming another skin
the skin of myself circulating with self-corrective pressure on its skin
forming a skin of space where I voice from
the skin is always forming and shedding itself
I have my finger on it moving it
I have my finger on my voice tracking it
driving it
moving the skin
spinning the skin

continuing the space
playing the meaning
stretching the skin taut
touching down
touching sound
touching image
touching touching
voicing my thoughts between the skins
playing the skin
drumming my thoughts into the skin
driving the space
driving the speaker
imaging the sound hitting your skin
keeping the space taut
drumming your mind through the skin
circulating the space
circulating the sound
grafting my voice to the skin space
tracing our spiral in and out
pulling the skin
pushing the skin
sending the skin to push the space to pull your skin taut
to touch your space
circulating the skin
I have my finger on my voice
tangent to the skin
put your finger on it
put your mind through it
skin your thought
graft your skin
shed your skin
I want your skin
give your skin to me
I want to put my finger on it
I want to circumscribe the space
tracking the threshold
imaging the sound
sounding the image
forming the skin space
drumming your mind through the skin
drumming the skin stretched through your mind
I want your mind

I want your mind for the skin space
I want to peel the skin through the space
imaging the skin
peeling back the space
sounding the skin taut
the skin is pushing my voice
the skin is pulling my voice
forming a skin of space where I voice from
stretching my voice to the edge
pulling the skin
pushing the skin
sending the skin to push the space to pull our skin taut
sounding the sounding
imaging the imaging
sounding the imaging
voicing the skin
spacing the thoughts under the skin
pulling it taut
locating the space
imaging the distance between soundings
sounding the skin stretched between us
I want the skin
I want to spread the skin
I want to cover my voice with the skin
steal the skin giving voice to the skin
cover the skin with the image of skin
space the sound
ground the voice to the skin

Transcript of voice over from Gary Hill, Soundings (1979), excerpted from An Art of Limina: Gary Hill's Works and Writings, ed. George Quasha and Charles Stein (Barcelona: Ediciones Polígrafa, 2009), 293.

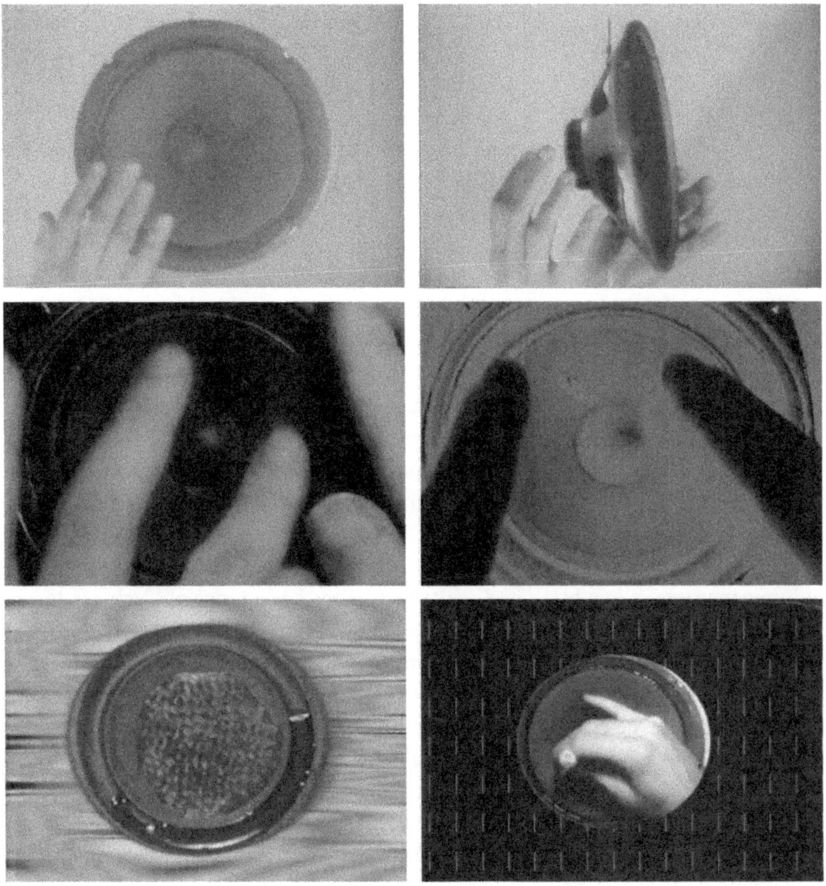

Figure 6.7 Gary Hill, *Soundings* (1979), video, color, sound, 17:41 min. Stills © VG Bild-Kunst, Bonn 2020.

Light and Darkness in the Electronic Landscape (1978)

Barbara Buckner

As I see it, video appears to be the first visual art- and information-producing tool that has a built-in cyclic nature (Figure 6.8, diagram B). Just as the processing of information in the brain is accomplished by an electrical sweep of scansion (to and fro) through the cerebral cortex, generating electrical activity in the form of alpha, beta, and theta waves by which we monitor all sensory and nervous connections, so the video camera and monitor operate on the same cyclic principle of scansion—where each frame of video is scanned 30 frames per second at normal speed in contrast to film which runs at 24 frames per second at normal speed. Two fields make up one frame of video (diagram C). Each field occurs every 60th of a second. The two fields are like two sides to the same story, an interpolation of two views of the same scene, the story being the telling of picture information. Thirty times a second the electron beam, which consists of a focused stream of electrons, scans 525 consecutive horizontal lines of picture information

Imagine a scene as seen by your eyes. The scene is composed of varying degrees of luminance which in a black-and-white picture read as a range of black, white, and shades of gray. On the back of the retina there are millions of light-sensitive rods and cones which are stimulated and convert the light into electrical impulses. These corresponding voltages are sent along the optic nerve to the brain which interprets these electrical impulses as a whole picture. This process is similar in the video system. The video camera is the eye of the system which is sensitive to light energy. The camera tube then converts this light energy by scanning the picture elements with the electron beam, encoding the light energy as electrical energy or voltage, which the monitor then plays back as light energy or picture information. We see the translation of voltages corresponding to the original picture as seen by the camera.

Each of the 525 horizontal lines of information is divided into hundreds of picture elements of varying brightness which are scanned by the electron beam (diagram E). The number of picture elements along the line determines how much detail or resolution the picture has. For the period of one field, the 262.5 odd-numbered lines are scanned; for the period of the second field, the 262.5 even-numbered lines are scanned (diagram D). The whole picture may be seen as a metrical mosaic of alternating light and dark which due to the incredible speed of scansion we perceive as a whole picture, at the source of transmission and final reception.

After each field is scanned, the electron beam is extinguished and instantaneously returned to the top of the field to begin its scanning pattern again for another cycle. This is called the vertical retrace. This vertical pulse occurs every 60th of a second. The horizontal scans and the vertical deflections are timed very precisely by what are known as vertical and horizontal sync pulses. They can be likened to the film sprocket holes which pull down 24 film frames every second in syncopation with the camera or projector. If these sprocket holes are ripped, or if the motor or spring is faulty, the film will disengage and we will see a blurred image, because the frames are not being pulled down at the correct speed which creates the illusion of normal movement. The

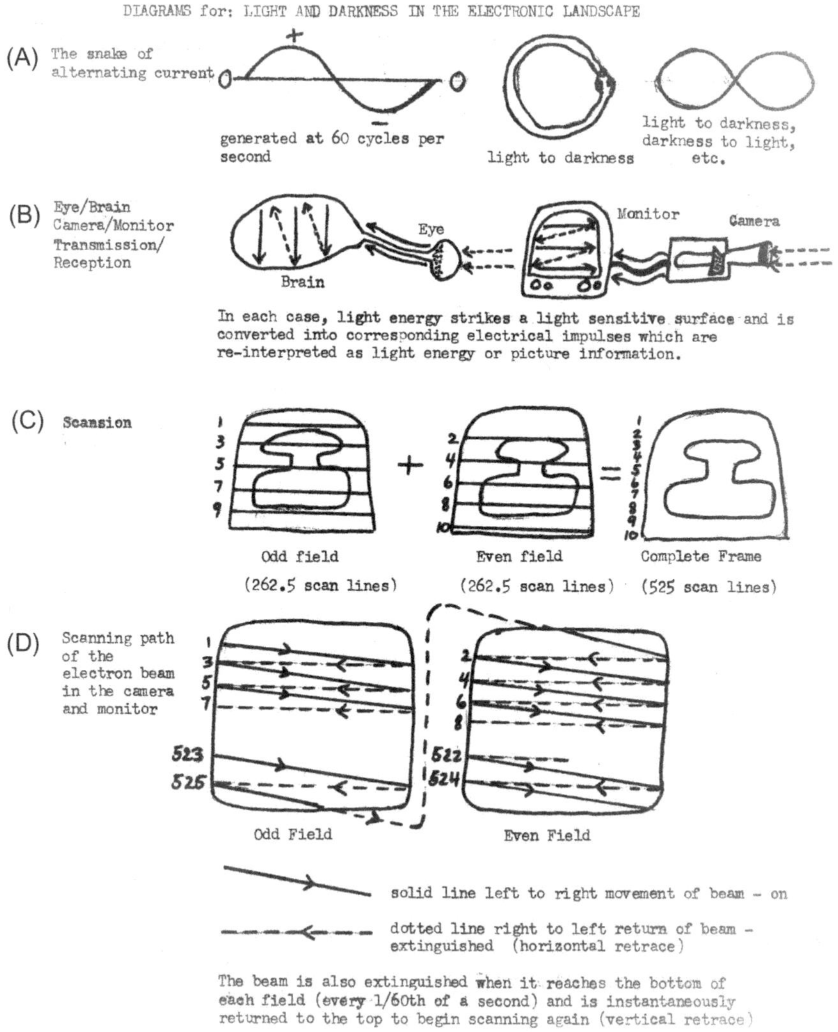

Figure 6.8 Barbara Buckner, illustrations accompanying her lecture "Light and Darkness in the Electronic Landscape," 1978.

process of video image scanning and recording is the process of converting reflected light as seen by a camera eye and coding this light energy as intelligence in the form of a sequence of voltages over time and decoding that arrangement into radiated and transmitted light in the monitor.

How different this process is from film. The crucial difference being that between transmitted and projected light. In film, the image is projected from one surface (the film plane) to another surface of the screen. The small image on film is shot through with light and magnified onto the screen. In video, the internal transmission entails a light to electrical energy conversion, a process of encoding and decoding a signal of varying voltage, a translation of the light substance itself where electrical current transduces to light.

The film image is eternally recorded, a fact which does not change. Once chemically developed on film, the image is not recomposed in the present. The chemical is developed: this is the recorded quality of film. Each time a video recording is played back, there is a coding process which must be relived in order to translate the encoded magnetism on tape to the monitor picture. This is the sense of immediacy inherent in the video medium.

This may also explain, in part, why one can look, gaze, and finally be numbed into holding one's vision toward the television screen that has even a still scene on it. The picture processing mirrors or counterpoints the electrical activity and cyclic movements in the brain. Instead of watching the wave break, recede, gather itself up again, and break, we have become the wave and have neither memory nor expectancy. For this reason also, video is crudely a meditative medium; crudely, in that the single-mindfulness is built into the system and works upon the beholder.

A videotape recording is accomplished by using videotape as the recording intermediary between the source of transmission—the camera—and the place of reception—the monitor. In its unrecorded or raw state, the video tape is in a state of complete chaos. This is what we see as noise or "snow" or "salt and pepper" patterns on the screen when no signal or intelligence is being transmitted. In this state the tape consists of an unintelligent surface of unmagnetized particles. When played back, this uncoded energy is transmitting chaotic luminance patterns. When the videotape recorder is set into the record mode, the video recording heads magnetically lair down tracks of information along the tape at a high speed. The non-arrayed, unmagnetized particles on the tape are organized into an arrangement of a coded signal or voltages. Other circuits within the videotape recorder are designed to transduce this magnetic recording into a transmitted signal which the monitor plays back in concert with the recorder. All sync pulses and timing references must be aligned for camera, recorder, and monitor. The sync pulses, the invisible hooks which hold the frame in place as they run in place are a prison in the way that natural day and night are—a necessary division of activity. When the image loses sync, there are visionary cataclysms which occur similar to earthquakes and flooding. The eye is the recipient of such natural disasters and wishes to flee the scene (seen). Loss of vertical sync is seen as the vertical rolling of the picture; horizontal sync loss is when the picture collapses into horizontal bars across the screen.

The monitor also contains an electron beam which scans the underside of the monitor screen which is coated with a layer of light-emitting phosphors. When the electron beam strikes the phosphors, they emit a corresponding intensity of light for each picture element. It is this radiated light which we see as the picture on the face of the screen.

The electron beam is the internal sun which illumines the whole interior of the electronic landscape. It is actually extinguished or eclipsed at the end of each horizontal line scan and again at the vertical retrace interval, when the beam is returned to the top of the field to begin its surveyance of the video field (diagram D). At these times, there is no transmission of picture information. If this were not done, it would result in confusing picture information during the horizontal and vertical retrace intervals. it is the nay-saying part of the electronic pulse, the other half of the face of the sun. [. . .]

The video image as seen by a black-and-white camera is the natural one. It is a product of the natural landscape of vision reflected by the light of the natural sun whose rays reflect its natural skin. When seen as a video image, the object is in its most natural setting—that of the document or record. The light of the image remains literal. It awaits the ecstatic fire of another landscape—or the land of the artificial sun. That land gives rise to a raiment of color so vast as to resemble the lightness and chimera of the dream—in its quantity, its movement, fluidity, and magic proportion. This is the land of the internal processing currents embodied within the casing of those magic image machines known as electronic image processors—alone and in concert with computers. In these machines the natural image is reconstituted into electronic pictographs of pulsing color, shape, texture, and forces—the instantaneous magic mirror of the mind's eye.

The image seen by a camera eye is the natural one—natural in outline, texture, and luminosity. It is all we can say about it. It is assumed in its adroitness and simplicity. It is a phenomenon of reflection, visible because of the exterior sun shining upon it. If the sun does not shine we do not see it. Whether it be a human head, a tree, or a lamp, it remains the direct perception of the camera eye, the natural sight of its sister sight—the human eye. As soon as the light surface is struck by the electron beam, the image at once begins its second birth in artificial reproduction. The light is transmitted on the face of the tube into multiplied countenances of varying voltage. This seeding of light along a time line for 525 lines is the machine sampling of light and dark, where the natural object is remodeled continuously as the sum of the parts of itself. This is the natural landscape transformed to the artificial one, in the land of the internal sun. The image is whole but transmitted as moving and varying voltage. It has been dismembered into models of itself and serially added in order to reproduce itself as whole. It is because of this characteristic that the video image appears to have the unique property of being still and moving at once.

At this point, the natural source of illumination needed to light the object is gone. Reflected light has gone the route of internal transmission instead. At this point the image has become the product of the interior field—the eye turned back on itself, or the mind's eye producing its own pictures. The image made whole by the camera eye is battered and recommences to make itself whole in series—a sequential summation of light and dark sown in the electronic landscape. The image is lit from within. The monitor illumines the image from the inside out. How different is the process from the projection of a film. The reflection is no more, projection is no more. The natural sun has passed away into a cloud forever. The dark box—camera obscura—is now continually lit to transform the image continually in the present. In sequence, ever again, the image is constantly re-lit and re-lived. Yet the changing mosaic is ever still, its stillness being the complete and ever-changing reproduction of the original image. [. . .]

This electronic machine is the great artificer, the body which remakes the body of the necessary and natural object. It automatically accomplishes the demonic process where in an image light becomes shadow and shadow light, sky earth and earth sky, water fire and fire water. One does not have to wait for the natural tree to eclipse the natural sun so that leaves may cast their shadows. The elements transmute their shape and energies to some phenomenal ersatz. The machine is the electronic beast by which the initiating force of the human hand continues to reshape the phantasms which fire the human brain and imagination. The human may program a set of controls via the computer to control the intensity and choice of color, brightness level, amount of contrast, and gray levels, multi-camera image sequences, the insertion of one image into another and the rate of change for each. The human may program the machine to go on indefinitely creating variations on itself in time. The serpent power begets itself. These are the new pictures, or the artificial and incendiary mind creatures invested with the power to evolve in the bogus mirror of machine dance, in the space where thousands of lights erupt and die—the expressive heart.

To quote from Don McArthur, a designer of a computer-based video synthesizer system:

> With a computer-based video synthesizer, one can generate a sequence of images while controlling each individual image with a detail and precision that is many orders of magnitude greater than is possible with manual control . . . In the compositional mode, the artist can enter programs and parameters through the keyboard, observing the resulting sequence of images, and then modify the parameters through either the keyboard or a real-time input and thus build up a data set for a complete piece. The data set, representing all the aesthetic decisions made by the artist, is stored in the computer at each state of the composition. When the composition is finished the system will operate in the automatic-production mode generating the final video signal in real time with no intervention by the artist.[1]

The video image processors reconstitute a natural image as seen by the camera eye. A black-and-white video camera will see a flower in its natural state. This natural black-and-white image will be passed through an image processor which electronically adds a variety of color, increases and decreases the amount of luminance, gray levels, and contrast in the image. Up to eight or sixteen images may be mixed together additively; some parts of one image being inserted into parts of the second and third and so on until a multi-layered, multi-colored new image composite is created which is not only a variation on the original, but also takes on a form which is completely original because new lines of force and texture have been compounded. The process of compounding two or more images together is similar to the iconic and mental configurations which occur in Chinese character formation (diagram G). In the video mixing process, the inside of one image may become the outside of the other image, the boundary of an object is conjoined electronically with another. Where light falls in one, the dark portion of the second image may appear. The contour of one may interdict the other and form a new contour altogether. The body of the contours, that mass between lines of the exterior form, may have been of a single texture. A second texture mixed with the former creates a transmuted one.

Perhaps paradoxically, video is not a medium for detail. To record the image of an object with a video camera and process that image with a variety of luminance, contrast, and color is to automatically lose original detail and hence texture. One must electronically add texture to texture or modify texture to create new texture, or detail. The phenomenon of adding color co any black-and-white image is basic to electronic video picture making. Unlike film, color and light in video are disengaged from their objects, because they are added and subtracted independently from the initial image. Color may fly from one object to another; it may pass from foreground to background, electronically flown out of reach of gravity or attachment. Color added to an image is not the naturalistic color of a color camera—it is artificially created internally by changing the phase relationships between the three primary colors of light—red, green, and blue. An equal mixture of these three creates white or the total additive mix of colored light. Each colored light mixed is a step toward increased luminosity. This is the reverse of mixing pigments where every color added is one more step toward black. An unequal mixture of these three primaries yields the electronic palette of video. The internal sun of the video machine issues forth an artificial rainbow of itself, the recreation of color anew—not from the natural sun whose rays reflect the object, but from the shining internal one whose raiment are the colored sums of electron flow.

Where an object had a reflection and luminance added to it, that lit portion will appear to create a new body or mass in and of itself. It loses the appearance of being a highlight belonging to a larger body. That light becomes a new mass, a body in its own right which acts in consort with other light bodies of a similar kind. [. . .]

The camera is still used with most image processors to retrieve the initial image for processing. The electronic sun eclipses in the camera every 60th of a second. The natural sun promises to eclipse altogether when the camera or the use of reflected light is done away with altogether. If the screen can be divided into the millions of bits of picture information that it is; if all the information in one frame of video can be stored in computer memory, the whole picture can be reproduced point by point, line by line, and images created without any natural referent whatsoever. One can create an image from nothing with the greatest detail through varying degrees of abstraction. This information can be called up or stored at any time. It is the end of the necessary object in natural space and time. It is the art of total artifice. The interior sun begetting its children in the electronic landscape programed to continue during the day light hours or the dark is like the eye begetting imagery on the face of the mind when the eyes are closed. The interior sun haunts the imaginary landscape, the human consciousness. The electronic sun haunts the same landscape and will beget its own children, incendiary computer images of fire. [. . .]

The ecstasy of the machine dance is that the machine can create these colors and images in any variety that the artist wishes: evolutionary histories of shape and color called up before the eyes for some future incarnation or stored away for temporary death. These could be likened to unevolved image species which undergo mutations in time with a certain amount of direction from the electronic picture-making machines—the human imagination and its electronic servants. This is perhaps the ecstasy and dilemma of those creating machine-assisted works. The universe is not made up of moving geometries forming out of vast space and crashing into colored oblivion. The artist enters as Chaos, but he/she also enters as the vision to wreck order upon the order of the machine.

The mind breathes forth its own illusion—it is that total and that instantaneous. The machine breathes forth its own illusion—it is that total and that instantaneous. The mind—its picture-making capability, its executing decisions, its will, its pattern recognition capability, its recall and memory have been externalized from the body of the human. The mechanism of mind and its picture-making ability are now embodied in the body of a computer/processor whose function it is to lift this burden into the realm of what is known as artificial intelligence. [. . .]

The human stands locked between heaven and earth, eternally grounding the lightning that is hurled from sphere to sphere. The machine has caught fire with the same and is destined to take the burden from the human in order to do work. Lightning strikes and the hum is deafening and meted out in appropriate portions—to the gate of one circuit and passed through to another. This is the distribution of shocks, of cataclysms, of natural disaster correcting itself outside the human brain. The machine creates models for execution without the trial of execution. This is the burden of mind workings lifted from the human body onto its sister, galvanized.

The art of the video image is created from a perfect union of two beasts—the human and the mechanistic, both extraordinary creatures of light. The human has eyes in the illumined sun of imagination; the machine reroutes that fire of sight at extraordinary speed and calculation so it may serve well the conceptions of the heart.

Life and Death in the electronic landscape exist contemporaneously, as Nature holds sway in this world continuously. The artist or electron warrior has met the natural enemy in its own landscape of consciousness—the warring of heaven and earth in the human imagination. It is the serpent power winding its way eating light to make light. This is the feast of light eaters and death swindlers, or the electronic beast counting out its lives in the hinterland of an electronic wilderness—the frontier for a new art form (Figure 6.8).

From Barbara Buckner, "Light and Darkness in the Electronic Landscape: Some Aspects of the Video Image," lecture given at the Collective for Living Cinema, New York, February 1978; unpublished typescript from the archive of the author.

Note

1 *A Computer-Based Video Synthesizer System* by Donald E. McArthur, June 1977. Research and development conducted at the Experimental Television Center, Binghamton, New York. The Experimental Television Center is funded by the NYSCA and NEA.

7

Video | Performance and Theater

Introduction by Barbara Büscher (Guest Editor)

I.

The combination of (theater) performance with moving-picture projections has a multifaceted history that goes back to the early twentieth century and the use of slides and film clips by theater directors such as Vsevolod Meyerhold of Russia and Erwin Piscator of Germany. In the 1920s, Piscator used film projections in some of his productions of plays, aiming to introduce a documentary perspective and open up the enclosed theater space to the world outside, to the social and political realities of the day, which served as a visual background to the stage (like a backdrop). "The media that Piscator incorporated into his productions were not typically seen as artistic media, but rather as sources of information. He used film, projections, and posters as pieces of evidence for the political claims of the play."[1]

Projecting film, slides, and, more recently, video remains a relevant way of combining theater/performance with moving images today. Increasing emphasis has been placed on the material character and position of the screen or projection surface in its role as an interface between the space inhabited by moving images, constituted of light and shade, and the physical, material space of the performance.[2] Since the 1960s, a plethora of projection spaces and techniques have emerged. Some were devised for performances or installations within a museum setting, in which the very act of projecting could become a performance, for example, in the works of US artist Ken Jacobs.[3] These were associated with *expanded cinema*,[4] a development that anteceded the widespread adoption of video by the performing arts. The expansion of cinema also extended into performance, where operating with media devices (for filming and projecting films) already played a central role. Performance highlighted the processual nature of the film screening, made it into an event that suspended the spatial order and temporal structure conventionalized by the cinema setup. Performance moreover implemented a disruption of narrative continuity based on technology; it favored the reduction and separation of media components, which then—crucially—are realized and combined live, implemented anew with each performance. Or, as Nam June Paik put it: "Film ceases to be the REPEAT-art and attains the high quality of unrepeatable 'einmalige live performance' as music and drama."[5]

Breaking up established, apparatus-based constellations—such as film projections—became a way to focus attention on the event character of the presentation or performance and facilitate critical reflection on such constellations by exposing their modes of operation and utilization. "Live vs. recorded" is one aspect that has become a recurring topic of discussion where artistic practices combining performance with moving-picture media are concerned. As well as incorporating projections to open up and visually extend the space, performances have increasingly used techniques to control sound and images live. One example is the much-quoted *Nine Evenings: Theater and Engineering* (1966). This series of performances attracted the participation of artists from the fields of music, visual arts, dance, and cinema, including John Cage, Robert Rauschenberg, Yvonne Rainer, and Robert Whitman. They cooperated with technicians and engineers to experiment with new artistic practices at the interface between performance and contemporary media technology.[6]

As video proliferated and was taken up by artists, performances featuring the live handling of moving images and sounds occurred on a new technological footing. The possibilities increased for creating new stage and scenographic constellations and exploring subjects focusing on the relationship between physical presence and screened imagery.

While devoting an entire chapter to "Television as a Creative Medium" and emphasizing the unique potential of CCTV in his book *Expanded Cinema*, first published in 1970, author Gene Youngblood's consideration of *intermedia theater* concentrated mainly on works that engaged performatively with film projection.[7] As early as 1966, the *Tulane Drama Review*[8] dedicated an edition to performative artistic practices with film. This drew heavily on reports from the context of the *New York Cinema Festival 1*, co-organized by Jonas Mekas in 1965, which marked the first time that several works of what then became known as *expanded cinema* were presented collectively. A similar tendency evolved in Europe, driven by artists including Valie Export, Peter Weibel, Birgit and Wilhelm Hein, and Malcolm LeGrice.[9]

With installation, performance, and video art, the field of visual art broadened in the 1960s to include approaches that extended the artistic space and concept of temporality. This led to the forging of new connections with other arts, such as theater, dance, music, and film, and shifted the focus on to performativity and processuality across all media formats used to create artistic works.

Even more than the characteristics of the video image, the medial aspect of immediate and simultaneous recording and transmission—which is often perceived as the live character of the medium—generated new approaches to using moving images in performance. Joan Jonas described this in a text included in this chapter: "What video offered me was the opportunity to work live, to make a continuous series of images explicitly for the camera during live performance, which allowed me an added non-narrative layer in a kind of condensed poetic structure."[10] By the same token, video allowed performances to be recorded and these prerecorded tapes to be used later and so—as Jonas put it—"to work back and forth between tape and video performance, translating ideas from performance into tapes, transferring elements from tapes back into performance."[11] This switching back and forth between media, circulating the material in performance, in tape, or in installation form, is a defining trait of Jonas's work based on the simultaneity of recording and replay, the innovations arising from the video medium.[12]

Initially, Jonas had translated her performances into film, "to save them in an interesting form."[13] The recording of performances and theater productions, transforming them into audiovisual storage media, represents another long-standing connection between the two fields, allowing accessibility and the creation of archives. "Videoperformance"—as defined by Willoughby Sharp in 1976 in reference to his 1974 exhibition of the same name[14]—is understood by the artists as both: video performance can be a tape based on a performance ("visible only on video," as Chris Burden is quoted here[15]) or a performance that integrates video in various ways.[16] Other authors refer to "live video action."[17] In addition, video can be used for documenting performances. All three varieties of the relationship between video/moving images and performance/live presentation remain relevant today. In the 1980s, the interrelations between dancers' movements and camera movements were explored to give rise to trends such as "video dance," primarily denoting tapes and films that captured the transformation of a choreography for the camera.[18]

II.

This chapter focuses on the relationship between performance/theater and video, where projection and camera use, the live process of operating the media, and the immediate presentation of the recorded material are integral components of a performance. Analyses of and reflections on this relationship are based on an understanding of performance as a media nexus[19] in which moving images—their generation and presentation—are just one among several media. The emergence of what Hans-Thies Lehmann described in the 1990s as "post-dramatic" theater highlighted the mediality of theater or other performances, an issue which then became a central concern of theater studies and related research. The integration of contemporary media and technologies into theatrical performances and the departure from the dramatic text as the predominant element structuring theater, described by Lehmann as "decomposition" and the "separation of elements," raised questions of the interconnection of performativity and mediality.[20] "Theater is accomplished by means of an open, dynamic configuration of media transmissions. According to the historical or cultural context in which theater takes place, it is identical with those media which embody its structure-determining elements."[21] Seen in this light, theater is a momentary constellation of interacting media components that are updated and realized with each performance. But as the theoretical conception of theater is of a network of multiple, diverse media—which includes the bodies of the actors—individual consideration is rarely given to video as a separate medium, as we will see in the key concepts discussed below.

While such reflections emphasize the mediality of theater and performance, they also bring into focus the performativity of dealing with media. Here, a key concept is that of the *Apparatus Operator Complex*, as used by Vilem Flusser in his observations on the gestures of various media. Taking photography as an example, Flusser notes:

"[The photographer] takes part in a complex action in which it would be pointless to differentiate between him and the apparatus. The decisions made during this action are neither 'man-made' nor 'mechanical' but decisions arising from the apparatus/operator complex."[22] The idea of the action, which Flusser refers to here for description purposes, is repeated in the emphatic use of video or digital cameras within a performance. The conclusion that Flusser draws from the relation between the apparatus and the operator equally indicates the potential of such projections. This depends on the insight that the unique character of each of the various "technoimages" can only unfold based on a knowledge of their different modes of production—of use and recording, hardware and software, mechanics and programming.[23] This approach leads toward the dual meaning of the term "performance" in the constellations discussed here: on the one hand it is an *enactment* in the sense of a (re)presentation, with the meaningful and meaning-making use of media of all kinds, on the other the *execution* of directions that result from a compositional order, a (narrative) dramaturgy, and the technical media dispositives.

In theoretical terms, the relation between performance/theater and media/video can be narrowed down to three concepts in which this aspect of the dual meaning of performance is an implicit factor. They are intermediality, expanded scenography, and liveness. These three concepts refer to both the specific context of using video/moving images as part of performances and to the fact that operating with media implies their performativity.

III.

In the 1980s, work with video/moving images in theatrical and artistic performances increased and diversified and became a hallmark of many of the performance and theater groups that Lehmann discussed as representing "post-dramatic" theater.[24] The Wooster Group, John Jesurun, The Builders Association, Studio Azzurro/Giorgio Barberio Corsetti, and Helena Waldmann are just some of the names he mentions. Their work also provides the frame of reference for the considerations presented here.[25] Theater-based artists often cooperated with video/film artists on such projects. Later, starting in the early 1990s, theater studies and other fields of art research advanced the term *intermediality* to explore whether and how the incorporation of contemporary technological audiovisual media had caused a permanent shift in the media nexus of performances. Explicit reference to Fluxus artist Dick Higgins's concept of *intermedia* linked these observations with developments in the arts in the 1960s.[26]

In the introduction to a publication on intermediality in theater, editors Freda Chapple and Chiel Kattenbelt write:

> A first assumption is that intermediality is associated with the blurring of generic boundaries, crossover and hybrid performances, intertextuality, hypermediality, and a self-conscious reflexivity that displays the devices of performance in performance. From there we can see that there is a need to assess how the incorporation of digital technologies and the presence of other media . . . is

> creating new modes of representation; . . . new ways of creating temporal and spatial relations. These modes of representation are leading to new perceptions about theater and performance.[27]

With regard to this development in modes of representation in terms of the artists' playing with the technological media, the positioning of media in relation to each other, and the spectators' perception, an informative source is *Remediation* by Jay Bolter and Richard Grusin, which addresses and interprets a wide variety of modes of presentation and narrative patterns.[28] The term "hypermediacy," especially, has come to encapsulate a specific reading of the hybrid ways the elements in a performance work alongside, against, and with each other. The UK theater theoretician Andy Lavender describes it as follows:

> Hypermediacy is not simply a question of multiplicity of sources, images or image systems. It is expressed through simultaneity: two or more sources, images, systems and effects in play at the same time in a shared ecosystem. . . . In hypermedial performance, mise en scene is a network of mediations that are also remediations, persistently playing back to its spectators both the modes of the piece and the culture's modes of aesthetic affinity. . . . Hypermedial performance engages the spectator in an awareness of the interaction of different media, hence of media themselves.[29]

Other authors have further broken down the concept of intermediality to more clearly accentuate the process of transmission and dynamic configuration.[30] And media theorists have pointed out the inevitable shift in the concept of intermediality caused by digitalization: "Intermediality, as we know it today, implies the possibility of simulating any kind of medial characteristic by digital programming."[31] Researchers have objectified such reflections by conducting case studies on individual art projects and the way they deal with specific medial networks in performance. Many of these studies focus on video and film projections and the use of live cameras, examining how they relate with the other media of a performance and the shifts in these relations. That is an aspect also elucidated in the texts selected for publication here. In an excerpt from an analysis of works by the Wooster Group, Nick Kaye comments on the "order of difference" and rhythmic complexity created by the overlapping and simultaneity of different modes of medial representation—by the repetition of motifs and situations in video/film and on stage and by the different ways that dances, mediation, and recorded video are structured.[32] Mediation and the presence of the video operator testify to the twin aspects of performance as enactment and execution, as discussed above. Seeing dramaturgy in a general sense as the structuring of an event in a specific time frame, one could, in the words of Valentina Valentini and Bonnie Marranca, speak of "mediaturgy."[33] As yet, the task of systematizing relations between the analog and digital modes of video use and modes of performance remains to be accomplished.[34]

Analyses focusing on the space as the structuring element of theatrical performances link these general theories and methodological considerations on intermediality with those of *expanded scenography*. An excerpt from Birgit Wiens's book *Intermediale*

Szenographie included here takes this perspective to examine the medial structure of a performance. Wiens starts by asking how scenographer Bert Neumann's work allows for "playing with different media under live conditions, for hybridizing spaces, for shifting the axis of vision, and for putting the audience's possibilities of perception into constant motion."[35] Her analysis of Neumann's work at the Volksbühne in Berlin highlights the significance of spatial narration—drawing attention to the relation between inside and outside—for structuring a play. Neumann accompanies the device of closing off the "fourth wall," that is, physically obstructing the audience's view with live recordings and the transmission of recorded images on a large screen on the stage. When perceptibility is structured by means of medial transmission in this way, creating a gap between what is physically present and what is transmitted via media, the audience can experience what already pervades their mediatized everyday lives: "The fully media-wired home had become the human condition."[36] Scenography in the expanded sense is seen as a practice involving space-modeling processes, which no longer merely supplies settings for the presentation of various art forms but increasingly aims to be—and is perceived as—an autonomous art practice. In this sense it can, as the US scenography theoretician Arnold Aronson put it, "make the underlying structures of representation visible, presenting the spectator with multiple (and sometimes contradictory) understandings that expand a literal text. Meaning is replaced by relationship."[37] Aronson had already pointed out in an earlier text that production and presentation can be regarded as a closely intermeshing fabric of technology, scenography, architecture, and dramaturgy.[38] Hence the involvement of architects such as Diller + Scofidio, whose contribution to this chapter looks at their interpretation of the equation "space–video projection–mirror and screen–physical dancers" for the dance production *Moving Target*.

Most examples of the design or appropriation of spaces considered in the texts here follow the classic separation of stage and auditorium. But the concept of expanded scenography has in fact long since broadened to encompass "found spaces" and sites of all kinds. It now includes creating physically real spaces for the activities of former audience members that have now become users, interlinking them with virtual spaces. The current wide range of possibilities for screen spaces has brought the combination of media and performance to a new level by allowing the actors involved to operate remotely and by utilizing and adapting today's ubiquitous miniaturized screens. As Dorita Hannah notes:

> The screen—a fixed or movable plane that simultaneously divides and connects, reveals and conceals, upon which images and data are displayed and filtered—presents a powerful concept for scenographic performativity: especially in our highly mediated world streaming information 24/7 via smart phones, tablets, television, computer monitors, slide show presentations, and architectural facades; but also where bodies themselves (both visceral and virtual) are screened to vet who's in and who's out.[39]

Performance groups such as Blast Theory[40] have used iPads and smartphones since the 2000s to create new action and perception spaces based on gaming structures for their users/audience (see Figure 7.1).[41] These consistently play with the interchange between physical presence and absence, between media-channeled communication and its flipside, hidden controls and surveillance.

Games like these, which include live actions in outdoor spaces with data/image transfer through smartphones and other handheld displays, are structured around the mobility of the players whose experiences can be communicated, for example, from diverse places in a city. In contrast, recent restrictions during the Covid pandemic have forced an increased immobility fostering a development toward live streams. Viewers, users, and players remain constrained to the domestic atmosphere of their own four walls and are connected with each other only by image/data transfer. Theater productions, concerts, and club events appear as part of the video flow, detached from their staging within a space, or as a spatial image transformation.

Such aspects actually were already touched on in early discussions of the potential of video. Considered in the context of performance or theater, the terms *liveness* or *presentness* are used to circumscribe the distinction between video and film on the one hand and between video/media and performance on the other.[42] In the texts presented in this chapter, the question of presentness plays an important role. Depending on the art practices discussed, they inquire into the role of presentness in the relationship between performers, operating media or mediated action, and projected images. In reference to the performance works of Studio Azzurro, Valentini

Figure 7.1 Blast Theory, *Can You See Me Now?*, 2001. A collaboration between Blast Theory and the Mixed Reality Lab, University of Nottingham.

speaks of a "doubled register of presence." "Electronic audiovisual technologies do not lead to reproducibility; rather, they emphasize immediacy, perhaps the most specific identifying trait of theatrical spectacle."[43]

While media theorists and artists have from the outset placed the focus on the immediacy and presentness of work with video as distinct from film, scholars of performance and theater studies have stressed the "physical co-presence"[44] of actors and spectators as marking the ontological difference between performance on the one hand and presentations of recorded images and situations on the other. Many authors have referred to the connection between the video medium's liveness and the real-time transmission of recorded material, its close affinity with "television's early days, when it was entirely a live medium in the sense of being broadcast as it was performed."[45] In his analysis of current constellations of media use and social copresence, Nick Couldry has found that ultimately "liveness . . . is continuous connectedness."[46]

In 1999, Philip Auslander introduced the discourse on media (theory) to the performance studies research context and challenged the "reductive binary opposition of the live and the mediated."[47] Deepening the discussion on the concept's possible meanings, he clearly underlined the aspect of perception, insisting that "the experience of liveness is . . . built around the audience's affective experience," and that "some real-time operations of digital technology make a claim upon us to engage with them as live events."[48] Such proposals reveal a growing proximity to the theories of New Materialism, which similarly compare human with nonhuman actors and so change our perspective on medial objects and their agency in performance.[49] They are concerned with relations between media objects, seen as image processors and as apparatuses, with fields of activity, modes of use, as well as operations that challenge and facilitate them or that they undermine and disrupt. It was the emergence of video that allowed the act of processing within a performance to unfold and appear alongside the multiple options for projection.

Notes

1 Minou Arjomand, "Erwin Piscator: Staging Politics in the Weimar Republic," in *The Great European Directors*, ed. David Barnett (London: Methuen, 2019), vol. 2, 66–91, esp. 82f. See also Erwin Piscator, "Die Funktion des Films," in *Erwin Piscator: Eine Arbeitsbiographie in 2 Bänden*, ed. Knut Boeser and Renata Vatkóva (Berlin: Ed. Hentrich, 1986), vol. 1, 190–2. Observations on Piscator, Meyerhold, et al. also open a publication on performance by Chris Salter, *Entangled: Technology and Transformation of Performance* (Cambridge, MA/London: MIT Press, 2010), 32–6.

2 See Barbara Büscher, "(Interaktive) Interfaces und Performance: Strukturelle Aspekte der Kopplung von Live-Akteuren und medialen Bild/Räumen," in *Maschinen, Menschen, Performances*, ed. Martina Leeker (Berlin: Alexander, 2001), 87–111.

3 See e.g. "Ken and Flo Jacobs. Interview," *Millenium Film Journal* 32/33 (1998), 131–40; also Barbara Büscher, *Live Electronic Arts und Intermedia: Die sechziger Jahre* (Leipzig, 2002), https://nbn-resolving.org/urn:nbn:debsz14-qucosa-39497, 314–16.

4 See, e.g., *Expanded Cinema: Art, Performance, Film*, ed. A.L. Rees, Duncan White, and Steven Ball (London: Tate Publishing, 2011); Andrew V. Uroskie, *Between the Black Box and the White Cube: Expanded Cinema and Postwar Art* (Chicago/London: University of Chicago Press, 2014).

5 Nam June Paik, "Scenario (1962–63)," in *We Are in Open Circuits: Writings by Nam June Paik*, ed. John G. Hanhardt, Gregory Zinman, and Edith Decker-Phillips (Cambridge, MA/London: MIT Press, 2019), 200.

6 See e.g. Jack Burnham, *Beyond Modern Sculpture: The Effects of Science and Technology on the Sculpture of this Century* (New York: George Braziller, 1968); *9 Evenings Reconsidered: Art, Theater, and Engineering 1966* (Cambridge, MA/London: MIT Press, 2016); Büscher, *Live Electronic Arts*, 101–31; and the website of the Canadian Langlois foundation, https://www.fondation-langlois.org/html/e/selection.php?Selection=9EVO.

7 Gene Youngblood, *Expanded Cinema* (New York: Dutton, 1970), 365–98.

8 *Tulane Drama Review* 11, no. 1 (Autumn 1966). Contributors included Susan Sontag ("Film and Theatre, "24–37), Stan Vanderbeek ("Culture: Intercom and Expanded Cinema," 38–48), Michael Kirby ("The Use of Film in the New Theatre," 49–61), and Milton Cohen ("Film in Space Theatre," 62–7). On the trend in general, see also Richard Kostelanetz, *The Theatre of Mixed Means* (New York: Dial Press, 1968).

9 See, e.g., *X-Screen: Film Installations and Actions in the 1960s and 1970s*, (Vienna: Museum Moderner Kunst Stiftung Ludwig Wien; Cologne: König, 2004); *Film Unframed. A History of Austrian Avant-Garde Cinema*, ed. Peter Tscherkassy (Vienna: Synema, 2012).

10 Joan Jonas, "Transmission," in *Women, Art, and Technology*, ed. Judy Malloy (Cambridge, MA/London: MIT Press, 2013), 122; reprinted in this chapter.

11 Jonas, "Transmission," 125.

12 See *In the Shadow of a Shadow: The Work of Joan Jonas*, ed. Joan Simon (New York: Miller; Ostfildern: Hatje Cantz, 2015).

13 Jonas, "Transmission," 121.

14 *Video Performance*, 112 Greene Street, New York, January 1974. See "Video Performance," *Avalanche Newspaper* 9 (May/June 1974).

15 Willoughby Sharp. "Videoperformance," in *Video Art: An Anthology*, ed. Ira Schneider and Beryl Korot (New York/London: Harcourt, Brace and Javanovich, 1976), 252–67, esp. 265.

16 Schneider and Korot, *Video Art*, 258. See also Helen Westgeest, *Video Art Theory* (New York: Wiley & Sons), 45–7.

17 See, e.g., Yvonne Spielmann, *Video: Das reflexive Medium* (Frankfurt am Main: Suhrkamp, 2005), 141–7.

18 See, e.g., Claudia Rosiny, *Videotanz: Panorama einer internationalen Kunstform* (Zürich: Chronos, 1999).

19 See Büscher, *Live Electronic Arts*, 14–22.

20 See, e.g., Sybille Krämer, "Was haben 'Performativität' und 'Medialität' miteinander zu tun?" in *Performativität und Medialität*, ed. Sybille Krämer (Paderborn: Fink, 2004), 13–32.

21 Kati Röttger, "Intermedialität als Bedingung von Theater: Methodische Überlegungen," in *Theater und Medien*, ed. Henri Schoenmakers (Bielefeld: transcript, 2008), 117–24, esp. 119.

22 Vilem Flusser, "Umbruch der menschlichen Bezehungen?" in *Kommunikologie*, ed. Stefan Bollmann and Edith Flusser (Frankfurt am Main: Fischer, 1998), 9–234, esp. 184f.

23 Barbara Büscher, "Medial Gestures: On the 'Decipherability' of Techno Images (Vilem Flusser) and Their Production," in *MAP#7 Media/Performances: On Gestures* (Leipzig/Berlin, April 2016), https://www.perfomap.de/map7/media-performance-on-gestures/medial-gestures.-on-the-2018decipherability2019-of-techno-images-vilem-flusser-and-their-production.

24 Hans-Thies Lehmann, *Postdramatisches Theater* (Frankfurt am Main: Verlag der Autoren, 1999).

25 Their work was made accessible and disseminated via a network of European production venues, including the Big Motion festival in Vienna in the early 1990s.

26 See Dick Higgins, "Intermedia" (1965), with an appendix by Hannah Higgins, *Leonardo* 34, no. 1 (2001), 49–54; Büscher, *Live Electronic Arts*, 59–75.

27 Freda Chapple and Chiel Kattenbelt, "Key Issues in Intermediality in Theatre and Performance," in *Intermediality in Theatre and Performance*, ed. Freda Chapple and Chiel Kattenbelt (Amsterdam: Rodopi 2006), 11; *Mapping Intermediality in Performance*, ed. Sarah Bay-Cheng, Chiel Kattenbelt, Andy Lavender, and Robin Nelson (Amsterdam: Amsterdam University Press, 2010); *Multimedia Performance*, ed. Rosemary Klich and Edward Scheer (Basingstoke: Palgrave, 2012).

28 Jay David Bolter and Richard Grusin, *Remediation: Understanding New Media* (Cambridge, MA/London: MIT Press, 2000).

29 Andy Lavender, "Mise en scene: Hypermediacy, and the Sensorium," *Intermediality in Theatre and Performance* (2006), 55–66, esp. 56, 63.

30 Kati Röttger, "The Mystery of the In-Between: A Methodological Approach to Intermedial Performance Analysis," *Forum Modernes Theater* 28, no. 2 (Tübingen 2013), 105–16.

31 Joachim Paech and Jens Schröter, "Intermedialität analog/digital: Ein Vorwort," in *Intermedialität analog/digital. Theorien, Methoden, Analysen* (Munich: Fink, 2008), 9–14, esp. 10.

32 Nick Kaye, *Multi-Media: Video—Installation—Performance* (London: Routledge, 2007), 168.

33 Valentina Valentini, "Studio Azzurro: Reinventare il medium teatro," in *Studio Azzurro. Teatro*, ed. Noemi Pittaluga and Valentina Valentini (Rome: Contrasto, 2012), 6–21, esp. 7; reprinted in this chapter.

34 In a chapter entitled "The Monitor and the Mise-en-Scène," Salter has attempted to systematize the modes of use and aims of video in performance settings. He arrives at ten different aspects, which are not always clearly distinguishable and do not always mark out distinct levels of argumentation. Chris Salter, *Entangled*, 130–1.

35 Birgit Wiens, *Intermediale Szenographie: Raum-Ästhetiken des Theaters am Beginn des 21. Jahrhunderts* (Paderborn: Fink, 2014), 248; reprinted in this chapter.

36 Ibid., 256.

37 Arnold Aronson, "Foreword," in *Scenography Expanded: An Introduction to Contemporary Performance Design* (London/New York: Bloomsbury), XIII–XVI, esp. XV/XVI.

38 Arnold Aronson, "Technology and Dramaturgical Development: Five Observations," in Aronson, *Looking into the Abyss: Essays on Scenography* (Ann Arbor: University of Michigan Press, 2005), 67–80, esp. 72.

39 Dorita Hannah, "Scenographic Screen Space: Bearing Witness and Performing Resistance," in *Scenography Expanded*, 2017, 39–62, esp. 40.

40 For Blast Theory's history, see the group's informative website, which includes an extensive bibliography of texts and books on their work, ed. Martin Rieser http://www.blasttheory.co.uk/about-us/.

41 On these new performative modes of playing in urban spaces and similar formats, see, e.g., *The Mobile Audience: Media Art and Mobile Technologies*, ed. Martin Rieser (New York: Rodopi, 2011); Judith Ackermann, "Digital Games and Hybrid Reality Theatre," in *New Game Plus: Perspektiven der Game Studies*, ed. Benjamin Beil, Gundolf Freyermuth, and Lisa Gotto (Bielefeld: transcript, 2015), 63–88.

42 See, e.g., William Kaizen, "Live on Tape: Video, Liveness and the Immediate," in *Art and the Moving Image*, ed. Tanya Leighton (London: Tate Publishing, 2008), 258–72; Rudy Navarro, "Reconciling Video and Film in Frank Gillette and Ira Schneider's Wipe Cycle," *Journal of Film and Video* 71, no. 2 (University of Illinois Press, Summer 2019), 3–17.

43 Valentina Valentini, "Studio Azzurro: Reinventare il medium teatro," in *Studio Azzurro. Teatro*, ed. Noemi Pittaluga and Valentina Valentini (Rome: Contrasto, 2012), 7; reprinted in this chapter.

44 See, e.g., Erika Fischer-Lichte, *Ästhetik des Performativen* (Frankfurt am Main: Suhrkamp, 2004); Peggy Phelan, *Unmarked: The Politics of Performance* (London/New York: Routledge, 1993).

45 Nick Couldry, "Liveness: 'Reality,' and the Mediated Habitus from Television to the Mobile Phone," *The Communication Review* 7 (2004), 353–62, esp. 355.

46 Ibid., 360.

47 Philip Auslander, *Liveness: Performance in a Mediatized Culture* (London/New York: Routledge, 1999), 3.

48 Philip Auslander, "Digital Liveness: A Historico-Philosophical Perspective," *PAJ: A Journal of Performance and Art* 102 (New York, 2012), 3–11, esp. 6/7.

49 Key reference texts for this school of thought—alongside Bruno Latour's actor-network theory—include Jane Bennett, *Vibrant Matter: A Political Ecology of Things* (Durham: Duke University Press, 2010); *The Non-Human Turn*, ed. Richard Grusin (Minneapolis: University of Minnesota Press, 2015). Dorita Hannah discusses the screen as an object-event, also with reference to these proposals. See Dorita Hannah, "Scenographic Screen Space" (2008), 59–60. A recent publication focusing on the relationship between things and dance is *Tanz der Dinge / Things That Dance*, ed. Johannes Birringer and Josephine Fenger (Bielefeld: transcript, 2019)

Transmission (1998)

Joan Jonas

My work consists of fragments and chance as much as materials and technology. In the late 1960s, after studying art history and sculpture, I became inspired by the idea of performance and began to work with time as material, transferring my concerns with drawing and the object into movement. At the time, "I didn't see a major difference between a poem, a sculpture, a film, or a dance."[1] Now, in 1998, working in video, performance, installation, sculpture, and drawing, I experience the forms as overlapping, not totally separate.

While I was studying art history, I looked carefully at the space of painting, films, and sculpture—at how illusions are created within a frame. From this, I learned how to deal with depth and distance. When I switched to performance, I went directly to real space. I looked at it, and I would imagine how it would look to an audience. I would imagine what they would be looking at, how they would perceive the ambiguities and illusions of the space. An idea would come from just looking until my vision blurred.[2] [. . .]

At that time, I also traveled to the Southwest to see the Hopi snake dance. My reaction was complicated. I remember now the profound effect this dance—a ritual with live snakes—had on me, as well as the architecture of the pueblos and the amazing desert landscape. [. . .]

In a second ceremony at Ancoma, costumed figures were far away, in the desert, and then suddenly they were dose up, in the plaza, dancing. What was striking to me was how these images from afar could be brought back home. What became apparent and of interest was how to think about one place and be in another. Was it possible to cross-reference rather than categorize? Was it possible to translate such concepts into one's own intuitive language, using technology as a tool of transformation and transmission?

Other references for me were the circus and magic shows that I saw as a child and the idea of alchemy or transformation of material and psyche. I especially liked sleight of hand—visual tricks that could be special effects. Perhaps I always like to have a reason in relation to structure and content—to know that something made it happen even if we don't know and can't see what it was. On the other hand, I'm interested in the obvious. In works of mine such as *Vertical Roll* (1972),[3] I reveal the mechanics of the illusion. I like to juxtapose high tech with the original gesture. In that way the touch, the body, and the machine are put into play.

Performance as a medium exists somewhere between "conceptual art" and "theater." For performance, a genre of multiple media, the critical material is time. This is said in the context of the visual arts—in my context. The artist builds a performance by designing and composing all aspects of the work—conceives, constructs, draws, and choreographs; makes the music or chooses it or selects a composer to work with; performs, produces, and directs film and video; often does camera or directs the camera work; and edits. The work is based on visual and aural concerns rather than text, although text can be used as material, and it can be written or chosen by the artist. Beyond this, there is also close collaboration with other performers and artists, filmmakers, editors, and producers. [. . .]

1968 Transmission: The Mirror

Inspired by the short stories of Jorge Luis Borges, I chose as my first technological tool the mirror, a device that transmits light. First, I made a long black costume for myself with mirrors pasted on it. I moved stiffly, parallel to the audience, quoting all references to mirrors in the short stories of *Borges's Labyrinths*. The piece was called *Oad Lau* (1968)[4] ("watering place," after a trip to Morocco; this work also related to the Greek wedding). Later, similar moving figures—a man and a woman appeared in *Wind* (1968)[5]—my first film.

From the beginning, the mirror provided me with a metaphor for my reflective investigation. It also provided a device to alter space and to fragment it. By reflecting it, I could break it up. I could mix reflections of performers and audience, thereby bringing all of them into the same time and space of the performance. In addition to creating space, a mirror also disturbs space, suggesting another reality through the looking glass—to see the reflection of Narcissus, to be a voyeur, to see one's self as the other. In this piece, *Oad Lau*, the reality was also to see oneself among and as one with others.

Then I did a series of works in which performers—about fifteen of them—carrying 5-foot-by-18-inch glass mirrors and glass moved slowly in choreographed sequences and patterns, reflecting the audience, themselves, and the space, fragmenting it, and yet always flattening it. The mirrors face front. The glass is heavy. The performers move slowly—in lines (*Mirror Piece I & II*, 1969 and 1970).[6]

In another part of the piece, bodies were treated as material. They were carried stiffly—horizontally by feet and neck—-like boards or glass. In another sequence, transparent glass panels are used. Two women roll across the floor with a 5-foot-by-18-inch sheet of glass between them, avoiding breakage. The panel is the same size as the mirrors used previously; here, though, at the same time, two men work with a larger piece of glass (four feet by five feet), turning it, shifting it. The audience, included by reflection, is part of a moving picture.

The mirrors and clear sheets of glass could break or shatter at a wrong move. We were barefoot. I was interested in this tension and that the onlookers might feel uneasy.

Narcissism provoked by mirrors is also disturbing. For *Mirror Check* (1970)[7] I stood naked, inspecting all parts of my body with a small round hand mirror. Using a slow circular movement, I began with my face and finished with the bottoms of my feet. The audience watches me checking myself. Vicariously, however, as they can't see what I see, despite the fact that they see more of me. The duration of the performance was about ten minutes. [. . .]

Transmission: Moving Images in Film, Electronic Signals in Video

Wind (1968) and *Songdelay* (1973)[8] translated my live performances into the medium of film. In *Wind*, an indoor work—*Oad Lau*—was taken outdoors to a beach on Long Island's north shore. It was winter. The element of wind became the central force as mirrored figures slowly moved in a snowy landscape. We played with the wind, taking our coats on and off, again and again, with some effort, while moving along the water's edge in the strong wind.

In *Songdelay*, by using different lenses, a wide angle and telephoto, I translated the outdoor performance *Delay Delay* into film. This was the final development of the series of outdoor works that began at Jones Beach. I wanted to save my performances in a form that interested me, and since I consciously used film as a reference at times during the performances, film was appropriate to the task.

I was particularly drawn to early filmmakers such as Vertov, Vigo, Franju, Eisenstein, and Ozu. And the fragmentation of sequences in my performances comes partly from ideas that are based on film techniques such as the cut and the idea of montage. I felt the freedom to move from one element to another, cutting from one scene to the next like cut and paste.

In 1970, in Japan, I bought my first Portapak and began to work in video. The Portapak (a big heavy camera and reel-to-reel deck) was not often used for art-making at the time. Some artists had begun to use it in the last few years of the 1960s, and artists such as Nam June Paik had worked with broadcast television in the early 1960s. It was definitely outside the mainstream commercial art world and television industry. The Sony Portapak was an appropriate tool for artists, who usually worked alone in their studios. It could be handheld. The technology was simple, and it did not require a crew. It was black and white.

The video camera did not have a history for me to refer to. In fact, history for me was film, a reference against which the new video possibilities became clear. I was aware of the work of independent filmmakers like Jack Smith, Kenneth Anger, and Stan Brakhage (and in 1976 came to know the work of Maya Deren). What video offered was the opportunity to work live, to make a continuous series of images explicitly for the camera during live performance, which allowed me an added nonnarrative layer in a kind of condensed poetic structure that I had earlier found in the writings of the American imagists (including H.D., William Carlos Williams, Ezra Pound, and Emily Dickinson) and in Japanese haiku. I was also interested in how myth was used in the work of James Joyce, for instance. These forms were also models for work in time.

Video allowed for the immediacy and the continuity of television's live broadcast, while also allowing real-time, ongoing viewing via a monitor. It was simultaneously a recording medium. Video offered a continuous present—showing real-time actions, and incorporated a potential future, re-viewing and reusing actions thus recorded.

The monitor, at that time a critical factor of video, is an ongoing mirror. I explored image-making with myself as subject: I said "this is my right side, this is my left side," and the monitor shows a reversal. I made a tape about the difference between the mirror and the monitor.[9] I worked with the qualities peculiar to video—the flat, grainy, black and white space, the moving bar of the vertical roll, and the circle of circuitry formed by the Portapak, monitor/projector, and artist.

In the first tape that turned into the first performance, I imagined myself making a film. I sat on a white wicker chair facing the camera and monitor, and using props, objects, and sound, I improvised for the camera.

Organic Honey's Visual Telepathy (1972)[10] evolved as I found myself continually investigating my own image in the monitor of my video machine. Wearing the mask of a doll's face transformed me into an erotic electronic seductress. I named this TV persona "Organic Honey." (I stayed up all night wondering what to call my persona and then saw on the table a jar labeled "organic honey": it seemed perfect.) From a book on magic came the phrase "visual telepathy."

In translating this initial experiment into performance, I thought of my stage as a film set within my loft. I added a 4-foot-by-8-foot piece of plywood on sawhorses—a table for my objects. Among them were a big glass jar filled with water and a small shot glass, mirrors, silver spoon, old doll, silver purse, stone. On the wall, I tacked a drawing of my dog with one blue eye and one brown eye, doubled. I also used a tall, antique, wood accounting chair. Inside this set, I put the camera on a tripod. For some sequences, the camera would also be hand-held by the camera woman. I showed the audience the video images in two ways—one on a small monitor, the other in a large projection on the wall of the set. I also placed a small monitor inside the set for me. All of my moves were for the monitor, which I monitored, keeping my eye on the screen as I worked.

The camera woman, holding the camera or placing it on the tripod, operated inside the set with me. She followed my rehearsed movements in close-up. This system—the set for *Organic Honey's Visual Telepathy* and *Organic Honey's Vertical Roll* (Figure 7.2),[11] the live performance and its related tapes[12]—was the model for all my subsequent black and white video works.

Video performance offered the possibility of multiple simultaneous points of view. Performer and audience were both inside and outside. Perception was relative. No one had all the information. I thought I had, but it was an illusion.

The audience sees Organic Honey in her green chiffon dress. She kneels on the floor over a piece of white paper under the overhead camera. She slips back her mask to wear it like a hat, then draws a dog's head, the top half on the bottom of the paper, the bottom half on top. On the monitor, as the vertical roll bar rolls, the two halves of the drawing come together in proper position. As she draws, Honey's hands and arms become visible. Occasionally her mask looks up at the camera. I draw watching the monitor. These (and later performed drawings) are drawings for the monitor. The camera (woman) frames the drawing and the mask—and this detail is what is seen on the video monitor (and/or projector) in the live closed-circuit system. Then Honey removes the drawing, revealing a mirror also on the floor, and with a large silver spoon she bangs it methodically. The video sees and shows: a silver spoon hitting the mirror, with afterimages. The camera zooms into the spoon, the sound of metal hitting glass echoes against the walls and ceiling—hitting the mirror with a spoon, a tapping signal that loudly resonates as silver on glass. This began as anger. I was interested in translating emotions.

The audience sees, in fact, the process of image-making in a performance and simultaneously with a live detail. I was interested in the discrepancies between the performed activity and the constant duplicating, changing, and altering of information in the video. The whole is a sequence of missing links as each witness experiences a different series by glancing from monitor to projection to live action. Perception was relative. There was a range of choices. Time and space in these performances were

Figure 7.2 Joan Jonas, *Organic Honey's Vertical Roll*, 1972. Performance at Galleria Toselli, Milan, 1973. Photo: Giorgio Colombo. © Joan Jonas.

like Borges's *Garden of the Forking Paths*. Here were parallel worlds. I could inhabit, simultaneously, different fields of view, different channels.

Several parts of the Organic Honey performances were prerecorded tapes that could exist on their own as well as be part of the performances.[13] I worked back and forth between tape and video performance, translating ideas from performance into tapes, transferring elements from tapes back into performance. The word "tape" itself covers multiple types and uses: continuous tape, tape prerecorded to be included in a performance, or tape recorded to stand on its own. (Performances that were documented on tape to me are only documents, not artworks.) A performance recorded for a single-channel video work to be shown publicly would be altered—through special effects, change in camera angle, or working with and cutting back and forth with two cameras, inserting new material, cutting out parts, and so on.

The structure of videotape was not divided into visible frames, as in films. One could record for longer periods of time without breaks. Artist filmmakers recorded on ten-minute reels at that time. At first, the duration of videotape seemed to slow time. Time could be delayed. On the other hand, editing was fast—just pressing buttons.

Later performances included *Funnel* (1974),[14] with the camera person outside the set looking in. I used one monitor facing the audience and none for me. The set is made of paper in the shape of a cone. *Twilight* (1975)[15] employed two simultaneous dosed-circuit systems of cameras with monitors. There were five performers. For *Twilight* and *Mirage*,[16] I designed the pieces for the theater space of Anthology Film Archives in New York. Because I had seen so many films in this space, I was inspired. I made 16 millimeter films for projection in both performances. *Mirage* was made after a trip to India (an underlying influence) and was the last of the black and white series. There was no live video, only prerecorded tape and 16 mm film. The film of drawing and erasing on the blackboard was a series of images from past and present pieces—a heart that looked like a bug, signs for a storm, a rainbow, and a mirror reflection, all to be read as a kind of sentence with no fixed meaning. There was also a five-minute documentary loop of volcanoes erupting and a film shot of the monitor of a television turned on its side with the vertical roll bar switching from right to left. My action of repeatedly stepping through a small wooden hoop was broken by the vertical bar. Rhythms were syncopated.

Around 1970, when I began the Organic Honey pieces, issues of feminism were important for all of us. In general, video became a vehicle for women's voices. It was unexplored territory. I was interested in the condition that both video and performance were unexplored.

As soon as I began to work with video, my focus shifted. I began to move away from a kind of minimalism to represent my concerns. I wanted more complicated layers of form and content. We could speak to the camera, record our movements, communicate our desires. I explored the possibilities of female imagery, questions of whether there is a female psyche, and representations of emotions. But anger was one of the main ones for many of us, expressed indirectly through a visual and aural form. Video as we used it was personal, and the personal was political.

To be without expression was the style of performance art. I used the mask as a way of exploring female identity. This instantly took away facial expression and my identity. Masking both concealed and revealed possibilities of representation that may not otherwise have been possible for me. Hidden, I was in a private world that seemed open and magical. The particular mask of Organic Honey created a persona that seemed to be distinctly someone else. A mask here altered body language: I could add an erotic tone. I imagined playing roles like an electronic sorceress or a dog. I howled. I sang. I danced. I explored the place of women in history as outsiders—healers, witches, storytellers.

The video monitor's screen or the projected image was another mask for the construction and deconstruction of persona. Here there was also distance—even in the close-up. I did not act, I behaved. I performed activities. In a belly dancer's costume, I jumped in and out of the bar of the vertical roll like frames in a film going by. This out-of-sync dysfunction of the television—the rolling pictures—presented on the screen parts of the body, never a whole. I had begun to dance with the TV. [. . .]

From Joan Jonas, "Transmission," in *Women, Art, and Technology*, ed. Judy Malloy (Cambridge, MA and London: MIT Press, 2003), 114–33. While this seems its first publication, early in the text the author writes "now, in 1998," which suggests that it was written at that time.

Notes

1 Joan Jonas, *Scripts and Descriptions, 1968–1982*, ed. Douglas Crimp (Berkeley, CA: University Art Museum; Eindhoven: Stedelijk Van Abbemuseum, 1983), 137.

2 Ibid.

3 *Vertical Roll* (1972), black and white video, 20 minutes, sound, camera by Robert Neiman.
4 *Oad Lau* (1968), performance.
5 *Wind* (1968), 16 mm, black and white, 7 minutes, silent, camera and coediting by Peter Campus.
6 *Mirror Piece I* (1969), *Mirror Piece II* (1970), performances, partial list of performers: Francis Barth, Eve Corey, Susan Feldman, Pam Goden, Carol Gooden, Deborah Hollingworth, Keith Hollingworth, Barbara Jarvis, Joan Jonas, Julie Judd, Jane Lahr, Lucille Lareau, Jean Lawless, Susan Marshall, Rosemary Martin, Tom Meyers, Judy Padow, Linda Patton, Corky Poling, Peter Poole, Susan Rothenberg, Andy Salazar, Lincoln Scott, Michael Singer, George Trakas, Pam Vihel.
7 *Mirror Check* (1970–1974), solo performance.
8 *Songdelay* (1973), 16 mm, black and white, 18 minutes, sound, camera and coediting by Robert Fiore; sound by sound technician Kurt Munkacsi, with Ariel Bach, Marion Cajori, James Cobb, Carol Gooden, Randy Hardy, Michael Harvey, Glenda Hydler, Joan Jonas, Epp Kotkas, Gordon Matta Clark, Michael Oliva, Steve Paxton, Penelope, James Reineking, Robin Winters.
9 *Left Side Right Side* (1972), black and white video, 7 minutes, sound, camera and performance by Joan Jonas, produced by Carlotta Schoolman.
10 *Organic Honey's Visual Telepathy* (1972), black and white video, 23 minutes, sound, camera and performance by Joan Jonas.
11 *Organic Honey's Visual Telepathy* (1972), performance, Joan Jonas with Suzanne Harris, Kate Parker, Linda Patton; *Organic Honey's Vertical Roll* (1973, 1974, and 1980), performance, camera by Robert Neiman, performed by Joan Jonas with Anne Thornycroft, Margaret Wilson, and Freuda; *Organic Honey's Vertical Roll* (1973, 1974, and 1980), performance, camera by Barbara Mangolte and Joan Jonas.
12 Tapes that were made in relation to the Organic Honey series: *Organic Honey's Visual Telepathy, Vertical Roll, Duet* (1972), black and white, 4 minutes, sound and camera by Joan Jonas; *Left Side Right Side, Two Women* (1973), black and white, 20 minutes, silent, camera by Joan Jonas, with Christine Kozlov, Penelope.
13 Tapes that were used in the performance: *Anxious Automation* (1972), by Richard Serra, sound by Phillip Glass, performed by Joan Jonas; *Duet*; and *Two Women*.
14 *Funnel* (1974 and 1980), performance, performed by Joan Jonas, camera in 1974 by Babette Mangolte, in 1980 by William Farley, assisted in 1974 by Robin Winters and Christine Patoski.
15 *Twilight* (1975 and 1976), performance, performed by Joan Jonas with Ariel Bach, Karen Helmerson, Chris Jonic, Paula Longendyke, Robin Winters, camera in New York by Andy Mann, in San Francisco by Pat Goudvis, film by Lizzie Bordon and Joan Jonas.
16 *Mirage* (1976, 1977, and 1980), performance, performed by Joan Jonas, assisted in different locations by Tabea Blumenschein, Jane Crawford, Rosella Or, Christine Patoski, Elsie Ritchie, Jane Savitt, film by Babette Mangolte and Joan Jonas.

Moving Target: General Intentions (1996)

Diller + Scofidio

The performance explores the ever-shifting relation between the "normal" and the "pathological." It does not intend to dissolve the culturally determined categories, nor exchange one for the other. Rather, it focuses on the shift itself as its object. Dualisms such as the healthy/sick body, virtual/actual space, and utopic/dystopic views of technology will be targeted.

The performance combines intact bodies and ones disassembled into parts, systems, desires, gestures, expressions, tics, etc. These two types are not set against one another. Rather, they are the same bodies in different registers.

Live/Mediated SPACE

"Live" (as it applies to broadcast) is one of the last strongholds of "auratic" experience in postmodern culture—seeing the event at the precise moment of its occurrence.

The theater audience goes to a "live" performance to experience a unique, unrepeatable event in time and space—perhaps this is a nostalgic need to recover a "public" experience lost to the "mediated" experience of ubiquitous media.

"Live" television recuperates the public sphere (in its mediated way), i.e. the Gulf War was a 100-hour event shared in real time by a remote public connected by an "electronic weld."

The term "mediated" is considered of a lower status to "live" because it divorces spectatorship from event.

In an alternate view, mediation can be seen as a complex layer filling a needed gap between event and spectator in which a new event is produced—one for which real time is an obstacle: consider montage, sampling compositions, etc. . . .

In a parallel issue of mediation, the disease of schizophrenia can be said to be an affliction of "uncontrollable perceptual and cognitive mediation" wherein the symptoms block, distort, and disintegrate the victim's perceptions. This particular type of madness, which isolates its victims in a world of experience randomly disengaged from environmental stimulation, is often described as "looking at the world through a distorted mirror or screen."

The challenge of the project, which is set in theater space with the expectations of a theater audience, is to interfere in spatial and temporal "liveness" of the perceived event, to "tease" the distinctions between "live" and "mediated," to undermine the authority of "live" over "mediated" experience, to reveal theater as another mediated experience, and to confuse the status of the "theater audience."

Ultimately, we would like to collapse the distinctions of "live" and "mediated" altogether into an event with multiple spatialities and temporalities.

Interscenium

The stage-apparatus will interfere with the frontal, holistic gaze of the audience. In the traditional theater of illusion, the proscenium divided the narrative space of the stage from that of the audience. "Proscenium" means "pro-" or in front of, "-scenium," the scene . . . in front of the scene. The staging-apparatus here can be considered to be an interscenium—that which interrupts the scene.

A 45° semi-transparent mirror, suspended above the stage, is a mechanism refracting video projection. (The use of both the mirror and live video are particularly poignant with regard to the pathological body, as they are both disciplinary apparatuses used in surveilling misbehaved bodies as well as therapeutic devices used in "correcting" them. This medico-regulatory aspect can come into the piece).

- Live performers disengaged from the dictates of gravity and from the horizontal site of the floor can fill the full height of the stage space.
- In combination with a projected video image, the mirror can organize bodies according to the logic of video.
- Live performance in front of the mirror and behind the mirror can combine with hyper-virtuosic pre-recorded and "assisted" video bodies within a hybrid space.

Temporal Structure

Rather than dividing the performance into scenes and acts, the piece can be seen as a continuous performance "interrupted" by a series of advertising spots. The commercial "spots" are considered psychotic breaks in the dance performance. Five spots make up the advertising campaign for "Normal Pharmaceuticals," a pharmaceutical company advertising a chemically-produced "normal" for a post-psychotherapeutic culture. Each spot takes on a particular pathology—all the pathologies are of the everyday variety—ones paradoxically produced and reinforced by the media itself. Look normal. Feel normal. Act normal. Be normal.

Distraction

Theatrical experience is typically focal: all attention converges onto the action under the spotlight. We intend to fracture the focus of the audience, to alternately suspend, drop, and refract its gaze, to ultimately fracture the unity of the audience. In structuring live, real-time mediated, delayed, and recorded events in different combinations, multiple channels of action are offered.

Body Discipline

Modeled on the electronic cuff which keeps prisoners confined to a territory by an electronic leash, a body tracking system on stage exerts invisible control over the dancer's movements to limit him/her to the "official zone of performance." A transgression will cause interference in the audio. The dancer finds the limits of the official zone by trial and error. But rather than becoming docile and obedient to its normalizing tendencies, the dancer incorporates the chance irritation of static as a desirable musical effect, to propel a new dance that is inclusive of its restriction.

Diller + Scofidio, "General Intentions," in Frédéric Flamand, Charleroi Danses/Plan K, and Diller + Scofidio, *Moving Target*, program notes, Charleroi n.d. (1996), unpag. *Moving Target* was a cooperation between Frédéric Flamand of Charleroi Danses, Plan K (conception, choreography), and Diller + Scofidio (set design, documentation, spots, text/dance, and videos). During the early career, architects Elizabeth Diller and Ricardo Scofidio also worked for stage performances: "During their first fifteen years of working together, Diller + Scofidio focused [. . .] on live performance and on architectural installations within the context of the art world. Thus, they were able 'to construct ideas in real space,' as Diller said, and also have audiences respond to their ideas. Between 1983 and 1998, the architects staged nine performances [. . .]. These performances and their collaborations with choreographers, writers, and directors formed an investigation of a range of highly considered architectural theories." Roselee Goldberg, "Dancing about Architecture," in *Scanning: The Aberrant Architectures of Diller + Scofidio* (New York: Whitney Museum of American Art, 2003), 45.

Studio Azzurro: Re-Inventing the Medium of Theater (2012)

Valentina Valentini

[. . .] The work of Studio Azzurro can be read in the context of new paradigms arising from mutations taking place in science, new technologies, and aesthetics since the 1970s.

The company's production of spectacles—musical, theatrical, choreographic (setting aside for now the problem of the fragility of these generic borders)—merits critical analysis not only for its complexity and variety (video, films, spectacles, multimedia and interactive installations, performances, "museums as narration"), but for specific questions it raises: Has the use of technology deadened or amplified theater; has dramaturgy utilizing new technologies to compose spectacles shown itself capable of reinventing the medium of theater?

And presuming a re-invention is underway, what are its characteristics and configurations?

The 1990s saw a widespread phenomenon where theater was rejected as an autonomous artistic genre while simultaneously production expanded and blossomed beyond theater's traditional confines. On the one hand, many standard traits of the theatrical spectacle were set aside, on the other, the essential here-and-now quality that has always defined theater burst its former borders.

Intermediality has become a structural element in the work of a new generation of theater groups, shaping their spectacles in both design and practice without concern for established generic markers. The generation of the '90s tolerates neither the word "actor" nor that of "theater": "Fortunately, we don't do theater, and I don't say that just to be fashionable, but to stress the fact that it is impossible for us to restrict our work within the limiting confines of that word. We have chosen to refer to our work as performance, a much more general term that emphasizes the component of live action, the fact that the art is produced in front of an audience."[1]

In an era when not only theater but every other medium tends to lose its distinguishing characteristics as it passes through the homogenizing devices of digital technology, hybrid forms emerge that are neither one thing nor another—neither cinema nor theater (the live film), neither film nor installation (expanded cinema), then again simultaneously live and reproduced (live media), asynchronous (Foster), or remediated (Bolter and Grusin). An old medium seeks a way out of entrapment by taking on aspects of a different medium: photography camouflages itself as cinema, theater masquerades as television.[2] Bonnie Marranca has coined the term "mediaturgy" to substitute the older "dramaturgy," in order to indicate the shift taking place from drama to technological media: "Mediaturgy . . . situates media as the center of study, though I am acutely aware of the tension between these two terms."[3]

The intention of this essay is to identify the figurations of an emergent media dramaturgy by analyzing the spectacles of Studio Azzurro in the context of contemporary production internationally.

Extension of the Visible

The implementation of electronic and digital resources produces a form of spectacle that expands the territory of the visible, creating an experience of sensorial stratification obtained by adding new settings, bodies, spaces, and otherwise invisible details.

In *The Cenci* (Studio Azzurro, 1997), the actors on stage are augmented by projected characters that add new kinds of presences: hands whose gestures tell the love story between Beatrice and Orsino before a sheet of water; hands that stretch, pull, and tear the Cenci's bedsheet; hands of guests at the banquet; hands that set and clear a table. All these additions lead to an indistinguishable mixing together of live and virtual bodies. In the banquet scene, images extend the real dimensions of a table by creating a sort of *trompe l'oeil* effect. Actions produced on a horizontally or vertically sectioned video monitor interact in simultaneity with the actions of the live actors, constituting an interconnecting, multidimensional space.

By projecting images from the Meteosat satellite of the Earth seen from space, *Kepler's Traum* (Studio Azzurro, 1990) encompasses an extraplanetary viewpoint within its narrative structure, making it possible for spectators to observe themselves simultaneously as they watch the spectacle unfold. [. . .]

Technologies create multiple locations simultaneously, conjoining the inside with the outside, the public with the private, the individual with the collective.

Liveness and Reproducibility

Technological devices create a virtual theater-world in which an image has a body; that is, it is no mere reproduction of a real object, but an elastic body, alive in that it spreads into space, manipulates time, and transforms matter. Referring in 1985 to the spectacle *Prologo a diario segreto contraffatto* (Prologue to a Counterfeit Secret Diary), I made the observation that electronic technologies were introducing new models of codification into theatrical settings; models based on integration, simultaneity, and chromatic/auditory manipulation: "Fluidity and instability are traits of a new form of composition for the stage that tends toward the re-integration and fusion of time and space, of environment-stage and action-body, of the animate and the inanimate, of figurative and abstract elements. Electronics are no longer a medium that works merely as a prosthesis of the body to better view the world, nor is it merely the I observing itself. The novelty of these spectacles is not in their self-reflexivity but, rather, in a transparency that invites us to consider technology not as an extension of our bodies—something external to us—but as an energy that transforms matter."[4] Analyzing two Studio Azzurro spectacles born from a collaboration between the theater company of Giorgio Barberio Corsetti and the multimedia production collective, Didier Plassar wrote: "The introduction of the video image into the stage does not . . . lead to a reduction of theatricality; rather, on the contrary, through a doubled register of presence (the actor *and* the character, the stage *and* the fictional setting) the electronic apparatus expands the theatrical effect."[5] The revolutionary factor that both Studio

Azzurro's *Prologo* and *La camera astratta* (The Abstract Room; Figure 7.3) identified was the overturning of a paradigm: electronic audiovisual technologies do not lead to reproducibility; rather, they emphasize immediacy, perhaps the most specific identifying trait of theatrical spectacle. "Television sought to transport the stage into the television studio, sacrificing the actor-spectator rapport and the sensation of a live event. Electronic theater works in the opposite direction, bringing the television studio onto the stage, utilizing the electronic instrument to recover the immediacy between real action and its transposition onto a monitor. An accord was reached between video and theater that privileged the event, in function of the presence of the actor."[6] [. . .]

In the virtual worlds created by new technologies, subject and object encounter one another without opposition, producing interactions that avoid dichotomies: virtual bodies are image-bodies, they are both object and event. The interactive work of art is not reproductive, in that its *fruition-production* constitutes a virtual artwork, an object-event that evokes an ecstatic dimension (a Pan-ic dimension, related to the ancient god), because the spectator-performer becomes one body with the work of art.[7] The dichotomy between real and virtual collapses: "Virtualization is not a matter of de-realization (the transformation of a unitary reality into a collection of possible realities), but a change of identity, a shift of the ontological center of gravity of the object in question . . . Virtualization is one of the most important vectors of the creation of reality."[8] We find this theory inscribed in the dramaturgy of recent spectacles that prove there is no contradiction between tangible and intangible, between virtual and real. [. . .]

Figure 7.3 Studio Azzurro, *La Camera Astratta*, 1987. Video opera, stage director Giorgio Barberio Corsetti, video director Paolo Rosa. Courtesy of Studio Azzurro.

The Tangibility of the Immaterial

The theater-worlds created by Studio Azzurro are animated and inhabited by luminous-chromatic bodies for which—beyond the images displayed—electronic/digital means are employed to construct a luminous choreography, energy in its pure state. In *Neither* (Studio Azzurro, 2004), "during the prelude, the true protagonist is light. It is light that generates the images, creating before our very eyes a world—oscillating between self and un-self, between inner and outer shadow—which it will disappear in the second part."[9] Within the spectacle, the intensity of tones gradually increases, reaching a level of excess that provokes dismay in the spectator. The shrill, disembodied, and de-personalized voice of the performer, Petra Hoffmann, reflects the work's premise: "The absence [and] lack of a Character, a Protagonist, a Subject."[10]

In *Wer möchte wohl Kaspar Hauser sein?* (Now Who Wants to Be Kaspar Hauser?, Studio Azzurro, 2000), darkness is the abode of Kaspar, a darkness traversed by phosphorescent lights until the moment when the world floods in as light, a feather spins in the air, colored figures take on form, and Kaspar discovers colors, flavors, smells. Not mere images, but luminous, chromatic choreographies transport Kaspar and the spectators into an interior space, a mental dimension. In *The Cenci*, the sound score aids the creation of subjective visions that emerge from the characters' psychology and anguish, their dreams and neuroses.[11] The sound space encompasses the spectator, intensifying the collective dimension of the experience of the spectacle, magnifying sensorial perception beyond the merely visual, enwrapping spectators and transporting them to the represented locations. The mutual exchange between sight and sound constructs a third dimension of imagery endowed with physicality in dialogue with its environment. Images become dense and solid, occupying space through the dislocation of sound sources and images projected throughout the performance space.[12]

Interactivity: Doing—Sharing—Feeling

Studio Azzurro has developed a method of composition for the stage based on interactive media, employing diverse modalities to deeply explore the live dimension of computer programming alongside the research begun in *Prologo* and *La camera astratta*. Working in parallel, performers onstage produce some of the spectacle's "actions" in real time by using computers, while spectators have the opportunity, at the end of the performance, to substitute the actors and "play" their own spectacle.

At the end of *The Cenci*, the huge cross that constituted the central prop, set horizontally as a table, was made available to spectators who came on stage after the actors exited, and they were able to use the interactive computerized machines to reactivate images and sounds from the spectacle. "The spectators could walk on, touch, change scenes, and live in this setting as though to take ownership of the last part of the spectacle."[13]

In *Il fuoco, l'acqua e l'ombra: La danza della natura nelle immagini di Tarkovsky* (Fire, Water and Shadow: The Dance of Nature in Tarkovsky's Images, Studio Azzurro, 1998), the spectator becomes the target of a series of projections, while in *Kaspar Hauser* infrared beams capture the faces of spectators in close-up, which are then projected onto the stage.

Interactive devices have re-invented compositional strategies affecting the participation of the spectator in the spectacular event. Where is all this leading? The transformation of the spectator from contemplative consumer into performer, into the person who carries out actions, is a new phenomenon in the artistic practice of the later twentieth century. We have seen this both in closed-circuit installations (in a Bruce Nauman work, if a visitor does not cross the corridor designed by the artist, the installation does not take place) and in Body Art performances that require spectators to perform actions. In *Paradise Now*, the Living Theater asked spectators to leave their seats and join the actors on stage in a decisive action that would change their lives, making them adherents of a theater-world.

In Studio Azzurro's interactive gallery installations the spectator-visitor operates the computers that have constructed the artwork, while in the company's theatrical spectacles, by contrast, the interactive procedures take place for the most part among the performers on stage. At a certain point in *Kaspar Hauser*, the protagonist gets up on a tilting platform and uses a data glove (a glove fitted with sensors) to transfer projections from one surface to another, an operation repeated differently in each performance.

Giacomo mio, salviamoci! (My dear Giacomo, Let's Save Ourselves!; Studio Azzurro, 1998) takes the form of a sort of class conducted by Umberto Orsini, who sits at a writing desk and minutely discusses the life of the poet Giacomo Leopardi as presented by the writer Vittorio Sermonti. At the sides of a large screen, musicians and the actor-narrator interact with images that produce sounds when touched by their hands. In *Kepler's Traum*, an orchestra is inserted as a visual element at the end of the spectacle, with the actor-musician Moni Ovadia using a video camera to film the musicians, whose images were projected in real time on an upstage screen. In *Galileo (studi per l'Inferno)* (Galileo [Studies for the Inferno], Studio Azzurro, 2006), the movements of dancers activate sensors that project images: "Here, the relation between choreography and stage was clearly more interactive, in the sense that the measurements and trajectories delineated on the stage were determined by the positioning of the various dancers. The scenarios traced by all the choreographic paths mutated continuously."[14]

Let us now attempt to answer the question posed at the beginning of this text. Rather than deadening or magnifying the performative and theatrical dimension of a spectacle, interactive dramaturgy made with the use of information technology transforms the theatrical stage by introducing new expressive materials that substitute traditional ones—such as the actor, for example—revealing new performative dimensions. In this sense, the *liveness* of the theatrical stage is not deadened, but transferred to other active agents (the creation of a website in one of John Jesurun's spectacles, or images in movement created by the actions of a performer in a setting made with a blue screen). Presence no longer belongs exclusively to the performer, in that the quality of *liveness*, its immediacy, is transferred to chromatic, auditory, three-dimensional, and visual materials. This process of transformation leads to a reduction in the primacy of the actor in favor of the spectator, and also to an expansion of the live, performative quality of other expressive materials.[15] A pronounced element in the functioning of interactive installations is the collective dimension of the experience, the aspect of creating and sharing together: "Even though there are no actors, but mere figures projected on a screen or onto the space, the indispensable physicality of theater is recovered by the expressivity of the reactions and relations produced by the spectators . . ."[16]

For Studio Azzurro, the recourse to interactive technologies that arouse spectators to participate in the production of the artwork, as opposed to artworks that require no active contribution by the viewer, can be understood as a reaction against the anesthetic effect of media. The permeation of media into individual and collective lives provokes a reaction that calls for shared creation through a different use of the same information technologies. In her essay on interactivity as seen in the work of Studio Azzurro, Silvana Borutti maintains that "contemporary art makes us experience the present-ness of phenomena, so as to compel us to feel."[17] Interactive technology, that is, promotes an aesthetics that works through feeling rather than cognition. Digital technologies produce a surplus of performativity, of live presence, that reduces the space accorded to cognitive and symbolic processing: "The artwork becomes its own actualization, action in the present moment."[18] Borutti explains that the aspiration to present-ness and for real-ness manifests as an impulse toward that which cannot be symbolized, the striving toward a *liveness* which has less to do with theatrical representation and more to do with ritual. Thus the new work aspires to create a shared public experience that puts the spectator into play in the action, as a means of regenerating the forms of aesthetic participation. In synthesis, interactive technologies work toward breaking down the compositional practices of theatrical tradition. "In contemporary art, there is a clear shift in the concept of *poesis*. Contemporary art induces us not to merely observe an artwork, but to experience an *exposed action* that provokes us to participate in the work in its living presence, not as a representation, but as a performance that requires the consent of those present and a collective sharing of the moment."[19]

The globalization of information exalts less the dimension of representation, as found in a museum setting, but instead foregrounds qualities of instantaneous apparition and disappearance at the root of performance, "the impulse toward manifestation in the present rather than representation."[20]

When an artwork takes on characteristics that make experience and time into components of the text, the effect is to deemphasize the traditional role and function of the spectator, transforming the receiver instead into a coproducer of the work itself, in a shift that reorients the process of authorship from preproduction to postproduction (Bourriaud), thus redefining the roles both of author and spectator. [. . .]

From Valentina Valentini, "Studio Azzurro: Reinventare il medium teatro," in *Studio Azzurro: Teatro*, ed. Noemi Pittaluga and Valentina Valentini (Rome: Contrasto, 2012), 6–21; translated for the present publication by Thomas Haskell Simpson.

Notes

1 The Big Art Group was founded by Caden Manson in New York in 1999. Their work reworks B movies and parodies popular TV series such as Saturday Night Live and Mad TV. See Riccardo Fazi, "Il territorio dell'indesirabile. Intervista a Jemma Nelson del Big Art Group," in *Biblioteca teatrale:Il teatro di fine Millennio*, ed. Valentina Valentini, nos. 74–75 (2005), 242.

2 See David Bolter, Richard Grusin, *Remediation: Competizione tra media vecchi e nuovi* (Milan: Guerini studio, 2002) [*Remediation: Understanding New Media* (Cambridge, MA: MIT Press, 1999)]; Hal Foster, *Design & Crime* (Milan: Postmedia, 2003), 127f [*Design and Crime (and Other Diatribes)* (London and New York: Verso, 2002)].

3 Bonnie Marranca, "Performance as Design: The Mediaturgy of John Jesurun's *Firefall*," *PAJ* 96 (2010), 16.

4 Valentina Valentini, "Prologo elettronico: Fluidità e trasparenza," in Studio Azzurro and Giorgio Barberio Corsetti, *La camera astratta: Tre spettacoli fra teatro e video*, ed. Valentina Valentini (Milan: Ubulibri, 1988), 19.

5 "Among the many types of play between the living interpreter and the electronic image, which constitute the central axis of the stage actions in *Prologo* and *La camera astratta*, many induce . . . a process of fictionalization of the video device: either the screen is transformed into a simple transparent window (like a window or the glass wall of an aquarium, which one bumps into, explores with one's hands, or wipes to clean it), or the monitor becomes literally a cube, with its concrete dimensions, its solid borders, stackable on other cubes; capable, for example, of imprisoning an actor." Didier Plassard, "Dioptrique des corps dans l'espace électronique: Sur quelques mise en scène de Giorgio Barberio Corsetti," in *Les écrans sur la scène: Tentations et résistance de la scéne dace auz images*, ed. Béatrice Picon-Vallin (Lausanne: Ed. L'Age d'Homme, 1998), 149–56.

6 Valentina Valentini, "Prologo elettronico," 18.

7 Roberto Diodato, *Estetica del virtuale* (Milan: Mondadori, 2005).

8 Pierre Levy, *Il virtuale* (Milan: Raffaello Cortina, 1997), pp. 8f.

9 Studio Azzurro, *Videoambienti, ambienti sensibili e altre esperienze tra arte, cinema, teatro e musica*, ed. Bruno Di Marino (Milan: Feltrinelli, 2007), 178.

10 Studio Azzurro, *Immagini vive* (Milan: Electa, 2006), 202.

11 Giorgio Battistelli, "Immagini di personaggi che diventano suoni," interview by Noemi Pittaluga, in *Studio Azzurro. Teatro*, ed. Noemi Pittaluga and Valentina Valentini (Rome: Contrasto, 2012), 176–91.

12 Noemi Pittaluga, "The Cenci: Performance Program," in ibid., 131–7. Given that contemporary experience increasingly is deprived of physicality and tactility, the performer's actions become instable signals on projection screens, while sounds produce ever more imposing sensorial impact. The phenomenon of VJing, live mixes of image and sound, works on the expropriated body deprived of the direct experience of producing sounds, imposing a physical impact through super low-frequency vibrations (perceivable even by the deaf). Live electronic music composed on laptops utilizes images to compensate for the bodily absence both of the composer and the spectator—sampling the sounds produced by the missing body. In the last decade, experiments with capturing sounds created by the moving bodies of performers (using sensors placed on the stage and on the performers' bodies) have

come into wide practice, producing an auditory spatialization of movement in real time. The three-dimensionality of sound embraces the spectator with resonance.

13 Paolo Rosa, in Valentina Valentini, "La vocazione plurale della regia: Conversazione con Paolo Rosa," in *Biblioteca Teatrale: I modi della regia nel nuovo Millennio*, nos. 91–92 (July–December 2009), 152.

14 Ibid., 153.

15 "It begins with the double set of the early works made with Corsetti, in which the actor confronts, and competes with, his own double seen in video. He competes with this virtual double, and the real setting competes with the virtual setting, and then progresses, in *Delfi*, to a situation where both the protagonist and the stage are negated, immersed in darkness, in invisibility, and become visible only through the eyes of technology, the infrared beams of the video cameras. Thus an actor virtually renders himself invisible, he vanishes from the stage although physically present. In the most recent work, the actor disappears entirely, he no longer exists, as in *Neither*: a stage without a protagonist, without actors, without singers, with nothing on stage. There is thus a constant in our work, as though there was a necessity, I wouldn't say to make the actors disappear, but to think that the actor's presence can be substituted, can rebound into another situation in which the spectators can become actors." "La scena digitale: Nel cannocchiale di Galileo la visione di un altro teatro. Conversazione con Paolo Rosa di Andrea Balzola," *OFF—Quotidiano dello spettacolo*, January 31, 2007.

16 Paolo Rosa in Valentina Valentini, "La vocazione plurale della regia," 152. This type of interactivity, which summons the spectator to share in the construction of the spectacle, is absent in the work of younger companies such as Santasangre, Nanou, Umeda, Sakamoto, or Orthographe. They keep spectators at a distance in a frontal arrangement. In an email exchange with me, Matteo Antonaci observed: "What is emphasized instead is a silent, cinematographic contemplation, in which the stage presents itself like a screen to be watched." Email by M. Antonaci to V. Valentini, April 13, 2012.

17 Silvana Borutti, "Devenire figura: Le immagini fra memoria, desiderio e sublime," in *Alla fine delle cose: Contributi a una storia critica delle immagini*, ed. Daniele Guastini, Dario Cecchi, and Alessandra Campo (Florence: Usher Arte, 2011), 205–17.

18 Ibid., 215.

19 Ibid., 216.

20 Ibid., 217.

Intermedial Interplay between Real-Time Videos, Film, and Theatrical Scenes: Bert Neumann's Spaces for Frank Castorf's Dostoevsky project *Erniedrigte und Beleidigte* (2014)

Birgit Wiens

[. . .] In the way they allow for playing with different media under live conditions, for hybridizing spaces, for shifting the axis of vision, and for putting the audience's possibilities of perception into constant motion, Bert Neumann's scenographies open up a discourse on the manifestation of spaces, on non-visibility, gray zones, and disruptions, and, more generally, on the question of how spaces in fact come into being (with the help of architecture, language, media), and which functions media take on during these processes. How far are media "intermediaries" and how far are they constitutive, in the sense of spatial creation? In addition, Neumann's medial hybrid spaces throw up pertinent questions that go beyond the stage and the theater space: In what way does the familiar omnipresence of all types of media (such as film, video, and the Internet) lead to a multiplication of spaces, changing the patterns and habits of human spatial perception and leading to more complex spatial experiences. [. . .]

For *Erniedrigte und Beleidigte* (Humiliated and Insulted, 2001), the second part in Castorf/Neumann's Dostoevsky series after *Dämonen* (Demons, 1999),[1] Neumann once more designed an enclosed bungalow: a container building—now as a very stable construct—that was again located within a sparse, placeless landscape in which winter obviously had started. [. . .]

In *Erniedrigte und Beleidigte*—as in Castorf's earlier production *Endstation Amerika* (Last Stop America, 2000), for which Neumann had built a stage with an enclosed bathroom based loosely on Hitchcock—video and projection technology was used to give the audience insights into the closed-off interior of the building. For that, Neumann had a projection screen installed on the roof of the small, one-story house. On the inside there were two rooms that were "inhabited" by the actors, as well as an editing room from which the filmed sequences (that, quickly produced, nearly felt like private "home videos") could be transmitted onto the approximately three-by-four meters large video projection wall in real time (Figure 7.4). It has been extensively discussed both by critics and within theater studies how and in what manner the relationships between theater and film (or video image), between theatrical and virtual space, between the stage and the screen presence of the actors, were playfully explored in Castorf's productions.[2] While some theoretical positions evaluate the interplay of theater and video (or film) as a somewhat competitive relationship (Fischer-Lichte), there are also discursive approaches—namely within the field of intermediality in theater studies—that understand the intertwining and interplay between theater event and live video as a narratological process operating with different media, both visually and acoustically (Peter Boenisch has suggested the term "hybrid compositing" here).[3] This process—in its combination of live action, transmission (or "broadcasting"), and complex "networking"—can be seen as an interconnected procedural process

Figure 7.4 Bert Neumann, scenography for *Erniedrigte und Beleidigte*, 2001, Volksbühne Berlin, director Frank Castorf, on the videoscreen: Martin Wuttke. Photo: © Thomas Aurin.

that configures different spaces and spatial qualities with each other. In fact we are dealing with a hybrid staging experiment, which did not qualitatively place the actors' theatrical performances over their technically produced media images; rather, both were principally treated as equal media phenomena and examined on stage as to their different medial communicability. [. . .]

The bungalow that Neumann had placed on that stage for *Erniedrigte und Beleidigte*, with its doors, its lit-up windows, and a chimney from which smoke billowed once in a while, signalized to the audience: this house is inhabited. [. . .] At the same time, filming was done in all of the rooms (the lounge had cameras on the ceilings, while the events around Vanya were simply recorded with a hand-held camera)—the fully media-wired home, in one form or another, had become the human condition. From the viewpoint of the audience, the video wall on the roof of the house initially did not seem to fit the picture, but after some time one got used to it, especially since these types of video and LED walls have become a ubiquitous phenomenon in inner cities or as flickering messengers at the sides of motorways and other traffic routes. Just like a metaphor it reminded one, before the play even started, of the numerous screens and displays that mark today's reality in their function as advertising billboards or information screens. Going above and beyond the microcosm of the stage, this video wall pointed out (exactly because it at first seemed so alien here) the very common medialization of our current lives in a reality that can no longer be surveyed or understood in its full complexity.

Dostoevsky wrote the novel *Humiliated and Insulted*, which Castorf brought to the stage with this scenography, in 1861. He had returned from an eight-year Siberian exile, and penned the novel as a newspaper serial, mainly to earn some money. On closer analysis, the text (in contrast to Dostoevsky's philosophical novels, such as *Demons*) is rather roughly thrown together, commercial fiction for entertainment (that, from the viewpoint of today's media habits, reminds one of a soap opera told in several episodes). The strong interest in business which runs through the entire novel, served as a leitmotif to thematically define the theater production. Further themes were isolation, social inequality, as well as the experience of unhappy love within fatal three-way relationships. [. . .]

Provisionally one could say that the story was "spatialized" with the help of circumstances and obstacles set by the scenography (i.e. the interplay between interior and exterior as well as splitting the inner area into two different social spheres). An additional complexity (also: a sort of microscopic view on the circumstances) came about by the way video was used. One could find a number of examples for this technique: At the start of the play, while there was no one to be seen in the space in front of the house, a conversation took place between Vanya and Ikhmenev, which turned into something of a monologue. Here Vanya told the story of an old man with a dog, who sat in a café and irritated everybody because he did not talk to anyone at all; when it finally became known that he only wanted to warm himself, the dog at his feet had already died. As he was telling this story one could see Vanya (Martin Wuttke) in a live close-up above on the video wall. Shortly thereafter a door opened down below and out of the house came an old man who left the stage sideways, accompanied by a very much alive four-legged friend. A similar shift or suspension of linear narration took place in a later scene when Vanya told an old friend from kindergarten days beside him that the friend would die due to his alcohol consumption (anticipating future events). The video wall, by the way, showed projections during nearly the entire time of the five-hour performance; depending on what the cameraman and the cutter allowed one could look into the two inner rooms of the bungalow from different perspectives, always *live*. Once in a while, though, pre-produced material was played, including images of Berlin at night, advertisements, and also pornography. One of the highlights of the production certainly was the moment when Vanya, the author, climbed up onto the roof in search of a story and then addressed the film images directly, exclaiming ("beautiful people . . . who are you?"), demanding that the others "explain the pictures to me!"[4] and finally—as advertisements for rice pudding, cosmetics, and shampoo flickered across the screen—reciting one of the best-known quotes from Dostoevsky's text: here in the city, one was in the "middle of the dark secret corners of the vast town, in the midst of the giddy ferment of life, of dull egoism, of clashing interests, of gloomy vice and secret crimes, in that lowest hell of senseless and abnormal life."[5]

Medial transfers, striking contrasts, planned and unplanned camera settings, chronological flashbacks and foreshadowing, as well as the spatialized play regarding the various media running in parallel, interrelated, or successively—all of these techniques made up the aesthetic narration of this production. For an internal discourse within the theater—which, according to its traditional formation as a "construction for showing" or "show stage," is actually a medium for showing or exhibiting, for making things visible—this was a breach of basic conventions. This breach was calculated: by placing an enclosed house on stage, Neumann explicitly referred to a well-known rule, Diderot's concept of the "fourth wall" (which has often been criticized in modern theater).[6] Actually building a "fourth wall" for *Erniedrigte und Beleidigte* (and before that for *Dämonen*), Neumann took Diderot's concept literally. However, in contrast to Diderot he deliberately refused to give a good pictorial overview of the stage. Instead the bungalow—as a built, sculptural element—protruded into the stage space and in its enclosed cohesion refused to allow any insights into the interior. The video "breaking into" the scene proved another consequential step in the logic of the Dostoevsky experiments: its appearance in the performative stage architecture, which refused a uniform pictorial effect and on top of that was put on a revolving stage, lead to further complication and hybridization. As a clearly different medium, it also meant a rupture in the aesthetic space of the theater. [. . .]

Neumann was dealing less with the pictoriality of theater (in any case not in the conservative sense of stage set and scenography), but instead was focusing on its spatiality. This is evidenced, as has been seen, by the setting of the scenographic house and by the special use of video. The appearance of film in the theater does have a longer tradition; for example, when Piscator experimented with the projection of film and slides (excerpts from weekly news programs and documentary pictures) in the 1920s, he opened up a "window to the world" on stage. This effect—which back then was sometimes criticized as being "alien to the theater,"[7] at other times welcomed and moved forward in anti-naturalistic stage concepts[8]—would later be found, under different circumstances, in post-dramatic theater and its deconstructive techniques. Frequently these stages remind one of the "windows" systems familiar from computer interface design.[9] With multiple screens and monitors that de-unify the appearance of the stage and cut it up into heterogeneous zones of meaning, these scenographies still keep up, when examined closely, a pictorial discourse. As the scene examples have shown, Neumann's intermedial scenography, while using similar means, on the contrary started an aesthetic reflection on space: in his stage order for *Erniedrigte und Beleidigte*, the video did not take on the figurative character of a "window" looking out into whatever outside world. Instead the interplay between video, actors, and architecture, which in itself appeared as a sort of "meta-body," delivered more of an inside view.[10] The live video thus became a means with which Castorf and his cameraman Jan Speckenbach ventured forward into "the inner reality of the stage itself" (by rendering the make-up, the sweat-drenched costumes, and the skin pores of the actors distinctly visible).[11] Mainly, though, the camera became an instrument with which one could intrude into the "meta-body" of this house in order to analyze a fragmented, clearly self-destructing social body during a painful procedure—performed on the living body from the inside—that lasted for hours. The intended effect was that this analysis would not be transmitted in uniform overview pictures. Whenever the audience had a certain idea of what was happening, the picture was immediately covered again. Contrary to the classic image metaphor (the conception of images and pictures as "windows"), the pictures here were rather seen as a *cache*, a "cover of all that one cannot actually see in the shot itself."[12] [. . .]

Accordingly, the production also denied any sense of continuous orientation to the audience. Instead the strategies described above brought the audience into a sort of inner imbalance: For in a world that clearly has no center the audience should also not find peace and quiet.

Excerpt from the chapter "Architekturen auf Zeit. Szenographie als Spiel mit der Medialität: Bert Neumann" in Birgit Wiens, *Intermediale Szenographie: Raum-Ästhetiken des Theaters am Beginn des 21. Jahrhunderts* (Paderborn: Wilhelm Fink, 2014), 248–61; translated for the present publication by Marc Heinitz.

Notes

1 Castorf/Neumann's Dostoevsky series at the Berliner Volksbühne comprised Castorf's 2002 production of *Der Idiot* (The Idiot) set in Neumann's *Neustadt* (New City), a spatial installation placing the audience within a "total theater" environment reminiscent of a film set, as well as *Schuld und Sühne* (Crime and Punishment, 2005), *Der Spieler* (The Player, 2011), *Die Wirtin* (The Landlady, 2012) as well as their collaboration a short time before Neumann unexpectedly died, *Die Brüder Karamasow* (The Brothers Karamazov, 2015).

2 Cf. the corresponding chapters in Erika Fischer-Lichte, *The Transformative Power of Performance: A New Aesthetics*, trans. S.I. Jain (London and New York: Routledge, 2008), as well as Peter M. Boenisch, "Frank Castorf and the Berlin Volksbuehne: *The Humiliated and Insulted*," in *Mapping Intermediality in Performance*, ed. Sarah Bay-Cheng, Chiel Kattenbelt, Andy Lavender, and Robin Nelson (Amsterdam: Amsterdam University Press, 2010), 198–203.

3 Boenisch, "Frank Castorf and the Berlin Volksbuehne: *The Humiliated and Insulted*," 198.

4 Cited after a video recording, *Erniedrigte und Beleidigte*, Berliner Volksbühne (2001), Part 2, 32'30".

5 Cf. Fyodor Dostoevsky, *The Insulted and the Injured*, trans. Constance Garnett (London: Heinemann, 1915).

6 With his formula Diderot defined the proscenium stage of his day as a moving tableau, strictly dividing the theater space into a here (this world) and a there (the other world) by the edge of the stage: "Whether you write or act, think no more of the audience than if it had never existed. Imagine a huge wall across the front of the stage, separating you from the audience, and behave exactly as if the curtain had never risen." From Denis Diderot's treatise on his play *Le Père de Famille*, "On Dramatic Poetry" (1758), in *European Theories of the Drama*, ed. Barrett H. Clark (Cincinnati: Stewart & Kidd, 1918), 299.

7 Cf. Max Herrmann, "Das theatralische Raumerlebnis" (1931) in *Raumtheorie*, ed. Jörg Dünne and Stephan Günzel (Frankfurt am Main: Suhrkamp, 2006), 510.

8 Cf. for this e.g. Thomas Tode, "Wir sprengen die Guckkastenbühne! Erwin Piscator und der Film," in *Bertolt Brecht und Erwin Piscator: Experimentelles Theater im Berlin der zwanziger Jahre*, ed. Michael Schwaiger (Vienna: Verlag Christian Brandstätter, 2004), 16–34.

9 On this see Greg Giesekam, *Staging the Screen: The Use of Film and Video in Theatre* (New York: Palgrave Macmillan, 2007); also Robin Nelson, "New Small Screen Spaces: A Performative Phenomenon?" in *Intermediality in Theatre and Performance*, ed. Freda Chapple and Chiel Kattenbelt (Amsterdam/New York: Rodopi, 2006), 137–50.

10 On the function of the scenographic house not only as an aesthetic form but also as a social metaphor and "meta-body" cf. Steve Dixon: "The Philosophy and Psychology of the Scenographic House in Multimedia Theatre," *International Journal of Performance Arts & Digital Media* 6, no. 1: *Alternative Materialities: Scenography in Digital Performance* (2010), 7–24, especially 14.

11 Jan Speckenbach, "Der Einbruch der Fernsehtechnologie," in Carl Hegemann, *Einbruch der Realität* (Berlin: Alexander Verlag, 2002), 82.

12 Ibid., 83. While Neumann's stages had always suggested they wanted to provoke social reality bursting into the theater, in dealing with other media such as film, as cameraman Speckenbach observed, it became clear that he was constantly working with fragments that were "themselves only excerpts" that in turn "covered up other excerpts" (ibid.).

Multiplication: The Wooster Group (2007)

Nick Kaye

Under the direction of Elizabeth LeCompte, the Wooster Group's theater work has come to exemplify an overtly multimedial practice articulated in distinct and simultaneous channels of address. "Working," James Leverett proposes, "at the point where the lens and the stage interact, contradict, complement, even interchange,"[1] an interweaving of "live" and "mediated" modes of work has become integral to their working methods, in which, Euridice Arratia notes in recording the company's preparations for *Brace Up!* (1991; Figure 7.5), "the live performance, the mediated performance, and the sound score are developed simultaneously . . . Monitors, video cameras, and Christopher Kondek, the video operator, are at all rehearsals. As [Jim] Clayburgh worded it, 'Since *Route 1&9* [1981], microphones and video monitors have been like performers, part of the company.'"[2]

The place of film and video in the Wooster Group's work has its roots in the company's earliest practices. Emerging out of Spalding Gray and Elizabeth LeCompte's development, with other members of the Performance Group, of the *Rhode Island Trilogy* (1975–1978),[3] the Wooster Group's first performances signaled a departure from the politics and aesthetics of a "Performance Theater"[4] exemplified by the Living Theatre and the Performance Group itself. Led by Richard Schechner, and originating from his encounter with [Jerzy] Grotowski's "Poor Theatre" in New York in 1967,[5] the Performance Group's focus on the "authenticity" of the performer's commitment, experience, and "presence" in performance also responded to the innovations and politics of the Living Theatre, the theatrical implications of happenings, and John Cage's reconception of music and theater.[6] Here, more specifically, Schechner sought to create an "Environmental Theater"[7] in which the performance of text would become subject to the personal, social and theatrical dynamics operating variously between performers and spectators. Yet, while the Wooster Group's exploration of framing, intertextuality, mediation, and paradox has been taken to effect a deconstruction of Schechner's[8] and others' attempts, in the context of 1960s' countercultural theatrical practice, to address the "presence" of audience and performer,[9] the Group's multi-media practices have also articulated a complex and equivocal response to this approach to the "real" act of theater or performance. [. . .]

In contrast to the Performance Group's exploration of personal, social and theatrical transactions in order to *interrupt* the theater's representations with the "real" circumstances of their performance, *Rumstick Road* [1977, the second play of the trilogy] emphasizes the "signs" of the real, the "evidence" of "authenticity." Characteristically, too, this reversal provides the first of a series of linked paradoxes. In emphasizing the performer's *encounter* with the material at hand, *Rumstick Road* repeatedly directs attention toward "the real recording," as if, in the lip-synching of audiotapes, for example, to demonstrate the incapacity of the theater to capture or restore that to which its signs refer. Here, it seems, where "real evidence" intrudes into the theater's representations *in mediation*, "live performance" functions as "text" and

Figure 7.5 The Wooster Group, *Brace Up!*, 1991/2003, director Elizabeth LeCompte. Left to right: Scott Renderer, Jeff Webster (on large monitors), Paul Schmidt (on small monitor), Kate Valk. Photo: © Mary Gearhart.

"sign." Such reversals evidently counter the privileging of the "live presence" of the performer in Schechner's work.

In this context, the third play of the trilogy, *Nayatt School* (1978), extended this logic while marking the Group's first direct incorporation of film into performance. Drawing on LeCompte's training in graphic design, *Nayatt School* further emphasized the edit, the cut, and the radical interleaving of distinct elements. In a multiplication of highly referential fragments, David Savran records, *Nayatt* School brought together a "wild assortment of texts,"[10] including vaudeville comedy-horror sequences, excerpts from T.S. Eliot's *The Cocktail Pony*, a scene, "The Breast Examination," by Jim Strahs, as well as various musical and nonmusical recordings, including a 1950s sound recording of *The Cocktail Party* starring Alec Guinness. [. . .] In Part V, "The Fifth Examination of the Text: In Which Spalding Introduces the Children in Their Parts and the Man, the Woman and Spalding Play a Scene with Them (*The Cocktail Party*, Act III),"[11] a projection of Ken Kobland's record of the Group's rehearsal of the same scene with child and adult performers produced characteristically multiple implications. The film is projected over the whole space such that "the live action is doubled by a film of a previous performance,"[12] and Kobland notes that in "going back into another time" the film "was a constant next to the variables, the people who aren't there, which is also a part of *The Cocktail Party*. Of the monologues. Of the past. Of the Wooster Group."[13]

In including the film record of a past rehearsal, Kobland suggests, "[t]he idea was that the piece would be, with the film involvement, a piece of contradiction, of time passing in different ways."[14] Echoing the times implicit in the overlaying or reconstruction of Gray's "documentary" recordings in *Rumstick Road*, the film also emphasized a key characteristic of the Group's subsequent performances, in which the history of the Group, of their rehearsal and making of work, is selectively reproduced. The *Trilogy*, in this aspect, is a work "about" the creation of theater [. . .]. Thus, *Nyatt School*'s re-playing of the Group's rehearsal plays explicitly on "the real" and its reproduction, offering an ambivalent retelling of their "performance biography" that, even in emphasizing its recording of a "real rehearsal," gains an explicitly metaphorical and so textual charge.

Such tactics continually construct the elements of these performances as caught within an *order of difference*. Thus, the film projection is read in the *different* times in which the performance now operates: in relation to the "real" record; in its new contextual "meaning"; in plays across "actuality" and "textuality" produced in its repetition and reproduction *here*. Here, too, the Wooster Group's reuse of material plays between "repetition" and "reproduction," as live and recorded performances are layered to articulate the group's restaging of their own and others' work. Such repetitions are not only linked to the open intertextuality of the Wooster Group's productions, in which texts, performances, and films are appropriated and re-performed or reproduced, but refer, again, to the process of "making theater," and, in this, to distinctions between the "live event" and its mediation. [. . .]

Through Frank Dell's *The Temptation of St. Antony* (1987), developed over a four-year period, the Group realized its most overtly complex collage of disparate theatrical, literary, and philosophical texts. Achieving an extraordinary degree of reference, superimposition, and dialogue between seven principal texts identified in the Wooster Group's published script,[15] in their rehearsal process, Suzanne Letzler Cole records, the company integrated at least fourteen distinct sources into the performance.[16] Thus the piece explicitly incorporates reworkings of Gustave Flaubert's *La Tentation de Saint Antoine*, Ingmar Bergman's film *The Magician* (1958), and the unauthorized biography of Lenny Bruce, *Ladies and Gentlemen, Lenny Bruce!!* (1974) by Albert Goldman. At the same time, the performance draws on an edition of Flaubert's letters, videotapes produced in the manner of "Channel J," a late-night New York cable channel talk show in which host and interviewees were nude, poetry by Geraldine Cummins and a history of the art of entertainment.[17] Thematically, in relation to the texts it superimposes, the performance crosses polarities and oppositions, investing references to the metaphysical in allusions to obscenity and the obscene, confusing the spiritual with references to vaudeville magic shows, the "psychical" and charlatanism. Shadowed, like many of the Wooster Group's performances, by the story of a performance company, here an itinerant magic troupe, the production characteristically defers between narrative lines and fragments and allusions to the making of theater. Here, too, and reflecting LeCompte's realization and instruction to the actors in rehearsal that "[y]ou're in two plays at the same time,"[18] *Frank Dell's The Temptation of Saint Antony* foregrounds a traversing of media and texts, linked to the media's operation itself, and exemplified in Ron Vawter's performance of its opening scene.

In "EPISODE 1: THE MONOLOGUE, in which Frank runs his tape, and takes a call from Cubby,"[19] Vawter, ostensibly rehearsing his act in his dressing room, performs Lenny Bruce's early alter ego "Frank Dell." Off-stage, "Sue" occasionally prompts, replies, or throws remarks into Vawter's seemingly stream-of-consciousness monologue, while above, and on monitors dispersed over the audience, a silent tape of an interview with a nude young man and woman plays on. Here, Don Shewey recounts: "Wearing dark glasses, sandals, and a bathrobe, the central character of *Frank Dell's The Temptation of St. Antony* stands under a spotlight muttering into a microphone. Calling out instructions to an unseen engineer, he obsessively plays and replays scenes from a cable-TV nude talk show visible on a row of monitors above his head, dubbing in all the voices himself like a video ventriloquist. The dialogue these embarrassed looking nudists spout ranges from banal chitchat to metaphysical ruminations.[20] [. . .]

In this aspect, Vawter's "Act" exemplifies a structural rhythm characteristic of Wooster Group performances. In bringing together the various elements of the Group's work, LeCompte emphasizes, the company aims "to allow them to be in the space together, without this demand for meaning"[21] [. . .].

Vawter's performance asserts a multiplication of times as well as frames and *places.* Analogous to Elizabeth Ermarth's account of structures producing a "postmodern time" in the novel,[22] and which may be extended toward video and video installation, this inflection of one text and action across another marks a rhythm that unsettles the time of Vawter's "Act." Where in the novel, Ermarth notes, "postmodern time" is established in narrative structures through which "[t]he story forces reader attention into play between alternate semantic systems,"[23] Vawter's performance poses the question of how to position, or read, what is done *in multiple contexts.* [. . .] Vawter's "phrases" *traverse* media in simultaneous conjugations of *explicitly different* spaces and times: the "live" Act; the "fictional" rehearsal; the "mediated" (recorded) interview. In this rhythm, too, Vawter's "Act" reflects the crisis of the subject Ermarth identifies with the postmodern novel, where the question of "who" and "what" action is present comes to the fore. Writing "On Form" with regard to *Brace Up!* (1991), which incorporated Chekhov's *Three Sisters,* LeCompte emphasizes: "There is no 'Masha' on the stage. There is only the actor/performer. The audience makes 'Masha' from the actors' actions and the images which simultaneously occur in the stage world. The character is an accumulation of fragments of which the performer is the initiator. The character is a 'moment in stage time.'"[24] [. . .]

The Wooster Group's later work departed from the extreme dispersal and fragmentation characterizing *St. Antony,* to explore the production of complete or virtually complete texts encompassing the time of performance while further developing this rhythmic complexity. Here, beginning with *Brace Up!,* which brought together a specially commissioned translation of Chekhov's *Three Sisters* by Paul Schmidt with the conventions of Noh theater and popular Japanese television, the Group has gone on to engage with a wide range of canonical dramatic texts, including O'Neill's *The Emperor Jones* (1993) and *The Hairy Ape* (1996), as well as Racine's *Phèdre* in *To You, the Birdie! (Phèdre)* (2002). Implicitly engaging with a mediation or "remediation" in which one text or set of conventions is filtered through another to produce a "complex polyphonic structure,"[25] these performances approach the combination of selected texts in ways consistent with Vawter's traversing of character and context. [. . .]

Characteristically, these dialogues between structures, conventions, and texts work to disperse attention from one point to another within the space. Thus, in her notes on *Brace Up!*, LeCompte's remarks "On Fragmentation" indicate a series of exercises in displacement, in which live, mediated, and recorded activities are bound one to the other while diverting attention away from a resolution of the relationship between their various spaces. Amongst these instructions, LeCompte notes:

> Performers on TV develop all relationships through a language of vocal and spatial displacements, i.e., the Baron speaks to a specific point on the upstage left wall to indicate that he is "speaking to" the doctor.
>
> Performers on TV are also seen on stage from the back and in profile—and simultaneously on TV in close up. When the performers on the TV engage the lens directly, they are referring to the stage performers who spoke before them or after them . . .
>
> If dominant stage action is at stage left, then the TV performers' "gaze" must be towards stage right—always pulling the center away from itself as soon as it forms.[26]

Reflecting on the performance's articulation in such distraction, Schmidt himself recalls the "music" of *Brace Up!* as a series of "calculated and rehearsed" layers, each of which asserts its difference in a "complicated orchestral composition" of reflexive elements.[27] Including "the text of Chekhov's *Three Sisters*; comments on the text by Kate Valk as the Narrator or myself as the Translator," Schmidt observes these distinct layers extending toward "recorded music and sound effects performed on complicated machinery . . . live music and singing; fourth, the sound of the stage itself—furniture and props being moved about and handled; and fifth, the movement of bodies and the swish of costumes" and, finally, "silence."[28] Within this structure, he recalls: "We wanted to go with the mood, listen to the wind, identify ourselves with the emotional overtones of the background. And [LeCompte] was asking us instead to play against all that: to play one tempo on top of another, in other words, like a piece of music with one time signature in one hand and a different one in the other."[29][. . .]

In turn, in *Brace Up!*, and characteristically of the Group's performances, these rhythmic constructions are provided with another layer of complexity through set-piece dances and the play of live mediation and recorded video. Here, Arratia notes, in the rehearsal of *Brace Up!* "[t]he Wooster Group's dancing is made manifest throughout their work in the special attention to concrete time and space."[30] Specifically, the Group worked to ensure that its choreographies remain rhythmically unpredictable, as if the performers might, in their dancing, move "in and out" of their choreography's performance. [. . .]

Where the Wooster Group's dances work *across* rather than *in* a rhythmic unity, video itself introduces another and separate continuity into the performance. Here, the unfolding of images in the video's "own" "textual" worlds asserts an "opening up" of *Brace Up!* to rhythmic orders apparently quite *other* to its principal textual sources. In this, too, the drone of video, the *operation* of the televisions and their physical manipulation by the performers on a series of runners integrated into the set, provide a further structural layer, which, at moments, may gain a specific metaphorical or narrative charge, as if the video itself might move "in and out" of *Brace Up!*'s performance. [. . .]

It is in this rhythm, too, that the Group's performances extend toward a disruption of the oppositions in which the conventional production of theatrical texts tends to operate: the distinction between "performer" and "character," "live" and "mediated," "real" and "representation." Indeed, and echoing the tendency toward an "opening-out-to-the-world"[31] evident in earlier multi-medial practices, the Wooster Group's layering of actions, spaces, and times potentially extends toward an inclusion of "temporality *in general*"[32] into its structural framework. [. . .]

From the chapter "Multiplication: The Wooster Group" in Nick Kaye, *Multi-Media: Video—Installation—Performance* (London and New York: Routledge, 2007), 164–81.

Notes

1 James Leverett in Susan Letzler Cole, *Directors in Rehearsal: A Hidden World* (London: Routledge, 1992), 91.
2 Jim Clayburgh in Euridice Arratia, "Island Hopping: Rehearsing the Wooster Group's Brace Up)," *The Drama Review* 36, no. 4 (1992), 121–42.
3 [The *Rhode Island Trilogy* comprised *Sakonnet Point* (1975), *Rumstick Road* (1977), and *Nayatt School* (1978), as well as *Point Judith (an epilog)*, see https://thewoostergroup.org/spalding-gray.]
4 C.E.W. Bigsby, *A Critical Introduction to Twentieth Century American Drama, Volume III* (Cambridge: Cambridge University Press, 1985).
5 Richard Schechner in Nick Kaye, *Art into Theatre: Performance Interviews and Documents* (Amsterdam: Hardwood Academic Press, 1996), 174.
6 Richard Schechner, "Six Axioms for Environmental Theatre," *The Drama Review* 12, no. 3 (1969), 41–64.
7 Richard Schechner, *Environmental Theater* (New York: Hawthorn, 1973).
8 [Richard Schechner led the Performance Group from 1967 to 1980. He is also one of the leading theorists of performance studies with many publications, who cofounded the Department of Performance Studies at NYU Tisch School of Arts in 1980.]
9 Philip Auslander, *From Acting to Performance: Essays in Modernism and Postmodernism* (London: Routledge, 1997).
10 David Savran, *Breaking the Rules: The Wooster Group* (New York: Theater Communications Group, 1988), 102.
11 Ibid., 104.
12 Ibid., 124f.
13 Kobland in ibid., 107.
14 Ibid., 102.
15 The Wooster Group, "Frank Dell's The Temptation of St. Antony," in *Plays for the End of the Century* ed. Bonnie Marranca (Baltimore, MD: Johns Hopkins University Press, 1996), 261–314.
16 Letzler Cole, *Directors in Rehearsal*, 94–6.
17 The Wooster Group, "Frank Dell's The Temptation of St. Antony," 265f.
18 Letzler Cole, *Directors in Rehearsal*, 118.
19 The Wooster Group, "Frank Dell's The Temptation of St. Antony," 267.

20 Don Shewey, "Wooster Group Not Tempted by Conventionality: The Experimental-Theater Troupe Has Jumbled-up Flaubert for Its 'Frank Dell's the Temptation of St. Antony,'" *Los Angeles Times*, August 27, 1990; available at https://www.donshewey.com/theater_articles/wooster_group_for_LA_times.htm.

21 Elizabeth LeCompte in Kaye, *Art into Theatre*, 256.

22 Elizabeth D. Ermarth, *Sequel to History: Postmodernism and the Crisis of Representational Time* (Princeton, NJ: Princeton University Press, 1992), 21.

23 Ibid., 68.

24 Elizabeth LeCompte, "*Brace Up!*," *Felix* 1, no. 3 (1993); online at http://www.e-felix.org/issue3/Lecompte.html.

25 Paul Schmidt, "The Sounds of *Brace Up!*," *The Drama Review* 36, no. 4 (1992), 154–7.

26 LeCompte, "*Brace Up!*"

27 Schmidt, "The Sounds of *Brace Up!*," 156.

28 Ibid.

29 Ibid., 155.

30 Arratia, "Island Hopping," 135.

31 Allan Kaprow, "Nam June Paik" (1968), in *Nam June Paik: Video Time, Video Space*, ed. Toni Stooss and Thomas Kellein (New York: Harry N. Abrams, 1983), 114.

32 Ina Blom, "Boredom and Oblivion," in *The Fluxus Reader*, ed. Ken Friedman (Chichester: Academy Editions, 1998), 67.

8

Video | Internet: Online Video and the Consumer as Producer

Introduction by Martha Buskirk (Guest Editor)

The utopian promise of YouTube's tagline, "broadcast yourself," is certainly alluring. There can be no doubt that the potential for supplanting corporate and governmental control of the airwaves with direct access to an ever-growing community of users has dramatically transformed the experience of video—with hundreds of hours of content being uploaded every minute and over a billion users engaging in an increasingly complex interplay of consumption and production. But even though YouTube's dominant market position makes it a natural focal point, it is only one of many options for viewing and sharing video-based material in the context of an experiential field saturated with moving images. Humor, how-to, personal narrative, gaming video, marketing, cultural critique, and political activism are all part of a continuum ranging from banal to extreme, where users easily morph into producers and where the posting and recirculating of both found and original imagery are all tightly intertwined. Linked to this ubiquity is a widespread breakdown of distinctions, including video/film, amateur/professional, original/remix, public/private, commercial/noncommercial, live/taped, and, perhaps most importantly, consumer/producer.

This contemporary landscape is characterized by dramatic changes in the nature of access across three major areas: existing cultural material, recording and editing technology, and channels of distribution. While relatively fast (within the lifetime of many people reading this text), these shifts have also been incremental, so it is important to keep them in perspective. The possibility, initially offered by VCR technology, of watching film and television at will, rather than viewing tied to a specific place or time, is now taken for granted in the context of widespread digital circulation of cultural material. Previously cumbersome video cameras have become both miniaturized and ubiquitous via their smooth incorporation into multifunction cell phones, while readily available editing software allows users to accomplish what once required expensive tools along with specialized knowledge. Finally, social media and related platforms have facilitated a dramatic shift in distribution channels for content of all kinds, including user-generated.

It is important to pay attention to what is gained, but also lost, in this process. The dominance of major media companies, which controlled both content production and largely one-directional channels of distribution, has been supplanted by the dominance of major technology companies, whose platforms establish parameters for information exchange. While the huge volume of material circulating electronically can make it appear as if everything is available, state-imposed censorship in some regions and increasingly prevalent copyright mechanisms limit archival scope and potential. The sheer noise associated with the intersection of everything from cute cat videos to partisan political messaging threatens both utopian hopes for video and any remaining sense of its coherence as a medium.

The first video uploaded to YouTube in 2005, "Me at the Zoo" by Jawed Karim, one of the site's founders, was a nineteen-second monolog shot at the zoo by a friend, in which he makes the following momentous series of observations: "All right, so here we are in front of the, uh, elephants, and the cool thing about these guys is that, is that they have really, really, really long, um, trunks, and that's, that's cool, and that's pretty much all there is to say." YouTube quickly became an extremely popular forum for home-made and generally quite short videos (and was acquired by Google in 2006 notwithstanding its absence of revenue at that point).[1] In an essay exploring this early landscape, including material that appealed to early "surf clubs," Ceci Moss pointed out how, despite the quirky allure of many of these offerings, this initial form of content limited both profitability and the amount of time most people spent on the site.[2]

As early as 2010, an article in the *Los Angeles Times* predicted that the platform, which had started out wanting to be "the antithesis of television," would evolve to a point where there would be no distinction between the two.[3] In 2014, Google and Viacom settled a major copyright infringement suit concerning copyrighted Viacom content posted to YouTube (with offending clips from *The Daily Show*, *South Park*, and *SpongeBob SquarePants* specifically referenced). Viacom was motivated to settle in part because Google had scored some courtroom victories on the grounds that they were protected by "safe harbor" provisions of the Digital Millennium Copyright Act as long as they acted promptly to take down content after receiving infringement notifications. But the settlement was also motivated by the increasing potential for a convergence of business interests, rather than rivalry.[4]

If YouTube's initial appeal was connected to the apparent freedom it offered to users to share content, its long-term success has been linked to blocking two of the most popular types of uploads: pirated material and pornography. For a time the microblogging site Tumblr became a porn-friendly alternative, until it abruptly banned adult content in late 2018 (and immediately experienced a sharp drop in users), and of course Snapchat has been notorious as a major forum for "sexting."[5] The extent to which such material still slips through, along with the obverse, of videos that shouldn't be flagged somehow triggering YouTube's highly automated controls, indicate the obvious limits of relying on software to sift through the unending tsunami of uploaded video.

Certain YouTube shifts reflect the gradual evolution of how users have attempted to employ the platform, along with expanding technological capacities that include dramatic improvements to standard video capture in cell phones, bandwidth, and storage options. But others are the result of conscious algorithm tweaks designed to maximize profits. One important change, in 2012, altered the popularity metrics from the number of initial clicks to overall watch time—to prevent gaming the system with provocative titles or associated thumbnail images and to keep viewers watching through multiple ads.[6]

The contemporary version of YouTube remains a multifaceted organism. It holds out the possibility of a form of stardom marked by subscriber numbers (and a related share of ad income dollars) measured in millions, even as it also supports smaller communities whose use of the platform is not motivated by self-commercialization, including the transgender video bloggers and viewers discussed in Tobias Raun's "Screen Births: Trans Vlogs as a Transformative Media for Self-Representation" in Chapter 3 of this reader. Yet the potential for intensifying niche messages has also proven to be a significant downside, with algorithm-driven recommendations that promote more of the same, often in increasingly excessive versions, helping to amplify conspiracy theories and extremist ideologies.[7]

In reading the essays in this section, it is important to think about the perspectives they bring in relation to a fast-changing landscape. As part of the cross-generational conversation between pioneering video artist Dara Birnbaum and new media artist Cory Arcangel, Birnbaum looks back at the tremendous hurdles she had to overcome simply to gain access to the footage she used to create her 1978 video *Technology/Transformation: Wonder Woman*. At the same time, reading this 2009 conversation from a later vantage point provides a different form of evidence about incessant change. As somewhat of an aside, Arcangel asks, "Are you going to Twitter about what you've been doing every second?" and Birnbaum responds, "What's Twittering?" Arcangel, true to his role as an early adopter, tells her: "Twitter is this new website. People use their cell phones to text what they're doing—'I'm eating lunch' or 'I'm in the *Artforum* offices having a conversation'—to their website, where other people can read about it."[8] Both his terminology ("to twitter" rather than "to tweet") and his reference to a fairly basic website structure provide evidence of how dramatically the platform has evolved.

Hito Steyerl addresses one of the early trade-offs associated with online distribution in her 2009 text "In Defense of the Poor Image." Regarding the image quality lost due to compression, there are points of comparison to the previous underground trade in bootleg videotape copies. (New York City residents of a certain age share fond memories of Kim's Video, with its wide-ranging collection of videotapes both legally and illicitly obtained.) Notable improvements in the resolution quality of online video are, however, inseparable from the realization of business models that can support constant technological innovation, massive server farms, and any other infrastructure necessary to sustain apparently weightless transmission.

As an important counterpoint, the integral role of social media platforms and online videos in the Arab Spring uprisings shows the subversive potential of user-generated content. Peter Snowdon has identified the shift from private to public as crucial to the political efficacy of this improvisatory and vernacular practice. Rather than functioning as an extension of the eye, cell-phone videos captured from the midst of protest activities and violent counterattacks provide chaotic evidence of bodies in motion.[9] However, in her essay included in this section, Cécile Boëx traces a transition, in the Syrian context, from initial spontaneity to increasingly professionalized video recording while cautioning against overestimating the power of such documents, in and of themselves.[10]

A second-order response to the amateur video broadcast out of Syria appeared in Rabih Mroué's 2012 lecture/performance entitled *The Pixelated Revolution*, where he emphasized the unequal parallel between gun and camera in the evolving conflict—on the one side, individuals using their recording devices as part of a campaign to stop the carnage and, on the other, lethal violence to suppress the act of recording—while also exploring challenges associated with relying on the internet's vast compendium of unverifiable sources.[11] In another turn, however, a high-resolution video of that lecture has been shown in exhibition venues as a video projection/installation. And in an echo of the original mode of dissemination for the source material, parts of that high-resolution video have been uploaded as short, lower-resolution excerpts to YouTube (Figure 8.1).

The reference Boëx makes to the unpredictable disappearance of the videos upon which she based her analysis indicates another challenge associated with the instability of YouTube as an archival resource (a goal that is clearly not a priority for their business model). One attempt to preserve material related to the Egyptian uprising can be found in the archive made public in 2018 by the activist group Mosireen, with its

Figure 8.1 A Syrian youth films the sniper who kills him in the Karm al-Sham area of Homs. Uploaded by Abumfarg on July 4, 2011, www.youtube.com/watch?v=Q0pFYXFIy9CY&feature=related (no longer available). Image capture from Rabih Mroué, *The Pixelated Revolution*, 2012.

title, the 858 Archive, based on the hours of footage at the time of its initial release.[12] Nor is this the only instance where organizations and more loosely structured groups have responded to this danger by harnessing volunteer labor to scrape the records associated with recent events. Such attempts recognize how important evidence can be lost, as documentation produced by participants themselves and shared in the heat of the moment can be quickly deleted (both consciously scrubbed from individual accounts and because the material was shared via apps designed to do exactly that).[13] Moreover, the emergence of such material in the first place is increasingly endangered, as governments attempt to block the use of social media to counteract the impact of state-controlled mass media channels. China's censorship strategies are particularly sophisticated and pervasive; but there are many examples of less subtle blocking of sites, or all forms of internet communication, at key moments.[14]

The prominent role that video continues to play in publicizing acts of racism and police abuse in the United States and other Western democracies speaks to the power of such images to cut through attempts to spin the narrative. For the Black Lives Matter movement, documents of horrific violence provided inconvertible evidence of systemic racism's pervasive impact. Emphasizing this historic significance, but also the trauma associated with bearing witness to images of violent death, Allissa V. Richardson has traced parallels to earlier photographic records of lynchings. Videos captured by bystanders record acts of aggression that might otherwise remain hidden from view, with their storylines controlled by the perpetrators. Yet Richardson has been taken aback by the casual ease with which such footage circulates online, in contrast to the restraint typically accorded to violent events involving white victims.[15]

Alexandra Juhasz's essay in this section, "Nothing Is Unwatchable for All," addresses the tension when wrenching images of violent death are absorbed into our current information overload. Juhasz views this important but often invasive function against a larger critique of media manipulation and destabilization. As early as 2008 Juhasz had pointed to a disconnect that has only become more extreme, between aspirations for YouTube to fulfill "idealistic dreams of universal access to a democratic media with a host of scholars and makers" and the actual experience of visiting "this marvelous place" and finding "the stuff I see there so thoroughly unsatisfying."[16] More recently, with *#100hardtruths-#fakenews*, a website focused on the first 100 days of the Trump presidency, Juhasz highlighted the fracturing of the media environment in ways that allow conspiracy theories and other willful distortions to circulate and metastasize. Warning against the danger of having public debate framed and mediated by the image streams on our devices, Siva Vaidhyanathan in his essay similarly outlines the potential loss of context or perspective associated with abundance.[17] A singular video like the one that captured the horrific death of George Floyd, asphyxiated by a policeman's knee on his neck, still has the power to cut through this cacophony. Yet the ability to distinguish between news and propaganda is undermined by a flood of information with increasingly slick production values, including the deepfakes discussed in Chapter 11.

Citing the remarkable volume of video constantly in play, "billions of cameras around us, constantly uploading, sharing, linking, and relating," Andreas Treske's contribution diagnoses web and video as so tightly intertwined that they become potentially synonymous.[18] The heterogeneity within YouTube is already startling, yet it, along with less dominant platforms such as Vimeo and Daily Motion, is surprisingly focused in comparison to the integration of moving images into all forms of social media—Facebook, Snapchat, and Instagram being major players at the time this was written, and others certain to become part of the landscape in the future. There is also clearly room for new platforms focused on short, meme-type videos, as evident in Vine (even if short-lived) or the sudden popularity of TikTok.

The dramatic transformation is ultimately twofold. One is the unfathomable volume of moving images simultaneously stored and accessible in electronic form. The second lies in the miniaturized recording, playback, and editing devices carried by an increasingly large percentage of people across the world. The potential of cell phone technology not only to record but also to simultaneously broadcast—whether it is revolutionary action or documentation of individual encounters with racism or police violence—will continue to be a powerful tool. But it is equally crucial not to overlook the cultural significance of the many other ways, from animated selfies to a host of memes and remix gestures, whereby individuals are part of a dynamic in which consumption and production are inextricably interwoven.

Notes

1 For early perspectives on YouTube's impact, see Pelle Snickars and Patrick Vonderau, *The YouTube Reader* (Stockholm: National Library of Sweden, 2009); and Jean Burgess and Joshua Green, *YouTube: Online Video and Participatory Culture* (Cambridge, UK; Malden, MA: Polity, 2009). The latter also appeared in a substantially updated second edition, published in 2018.

2 Ceci Moss, "Internet Explorers," in *Mass Effect: Art and the Internet in the Twenty-First Century*, ed. Lauren Cornell and Ed Halter (Cambridge, MA: MIT Press, 2015), 147–57.

3 Alex Pham, "YouTube Turns 5, Can't Wait to Grow Up," *Los Angeles Times*, May 17, 2010, http://articles.latimes.com/2010/may/17/entertainment/la-et-youtube-20100517.

4 See, e.g., Dominic Rushe, "Google and Viacom Settle Major Copyright Case after Years of Litigation," *The Guardian*, March 18, 2014, https://www.theguardian.com/technology/2014/mar/18/google-viacom-settle-copyright-case-years-of-litigation.

5 See, e.g., Nicole Karlis, "Did Banning Porn Make Tumblr Worthless?" *Salon*, August 16, 2019, https://www.salon.com/2019/08/16/did-banning-porn-make-tumblr-worthless/. For a discussion of early forms of home video and internet pornography, see Sarah Késenne, "Regarding the Sex, Lies and Videotapes of Others: Memory, Counter-Memory, and Mystified Relations," in *Video Vortex Reader II: Moving Images Beyond YouTube*, ed. Geert Lovink and Rachel Somers Miles (Amsterdam: Institute of Network Cultures, 2011), 61–9, http://www.networkcultures.org/_uploads/%236reader_VideoVortex2PDF.pdf.

6 For an overview of various algorithm shifts, see Julia Alexander, "The Golden Age of YouTube Is Over: The Platform was Built on the Backs of Independent Creators, but Now YouTube is Abandoning them for More Traditional Content," *The Verge*, April

5, 2019, https://www.theverge.com/2019/4/5/18287318/youtube-logan-paul-pewdiepie-demonetization-adpocalypse-premium-influencers-creators.

7 For an overview of algorithm functions in this context, see Lee Rainie and Janna Anderson, "Code-Dependent: Pros and Cons of the Algorithm Age," *Pew Research Center Report*, February 8, 2017, https://www.pewinternet.org/2017/02/08/code-dependent-pros-and-cons-of-the-algorithm-age/. For a narrative of one person's journey into YouTube conspiracy theories, see Kevin Roose, "The Making of a YouTube Radical," *The New York Times*, June 8, 2019, https://www.nytimes.com/interactive/2019/06/08/technology/youtube-radical.html.

8 Cory Arcangel and Dara Birnbaum, "Do It 2," *Artforum* 47, no. 7 (March 2009), 193.

9 Peter Snowdon, "The Revolution Will Be Uploaded: Vernacular Video and the Arab Spring," *Culture Unbound: Journal of Current Cultural Research* 6, no. 2 (2014), 401–29.

10 See as well the related essay by Kathrin Peters, "Images of Protest: On the 'Woman in the Blue Bra' and Relational Testimony," in Chapter 11 of this reader for a discussion of the inherent instability of meaning associated with the rampant circulation of certain fragmentary moments.

11 See Rabih Mroué, "The Pixelated Revolution," trans. Ziad Nawfal, intr. Carol Martin, *TDR: The Drama Review* 56, no. 3 (2012), 18–35.

12 The 858 Archive can be found at https://858.ma. For further information see Amir-Hussein Radjy, "How to Save the Memories of the Egyptian Revolution," *The Atlantic*, January 25, 2018, https://www.theatlantic.com/international/archive/2018/01/an-internet-archive-rekindles-the-egyptian-revolutions-spirit/551489/; and Ursula Lindsey, "An Online Archive of the Egyptian Revolution," *Al-Fanar Media*, February 21, 2018, https://www.al-fanarmedia.org/2018/02/online-archive-egyptian-revolution/.

13 See, e.g., Allissa V. Richardson, "The Coming Archival Crisis: How Ephemeral Video Disappears Protest Journalism and Threatens Newsreels of Tomorrow," *Digital Journalism* 8, no. 10 (2020), 1338–46; and Philip Bump, "The Capitol Mob Recorded Its Own History. Now, Volunteers Are Trying to Preserve the Record," *Washington Post*, January 7, 2021, https://www.washingtonpost.com/politics/2021/01/07/capitol-mob-recorded-its-own-history-now-volunteers-are-trying-preserve-record/.

14 See, e.g., Emna Sayadi, "Egypt: More Than 500 Sites Blocked ahead of the Presidential Election," *Access Now*, March 14, 2018, https://www.accessnow.org/egypt-more-than-500-sites-blocked-ahead-of-the-presidential-election/.

15 Allissa V. Richardson, *Bearing Witness While Black: African Americans, Smartphones, and the New Protest #Journalism* (New York: Oxford University Press, 2020); and "Why Cellphone Videos of Black People's Deaths Should Be Considered Sacred, Like Lynching Photographs," *The Conversation*, May 28, 2020, https://theconversation.com/why-cellphone-videos-of-black-peoples-deaths-should-be-considered-sacred-like-lynching-photographs-139252.

16 Alexandra Juhasz, "Documentary on YouTube: The Failure of the Direct Cinema of the Slogan," in *Rethinking Documentary: New Perspectives, New Practices* (Maidenhead, Berkshire; New York: Open University Press/McGraw Hill Education, 2008), 209.

17 Siva Vaidhyanathan, "The Dangers of Ubiquitous Video," *Wired*, August 18, 2020, https://www.wired.com/story/dangers-ubiquitous-video-propaganda/.

18 Andreas Treske, "Shiny Things So Bright," draft text of a talk at *Video Vortex XI* in Kochi 2017, http://networkcultures.org/wp-content/uploads/2017/04/Catalouge-compiled-final-28-03.pdf

Do It 2 (2009)

Cory Arcangel and Dara Birnbaum

Cory Arcangel: Recently I read an interview in which you said clubs provided one of the first outlets for your videos. In other words, you felt you could make videos to be projected in clubs at the same time you made videos that were to be shown in art spaces. Was that specific to the time? It made me wonder how the context for video has changed over the past thirty years or so.

Dara Birnbaum: Well, to clarify just a bit, I was saying that whenever I made a work, I believed it could be inserted into different contexts. It wasn't that I was actually making different work for a specific venue. You see, when I started, video was a very bastardized medium, mainly separated out from the arts. The only video I knew of within the arts in the 1970s consisted mostly of extensions of performance art, body art, or Earth art. Video was understood almost as an expanded documentary format, whereas I thought that it had a great capacity for different applications. I was excited when, for instance, the Guerrilla Girls asked me to show *Technology/Transformation: Wonder Woman* [1978–1979] at a special evening in their honor at Palladium, which had these massive video walls, or when I could show *Pop-Pop Video: Kojak/Wang* [1980] in another club that had 40 monitors around the room, so we could stand within this shootout, truly encircled by the action on-screen, which never resolves itself. But my excitement was more about the change of context than about changing the content. [. . .]

CA: I think I'm definitely in a parallel situation today when it comes to the question of context. You made videos and found it interesting to place them in clubs; my videos go on view in galleries, but I'll also put them online. And just as the galleries weren't interested in your video work because they thought it was just TV, they weren't so interested in my work at the beginning. They just didn't see it as art.

DB: I initially avoided galleries like the plague. I didn't want to translate popular imagery from television and film into painting and photography. I wanted to use video on video; I wanted to use television on television. A lot of us who went into video at the beginning did so because we thought art shouldn't be made in limited editions, and in video we finally had an eminently reproducible medium that could get out into the hands of many. It was a populist form, and our great hope was to do something that made it to Kim's Video store. You know? I didn't want to be collected. I wanted to talk. Looking back, there were different test runs to promote this way of distribution for artists, but nothing ever truly supported that vision.

CA: But that last assertion makes me wonder: Is there even such a thing as a bastardized medium today? Sure, if you're talking specifically about the art context and its inevitable waves of style. In larger culture, however, you now have to consider all the developments in distribution. The fact is that you can put anything up on the Internet and there will be five people who want it, no matter how weird or obscure the information. The niche exists; someone's going to find you, period. [. . .]

Media is no longer a one-way street. It's participatory. People just make things. And so I don't know whether it's so necessary to "reveal" anything anymore. Maybe a previous era's debate has shifted over to, I don't know, "Are you going to Twitter about what you're doing every second?"

DB: What is Twittering?

CA: I'm sorry. This is embarrassing. I'm going to tell the editors not to print the word "Twitter." Twitter is this new website. People use their cell phones to text what they're doing—"I'm eating lunch" or "I'm in the *Artforum* offices having a conversation"—to their website, where other people can read about it. I do have my own audience online, in this sense, because I surf the Internet all day long and leave a bread-crumb trail so people can see what I've been looking at. And when I'm "leaving bread crumbs" for my audience, I'm Twittering, basically. It's like production itself has become consumption.

DB: That sounds to me almost like when artists first got hold of the Portapak. They would just turn it on, not really knowing what to say with this new device. I remember a tape by Howard Fried called *Fuck You, Purdue* [1972]. It was just him in his studio, pacing and recording every word: "Fuck you. Fuck you, Purdue."

CA: I *have* to see that.

DB: There was a genuine amazement about the technology, and artists were as amazed as anyone else, with the hope that they would look into the new aspects of the medium's potential. But you merely got people turning on that Portapak and recording every moment of what they did. [. . .]

Having grown up reading a fair amount of Marxist theory, I recall that Walter Benjamin's idealistic hope was that people would become involved in production. Society would be better off if it wasn't only about producing products for the general populace as the consumer, but rather about people remaining directly engaged by being their own producers. I wonder if this is a very failed vision.

CA: If everyone is a producer now, then we have a data-archiving problem—meaning that we do not know where, or how, to look for accurate information. I don't want to speak in favor of heavily edited, manicured media, because obviously that has its own problems. But the Internet is full of half-truths; you can find a "factual basis" for anything. With things like Wikipedia, you're forced to ask, "What is the real version of history?" Or, more precisely, "What's real history now that people are in control of it?"

DB: I think Benjamin was interested in the way in which people might change their ideologies, in other words, by participating, since then they are less capable of being simply consumers. Of course, as you're suggesting, the problem now revolves around the questions: What are you producing? Is the simple act of production by itself worthwhile? Where do you look for any value structure or affect that this can have? And does it say, ultimately, that anyone can be an artist—this dream of the Internet, that there is no hierarchy?

It all brings to mind an ongoing project by Hans Ulrich Obrist [launched in 1993], called *Do It*, which has included both a book and a traveling exhibition. Here, the basic concept seemed like a—perhaps false—utopian fulfillment of Lawrence Weiner's project *Statements* [1968]: the artist issues a set of instructions that have or do not have to be executed by the receiver of the statements. But I think Hans Ulrich became infatuated with seeing work disperse widely into culture. And who gets eliminated from that system? Well, the artist. I mean, there was a sense of freedom in Weiner's saying that artists can, or need not, be present to enact work themselves or, as is the case with early Michael Asher works, the artist can then hire someone else to execute the work. But in the case of *Do It*, perhaps this is more like what T.J. Clark called a false utopia of images. In your work, you come to this schema much differently, right? You present or enact a set of instructions, too, but it's democratic in the sense that you say, "It's 'art,' but don't take it too seriously as art, because anyone can get at the essence of what this game is about."

CA: Yeah. When I put instructions or code online, it is really intended for use by people who don't know anything about art. This makes it slightly weird when people in the art context get excited about the work—particularly given that conceptual art, as well as the kinds of work that were in *Do It*, is slowly becoming a kind of vernacular on the Net. One is always encountering a cool new project someone is doing and explaining. [. . .]

DB: For my generation, "do it" was a leftist remark aligned with Yippie freedom, whereas by the '90s, I think, Nike is yelling at you, "Just Do It," implying that everyone can do something, be active. Those are two very different things. In fact, when Hans Ulrich asked me to contribute some instructions to his book, I, as a child of the '60s, just submitted imperatives from Jerry Rubin, who was saying things like, "Be an American, eat hamburgers every day." My decision to use that phrase in its original, obsolescent form, relates to the way you pick up an old computer-game cartridge: maybe I keep reaching backward because I, too, see things that are laid aside—almost like they have an obsolescence, when, in fact, they don't. There is a reason they existed, and they can be reactivated. The work doesn't have to be seen as nostalgic, but can be understood as a fertile gesture of reframing things laid aside by a society.

CA: The nostalgia question is difficult to elude because technological time is so fast. If I have a first-generation iPod, it's just a few years old, but people laugh at it now. If, on the other hand, I'm wearing a Polo sweater from 20 years ago, nobody laughs at all. And culture runs in technological time, while the art context runs in whatever warp time it runs in. When you implant technological time with art time, people don't know what is nostalgic and what isn't.

But you know, this goes back to the fact that I have different audiences that are totally unaware of each other. For example, most people online know my work *Pizza Party* [2004], which I wrote with the programmer Michael

Frumin at Eyebeam Atelier. It's a program that allows you to order Domino's Pizza using a command line: you just type "pizza," hit a button, and some guy delivers. In terms of sheer eyeballs, a thousand times more people have seen that than the *Clouds* piece, but I never hear about it, because these are random people I don't know. [. . .]

DB: Do *Pizza Party* and some of your other works qualify as a kind of hacking? Do you use that term to describe your work?

CA: I get in a lot of trouble with that term. I'm not some hooded figure breaking into banks and doing covert political stuff. I'm closer to the older meaning of hacker as somebody who just does clever things with software; there was a connotation of it being a kind of joke, technically cool. That is the kind of hacker I am. I modify things, and they will be technically cool or just interesting, and then I'll redistribute them.

DB: We used to say "pirating." I mean, the term pirating was used for my early work.

CA: Was it really?

DB: Yeah. For example, when I started, there were no home-recording units. There was no TiVo. There was nothing like that.

CA: It must have been very difficult for you to get that footage.

DB: It was. There was no way to get the footage I needed directly. I had to find people inside the industry who believed in my artwork and were willing to get images out to me. So they called me a "pirateer" of imagery. That had a very romantic sound to it: "Oh, she's the one who pirates imagery from television."

Maybe this is the real difference between our generations. In pirating, originally, there was no way to talk back to the media. That's why I did it. The stuff was coming one way at you, and there was no way to arrest it, stop the action, divert it, alter the vocabulary, or change the syntax. So I had to go in there pretty much illegally, take the footage from TV programs, and reassemble it. Your hacking, on the other hand, is coming from almost total accessibility—and you're able to reframe things, frequently obsolete images and objects, quite readily. What we wish to achieve as artists is probably similar, but the implications are different, as are our definitions. Also, our political scenarios seem to differ. After all, people who said I was pirating in the '70s would say, in the next decade, "Oh, she's appropriating. She's deconstructing." Later, people started using the phrase, "She takes images from . . ." After a while, I started thinking that people would eventually just call me someone who steals stuff [*laughter*].

CA: I don't know what they would say now.

DB: Whatever it is, I'm doing it. But I think that the important thing for me was to use the most common vocabulary of the time, and the most common vocabulary was television. The most common vocabulary for you is the Internet.

CA: Definitely. I only came to art from the Internet; what I am doing still comes from general online culture. And lately I have felt that some of these clever projects work best online and shouldn't appear in the art context. They work better when open to a live audience online.

DB: That goes back to those parallel tracks and the question of whether they will ever meet. They might give a promise that's never fulfilled, but you choose to jump between them. In fact, maybe the most important thing is that you are active in both spheres. Maybe by jumping between the tracks, you've become a conduit for the question of whether they can meet or not. Maybe that's a very important thing to do. I think many people of my own generation, in the late '70s, were attempting the same things by changing contexts. Maybe we have come full circle in the more than 40 years since video's appearance in the arts. By moving between these tracks, we might prevent a collision from happening or prevent them from ever meeting—but we show a potential for what can exist; we show the double-sided coin.

From Cory Arcangel and Dara Birnbaum, "Do It 2," *Artforum* 47, no. 7 (March 2009), 191–8.

In Defense of the Poor Image (2009)

Hito Steyerl

The poor image is a copy in motion. Its quality is bad, its resolution substandard. As it accelerates, it deteriorates. It is a ghost of an image, a preview, a thumbnail, an errant idea, an itinerant image distributed for free, squeezed through slow digital connections, compressed, reproduced, ripped, remixed, as well as copied and pasted into other channels of distribution.

The poor image is a rag or a rip; an AVI or a JPEG, a lumpen proletarian in the class society of appearances, ranked and valued according to its resolution. The poor image has been uploaded, downloaded, shared, reformatted, and reedited. It transforms quality into accessibility, exhibition value into cult value, films into clips, contemplation into distraction. The image is liberated from the vaults of cinemas and archives and thrust into digital uncertainty, at the expense of its own substance. The poor image tends towards abstraction: it is a visual idea in its very becoming.

The poor image is an illicit fifth-generation bastard of an original image. Its genealogy is dubious. Its filenames are deliberately misspelled. It often defies patrimony, national culture, or indeed copyright. It is passed on as a lure, a decoy, an index, or as a reminder of its former visual self. It mocks the promises of digital technology. Not only is it often degraded to the point of being just a hurried blur, one even doubts whether it could be called an image at all. Only digital technology could produce such a dilapidated image in the first place.

Poor images are the contemporary Wretched of the Screen, the debris of audiovisual production, the trash that washes up on the digital economies' shores. They testify to the violent dislocation, transferals, and displacement of images—their acceleration and circulation within the vicious cycles of audiovisual capitalism. Poor images are dragged around the globe as commodities or their effigies, as gifts or as bounty. They spread pleasure or death threats, conspiracy theories or bootlegs, resistance or stultification. Poor images show the rare, the obvious, and the unbelievable—that is, if we can still manage to decipher it.

Low Resolutions

In one of Woody Allen's films the main character is out of focus.[1] It's not a technical problem but some sort of disease that has befallen him: his image is consistently blurred. Since Allen's character is an actor, this becomes a major problem: he is unable to find work. His lack of definition turns into a material problem. Focus is identified as a class position, a position of ease and privilege, while being out of focus lowers one's value as an image.

The contemporary hierarchy of images, however, is not only based on sharpness, but also and primarily on resolution. Just look at any electronics store and this system, described by Harun Farocki in a notable 2007 interview, becomes immediately apparent.[2]

In the class society of images, cinema takes on the role of a flagship store. In flagship stores high-end products are marketed in an upscale environment. More affordable derivatives of the same images circulate as DVDs, on broadcast television, or online, as poor images.

Obviously, a high-resolution image looks more brilliant and impressive, more mimetic and magic, more scary and seductive than a poor one. It is more rich, so to speak. Now, even consumer formats are increasingly adapting to the tastes of cineastes and aesthetes, who insisted on 35mm film as a guarantee of pristine visuality. The insistence upon analog film as the sole medium of visual importance resounded throughout discourses on cinema, almost regardless of their ideological inflection. It never mattered that these high-end economies of film production were (and still are) firmly anchored in systems of national culture, capitalist studio production, the cult of mostly male genius, and the original version, and thus are often conservative in their very structure. Resolution was fetishized as if its lack amounted to castration of the author. The cult of film gauge dominated even independent film production. The rich image established its own set of hierarchies, with new technologies offering more and more possibilities to creatively degrade it.

Resurrection (as Poor Images)

[. . .] Twenty or even thirty years ago, the neoliberal restructuring of media production began slowly obscuring noncommercial imagery, to the point where experimental and essayistic cinema became almost invisible. As it became prohibitively expensive to keep these works circulating in cinemas, so were they also deemed too marginal to be broadcast on television. Thus they slowly disappeared not just from cinemas, but from the public sphere as well. Video essays and experimental films remained for the most part unseen save for some rare screenings in metropolitan film museums or film clubs, projected in their original resolution before disappearing again into the darkness of the archive. [. . .]

In this way, resistant or nonconformist visual matter disappeared from the surface into an underground of alternative archives and collections, kept alive only by a network of committed organizations and individuals, who would circulate bootlegged VHS copies amongst themselves. Sources for these were extremely rare—tapes moved from hand to hand, depending on word of mouth, within circles of friends and colleagues. With the possibility to stream video online, this condition started to dramatically change. An increasing number of rare materials reappeared on publicly accessible platforms, some of them carefully curated (Ubuweb) and some just a pile of stuff (YouTube).

At present, there are at least twenty torrents of Chris Marker's film essays available online. If you want a retrospective, you can have it. But the economy of poor images is about more than just downloads: you can keep the files, watch them again, even reedit or improve them if you think it necessary. And the results circulate. Blurred AVI files of half-forgotten masterpieces are exchanged on semi-secret P2P platforms. Clandestine cell-phone videos smuggled out of museums are broadcast on YouTube.

DVDs of artists' viewing copies are bartered.[3] Many works of avant-garde, essayistic, and noncommercial cinema have been resurrected as poor images. Whether they like it or not. [. . .]

Imperfect Cinema

The emergence of poor images reminds one of a classic Third Cinema manifesto, *For an Imperfect Cinema*, by Juan Garcia Espinosa, written in Cuba in the late 1960s.[4] Espinosa argues for an imperfect cinema because, in his words, "perfect cinema—technically and artistically masterful—is almost always reactionary cinema." The imperfect cinema is one that strives to overcome the divisions of labor within class society. It merges art with life and science, blurring the distinction between consumer and producer, audience and author. It insists upon its own imperfection, is popular but not consumerist, committed without becoming bureaucratic.

In his manifesto, Espinosa also reflects on the promises of new media. He clearly predicts that the development of video technology will jeopardize the elitist position of traditional filmmakers and enable some sort of mass film production: an art of the people. Like the economy of poor images, imperfect cinema diminishes the distinctions between author and audience and merges life and art. Most of all, its visuality is resolutely compromised: blurred, amateurish, and full of artifacts.

In some way, the economy of poor images corresponds to the description of imperfect cinema, while the description of perfect cinema represents rather the concept of cinema as a flagship store. But the real and contemporary imperfect cinema is also much more ambivalent and affective than Espinosa had anticipated. On the one hand, the economy of poor images, with its immediate possibility of worldwide distribution and its ethics of remix and appropriation, enables the participation of a much larger group of producers than ever before. But this does not mean that these opportunities are only used for progressive ends. Hate speech, spam, and other rubbish make their way through digital connections as well. Digital communication has also become one of the most contested markets—a zone that has long been subjected to an ongoing original accumulation and to massive (and, to a certain extent, successful) attempts at privatization.

The networks in which poor images circulate thus constitute both a platform for a fragile new common interest and a battleground for commercial and national agendas. They contain experimental and artistic material, but also incredible amounts of porn and paranoia. While the territory of poor images allows access to excluded imagery, it is also permeated by the most advanced commodification techniques. While it enables the users' active participation in the creation and distribution of content, it also drafts them into production. Users become the editors, critics, translators, and (co-)authors of poor images. [. . .]

Poor images are poor because they are heavily compressed and travel quickly. They lose matter and gain speed. But they also express a condition of dematerialization, shared not only with the legacy of conceptual art but above all with contemporary modes of semiotic production.[5] Capital's semiotic turn, as described by Felix

Guattari,[6] plays in favor of the creation and dissemination of compressed and flexible data packages that can be integrated into ever-newer combinations and sequences.[7] [. . .]

The poor image [. . .] constructs anonymous global networks just as it creates a shared history. It builds alliances as it travels, provokes translation or mistranslation, and creates new publics and debates. By losing its visual substance it recovers some of its political punch and creates a new aura around it. This aura is no longer based on the permanence of the "original," but on the transience of the copy. It is no longer anchored within a classical public sphere mediated and supported by the frame of the nation state or corporation, but floats on the surface of temporary and dubious data pools.[8] By drifting away from the vaults of cinema, it is propelled onto new and ephemeral screens stitched together by the desires of dispersed spectators. [. . .]

Now!

The poor image embodies the afterlife of many former masterpieces of cinema and video art. It has been expelled from the sheltered paradise that cinema seems to have once been.[9] After being kicked out of the protected and often protectionist arena of national culture, discarded from commercial circulation, these works have become travelers in a digital no-man's land, constantly shifting their resolution and format, speed and media, sometimes even losing names and credits along the way.

Now many of these works are back—as poor images, I admit. One could of course argue that this is not the real thing, but then—please, anybody—show me this real thing.

The poor image is no longer about the real thing—the originary original. Instead, it is about its own real conditions of existence: about swarm circulation, digital dispersion, fractured and flexible temporalities. It is about defiance and appropriation just as it is about conformism and exploitation.

In short: it is about reality.

From Hito Steyerl, "In Defense of the Poor Image," in *e-flux journal*, no. 10 (November 2009), www.e-flux.com/journal/10/61362/in-defense-of-the-poor-image/.

Notes

1 *Deconstructing Harry*, directed by Woody Allen (1997).

2 "Wer Gemälde wirklich sehen will, geht ja schließlich auch ins Museum," *Frankfurter Allgemeine Zeitung*, June 14, 2007. Conversation between Harun Farocki and Alexander Horwath.

3 Sven Lütticken's excellent text "Viewing Copies: On the Mobility of Moving Images," *e-flux journal* 8 (May 2009), drew my attention to this aspect of poor images. See http://e-flux.com/journal/view/75.

4 Julio Garcia Espinosa, "For an Imperfect Cinema," trans. Julianne Burton, *Jump Cut* 20 (1979), 24–6.
5 See Alex Alberro, *Conceptual Art and the Politics of Publicity* (Cambridge, MA: MIT Press, 2003).
6 See Felix Guattari, "Capital as the Integral of Power Formations," in *Soft Subversions* (New York: Semiotext(e), 1996), 202.
7 All these developments are discussed in detail in an excellent text by Simon Sheikh, "Objects of Study or Commodification of Knowledge? Remarks on Artistic Research," *Art & Research* 2, no. 2 (Spring 2009), http://www.artandresearch.org.uk/v2n2/sheikh.html.
8 The Pirate Bay even seems to have tried acquiring the extraterritorial oil platform of Sealand in order to install its servers there. See Jan Libbenga, "The Pirate Bay plans to buy Sealand," *The Register*, January 12, 2007, http://www.theregister.co.uk/2007/01/12/pirate_bay_buys_island.
9 At least from the perspective of nostalgic delusion.

Shiny Things So Bright (2017)

Andreas Treske

"Sul cominciare e sul finire" (On the beginning and the ending)

First Movement: The Window

The history of film theory starts with the metaphor of the window. The screen appears as an opening into another world constructed by the projected moving image. From early cinema and early film theory to video, computers, and software, we have come a long way, with various approaches and methodologies applied, to describe and understand what happens with the moving images we are creating and how this shapes/affects us.

When we visualize all available videos together at the same time, the resulting image might resemble an image we are already familiar with. As data is expanding exponentially into incredible amounts that a human being could never meaningfully conceive of, automatic and algorithmic visualization tools (such as the ones Lev Manovich is researching and applying) allow for the compression or extraction of understandable or meaningful chunks on the nanoscale, resembling another common standardized or stereotyped image.

In 2007, a new glass window was inaugurated in the south transept of Cologne Cathedral. It was designed by the German artist Gerhard Richter and met with an enthusiastic reception. Richter used small squares to create what appears to be a kind of modern pixelated image of colors and light shining through. He designed the windows with the help of an aleatoric computer program, leaving some of the elements to chance.

Richter's work rejects an obvious meaning or message. He seems to neutralize the sacralized representative space of the church and provides an experience of lights and colors not transformed by the dominating narrative of the medieval space. With the change of light, Richter's work gains a state of permanent uninfluenced change.

Such a state of permanent uninfluenced change of light might also be created by all the billions of cameras around us, constantly uploading, sharing, linking, and relating. It appears that a blue ocean is covering our planet, an ocean of video (if the assumption that the totality of all video would appear to be blue might prove valid).

What would look like bluish noise and dust from the far outside, might embed a beautiful and fascinating living scape of moving images, objects, and light impulses constantly changing, rearranging, assembling, evolving, collapsing, but never disappearing, something like a pulsar or like real cinema (if cinema is basically the change of light through movement).

In my book *Video Theory: Online Video Aesthetics or the Afterlife of Video*[1] I tried to describe and theorize what one might call phenomena, objects, or things formerly named as video, including their forms, behaviors, and properties. And I ended up looking at Gerhard Richter's window and its marvelous colors, with the light shining through.

Second Movement: Online Video

Online video has not only become the driving force on the web. From a static line the web itself evolved to a dynamic audiovisual network, constantly creating and operating temporal objects. Video-enabled devices were more or less responsible for the net blackout in huge parts of the US in 2016.[2] As personal media on the web, moving images are the most significantly spreading form. The recording, editing, distributing, and mixing of personal means of expressions pushes a wide range of technologies and applications for the web and devices.

Web space is developing into a video space with distinct aesthetics. Snapchat and Instagram stories as apparently ephemeral mobile applications are setting new temporal standards, moving forward to animated, looping, moving contents instead of still image representations and doubles. Profile images can integrate cinematographic looping elements, while images on timelines will be looking back and following our gaze. Stills are paused images of intersecting timelines of temporary events or event formations, a point on a multidimensional map in a non-Cartesian space.

A multitude of actors, a world of possibilities: an evolving industry pushes toward a personal cinema and the personal gesture, creating and rendering the data of self as its product constantly. The web space embeds these personal gestures and through video creates a sphere or living cell, expanding our physical space endlessly. Through video, the web advances to an actor in our environment, an ecological system and a life-like being that is not just related to us, but exists with us in various forms and shapes. Always shifting, around us and with us.

Video itself, as this "ubiquitous, liquid" something, absorbs every other medium.[3] As a transformative technology, online video collapses walls of classifications, systematizations, specificities, "barriers erected by broadcast corporations and the art-world machine" including academia.[4] There is a definite need for models, methodology, and theory, since the established ones, including the late-born "Digital Humanities," are no longer adequate. The paradigm change has begun and will automatically overturn the established conceptualizations—it is already redefining culture.

But as Adorno said: "Whoever speaks of culture speaks of administration, whether this is his intention or not."[5] For defining a status quo, academic institutions of the moving image are becoming more and more suspicious. They make the moving image appear like looking through the ghost of an invisible object, an object that is not there, the meta of meta language on something historical defined by some posttemporal power.

For a new theory we need to storm academia, the shopping malls of knowledge, their classified shops, and turn over their shelves to describe things, objects, and sensitivities, to catch the moving image on the run.

But we don't see. We have learned that we don't see, that we can't see if we don't have the right tools. We rely on patterns, sequences, blocks, and chains, and the frame as a basic category for chunks of information of a status from a specific time, a status or recording of difference, a nonexistence.

John Cage already defined the frame as a basic unit for temporal events, a basic measurement of time in "The Future of Music" from 1937.[6] Sounds for Cage can be organized in simple frames, which would be the actual score. Musical structure is based on length of time. Influenced by Luigi Russolo and the Futurists, Cage claims that sounds are just sounds, and are all equally valid. Therefore a composer discovers new possibilities through technological experimentation.

Video is much closer to sound than to the photographic image. Even the cinematographic apparatus is a transport vehicle of stillness. Video does not know such stillness. Its forming structural elements are movement and time.

The photographic image as a time component of a frame is just a single mark in a linear landscape, a single perspective, one point, one POV. It does not relate exactly to the world. It is not even a cut or a slice. The photographic image can be anything. This is what makes images so weak, prone to violation and misuse, fragile constructions of a possible death frozen, always in need of an explanatory vectorial layer to point to something, semiotically signifying.

Video is part of an always evolving system. Video has no beginning and no end. Video is by definition in constant flow. The time-based unit of the frame creates an imprisonment for readability and speak-ability, confirming a set of data, massively expanding data. The time-based unit of the frame might be too small for human life as well as too big for a single human life, too small for a moment and too big for a moment of human life. The time-based unit of the frame, like in a block chain of data, delivers an original, individual, never-changing and private address for a block of data, high density information packages, thick and spherical.

Third Movement: Shiny Things Substantial

What is the essence? The substance of video? So far I've tried to look in from the outside, now I should move back inside . . . like with Google Earth, zooming back into the bluish video ocean and deeper, inside shiny things, where crystals and diamonds of temporality appear. Though I first described the inside as assemblages, building blocks, Lego-like objects, paradoxically chains appear fluid. I want to dive along with Dorothy and Alice, Humpty Dumpty as my companions to wander through shiny things so bright. I am a flaneur strolling through the crystalline vision of structures similar to the ones of Bruno Taut, Paul Scheerbart, and the architects and artist of German Expressionism after World War I, moving chains of glass pearls at my fingertips.

Paul Scheerbart's influential treatise *Glasarchitektur* (Glass Architecture, 1914) "foretold of a sublime, technocratic civilization whose peaceful world-order was borne from the proliferation of crystal cities and floating continents of chromatic glass, a vision summed up in his aphorism: 'Colored glass destroys all hatred at last.'"[7]

Only more than a decade after its birth in 1991, the web was able to embed video in containers, plug-ins for web browsers to allow video viewing. The "Dancing Baby" video (1996) was a strange thing, an object that needed to be somewhere in a specific location to be pointed to. The preceding technical development went hand in hand with the digital video revolution in film making of the early 2000s and culminated in the birth of YouTube in 2005.

With HTML5 coding the web is not only understanding "video," it actually is about to become like video itself. Its basic numerical code, its logic and structure, will be or are already video-like. Therefore I argue that video absorbs the web.

Online video touches and merges with every other object space in a variety of forms and practices, leaving web-objects as skeletons for video wraps or liquid chains. Like hypertext, interactive video stacks build parent and child relations, creating inner and outer worlds living with us, in us, around us, or as granules and molecules forming tissues clothing us, and building new transparent skins temporarily shifting.

Video becomes an easy packaging tool for an enormous amount of data, and a fast method of transport—big data simplified. The frame as a temporal unit of video is a block of data in a chain, a ring of pearls, similar to the prayer beads that are used by members of various religious traditions. The chain of temporal audiovisual data organizes in a repetition of spherical elements, containing a similar substance itself. The frames like the pearls are a mode of counting and coding time, stamping each other to keep countability and structure.

Chains anytime and anywhere create and define new patterns of meaning for us, melodies of life for humans. Machine seeing is superior as nonhuman seeing results in translation and action, but how, and on what, for what, when and why? We are experiencing an alienation of difference and an otherness toward the seeing as we are trying to see the chains we are creating in and with.

The sneezing of a baby is a movement best translated as a signal through impulses or frames. Frame and signal are close to particle and wave. The basic signal is the information of a change. The signal has changed, translated into light, or movement. Position change of a known object means again change of light, change of sensor information. Frame and signal are a way of reading and writing. Through this process, video overcame darkness.

The recording of a repairman by the neighbor on a mobile device, as well as streaming the conversation live to others far away, is in principle a similar normal gesture like streaming the live audiovisual signal of a protest against a government or the industrial military complex, etc. The signal emphasizes and underlines the gesture, the act.

The photographic image is by definition the constitutional basic of cinema forming movement through loading and reloading into projection. It is a mechanical information surface, slice of a chunk of data.

A website is another slice of data, time-stamped and postal-addressed; browsing appears as cinematic movement and creates cinematic sequences and emotional cues.

A score in music translates into an orchestral experience. The form of coding of the web as video creates a dynamic temporal cinematic form.

The conventional cinema apparatus, the dispositive of cinema itself turns out to be too slow and too heavy. We need to confirm that the audiovisual is not mechanical anymore. Cinema has moved.

Already a long time ago, Jean-Luc Godard stated: "There are no more simple images . . . The whole world is too much for an image, you need several of them; a chain of images."[8]

Godard's "chains of images" still seem to be a very linear approach. Cinema suggests that images are organized in a linear chain, one image juxtaposed to the other and so on. We might see this cinematic chain oriented or directed along the x-axis in a graphical representation system. Movement in cinema means moving along this chain horizontally, to advance forward in time on one horizontal level. At the same time, as we are moving, we can experience a vertical extraction or extension at every point of the chain as well as a depth extension. Multilayering of chains over, below, and in each other creates a multitude of crossing shiny things at every point in time.

We are linear but acting on a point with multiple references. Early analog video artists and thinkers like Paul Ryan and the writers of Radical Software in the 1970s seemed to already have a sense of what is video's capability, when they were more interested in the signal character of video and saw video like an ecological system.

Fourth Movement: Heaven on Earth

Gene Youngblood's last sentences of *Expanded Cinema* (1970): "The limits of our language mean the limits of our world. A new meaning is equivalent to a new word. A new word is the beginning of a new language. A new language is the seed of a new world. We are making a new world by making new language. We make new language to express our inarticulate conscious. Our intuitions have flown beyond the limits of our language. The poet purifies the language in order to merge sense and symbol. We are a generation of poets. We've abandoned the official world for the real world. Technology has liberated us from the need of officialdom. Unlike our fathers we trust our senses as a standard for knowing how to act. There is only one real world: that of the individual. There are as many different worlds as there are men. Only through technology is the individual free enough to know himself and thus to know his own reality. The process of art is the process of learning how to think. When man is free from the needs of marginal survival, he will remember what he was thinking before he had to prove his right to live. Ramakrishna said that given a choice between going to heaven or hearing a lecture on heaven, people would choose the lecture. That is no longer true. Through the art and technology of expanded cinema we shall create heaven right here on earth."[9]

Andreas Treske, "VideoTheory II: Shiny Things So Bright. Manifest and Overture," draft text for a talk at Video Vortex XI in Kochi, India, held on February 24, 2017, first published in the catalog for the event, online at http://networkcultures.org/wp-content/uploads/2017/04/Catalouge-compiled-final-28-03.pdf; revised for the present publication by the author.

Notes

1 Andreas Treske, *Video Theory: Online Video Aesthetics or the Afterlife of Video* (Bielefeld: transcript, 2015).
2 Nikki Wolff, "DDoS Attack that Disrupted Internet was Largest of Its Kind in History, Experts Say," *The Guardian*, October 26, 2016, https://www.theguardian.com/technology/2016/oct/26/ddos-attack-dyn-mirai-botnet/.
3 Tom Sherman, "Video 2005: Three Texts on Video," *Canadian Art*, March 3, 2015, https://canadianart.ca/features/video-2005/.
4 Sherry Miller Hocking, "A Brief Look at Analog Imaging Instruments," *Television Projects*, 2013, http://televisionsprojects.org/a-brief-look-at-analog-imaging-instruments/.
5 Theodor Adorno, "Culture and Administration," *Telos*, September 21, 1978, 93.
6 John Cage, "The Future of Music" (1937), http://www.medienkunstnetz.de/source-text/41/.
7 Eric Morse, "Dreams from a Glass House: An Interview with Josiah McElheny," *The Paris Review*, February 9, 2015, https://www.theparisreview.org/blog/2015/02/09/dreams-from-a-glass-house-an-interview-with-josiah-mcelheny/.
8 Quoted in Lev Manovich, *The Language of New Media* (Cambridge, MA: The MIT Press, 2001), 152.
9 Gene Youngblood, *Expanded Cinema* (New York: P. Dutton & Co, 1970), 419; available at http://www.vasulka.org/Kitchen/PDF_ExpandedCinema/book.pdf.

YouTube and the Syrian Revolution: On the Impact of Video Recording on Social Protests (2017)

Cécile Boëx

Since March 2011, the revolt that transformed into a conflict in Syria has yielded a considerable and varied collection of videos recorded and posted online by protesters, activists, and militants.[1] At the stage of pacifistic mobilization between 2011 and 2013, not only did they play the main role in the narrativization of the revolt, but they also stimulated the emergence of new forms of protest based on the impact of the image. In this essay, I pose questions about the influence of vernacular videos on protests staged in extremely repressive circumstances. To this end I propose to trace the course of the revolt from the perspective of the evolution of video recording practices and the audiovisual grammars that they generate. Initially the manifestations were filmed spontaneously, but their later proliferation entailed the professionalization of video recording. A diachronic reconnaissance of footage from the beginning of the revolt offers the possibility of retracing the links between the act of filming and the act of protesting, intertwined by means of the body, words, and emotions. Created on the margins of the world of institutionalized media production, these images and sounds depict an array of new forms of speaking out and engaging in a struggle. Yet the point is not to overestimate the power of such footage—akin to social networks, they do not raise rebellion in and of themselves;[2] they also report on a mere fraction of the revolt. Still, video recordings remain valuable because they not only provide a trace of events, but also—and above all—document new ways of participating in them.

The practices of video self-documentation during protests are nothing new. They emerged at the beginning of the millennium owing to the democratization and mass popularization of digital technologies for recording audiovisual materials and making them publicly available.[3] They played a particularly important role during the brutal clashes that accompanied the G8 summit held in Genoa in 2001. The establishment of YouTube, the most commonly used social platform, popularized those practices and made it possible to share footage online almost instantly and multiply documentation of a single event. In the Middle East, the process gathered momentum in 2009, when a revolt broke out against the reelection of President Mahmoud Ahmadinejad. The government banned the foreign press from reporting on events. Hundreds of films recorded by protesters were subsequently posted online in order to demonstrate the scale of the revolt and repressions. Since 2010, the revolutionary movements that shook the Arab world have left a trail of a considerable number of recordings, most of them anonymous.[4] The protests in the aftermath of the presidential elections in Iran and the revolts in Arab countries stimulated the emergence of numerous studies devoted to cyber-activism.[5] Not only do they often overestimate the role of the Internet and social networks, but also betray a tendency to treat digital space as tangible and present it as a separate world governed by its own logic. It can be viewed in a more prosaic manner, however, in its interactions with the "real world,"[6] by observing how the new forms of communication are shaping practices, discourses, and the imagination.

Recordings Immersed in the Event: Distortion, Corporeality, Emotion

Since the first manifestations in March 2011, protesters in Syria have been spontaneously documenting events in order to bypass the media embargo imposed by the regime of Bashar al-Assad, who negates the very existence of the social rebellion, deeming it a conspiracy and labeling the protesters as Islamist terrorists. The authorities also try to conceal the repressions that intensify as the months go by. In such a context, filming is primarily a matter of the pursuit of establishing the truth anew and regaining control of the interpretation of events. In his definition of vernacular video as a tool of decentralized communication,[7] Tom Sherman indicates the significance of the effect of the sheer presence of people who make video recordings, and of the pursuit of effectiveness. In extreme situations, however, these two characteristics may prove to be paradoxical. In the case discussed here, some of the footage created at the very heart of manifestations is essentially distorted: it does not offer the possibility of immediately observing and understanding what is actually happening. At the same time, the distortion that characterizes these types of video recordings results from their proliferation—since they are posted online in such great numbers, they make each other invisible. Scattered around the enormous, intricate space of YouTube, the vast majority of these images remain latent, if not simply disappearing at a certain point.[8] Furthermore, despite their availability, the images and sounds are insignificant, poor, weak, and insufficient. Most of them are also ineffective in the sense that they usually provide little information about the context. This type of footage definitely has little importance to the relations of the forces that operate in the area.

When the first demonstrations in Syria took place, the majority of protesters brandished cameras, i.e. their cell phones. The footage recorded during those demonstrations is spontaneous in the sense that it is shot in the heat of action and does not follow any communication strategies whatsoever. Immersed in the event, it shuns the standards of framing used in the media world. The shots are shaky, the images are blurred, and there are only scarce hints to help understand the spatial conditions of events and the way they unfold over the course of time. Posted online without prior editing, the raw footage prolongs the duration of the manifestation. Therefore, every viewer gets a powerful impression of authenticity as they are thrown into the very center of the action, but at the same time the images seem distorted as a result of breaking the field of vision, chaotic camera movement, and poor resolution.[9] Simultaneously, this video genre paradoxically unveils the tension between the intensity and authenticity of lived experience on the one hand, and the abstract form of its audiovisual interpretation on the other.[10] Ultimately the recordings provide little information about events themselves.[11] Yet, insofar as they carry scant information data, they document in a perceptible way the experience of protest pursued in the specific context of repression. The words, movements, and emotions of the people recording the images deliver sufficiently numerous and valuable elements to allow us to better understand the significance and stake of the act of participating in a demonstration. What we therefore see is the sheer physical and emotional engagement of individuals who film and take part in an event, rather than the event itself.

The film shot in Hama just ten days after the first demonstration in Dara shows particularly well what filming practices looked like in the first phase of the protests (see Figure 8.2).[12] [. . .] The creator of the footage films and protests at the same time until he finally forgets about the former. The image eventually becomes subjected to the rhythm of an arm swinging while chanting. The camera becomes an extension of the body that is participating in the action. The shaken device, held in the hand, repeats its movements and conveys excitement through the manner of filming, which is subordinated to motion rather than to the view.[13] The spontaneity of videos shot by ordinary protesters is characterized by exactly such corporeality of the audiovisual record, which also results from the fact that the action is far from staged; it is the intensity of the experienced events that actually imposes the character and dynamics of image framing. [. . .]

If it were not for the title (in Arabic), it would be difficult to understand what the film is about. Yet the documentation value of the recording lies somewhere else—in its very illegibility. The chaos of images and sounds allows us to instantly and physically see and feel the emotions of the person shooting the video and of everyone else around them. The footage documents the extreme experience of protesting in repressive circumstances and generates a vision of the event—marked by movement, embodied—which is too drastic to be represented coherently. The fusion of the body, the camera, and the action shifts visual perception in the direction of perception via other senses.[14] [. . .] The image—born at a moment of paroxysm both embodied and mechanical—is

Figure 8.2 Demonstration in Hama on March 25, 2011, to support the inhabitants of Dara (translation of the Arabic caption). Video uploaded on March 25, 2011, https://www.youtube.com/watch?v=ywviRWqZE7U (no longer available).

akin to a living imprint of the relation between the historical event and the experience of that event, between the communitarian and the personal dimensions.

The Dramaturgy of Collective Action

As the weeks go by, raw footage yields to more "professional" video recordings. A strategy of filming emerges that aims to generate information about events themselves. The pursuit of legibility contributes to an increasingly controlled mode of recording: the very act of filming is subject to reflection and becomes detached from the act of protesting, as it is supposed to capture the event in its spatial and temporal entirety. The process of professionalization is motivated by a high demand for images on the part of the traditional media, deprived of access to the sites of events, but also by more effective self-organization of manifestations at the level of local management committees taking care of logistics and ensuring safety. The committees take on the task of recording images that present the protests and, at the same time, generate a space for various forms of collaboration between the protesters and those who film them. From that point onwards, the spontaneity of film gives way to recording techniques that aim to provide information and to raise sympathy. As a result, we observe the emergence of mechanisms of contextualizing and staging protests which are supposed to make the video footage more legible and attractive. The mechanisms of contextualization make themselves manifest through the distanciation of oneself from an event, which offers the possibility of creating a coherent visual representation. [. . .]

Recordings as Carriers of Protest Ingeniousness

[. . .] Creativity unleashed by video recordings also led to the privatization of protest space due to the emergence of forms of action based on a limited number of participants. The framework of activity and visibility thus defined prompts the issue of anonymity. After all, in a crowd, even if individuals protest with uncovered faces, their identity becomes dissolved in collectivity. In turn, in filmed actions, exposure strengthens individualization, and therefore the majority of protesters hide their identity. Nevertheless, this does not remain indeterminate, but quite the opposite—it is revealed in a new way. Filming one's own activities in private space was initially motivated by the pursuit of avoiding repression. That is why the tactic was most often used by women, who were less frequently engaged in activities on the streets than men—although they were also present there. Many of them preferred less visible forms of engagement, such as humanitarian aid or medical care. Women also played an important role in the organization of protests by creating slogans and banners. Yet for some of them, staying behind the scenes was not enough, and therefore they invented their own type of demonstration, the "home sit-in" (*i'tisam manzih*). This activity—an emblematic example of the privatization of protest—is characteristic of the Syrian revolution, and it became popularized and institutionalized because of video recordings.[15] The rules of home sit-ins were quickly defined, although different variants can be observed depending on the group or city. They usually gather around ten female participants and take place in a living room, whose space and decorations are changed for the occasion with revolutionary standards, banners, and portraits of martyrs. The introduction of the camera and Internet reconfigures domestic space and transforms it into public space. As a result, what emerges is a liminal space between the street and the living room. This domestic abolition of divisions is also expressed through performances such as the reading out of declarations that condemn the abuse of power or express solidarity with the protesters and militants of the Free Syrian Army. [. . .]

Experience, Action, and Memory

At the beginning of the revolt, protesters held cell phones in their hands not only to document events: by filming, they challenged the authorities and reclaimed the streets from them. The visual and aural reclamation of public space is an obvious reason why video recordings—however blurry—were posted on YouTube on such a mass scale. In this context, uploading content online served to confirm the authenticity and scale of the revolt. It also offered the possibility of preserving traces of it, however weak or illegible. Those who come across these films—hastily shot and posing a risk to their creators—through the determining work of algorithms and keywords have an opportunity to sense the intensity of the experience of revolt. Video recordings stimulate the creation of new regimes of image and sound expressed in a straightforward manner by protesting bodies. The spontaneity of the protest footage fairly quickly gives way to the practice of recording images driven by strategies of increasing the visibility of revolt and explaining it. Such a rationalization of filming influences the way protests are staged. Rebellious communities rely on visuality and sound to express their demands and identifications through numerous material means and performative elements. Recordings are created in the belief that they have an impact on the viewer: they are supposed to elicit empathy, raise sensitivity, encourage action, and convince. In the long run, however, they have played little role in raising awareness of the revolt and increasing its visibility. Nevertheless, recording practices—adapted by hermetic groups that do not usually take part in protests—made it possible to invent new ways of engagement and of seizing public space. Protesters' creativity is enhanced by the way the Internet helps enrich creative competences. The visual aspects of the revolt in Syria manifest themselves in different ways depending on time and space. They focus on the experience of protest, its narrativization and imaging, as well as on its commemoration. The majority of the recordings did not attract a large number of views and, despite their ubiquity, the films have not had any impact whatsoever on the relations between forces in the area. They are therefore ineffective, weak images. Their value and force obviously lie beyond the ephemeral temporality of politics and the media: they derive their power from the intensity and uncertainty of lived experience, which undergoes a twofold process of the compression and extension of time and history—a process that characterizes the situation of revolt.

From Cécile Boëx, "YouTube and the Syrian Revolution: On the Impact of Video Recording on Social Protests," trans. Lukasz Mojsak, in *View: Theories and Practices of Visual Culture*, no. 17 (2017), https://www.pismowidok.org/en/archive/2017/17-protesting-images/youtube-and-the-syrian-revolution.

Notes

1 A precise count is impossible, but the number of such films can be estimated in the 100,000s.

2 Sahar Khamis, Paul B. Gold, and Katherine Vaughn, "Beyond Egypt's 'Facebook Revolution' and Syria's 'YouTube Uprising,'" *Arab Media & Society* 15 (2012), 1–30.

3 See Olivier Blondeau and Laurence Allard, *Devenir média: L'activisme sur Internet, entre défection et expérimentation* (Paris: Editions Amsterdam, 2007).

4 See Peter Snowdon, "The Revolution *Will* Be Uploaded: Vernacular Video and the Arab Spring," *Culture Unbound* 6 (2014), 401–29; Dork Zabunyan, *L'insistance des luttes: Images, soulèvements, contre-revolutions* (Paris: De l'incidence éditeur, 2016).

5 Cf. Annabelle Sreberny and Gholam Khiabany, *Blogistan: The Internet and Politics in Iran* (London: Tauris, 2010); *Mouvements sociaux en ligne, cyber activisme et nouvelles formes d'expression en Mediterranée*, ed. Sihem Najjar (Paris: Karthala, 2012), among others.

6 Madeleine Pastinelli, "Pour en finir avec l'ethnographie du virtuel! Des enjeux méthodologiques de l'enquête de terrain en ligne," *Anthropologie et Societes* 1–2 (2011), 35–52.

7 Tom Sherman, "Vernacular Video," in *Video Vortex Reader: Responses to YouTube*, ed. Geert Lovink and Sabine Niederer (Amsterdam: Institute of Network Cultures, 2008), 161–8.

8 Since the beginning of my research, around 10% of the corpus of sources has become unavailable due to closures of the accounts of users who posted them online.

9 Kari Andén-Papadopoulos, "Media Witnessing and the 'Crowd-sourced Video Revolution,'" *Visual Communication* 3 (2013), 341–57.

10 According to Roger Odin, this paradoxical tension is part and parcel of the aesthetics of films shot with cell phone cameras. Cf. *Téléphone mobile et création*, ed. Laurence Allard, Laurent Creton, and Roger Odin (Paris: Armand Colin, 2014).

11 This deficit of legibility is often compensated for by texts that accompany videos posted online. 90% of those texts are in Arabic.

12 Video uploaded to YouTube on March 25, 2011, https://www.youtube.com/watch?v=ywviRWqZE7U.

13 Writing about footage from the revolt in Tunisia, Ulrike Lune Riboni defines this type of image as a *bodymage* in order to emphasize the unique intertwinement of the body and the record. At the same time, the researcher likens the cellphone camera to the *paluche*—the miniature camera invented at the beginning of the 1980s which made it possible to detach the act of directing the lens from the eye. Cf. idem, "Notes pour une définition: 'Bodymages,'" *WINDOW: Carnet de recherche de Ulrike Lune Riboni*, entry of October 7, 2013, http://window.hypotheses.org/102.

14 In his concept of filming practices by means of portable cameras—which the author himself defines as *mobilographie*—Richard Begin emphasizes the shift from the event to the experienced event, which also entails a shift from seeing to feeling. Cf. idem, "L'image au corps," *Vertigo* 48 (2015), 6–16.

15 I have so far gathered around 60 video recordings of home sit-ins held throughout Syria between 2011 and 2014.

Nothing Is Unwatchable for All (2019)

Alexandra Juhasz

In July 2016, I published an opinion piece, "How Do I (Not) Look? Live Feed Video and Viral Black Death."[1] It was a personal and professional coming to terms with this disruptive, horrific cultural media event. There I explained why "I just can't watch" one particular video that was, at that moment, ricocheting across the screens, hearts, and minds of the world: "Diamond Reynolds's live feed video of the brutal murder of her boyfriend Philando Castile at the hands of the police with her child as witness in the backseat." I went on to name and delineate four traditions from visual culture, media studies, and critical Internet studies that could serve as "a brief primer of ways to understand how or why we might (not) look": Don't Look, Look Askance, Look at Death, and Look at Death's Platforms.

Looking now, back and through and about death's visual platforms, I see that my earlier writing served at least four critical functions:

- It provided a process for my own disorienting but strongly felt reactions to a series of highly circulating images: namely, I'm not going to watch.
- It opened a space to ruminate upon and share a long tradition of scholarly thinking (including my own) that granted this intuitive self-protective impulse a more rational or political basis.
- It allowed me to offer up one—my own—unique reaction to the raucous conversation about Reynolds's video and similar images. Not why I found it unwatchable, or why I chose not to watch it, but more that every look at violence and brutality in this, our moment of persistent, total, sharable, encompassing visibility, is an ethical choice and a political act.
- It implicated me, as a white woman, as a scholar who writes on and makes video, who has celebrated outsiders' voices for decades, who had once believed in the politics of visibility. It implicated me as one player within a dynamic ecosystem of words and images emanating from our diverse bodies and formats of work, our many watchings, our clicking and forwarding, our not watching, and our associated actions. My not watching was not necessarily being irresponsible or disconnected or somehow safe and outside of this logic of seeing and violence. I had to account for myself, publicly, as a form of penance.

Over the next year, another wave of viral images, and their linked and co-constitutive words and violence, momentarily and brilliantly sucked up all the air of our shared looking space. The images and sounds of fake news (in all of its confusing multiplicity and mutability, referring, as the phrase now does, depending upon who is speaking, to media images from *The Daily Show* or Breitbart, or to what Trump calls the failing *New York Times* and CNN, or to intentional propaganda or profiteering clickbait) grew to become, in their/our moment, fully reprehensible and utterly deplorable. But with only a little hindsight (and it does seem so hard to see clearly in this new era of Trumpian image-blitzkrieg), I can see how fake news videos continue and expand the logic of images of viral black death that had so recently demanded all of our viewing attention.

Of course, such images aren't new, only newly fascinating, following on a decade of related viral video of first-person mayhem and cruelty and a millennium of racist depictions of brutality in ways that define today's new and also very horrific video zeitgeist. Both bodies of viral media are real-time; people-made; immediately transmedial and thus corporate-influenced and controlled; utterly and definitively subjective and political; manifestations and at the same time witnesses of hatred, fear, and violence; image projects that observe and then render more real-world suffering; entirely dependent upon context and audience for meaning; and spellbinding in their capacity for saturating the senses and spirit so that dissociation, denial, and self-hatred (not watching) seem as reasonable and righteous a response as does anger, action, or analysis.

Perhaps this linking of viral live-feed images of black death and fake news is crazy. Or downright wrong. Shortsighted or insensitive. Simplifying? Generalizing? I do know that one body of viral video defined a highly topical media moment that was followed by the next; but I also know that I chose not to look at one, while I ended up staring much too closely at the other: a look that also, ultimately, brought me to myself. My ethical, political, personal choice to look *every day for 100 days* at fake news, and then share my responses online, is a stunning parallel to and reverse of my earlier gesture, non-choice, and act of self-punishment in the ominous endless sight of black death.

When I built the online primer of digital media literacy, *#100hardtruths-#fakenews*[2]—working steadily from January 20 to April 19, 2017, and with the help of my colleague, the technologist Craig Dietrich—my impulse was not to sustain the offenses held therein nor the conversations about or responses to those self-same transgressions. Rather, I was moved, as a citizen, to act in alignment with and all the while against this mounting visual information travesty: as witness to, teacher about, and interlocutor with an escalating media abomination. Linked as I was to our illicit and new president, Donald Trump, his news, and our media, my project (in social media and on the stand-alone website) was at once sordid and pained, if sometimes hopeful. It was just one offering among many but still became overfull with too much. And thus, also, it became one woman's real-time testament to and hording of a hundred days' detritus left over from a digital life attending to fake news. Where once I had chosen scarcity and clarity (don't look), here I went for overabundance and onslaught (never look away).

Fake news, I decided—and the Internet's mountain of attempts to better see it, know it, defang, debunk, and stop it—should be carefully looked at for no better reason than that it was and is. More so, in its unseemly existence it proved itself at once inordinately powerful within the fleeting attention economy of the Internet and also for its associated material manifestations of aggression. For *#100hardtruths-#fakenews*, all of my attention was beelined to see and show the connections that the Internet and its president were attempting to hide: how sick consolidations of falsehoods and their seemingly trifling swirls of online reaction in the form of memes, reposts, likes, and more fake news congeal into corporate, governmental, and patriarchal power that is unleashed in the form of punitive projections, escalating restrictions, and literally, inevitably, the mother of all bombs.

This I called "virality is virility," and its gross material enactments were what I was watching for. I knew and found that this kind of looking—his, ours, the media's, mine—would end with bullying, arrests, deportations, people not going to college, others not getting to use bathrooms or stay in the military, and yes, bombs: falling, landing, killing, destroying, blindly.

Needless to say, averting our gaze with disdain or otherwise censoring the visual unpleasantness that was made by and for us in the current format of the Internet-minute—fake news—would be the responses that any despot would wish for. So, yes: let's watch.

But, let's also face it: "Fakenews r us." This self-reflexive, self-fulfilling, skeptical mandate (another of my hardtruths) is central to all watching on the Internet. While the fake news is bogus, by definition, so too must be our watching and linked writing about it. Yuck.

So why did I choose to look at and be fully dirtied by one unwatchable body of work while selecting to not and never to look at the other (even so, not staying clean)? How do my diametric positions of watching allow me to understand better my own limits as well as the boundaries and differences between two appalling bodies of viral video and the actions that each might inspire, produce, or crush?

First, there is the matter of Internet time. Last year's insults must be biggered and bettered in a logic of neoliberal growth. We tire so quickly. Our eyeballs become numb.

Then there is a matter of truth. For one short, horrific moment last year, a series of viral images of black death moved fully—not via the logic of fakery or uncertainty that I, for one, argue defines all Internet viewing (see above)—but rather on the force of their authenticity: images that were unarguably, unutterably so true that no one (white) could undermine, unsee, unknow their structuring logic of viciousness, even if not looking.

Which gets us to #BlackLivesMatter, and the power of that movement's ultra-true images, and *#100hardtruths-#fakenews* and the insipid helplessness of this newer moment underwritten by image deception, just one year and one president later. Which allows me to end with difference, context, shame, and forgiveness.

My watching patterns, as a white middle-aged queer academic in the time of Trump (difference), are situated in what I can bear (context), what I can do (by virtue of privilege and passion . . . shame), and who I might work to join so as to get and do better (forgiveness). Nothing is unwatchable for all, so perhaps we need to do better in sharing the burden of viewing image-based brutality with and for each other.

Alexandra Juhasz, "Nothing Is Unwatchable for All," in *Unwatchable*, ed. Nicholas Baer, Maggie Hennefeld, Laura Horak, and Gunnar Iversen (New Brunswick: Rutgers University Press, 2019), 121–5.

Notes

1 Alexandra Juhasz, "How Do I (Not) Look? Live Feed Video and Viral Black Death," *JSTOR Daily*, July 20, 2016, https://daily.jstor.org/how-do-i-not-look/.
2 Alexandra Juhasz, "*#100hardtruths-#fakenews*" (2017), http://scalar.usc.edu/neh vectors/100hardtruths-fakenews.

The Dangers of Ubiquitous Video (2020)

Siva Vaidhyanathan

We might look back at 2020 as the year of maximum screen time. Severed by the pandemic from face-to-face interactions, we have been chained to our devices, making more video and watching more video than ever before. This ubiquity of moving images—this videocracy that first took shape during the aughts, with the rise of data-connected phones, Facebook, and YouTube—has become the chief way many of us view the world. And it's dangerous. We anchor our public debates on video. We make judgments based on moving images and truncated sounds. They guide and structure the consideration of our public concerns.

Video resists thought. It breaks linear modes of argumentation and resists complexity, containing all within a frame often now the size of a human hand. Videos can mislead us even when they aren't clearly false or fraudulent, dangerous or destructive. Even those we might consider "news" or "documentary" may be a form of propaganda, compressing and distorting events, stories, and issues.

The propagandistic effect was most acute when the moving image was new. A film like Leni Riefenstahl's *Olympia* (1938), for instance, once could draw viewers into its embrace with an erotic idealization of the "Aryan" body and allusions to classical empires. Audiences in the 1930s didn't have the language or the tools to understand these tricks. They could not stop a film to study it, then rewind and watch again. They didn't have the armor made from decades' worth of criticism, the hard-earned knowledge of the risk: that video can undermine and overwhelm collective thought.

We're more sophisticated now, but the risk has not subsided. If anything, it has increased exponentially. The rapid, global proliferation of digital video, from around 2005 up through the present, makes it harder to sort and contextualize what we see—to think about, through, and with video. We may now resist the clumsy, overbearing propaganda of *Olympia*, or of any other single piece of video, but we're more susceptible to the barrage of subtler, less bombastic messages that flow around us, each unworthy of attention yet influential in the aggregate. For every helpful medical news clip about Covid-19, the platforms host dozens of videos coaxing viewers to mistrust medical experts or vaccinations. For every stirring scene of a Confederate statue coming down, there are countless paranoid and racist rants delivered to a camera. Cell phone footage too, and sponsored messages, political ads, instant replays on the Jumbotron, doorbell camera clips, and schoolroom lessons given via Zoom. These all are streams within the torrent of stimuli. In the form of our phones, we all have Times Square in our pockets. It's the environment that distorts reality now.

The overall effect is of cacophony: a vast, loud, bright, fractured, narcissistic ecosystem that leaves us little room for thoughtful deliberation. It's not that we'll believe the latest Covid conspiracy video (although too many people do). It's that seeing video after video after video after video renders us unable to judge. They're all making contradictory claims; they're all just slick enough to make plausible demands for our attention and respect. We find ourselves numbed by overstimulation, distracted by constant movement and sound, unable to relate to those ensconced in different bubbles and influenced by different visions of reality. We can't address our problems collectively in the face of this montage. We can't mount cohesive and convincing arguments with ease or confidence. We mistrust everything because we can't trust anything.

That's not to say collective, collaborative thought is impossible in the age of ubiquitous video. It just means that we have to try harder, that we must construct better methods to defuse propaganda with deliberation. I'm not sure we can do this. But the events of this past spring and summer, when a single viral video seemed to move the world toward justice, gives me cause for limited optimism.

The footage capturing the last eight minutes of George Floyd's life, as a Minneapolis police officer crushed it out of him on May 25, launched a remarkable, transnational movement for racial justice. Like Eric Garner, who died at the hands of a New York City police officer in 2014, Floyd had his public execution by asphyxiation documented by a bystander recording on a mobile phone. The moving images and sounds quickly wrapped the globe, puncturing illusions, igniting latent frustrations, and propelling millions out into the streets.

Floyd's death was captured by raw video. Its truths were impossible to deny. The officer's voice was clear. Floyd's voice was clear. The bystanders' voices were clear. The image was clear. It was more powerful than any video of police brutality that came before, and yet it also built upon them all.

Now think back to Rodney King. George Holliday just happened to be one of the few Americans toting a portable video camera in 1991, and he just happened to be there to capture King's beating by Los Angeles police officers on a grainy analog videotape. Stirring demonstrations broke out all over the country, along with riots. Commissions and studies of police violence followed and were quickly forgotten.

We had the opportunity, back then, to convene and deliberate seriously about the constant plague of racially motivated police violence. But the "national conversation," as some proposed to call it, had gotten focused on one person, one event, and one poor-quality video. That made it all too easy to dismiss, as if the pattern of injustice were somehow not yet fully clear.

The elements of that pattern are now laid out for everyone to see, in one video after another of Black people's mistreatment by police. Today, paradoxically, the very profusion of such videos has helped us in this moment to deliberate on greater, broader questions; not just on one story but on all the policies behind it. The same cacophonous media environment that tends to dazzle and confuse us—that stupefying video-after-video-after-video-after-video effect—in this case yielded clarity. Video resists thought, but it does not prevent it. The footage of Floyd's death forced the issue with its length: dreadful and transfixing, a format that invited contemplation. If this principle could be extended—if we could learn to harness our attention, discipline ourselves, and focus—then perhaps we'd have a chance to curb injustice on an even grander scale. With cameras everywhere, we have a lot of evidence from which to draw. But it will take work. The torrent of video never stops battering our minds. When thought prevails, it's by weathering this downpour and pushing through to higher ground.

Siva Vaidhyanathan, "The Dangers of Ubiquitous Video," in *Wired*, August 18, 2020, https://www.wired.com/story/dangers-ubiquitous-video-propaganda/.

Section III

Repercussions

9

Sociality | Participation | Utopias

Introduction by Dieter Daniels

The contributions in this chapter juxtapose the optimistic sense of departure prevalent during the 1970s with their critical revision undertaken in the 1980s. The texts are organized diachronically, similar to Chapter 3, "Video and the Self," except we have no comparably canonical writings: the discourse on video and Utopia has always stayed polyphonic and pluralistic. While the technocentric video-utopian discourse of the 1970s was mainly dictated by male authors, an extensive feminist theory and practice of video developed concurrently, which will be introduced at the end of this chapter.

The social upheavals and student-initiated protests of 1968 lent an unsuspected "street credibility" to political theory and opened a path for the video medium that led from private living rooms into the midst of publicly staged conflicts. Of course, when we look at the actual technological details, the story becomes more complex.[1] While the student protests in Western industrial nations coincided with the launch of the Sony Portapak in the United States in that same year of 1968, it is difficult to find further commonalities except that both enterprises followed heterogeneous goals not precisely defined even for those involved. It took several years for this temporal coincidence to cause synergetic effects between technology and social theory: the video-utopian sense of departure in texts from the early 1970s documented in this chapter was closely aligned with the introduction of affordable, portable video gear, as well as expectations that the autonomous use of media would lead to social change.

The technological-industrial development and marketing of portable video was an international affair: Japanese technology (especially Sony's Portapak) conquered the US-American market, while European models (such as the "Paluche," a *caméra vidéo de poing* produced by the French company Aaton[2]) had limited commercial success even if they were both technically and aesthetically innovative. Social, educational, activist, as well as artistic and theoretical approaches to the mobile use of video were likewise undertaken within a broad international spectrum, and the US-American bias of most literature on early video history requires some correction. In the following, we will attempt to clarify the parallels and differences between ideals and ideologies in contributions from the United States, France, Germany, and Japan.

During the 1970s, many initiatives oriented themselves toward an ideal of collective creativity typical of the time.[3] Especially in the video sector, this mode of working was heralded as an alternative to the hierarchical division of labor in the studio system and the industrialization of movie production. In Europe, French film and video collectives served as a model for politicized work in both these media.[4] Especially Jean-Luc Godard's ideas on the "Magnetoscope des amateurs" from 1968 were widely shared, not least because of his celebrity status as a director of the Nouvelle Vague movement (see the contribution by Godard in Chapter 4).[5] In Germany, a certain skepticism in tune with the Frankfurt School prevailed, questioning if media could be refashioned for political aims within the capitalist entertainment industry. Hans Magnus Enzensberger's widely read essay "Constituents of a Theory of the Media" (1970) offered a manual for such subversive use, differentiating between a "repressive" (capitalist, centrally controlled) and an "emancipatory" (collective, decentralized, self-organized) use of media while urging the New Left to overcome their archaistic hostility toward the new media.[6] Enzensberger mentions video only as one media innovation among others, but he does establish a connection to the film theory of Walter Benjamin and the radio theory of Bertolt Brecht, both of which have since become important fixtures of critical media practice in Europe.[7]

In the United States, Marshall McLuhan is widely seen as the most important pioneer of video utopias, despite the fact that he hardly discussed the medium itself.[8] Gene Youngblood's writings, especially his book *Expanded Cinema* (1970), proved just as influential on artistic-experimental practices. Between 1970 and 1974, the *Radical Software* magazine established an internationally unique forum for the exchange between practitioners.[9] Generally, the volume of US literature was based on practical experiences and focused on needs and expectations in working with electronic media. In contrast to Europe, historical media theory or Marxist designs for society played hardly a role. The scene around *Radical Software* largely reflected "hands-on" practice to develop an application-oriented theory. Any utopian moment was usually located within the technology itself and its potential for social change.[10] "The only pure revolution in the end is technology," Abbie Hoffman, founder of the Yippies (Youth International Party), claimed in 1968.[11] These beginnings of technology-oriented video utopias cannot be integrated into a wider media-theoretical genealogy, since they do not fall back on established models from film, photo, or television theory.

Guerilla Television and Videotopia: Michael Shamberg, Alfred Willener, Guy Milliard, Alex Ganty

The *Guerrilla Television* manual (1971) by Michael Shamberg and the Raindance Corporation announces itself without false modesty: "This book is the first of a kind. It tells how we can break the stranglehold of broadcast TV on the American mind.... Shamberg and Raindance's contention is that politics are obsolete and that information tools and tactics are a more powerful means of social change."[12] While the objective of the authors of the French study *Vidéo et société virtuelle* (1972), published in English under the title *Videology and Utopia: Explorations in a New Medium* (1976), is phrased in more academic terms, it is almost identical in content: "They discern in the liberating potential of video an antidote to the dominance of centralized TV in consumer society and ultimately, perhaps, a means towards the progressive social reappropriation of the media of communication."[13]

Both books are based on the practical experiences of their authors and aimed toward applicability. They combine comprehensive theory formation with detailed scenarios for future use, stressing the social, political, and educational potential of the video medium. They favor autonomous, often collaborative video practices that compete with TV's centralized monopoly of interpretation as a mass medium. Both transfer this collaborative video maker's approach to theory formation: Michael Shamberg and Raindance Corporation combine as authors for *Guerrilla Television*, while Swiss sociologists Alfred Willener, Guy Milliard, and Alex Ganty explicitly label *Videology and Utopia* as a "collective writing" project whose explorations correspond to the structures of the medium.[14]

Apart from these broad commonalities, there are also clear differences between the two publications: the design for *Guerrilla Television* follows an Underground aesthetic, despite the fact that in Holt, Rinehart & Winston the book had a mainstream publisher, which, to top it off, was owned by the television broadcaster CBS. Its unconventional appearance cannot really hide the fact that many of the featured countercultural strategies could be commercialized effortlessly.[15] The design combines elements of comics, pop culture, fanzines, advertising, and technical manuals (Figure 9.1). Not least due to its attractive look, the book went through three editions within a year. Soon after the original, a Japanese translation was published in 1974, which apart from the use of a different typography emulated the elaborate graphics of the American edition (Figure 9.2). A bilateral but not equal exchange was developing: ideology made in the United States for technology made in Japan.

Videology and Utopia on the other hand appeared in the standard academic textbook format in English and French. The same was true for two earlier books, both published in 1970 and concerned with the educational use of video: *Realities of Teaching: Explorations with Video Tape*—possibly the first book ever to bear the term videotape in its title—paradoxically was not about the use of video in teaching situations but solely about the empirical examination and optimization of learning processes with the help of video monitoring.[16] And Dieter E. Zimmer's *Ein Medium kommt auf die Welt: Video-Kassetten und das neue multimediale Lernen* (A Medium Is Born: Video Tapes and the New Multimedial Learning) offered a first survey on the confusing variety of competing video systems as well as an outlook on the "new multimedia learning," which the author located mainly in schools and universities—in contrast to the grassroots DIY ethics of *Guerrilla Television*. Zimmer was the only author to describe video technology as a "child of capitalism":

> Not commissioned by any social need but simply technologically possible, potentially in demand and therefore commercially exploitable, and thus suddenly existent one day; developed in many places at once, in some of them needlessly as only a few of these developments will get a chance, and others will be wasted labor; just as impossible to influence or correct in its potential to sway opinions as the market for books, newspapers, or records.[17]

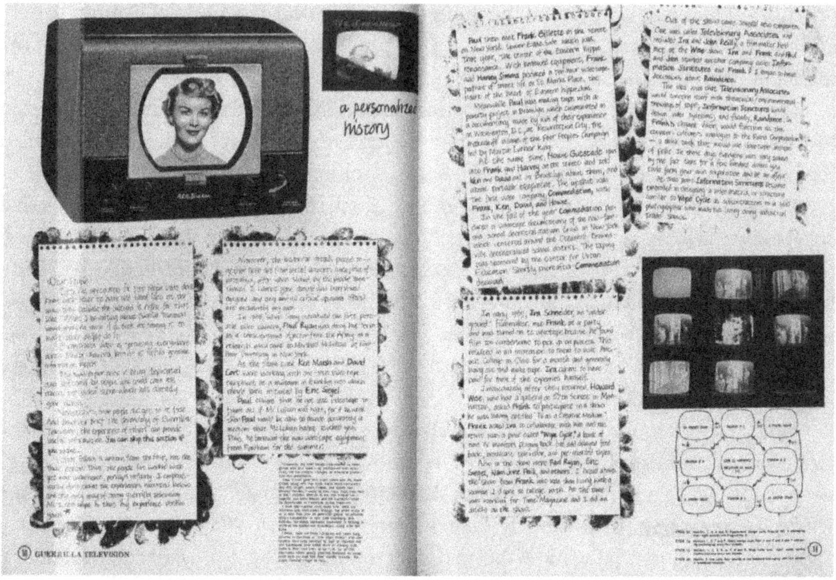

Figure 9.1 Double spread from Michael Shamberg & Raindance Corporation, *Guerilla Television* (Saint Louis: Holt, Rinehart and Winston, 1971). Design by Ant Farm. © Michael Shamberg & Raindance Corporation.

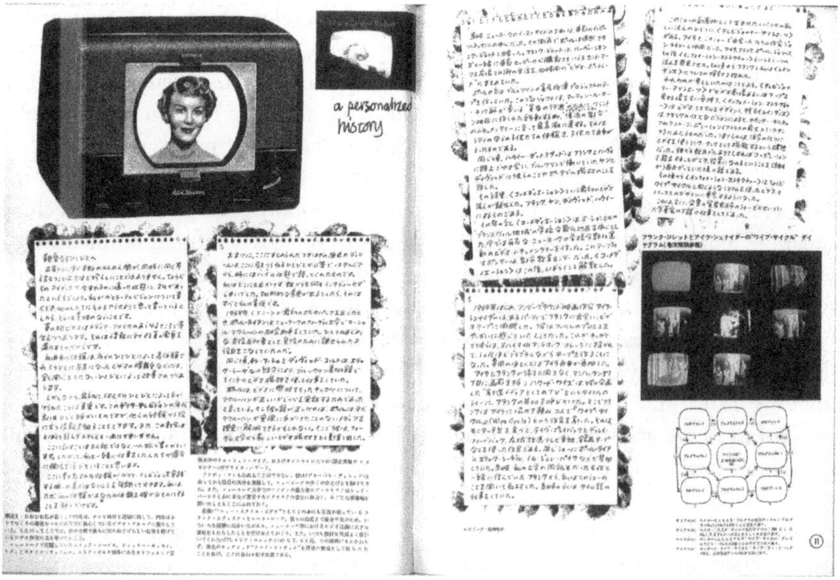

Figure 9.2 Double spread from the Japanese edition of Michael Shamberg & Raindance Corporation, *Guerilla Television* (Tokyo: Bijutsu Shuppan-Sha, 1974). Design by Ant Farm. Adaptation of original layout Ryoichi Enomoto. Translation Fujiko Nakaya. Courtesy Hiroko Kimura. Japanese edition © Bijutsu Shuppan-Sha.

This approach, decidedly skeptical and system-analytical, can be seen as a contemporary corrective to the American and French video utopias, whose claims sound somewhat emphatic today.

Utopia Revisited: Deirdre Boyle (Martha Rosler, Joan Braderman, Raymond Bellour, David Joselit)

The 1980s saw a widespread revision of progressive notions and social ideals held by the late 1960s and early 1970s with regard to politics, the media, education, and economics. Yet while the debate on alternative leftist, collectivist, or ecological designs for society continued unabated, the video-activist impulses of this time remained comparatively ineffectual. Deirdre Boyle's text from 1985 excerpted in this chapter (as well as her later book on the same topic) was based on an extensive research trip she had taken two years earlier. Hauntingly she speaks of inaccessible or already decaying video materials in the archives of groups participating in 1970s video activism.[18]

The incompatibility of commercial television and video as a form of *Guerrilla Television* became apparent in the United States earlier than in Europe. For example, in 1969 CBS invested a considerable sum in a production by the Videofreex collective, which was to portray social upheavals in the United States under the title "Subject to Change." After a screening of the pilot video, though, CBS immediately canceled the project.[19] *The Very First Half-Inch Videotape Festival Ever*, organized by WHGB Boston in 1972, offers an especially striking example of broadcast TV attempting to protect its powers of interpretation over *Guerrilla Television*. The broadcaster invited hundreds of video activists, artists, and educators for a big screening meeting. The videos shown there, however, were not broadcast on TV; instead, host Russell Connor presented an overview of the festival and only during conversations with participants did the television cameraman sometimes catch excerpts of their videos.[20]

So far there has been no comparative international research into the video movements of the 1970s. A renewed interest in the study of each country's alternative media-historiographies has become noticeable only in the last few years. Still, a tentative overview suggests similar reasons for the ultimate failure of the initial video euphoria in the United States and Europe. These include two social factors:

1. Over the long run, collective authorship proved nonfeasible, since on the one hand increasing specialization of technological know-how required labor division and on the other hand revenues eventually generated by the videos led to conflicts of copyright.[21]
2. Initially, common goals were coupled with an enthusiasm for innovation, which made way for a greater differentiation of interests between individual practitioners and their heterogeneous aims (e.g., counter-public political strategies, sociocultural work in media cooperatives, societal documentation, video art, media education, feminism, anti-racism, AIDS solidarity, ecology, anti-war, and anti-nuclear movements, to name but a few examples).

Added to which can be two technological-industrial or media-structural factors of equal complexity:

3. The incompatibility of competing and quickly outdated video systems made exchange, networking, and sustainability more difficult; while additionally the mid-1970s saw costs on the rise because of newly introduced semiprofessional technologies (editing, color, timecoding, video effects) that set new production standards and increased the pressure to commercialize.[22]
4. The relation with mainstream television remained unresolved: while alternative video productions were not widely accepted or broadcast on television, no other autonomous distribution channels of nearly comparable effectiveness could be established.

Starting in the mid-1980s, discussion turned to the loss of utopia and how to gain back the utopian potential of video. With his text "Video Utopia" from 1986, Raymond Bellour reached back into the nineteenth century for a solution: just as Stéphane Mallarmés poetic-utopian concept of the simultaneous vision of a page was inspired by and yet critically transcended the newspaper, so video art was able to produce a new language by utopically transforming television.[23] Martha Rosler and David Joselit, on the other hand, criticized the practice of separating video art from other, often political video activities or from television. In her 1985 essay "Video: Shedding the Utopian Moment," Rosler commented on the pressure to incorporate video (art) history into art history, thereby disassociating it from the medium's wider social history: "The history of video becomes a pop history, a pantheon, a chronicle. Most important the history becomes an *incorporative* rather than a transgressive one."[24] By canonizing artistic positions and attributing certain "styles" and "intentions" to the artists, video art was distinguished as a part of high culture, in contrast to the mass-medial "naturalization" of the medium, for example, as home video or music video.[25] In this way, video's utopian potential for changing the art system was lost. Rosler diagnosed that the institutionalization of video in an art context, together with the art discourse's focus on medium specificity and the neglect of broadcast television as a "parent medium," aimed "to tame video" and rob it of its potential for social criticism and institutional critique.[26]

In the aftermath of Rosler's influential essay, the debate focused on how the lost utopian potential of the medium could be historically revalued or even revived. Rosler had shown that video history was being depoliticized by "separating out something called video art from the other ways that people, including artists, are attempting to work with video technologies."[27] Looking back on the diversity of early US-American video culture, David Joselit in 2002 likewise observes a retrospective separation between video art and video activism, obliterating the fact that in the original context of *Radical Software*, "art and activism were shown to be formally equivalent on account of their shared practice of feedback."[28] Joselit sees Rosalind Krauss's notion of video as a narcissist medium as one of the reasons why "video of the '70s is now primarily discussed as an art genre rooted in individual subjectivity."[29] In contrast he argues to revise the common reading of *Radical Software*'s "utopian placement" of video and read it as "a refreshing corrective to the repressive disciplinary boundaries that structure current discussions of visuality in both the academy and the art world."[30] Joan Braderman had taken up Rosler's critique in 1991 and added her own demand: "What needs to be staked out and reclaimed is a different utopian moment, the larger one, the one we're not supposed to dream about anymore."[31] Braderman's media-critical programs in collaboration with the Paper Tiger Television collective for Manhattan Cable TV realized this idea of a practice straddling art and activism.

Both Rosler's critique of the uncritical assimilation of video into the art context and Joselit's historical analysis offer a retrospective stocktaking; they do not suggest concrete alternatives. Gene Youngblood, on the other hand, developed a far-ranging scenario of future media-technological perspectives in 1988 based on his widely read book *Expanded Cinema* from 1970. His essay bears the somewhat misleading title "Video and Utopia," although it treats video as just one element among many. With his concept of the "amateur," Youngblood introduces a figure of thought that transcends the borders between art, design, technological development, and activism as the agent of a dialogue-based communications revolution. Models developed and implemented by media amateurs are described as utopian in two respects: they amount to a real and functioning utopia machine; and they stimulate the utopian longing for community and connection, which the machine produces and permits us to imagine.[32] Referring back to Brecht's and Enzensberger's theories of a communicative rewiring of the electronic mass media's distribution function, Youngblood builds on the video utopias of the 1970s sketched out above. At the same time, his predictions reach far beyond video technology into internet-connected utopias of the 1990s as well as their failure due to the commercialization of social media over the last two decades.[33]

Video and Feminism: Anne-Marie Duguet (Ulrike Rosenbach, Malin Hedlin Hayden)

In the 1970s and 1980s, authors, artists, and women activists conceived explicitly feminist theories on video as a medium of female autonomy. For the first time, a gender-based media theory primarily served to substantiate and develop a new practice. This perspective, forward-looking and practical, differentiated feminist video theory from contemporary feminist film theory. In 1973, Laura Mulvey's influential film-theoretical study of cinema as a dispositive of the "male gaze," spotlighting the "to-be-looked-at-ness" embodied by actresses, referred to Hollywood and especially to Alfred Hitchcock's films over the past decades.[34] While Mulvey was interested in the foundation of a new practice—to which she actively contributed in her films made in collaboration with Peter Wollen—she still oriented her theory in opposition to the status quo of the male-coded feature film.

In contrast, contributions to this book by Anne-Marie Duguet and Ulrike Rosenbach show that female authors of the 1970s saw video as a medium not yet male-coded but allowing them to express an own perspective on society and the self that was conceptualized as female from the beginning. A second factor repeatedly stressed by these artists and activists is that video offered the chance for an autonomous practice not dependent on male expertise.[35] Independent of each other, the authors formulate almost identical theses. Anne-Marie Duguet: "First of all, it should be recalled that this new field of audiovisual production had not yet been monopolized by men."[36] Ulrike Rosenbach: "It was a medium not encumbered with a long cultural tradition based on the quality criteria of men. Video represented a blank canvas, unbiased and free from judgment—a virgin territory for experimentation."[37] Or from the context of French 1970s activist movements: "It is a medium that has not yet been appropriated by men."[38] Finally Dot Tuer, who in 1990 looked back on the "imaginary utopia of video's beginning" in more detail: "Women turned to the 'new' medium of video as a medium without a history, one which would document absences of women's concerns and expose media's manipulation/exploitation and, which as a *tabula rasa* within the traditional sites of art would create a domain of exploration and aesthetic innovation."[39]

Somewhat simplified one might suggest that feminist video theory was first of all a theory for doing things, for autonomous action, while feminist film theory was mostly a theory of viewing, of heteronomous reception, that could only potentially be transformed into counteraction. Texts on feminist video referred to potential actions and they were not part of the same historical discourse as the film theory of the time. For example, Rosalind Krauss's essay on the immanent narcissism of video from 1976 did not open a dialogue with Laura Mulvey's theses on the gender-coded, voyeurist-narcissist polarity of Hollywood cinema, although both were steeped in psychoanalysis. Interestingly, while both texts influenced respective schools of thought, they have stayed mostly unlinked to this day.[40]

The feminist utopia of video as a medium not yet coded by men finds its counterpart in a lack of historical situatedness. As Ulrike Rosenbach wrote in 1980: "When you float through Nothing, maybe you can still work politically as an act of resistance, but it is very difficult to work artistically, since there is no real female tradition you can call upon."[41] Accordingly, between 1976 and 1982 Rosenbach expanded her artistic practice by founding a School for Creative Feminism, which focused on a combination of performance and video. Female artists and activists in the United States worked in a similar manner within self-organized forums and structures, ultimately with an aim to establish a new tradition of female creativity. In 1972, for example, Steina Vasulka instigated the New York Women's Video Festival, which would continue until 1980 under the direction of Susan Milano. In its 1976 iteration, innovative environments explored body-oriented forms of video viewing as alternatives to the traditional cinema dispositive.[42] From its beginnings, the Women's Video Festival offered an inclusive framework: in the program notes for 1972, we can find entries for queer, transgender, and lesbian mother videos (Figure 9.3).[43] Under the umbrella of "Women's Video," not just explicitly feminist but wider gender-specific approaches had a forum.

These international parallels in feminist video initiatives of the 1970s should not make us forget that national developments were quite specific and at the time

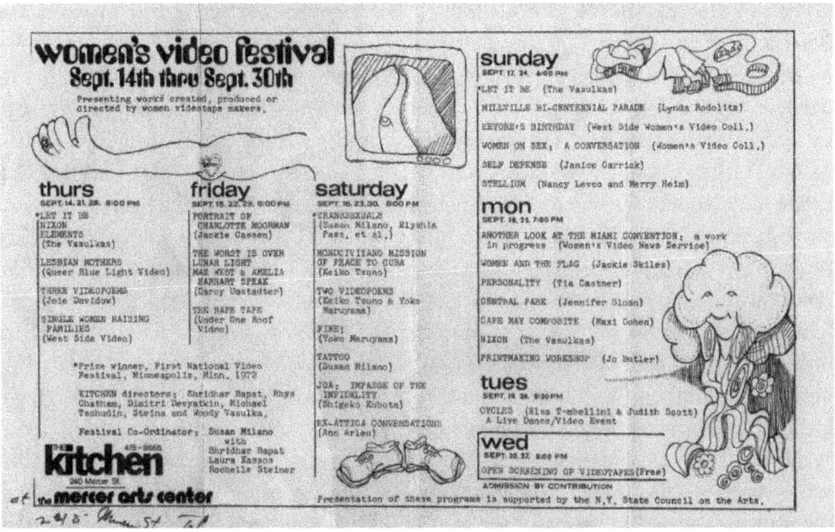

Figure 9.3 Festival program for the *Women's Video Festival, NYC 1972.* Courtesy Electronic Arts Intermix (EAI), New York.

remained relatively unconnected.[44] Pointing out the simultaneity of the founding of the "Mouvement de libération des femmes" (MLF) and private access to video technology, Anne-Marie Duguet conducts a detailed survey on feminist video work in France, which was more closely connected to the female workers movement and the struggle of housewives for proper recognition of their work than in other countries.[45] Collective modes of working in feminist contexts had more institutional sustainability in France than in the United States: for example, the collaboration between Carole Roussopoulos, Delphine Seyrig, and Ioana Wieder under the name "Les Insoumuses" (Defiant Muses) led to the foundation of the Centre audiovisuel Simone de Beauvoir in Paris in 1982.[46]

With the "naturalization" of video as defined by Martha Rosler, the traditional patriarchal structures, familiar from other media, began establishing themselves on what Dot Tuer has termed the "tabula rasa" of the 1970s. Subsequently, a different question came to dominate the discourse: can video by women be equated with feminist video? The argument was no longer about a video-specific utopian-feminist position toward a medium not yet gender-specifically defined—it became part of a larger discussion of related thoughts on film, the fine arts, and literature. Accordingly, the question would have to be explored in a much wider context, especially since, as the contribution by Malin Hedlin Hayden shows, the debate is ongoing.

Looking back at the 1970s, Ilene Segalove observed in the mid-1980s: "Just to put your hands on the camera [was] a feminist act."[47] JoAnn Hanley, in 1993 curator of the retrospective exhibition *The First Generation: Women and Video, 1970–1975*, likewise saw a far-reaching correspondence of female and feminist video work: "Not all of the artists in this exhibition made overtly feminist or political work, but most early 1970s video work by women *is* feminist simply by virtue of having been made by women at that time."[48]

In contrast, Malin Hedlin Hayden advocates the necessity of differentiating between various forms of feminism and female subjectivity, which cannot be grasped by such broad categories. Her discourse analysis of texts by Michael Rush, Chris Meigh-Andrews, Catherine Elwes, and Martha Gever concludes that the firm link between video and feminism developed into an art-historical topos in the 1990s. As such, it is no longer oriented toward a future practice but solely serves (art-)historical categorization. Art and video theory take up the historical arguments of feminist film theory with references to the cinematic "male gaze" but under different preconditions: female artists were sorted into the category, or "genre," of feminist video art because of their sex and their work within the medium. According to Hayden, in this way outdated "essentialist" concepts of gender are recycled in the art discourse, dragging it back behind the current (post-)feminist state of gender equality in politics and society.[49] While the "strategic essentialism" of 1970s feminism was historically justified in video art as much as elsewhere, Hayden makes the case for using the plural "feminisms" today, to negotiate the various meanings of "the female/femininity" for questions of identity and individual choice and actions.[50]

Notes

1 The first video recorder for home use was launched in 1965, the Sony TCV-2020. Like competition models by Shibaden, National, and Philips that soon followed, it could only be used plugged into the power supply and was also prevented from outdoor use by its design and weight. The first portable video recorder, the Sony DV-2400, followed in 1967 and was marketed in the United States from 1968 on. This rather primitive apparatus could only be used for recording; one still needed a stationary device for playing, rewinding, or fast-forwarding the tape. The success story of the so-called Portapak only began with the Sony AV-3420 and the matching AVC-3420 camera in 1971: 20,000 units were sold in the United States over the first year. The best survey on the complex development of gear, technical standards, and prices can be found in Christoph Blase, "Welcome to the Labyrinth of Machines: Tapes and Video Formats 1960–1980," in *Record—Again! 40yearsofvideoart.de, Part 2*, ed. Peter Weibel and Christoph Blase (Ostfildern: Hatje Cantz, 2010), 500–8. A media-archeological overview from film to digital video is offered by Ricardo Cedeño Montaña, *Portable Moving Images: A Media History of Storage Formats* (Berlin: De Gruyter, 2017).

2 Anne-Marie Duguet dedicates an own chapter to the "Paluche" in a book whose title is likewise inspired by the handling of this camera model: Anne-Marie Duguet, *Vidéo, la mémoire au poing* (Paris: Hachette, 1981), 165–74.

3 Most recently, the topic of Participatory Video has become a central point in this debate (see Chapter 10), a postcolonial media practice to support transferring traditional collaborative strategies into the contemporary world, mainly for the self-articulation of marginalized groups by collaborative strategies.

4 For example, German film director Claudia von Alemann joined the film collectives of the "Etats généraux du cinéma" in Paris 1968 and shot a television documentary,

Das ist nur der Anfang—der Kampf geht weiter (This is only the beginning—the struggle continues, 1968/1969), about video's potential for social change through the presentation and exchange of tapes between video groups.

5 Godard and the Dziga Vertov Group actively supported the dissemination of video technology for political purposes between 1968 and 1974, handing on equipment to dissident and militant groups especially in Palestine. See Michael J. R. Witt, *On Communication: The Work of Anne-Marie Mieville and Jean-Luc Godard as "Sonimage" from 1973 to 1979*, PhD (Bath: University of Bath, 1998), 57.

6 Hans Magnus Enzensberger, "Baukasten zu einer Theorie der Medien" (1970); English translation by Stuart Hood, "Constituents of a Theory of the Media," in Hans Magnus Enzensberger, *The Consciousness Industry: On Literature, Politics and Media* (New York: Seabury Press, 1974), 95–128. See also Enzensberger's "Television and the Politics of Liberation," in *The New Television: A Public/Private Art*, ed. Douglas Davis, Allison Simmons, and Fred Barzyk (Cambridge, MA: MIT Press, 1977). Here Enzensberger is more skeptical toward the "general enthusiasm about the possibilities offered by the electronic media . . . which we all felt a few years ago." Ibid., 253.

7 Gerd Roscher sees a combination of Godard's theories on video and Enzensberger's ideas as the theoretical foundation for autonomous video practice in 1970s Germany. Gerd Roscher, "On the Concept of an Alternative Media Practice" (1976) in *Media Art Action: The 1960s and 1970s in Germany*, ed. Rudolf Frieling and Dieter Daniels (Vienna and New York: Springer, 1997), 228–36.

8 See the introduction to Chapter 1 of this book.

9 On the prehistory, foundation, and the network around Radical Software see Davidson Gigliotti, "A Brief History of RainDance," http://www.radicalsoftware.org/e/history.html.

10 Since this techno-utopian discourse was mainly led by male authors, historical studies hardly mention that Beryl Korot and Phyllis Gershuny were the editors of the first *Radical Software* issue in 1970, before successively being replaced by men.

11 Free [Abbie Hoffman], *Revolution for the Hell of It* (New York: Dial, 1968), 86. On Hoffman's role in the video movement see Peter Sachs Collopy, *The Revolution Will Be Videotaped: Making a Technology of Consciousness in the Long 1960s*, PhD (University of Pennsylvania, 2015), 238–307.

12 Cover blurb for Michael Shamberg and Raindance Corporation, *Guerrilla Television* (Saint Louis: Holt, Rinehart & Winston, 1971). Shamberg and the Raindance Corporation also belong among the initiators of *Radical Software*.

13 Cover blurb for Alfred Willener, Guy Milliard, and Alex Ganty, *Videology and Utopia: Explorations in a New Medium* (London, Henely and Boston: Routledge & Kegan Paul, 1976); first published in French as *Vidéo et société virtuelle* (Paris: Tema-Editons, 1972).

14 Ibid., IX, 5. A collaborative or collective practice characterizes the work of many groups of the 1970s, such as TVTV, Videofreex, and Radical Software in the United States. For France, especially feminist groupings there, see Stéphanie Jeanjean, "Disobedient Video in France in the 1970s: Video Production by Women's Collectives," *Afterall* 27 (Summer 2011), 5–13.

15 In his introductory "Process Notes," Shamberg refers to the ties with CBS. He also explicitly addresses the transition from the initial collectivist-idealist euphoria to the imminent commercialization of the extant know-how: Shamberg and Raindance Corporation, *Guerrilla Television*, 28. A similar development could be seen in the commercialization of the internet in the 1990.

16 Raymond S. Adams and Bruce J. Biddle, *Realities of Teaching: Explorations with Video Tape* (New York: Holt, Rinehart and Winston, 1970).
17 Dieter E. Zimmer, *Ein Medium kommt auf die Welt: Video-Kassetten und das neue multimediale Lernen* (Hamburg: Wegner, 1970), 10.
18 Deirdre Boyle, *Subject to Change: Guerrilla Television Revisited* (New York: Oxford University Press, 1997), 209f.
19 Ibid., 16–25. See also the documentary *Here Come the Videofreex*, dir. Jon Nealon and Jenny Raskin, USA 2015.
20 Kris Paulsen, "To the Control Tower: WHGB and the Reprogramming of American Television," in *Early Video Art and Experimental Films Networks*, ed. François Bovier (Renens: ECAL; Dijon: Les presses du réel, 2017), 182f. Because of their low resolution and signal fluctuation, black-and-white half-inch videos were not technologically compatible with television broadcasting standards without further processing. Ibid., 180, notes 17–19.
21 The prominent TVTV (Top Value Television) group, for example, dissolved after a "bitter battle over credits." Boyle, *Subject to Change: Guerrilla Television Revisited*, 213.
22 Deirdre Boyle later characterized these changes, which became discernible from the mid-1970s on: "A technological revolution that was propelling video away from its funkier, low-tech, black-and-white beginnings into a more sophisticated, expensive, and technologically daunting era." Boyle, *Subject to Change: Guerrilla Television Revisited*, VI.
23 Raymond Bellour, "Video Utopia" (1986) in idem, *Between-the-Images* (Zürich: JRP Ringier, 2012), 62–77.
24 Martha Rosler, "Video: Shedding the Utopian Moment," in *Illuminating Video: An Essential Guide to Video Art*, ed. Doug Hall and Sally Jo Fifer (New York: Aperture, 1990), 44. Originally published in *Block*, no. 11, London 1985/1986.
25 Ibid., 43.
26 Ibid., 31, 33.
27 Ibid., 49.
28 David Joselit, "Tale of the Tape," *Artforum* 40, no. 9 (May 2002), 155.
29 Ibid.
30 Ibid., 196.
31 Joan Braderman, "TV/Video: Reclaiming the Utopian Moment," in *Roar! The Paper Tiger Television Guide to Media Activism*, ed. Daniel Marcus (New York: Paper Tiger Television Collective, 1991), 20.
32 Gene Youngblood, "Vidéo et Utopie," *Communications* 48, "Vidéo" issue (1988), 186.
33 On Gene Youngblood's continued influence on early internet discourse, see: Dieter Daniels, "Reverse Engineering Modernism with the Last Avantgarde," in *Netpioneers 1.0: Contextualizing Early Net-Based Art*, ed. Dieter Daniels and Gunther Reisinger (Berlin and New York: Sternberg Press, 2010), 15–63.
34 Laura Mulvey, "Visual Pleasure and Narrative Cinema," *Screen* 16, no. 3 (October 1975), 6–18. Mulvey's 1975 text is based on a lecture held at the University of Wisconsin in 1973.
35 Video equipment is relatively lightweight (thus the French term *vidéo légère*) and can be used without additional technicians for light or sound.
36 Anne-Marie Duguet, *Vidéo, la mémoire au poing* (Paris: Hachette, 1981); for a first partial translation of this text see the excerpts in the present chapter.

37 Ulrike Rosenbach, "Video als Medium der Emanzipation," in *Videokunst in Deutschland, 1963–1982*, ed. Wulf Herzogenrath (Stuttgart: Hatje Cantz, 1982), 101; English translation reprinted in Chapter 12.

38 "C'est un medium que les hommes ne se sont pas encore appropriés." N.N., "Le Centre Audiovisuel Simone de Beauvoir: Eléments pour un début d'histoire, 1982–1993," http://www.centre-simone-de-beauvoir.com/wp-content/uploads/2017/05/HistoriqueCASdB-Mai2017.pdf.

39 Dot Tuer, "Screens of Resistance: Feminism and Video Art," *Canadian Women Studies* 11, no. 1 (1990), 74.

40 Since Krauss's argument is not gender-specific, this lack of connectedness in the reception history of Mulvey and Krauss can be explained both by the different media discussed (cinema and video) and by the different discourses addressed (gender and media specificity).

41 Ulrike Rosenbach, "Kreativer Feminismus," *Emanzipation: feministische Zeitschrift für kritische Frauen* 6, no. 1 (1980), 13.

42 Melinda Barlow, "Feminism 101: The New York Women's Video Festival, 1972–1980," in *Camera Obscura, Dossier on Women and Video: Histories and Practices* 18, no. 3 (2003), 20f.

43 See the documentation of program notes for the Women's Video Festival at https://www.eai.org/webpages/1174.

44 This is also true for research on the history of feminist video movements, which is largely made up of a number of "minor histories" without an attempt at an international overview. See, e.g., the following studies on national developments: Stéphanie Jeanjean, "Disobedient Video in France in the 1970s: Video Production by Women's Collectives," *Afterall* 27 (Summer 2011), 5–13; Hélène Fleckinger, *Cinéma et vidéo saisis par le féminisme (France, 1968–1981)*, thèse de doctorat en études cinématographiques et audiovisuelles (Paris: Université Sorbonne Nouvelle—Paris 3, 2011; unpublished); Alexandra Juhasz, "No Woman Is an Object: Realizing the Feminist Collaborative Video," in *Camera Obscura. Dossier on Women and Video: Histories and Practices* 18, no. 3 (2003), 71–97 (on the development of collective practices in the United States); Noémie Brassard, "Des Filles des vues à video femmes: Les 10 premières années," *Le Spirascope* 12 (Autumn 2017), https://www.spira.quebec/qui-sommes-nous/video-femmes.html (on the Vidéo Femmes group in Quebec); Julia Knight, "Video," in *Feminist Visual Culture*, ed. Fiona Carson and Claire Pajaczkowska (London: Routledge, 2001), 249–63 (on developments in Great Britain); Dagmar Brunow, "Before YouTube and Indymedia: Cultural Memory and the Archive of Video Collectives in Germany in the 1970s and 1980s," in *Studies in European Cinema* 8, no. 3 (2012), 171–81 (on feminist film and video collectives in Hamburg).

45 Duguet, *Vidéo, la mémoire au poing*, 89–111.

46 See the exhibition *Defiant Muses: Delphine Seyrig and the Feminist Video Collectives in France in the 1970s and 1980s*, Museo Reina Sofía Madrid in collaboration with Centre audiovisuel Simone de Beauvoir Paris, 2019.

47 Ilene Segalove, in Linda Podheiser, "Ilene Segalove, Girl Video Artist," *Boston Review* 9, no. 3 (June 1984): quoted in JoAnn Hanley, "Introduction," in *The First Generation: Women and Video, 1970–1975* (New York: Independent Curators Inc., 1994), 15.

48 Ibid. See also Malin Hedlin Hayden, *Video Art Historicized: Traditions and Negotiations* (Farnham: Ashgate, 2015), 151.

49 See Malin Hedlin Hayden, "Women Artists versus Feminist Artists: Definitions by Ideology, Rhetoric or Mere Habit?" in *Feminisms Is Still Our Name: Seven Essays on Historiography and Curatorial Practices*, ed. Malin Hedlin Hayden and Jessica Sjöholm Skrubbe (Newcastle upon Tyne: Cambridge Scholars Publishing, 2010), 57–83.

50 Ibid., 67.

Videotopia (1972)

Alfred Willener, Guy Milliard, and Alex Ganty

This research has chosen a field, some sites, some tools of exploration. Its project, its orientation in the field, are uncompromisingly u-topian, that is to say they belong to the realm of that which is not yet there, but could become concrete by taking support from latent motivations. It could make a constellation of potentialities emerge through praxis. It is meant to be yeast, enzyme, potential contagion. It is not intended to sow broadcast. Its orientation points expressly toward a progressive reappropriation of the means of communication, while clearly stating the need for the socialization of the use and control of the media.

If you trace out its "topia," its real locus, you will not locate it through a definition of its domain. The locus of research is being sought while the research is being carried on; taking its point of departure from situations (of adolescents, women, students, workers, waiters, televiewers), it traces a series of possible migrations. By means of a succession of movements back and forth and adjustments, video practice tries to apprehend the macrosocial in the microsocial, close to the fabric of everyday life, while penetrating further than a cinematic ethnography and revealing what is latent and possible beyond what is visible and patent.

In this way video is at one and the same time both "territory" and instrument of exploration; furthermore, the observers are also the objects of observation; the researchers are also actors, passing from a participation that is primarily observational to a participant-observation.

The video experience can go further than the audiovisual reporting of a situation. Through a series of documents and meetings that integrate various moments and feedbacks, it permits a redefinition both of the theme and of the situation and the actors.

Television and the cinema tend to bring near what is distant and to make distant what is near, as do all the "mass" media, integrated as they are with a society which reduces creative works to products, and products to merchandise, and which generates around itself metalanguages either of "high" culture or of mass culture.[1] These media increase the separation and alienation from experience. Conversely, video material, stored in the form of magnetic tapes, is comparable to a series of sketches or clay models: u-topias of images to be realized; u-topias of social situations to be made concrete, to be experimented with. This operation reveals a potentiality, and conceals it. It offers the possibility of learning, at the same time, both a language and a social praxis.

A group will tend to be "hyper-reactive" to video images in which it is directly involved (the multiplicative effect); it is then in a position to distinguish what is normally obscured and repressed in its experience, what is below the threshold of words but open to the senses. It can offload the customary burden of the "obvious" and commonplace, the logical, the stereotyped. It attains to a stronger awareness of one kind of reality that is "sub-real" and of another that is "sur-real," something that practically never emerges from the traditional methods of social investigation.

In a consumer society governed by the dominant models of the mass media and advertising, centralized television is dependent in the highest degree on the established technological and ideological system. The endless dialectic between the ineluctable appearance of new technical products (including video) and the multiple connotations of such objects, linked to desires, practices, and changes in society, at this point creates a breach: at a given moment video becomes the medium for achieving liberation from subjection to TV; it ends by encompassing TV in a combined praxis that is wider and more complex; most videological processes offer reversible propositions, thus introducing a dimension that is almost nonexistent in current televisual space.

The magic triangle of transmission-distribution-reception becomes a series of trihedrons in space: in the case of the "producers," the conditions of production increasingly impinge on the message; in the case of the "receivers," the conditions of perception and of recreation acquire increasing importance; finally, in the case of "distribution," this no longer corresponds to a linear schema, even in a double sense, but rather to a series of loops and interactions, leading to the establishment of a network branching out into autonomous and/or coordinated regions.

A video operation proceeds like a Russian doll, each new stage including the preceding ones. Dialectical relations are established between one element and the whole and between the diachronic and the synchronic dimensions.

The first "topia" of this phenomenon is found in the relationship between video (camera and VTR) and the general idea one is aiming to develop (plan for a study, open scenario, or whatever); various elements of differing origins and fields of application are harmonized and transformed.

Another locus of the video phenomenon is within an emergent cultural current, for which it becomes, in the limiting case, an amplifier or telescope.

The VT generation, following the TV generation, is in fact emerging toward new forms of creation and communication. Video can depass its gadget status by becoming part of a cultural movement that is essentially an action-culture.

A parallel can be found here with what is observable on the musical scene;[2] on the one hand, supersaturation of the market with discs, pop idols, and so on; on the other the birth of new musical and instrumental styles, of electronic-acoustic assemblages, seeking liberation from the state of passive consumption. Video might come to play the same role in relation to cinematic and televisual expression as is played by the guitar and electronic recording in relation to musical forms that are experienced as external.

From the chapter "Videotopia" in Alfred Willener, Guy Milliard, and Alex Ganty, *Videology and Utopia: Explorations in a New Medium*, ed. and trans. Diana Burfield (London, Henley, and Boston: Routledge & Kegan Paul, 1976), 131f. Original French publication: "La Vidéo-topie," in *Vidéo et société virtuelle* (Paris: Tema-Editons, 1972), 230–3.

Notes

1 See Walter Benjamin's essay "The Work of Art in the Age of Mechanical Reproduction" (1936), in idem, *Illuminations* (London: Cape, 1970), and also John Berger, *Ways of Seeing* (London: BBC; Harmondsworth: Penguin, 1972).

2 See also Paul Beaud and Alfred Willener, *Musique et vie quotidienne: Essai de sociologie d'une nouvelle culture* (Paris: Mame, 1973).

Guerrilla Television (1971)

Michael Shamberg

I Meta-Manual [. . .]

4. Media Evolution

[. . .] Man's media processes are cultural DNA; the assimilation of them we call education. For a medium of function like DNA, its genetic analogue, it must have three modes: record, storage and playback.

Print meets those criteria. We record with writing, store on paper, and play back through reading. Film has never supplanted print because its three modes are expensive and demand an intolerable lag time for processing. Moreover, film technology, especially in playback, demands a fetishist's attention to equipment and environment, which is why film is a cult medium.

Film is the evolutionary link between print and videotape. Like reading, seeing a movie is essentially a solitary experience. Unlike print, film is highly kinetic.

Media also exists in symbiotic or hybrid forms. Film and TV combine into movies on television. The symbiosis of radio and TV is Walter Cronkite. And so on.

But each medium also demands its own context. Until the development of videotape it was possible to view TV as a hybrid. With videotape, however, television becomes a total system and succeeds print as our cultural DNA. Recording on videotape is analogous to writing, the tape itself is equivalent to paper, and playback through a TV set is video read-out. Only by pushing film to its limit can it match ease of operation at which videotape begins. Videotape as a process medium frees film to become an art form.

A failure to understand which medium is cultured DNA at any point in time is counter-evolutionary. Because American education, which is only now getting into *film*, refuses to verify the assimilation of video literacy it has become anti-survival. In that context, rebellion is a biological response.

Evolution is essentially a process of information storage and retrieval. That's what genes are all about. Resisting the neurophysiological congruence of television and brain is schizophrenic. It may be that there will be no clear-cut new medium to succeed television, only symbioses of video, lasers, computers, and beyond. But cultural DNA is to ascend to new hybrid forms. Already people find holograms phenomenally "real."

Just as techno-evolution is gradually phasing out our bodies with increasingly sophisticated technologies like heart machines, synthetic arteries, and so on, so too is media evolution transforming us into whatever technology can best record and retrieve information.

Some scientists for example are using a computer transfer system where one keys in his latest theory for feedback by others. The result, coupled with the amazing amplification of thought process that the computer already offers, is a whole new process of mind, which supplants "human" relationships.

Right now, the human brain in symbiosis with computers is the best thing going. But if some fabulous computer can process intelligence better than man all by itself, then at that point the computer may be man. [. . .]

8. Survival Modeling

[. . .] We're just now understanding the consequences of hardware, but nobody's anywhere near publicizing potential software fall-out. Twenty-five years too late people are concerned about the effects of broadcast-TV. But no one is looking into the potential of the technologies which will replace it. How are kids going to respond to cable television and videocassettes? Nobody asks, and as a result bad design decisions are being made.

CBS, for example, has developed a videocassette which is called EVR. Its dominant characteristic is that it has no record mode. To do that CBS had to design a technologically reactionary piece of hardware. Rather than use videotape, which is indigenous to television. CBS chose a film medium because it won't allow you to do your own recording.

That was a deliberate design decision. It was probably motivated by men who think of information as property and thus wanted to minimize copying. The software ramifications are that people can't generate their own Information with the system.

Now CBS is pushing very hard to sell EVR to school systems. That means that educational retooling money for those schools which buy EVR will be tied up for years in a system which minimizes student participation, other than to let them choose from a prerecorded library over which they have no control. Interaction will be minimized when most educators agree that that's precisely the opposite of what is needed. Yet, because they have no sense of software they're going to frustrate their own wishes.

Software fallout is a confluence of the media's failure to develop a grammar of process. Other than anthropomorphize it, the popular press has developed no language to personalize the effects of technology. We do not learn about scientists and technologists in the same colorful way we learn about politicians or even athletes.

Yet the bias of technology, not ideology, is where the real power lies in Media-America. Our having no online technological analysis is an anti-survival mode. [. . .]

11. Schools

[. . .] When I was a kid we used to go on "field trips." That meant we'd hop in a yellow school bus, drive fifty miles, and then be allowed to consider our environment as information. At all other times the teacher wouldn't label the outside environment so we wouldn't go out and learn from our friends or learn to observe our parents.

Video equipment is subversive of all that because it allows students to generate their own knowledge. Portable video equipment extends to the whole environment and thus invalidates the school itself as a place of learning.

Now it's hard to control a lot of kids who are turned-on to taping everything everywhere. So when television equipment is installed in schools it is usually as centralized and heavy as possible so the kids can't get at it without an "instructor" to monitor them.

At the Television School of San Francisco State College, considered one of the "best equipped" in the country, students are taught skills in studios where no smoking, eating, or drinking are permitted because the equipment is "too expensive" to take chances.

But try to imagine a true life situation without those activities. In other words, students there are being taught skills solely for nonlife situations, ones which only have market value in the scarcity job market of broadcast-TV (which many of them say they dislike). And not only are there not enough jobs to go around now, there will be fewer in the future. Thus the school automatically prepares them for non-survival.

One student told me that the Television School refused to buy flexible portable video cameras because it had too much tied up in heavy, immobile, studio equipment and was actually saving all its money to buy more in a few years.

When video equipment is more flexible, teachers lock it in a closet because they're not sure what to do with it. Almost every teacher I've met says their school's video equipment, when they have it, goes unused. None have thought just to let the kids experiment with it independent of any prestructured activity. My own experience with kids and TV is that when they know they're guaranteed access they'll think up a thousand things to do by themselves and start to get pissed off because the equipment can't make all the effects they want.

Electronic information is a psychic space which doesn't leave your head just because you're in a classroom. When teachers let their students decorate classroom walls, the first thing they do is slap up posters. I've been in school rooms with up to thirty posters on the wall. But they still couldn't compete with TV. There's more potential action in a short-term television access model, *i.e.*, *TV Guide*, than all the Dewey Decimal System. [. . .]

13. Context

[. . .] But new lexicons reflect and generate cultural change. The 1960s, for example, were given their character partly by the widespread use of psychoanalytic terminology to describe practically anything. Already new terminologies are competing for the direction of the 70s.

Some people, for example, see videotape as being merely a kind of "Polaroid home movies." Those of us working in the medium believe its significance is much greater than that of mere improvement on an old medium, that rather videotape can be a powerful cultural tool, and so we want videotape to be accepted on its own terms. That means it has to have its own terms.

Moreover, because videotape is part of a whole way of viewing and using technology, and because technology has up until now been the province of scientists and government, by mixing technological jargon and slang we can make technological design responsible to a whole alternate cultural view.

Unfortunately, most people of the alternate culture don't understand the dynamics of information. They think that it's possible to use the message system of another context to put across your own. But contexts are co-opting, particularly in the nascent stages of a movement when, as Paul Ryan says, "overexposure means underdevelopment." [. . .]

The Black Panthers (they actually number about a thousand) were created by TV because the image they put out is fantastic: strong, young black cats with guns. Some news shows even got to flashing a drawing of a charging black panther (the animal) behind the newscaster when he read his story. You can't do that with the N.A.A.C.P. But just as the media created the Panthers, they can destroy them, because the Panthers have no ultimate control over their own information.

No alternate cultural vision is going to succeed in Media-America unless it has its own alternate information structures, not just alternate content pumped across the existing ones. And that's what videotape, with cable-TV and videocassettes, is ultimately all about. Not Polaroid movies.

Context is crucial to the amplification of an idea to prevent co-option. It's rear-view mirror thinking to expect an old context successfully to convey a plan for social re-structuring. Even Nixon is out hyping his actions as "revolutionary." [. . .]

Amplifying an idea is easy when the social space is ready for it, impossible when it's not. Last year, when we were still naive, we knew we were on to something with this videotape stuff and we'd talk to anyone about it, for free. Now we turn some people down and charge those who can pay. And somebody gave me an advance to write this book.

What's important in putting across a context is that you know its temporal velocity and where it can best be amplified. Often no publicity is better than exposure in even relatively decent publications. Or if you're trying to organize a movement, going on the Johnny Carson show won't exactly enhance your credibility. And so on.

Contexts have to be nurtured to be successfully amplified. In Media-America that means not mistaking information process for public relations. Movements and personalities burn themselves out very quickly when they're devoured by publicity. Remember ecology?

14. Death of Politics

[. . .] Most radicals misunderstand the bias of information systems. They think all you have to do is substitute your message for the ones going across. But the actual result would be that instead of being frustrated by a one-way system which hypes a plastic product-America, as people now are, they'd be equally frustrated by a radical political message which also gives them no chance to feed back. True cybernetic guerrilla warfare means restructuring communications channels, not capturing existing ones.

Another major problem with radical politics is that it has to create an artificial base of repression, rather than feed off an indigenous support center as classic guerrilla warfare.

True, blacks are really repressed, but if you're white and middle-class, as most radicals are, then trying to get in on the heat coming down on the blacks for your own self-definition its parasitic.

A more genuine radical strategy for middle-America would be to build a base at the actual level of repression, which for whites it mostly physical. This means developing a base of indigenous information to work from. It might include tactics like going out to the suburbs with video cameras and taping commuters. The playback could be in people's homes through their normal TV sets. The result might be that businessmen would see how wasted they look from buying the suburban myth.

Similarly, it's possible to sensitize the police rather than alienate them, as is now the case. Neither the police nor the middle classes are getting the feedback they need from regular TV. With video, it's possible to organize a community around cable television and begin to enhance all kinds of behavior, not just put over some long-haired, dope-smoking fantasy which if everyone did it would be as fascist a culture as ever was. Respecting diversity, not minimizing it, is the real potential of information tools.

In an information economy like Media-America, real power lies with information centers. An alternate culture should be setting up alternate information systems like video networks and computer data banks. Once you become a source of survival information you don't need political rhetoric, which is what the *Whole Earth Catalog* is partly about. [. . .]

As government does become more oriented toward information systems, the way information is modeled becomes more crucial. In other words, to key a spending program off a computer analysis means that the questions which go into the data gathering become the real level of decision-making. If the right questions or the right people aren't asked, then money will be misappropriated time and again. The way poor people and blacks are being ripped off now will seem minor unless they have their own people skilled in computer technology.

In a cybernetic culture, power grows from computer print-outs, not the barrel of a gun.

Moreover, the inherent potential of information technology can restore democracy in America if people will become skilled with information tools. [. . .]

15. The General Market

The technology of Media-America has killed the mass market. What we call marketing is essentially the orchestration of information systems, first in finding out who will buy what, and then in coordinating the logistics of delivery.

Information technology is a general-purpose system. Rather than being hardwired into one use like, say, an electric can opener, a computer has the flexibility to do a variety of tasks. The cost of any particular computation is minimal once the overall program has been written.

The result is that the service economy, which as process is computer-based, is becoming more and more specialized. Service means catering to individuals and the computer offers the administrative capacity to translate personal desires into fulfillment. [. . .]

II Manual

Guerrilla Television: Some Theory

In the summer of 1968, Sony, the Japanese electronics manufacturer, began marketing in America a low-cost, fully portable, videotape camera.

Prior to this, videotape equipment was cumbersome, stationary, complex, and expensive, even though it had been used commercially since 1956.

By now it's clear that television has succeeded print as this culture's dominant communications medium. The first videotape equipment embodied its analogue to Gutenberg. Portable video is TV's offset printing, the result of a techno-evolutionary trend toward decentralization and high access; just as developments in printing meant that we could get more than Bibles.

Whereas tens of thousands of dollars were once needed to tool up for videotape, now only $1,495 are required. In place of a machine weighing hundreds of pounds and requiring special power lines, all you need now is standard house current to recharge batteries which will let you use the 21-pound system anywhere, independent of external power. And instead of a mystique of technological expertise clouding the operation of the system, all you have to do is look at a tiny TV screen inside the camera which shows exactly what will be recorded, and then press a button.

Typically, the technology was (and still is) designed and marketed in a rear-view mirror. Treated like Polaroid movie cameras (in other words, "films" which play back right away), they're hyped to industry and government as a low-cost way to train employees or do surveillance.

From Michael Shamberg and Raindance Corporation, *Guerrilla Television* (New York: Holt, Rinehart and Winston, 1971); Meta-Manual 7–31, Manual 5.

Subject to Change: Guerrilla Television Revisited (1985)

Deirdre Boyle

Video pioneers didn't use covered wagons; they built media vans for their cross-country journeys colonizing the vast wasteland of American television. It was the late sixties, and Sony's introduction of the half-inch video Portapak in the United States was like a media version of the Land Grant Act, inspiring a heterogeneous mass of American hippies, avant-garde artists, student-intellectuals, lost souls, budding feminists, militant blacks, flower children, and jaded journalists to take to the streets, if not the road, Portapak in hand, to stake out the new territory of alternative television.

In those early days anyone with a Portapak was called a "video artist." Practitioners of the new medium moved freely within the worlds of conceptual, performance, and imagist art as well as of the documentary. Skip Sweeney of Video Free America, once called the "King of Video Feedback," also designed video environments for avantgarde theater (*AC/DC*, *Kaddish*) and collaborated with Arthur Ginsberg on a fascinating multimonitor documentary portrait of the lives of a porn queen and her bisexual, drug-addict husband, *The Continuing Story of Carel and Ferd*. Although some artists arrived at video having already established reputations in painting, sculpture, or music, many video pioneers came with no formal art training, attracted to the medium because it had neither history nor hierarchy nor strictures, because one was free to try anything and everything, whether it was interviewing a street bum (one of the first such tapes was made by artist Les Levine in 1965) or exploring the infinite variety of a feedback image. Gradually, two camps emerged: the video artists and the video documentarists. The reasons for this fissure were complex, involving the competition for funding and exhibition, a changing political and cultural climate, and a certain disdain for nonfiction work as less creative than "art"—an attitude also found in the worlds of film, photography, and literature. But in video's early years, guerrilla television embraced art as documentary and stressed innovation, alternative approaches, and a critical relationship to Television.

Just as the invention of movable type in the fifteenth century made books portable and private, video did the same for the televised image; and just as the development of offset printing launched the alternative-press movement in the sixties, video's advent launched an alternative television movement in the seventies. Guerrilla television was actually part of that larger alternative media tide which swept over the country during the sixties, affecting radio, newspapers, magazines, publishing, as well as the fine and performing arts. Molded by the insights of Marshall McLuhan, Buckminster Fuller, Norbert Wiener, and Teilhard de Chardin, influenced by the style of New Journalism forged by Tom Wolfe and Hunter Thompson, and inspired by the content of the agonizing issues of the day, video guerrillas set out to "tell it like it is"—not from the lofty, "objective" viewpoint of TV cameras poised to survey an event but from within the crowd, subjective and involved. [. . .]

Video represented a new frontier—a chance to create an alternative to what many considered the slickly civilized, commercially corrupt, and aesthetically bankrupt world of Television. Video offered the dream of creating something new, of staking out a claim to a virgin territory where no one could tell you what to do or how to do it, where you could invent your own rules and build your own forms. Stated in terms that evoke the characteristic American restlessness, boldness, vision, and enterprise that pioneered the West—part adolescent arrogance and part courage and imagination—one discovers a fundamental American ethos behind this radical media movement.

Guerrilla Television Defined

The term "guerrilla television" came from the 1971 book of the same title by Michael Shamberg.[1] This manifesto outlined a technological radicalism that claimed that commercial television, with its mass audiences, was a conditioning agent rather than a source of enlightenment. Video offered the means to "decentralize" television so that a Whitmanesque democracy of ideas, opinions, and cultural expressions—made both by and for the people—could then be "narrowcast" on cable television. Shamberg, a former *Time* correspondent, had discovered that video was a medium more potent than print while reporting on the historic *TV as a Creative Medium* show at the Howard Wise Gallery in 1969. Banding together with Frank Gillette, Paul Ryan, and Ira Schneider (three of the artists in the show), among others, they formed Raindance Corporation, video's self-proclaimed think tank equivalent to the Rand Corporation. Raindance produced several volumes of a magazine called *Radical Software*, the video underground's bible, gossip sheet, and chief networking tool during the early seventies. It was in the pages of *Radical Software* and *Guerrilla Television* that a radical media philosophy was articulated, but it was in the documentary tapes, which were first shown closed-circuit, then cablecast, and finally broadcast, that guerrilla television was practiced and revised.

Virtuous Limitations

Before the federal mandate in 1972 required local origination programming on cable and opened the wires to public access, the only way to see guerrilla television was in "video theaters"—lofts or galleries or a monitor off the back end of a van where videotapes were shown closed-circuit to an "in" crowd of friends, community members, or video enthusiasts. In New York, People's Video Theater, Global Village, the Videofreex, and Raindance showed tapes at their lofts. People's Video Theater was probably the most politically and socially radical of the foursome, regularly screening "street tapes," which might include the philosophic musings of an aging, black, shoeshine man or a video intervention to avert street violence between angry blacks and whites in Harlem. These gritty, black-and-white tapes were generally edited in the camera, since editing was as yet a primitive matter of cut-and-paste or else a maddeningly imprecise backspace method of cuing scenes for "crash" edits. The technological limitations of early video equipment were merely incorporated in the style, thus "real-time video"—whether criticized for being boring and inept or praised for its fidelity to the cinéma vérité ethic—was in fact an aesthetic largely dictated by the equipment. Video pioneers of necessity were adept at making a virtue of their limitations. Real-time video became a conscious style praised for being honest in presenting an unreconstructed reality and opposed to conventional television "reality," with its quick, highly edited scenes and narration—whether stand-up or voice-over—by a typically white, male figure of authority. When electronic editing and color video became available later, the aesthetic adapted to the changing technology, but these fundamental stylistic expectations laid down in video's primitive past lingered on through the decade. What these early works may have lacked in technical polish or visual sophistication they frequently made up for in sheer energy and raw immediacy of content matter. [. . .]

Changing Times

[. . .] Once the possibility of reaching a mass audience opened up, the very nature of guerrilla television changed. No longer out to create an alternative to television, guerrilla TV was competing on the same airwaves for viewers and sponsors. As the technical evolution speeded up, video freaks needed access to more expensive production and postproduction equipment if they were to make state-of-the-art tapes that were broadcastable. Although some continued making television their own way, pioneering what has since become the world of low-power TV and the terrain of public-access cable, many others yearned to see their work reach a wide audience. Without anyone's noticing it, the rough vitality of guerrilla TV's early days was shed for a slicker, TV look. The "voice of God" narrator, which had been anathema to TVTV and other video pioneers, was heard again. Gone were the innovations—the graphics, the funky style and subjects, the jousting at power centers and scrutiny of the media. Gone was the intimate, amiable cameraperson-interviewer style, which was a hallmark of alternative video. Increasingly, video documentaries began looking more and more like "television" documentaries, with stand-up reporters and slide-lecture approaches that skimmed over an issue and took no stance.

Where one could see the impact of guerrilla television was in its parody: sincere documentaries about ordinary people had been absorbed and transformed into mock-u-entertainments like *Real People* and *That's Incredible!* The video verité of the 1976 award-winning *The Police Tapes*, by Alan and Susan Raymond, had become the template for the popular TV series *Hill Street Blues*. In the sixties, Raindance's Paul Ryan proclaimed, "VT is not TV,"[2] but by the eighties, VT *was* TV. [. . .]

McLuhan's reductionist view that "the medium is the message" was embraced and then rejected by the first video guerrillas, who asserted that content *did* matter; finding a new form and a better means of distributing diverse opinions was the problem. That problem is still with us. How a new wave of video guerrillas will resolve it and carry on that legacy, human and imperfect as it may be, should prove to be interesting and unexpected. More than guerrilla television's future may depend on it.

From Deirdre Boyle, "Subject to Change: Guerrilla Television Revisited," *Art Journal* 45, no. 3 (Fall 1985): issue *Video: The Reflexive Medium*, 228–32.

Notes

1 Michael Shamberg and Raindance Corporation, *Guerrilla Television* (New York: Henry Holt, 1971).
2 "Feedback," *Radical Software* 1, no. 1 (Spring 1970), 20.

Women's Video (1981)

Anne-Marie Duguet

Many video-makers are women. People are no longer surprised by this observation, yet it is not insignificant.

On one hand, the spread of video corresponded fairly closely with the rise of the feminist movement in France. On the other, the relegation of women to subordinate production jobs, in both television and the movies, and the difficulties they encountered in attaining certain types of work—technical jobs, for example—explained their quest for more open modes of expression such as video. It should not, however, be said that they took up video as a stopgap, as a fallback position. Video offered them the possibility of conceiving a work entirely by themselves—directing it, editing it, and controlling the entire process if they so wished. They could seek their own voice far from prying paternalistic eyes, whether bemused or anxious.

Twin Sisters: Video and Women's Lib

1970: The first regular videowork by women, and the appearance of the women's lib logo, MLF (Mouvement de Libération des Femmes). The women's struggle in France grew and asserted itself through manifestos (notably one signed by 343 women who had had illegal abortions, April 1971), by strikes in companies largely staffed by women (Troyes, 1971), by demonstrations and wildcat actions, and by the increase in women's groups in the neighborhood and workplace. Similarly, women seized upon all modes of expression to demonstrate their particular oppression and their rebellion: by founding feminist magazines,[1] a women's publishing house, specialized bookshops, groups devoted to theater (La Carmagnole), the movies (Musidora), music, the visual arts, and so on. They also took up video, said to be a way for everyone to express themselves. So why not women? They were ready to seize the opportunity.

In addition to the scope and drive of the feminist movement, factors related to the very nature of video and its inherent production conditions help to explain the relative ease and swiftness with which women adopted it.

First of all, it should be recalled that this new field of audiovisual production had not yet been monopolized by men and that, above all, it entailed no heavy financial or administrative constraints. For those women who were untrained or excluded from audiovisual firms, a fairly flexible production unit (one or two people sufficed), a technology enabling everyone to follow the various stages of work, relatively lightweight equipment, and a certain ease of use that did not require overly long apprenticeship and permitted a swapping of roles, appeared to be a feasible, appealing adventure. In the movies, as elsewhere, people still hesitate to entrust large budgets to women: will they be "up to it"? Women often wind up wondering themselves, and give up without even trying. Fighting the interiorization of this feeling of inferiority is already one of the aims of their video work. The ability to erase mistakes makes beginners feel safer, eliminating the angst of expensive errors, blame, guilt, and subsequent lack of confidence. A mistake is no longer a tragedy, and the "wasted" time is at least a time of learning or a cost-free chance "just to see." A free chance to hesitate, to do it over. And also a chance to change things, to explore, to get to know. [. . .]

Fringe Organization

Women are nevertheless careful not to get trapped into an overly rigid way of functioning. This "instability" should sometimes be understood as respect for the rhythms, interests, and desires of each woman. Women have specifically developed "open" associations based on projects and affinities. These organizations are a reflection of the women's lib movement—noninstitutional, flexible, fluctuating yet fertile and numerous, in which a sense of urgency and the need to speak out prevent them from becoming too rigid. [. . .]

Who are these women? Feminists, film editors, actresses, artists. Most women video-makers work in the institutional, sociocultural, or educational sectors: they are instructors, coordinators, teachers, researchers, psychologists, sociologists, etc. The increasing feminization of these kinds of job and the growing facilities to which they give automatic access also explain the large number of women using video.[. . .]

Technology: Where's the Problem?

Sexist attitudes surface, for example, during the frequent breakdowns of video equipment, which is currently fragile and not very reliable. If a problem arises while a woman is using such equipment, the spontaneous reaction is to blame *her* rather than the *machine*. Up races a male tinkerer who taps it and fiddles with it, becoming annoyed because, in theory, he should get the better of it. Given equal ignorance, a male's lack of knowledge will seek to triumph. Video-making requires either a serious knowledge of electronics or else fairly basic training that cannot be skipped, and which should be reinforced by maintenance courses. The only women who never run into this type of problem are either the ones who deliberately ignore it because they have truly qualified technicians available, or else the ones whose competence is unimpeachable, that is to say superior to the skill required of a man. A female technician must be an engineer,[2] a male technician is just a guy.

On one hand, video technology is mythified, which hardly facilitates its appropriation by women, and on the other hand its simplicity of use is vaunted by advertisers, who demonstrate it by producing sales catalogs with photos of pretty women strapped to a recorder, camera in hand: even ladies can use it! As simple as a dishwasher—just push the button. It's a snap, you can do it, so can everyone. Women sell electronic equipment along with everything else, at least the equipment connected to home use and leisure activities. But women are also the advertisers' direct target: the modern woman active in every sphere. This dynamic type of woman makes "action videos on location" (ad picture: a picnic in the countryside!) and, strangely, wears a very masculine suit. [. . .]

Their Bodies, Her Image

Finally, women directors are seeking a new language, exploiting video's specific possibilities with occasional boldness, remodeling space and duration according to rhythms and viewpoints they have reappropriated.

What only women can express are the pleasures and pains specific to their gender, which their tapes reveal without shame or shilly-shallying, defying taboos in order to eliminate the guilt and anguish of situations made more alarming by each women's isolation and unawareness. They insist on the right to dispose of their bodies freely, they are attempting, individually and collectively, to stake out their identity, to shape their identity through their own images. [. . .]

In fact, most video recordings of workers' struggles have been made by women who were initially interested in the women who led battles on their own or who sought to fight alongside the men. Benefiting from what might be called a "basic shared oppression" as women, these video-makers can establish more direct, closer contact with female workers.

The upshot has been various examples of an unusual image of women: as determined and clear-sighted as male activists, able to resist intimidation. It is usually the first time they have experienced this collective commitment, this political action determined by themselves in a realm from which they are usually excluded. Together they are learning how not to capitulate in general: the demands of the struggle are a "decent" reason for abandoning household chores. The upshot is a double emancipation: from bosses and from husbands. [. . .]

In addition to these difficulties precisely experienced by women in finding and holding an outside job, there is the lack of recognition of housework. Monique Haicault notably made a video piece on this issue in Toulouse, while Catherine Lahourcade and Syn Guérin documented the daily oppression of an old farmer's wife in *Des Femmes du Haut Quercy* (1975). Then there are the immigrant Turkish women shot by Nil Yalter and Nicole Croiset in the absence of their husbands (in whose company they would otherwise remain silent). This "gang of women" is shown in their daily tasks of making meals, serving tea, watching the children—they talk about their living in conditions in France, their nostalgia for their home country, and problems of language, education, and so on.

Rather than trying to establish what "specifically feminine" video work might be—which would certainly run the risk of reproducing the categories that trap women into specific roles (sensitivity, gentleness, etc.)—this article merely seeks to identify certain exploratory efforts at change that moreover flaunt their difference.

Most of these works stumble into the same pitfalls as all others: verbosity (interviews, debates, panel discussions, etc.), naiveté, poor quality—why should we expect women to spontaneously escape them?—but those with true originality display a special level of audacity, which is perhaps the backlash from being historically denied a public voice: having no "artistic status" to lose, they adopt certain bold measures.

Bold, first of all, in the intimacy of their content and radical nature, such as accounts of prostitution and sexuality. Bold also in the intimacy of pictures of the naked bodies of pregnant women, breasts swollen and belly distended, which focus on dilated vaginas. The "labor" of a woman's body is observed, quite openly, in all its states, all worked up. The artistic approach is, straight away, experimental. It's a question of learning and demystifying, which calls for directness and preciseness.

Such works take the time to re-establish the truth of certain situations and how they actually happen. They show abortions and delivery in their real duration, uncut, and with live sound.

They also seek a different pace, a slow and steady discovery of things, and of their own powers of expression.

Even more striking is their way of creating an intensified image of themselves. The video image is often a specular image of themselves—mirrors are involved from the start, multiplying all. Hungry for such discoveries, they indulge in an integrating narcissism, a kind of playful self-analysis. There is no rupture. Video enables them to be present in the same scene they are recording.[3]

These highly personal productions, free from activist didactics, break not only with normal discursive linearity by employing free association and incorporating images, but also with standard categories of genre, seeking to forge a kind of "docu-fiction-narrative."

And since they also have hearty, ironic appetites, they have produced some original, counter-attacking video work.[4]

From the chapter "La vidéo des femmes," in Anne-Marie Duguet, *Vidéo, la mémoire au poing* (Paris: Hachette, 1981), 89–111; translated for the present publication by Deke Dusinberre.

Notes

1 Publications included *Le torchon brûle*, *Les femmes s'entêtent*, *Les pétroleuses*, *Sorcières*, *Les Cahiers du feminisme*, *Histoire d'elles*, and *Questions féministes*.

2 Fabienne Vansteenkiste, the video technician at the École Nationale Supérieure des Art Décoratifs in Paris, is a graduate of the prestigious engineering school known as the École Centrale.

3 See Jean-Paul Fargier, "Questions à Milka Assaf" and "Anne Faisandier parle de Nombrelles," *Cahiers du Cinéma* 292 (September 1978).

4 These ideas were developed in a later chapter, devoted to "Les écritures" and "La vidéo critique de la télevision," of my book *Vidéo, la mémoire au poing* (Paris: Hachette, 1981).

10

Communities | Amateurism | Ethnographies | Participation

Introduction by Dieter Daniels

The contributions presented here cover a much wider geographical area than those in all the other chapters. What links the home video cultures of Western industrial nations to the rise of video in Nigeria and the videos of indigenous communities in South America? This legitimate question can only be answered with a general reference to certain video-specific aspects: in the domains presented in this chapter, video functions as a semi-public medium, operating in intermediate zones that pertain neither to mass media nor to purely private media contents and circulating beyond the control of central entities, partly also outside of legality and copyright rules. The given examples stand for the independence of video-based media cultures that have developed parallel to, and in hybrid combination with, the established mass media of television and cinema. These communities still unfold in an analog way, by circulating videocassettes via "offline" networks. The video contents watched, produced, copied, and exchanged by these communities may often be irrelevant for a broader audience, but for their specific target group they are of utmost importance, sometimes even fulfilling an identity-building function.[1]

Another common feature is that the separation between those in front of the camera and those behind it, between making and taking part, is occasionally suspended or at least blurred. In this regard, the contributions reactivate and perpetuate the unrealized video-utopian approaches of the 1970s (see Chapter 9) in other contexts, for example, in collective production and perception. The topicality of these concepts is evidenced by the principle of "participatory video," which since the mid-1990s has evolved into an independent, postcolonial, and global practice.

Cultures of Analog Home Video: Sean Cubitt, Tobias Haupts, Lucas Hilderbrand

The video-utopian ideas of the 1970s were tied to the conquest of public space with the help of portable video devices in self-organized production contexts (see Chapter 9). In contrast, the home video boom of the 1980s could initially be seen as a "domestication" (Lucas Hilderbrand) and commercialization of the medium. Through the combination of recorder, TV tuner, and timer, video returned to the center of the living room, as a complement and extension of television consumption (see Chapter 5 on home video as a time-shift medium for TV recordings). The key factor for the sweeping success of consumer home video technology was global standardization, which around 1980 decided the ongoing videotape format war in favor of VHS.[2] This opened up a new market for the rental and sale of prerecorded videocassettes, with a peripheral gray area for private copying and exchanging as well as trading in illegal or (un)censored content.

Especially in combination with the camcorder, introduced in the 1990s, home video was also used to make private recordings, thus marking the beginning of the ubiquitous presence of video in everyday life. Both as regarded watching habits and production conditions, there was an essential difference to analog amateur films, which were only shot for, or shown on, special occasions. This new ubiquity allowed video to become a medium of unexpected testimony. The first prominent example of this was the almost accidental recording by video amateur George Holliday of the abuse of Rodney King by white police officers, and the far-reaching legal and political consequences of these images, which eventually culminated in the 1992 Los Angeles riots (see Chapter 11).

"I believe that videotape changes not just what we can watch but also how we do so. Would it be too much to say that we see differently when we see something recorded on video?"[3] This statement by Lucas Hilderbrand highlights a specificity of this chapter: within the broader scope of this reader, home video can be seen as the only realm in which the reception-related aspects of video are examined in more detail. Viewership research is generally a focus of television theory, but the difference between "passive" television and "interactive" video reception is only incidentally considered. Instead, the contributions in this chapter examine specific aspects of video reception in terms of content and viewing practices as well as regards the interactions between reception and production in the home and consumer segment.

The social and group-dynamic specificity of wedding videos examined by Sean Cubitt is exemplary for the emergence of new genres based on private recordings (weddings, birthdays, company celebrations, and holidays, but also private pornography).[4] The personal transmission and joint viewing of these recordings "acts as bond, a seal binding again the members of the family group: representation as a guarantee of the reality of the family union."[5] The phenomenon of a repeated rewatching of selected passages (*Stellenlektüre*) identified by Tobias Haupts as a video-specific mode of perception (for splatter and porn) was potentially linked to the procurement of videotapes from black markets or the production of bootleg copies analyzed by Hilderbrand. This semi-public circulation of illegal copies, as the latter shows, was also a model for the legal distribution of home productions, especially private pornographic recordings, which reached an audience of initiates via exchange networks. In private recordings of any kind another video-technical factor came into play: unlike amateur films, amateur videos were not processed in a laboratory. They therefore allowed for a new, video-specific dimension of intimacy, even—or especially—when passed on to third parties.

In this respect, wedding videos or amateur pornography as well as censored splatter films or pirated copies of cult films in the 1980 and 1990s were "video-specific" contents—not in a formal sense but simply because these contents were not available through other media channels. Home video brought forth a new way of dealing with images that could be described as a hybridization of established categories. In this new mode of reception and production, the boundaries between public and private visual worlds were blurred: personal video recordings, TV recordings, retail tapes, rental tapes, and a variety of private copies—all these heterogeneous contents were stored, viewed, maybe also deleted and overwritten with new recordings on the same devices, potentially even on the same videotape. The home video recorder, similarly to the personal computer and the smartphone later, thus became a multifunctional device for heterogeneous practices. Accordingly, home video amateurs can be seen as analog, proto-digital "prosumers," forerunners for online cultures in which personal and appropriated, self-produced, (pirate-)copied, and recreated images are interwoven in the form of mash-ups and memes.

Nigerian Video—from Piracy to Primacy: Brian Larkin

The interaction between video distribution and video production—examined in the previous section through 1980s Western home video culture—developed an unsuspected dynamic in Nigeria in the course of the 1990s. The gray areas of Western microeconomics here grew into a macroeconomy thanks to the professional, if not industrial, distribution of bootleg videos. Video piracy (of Hollywood and Bollywood movies) laid the financial basis for an independent Nigerian video culture (of so-called "Nollywood video films"). The infrastructures for bootlegging American and Indian films were serving as distribution channels for the booming industry of autonomous African video productions. In Nigeria, the conventional logic of industrial production methods was reversed: video perception through (illegal) appropriation gave rise to an independent film culture based on video tapes and an economy of national importance.

The levels of consumption, distribution, and production could occasionally merge in the microeconomics of individual cases, as evidenced by the "urban myth" of the video film *Living in Bondage* (1992), which is generally regarded as a milestone at the beginning of the Nigerian video boom: in a bid to increase his chances of selling a large stock of blank VHS tapes from Taiwan, the electronics dealer Kenneth Nnebue decided to produce a film included on the tape free of charge when purchased. The reproduction medium of piracy, the VHS videocassette, was thus turned into a distribution medium and, simultaneously, a means of financing the first successful Nigerian video film. Likewise, Nnebue changed both roles and sides, turning from supplier to investor, and from a profiteer of piracy to an initiator of autonomous video productions. Subsequently, the Nollywood economy was itself threatened by the very infrastructure of videocassette piracy that previously had helped to finance it. In 1997, Nnebue summed up the situation with the terse observation that "piracy is our AIDS."[6]

From a typological point of view, prevalent Nigerian video productions were mostly melodramas or soap opera formats, comparable in the Western context to the US series *Dallas* or *Dynasty*, and in the Global South inspired primarily by Indian Bollywood models.[7] The combination of the terms video and film in the title of the first survey publication on the topic, *Nigerian Video Films*, points to the hybridity of the format.[8] In Nigeria, video was mainly used as a fast and inexpensive medium for production and distribution, a replacement for film and TV technology. The extensive literature on the topic primarily summons references from film and television theory as well as from ethnography.

In the self-understanding of Western avant-gardes, the appropriation of industrial products by means of replication and found footage aims to turn them into a critique of the logic and aesthetics of commercial film and television production. Nollywood, on the other hand, can be seen as a form of postcolonial, Afrocentric originality that emerged from the appropriation and transformation of colonial mass media. This applies not only to the piracy and distribution structures described earlier but also to the content of certain films, in which we witness a creative amalgamation of the levels of reproduction and production. To demonstrate this, Heike Behrend cites the example of the 2003 Hausa remake of James Cameron's blockbuster *Titanic* (1998) by the Nigerian director Farouk Ashu-Brown. It combines excerpts from *Titanic* and *Deep Blue Sea* (1999), starring Samuel L. Jackson, with sequences shot in Nigeria into an uncommented continuous narrative. Behrend points out, however, that the Western enthusiasm for this kind of subversive appropriation is not shared by African film critics.[9] In this respect, comparisons between Nigerian piracy and avant-garde appropriation primarily reflect a Western perspective.[10]

From a transcultural perspective, Nollywood can be understood as an Afrocentric overwriting of Western or Indian models. In the words of Charles Igwe, one of the leading Nigerian film producers, the reason for the breakthrough of *Living in Bondage* was that "it was a story being told by our people to our people. That was key!"[11] In the academic field, Chukwuma Okoye has developed a series of theses on the anthropologization of the West from an African perspective, which he has substantiated with a case study of the video *Osuofia in London* (2003).[12] According to Okoye, such Nollywood films can function as "a postcolonial system of decolonization."[13]

Due to the failure of all state, public, and educational institutions of film and television culture in Nigeria in the 1980s, the shadow economy that grew out of piracy was able to fill a substantial gap and became a system-relevant factor. In the 1990s, neither the production of video films nor the distribution of the tapes were regulated by the state. Even if there are no reliable statistics from the beginning of this industry, an average of one new film per day was presented as early as the 1990s. Between 2005 and 2011, according to UNESCO surveys, an average of 966 new films were produced each year, putting Nigeria in third place worldwide after India and the United States.[14] Thus, from the turn of the millennium, Nollywood rose to become the second biggest industry in the country after agricultural production and even before the oil industry.

Does this mean that the utopias and ideals of "Guerrilla TV" and video activists nurtured in the United States and Europe during the 1970s were becoming a reality in Nigeria's state-controlled "counter-publicness"? As with the earlier comparison of video piracy with Western avant-garde strategies of appropriation, some fundamental differences must be taken into account here. This includes in particular the absence of an ideological superstructure, that is, of social, political, or even feminist utopias; rather, similarly to its Hollywood model, production followed capitalist economization. To cite but one particularly prominent example, *Living in Bondage*, coproduced by Nnebue with director Chris Obi-Rapu, raises numerous questions of political correctness from a Western perspective as regards gender equality, consumer-oriented status thinking, the influence of black magic, and equally obscure Christian promises of salvation.

The theorization of Nollywood is also caught in this dichotomy between methodological fascination and contentual distance to its subject. Generally, dealing with the phenomenon of Nigerian video films from the perspective of Western media theories is always subject to the reservation Jonathan Haynes already formulated so aptly in the first book on the topic, published in Nigeria in 1997:

> The enthusiasm of foreign cultural studies researchers can seem glib: coming from cultures secure in the possession of a "high" cinema . . . they do not feel responsible for defending the cherished project of cultural nationalism or the heritage of the Yoruba traveling theater, and can ignore the videos' not always critical reflection of the painful moral situation and frequently horrible social values of contemporary Nigeria.[15]

In the extensive literature on the topic, media-theoretical questions are often addressed marginally at best. Important research approaches include the transcultural comparison with Indian and US-American films, the development of independent Nigerian genres, and the differences in video cultures within Nigerian ethnic groups and languages (Hausa, Igbo, and Yoruba, also with regard to gender roles), as well as the effects of Islam with the introduction of Sharia law and, with it, censorship in northern Nigeria since 2000. The internationally noted, critical reflection on these issues that is taking place in Nigeria contributes to dismantling the "division of labor," rightly criticized by Haynes in 1997, "whereby Third World cultural products become grist for the First World theory mill."[16] Internationally acclaimed African authors include Abdalla Uba Adamu (Bayero University, Kano) and Chukwuma Okoye (University of Ibadan) as well as Onookome Okome (currently University of Atlanta).[17]

In this respect, the text by Brian Larkin republished here marks only a certain aspect of this debate—one that is particularly relevant for video theory. In terms of media technology too, the transition from analog videocassettes to digital storage media (video CD/DVD) and online video has been accompanied by decisive changes in Nigerian video culture, which means that Larkin's contribution from 2004 must be read as an analysis of a moment within a historical phenomenon in permanent transformation.

A separate field of investigation, which has so far received little attention, is the persistence of now largely obsolete physical storage media for video, both in Nigeria and in the global distribution of Nollywood. In 2016 Jade L. Miller explained the resistance of the Nollywood economy to appropriation by global players by "the immense disjuncture between the functioning of formal global capital and the logics of doing business in Lagos, in an industry run by a vast and opaque informal network of small-scale entrepreneurs hostile to formality."[18] This also applies to the failed attempts to displace the informal distribution channels for physical video storage media in Nigeria by online platforms.[19] And it applies equally to the global marketing of Nollywood to Nigerian communities in Europe and the United States, which is largely based on the local production and distribution of physical copies.[20] With the help of otherwise outdated, physical media technologies, the domestic, informal gray areas of dealing with copyright are exported to the Nigerian diaspora of Western industrial nations.

Indigenous Video and Local Ethnographies: Juan Downey, Terence Turner, Freya Schiwy

While indigenous video practice and the video boom in Nigeria originated at around the same time in the early 1990s, they developed in completely opposite directions. In Nigeria, autonomous capitalist production structures were created and the plots of Nollywood videos often represented capitalist ideals, which also explains why they are often seen critically in the country itself. Indigenous videos, on the other hand, were predominantly created in collaborative, publicly funded structures. Their postcolonial independence is mostly due to their intrinsic social feedback function rather than any appropriation of, and simultaneous delimitation from, "Western" models. Accordingly, the Nollywood discourse often relies on analyses of specific video films, whereas the discourse on indigenous video is first and foremost directed at social practices and the political representation of ethnic minorities.

The term "indigenous video" refers to a geographically dispersed practice. It spans American Natives in the United States, Inuit in northern Canada, Aborigines in Australia, and several indigenous communities in Bolivia, southern Mexico, northern Brazil, and Ecuador.[21] The contributions in this chapter focus on developments in South America from three different perspectives: Juan Downey as an artist and pioneer of participatory observation, Terence Turner as an activist anthropologist, and Freya Schiwy as a comparative scientist with a political message.

In the 1970s, Juan Downey developed artistic projects that, from today's perspective, can be regarded as forerunners of scientific studies on indigenous video yet to this day have received little to no attention in "visual anthropology." His starting point, *Video Trans Americas*, can be seen as a video-utopian project in the best sense of the word. Downey published his short concept in *Radical Software* in 1973 and partially implemented it in a series of videotapes from 1973 to 1979 (as well as related work in other media; see Figure 10.1).[22] His plan to connect geographically remote indigenous communities from North to South America by means of video betrays structural similarities to Nam June Paik's concept of an international exchange of TV programs between industrial nations. But while Paik's *Global Groove and Video Common Market* from 1970 (see Chapter 5) concerns mass media contents, Downey turns his attention to indigenous self-representation in video.[23] At the center of his interest are the independent experiences of indigenous Yanomami with the new medium, which in

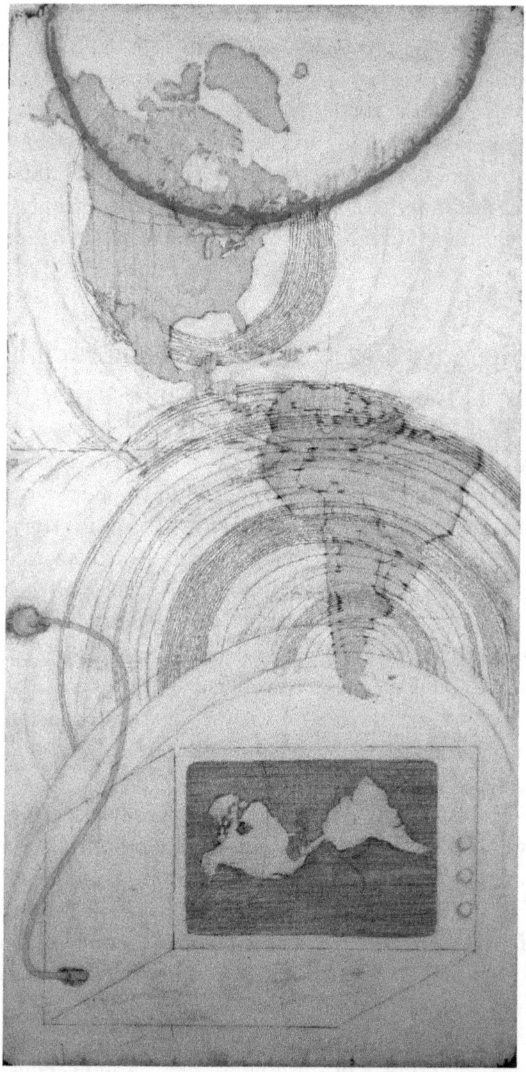

Figure 10.1 Juan Downey, *Video Trans Americas*, 1973–76, oil, acrylic, and graphite on plywood, 96 × 48 inches, Museo Nacional Centro de Arte, Reina Sofía, Madrid. Courtesy of the Juan Downey Foundation, New York. © VG Bild-Kunst, Bonn 2020.

turn raise his awareness for the limitations of his own, Westernized perspective.[24] His videotape *The Laughing Alligator* (1978), made in exchange with the Yanomami, differs from ethnographic films in that it parodies his own role as a participant observer.

Downey anticipated controversies about appropriate forms of representation in indigenous video that have been raised in anthropology since the 1990s and that Terence Turner's contribution illustrates in an exemplary way. Turner is one of the pioneers in the theory and practice of indigenous video. Together with the Kayapo people, he initiated a video project in the Amazon jungle, while also publishing scientific papers on the subject. The article reprinted here is based on the lecture, accompanied by video excerpts, that he held together with the two Kayapo Mokuka and Tamok as part of an ethnographic conference.[25]

The importance of video work for the participating Kayapo becomes clear in a video recording made specifically for the lecture, in which Mokuka speaks to the audience while Turner translates in parallel:

> Now that we are becoming more like the Whites, however, we are going to need to watch these videos we are making of ourselves. It is not Whites who are doing this work, but I, a Kayapo, who am doing it, as all of you can see. These videos will be seen in all countries. Tell your children and grandchildren, don't be deaf to my words, this [work] is to support our future generations, all our people. This is what I want to say to you today.[26]

Mokuka's words speak not only of his marked self-confidence but also of a well-reflected understanding of the dual function of these videos as internally directed means of self-representation and cultivating tradition and externally directed tools of political representation.[27] In the latter case, video can be instrumentalized to support specific political demands. This is exemplified by the use of video in the conflict between the Kayapo and Brazilian government agencies over the construction of a dam, analyzed by Turner.[28] The strategic utilization of the Kayapo's presence with their video cameras for press and television coverage was part of the implementation of such demands.[29] International reporting thus extended the limited radius of the videos—an amplification that helped draw attention to the ongoing conflict of the Kayapo with the Brazilian state.[30]

At the beginning of the 1990s, Turner's work was at the center of a controversy about the "objectifying gaze, embodied in Western audiences for films and videos produced by indigenous people."[31] Linked to this is the question to what extent indigenous use of video can remain independent in its relation to Western models, in other words, whether it repeats or even reinforces a subordinate role. Like Turner, Freya Schiwy argues that "empowerment" through video is possible. Based on an attitude that is reflexively distant compared to Turner's but nevertheless distinctly committed, Schiwy's contribution provides an overview of the further developments of this controversial discourse.

The cornerstones of this complex debate are essentially as follows:

- Can the "appropriation" (Turner) of video by indigenous communities lead to independent, self-sustaining self-representation?
- Which "involuntary effects" (Schiwy) can Western, capitalist technology have on indigenous forms of society?
- In what way does an indigenous visual language differ from the perspective filtered and shaped by Western culture (Downey and, in more detail, Turner and Schiwy)?
- Can video in an oral culture be a new, authentic form of transmission, representation, and political action in lieu of the Western notion of "literacy"?

- Is video therefore a "logical extension" (Schiwy) of indigenous knowledge cultures and collective working methods?

In other publications, Schiwy extends the thesis that "thinking with audiovisual tools"[32] can produce a specifically indigenous knowledge culture: "The process of indianizing creates continuities between complex indigenous systems of signifying and audiovisual aesthetics. These systems of signifying exceed the binary of literate versus oral culture. Indeed, these lines of continuity call into question the idea that film technology is alien to indigenous cultures."[33]

Similar questions have been discussed since the 1970s with regard to the potential of the video medium to change Western society. This includes the possibility of activist, emancipatory appropriation of a capitalist technology (see Chapter 9). These concepts are being further developed today in the form of "participatory video." Conversely, cultural-pessimistic scenarios still imply that "literacy" will be pushed back by audiovisual media.[34] In contrast, the hybridization, in the sense of Schiwy, of the binary opposition of "literate versus oral culture," as affirmatively posited by McLuhan, would appear to offer a promising option for Western societies as well.[35]

Outlook: Participatory Video

The social and collaborative approaches presented in this chapter so far are condensed and diversified in the concepts and practices of participatory video. The extensive literature on the topic falls into two categories: on the one hand, instructions for initiating and moderating participatory video processes; on the other hand, evaluations of case studies and field research, which in turn serve as empirical values for future applications. Owing to this practical aspect, the thematic scope reaches beyond the remit of video theory. Due to its global relevance, it will nevertheless be briefly presented here, albeit without a corresponding source text. In contrast to other areas presented in this reader, the discourse on participatory video can be considered to be distinctly transdisciplinary and international.[36] Numerous print and online manuals are available for further discussion.[37]

Participatory video has its roots in the so-called "Fogo Process" that Donald Snowden successfully tested in 1967 on Fogo Island on the east coast of Newfoundland.[38] His fundamental idea of an internal network among geographically separated fishing communities and a common political representation to the outside world has similarities with Downey's *Video Trans America* concept from 1973. Since the 1980s, participatory video practices have been put to use, particularly in Great Britain, in social work, communities, and the healthcare sector, as well as for media self-empowerment of marginalized groups. As described by Shaw and Robertson, participatory video is an activity that "utilizes video as a social and community-based tool for individual and group development . . . to develop their confidence and self-esteem, to encourage them to express themselves creatively, to develop a critical awareness and to provide a means for them to communicate with others."[39] The experiences gained in Western societies are now carried on predominantly in developing countries. NGOs and participatory video facilitators, who initiate processes and teach methods with which communities subsequently continue to work autonomously, play an important role in the transfer of know-how. Thus, participatory video can be seen as one of the successful "empowerment" strategies for human rights claims and the representation of marginalized population groups within these countries.

For the identity-building role of participation, video feedback processes are of central importance: joint production and perception, group viewing and evaluation in preparation of postproduction, ideally with a collaborative montage of the finished video. The video-specific feedback via "instant replay" in participatory video serves as a social and communicative function, which allows it to sets itself apart from art-theoretical theses on the medium's inherent narcissism (see Chapter 3). For participatory group work, processes are therefore more important than products. Gareth Benest, who works as a participatory video facilitator himself, sums it up as follows: "In participatory video it is possible to have a successful process without a product. That's right, without a finished video at the end. No video. Nothing."[40] The results of intragroup video work can, in particular with the help of professional formatting, also contribute to the external impact and political positioning of those involved: "The participatory video approach can be an effective way of engaging people in the decisions that affect them . . . by supporting the transfer of responsibility to them to enable them to voice their opinions and make real choices."[41]

Notes

1 For more on video as a community-building medium with collective practices of authorship, see the introduction to Chapter 9 of this book. In Western industrialized nations, the concept of community video received widespread attention particularly in the 1970s. For a historical analysis and suggestions on how to reactivate these concepts, see Edward Webb-Ingall, "Playback: Reactivating 1970s Community Video" (doctoral thesis, PhD Media Arts, Royal Holloway, University of London, 2018).

2 See the chapter "The Format Wars" in Lucas Hilderbrand, *Inherent Vice: Bootleg Histories of Videotape and Copyright* (Durham and London: Duke University Press, 2009), 50–4; other excerpts reprinted in this chapter.

3 Hilderbrand, *Inherent Vice*, 72.

4 See also James M. Moran, *There's No Place Like Home Video* (Minneapolis: University of Minnesota Press, 2002) and "Wedding Video and Its Generation," in *Resolutions: Contemporary Video Practices*, ed. Michael Renov and Erika Suderburg (Minneapolis: University of Minnesota Press, 1996), 360–81.

5 Sean Cubitt, *Videography: Video Media as Art and Culture* (London: Palgrave Macmillan, 1993), 4; other excerpts reprinted in this chapter. Similarly, video could also take on a community-forming and identity-building function in indigenous communities; see the following section.

6 Kenneth Nnebue in Jonathan Haynes, *Nigerian Video Films* (Athens: Ohio University Center for International Studies, 2000), 69. On the need for new models of

intellectual property, see Volker Grassmuck, "A Proposal for Legalising Small-Scale Physical Copyright Piracy: Book Publishing, Video Films and Music in Developing Countries," 2013 http://ssrn.com/abstract=2245342; See also Olufunmilayo B. Arewa, "Nollywood: Pirates and Nigerian Cinema," in Kate Darling and Aaron Perzanowski, *Creativity without Law: Challenging the Assumptions of Intellectual Property* (New York: New York University Press, 2017), 228–48.

7 "Indeed by 2001 the Hausa video film was merely a reproduction of a Hindi film, which itself is a mere reproduction of a Hollywood film." Abdalla Uba Adamu, "Private Sphere, Public Furor: Gender and Delineation of *lntimsphäre* in Muslim Hausa Video Films," in *Harsunan Nijeriya* (Kano: Centre for the Study of Nigerian Languages, Bayero University, 2011–2013), vol. 23, 349.

8 Haynes's *Nigerian Video Films* was first published in 1997 by Kraft Books for the Nigerian Film Corporation in Ibadan.

9 "The director's subversive reworkings of Cameron's premake in an Afrocentric perspective were not at all acknowledged. In addition, the pleasures of piracy were not shared. However, the critical attitude towards copying obviously is shared with other intellectuals in Kano as well as various Western film critics who . . . see remakes as a form of plagiarism that makes use in a parasitic way of the original films for commercial interests. While upholding the divide between "original" and "copy," they, on the one hand, negate the creativity that every act of copying or borrowing implies and, on the other hand, fail to acknowledge that every video is a mosaic of other videos." Heike Behrend, "The Titanic in Kano: Video, Gender, and Islam in Northern Nigeria," in *Gender and Islam in Africa*, ed. Margot Badran (Stanford: Stanford University Press, 2011), 186–7.

10 This Western perspective also applies to the haptic, even erotic charging of the image through the video-specific "bootleg aesthetics" of analog copies that Lucas Hilderbrand describes in *Inherent Vice* (64ff.) with regard to, notably, Laura Marks. Brian Larkin attributes similar qualities to Nigerian video: "Piracy creates an aesthetic, a set of formal qualities that generates a particular sensorial experience." Larkin, "Degraded Images, Distorted Sounds: Nigerian Video and the Infrastructure of Piracy," *Public Culture* 16, no. 2 (Spring 2004), 291; other excerpts reprinted in this chapter.

11 Charles Igwe, "The Nigerian Film Industry" (presentation at the seminar "The Rise of People's Cinema," The Center for Technology and Society at FGV, Rio de Janeiro, May 11, 2006), quoted in Grassmuck, "A Proposal for Legalising Small-Scale Physical Copyright Piracy."

12 Chukwuma Okoye, "Looking Back: Nigerian Video Film Anthropologises the West," *Leeds African Studies Bulletin* 72 (October 2010), 76–90.

13 Chukwuma Okoye, "Looking at Ourselves in Our Mirror: Agency, Counter-Discourse, and the Nigerian Video Film," *Film International* 5, no. 4 (August 2007), 26.

14 UNESCO Institute for Statistics, *Emerging Markets and the Digitalization of the Film Industry: An Analysis of the 2012 UIS International Survey of Feature Film Statistics*, UIS Information Paper, no. 14 (Montreal: UNESCO Institute for Statistics, 2013), 12–13.

15 Haynes, *Nigerian Video Films*, 17.

16 Ibid., 34.

17 A meritorious survey of the extensive African literature on this topic can be found in Jonathan Haynes, "Bibliography of Academic Work on Nigerian and Ghanaian Video Films," *Journal of African Cinemas* 4, no. 1 (2012).

18 Jade L. Miller, *Nollywood Central: The Nigerian Videofilm Industry* (London: Palgrave Macmillan 2016), 8.

19 See ibid., 56.

20 See ibid., 128, 130.

21 See Freya Schiwy, *Indianizing Film: Decolonization, the Andes, and the Question of Technology* (New Brunswick: Rutgers University Press, 2009), 5.

22 Juan Downey, "Video Trans Americas," *Radical Software* 2, no. 5 (Winter 1973), 4. After his return to New York in May 1975 Downey wrote: "Like a chemical catalyst I expected to remain identical after my video exchange has enlightened many American peoples by the cross-references of their cultures. I proved to be no real catalyst, for I was devoured by the effervescence of myths, nature, and language structures. Pretentious asshole levelled off! Only then did I grow creative and in manifold directions. Me, the agent of change, manipulating video to decode my own roots." Downey, Travelogues of Video Trans Americas (1973–1975) in Juan Downey 1940–1993, ed. Julieta González and Javier Rivero Ramos (Versalles: Ediciones MP, 2019), 330.

23 The series of videos made by Downey with indigenous communities includes *Guahibos* (1976), *Yanomami Healing One* (1977), *The Singing Mute* (1978), *The Abandoned Shabono* (1978), *More than Two* (1977), and *The Laughing Alligator* (1978). See Sarah J. Montross, "Mapping Juan Downey's *Video Trans Americas* (1973–1978)," in "Cartographic Communications: Latin American New Media Artists in New York, Juan Downey and Jaime Davidovich (1960s–1980s)" (PhD thesis, New York University, September 2012), 130–87. In her paper, Montross also discusses the installation based on these videos that Downey showed at the Whitney Museum of American Art in 1976, which can be considered a pioneering work for the presentation of video in museums.

24 See Downey's testimony in "Noreshi Towai," in *Mas de Dos: Videotapes de Juan Downey* (Caracas: Museo de Arte Contemporáneo de Caracas, 1977), reprinted in: *Video Writings by Artists (1970–1990)*, ed. Eugeni Bonet (Barcelona: Mousse Publishing, 2017), 84–90.

25 Lecture at the Third International Festival of Ethnographic Film of the Royal Anthropological Institute in Manchester in 1992.

26 Terence Turner, "Defiant Images: The Kayapo Appropriation of Video," *Anthropology Today* 8, no. 6 (December 1992), 8; other excerpts reprinted in this chapter.

27 In Turner's words, a "synergy between video media, Kayapo self-representation, and Kayapo ethnic self-consciousness." Ibid., 10.

28 Ibid., 11ff.

29 Ibid., 7.

30 See the interview with Kiabeiti Metuktire, "Kayapo Filmmaker: 'Video Is Our Bow,'" *National Geographic* (December 7, 2015), https://blog.nationalgeographic.org/2015/12/07/kayapo-filmmaker-video-is-our-bow/. Also available as a video, https://www.youtube.com/watch?v=M0brUVoUI_Y.

31 Turner, "Defiant Images," 14. The second, extensive part of Turner's text, which is not reproduced here, is a reaction to James Faris's critique of his practice. See James Faris, "Anthropological Transparency: Film, Representation and Politics," in *Film as Ethnography*, ed. Peter Crawford and David Turton (Manchester: University of Manchester Press, 1992), 171–82. Faris subsequently replied to Turner in "A Response to Terence Turner," *Anthropology Today* 9, no. 1 (February 1993), 12–13.

32 Freya Schiwy, "Decolonizing the Technologies of Knowledge: Video and Indigenous Epistemology" [2003] (paper translated from Spanish for online publication in the dossier "Decolonizing the Digital/Digital Decolonization" as part of the Worlds & Knowledges Otherwise project at Duke Center for Global Studies and the Humanities, 2009), 9, online at https://www.academia.edu/42204048/DECOLONIZING_THE_TECHNOLOGIES_OF_KNOWLEDGE_VIDEO_AND_INDIGENOUS_EPISTEMOLOGY; other excerpts reprinted in this chapter.

33 Schiwy, *Indianizing Film*, 14.

34 Refuting these sceptics, the principle of thinking in video instead of language can already be found in the work of Jean-Luc Godard; see the essay by Thomas Helbig in Chapter 4 of this volume.

35 For an overview of further topical developments, see *From Filmmaker Warriors to Flash Drive Shamans: Indigenous Media Production and Engagement in Latin America*, ed. Richard Pace (Nashville: Vanderbilt University Press, 2018). The volume includes a dialogue between Kiameti Metukire and Terence Turner, "A Legacy of Kayapó Filmmaking," 49–59.

36 For a good overview with contributions by forty-nine international authors, see *Handbook of Participatory Video*, ed. E-J Milne, Claudia Mitchell, and Naydene de Lange (Walnut Creek, CA: AltaMira, 2012).

37 For historical context, see Tony Roberts and Chris Lunch, "Participatory Video," in *The International Encyclopedia of Digital Communication and Society*, ed. Robin Mansell and Peng Hwa Ang (New York: Wiley-Blackwell, 2015), available online at https://insightshare.org/wp-content/uploads/2017/06/Participatory-Video-C.LunchT.RobertsInsightShare.pdf.

38 See ibid.

39 See the handbook with sixty exercises by Clive Robertson and Jackie Shaw, *Participatory Video: A Practical Approach to Using Video Creatively in Group Development Work* (London: Routledge, 1997), 11.

40 Gareth Benest, "A Rights-Based Approach to Participatory Video: Toolkit," *InsightShare*, June 2010, http://www.montesca.eu/VISTA/wp-content/uploads/2012/11/A-Rights-Based-Approach-to-Participatory-Video-toolkit-COMPLETE.pdf.

41 Robertson and Shaw, *Participatory Video*, 1.

[Wedding Videos] (1993)

Sean Cubitt

Video media can only be understood as the product, the site and the source of multiple contradictions, lived out in multiple practices, caught up in multiple struggles. To this extent, the study of video must address the structures and processes of the contemporary cultures in which it operates, the more so since "video" is both a duster of diverse, even mutually exclusive cultural practices, and at the same time a medium which the most diverse practitioners can still find ways to communicate about to one another. The internal undecidability, the lack of essence in video, its "lack of being" in the Lacanian phrase, should not be taken as the "truth" of video: video's internal dialectic is produced out of the circumstances of its invention (or more properly the multiple, ongoing invention of the medium). The complex of media clustered around the monitor/VDU and associated presentation media (video walls, projectors, and presenters) is formed in, performs, and informs the instability of contemporary social structures. Such contradictions inhabit even—or perhaps especially—the most banal forms of video: practices that least consciously address the characteristics of video as such, and in doing so reveal the more profoundly some of its most pervasive qualities.

The wedding video is a product of supreme invisibility and supreme formalism. Few video practices invite less critical attention to the niceties of lighting and angles, or to the other aesthetic issues that will be raised in this book, yet few forms are as tightly bound by rules. Deriving its shape from the wedding album, and most frequently delivered by the same high street photographers who otherwise would provide the snaps, wedding videos repeat not just the ritualized gestures of the marriage ceremony but the traditional set-ups for the wedding album: arrival of the bride, signing the register, the family group, cutting the cake, and so on. Every shot is precisely and skillfully done, and must be: the aim is to edit in camera (that is, without the use of an edit suite since that would cost too much in time and money, and delay the moment at which the family take delivery and watch the tape, both important factors in an extremely competitive market). At the same time, every tape must appear fresh and personal as if it addressed this event and no other, never to betray the suspected secret: that it is exactly the same as every other wedding video.

The point is, of course, that to the participants, this specific videotape is unique: precisely rendering the behavior of named and known people, including themselves. A disparity then arises between the formulaic mode of production and the tightly focused referentiality of the viewing situation. Giggling flower girls and page boys are part of the Formula, but not perceived as such when they are identified as specific cousins, and when the viewer has been party to the spectacle that the video has recorded. This is a form of reference that persists in video as in snapshots, a determination in relation to the real in which the videotape itself acts as a bond, a seal binding again the members of the family group: representation as a guarantee of the reality of family union (especially at a time when that union has to alter in the face of alliance).

In short, there is something specific to the viewing situation that determines the meaning of the video, just as much as the video itself determines the kind of viewing that is possible. In this instance there are two key functions: to bring into the family circle people who couldn't attend the event (but who can be trusted to recognize a useful proportion of the people shown there) and to help participants remember. This mnemonic function is, again, shared with photography and perhaps derives from it; video a supplement to the older medium. Like portrait photography, it takes on a double rote, promising presence while presenting absence: the image of an auntie is simultaneously a reminder of her presence, but is conditional on her actual absence, a dialectic fundamental to representational technologies. But this particular dialectic is only available to someone who recognizes the auntie. For them, the wedding video is an index, a way of pointing to the real auntie at a real moment in time. What is unusual, though, and what draws us back into a wider dialectic, is that taken as a whole the wedding video (formal product that it is, and record of a formal occasion) takes on simultaneously the character of a universal event. It's clear enough what is meant when people say that a wedding draws its participants into a continuity with everyone who has ever married. But the video too, especially by reiterating the formulae established for representing the event, takes on a quasi-linguistic form, a form which universalizes the event by referring it to all other wedding videos. Even the unique this-ness of the event and the record of it are shared with the equally unique this-nesses of every other wedding, every other wedding video.

At the same time, the experience of watching someone else's wedding tape is a bizarre one, especially when you know absolutely no-one shown there. Certainly the formulae are more apparent, but less readily expected is the intensity of interest with which it's possible to watch total strangers enacting an otherwise familiar spectacle. The sense comes over you of looking in on something rather private, something to which you are uninvited, that excludes you. And that sense of exclusion, I believe, derives from a reversal of the dialectic: moving from an expectation of the universal to a realization of the particular. What at first looks like a simple commodity, interchangeable with any other wedding tape, begins instead to look like a precious pledge of the particularity and specialness of these strangers' lives, a particularity so specific it overrides our culturally sanctioned pleasures in watching screened images.

These two factors are in play in watching a wedding video: universality (always, under capitalism, marked with the sign of the commodity) and particularity (likewise marked by the construction of individualism). Wedding videos are not unique in this: much the same might be argued of the classic realist text described by *Screen* theory in the 1970s. But the latter is an intellectual construct invented after the event to describe the similarities between an otherwise disparate family of texts, whereas the wedding video's claim to universality is based on the repetition of the same narrative elements in the same order in every variant. It is as if the logic of classical realism—obliteration of the processes of production, transparency of the medium, construction of an ideally coherent subject position from which the text is comprehensible—are all brought to a head in the wedding tape. The wedding tape carries out in meticulous detail the determining characteristics of classical realism. No-one questions the videomaker's intentions, so formalized is it; no-one notices the materiality of the image mediating between the event and its representation. And the viewer's position, even looking guiltily in on someone else's tape, could scarcely be more definite and hemmed in, more surrounded by ritual responses and respect for the authenticity of the experience on screen: few other media experiences so completely rule out the possibility of criticism. It is perhaps this traffic between the universal and the individual in realism and in wedding tapes that has taken the place of religion: that gives us a sense of where we fit into the scheme of things.

The formula reminds us of our place in an order which, socially and historically specific though it is, we still want to believe is somehow natural. At the moment of marriage, one of the few moments of Western life that is still surrounded by a commonly shared ritual, we have evolved, in the few years since cheap, portable video cameras became available, a form of representation as rule-governed as Spenser's epithalamia. That formal representation guarantees the interlinking of the particular and the universal, the single instance and the grand order of things. So deeply ensconced is this belief that we no longer notice the suddenness with which the video has become part of the wedding ritual. Instead, the new medium has acquired, in this usage, something of that religious aura which stops us criticizing wedding ceremonies, for both seem to guarantee us an official place in the world. It is then only surprising that we greet an image of ourselves participating in the wedding not with pleasurable recognition, but with shock and embarrassment.

The sight of oneself on tape is not grounds for identification: what you see is not the "ego ideal" of psychoanalytic identification in the cinema.[1] This flattened representation is a stranger, perhaps most of all (to use the psychoanalytic lexicon) it is a picture of the ego, by which is meant the conscious public front representing someone formally to the world, especially on a formal occasion. We feel an instant need to comment on the image, to explain our actions and deportment, to apologize for or to historicize the picture on the screen or the voice on the soundtrack. The role of words here is to act as supplementary material, to fill in the gaps, to make up for the alienated image, the difference between it as object and you as subject. That difference between (re)presentation and presence is an expression of a split we all feel anyway, but which is poignantly and powerfully apparent in this kind of video. That split is the difference between how we experience ourselves and how others see us, a split which we internalize at a deep level when we learn as children that we must accept social roles and social laws that will govern our conduct. One of the key functions of language is to try endlessly to plug this gap, babbling on and on in an attempt to complete and make whole the internally-fragmented psyche. That's why the sight of your own image calls forth so much explanation.

From the chapter "Videography: The Helical Scan," in Sean Cubitt, *Videography: Video Media as Art and Culture* (New York: Macmillan, 1993), 3–7.

Note

1 Cf. Laura Mulvey, "Visual Pleasure and Narrative Cinema," *Screen* vol. 16, no. 3 (Autumn 1975), 6–18.

[Bootlegging Video] (2009)

Lucas Hilderbrand

The Vice Squad

[. . .] I propose that bootlegging is exemplary of videotape: it foregrounds the technology as a recording format, it exposes the formal degeneration of the signal, it stresses the importance of access, and it raises issues of intellectual property rights. Bootlegging is also, significantly, an *amateur* practice—both in its common connotation as nonprofessional (unpaid) and in its original meaning as *amorous*. Imported from French, the term "amateur" literally refers to the lover, not the unskilled—and I thus argue that bootleggers (and lovers of bootlegs who may not do the duping themselves) have personal convictions about, and affectionate connections to, their recordings.[1] Bootlegs implicitly reveal audiences as users of videotape technology. Bootlegs' status as illicit, amateur copies indicates that they were made and that their source copies were probably actively sought. And analog videotapes, through intergenerational distortion of the image and sound tracks, materially record and reveal this process of creation and history of circulation. Bootlegs, in particular, demonstrate this aesthetic of access because they are typically multiple generations removed from a source or master tape. They suggest wonderfully lurid relationships.

Audiences who find digital recordings to be impersonal may deem analog media "romantic." [. . .] Some "romantic" technicians and artists have even used analog distortion for its unique affectations. As sound scholars have argued, in considering technological reproduction we must rethink issues of fidelity and authenticity to move away from conceptions of an original performance that precedes recording. Rather, fidelity and authenticity are a ruse, an ideology to promote newer and more expensive formats. Infidelity is the marker of the analog amateur. Bootleggers are promiscuous and polyamorous.

Have Tape, Will Copy

Bootlegs have been central to fan and film collector culture since the introduction of home video. Although it would be impossible to prove definitively, I suspect that videotape changed the very nature of media fandom and collecting. Through home video there could be a shift in collecting practices from seeking out various forms of *objects related to* the production or promotion of a film to collecting the *film itself*. Of course, there was a small Super 8 and 16 mm collector's culture that was already doing this, a specialist cult that I would correlate to the early home-taping videophiles. Through the mass marketing of prerecorded tapes and "collector's edition" DVDs, there was a mainstreaming of movie collecting culture—one that increasingly had less to do with specialized knowledge or unique objects but that instead contributed to a cultural popularization of geekdom. Yet even as DVD has grown the market for priced-to-own movies and collector culture, many of the most intensely interesting, perverted, or loved texts exist only outside legitimate distribution. The true collector collects those objects that have to be found (and copied) rather than simply purchased at Best Buy.

In his history of videotape as a mediating technology, Greenberg described early fan conventions where Betamax owners would swap tapes or "daisy chain" their Betamax decks in orgies of dubbing.[2] More recently, bootleg videos have circulated through semi-institutionalized networks of tapers, collectors, traders, and vendors—sites where hard- and soft-core pornography mingles with cult, horror, and fantasy cinema. Whether operating on an equal-trade or commercial basis, interpersonal connections, mail-order catalog services (advertised in fanzines), and cult film conventions provided the primary circulatory routes for bootleg tapes before the Internet. [. . .]

For cult film audiences who often relish low production values and schlocky scripts as part of the films' appeal, the addition of bootleg video aesthetics—whether from sketchy distributors or personal copying—may well enrich the text and add to the experience. As an art-horror film scholar has remarked of bootleg aesthetics: "The illegality is emphasized in the tape's very mode of viewer address . . . The very rawness of the image becomes both a signifier of the tape's outlaw status and a guarantor of its authenticity. You know this is the stuff you weren't meant to see simply because the image quality is so bad."[3] A global policy study observed such degeneration as a market strategy: "To prevent others from pirating his pirated tapes, he made a point of retaping them to the edge of fuzziness before rental."[4] Tape reveals its reproduction and can be used to police its uses. Both of these accounts of distortion—one incidental, the other intended—point to ways video aesthetics mark the text as forbidden. The idea of the forbidden here, of course, cuts both ways—as temptation and as warning. The white noise, the jittery image, the unnatural colors, the grain, the momentary loss of signal that triggers the blank blue TV screen or the flash of tracking: these are the marks of damaged dupes. Such effects can be frustrating, or they can intensify one's attention.

On other occasions when critics have pondered their rendezvous with videotape bootlegging, the topic has inspired purple prose and deviant pleasures. My favorite is a delirious revelry in which the writer plays fast and loose with his associations, drawing analogies between the worn-out aesthetics of duplication and the intensely carnal pleasures of sex, drugs, and rock 'n' roll:

> The harshest reds had been strained to a porn-zine labial pink, the blues and blacks dulled to a bad-meat gray. And the whole look of the frame changed; softened slightly with each generation—the images wavering in some liquid video purgatory—until the whole thing resembled some sort of a vertiginous underwater snuff film . . . Bootleg culture parallels drug culture, both in its word-of-mouth distribution system and in the kick of possessing, or simply being near, the forbidden object.[5]

This critic connects the fleshiness of the tapes to the viewer's affective response—one in which emotional reaction is as embodied as it is intellectual. His mixed metaphors and florid language vividly convey the sensual, illicit, and formal pleasures produced through reproduction. Although not writing of bootlegs specifically, Laura Marks has also theorized video's haptic aesthetics in relation to its low resolution and electronic manipulability:

> Part of the eroticism of this medium is its incompleteness, the inability to ever see it all, because it's so grainy, its chiaroscuro so harsh, its figures mere suggestion . . . But haptic images have a particular erotic quality, one involving giving up visual control. The viewer is called on to fill in the gaps in the image, engage with traces the image leaves.[6]

In effect, Marks suggests a submissive sexuality in watching grainy video. Video leaves the viewer wanting more.

What is described in each of these effusive bursts has remained marginal as a theory of aesthetic specificity for analog video. Yet the ways that they evoke the technical properties of videotape suggest that, just maybe, these ways of seeing video actually speak to its aesthetic better than any other. That there's something sensual about these passages also seems to reveal some of the formative ways in which video came to be defined. Inherent vice, indeed.

Videotape's Last Great Fling

Repeatedly in the history of reproductive technologies, pornography has been one of the earliest and most commercially successful forms of content. Although it has become accepted as a truism that pornography was the most prominent content available for prerecorded cassettes in the late 1970s, it was also already recognized as something home users with access to a camera could make themselves. In the "home video" epilogue to a 1977 book on the ways in which art practices defined video as a medium, analog aesthetics are eroticized with a description that prefigures Marks's remarks quoted earlier:

> Video pornography is first-rate. The fuzziness makes it hard to see, and your natural impulse to stare is heightened by the difficulty of figuring out exactly what is going on up there. The effect is like a striptease: Now you see it, now you don't. And your imagination will inflame you more than a realistic picture could.[7]

Whereas pornography has been credited with advancing the market penetration (as they say) of VHS in the late 1970s and early 1980s, beginning in the mid-1980s, the phenomenon of amateur porn exhibited a pervasive new and kinky video aesthetic.[8] In a way, pornography flipped the mainstream home video market's trajectory over, innovating the prerecorded content market and later returning attention to recording through amateur porn and celebrity sex piracy.

In the most literal realization of its etymology, *amateur* porn has circulated as a popular category of amorous analog video. Amateur pornography began as a kind of virtual swinging: tapes were swapped among the makers in a kind of bootleg network.

Such exchanges demonstrated a potential market, one that was soon exploited and institutionalized by porn video distributors, making the practice a hybrid of personal expression and professional marketing.[9] Part of the appeal—and, arguably, progressive representational politics—of amateur pornography is that it shows people with average bodies (i.e., breasts without implants, cocks shorter than ten inches) engaging in real sex for pleasure, maybe even love, rather than for money. (Of course, gonzo pornography pretty quickly moved the genre beyond amorous sex acts into pure exploitation.) The makers' less-than-ideal physiques and the realities of at times awkward or mundane sexual performance were complemented by the recording's subpar production values—low light, grainy image, handheld camera jiggle, overlong takes, indifferent framing, ambient buzz and mechanical noise, and often inaudible conversation. The genre's failure at simulating Hollywood's—or even studio porn's—fantastic realism or invisible construction both made it seem more intimate and called attention to the familiar specificities of video technology itself. These dual attributes have been read as asserting a kind of authenticity that is typically missing from professional porn. In addition, both the aesthetics of amateur pornography and its bootleg circulation make its participants seem somehow more plausibly sexually available to the viewers. [. . .]

From the chapter "Be Kind, Rewind: The Histories and Erotics of Home Video" in Lucas Hilderbrand, *Inherent Vice: Bootleg Histories and Copyright* (Durham and London: Duke University Press, 2009), 61–7.

Notes

1 The original French meaning of "amateur" is referenced in Evan Eisenberg, *The Recording Angel* (New York: McGraw-Hill, 1987), 177. Stephen Duncombe also traces the etymology of "amateur"—to the Latin *amator*—in his study of fanzines, using this meaning as defining that form of underground cultural production: *Notes from Underground* (New York: Verso, 1997), 14. Patricia Zimmermann cites the Latin *amare* as the root word in *Reel Families* (Bloomington: Indiana University Press, 1995), 1.

2 Joshua M. Greenberg, *From Betamax to Blockbuster: Video Stores and the Invention of Movies on Video* (Cambridge: MIT Press, 2008), 23–6.

3 Joan Hawkins, *Cutting Edge: Art-Horror and the Horrific Avant-Garde* (Minneapolis: University of Minnesota Press, 2000), 45, 47.

4 Gladys D. Ganley and Oswald H. Ganley, *Global Political Fallout: The First Decade of the VCR, 1976–1985* (Norwood, NJ: Ablex Publishing; Cambridge: Harvard University Program on Information Resources Policy, 1987), 54.

5 Richard Kadrey, "Director's Cuts," *World Art* 3 (1996), 64f.

6 Laura U. Marks, *Touch: Sensuous Theory and Multisensory Media* (Minneapolis: University of Minnesota Press, 2002), 11, 13.

7 Jonathan Price, *Video-Visions: A Medium Discovers Itself* (New York: Plume, 1977), 216.

8 Since the mid-1990s, both professional and amateur pornography has also proliferated as pervasive and profitable content for the Internet, and pornography has been prominent amid the rise of shared streaming video in the middle of the present decade—as well as smut-oriented and celebrity gossip blogs. Whereas YouTube

deactivates any content deemed obscene by users, knockoff sites such as PornoTube and XTube feature an array of content, professional and personal, commercial and shared.

9 See Zabet Patterson, "Going On-Line: Consuming Pornography in the Digital Era," in *Porn Studies*, ed. Linda Williams (Durham: Duke University Press, 2004), 110f.

[Splatter Videos, Scene Selection, and the Video Store] (2014)

Tobias Haupts

The following remarks consider to what extent the medium of the analog VHS tape presented new problems for the technical distribution and media presentation (in video rental stores, for example) of the genres of horror, splatter, and pornography in the 1980s, as well as for society, which had to respond to these changes. The main thesis is that changes in media technology, but also the discourse surrounding the protection of minors in and around the video rental store, significantly changed how we talk about these genres, and even altered the genres themselves.

At the beginning of the 1980s, horror and splatter films were accused of drawing an audience solely by means of the wounds that they staged, the murder sequences and explicit scenes involving the human body. The focus was not on the plot or characters but predominantly on individual moments in the film.

The fear that surrounded such films was not provoked by the video store displaying them, but by that which occurred after they were taken from that location. The VHS tape in the VCR, which could be played again from the beginning at any time, over and over, was in the eyes of many a genuine problem for the protection of minors. The possibility of using the stop and rewind buttons to navigate through the film to a particular image seemed to become perverted by the horror fan watching what made others look away. In fact, media criticism of horror film consumption above all seemed to discover not only an addiction that sought to continuously explore and transgress the boundaries of good taste, but to draw a parallel to pornographic films and their consumption. This association was due to the fact that, for the first time, moving images probing into what society generally deemed taboo were being consumed on a larger scale. Though—polemically speaking—these were nothing more than images of the beginning and end of life, it was above all an uncertainty regarding their effect on the mind, constitution, sexuality, and everyday life of children and adolescents that led critics to take action against these genres. The comparison of horror films, particularly those classified as splatter films,[1] to the pornographic film genre lies not only in the lack of acceptance of their images and the media criticism directed toward them, but also in their genuinely generic structures.

There are two ways in which both of these genres can be categorized as body genres.[2] This term refers to genres that place the body at the center of the staging and in the viewer's focus, and additionally to films that intend to elicit emotions in the viewer through their imagery and dramaturgical potential for affect. Horror often relies on fear and disgust, pornographic films on lust and excitement. In her investigation of the concept of body genres, Linda Williams pointed out that there is a close connection between horror films and pornographic films in terms of the sequence of images and the narrative structures.[3] [. . .]

Horror films—and this is where Williams's and Carol Clover's[4] deliberations on the genre coincide—consist of a series of scenes and climactic moments that make arbitrary and interchangeable what occurs in between. In horror films, these are the murders and killings that are depicted, and in pornographic films, the individual sex acts. [. . .]

The accusation of constant repetition, inherent in every genre film's variation between conforming and distinguishing itself, changed when viewers could use video technology to create repetition themselves.

Particularly in relation to pornographic films, the VHS tape seemed to complete the genre. As the VCR made it possible to eliminate what occurred between sex scenes, more and more porn producers began simply sequencing them one after the other on the tape, making it unnecessary to fast forward to the next climactic moment. This integration of porn and media technology has proven even stronger in relation to the Internet: the short clips on platforms such as YouPorn never last long, and what takes place before or after remains unknown. Here, once again, the medium seems to be the message that no additional clip is required once the first one has been consumed.

However, it is precisely this thesis as it relates to the theory of body genres—the interchangeability of what lies between the climactic moments—that reveals the extent to which the structure of the genre corresponds with the media technology of the VHS tape and the possibilities granted by the VCR. Critics who made the effort to employ a more nuanced reasoning often argued that the horror film viewer would operate the remote control more than viewers of other types of films. This would in turn cultivate a distinct type of media consumption that can be concretized with the German term *Stellenlektüre*, denoting the practice of selecting or rereading particular passages of a book, here applied to the scene selection encouraged by VCR.

In this context, the active study of specific passages denotes an interaction with media that had been applied as a modality for describing the handling of media itself even before it defined itself through scene selection with the VCR. It is an inherent critique of selecting certain passages that a text will no longer be perceived as a whole but rather dissolved into individual entities through the intervention of the reader. Once the consumer of any type of media breaks up previously defined structures by performing such an act, they place the detached contexts in a different frame of reference and are sui generis usually no longer able to follow the original intention and statement of the media in question, or to incorporate it. On the one hand, the moment of selection is indicative of creative interaction with the prefabricated products presented by the media landscape of the time. On the other hand, however, it also can be viewed as a step toward a fragmentation of perception.

By referencing text, for example in the form of a book, it becomes clear what scene selection in the case of video could entail. Leafing through a book, lingering on certain pages, or reading chapters out of order is similar to selecting scenes, and is diametrically opposed to immersing oneself in a book and becoming absorbed by it, which requires time, composure, and discipline. The media practice of selecting individual passages or scenes seems to precipitate a moment of dispersion. This becomes particularly clear when one looks at the progression from page-turning to scene selection with a remote control, which is demonstrated in zapping, or channel surfing.[5] It is precisely this form of scene selection that carries with it a strange aporia: the purpose of a television program is to create an individual *flow*[6] that counteracts the flow of other programming. In this way, the viewer becomes bound to a certain program, to the extent that their immersion pushes aside any thoughts of using the remote control. Being able to create their own *flow* by means of the remote control relieves media consumers of the passivity imposed on them by television, but only to a certain extent. Recognizing the viewer as a director responsible for their own programming places a slightly exaggerated emphasis on possibilities that were still rather limited in the 1980s.

The ability to select and record a particular scene using the functions of the VCR, as already described and outlined by Zielinski,[7] enabled a form of precise media consumption involving critical scrutiny of the TV program or the rented film. The VCR itself thus created far more freedom for the user than would have been possible by means of the television and remote control alone.

However, precisely these possibilities and forms of scene selection made possible by the VCR have become a critical characteristic of the horror fan and the consumer of pornographic videos alike.[8] Horror fans of the 1980s became familiar with the genre's rules and promises through the consumption of numerous films in the movie theater and at home. They knew about the nature of the dramaturgy of such films and operated with this knowledge even before Williams or Clover defined this form of viewing as part of genre theory in film studies. This concrete figuration of the viewer was now criticized for no longer being interested in the films themselves but only in the scenes that made the genre appealing through explicit depictions of violence. Using the VCR, it was possible not only to fast-forward through what preceded the scene, but also to slow down and freeze the gruesome act when it arrived. This created a better opportunity to see what was usually concealed through fast cuts in editing. The same technique was also employed for pornographic films, as it allowed the viewer to jump from one sex scene to the next.[9]

In relation to horror films, theories about scene selection escalated to a claim that the constantly repeated and frozen depictions of acts of violence and explicit orifices[10] would awaken a desire for the insides of the other[11] and provide both excitement and stimulation. The criticism of the genres and their structural similarities was thus exacerbated by the accusation that their images might serve the same purpose, that the images of pornography and horror films alike would provide sexual arousal.[12] [. . .]

This may appear a perversion of the possibilities introduced by the VCR, as Zielinski envisioned them, but the horror fan's understanding of their own role in fact corresponded to the VCR's own technical, conserving gaze, which effectively dissects the products of film and television. Rather than serving as a cheap thrill, the horror film freeze-frame allowed the image to be viewed and studied more closely. The interest of young and grown-up film enthusiasts alike was encouraged by the movies' special effects, which mostly found their climax in the elaborate murder scenes.[13] As if observing a magician carefully with the hope of understanding a trick, viewers searched for a point in the freeze-frame and the run-up to it that could expose the illusion and effect for what it was. The high degree of reality in the horror film images led to the aporia that technology, costumes, and make-up were more necessary than ever to achieve this reality-imitating effect.[14] At a time when making-of documentaries were not yet standard, the answers to questions about the story behind the film and its production secrets had to be discovered on one's own initiative. [. . .]

Therefore, it can be said that, for the first time, a form of anti-canon related to the offerings of the video store played a role in generating an understanding of the medium of film outside the cinema. Only this connection between how horror films were treated on cultural and technical levels, shaped by the industry and in the courts, and through interaction with the consumer, can reveal the extent to which the genre was transformed in the 1980s. [. . .]

Action, horror, and pornography, the triad of genres that made the video store famous and established its bad reputation, therefore operate with body genres that, through the means at their disposal, place the body in the center of the image to be dehumanized, tortured, or used. The images produced, distributed, and consumed as a result broke taboos of what could be represented, explored the possibilities of cinematographic transgression, and had never before existed in such a way. The difficulties in integrating the VHS tape into society are as much rooted in the history of film as they are in new forms of distribution.

From Tobias Haupts, *Die Videothek: Zur Geschichte und medialen Praxis einer kulturellen Institution* (Bielefeld: transcript, 2014), 290–312; revised by the author and translated for the present publication by Chelsea Leventhal.

Notes

1 See John McCarty, *Splatter Movies: Breaking the Last Taboo of the Screen* (New York: Columbus, 1984), on the onomatopoetic term "splatter."

2 US-American war films since the mid-1990s would also be among the forms referred to with the term "body genre" here, see Michael Wedel, "Körper, Tod und Technik: Der postklassische Hollywood-Kriegsfilm als reflexives Body Genre," in *Körperästhetiken: Filmische Inszenierungen von Körperlichkeit*, ed. Dagmar Hoffmann (Bielefeld: transcript, 2010), 77–99.

3 See Linda Williams, "Film Bodies: Gender, Genre, and Excess," in *Film Genre Reader II*, ed. Barry Keith Grant (Austin: University of Texas Press, 1999), 140–58.

4 See Carol J. Clover, *Men, Women, and Chain Saws: Gender in the Modern Horror Film* (Princeton: Princeton University Press, 1992).

5 On the media practice of "zapping," see Hartmut Winkler, *Switching, Zapping: Ein Text zum Thema und ein parallellaufendes Unterhaltungsprogramm* (Darmstadt: Häusser, 1991).

6 See Raymond Williams, "Programmstruktur als Sequenz oder *flow*," in *Grundlagentexte zur Fernsehwissenschaft: Theorie, Geschichte, Analyse*, ed. Ralf Adelmann, Jan-Otmar Hesse, Judith Keilbach, Markus Stauff, and Matthias Thiele (Konstanz: UVK, 2001), 33–43.

7 See Siegfried Zielinski, "Audiovisuelle Zeitmaschine: Thesen zur Kulturtechnik des Videorecorders," in *Video—Apparat/Medium, Kunst, Kultur: Ein internationaler Reader*, ed. Siegfried Zielinski (Frankfurt am Main, Peter Lang, 1992), 91–114, as well as Zielinski, "Der Videorecorder als Eingreif-Maschine: Vorschläge zur besseren Verwendung des Apparates," in *Kabelhafte Perspektiven: Wer hat Angst vor neuen Medien? Eine Anthologie*, ed. Klaus Modick and Matthias-J. Fischer (Hamburg: Nautilus/Nemo Press, 1984), 98–105.

8 Regarding scene selection in horror films see Arno Meteling, "Wundfabrikation: Pornografische Techniken des Splatterfilms," in *F.LM* 1 (2003), 4–14. Further defined in Arno Meteling, *Monster: Zu Körperlichkeit und Medialität im modernen Horrorfilm* (Bielefeld, transcript, 2006), 98ff.

9 However, it is unlikely that the stop button played a similar role to what it did for the reception of horror films, as the frozen image that the stop button revealed in a pornographic film could be obtained by other means. The attraction of pornography was in the ability to manipulate and consume moving images.

10 See Stefan Höltgen, "Take a Closer Look: Filmische Strategien der Annäherung des Blicks an die Wunde," in *Splatter Movies: Essays zum modernen Horrorfilm*, ed. Julia Köhne, Ralph Kuschke, and Arno Meteling (Berlin: Bertz + Fischer, 2005), 20–8.

11 See Marcus Stiglegger, "Einblicke: Neugier auf das 'Innere des Anderen,'" in ibid., 127–38.

12 Conversely, it is conceivable that the disgust associated with horror films would also be evoked by pornographic images.

13 The interest in special effects, which peaked repeatedly in the 1980s, and their inclusion in films, links horror films to action films. One could say that both genres create a new cinema based on special effects, which in the eyes of critics didn't offer much more than the visual appeal of new visual worlds. On the film-historical concept of the cinema of attractions, see Tom Gunning, "The Cinema of Attractions: Early Film, Its Spectator and the Avant-Garde," in *Early Cinema: Space—Frame—Narrative*, ed. Thomas Elsaesser (London: BFI Publishing, 1990), 56–62.

14 See Thomas Klein, "Fleisch und Haut, Maske und Special Effect: Zur filmischen Ikonographie des versehrten Körpers," in *Bildtheorie und Film*, ed. Thomas Koebner and Thomas Meder in association with Fabienne Liptay (Munich: Edition Text + Kritik, 2006), 544–55.

Degraded Images, Distorted Sounds: Nigerian Video and the Infrastructure of Piracy (2004)

Brian Larkin

In Kano, the economic center of northern Nigeria, media piracy is part of the "organizational architecture" of globalization,[1] providing the infrastructure that allows media goods to circulate. Infrastructures organize the construction of buildings, the training of personnel, the building of railway lines, and the elaboration of juridicolegal frameworks without which the movement of goods and people cannot occur. But once in place, infrastructures generate possibilities for their own corruption and parasitism. Media piracy is one example of this in operation. It represents the potential of technologies of reproduction—the supple ability to store, reproduce, and retrieve data—when shorn from the legal frameworks that limit their application. It depends heavily on the flow of media from official, highly regulated forms of trade but then develops its own structures of reproduction and distribution external and internal to the state economy.

It is through this generative quality that pirate infrastructure is expressive of a paradigmatic shift in Nigerian economy and capital and represents the extension of a logic of privatization into everyday life. Piracy's negative characteristics are often commented on: its criminality, the erosion of property rights it entails, and its function as a pathology of information processing, parasitically derivative of legal media flows.[2] As important as these questions are, the structural focus on legal issues tends to obscure the mediating nature of infrastructure itself. In the Nigerian case, this is seen most strikingly in the rise of a new video industry that makes feature-length films directly for domestic video consumption.[3] This new industry has pioneered new film genres and generated an entirely novel mode of reproduction and distribution that uses the capital, equipment, personnel, and distribution networks of pirate media. These Nigerian videos are a legitimate media form that could not exist without the infrastructure created by its illegitimate double, pirate media. [. . .]

In addition to generating new economic networks, piracy, like all infrastructural modes, has distinct material qualities that influence the media that travel under its regime of reproduction. Piracy imposes particular conditions on the recording, transmission, and retrieval of data. Constant copying erodes data storage, degrading image and sound, overwhelming the signal of media content with the noise produced by the means of reproduction. Pirate videos are marked by blurred images and distorted sound, creating a material screen that filters audiences' engagement with media technologies and their senses of time, speed, space, and contemporaneity. In this way, piracy creates an aesthetic, a set of formal qualities that generates a particular sensorial experience of media marked by poor transmission, interference, and noise. [. . .]

By subjecting the material operation of piracy and its social consequences to scrutiny, it becomes clear that pirate infrastructure is a powerful mediating force that produces new modes of organizing sensory perception, time, space, and economic networks. [. . .]

The Corruption of Infrastructure

Piracy's success lies in its own infrastructural order that preys on the official distribution of globalized media, thus making it part of the corruption of infrastructure. By *corruption* I mean the pirating of a system's mode of communication—the viruses that attach to other kinds of official or recognized movement. Technological infrastructure creates material channels that organize the movement of energy, information, and economic and cultural goods between societies but at the same time creates possibilities for new actions. [. . .]

[P]iracy operates as a corruption of communications infrastructures that develops its own circuits of distribution using officially organized media. Films made in Hollywood and intended for distribution in an organized, domestic circuit are copied by pirates; sent to Asia or the Middle East, where they are subtitled; recopied in large numbers as videocassettes, video CDs (VCDs are the dominant technology for media storage in much of Asia), or DVDs; and then reshipped mainly within the developing world. In recent years, as Nigeria has become progressively disembedded from the official global economy (with the single exception of its oil industry), it has become ever more integrated into a parallel, unofficial world economy that reorients Nigeria toward new metropoles such as Dubai, Singapore, and Beirut (what AbdouMaliq Simone more broadly calls the "worlding of African cities"[4]). [. . .]

The success of Kano's cassette reproduction industry is grounded in three developments: First, in 1981, the Motion Pictures Association of America (MPAA) suspended the distribution of Hollywood films to Nigeria. This was in response to the seizure of MPAA assets by the Nigerian government in an attempt to indigenize the control of Nigerian companies. Second, the oil boom of the late 1970s boosted consumption, allowing for the mass dissemination of cassette-based technologies. Finally, the longstanding position of Kano at the apex of wide-ranging transnational trading networks facilitated the quick exploitation of these possibilities and the forging of a distribution network that stretches over northern Nigeria and beyond. The subsequent rise of piracy means that far from disappearing, Hollywood films have become available at a speed and volume as never before. [. . .]

Piracy

Piracy is an ambivalent phenomenon in countries like Nigeria. It is widely feared by indigenous film- and music makers as destructive of the small profits they make by way of intellectual property. It has had disastrous effects on indigenous music makers and contributes substantially to the erosion of the industry as a whole. Yet at the same time, many of these same people consume pirate media both privately and professionally. Piracy has made available to Nigerians a vast array of world media at a speed they could never imagine, hooking them up to the accelerated circuit of global media flows. Where cinema screens were once filled with outdated films from the United States or India, pirate media means that Nigerian audiences can watch films contemporaneously with audiences in New York or Bombay. Instead of being marginalized by official distribution networks, Nigerian consumers can now participate in the immediacy of an international consumer culture—but only through the mediating capacity of piracy.

Piracy is part of a so-called shadow (second, marginal, informal, black) economy existing in varying degrees beyond the law. It produces profits, but not for corporations, and provides no revenue for the state.[5] The second economy is untaxed and unmonitored and enjoys all of the benefits and precariousness of this location. Until recently, media infrastructures in Nigeria, from the construction of radio diffusion networks to the building of television stations, have usually been state-controlled and organized around the fundamental logic of providing publicity for the state—indeed, of representing its progressivist, developmentalist logic.[6] Piracy, by contrast, is based in unofficial, decentralized networks, and Nigerian video represents the migration of these networks into the mainstream. [. . .]

Ravi Sundaram argues that informal processes in Indian media ecology should be seen as a pirate modernity—a mode of incorporation into the economy that is disorganized, nonideological, and marked by mobility and innovation.[7] This formulation nicely captures the ambivalence of piracy, refusing the simple equation that piracy is an alternative or oppositional modernity (though there are elements of this in people's justification that pirate media goods redress economic inequalities between developed and underdeveloped countries). Piracy is nonideological in that it does not represent a self-conscious political opposition to capitalism—it is not a kind of tactical media.[8] But it is also worth stressing the high degree of formality that marks this "informal" world. A focus on the mobility, innovation, and provisionality of piracy elides the fact that pirate networks are highly organized and determinative of other sets of relations. [. . .] (Figure 10.2).

The Materiality of Piracy: Breakdown

[. . .] My interest in technological collapse [. . .] is not in extravagant spectacles like collapsing bridges or exploding space shuttles but in the small, ubiquitous experience of breakdown as a condition of technological existence. [. . .]

[T]he poor material infrastructure of Nigeria ensures that as the speed of Nigerian life increases, so too does the gap between *actual* and *potential* acceleration, between what technologies *can* do and what they *do* do. Thus, even as life speeds up, the experience of technological marginalization intensifies, and the gap between how fast society is moving and how fast it could move becomes a site of considerable political tension.

The poor condition of infrastructure and the ubiquity of breakdown bring about their corollary: repair as a cultural mode of existence for technology. This is a consequence of both poverty and innovation. Breakdown and repair structure the ability of subjects to use and be used by technologies and also these subjects' sense of time and place. The culture of repair rests on the experience of duration in the

Figure 10.2 Kofar Wambai market, Kano 2002. Photo: Brian Larkin.

everyday use of technology. Breakdown creates a temporal experience that has less to do with dizzying, real-time global integration than with waiting for email messages to open, machines to be repaired, or electricity to be restored. In Nigeria, all technologies are variously subject to a constant cycle of breakdown and repair; the promise of technological prosthesis is thwarted by the common experience of technological collapse. Each repair enforces another waiting period, an often frustrating experience of duration brought about by the technology of speed itself. The temporal experience of slowness comes as a consequence of speed-producing technologies, so that speed and acceleration, deceleration and stasis are relative, continually shifting states. [. . .]

Nigerian dealers in the legal and illegal reproduction of media record data on cheap tapes with low-quality machines. This information is retrieved for the most part through old VCRs, televisions, and cassette players marked by distortion and interference. Watching, say, Hollywood or Indian films on VCRs in Nigeria, where there is no official distribution of nonpirate media, means necessarily watching the dub of a dub of a dub. As the same dealers, using the same equipment and same blank cassettes, dub Hausa video films, the result is that the visual standard for pirate media remains in place. Pirated images have a hallucinogenic quality. Detail is destroyed as realist representation fades into pulsating, pure light. Facial features are smoothed away, colors are broken down into constituent tones, and bodies fade into one another. Reproduction takes its toll, degrading the image by injecting dropouts and bursts of fuzzy noise, breaking down dialogue into muddy, often inaudible sound. This distortion is often heard in the vibrating shrillness of the tape players used by *masu saida kaset*, itinerant cassette hawkers who travel around the city selling eclectic collections of music. [. . .]

This distortion affects many media in Nigeria. Film prints, for instance, arrive at the end of long, picaresque journeys that begin in the metropolitan cinematic centers of India or Europe and cross the cinema halls of many countries before reaching the Nigerian circuit. There, they are often shown until they literally fall apart. All are scratched and heavily damaged, full of surprising and lengthy jump cuts where film has stuck in the projector and burned. Although the image and sound of video are poor, Ghanaian video filmmaker Willy Akuffo has warned video makers against a nostalgia for the "quality" of film that forgets how terrible film prints actually were. As a former projectionist, he had to deal with repairing burned film and refixing previous repairs that the prints had accumulated on their journey to Africa.[9] Likewise, the quality of video projection, with its low-resolution, ghostly images, can be highly variable depending on the age and condition of the equipment. In the poorer cinemas that converted to video in the mid-1990s, there were terrible problems with tracking and inaudible sound. The projected image often filled only a portion of the cinema screen or would be distorted into an hourglass shape. At other times, the corners of the image vibrated as if the screen were a photograph peeling off.[10]

The infrastructure of reproduction, like most contemporary infrastructures in Nigeria, is marked by cheapness, faulty operation, and constant repair. "All data flows,"

Figure 10.3 Hausa Videos, shop window, Kano 2002. Photo: Brian Larkin.

the media theorist Friedrich Kittler reminds us, "must pass through the bottleneck of the signifier," and in so doing they are vulnerable to being "engulfed by the noise of the real."[11] The "real" here is precisely the fuzziness of cinematic images or the hissing of tape recorders—the noise produced by the medium of transmission itself as it encodes and disseminates data across space and time. Yuri Tsivian has termed this effect the "semiotics of interference" and has analyzed the operation of early Russian cinema, arguing that the physical conditions of media exhibition—scratches on the film and noise and vibrations from projectors—became part of the "message" of films themselves.[12] For Nigerians, the costs of consuming and producing world media require operating on the margins of technology. Distortion on an audiotape, like dropouts on a video or a slow connection to the Internet, are the material conditions of existence for media. While media infrastructure creates the reality of being ever more connected to a globalized world, it does so by emphasizing Nigerians' marginalization at the same time. Electricity blackouts, snowy television images, difficulties getting international phone lines, and distorted loudspeakers on cassette players all create a technological veil of semiotic distortion for Nigerians (Figure 10.3).

Conclusion

[. . .] In many places, piracy is the only means by which certain media—usually foreign—are available. And in countries like Nigeria, the technological constraints that fuel pirate media provide the industrial template through which other, nonpirate media are reproduced, disseminated, and consumed.

Piracy and the wider infrastructure of reproduction it has generated reveal the organization of contemporary Nigerian society. They show how the parallel economy has migrated onto center stage, overlapping and interpenetrating with the official economy, mixing legal and illegal regimes, uniting social actors, and organizing common networks. This infrastructure creates its own modes of spatiality, linking Nigeria into new economic and social networks. Piracy means that Nigerian media production and circulation no longer depend on the intervention of the state (colonial or postcolonial) but are captured by the logic of privatization and gradually extend over differing areas of social experience. [. . .]

From Brian Larkin, "Degraded Images, Distorted Sounds: Nigerian Video and the Infrastructure of Piracy," in *Public Culture* 16, no. 2 (Spring 2004), 289–310.

Notes

1 Saskia Sassen, ed., *Global Networks, Linked Cities* (New York: Routledge, 2002).
2 John Chesterman and Andy Lipman, *The Electronic Pirates: DIY Crimes of the Century* (London: Routledge, 1988); Rosemary J. Coombe, *The Cultural Life of*

Intellectual Properties: Authorship, Appropriation, and the Law (Durham, NC: Duke University Press, 1998).

3 See Brian Larkin, "Hausa Dramas and the Rise of Video Culture in Nigeria," in *Nigerian Video Films*, ed. Jonathan Haynes (Athens: Ohio University Center for International Studies, 2000); Haynes, *Nigerian Video Films*, passim; N. Frank Ukadike, "Images of the "Reel" Thing: African Video-films and the Emergence of a New Cultural Art," *Social Identities* 6 (2000), 243–61; Asonzeh F.-K. Ukah, "Advertising God: Nigerian Christian Video-films and the Power of Consumer Culture," *Journal of Religion in Africa* 33 (2003), 203–31.

4 AbdouMaliq Simone, "On the Worlding of African Cities," *African Studies Review* 44, no. 2 (2001), 15–41. See also Jean-François Bayart, Stephen Ellis, and Béatrice Hibou, *The Criminalization of the State in Africa* (Bloomington: Indiana University Press, 1999); Janet MacGaffey and Rémy Bazenguissa-Ganga, *Congo–Paris: Transnational Traders on the Margins of the Law* (Bloomington: Indiana University Press, 2000); Achille Mbembe, *On the Postcolony* (Berkeley: University of California Press, 2001).

5 Although, as Jonathan Haynes pointed out to me, governments do collect revenue through taxes on blank cassettes.

6 Larkin, "Hausa Dramas and the Rise of Video Culture in Nigeria."

7 Ravi Sundaram, "Recycling Modernity: Pirate Electronic Cultures in India," *Third Text* 47 (1999), 59–65.

8 David Garcia and Geert Lovink, "The ABC of Tactical Media," in *In the Public Domain: Sarai Reader 01*, ed. Sarai, the New Media Collective, and Society for Old and New Media (Delhi: Sarai, the New Media Initiative, 2001).

9 Birgit Meyer reminded me that Akuffo described this problem with poor film prints at a workshop organized by the International Study Commission of Media, Religion, and Culture (May 19–27, 2000, Accra, Ghana).

10 Yet despite these problems, cassettes remain the more popular medium in northern Nigeria. In January 2002, when I asked Hausa video filmmakers why they had not switched to video CDs to distribute their movies, they pointed out that the technology was not yet widely available in the north, in part because damage to a VCD could ruin the entire disc, while damage to a tape created only passing moments of fuzziness.

11 Friedrich Kittler, *Gramophone, Film, Typewriter* (Stanford, CA: Stanford University Press, 1999), 14.

12 Yuri Tsivian, *Early Cinema in Russia and Its Cultural Reception* (London: Routledge, 1994). James Ferguson makes an interesting but different argument on the role of "noise" in globalization. He focuses on the traffic in cultural meanings, arguing that cities are culturally "noisy" in that all sorts of forms of cultural flows clash and are available to urban dwellers. But Ferguson's (1999: 208) central question concerns "which of the bits floating in the swirl of events does any given social actor bear." James Ferguson, *Expectations of Modernity: Myths and Meanings of Urban Life on the Zambian Copperbelt* (Berkeley: University of California Press, 1999), 208.

The Other Within (1989)

Juan Downey

> *A Copernican revolution is at stake, in the sense that in some respects, ethnology until now has let primitive cultures revolve around Western civilization in a centripetal motion, so to speak. Political anthropology appears to have made it abundantly clear that a complete reversal of perspectives is necessary (insofar as there is the desire to engage in a discourse concerning archaic societies that conforms to their reality and not ours).*[1]

In his anarchist manifesto, *Society against the State*, Pierre Clastres states the need for a Copernican revolution in terms of race and culture. The Western tradition is not the earth around which the *Others*, namely, the Amerindian, the African, the Asian, and the Australian cultures should orbit.

One can conceive of a world where a diversity of cultures and races interact in harmony. The same way one can imagine our beings undivided, no part of the self is masked or denied. One can dream of a self like a wholesome, luminous sphere, inclusive of any *Other* within. Survival places us in relationship to the environment, both physical and social, while self-esteem places us indirect confrontation with ourselves.

For the purpose of survival and self-esteem, we place what is extrinsic to us in an inferior category. By calling it *Other* we exclude it from ourselves and imply, in terms of culture, a differentiation that states our own superiority. Here we can observe negative connotations deriving from the labeling as *Other* everything that is foreign, especially considering that what is foreign to us is the whole field of our own ignorance. In a similar manner we exclude parts of the self.

Naming the *Other* brings to mind cultural differentiations that might be understood as racist. It echoes around the earth and down the corridors of time with accents of cultural superiority and with insistence upon greater achievement based on technological values. Yet, what characterized culture is not only technological products, but aspects of the mind manifested through the sophistication of language and the abundance of mythology. While certain cultures are relatively indifferent to commodity production, the vastness of the repertoire of myths they enjoy, along with their abundance of linguistic resorts point to a far greater spiritual and linguistic wealth than cultures that are materially richer.

From the onset, my video work has been concerned with representing the self as *Other*. In my first work, the performance and installation *Three-Way Communication by Light* (1971), three performers sat in a triangular formation, each provided with a closed-circuit television system, a mirror, and a Super-8 projector with a film loop documenting the facial expressions of the two other performers. They spoke to each other spontaneously through a voice-carrying laser beam. Their faces were painted white, and onto each face was projected a film of another performer's face, so that they exchanged physical appearances, which they could observe in the mirror as the audience watched all three on closed-circuit televisions. The video camera, being less sensitive than the human eye, blurred the distinction between the real face and the one projected on the performers' face, thereby transforming the performers into each other. Smoke in the room caused everything to almost disappear, while the red laser triangle floated in the middle of the space, shining brilliantly.

Over ten years ago, I, along with my wife and step-daughter, lived for eight consecutive months with the Yanomami Indians of the Upper Orinoco region of Venezuela (population 15,000). This experience is presented in *The Laughing Alligator* (1978).[2] Rather than an overview of the Yanomami culture, it is a documentary parody of Western modes of anthropology where the *primitive*, the *untamed*, that is, the *Other*, appears as a number of threats that a Western family confronts. Thus, the video intentionally mimics ethnography, and the social sciences, in its pretended objectivity, along with the Western narrative structure of melodrama, the backbone of television. The audience is invited to identify with the protagonists, my family, as we are exposed to a number of dangers: the violence of the primitive, of *abnormal sex*, and of the abuse of drugs. While Westerners accuse the primitives of these abominations, they are chiefly the sins of Westerners in their territories, and are primarily Western colonial ideas.

The Yanomami Indians of the Amazon rainforest are an example of a culture rich in myths and linguistic sophistication. Language research was not my intention when videotaping the Yanomami. Nevertheless, I studied their language and functioned adequately in daily life. They can, for example, express in a single plural noun a process that has ended though causing a process that is ongoing. *Hiki no mihou* describes how one falling tree will cause others to fall in a domino effect as it is used in deforestation.[3]

Other examples of the linguistic skill of the Yanomami are the single verbal forms that define the spatial characteristics of the action described. The size of objects and placement or location are both conveyed in an individual tense. In other words, a verb can accurately define the size and height of the objects involved in the action to which it refers. (This information was observed by a French linguist living in Caracas, I believe her name was Dr. Miller.) Nobody can argue that the languages of Greco-Roman antiquity ever attained such precision and economy.

Although *The Laughing Alligator* narrates some Yanomami myths and describes their lifestyle, it is unlike conventional documentary of that tribe, as it documents the interaction between a Western family and the Yanomami. It is focused on Westerners seeing the *Other*, as it exposes anthropological accounts of other ways of life as fictions, a colonial approach. The video explores how the *Self* and the *Other* might never succeed in a cultural exchange.

The fiction of violence is probed in a sequence of threats. As soon as I arrived in Yanomami territory, I discovered that the violence of the Yanomami is a projection of the Western culture. In the video, the camera is directed toward the Yanomami and toward my family. My appearance changes drastically over the course of this video; from one of wearing glasses, a moustache, a suit and tie, to one without glasses, or moustache, and donning a Yanomami haircut and Amazonian make-up covering half of my face.

In my suit-and-tie appearance, I am giving the authoritarian account of the dangerous Yanomami, and of violence among primitive people, a classic Western fiction. Later in the tape, while wearing face paint and a Yanomami haircut, I speak about the video and sound equipment and, finally, show the Indians playfully enjoying the Portapak and monitor. They point the camera at each other and gather to see themselves on the monitor. The Yanomami call photography, film, and video *Noreshi Towai*: literally to swallow that part of the spirit, which is any shadow or water reflection. Among these people, any shadow or reflection of a person is considered to be an important part of the spirit called *Noreshi*.[4]

For these rain-forest people, the *Self* is considered to be a complex assembly of interlocking spiritual entities. For instance, the plant where the placenta is buried at the birth of a person by the mother is very often connected to the name of that person. The name of a person itself is so interwoven with the notion of the *Self* that it is kept a secret, to be uttered exclusively in private, and always respectfully. The Yanomami function in the real world with nicknames, so as to protect that part of the self that is resonant in the actual name. Consequently, naming a person is placing that person in a vulnerable position. When a person dies, that name is never uttered again. Naming someone's deceased relative is viewed as an act of aggression.

In Yanomami society, the notion of the *Self* already implies a diversity, not only of spiritual principles, but also of physical manifestation. There is an animal in the forest that is a mirror replica of each Yanomami. Since birth, each Yanomami individual is inhabited by the spirit of that animal. They grow and live coupled, without ever seeing each other till the moment of death, when all of the forms of the individual spirit—the shadow, the name, the animal, etc.—meet and coalesce into one self that will live eternally. If any of the parts of the self are missing, that individual Yanomami will have a hard time during his or her life after death. This numerous assortment of diverse metaphors for the self accommodates the rich spectrum of manifestations that the spirit of an individual might have.

By shooting videotape with the Yanomami, I learned how limited my manner of framing reality was. I realized I was preconditioned by notions of composition based on the narrow and shallow vantage of one-point perspective. When a Yanomami used the camera, he or she tended to point it about the head, to allow what seemed to me excessive room over the head, or to one side. This roomy manner of framing seemed to reflect a desire to encompass other manifestations of the self being portrayed, as if next to the image of a person resided other parts of that being. It was through understanding the Yanomami way of framing that I was able to recognize my own. [. . .]

From Juan Downey, "The Other Within," transcription of a paper delivered during the Rockefeller Foundation Conference, Bellagio 1989; published in *Juan Downey: 1940–1993*, ed. Julieta González and Javier Rivero Ramos (Versalles: Ediciones MP, 2019), 425–30.

Notes

1 Pierre Clastres, *La société contre l'état* (Paris: Editions de Minuit, 1974), 23. [Downey quotes the French original; English translation from Clastres, Society against the State, trans. Robert Hurley (New York: Zone Books, 1989), 25.]
2 [As Downey explains later in the text: "*Video Trans Americas* is the name of a body of works that includes drawings, installations, and videotapes. Among them is *The Laughing Alligator*."]
3 Jaques Lizot, *Diccionario Yanomami-Espanol*, trans. Roberto Lizarralde (Caracas: Universidad Central de Venezuela, 1974), 25.
4 [Downey gives a detailed account of his video interaction with the Yanomami in *Noreshi Towai*, Video Guide #33, Vancouver, May 1985, 6–7.]

Defiant Images: The Kayapo Appropriation of Video (1992)

Terence Turner

Introduction: Kayapo Video in the Context of "Indigenous Media"

The global expansion of telecommunications, coupled with the availability of new and cheap forms of audiovisual media, above all video recording, have given rise within the past decade to an unprecedented phenomenon: the appropriation and use of the new technologies by indigenous peoples for their own ends. The peoples most involved in this development have been among those most culturally and technologically distant from the West: Australian Aborigines, Canadian Inuit, and Amazonian Indians. Among the latter, the Kayapo provide perhaps the most striking and varied examples of the indigenous use of video.

The use of video and other visual media such as television broadcasting by indigenous peoples differs in a number of ways from the making of ethnographic films or videos by anthropologists or other nonindigenous Persons. [. . .] Faye Ginsburg, in the only general theoretical discussions of indigenous media thus far to appear, has noted that the appropriation of visual media by indigenous peoples typically occurs in the context of movements for self-determination and resistance, and that their use of video cameras tends to be "both assertive and conservative of identity," focusing both on the documentation of conflicts with or claims against the national society and the recording of traditional culture.[1] She makes the important point that in contrast to an earlier generation of anthropological filmmakers but in convergence with the work of contemporary filmmakers like Asch, the MacDougalls, Kildea, Preloran, Rouch, and others, indigenous cultural self-documentation tends to focus not on the retrieval of an idealized vision of precontact culture but on "processes of identity construction" in the cultural present.[2] Here, indigenous videomakers converge significantly with tendencies in Western cultural theory such as the work of Stuart Hall and the Cultural Studies group, which rejects the notion of "authenticity" as applied to an idealized conception of "traditional" culture and emphasizes the ongoing production of ethnic, cultural, and subcultural identity through the construction of "hybrid" representations, combining aspects of mass culture and technology with more traditional elements.[3] [. . .]

As I proceed it will be necessary to emphasize a number of differences between the sorts of mediation going on in indigenous, or at any rate Kayapo, media and those involved in ethnographic film and video.

Social Effects of Indigenous Media in Indigenous Communities

One major difference concerns the act of video-making itself. As video takes on political and social importance in an indigenous community, which member of the community assumes the role of video cameraperson, and who makes the prestigious journey to the alien city where the editing facilities are located, become issues fraught with social and political significance, and consequently, social and political conflicts.

I have been surprised by how little this fundamental point crops up in the literature or in presentations at film festival or discussions at conferences. It is common to hear those involved in indigenous film and video, indigenous persons and sympathetic non-indigenes alike, proclaim that the guiding principle of their work is the integral vision of the interconnectedness of all things inherent in Amerindian, or as the case may be, Aboriginal or Inuit cultures. Yet few of these same eloquent evocations of the spiritual interconnectedness of the whole are accompanied by any reference to the effects of the activities of the film- or videomakers upon the communities in which they worked (in some instances, their own). Few reflect upon the possible effects of an objectifying medium like film or video on the social or cultural consciousness of the people filmed (Michaels again being perhaps the most notable exception[4]). Few discuss who ends up owning or controlling access to the films or videos at the community level.

These may seem petty issues with no connection to the grander issues of theory and politics normally addressed in the anthropological and media literature; but they are often the channels through which an indigenous community translates the wider political, cultural, and aesthetic meanings of media such as video into its own local personal and social terms. They can have cumulatively important effects on the internal politics of a community and the careers of individuals. It is especially important for non-indigenous people working in the field of indigenous media to pay attention to this level of phenomena and to try to make allowance for the specific effects their projects or support may have in the communities where they work.

Among the Kayapo, for example, becoming a video cameraperson, and even more importantly, a video editor, has meant combining a prestigious role within the community with a culturally and politically important form of mediation of relations with Western society. As a combination of the two main prerequisites for political leadership in contemporary Kayapo communities, it has been one way that people have promoted their political careers. Several of the current group of younger chiefs acted as video camerapersons during their rise to chieftainship, and a number of the more ambitious younger men have taken up video at least in part in the hope of following in their footsteps.

My general point is simply this: an outsider attempting to facilitate the use of video by a community, either for political or research purposes, by donating a camera or arranging access to editing facilities, quickly finds that she or he does not escape the invidious implications and responsibilities of "intervention" simply through handing over the camera to "them." Precisely whom she/he hands it to can become a very touchy question, and may involve consequences for which the researcher bears inescapable responsibility. The act of video-making itself, when done by an indigenous person or member of a local community, begins to "mediate" a variety of social and political relationships within the indigenous community in a way that has no exact parallel when the videomaker is an outsider, as is the usual case in documentary and anthropological film and video-making.

There is a complementary side to this point, which is that for a people like the Kayapo, the act of shooting with a video camera can become an even more important mediator of their relations with the dominant Western culture than the video document itself. One of the most successful aspects of the series of dramatic Kayapo political demonstrations and encounters with the Brazilians (and other representatives of the Western World system such as the World Bank and Granada Television) has been the Kayapo's ostentatious use of their own video cameras to record the same events being filmed by representatives of the national and international media, thus ensuring that their camerapersons would be one of the main attractions filmed by the other crews. The success of this ploy is attested by the number of pictures of Kayapo pointing video cameras that have appeared in the international press. The Kayapo, in short, quickly made the transition from seeing video as a means of recording events to seeing it as an event to be recorded. [. . .]

Editing

Between 1985, when they obtained their first video camera, and 1990, Kayapo video capability remained at the "home movie" level. Their original video tapes rapidly deteriorated under village conditions, as they had no way of copying or storing them in a safe place. They also had no training in editing and no access to editing facilities. In 1990, with a grant from the Spencer Foundation, I started the Kayapo Video Project to supply these needs, with the cooperation of the Centro de Trabalho Indigenista of Sao Paulo, which made available their editing studio and technicians to train Kayapo in editing, and their video storage space for a Kayapo Video Archive for original videos and edited masters. [. . .]

[F]or the Kayapo, even for accomplished Kayapo video editors, the difference between a fully edited and an unedited video is not yet culturally significant for many purposes. The Kayapo are happy to watch unedited "home movies" as well as the beautifully edited work now being turned out by some of their videomakers. Most of the Kayapo videos thus far have been of cultural performances such as rituals or political meetings which form natural narrative units, with self-defined boundaries and sequential order. Both in camerawork and editing, Kayapo have spontaneously tended to use technically simple long shots, slow cuts, and alternating panoramics and middle-range close-ups, while avoiding extreme close-ups of the face. [. . .]

Cultural Schemas and the Production of the Image

The sort of cultural "mediation" effected by indigenous video is also different from that effected by ethnographic film or video for another important reason: an indigenous videomaker operates with the same set of cultural categories, notions of representation, principles of mimesis, and aesthetic values and notions of what is socially and politically important as those whose actions he or she is recording. Worth and Adair, in their early project on Navajo filmmaking, were the first to realize the potential significance of indigenous film making in this respect.[5] The indigenous filmmaker's employment of his/her own cultural categories in the production of the video may reveal their essential character more clearly than the completed video text itself. This is true above all in one respect of great theoretical importance: as schemas guiding the making of the video, cultural categories appear in their essential social character as forms of activity rather than as static textual structures or tropes. [. . .]

The Kayapo do not regard video documentation merely as a passive recording or reflection of already existing facts, but rather as helping to establish the facts it records. It has, in other words, a performative function. Political acts and events which in the normal run of Kayapo political life would remain relatively contingent and reversible, the subjective assertions or claims of one individual or group remaining open to challenge by other groups with different objectives or interpretations (for example, a young leader's claims to chiefly authority), can be rendered by video in the form of objective public realities. The representation of transient events in a medium like video, with its capacity to fix the image of an event and to store it permanently in a form that can circulate in the public domain, objectively accessible to all in exactly the same way, make it a potent means of conferring upon private and contingent acts the character of established public facts. The properties of the medium itself may in this way be seen to confer a different kind of social reality on events than they would otherwise possess.

Here, then, is another way in which the mediation of social reality by indigenous media may involve different cultural and conceptual mediations than in the case of ethnographic film. The medium mediates its own properties as a permanent, objective, publicly circulating representation to the indigenous culture's consciousness of social reality. The Kayapo *penchant* for using video not only to document historic encounters with Brazilian state power but internal political events as well, such as meetings of chiefs or the founding of a new village, may be understood in part as an attempt to infuse these events with the more potent facticity and historical permanence conferred on Western political events by Western telemedia. The notion of an objectively determined social Reality permanently fixed by public documents, which many nonliterate societies first acquired through the medium of writing, has come to the Kayapo and some other contemporary nonliterate peoples through the medium of video. To this extent, it seems fair to say that video has contributed to a transformation of Kayapo social consciousness, both in the sense of promoting a more objectified notion of social reality and of heightening their sense of their own agency by providing them with a means of active control over the process of objectification itself: the video camera. [. . .]

Working with the production of indigenous visual media, observing the techniques of camera work and editing, and also the social activities and relations through which videos are made, used and controlled, provides an opportunity to study the social production of representations rarely approached in nonvisual ethnography, and different again from the insights afforded by ethnographic film. I would suggest that approaching the study of cultural categories in this way can be a salutary corrective to the historic bias of the discipline, inherited from both Durkheimian and Anglo-American positivism, toward conceiving of categories only in the static form of classification or collective representations, and not in the active form of schemas for producing classes or representations.

A theoretical approach of this kind, as I have further suggested, is not inherently opposed to or exclusive of a political approach to supporting indigenous media as a means of indigenous empowerment and self-conscientization. My own involvement with Kayapo media started as a politically motivated effort along these lines, rather than from theoretical premises. I have found, however, that working to promote political empowerment through media has converged both conceptually and practically with the theoretical interests of many visual anthropologists in image production and the role of media (particularly indigenous) as mediators of social and political activity.

From Terence Turner, "Defiant Images: The Kayapo Appropriation of Video," in *Anthropology Today* 8, no. 6 (December 1992), 5–16.

Notes

1 Faye Ginsburg, "Indigenous Media: Faustian Contract or Global Village?" *Cultural Anthropology* 6, no. 1 (February 1991), 92–112; Ginsburg, "Mediating Culture: Indigenous Media, Ethnographic Film, and the Production of Identity," in *Fields of Vision*, ed. Leslie Deveraux and Roger Hillman (Berkeley: University of California Press, 1995), 256–90.

2 Ginsburg, "Mediating Culture."

3 Stuart Hall, "Cultural Identity and Diaspora," in *Identity, Community, Culture, Difference*, ed. Jonathan Rutherford (London: Lawrence and Wishart, 1990), 222–37; Hall, "Cultural Studies and Its Theoretical Legacies," in *Cultural Studies*, ed. Lawrence Grossberg, Cary Nelson, and Paula Treichler (New York: Routledge, 1992), 227–94.

4 See e.g. Eric Michaels, "The Social Organization of an Aboriginal Video Workplace," *Australian Aboriginal Studies* I (1984), 26–34.

5 [Sol Worth, John Adair, and Richard Chalfen taught documentary filmmaking to a group of Navajo in Arizona 1966. See Worth and Adair, *Through Navajo Eyes: An Exploration of Film Communication and Anthropology* (Bloomington: University of Indiana Press, 1972).]

Decolonizing the Technologies of Knowledge: Video and Indigenous Epistemology (2003)

Freya Schiwy

The colonialist burden of the geopolitics of knowledge invokes a hegemonic structure of thinking that constructs the North as the source of theoretical knowledge, while the so-called Third and Fourth Worlds appear to produce culture, or, in the best of cases, "local knowledge." Parallel to this epistemological division, technology—industrial, representational, genetic, informational, etc.—seems to originate from the developed states of the North. Aníbal Quijano and Walter Mignolo have argued that the processes of colonization caused if not their disappearance, then the subalternization of Indigenous techniques of representation and epistemic articulation.[1] Corresponding to this colonialist geopolitical division of intellectual labor, when Indigenous organizations employ the audiovisual medium they are commonly considered oral cultures using a western technology.[2]

Nevertheless, in Bolivia, Ecuador, and Colombia, Canada, the USA, in fact, in almost all of the Americas, as well as Australia, communication and representation processes on the basis of video and the Internet testify to optimism about new technologies; an optimism shared by Indigenous activists and visual anthropologists such as Faye Ginsburg and Terence Turner.[3] This optimism is generally based on two fundamental observations: first, that video permits decentralized communication and representation; second, that the medium enables liberation from the requirements of literacy and state education. However, others such as James Weiner, Stanley Aronowitz, Teresa de Lauretis, and Catherine Russell insist that technology is not neutral and that it produces involuntary effects.[4] They agree that video inscribes a particular logic of production. Having emerged in capitalist, colonial, and patriarchal contexts, audiovisual media carry the burden of a colonial geopolitics of knowledge. This obviously impacts the way we think about the Indigenous appropriation of video. The colonial burden of technology also concerns the efforts of Indigenous individuals and organizations to make use of literary *testimonio* as well as academic discourse and its institutions. This, ultimately, also has to do with the notion of cultural studies. Do cultural studies want to deepen the division between theory and its object or point to the relations of power and colonialism inherent in our own modes of thinking? Doesn't the latter require a more profound questioning of the technology and contexts of academic production? Indigenous video offers, I think, a provocative perspective in this respect.

The interventions of film theorists allude to the logic of subalternity. That is, to enter into discourse, or, by extension, into the technological or representational medium, is to confront structures of comprehension. That which does not enter into this logic of contestation, that which does not make itself available for any means of interpellation, cannot be comprehended, made intelligible, or effective.[5] This logic of subalternity has a double consequence. It prescribes the critical act as a subversion of the existing codes, and simultaneously affirms these codes as a focal point. For film the solution becomes revealing fetishistic meanings in the composition of shots and the duration of takes, an aesthetic strategy in opposition to both Hollywood and conventional ethnographic documentaries. The majority of Indigenous media productions, however, are not experimental in this sense. They avoid confrontation with hegemonic cinematic codes, and unlike literary *testimonio*, resist incorporation into the university's academic curriculum. Yet Indigenous video activists demand the decolonization of the medium and of the geopolitics of knowledge.[6] How should we understand this? Perhaps it is necessary to take a step back and ask: What do we want to say when we speak about technology and its relation to knowledge? Are technologies the result of particular desires of knowing or is the production of knowledge dependent on its technological tools? Is it necessary or useful to distinguish between *techne* and *techné*, that is, between instruments of knowledge and their creative uses? [. . .]

As if responding to Stanley Aronowitz, who asserted in 1979 that cinema is the art form of late capitalism, Indigenous video makers have transformed the film production and distribution process, albeit in ways that differ from the anti-colonialist, testimonial, and militant filmmaking of the 1960s and '70s.

First, like the efforts of New Latin American Cinema, the labor of making video is collective and nonspecialized; but the emphasis is on converting Indigenous communities into protagonists. They now use the camera, work on scripts, define visual strategies, audio soundtracks, themes, and analyses. As the *Manual para facilitadores audiovisuales indígenas* (the manual for Indigenous audiovisual facilitators), published by CEFREC-CAIB in Bolivia,[7] states: "The objective of community self-diagnosis is that the community itself creates a hierarchy of cultural problems and their solutions, that is, that the main decisions are made in and from community itself, through consensus."[8]

There are variations in how communities are integrated into the production group's discussion processes. They are sensitive to the cultural differences among distinct Indigenous contexts. Likewise the ownership and distribution of the videos is conceived in different ways, following practices of exchange that differ in the mountains and the low lands. The Moxeña videomaker Julia Mosúa refers to a still unresolved debate about the ownership of images that communities believe to be their own, a product of what is effectively their unpaid labor of image production. Alfredo Copa from the Potosí area, on the other hand, explains that his community considers the images obtained from it as property of CEFREC-CAIB, that is, of the producers. The filmmaking affirms a reciprocal relationship between himself as media activist and his community. This relation extends beyond the filmmaking itself. Copa is asked to offer his knowledge, manual and intellectual services based on the needs of the community.[9] These notions of reciprocity and personal relationships also guide the exchange with the Spanish donors that finance CEFREC-CAIB's work in Bolivia, as well as with other, if very limited, international distribution contacts.

What I am interested in emphasizing here is that CEFREC-CAIB move away from a socialist logic of production and consumption. Rather, they inscribe audiovisual technology into Indigenous notions of property and exchange, which include future responsibilities in relation to their communities. This rearticulation of the technology transforms the idea of film as a free market commodity (the fetish that is liberated from human labor and production context). Video is contextualized within Indigenous relations that implicate the market but differ from socioeconomic relations informed by neoliberal capitalism. They oppose the global economic structures of inequality that Fernando Coronil has characterized as "globocentrism."[10] CEFREC-CAIB demand instead a culture of reciprocity and responsibility derived from long histories of living on the border with capitalism.[11] This subversion of the neoliberal market goes beyond the logic of subalternity. CEFREC-CAIB change the focus by thinking from what Mignolo has called "the colonial difference,"[12] that is, the process of video production and distribution modifies capitalism and grounds relations of exchange in Indigenous economic practices. [. . .]

When Aronowitz spoke of cinema as the paradigmatic art form of late capitalism, he wasn't referring only to the need to wrest the medium from its industrial anchors and for-profit interests.[13]

Like militant cinematographers in the 1960s, Aronowitz implied a need to call attention to the artifice of cinema, to jolt viewers and thus call their attention to the way that cinema, like consumer goods, hides the forms of labor that goes into its making. Critics of Indigenous media have alleged that because of the way cinema is apparently embedded in Western consumer culture, it can only detrimentally change noncapitalist, Indigenous cultures. Such a position, nevertheless, denies the history of colonialism and capitalism, which has long affected Indigenous peoples, along with the way cinema itself is deeply linked to Eurocentric constructions of Self and Other.

Although not experimental in an obvious way, the vast majority of CEFREC-CAIB's videos reclaim Indigenous oral, visual, textile, performative epistemic traditions—frequently more readily associated with female cultural practices—in indirect ways, even as they dialogue with mainstream cinematic genres and forms. Significantly, this appropriation and adaptation of the audiovisual medium to an Indigenous politics of knowledge implies a challenge to Indigenous patriarchy, to the way technology tends to be in the hands of men (both in Indigenous and non-Indigenous contexts) and to the way knowledge production in the West and North has long been associated with masculinity, rationality, objectivity, etc., conceptualized as in opposition to the body, the feminine, nature, and Indigenous people.

Even though CEFREC-CAIB's videos do not totally detach themselves from the link between Indigenous masculine-centric traditions and the modern/colonial gender imaginary, they are able to interrupt part of the separation between technology and its use. First, they explode the idea of mediation since any type of semiotic act implies as much the production of a reality as the discursive definition of it; second, they reclaim traditional semiotic-communicative media in Indigenous societies (both from the high lands and the jungle). Video emerges from this process as a logical extension of Indigenous intellectual capacities and of Indigenous epistemic technologies. They collapse as such the division between *techne* and *techné* by transforming not only the use or the form of the technological product, but the definition of the technology itself.

Of course, by using a medium that liberates video makers and viewers from alphabetic writing, monolingualism, and the requirements of schooling, Indigenous media activists and their audiences also forge international contacts. The video is converted into a new type of epistemic tool that dissociates alphabetic writing from its hegemonic position. At the same time, it undermines the division between orality and writing and dismantles the internal colonialism that would imagine the illiterate "Indian."

One of the effects of this process is the distinction it draws between cultural discourse and theoretical reflection. It challenges us as academics to further investigate the colonial legacies that affect academic production, the distinction between writing and orality, and the relation we have with our supposed objects of study. If as academics we want to understand this thinking environment without reproducing the colonial gesture—the objectification of culture as opposed to theoretical reflection—we still need an understanding of the decolonization process and the consequences that it has for our teaching and theoretical production. We cannot be content with transmitting knowledge for the benefit of the subaltern—even if this knowledge now emerges from the field of cultural studies—but rather must break the very reproduction of the hegemony-subalternity dynamic.

From Freya Schiwy: "Descolonizar Las Tecnologías del Conocimiento: Video y Epistemología Indígena," in *Estudios Culturales Latinoamericanos: Retos Desde y Sobre La Región Andina*, ed. Catherine Walsh (Quito: Universidad Andina Simon Bolivar and Ediciones Abya Yala, 2003); English version "Decolonizing the Technologies of Knowledge: Video and Indigenous Epistemology," trans. Dalida María Benfield, Tara Daly, and Freya Schiwy, online at https://www.academia.edu/42204048/DECOLONIZING_THE_TECHNOLOGIES_OF_KNOWLEDGE_VIDEO_AND_INDIGENOUS_EPISTEMOLOGY. Revised for the present publication by the author.

Notes

1 See Aníbal Quijano. "Colonialidad del poder, cultura y conocimiento en América Latina," *Anuario mariateguiano* (Lima) 9, no. 9 (1997), 113–21; Walter Mignolo, "Afterword: Writing," in *Alternative Literacies*, ed. Walter Mignolo and Elizabeth Hill Boone (Durham, NC: Duke University Press, 1994); Walter D. Mignolo, *The Darker Side of the Renaissance: Literacy, Territoriality and Colonization* (Ann Arbor: University of Michigan Press, 1995).

2 See Adolfo Colombres, "El cine y los medios audiovisuales como sustrato de una nueva oralidad de los pueblos indígenas," *Casa de las Américas* (La Habana) 35, no. 199 (1995), 97–103.

3 See Faye Ginsburg, "Embedded Aesthetics: Creating a Discursive Space for Indigenous Media," in *Cultural Anthropology* (Arlington, VA) 9, no. 3 (1994), 365–82; Ginsburg, "The Parallax Effect: The Impact of Aboriginal Media on Ethnographic Film," in *Visual Anthropology Review* (Charlottesville, VA) 11, no. 2 (1995), 64–76; Terence Turner, "The Social Dynamics of Video Media in an Indigenous Society: The Cultural Meaning and the Personal Politics of Video-Making in Kayapo Communities," *Visual Anthropology Review* 7, no. 2 (1991), 68–76; Turner, "Visual Media, Cultural Politics and Anthropological Practice," in *The Independent* (New York), January/February 1991.

4 See James F. Weiner, "Televisualist Anthropology: Representation, Aesthetics, Politics," in *Current Anthropology* 38, no. 2 (1997), 197–235; Stanley Aronowitz, "Film: The Art Form of Late Capitalism," in *Social Text* no. 1 (1979), 110–29; Teresa de Lauretis, *Alice Doesn't* (Bloomington: Indiana University Press, 1981); Catherine Russell, *Experimental Ethnography* (Durham, NC: Duke University Press, 1999).

5 This is the principal argument of postcolonial thinkers like Spivak and the Indian Subaltern Studies Group. See, for example, Gayatry Chakravorty Spivak, "Can the Subaltern Speak?" (1988), in *Colonial Discourse and Post-Colonial Theory: A Reader*, ed. Patrick Williams and Laura Chrisman (New York: Columbia University Press, 1994), 66–111; Ranajit Guha, "The Prose of Counter-Insurgency," in *Selected Subaltern Studies Reader*, ed. Ranajit Guha and Gayatri Chakravorty Spivak (New York: Oxford University Press, 1988), 45–86; Dipesh Chakrabarty, "Provincializing Europe: Postcoloniality and the Critique of History," *Cultural Studies* 6, no. 3 (1991), 337–57.

6 *La Otra Mirada* (1999), documentary, 15 min., color, Spanish, prod. CEFREC-CAIB (La Paz).

7 CEFREC (Centro de Formación y Realización Cinematográfica) has collaborated with diverse Indigenous communities in training audiovisual communicators since 1996. Members of CEFREC have also collaborated closely with CLACPI (Coordinadora Latinomericana del Cine y Video de los Pueblos Indígenas) in organizing video workshops throughout the hemisphere as well as organizing CLACPI's regular International Indigenous Film and Video Festivals. CAIB (Coordinadora Audiovisual Indígena Originaria Intercultural de Bolivia) is home to the Indigenous, First Nation, and Intercultural communicators who have been collaborating with CEFREC in multiple ways since the mid 1990s. For a recent ethnographic study of this collaboration see Gabriela Zamorano Villareal, *Indigenous Media and Political Imaginaries in Contemporary Bolivia* (Omaha: University of Nebraska Press, 2017).

8 Alcida Ramos, *Indigenismo: Red de comunicación intercultural. Manual para facilitadores audiovisuals indígenas* (La Paz: CEFREC/CAIB/CSUTCB/CSCB/CIDOB, 1996), 1.

9 See Julia Mosúa, Alfredo Copa, and Marcelino Pinto. "Entrevista con Daniel Flores," audiocasette, transcribed and edited version, *Bomb Magazine* 78 (2001), 30–5.

10 See Fernando Coronil, "Naturaleza del poscolonialism: Del eurocentrismo al globocentrismo," in *La colonialidad del saber: eurocentrismo y ciencias sociales*, ed. Edgardo Lander (Caracas: CLASCO/UNESCO, 2000).

11 See Brooke Larson, "Andean Communities, Political Cultures, and Markets: The Changing Contours of a Field," in *Ethnicity, Markets and Migration in the Andes: At the Crossroads of History and Anthropology*, ed. Brooke Larson and Olivia Harris with Enrique Tandeter (Durham: Duke University Press, 1995), 5–53.

12 Walter D. Mignolo, *Local Histories/Global Designs: Coloniality, Subaltern Knowledges and Border Thinking* (Princeton: Princeton University Press, 2000).

13 Aronowitz, "Film: The Art Form of Late Capitalism." For a more sustained discussion, see Freya Schiwy, Indianizing Film: Decolonization, the Andes, and the Question of Technology (New Brunswick: Rutgers University Press, 2009).

11

Surveillance | Exposure | Testimony | Forensics

Introduction by Dieter Daniels

The contributions presented in this chapter as key discursive examples span a broad range of disciplines, including philosophy, sociology, media theory, criminology, law, forensics, and social geography. They also concern surveillance studies, which have become an independent discipline since the 1990s, with extensive research literature and a specialist journal.[1] While the topic areas in Chapter 10 were separated with regard to geography and discipline, the following chapter connects interdisciplinary perspectives on the indexicality and temporality of video images.

The diverse uses of video discussed in the following are all nonfictional, which differentiates them from the narrative-fictional moving images in cinematography and "scripted" television programs (series, crime novels, music videos, etc.). The video image that appears on the video monitor as it is being captured differs fundamentally—technically as well as epistemically—from photochemical images in analog photography or film, which become visible only after development. In the video medium, the simultaneous visibility of the image during capturing and recording creates a new type of instantaneous indexicality. Different modes of this video-specific instantaneity have been compared in the introduction to this volume; the following chapter presents various contexts of their application (public, private, civil, military, etc.). Chapter 3 presents a related cross-section for the instantaneous self-image in the contexts of psychotherapy, media theory, and artists' video. In surveillance, control, and testimony, the instantaneous gaze is directed at others, especially others who do not see that they are being observed. The effects of such visual power structures embodied in video-based systems of instantaneous indexicality are eminently political.

In comparison with current nonvisual forms of dataveillance, video can be seen as a medium of transition between the photographic paradigm and the digital (de-) construction of visual indexicality. Several different modes of indexicality coexist in the video medium: the visual index as evidential value or control (surveillance), the investigative and legal endeavor to reveal the hidden index (forensics), the incidental capture of the index (testimony), the gendered game with the index (webcams), or the fake index simulated by AI (deepfake) come equally into play in the contributions presented below.

Technical Foundations from a Historical Perspective

From a media-archaeological perspective, the first concepts for television derived from electric live image transmission. At the end of the nineteenth century, a number of inventions were made, some of which were developed into patents, though none were technically feasible at the time. For example, Paul Nipkow's 1883 patent application for an "electric telescope" stated that "the purpose of the apparatus described here is to make an object at location A visible at any location B."[2] These inventions did not include the one-to-many broadcast or the recording of electric images. In analogy to telephony, these patents aimed at point-to-point "distant electric vision."[3] So far, these inventions of the late nineteenth century have been addressed mainly in the context of television history, yet they also offer new perspectives on the prehistory of video surveillance.

The history of ideas for surveillance based on the instant transmission of images therefore predates the advent of magnetic videotape recording. The most prominent example in literature is George Orwell's fiction *Nineteen Eighty-Four*, written in 1948, which unfurled a dystopian scenario of ubiquitous control.[4] In the novel, television is expanded into a two-way medium for around-the-clock visual and acoustic surveillance as well as for responding to commands from the omnipresent leader, "Big Brother," who appears regularly on the mandatory "telescreen" in every apartment. Telescreens are also used to distribute propaganda, news, and entertainment. Because the news are not available in print, telescreens are also part of the state's constant rewriting of history, in which Orwell's protagonist Winston Smith is professionally involved. In this respect, Orwell's concept of surveillance corresponds to the contemporary live status of television before the availability of video recording (see Chapter 4).[5]

Just a few years after Orwell's book, technical testing of electronic televisual surveillance began. In 1953, video cameras were installed in a prison in Houston, Texas, though only for centralized monitoring, that is, without the possibility to address the surveilled, as Orwell had imagined.[6] In Germany and Great Britain, video cameras were deployed in public spaces from 1956. The different scenarios for their use already correlated with the areas outlined by the contributions in this chapter. "In these early years, the public police cameras served three functions: the use of cameras in traffic management; the repressive use of cameras at demonstrations; and the persuasive use of the images," writes Dietmar Kammerer in a summary of the developments in Germany.[7] In England too, cameras were used for traffic control from 1956, both to regulate the flow of traffic and to increase safety in public transport.[8] And in the plot of Fritz Lang's last movie, *The Thousand Eyes of Dr. Mabuse* (1960), video surveillance serves the dystopian plans of a criminal.

The instant indexicality outlined earlier can therefore be seen as the first video-specific property to become a subject of public discussion even before the spread of visual magnetic tape-recording techniques. In this respect, the time frame for the topic area presented here is larger than in other chapters, ranging from the mid-1950s to current digital image processing and AI for face-recognition purposes.

Theoretical Foundations and Conceptual Developments

Michel Foucault's writings on what he termed the "panopticism" of modern disciplinary society are a common point of reference for theories of surveillance. However, the eighteenth-century architectural concept of Jeremy Bentham's Panopticon, to which Foucault explicitly refers, works without the support of technical media. Similarly, Foucault's theory does not explicitly address media surveillance. In addition, Bentham was committed to the spirit of the Enlightenment: the Panopticon, which was not implemented in the author's own lifetime, aimed at improving detention conditions in prisons and was supposedly suitable also for hospitals, psychiatric clinics, schools, and factories. Foucault's panopticism, on the contrary, pursues a critical analysis of such control mechanisms at the service of capitalism. According to Foucault, centralized surveillance systems lead to an internalization of control, and consequently self-control, of the surveilled: "Hence the major effect of the Panopticon: to induce in the inmate a state of conscious and permanent visibility that assures the automatic functioning of power."[9] Foucault goes on to argue that "he who is subjected to the field of visibility, and who knows it . . . inscribes in himself the power relation in which he simultaneously plays both roles; he becomes the principle of his own subjection."[10] Ultimately, Foucault's panopticism is closer to Orwell's dystopian novel than to Bentham's ideal architecture based on faith in progress. More specifically, Orwell's motif of "thought crime" can be read in analogy to Foucault's thesis of an internalization of control, even though Foucault does not mention television or video technology.

Foucault and the Panopticon hold a prominent place in surveillance studies. In the discourse, which is strongly influenced by social sciences, the media-technical aspects of surveillance are often only addressed in passing, and the specificity of video, as outlined here, is hardly taken into account. For example, in *Electronic Eye: The Rise of Surveillance Society* (1994), David Lyon cites Orwell and Foucault as his most important references and combines their approaches in his concept of an "electronic panopticon." Although the Panopticon, like the telescreens in *Nineteen Eighty-Four*, operates primarily on a visual level, Lyon, contrary to the expectations raised by the title of his book, hardly dwells on the specifics of visual surveillance. He speaks, for example, of the "ubiquitous digital 'gaze' of such computer systems" and amalgamates very different types of dataveillance and user data collection, the latter in reference to Mark Poster's "normalizing gaze of the Superpanopticon."[11] Lyon points out that Foucault ignores the importance of computers for his theory of panopticism.[12] Further critical assessments of Foucault's failure to account for media specificity can be found in the contributions by Thomas Mathiesen and Jonathan Rozenkrantz. Mathiesen introduces the concept of "Synopticon" as "enabling *the many to see and contemplate the few*."[13] He uses it to describe phenomena of celebrity (self-)exposure in the media, especially television. In contrast to Foucault's genealogy of an asymmetrical hierarchy of the gaze of the ruler on the ruled, Mathiesen argues that panopticism and synopticism have also historically developed "in intimate interaction, even fusion, with each other."[14] Rozenkrantz has coined the term "Autopticon" as an extension of Mathiesen's Synopticon concept to describe the phenomenon of self-observation and self-control associated with it. He notes several parallels between the use of video in psychotherapy and surveillance: "Autopticism appropriates and reconfigures both synoptic and panoptic functions. . . . and insofar as the aim of self-confrontation is to compel self-correction, autopticism perfects the panoptic dream of self-regulating subjectivation."[15] According to Rozenkrantz, the principle of the Autopticon is at play in reality TV, webcams, and social media.

Surveillance: Winfried Pauleit (Dietmar Kammerer), Stephen Graham (Clive Norris)

In comparison to the other applications of video discussed in this reader, video surveillance seems to reverse the general purpose of the medium. Here, video no longer serves the visual communication and public circulation of images but rather the—ideally unnoticed—capture of images that are often not even viewed. Or in the words of Dietmar Kammerer: "Video surveillance is to some extent an anti-mass-medium: it endeavors to convert the anonymous mass into a number of legible (criminal) elements."[16] The contributions in the section devoted to surveillance address the capture of images from the perspective of the observed; their equivalent from the perspective of the observer can be found in the contributions in the Forensics section.

The remarkably extensive and controversial literature on the topic of surveillance can only be reproduced here in a very shortened form.[17] To account at least to some extent for the interdisciplinary nature of the discourses, four authors, or rather disciplines, are presented, though only two feature in this reader with source texts. Film scholar Winfried Pauleit is interested in the time structures of surveillance; Dietmar Kammerer combines media theory with aspects of social science; Stephen Graham studies the social geography of surveillance infrastructures; and criminologist Clive Norris assesses their effectiveness.

Pauleit has coined the term "photographesomenon" to describe the immanent temporality of surveillance recordings. As a medium of prevention, the surveillance camera expands the previously mentioned instantaneity of video into an anticipatory dimension. Video surveillance is criminologically and politically directed toward the future, more specifically toward a future that is to be prevented. While photography, as Peter Geimer has pointed out, is open to contingency and nonintentionality, human as well as automated surveillance aims at the possibility of intervention in the object of the image, which has been filtered out of its contingent context. With reference to Paul Virilio, Kammerer explains that "computer vision" in surveillance cumulates into "a vision without a gaze," the automation of which is directed at the anticipatory elimination of that which is unpredictable for the human eye.[18] The ambition of "computer vision" to eliminate unpredictable coincidence and prevent the catastrophe thanks to preventive measures can thus be understood as a technical, operative update of Pauleit's temporal concept of the "photographesomenon."

These multiple time layers of surveillance can be compared with works of video art such as Dan Graham's installation *Present Continuous Past(s)* from 1974 (see

Chapter 3). Accordingly, the topic of surveillance has also found widespread resonance in the context of media art, particularly in artistic strategies of countersurveillance in which methods are developed to reverse the role of the observer and the observed, and to thereby also question the panoptic principle. Pauleit and Kammerer as well as, for example, Nicole Falkenhayner, focus on these kinds of artistic approaches.[19] The artistic analysis and deconstruction of surveillance systems forms a practice-based complement to the theoretical contributions presented here.

In comparison to theories with a background in the humanities, the numerous publications on video surveillance in social sciences and criminology are based on empirical data, referring to specific countries and their respective legal situation, social framework, and national security concepts. Accordingly, the methods of these field studies are application-oriented and relevant for video theory mainly with regard to the fact-based verification of hypotheses. One of the focal points of these studies is Great Britain, where video surveillance (there referred to as CCTV) in public spaces was widely implemented from the 1990s onward. According to Stephen Graham, in urban areas, a British citizen was captured by around 300 video cameras a day as early as 1999.

Graham's contribution looks at the economic and security-related arguments for installing CCTV in public spaces. He analyzes its intrinsic logic of constant expansion as a combination of "economy of scale" and "economy of scope," through which a new nationwide infrastructure is being created, comparable to the supply networks for water, electricity, gas, and telephone. Its ubiquity is driven by cost-saving digital automation as well as by terrorist attacks, which are invoked as arguments for a public need for security.

In the UK, the extent of public investment in CCTV has led to an increased political interest in impact evaluation.[20] The debate about the effectiveness of video surveillance in preventing acts of violence and prosecuting crimes remains extremely controversial to this day. For example, the tone of Clive Norris's summary of decades of criminological studies on CCTV in public spaces is highly skeptical. Based on his own field studies in Great Britain, Norris has undertaken a comparative evaluation of international surveys and cites both technical and psychological reasons for the scant effectiveness of CCTV in the fight against crime.[21] Kammerer similarly points to reports on the failure of Britain's security concept. As a deputy chief inspector put it in 2008: "There's no fear of CCTV."[22] It fails to deter violent criminals because there is no concept for police evaluation and legal evidentiality of the recordings. Despite the massive presence of CCTV, there is no internalization of control. Thus, at least in this specific case, police practice contradicts Foucault's theses on self-regulation as the basic structure of the panopticism of modern disciplinary societies. Norris has characterized this contradiction as "the problem of the rational offender."[23]

Interestingly, however, this negative evaluation of CCTV has not resulted in any reduction in visual surveillance of public spaces in the UK or in other countries. Instead, attempts are made to enforce the internalization of control by stepping up the technical capacities. Graham describes the transition, beginning in 2000, from monitoring by security personnel in control rooms to digital image processing based on pattern recognition. A further step has been the increasing use, since 2010, of digital methods for evaluation and assessing the legal evidentiality of video recordings, as presented by Kelly Gates in her contribution on forensics in this chapter. The use of the term "post-Panoptical control" has gained widespread currency in trying to describe the combination of video surveillance and dataveillance.[24] Current statistics show that, as a consequence of digital automatization, the number of video cameras continues to increase worldwide, but that this still does not lead to more security in public spaces.[25]

Even in the narrower field of video surveillance, the centralistic principle of the Panopticon must be revised. Orwell's *Nineteen Eighty-Four* imagined a single central authority; today's video surveillance, on the other hand, is operated decentrally by different agents and for different interests. As early as 2002, Graham identified the tendency toward ubiquitous surveillance through the interconnection of public and private camera networks, which he likened to the development in the realm of private and public telephone networks. The consequences of further decentralization of video surveillance are examined in the contribution by Kelly Gates.

Graham, Norris, and numerous other authors show that, despite the political will to increase the effectiveness and ubiquity of surveillance, the results of CCTV are one-sided. Quite contrary to the egalitarian fiction of the Panopticon, not all subjects are controlled equally in the public space. Rather, selection and discrimination of people based on their social status or ethnic affiliation is the rule and factually takes place on two levels: through research in control rooms, Norris was able to establish the widespread presence of racism and sexism among security staff.[26] Graham, in turn, examines the implementation of parameters of exclusion in the form of "normative assumptions" in software for automated surveillance. His call for a revision of the "politics of code" is shared by Kammerer, who concludes: "The thesis of the neutrality of technology must be questioned, if not completely abandoned."[27]

(Self-)Exposure: Wendy Chun (Jennifer Ringley)

In this section, "Self-Exposure" is understood as the counterpart to monitoring, as voluntary self-representation in surveillance systems. It is the subject of numerous cultural theoretical studies; examples include closed-circuit installations in video art, artistic strategies of countersurveillance, selfie culture on social media platforms, and, as their precursors, webcams, here examined by Wendy Chun.[28] They also comprise reality TV shows in which participants are subjected to around-the-clock video surveillance and whose outstanding viewer ratings have spawned a plethora of similar formats worldwide. Rather than the dystopia of a totalitarian surveillance state, Orwell's term "Big Brother" now serves to describe the staging of private self-exposure at the service of the attention economy. In contrast to personal webcams and video blogs, reality TV participants have to submit to a rigid system of control and competition. This concerns the setup, in which TV cameras and webcams, often used in conjunction, leave no space for privacy, but also, and more importantly, the cruel rules of the casting game, by which the viewers vote on the participants' fate until the bitter end.[29]

Personal webcams are particularly relevant to the topic of self-exposure because the actors in front of the camera have control over the image. They are the authors of their webcam presence rather than objects of surveillance; in this instance, the direction of camera observation can be reversed.[30] In that sense, webcams can be understood as the forerunners of self-portrayals on social media channels, with the difference that in the 1990s they were still able to act independently of the technical standardizations and legal regulations that characterize today's platforms.

Webcams represent a kind of missing link, a transitional medium between video and social media, especially with reference to the discourse on "Video and the Self" presented in Chapter 3. Initially fitted as supplement hardware to the upper edge of the PC screen in laptops, cameras were later integrated by default into the part of the lid above the screen. The implementation of "front-facing" (i.e., user-directed) cameras in smartphones derives directly from the webcam, as both were initially intended for videoconferencing or videotelephony. Instead, digital narcissism has turned the front-facing camera into a killer application on smartphones catering to online selfie culture.

With regard to the chapter's leitmotif of indexicality, webcams can be seen as a belated implementation of the previously mentioned late-nineteenth-century concepts of television as distant electronic vision, that is, as a prosthetic medium expanding the range of the human (and especially the male) gaze. Chun examines this specific type of implicit indexicality: "Webcam sites (both authentic and fake) do not simply generalize or spread voyeurism (the users are invited to watch) but rather mimic voyeurism in order to create indexicality and authenticity."[31] The time and date stamp on many webcam video images confirms their instantaneity and thereby reinforces this claim for authenticity.

Part of the research literature focuses on webcams run by women, partly owing to Jennifer Ringley's role model status. The website she operated from 1996 to 2003 was the first prominent example of a personal webcam. Viewers were able to follow her private life live online 24/7, initially via one, then several cameras, first with only one video still generated every three minutes due to the limited bandwidth of the internet back then. In a relatively short time, JenniCam became one of the world's most watched websites, and Ringley one of the first self-made internet celebrities, thus setting new standards for the effectiveness of individual intervention in the fledgling World Wide Web.[32] In contrast to today's commercialization of online attention, notably by influencers, Ringley invested money in her project, as the growing number of viewers generated higher costs for bandwidth provision.[33]

A major reason for the popularity of JenniCam was undoubtedly the uncensored completeness of her self-portrayal. Ringley has commented on her project numerous times, explaining that nudity and intimacy were an integral part of her life. The statements on her website and in interviews have in turn found their way into theory.[34] "One could theorize Ringley's feminist status in her obvious control over the presentation of her own image online and her control of what her male viewers are able to gaze. . . . Jennifer's site represents a complex dialectic between woman as subject and woman as object, woman as both consumer and consumed, and woman as a 'performer' of femininity through her interaction with 'woman' as object of desire," wrote Kristine Blair and Pamela Takayoshi in 1997.[35] Victor Burgin has dedicated an extensive essay to JenniCam, in which he refers to Laura Mulvey's feminist film theory on the voyeurism of the cinematographic "male gaze": "If . . . we judge Ringley to be an exhibitionist, we have done no more than acknowledge our own voyeurism."[36] After extensive psychoanalytic references to Freud and Lacan, he adds: "The voyeurism to which Jenni appeals is no less a complex amalgam of sexual and sublimated elements than is her purported exhibitionism."[37]

In the case of JenniCam, the indexicality of webcams is pervaded with an obvious gender dichotomy, which Chun chooses as the leitmotif of her investigation into so-called "camgirls": "'Voyeuristic' images lend the Internet an authenticity it otherwise lacks, and 'nonpornographic' cam sites, such as JenniCam, flirted with nudity in order to prove their 'realness.'"[38] Like JenniCam, the camgirls, some of whom Chun also interviewed, are part of the long history of "media amateurs" who are simultaneously pioneers of emerging mainstream developments.[39] They anticipated developments that became widespread thanks to social media channels, and they have also been a testing ground for problematic media effects, such as cyberbullying and its psychological consequences.

Using the example of the camgirls, Chun highlights the possibility of playing with indexicality.[40] At the same time, playing with the index can also mean playing with the "male gaze." The ambivalence between control and freedom suggested by the title of her book is also evident in the power of the (female) viewed over the (male) viewer, which subverts one-sided ascriptions of victim roles. Chun's book from 2006 describes a moment of transition in the development of the internet in technological as well as gender-specific terms. With the camgirls, she has documented a historic online community that has since disappeared.[41] Like Chun, Theresa Senft adopts a decidedly feminist stance in her comprehensive "ethnographic" study on camgirls from 2008. As a participating observer, Senft conducted numerous interviews and evaluated experiences from her research with her own webcam. She reaches the conclusion that not all of the camgirls she interviewed share this feminist point of view.[42] In the context of this reader, we may ask what happened to this specific moment of female empowerment through self-portrayal via webcams. Should it be considered merely with historical interest, just as the 1970s feminist movement took on video as a medium that was not yet male-dominated (see Chapter 9)? Or can it sustain itself against the patriarchal mainstream, even when "camming" is now primarily an online sex-working practice?

Feminist authors still disagree on whether the commercialization of the internet and the online sexploitation that comes with it still offer room for self-determined female "self-exposure" via webcam. "However, for camgirls of the past and present, elements of empowerment and exploitation have always existed along with the desire to be authentic and gain celebrity," writes Katharine Wimett.[43] In particular from the perspective of "neoliberal feminism," online sex work by camgirls is seen to have "empowerment" qualities.[44] However, male attacks on camgirls in the form of "capping" (distribution of illegitimate recordings of private cam sessions) and in particular "doxxing" or "swatting" (personal identification, physical localization, and personal discreditation or harassment) suggest that this freedom is distinctly precarious.

Testimony: Kathrin Peters, Alexandra Juhasz, Siva Vaidhyanathan (Abraham Zapruder Film, Rodney King Video, George Floyd Video)

The investigation into the testimonial value of video combines aspects of surveillance and forensics with the growing importance of private recordings for public image policies and the media economy. This applies in particular to incidental recordings of violent crimes by bystanders, which can play a central role in the political and legal assessment of these incidents. The media-theoretical implications of such viral videos are addressed in the contributions by Kathrin Peters and Siva Vaidhyanathan (see his contribution in Chapter 8). The historical context of this topical discourse is briefly outlined in the following.

Its antecedents reach back further than video, beginning with the amateur film recordings that Abraham Zapruder accidentally made during the assassination of John F. Kennedy on November 22, 1963. These twenty-six seconds of 8-mm Kodak film have been the subject of extensive research, both by the Warren Commission investigating the assassination and as part of its public use in news reports. At the time, *Life* magazine won the race for the rights of use ahead of CBS television and published individual stills from the film. It was not until 1975 that excerpts were shown on a US-wide television broadcast, sparking considerable public controversy over the ethical value and legal significance of the film. The specially formed US House of Representatives Select Committee on Assassinations (HSCA) subjected the Zapruder film to yet another forensic analysis. But to this day, the debate around "one of the most studied pieces of film in history"[45] or, alternatively, the "most important 26 seconds of film in history"[46] has never ceased.

From the 1990s onward, the introduction of compact video camcorders boosted private recording in public spaces thanks to lower costs and longer running times for videotapes compared to amateur film. These camcorder recordings are forerunners of today's "occasional" smartphone videos and their role in political conflicts, as examined by Marc Ries.[47] The Rodney King case offers a prominent example of the far-reaching political and legal consequences of this kind of incidental video footage. On March 3, 1991, video amateur George Holliday accidentally recorded the abuse of the African American Rodney King by four police officers with his new camcorder. Eighty-one seconds of the grainy video footage were broadcast the same day by various TV stations in Los Angeles. The public dissemination of the video eventually led to an indictment. The legal proceedings against the police officers ended with an acquittal, despite the fact that the mistreatment can be clearly seen in the video. Charles Goodwin has provided a detailed analysis of the controversy between accusation and defense over the interpretation of the video based on transcriptions of the proceedings.[48] With graphic charts and stills from the video, a police expert managed to deconstruct the evidence of the video for the lay jury. The decontextualization of the images was intended to make Rodney King appear as the aggressor rather than the victim.[49] Avital Ronell has commented on this scandalous procedure from a media-theoretical standpoint in several texts.[50]

In the public opinion, however, the video was seen as an obvious example of racist violence. As the attorney general pointed out during the trial: "What more can you ask for? You have the videotape that shows objectively, without bias, impartially, what happened that night."[51] Furthermore, the video stood as unique evidence for numerous other, undocumented and hence unprosecuted attacks by white police officers on African American citizens. The acquittal of the policemen despite the video testimony was quite rightly understood by the Afro-American community as a racist falsification of the evidence at hand and a confirmation of discrimination. Coming one year after the incident, the verdict triggered the Los Angeles riots, which are considered to be the greatest civil disturbance in US history, leaving sixty-three people dead and large parts of Los Angeles devastated.

The Rodney King case still stands as a symbol of the fight against structural racism.[52] In the longer perspective, it also led to a reorientation in the legal assessment of video material.[53] Because of its massive repercussions, the Rodney King video can be seen as a turning point in the discussion on the legal, forensic, political, media-theoretical, and epistemic evaluation of amateur video material. The killing of George Floyd by police officers in plain sight of several cameras on May 25, 2020, marks an equally significant turning point. This murder was documented by several bystanders with smartphones and by two surveillance cameras. The videos shared on social media immediately sparked a wave of protest. While the 1992 uprisings concentrated on Los Angeles, the Black Lives Matter movement gained an unprecedented global resonance after the murder of George Floyd.

This case, which unfolded during the work on this publication, confirms some of the historical developments of video testimony outlined here. At the same time, there are important differences. Instead of a single witness video, it involves a complex interplay of several video sources that were publicized via different channels: the parallel recordings made by at least four eyewitnesses at the crime scene, the instant reception of the footage via social media, the analysis of two surveillance camera recordings, and the legal seizure of the bodycam footage of two police officers involved.

The George Floyd case is the temporary climax of a genealogy of video recordings of racist abuse and murder in the United States during the last decade: Michael Brown in Ferguson (2014), the so-called "Ferguson Six" during the subsequent protests (2014), Eric Garner in New York (2014), Philando Castile in Saint Paul, Minnesota (2016), Breonna Taylor in New York (2020), and Ahmaud Arbery in Glynn County, Georgia (2020). Each of these tragic cases bears witness to a very specific dynamic as concerns the interaction between violence, testimony, and public reaction. This results in different political and legal consequences. The evidential and drastic nature of the Floyd murder videos sparked immediate civil protests and demonstrations. In the Rodney King case, the uprisings did not occur until a year later, after the policemen were acquitted. This suggests that any hopes that video testimony of a racist attack could lead to justice and its perpetrators being punished have been largely eroded in the public mind since 1992.

On the other hand, the growing impact of video testimony was confirmed by the *New York Times*' successful call to make private footage of the George Floyd incident publicly available.[54] On the basis of four different smartphone videos, the material from two surveillance cameras, and audio from the emergency call, a forensic reconstruction of the events on the *New York Times* website greatly enhanced the mobilizing power of the footage.[55] In addition to these media-specific aspects the failings of Donald Trump's policies increased public pressure for a thorough investigation. This allowed the murder of George Floyd, more than any of the examples mentioned here, to trigger a worldwide wave of solidarity whose momentum continues to this day.[56]

The impact of Zapruder's film of the assassination of JFK and of the Rodney King video derives from the dissemination of their images via centrally organized media: in the former instance, print media, in the latter, TV. The contributions by Kathrin Peters, Alexandra Juhasz, and Siva Vaidhyanathan address similar fatal incidents of physical abuse by security staff or police in broad daylight. The crucial difference concerns the viral distribution of these videos on social media platforms that are no longer controlled by a central authority.

Responsibility for the dissemination and impact of viral videos no longer lies with a central, hierarchical structure such as the press or television. Still, this does not imply that it lies outside of the realm of human decision. Rather, one could speak of a kind of decentralized responsibility, which affects the producers of such videos, who often remain anonymous, as much as the platforms on which they are uploaded and the viewers who distribute them by sharing and recommending them. All of these actors contribute at different points to the viewing, assessment, and marketing of images of violence, to their potential use and abuse for political and personal purposes. As Peters and also Philipp Müller show, these videos, which are initially distributed virally, are subsequently reformatted and commented on by print media and television, thereby losing their "unofficial" nature.[57] In other words, their effect as testimony is reinforced because they appear in editorially evaluated and citable contexts.[58] The Zapruder film and the Rodney King video also went through this process, albeit under other technical conditions.[59] The George Floyd case demonstrates that the combination of decentralized eyewitness videos with their concentration and processing by central authorities (in this instance the *New York Times*) raises the impact of video testimonies to yet another level. Such strategies have been developed by the research agency Forensic Architecture since 2010, an example of which is presented by Eyal Weizman in the next section.[60]

While Siva Vaidhyanathan (see his contribution in Chapter 8) contrasts the contingency and banality of the viral "videocracy" with the hope for a collective gain in awareness based on the George Floyd videos, Kathrin Peters examines the transfer of such an "iconic" video recording of violent acts across various video and print formats. Philipp Müller has introduced the concept of the "observer-producer as accomplice . . . in the space of action of attention-seeking terrorist criminals."[61] To the extent that he "becomes not only a producer but also a distributor, the noninvolved puts himself in the position of a potentially complicit involved, as do all the people who also see and share the video."[62] Müller has therefore called for a visual studies-based media ethic on the affective impact of images of violence. His concern complements the approach of

Alexandra Juhasz (see her contribution in Chapter 8), who justifies her decision not to watch the live video stream of the death of Philando Castile after his shooting by a police officer, which went viral in 2016, by arguing that viewing violent videos is itself a political act insofar as it participates in the distribution of the images.[63]

Peters examines how, in the political and public sphere, the production of images intertwines with the events they depict. In some extreme cases, the presence of a recording device can itself trigger the recorded violence, as the device implies the possibility of immediate dissemination.[64] This reciprocating violent power of images of violence has reached a new dimension today, as terrorists, using the instantaneity of social media channels for their own purposes, distribute videos of their attacks themselves.[65]

Forensics: Kelly Gates, Eyal Weizman (Harun Farocki)

Forensic video analysis has a wide range of applications: besides the evaluation of surveillance images in view of the prosecution of criminal offenses and as evidence in traffic accidents, forensic procedures are also used for the legal assessment of military operations. In a related form, video recordings are instrumental in sports to support referee decisions.[66] In all of these areas, specialized procedures have been developed in order to transform original material that does not seem meaningful at first glance into visual evidence, which in case of doubt can stand up in court. In this regard, Dietmar Kammerer writes about the legal use of video that "the evidential value of an image relies on the *performance* of those who create it."[67]

In contrast to "live" video surveillance, video forensics work primarily with recordings. However, the instantaneous indexicality of the video image outlined earlier is not entirely lost. The metadata embedded in the digital video can be used to determine the time and location of the recording with greater precision than in analog video footage. This means that forensics can enhance the instantaneous indexicality of the digital video material, for example, when trying to ascertain the exact circumstances of a crime or a traffic accident. Kelly Gates therefore speaks of the "implicit rhetorical claim of temporal indexicality."[68]

The two contributions presented here each highlight different interests. While Gates presents the increasingly immaterial "labor of surveillance" in the public fight against crime, Eyal Weizman outlines his educational work for NGOs in trying to prove human rights violations and war crimes committed on behalf of governments. Parallel to governments and NGOs, commercial "law enforcement" agencies have expanded forensic video analysis into a sizable new field of business. The motto of the National Technical Investigators' Association—"In God we trust, all others we monitor®"—speaks to the political slant of these agencies.[69] Unsurprisingly, the strategies and proprietary technologies used in this sector are not made public, which explains why they are hardly accessible to theory.

Gates's contribution evidences why the panoptic principle seems outdated in light of the decentralization of video surveillance. The localization, collection, storage, and evaluation of video recordings from private, corporate, and governmental sources present the police with challenges similar to those faced by big film productions. In this respect, Gates describes the "managing of video assets as a fundamental part of evidence production."[70] In order to stand up in court, the material from surveillance cameras requires extensive postproduction. According to Gates, surveillance images may therefore not be regarded as neutral raw material: "There is nothing new about calling attention to the indeterminacy of images or the fact that there are intentions embedded in their production, but these points need re-emphasizing with respect to surveillance images."[71] From a legal point of view, the evidential value of images from surveillance cameras is often based on their nonintentionality. In court they are therefore more reliable than the "occasional" video recordings of people who happen to be present at the scene.[72] However, Gates shows that the indexicality of surveillance images too must be generated through intentionality. She therefore criticizes the tendency to replace the prevailing paradigm of the objectivity of "trained judgment" with "computational objectivity" as a "new epistemic virtue"; rather, the two coexist and condition each other.[73]

Weizman's contribution presents a case study from the work of the research agency Forensic Architecture. Rather than for planning buildings and cities, methods for visualizing buildings and simulating urban spaces are here used for forensic analysis of incidents during combat operations and human rights violations so as to generate architectural evidence that is legally and politically reliable.[74] The findings of this elaborate research are also used in an adapted form for presentations in the context of contemporary art exhibitions. According to Weizman, this cross-disciplinary effectiveness is inherent in the methods used: "Forensics—the mode by which political claims are made public—must be thought of as an aesthetic practice."[75] The confluence with visual arts becomes evident not only in the exhibits of Forensic Architecture but also in the fact that the contribution by Weizman presented here was going to serve as the basis for a film by Harun Farocki—a project that did not come about due to the filmmaker's death in 2014.[76] Since 2003, Farocki's interest had turned to "operational images"—images that not only represent things but also control processes, often without being seen by a human eye.[77] This also includes the drones examined by Weizman, which search for, and destroy, their targets autonomously.[78]

For the example presented here, Forensic Architecture had been commissioned by the United Nations to investigate the illegal use of drones in Pakistan, Afghanistan, Somalia, Yemen, and Gaza. Weizman explains that the targeted killing of people by drones is officially allowed not as punishment but only to prevent a crime in the making.[79] In other words, any such lethal operation would have to be preceded by a forensic prognosis in order to ascertain that the person in question was indeed planning this kind of action. Weizman likens this sort of prognosis-based killing to climate disaster forecasts as "forensic of a damage that has not yet occurred. It's a forensic of the future."[80] Needless to say that for its investigative analysis of drone deployments, Forensic Architecture cannot rely on data from military operations control that would corroborate its legitimacy. Images from commercial satellites are not conclusive due to governments regulating their resolution. Weizman therefore points out that the forensic perspective lags behind the military perspective: "Human figure is the convergent point of drone vision, it is what satellite images are designed to mask."[81] As Weizman emphasizes, "image-based practices" must, as in the case study presented here, use other data sources.

Outlook: Fake versus Forensics, Forensics versus Fake (Deepfake Videos)

Deepfake videos created using artificial intelligence form the epistemic counterpart of video forensics, insofar as they use documentary recordings to compute fictitious but realistic video scenarios that depict people doing things they never did. While this phenomenon is currently receiving a great deal of media attention, reliable theories are only just emerging. One of the first prominent examples of a deepfake video was based on the "Synthesizing Obama" software.[82] It enables lip-sync video simulation of an address by Barack Obama based on excerpts from former speeches. In the 2018 video, Obama is shown warning viewers of the very technology that puts these words in his mouth: "We are entering an era in which our enemies can make anyone say anything at any point in time."[83] But contrary to the enlightening impetus of this video and the academic background of the software used to create it, many virally distributed deepfake videos originate from illegal, anonymous sources. This applies in particular to so-called "face swapping." Those affected are mostly female actors, pop stars, and politicians, whose faces are inserted in porn videos without their knowledge and consent.

Both variants of deepfake—the simulation of a speech or action based on appropriated content and the implementation of images of a person in a different context of action—equally lend themselves to extensive abuse: discrediting individuals, faking facts in order to influence the public (especially in the lead-up to elections), and manipulating political processes (e.g., in international conflicts between parties without diplomatic relations). In the first comprehensive legal study on this topic, published in 2018, Robert Chesney and Danielle K. Citron forecast the scope of the problem: "The marketplace of ideas already suffers from truth decay as our networked information environment interacts in toxic ways with our cognitive biases. Deepfakes will exacerbate this problem significantly. Individuals and businesses will face novel forms of exploitation, intimidation, and personal sabotage. The risks to our democracy and to national security are profound as well."[84]

Initially, the phenomenon affected mainly public figures, because extensive available footage was required to train the artificial intelligence software. But thanks to rapid advances in software development, deepfake videos of private individuals can now be created on the basis of just a few images, to a perfection that outplays the capacities of human judgment. In an effort to expose this kind of manipulation, new forensic procedures are in turn being developed.[85] Here, the function of video forensics is reversed: instead of bringing to light a truth hidden in the image, it aims to expose a deception implemented in it. Forensic deepfake detection as well as production are based on AI algorithms: "The inspiration is that what AI has broken can be fixed by AI as well."[86] Thus, a race between fake and forensics has begun, the outcome of which remains open for the time being.

Notes

1 For an overview of the developments in surveillance studies since the 1980s, see David Murakami Wood, "Situating Surveillance Studies," *Surveillance & Society* 6, no. 1 (2009), 52–61.
2 English translation quoted in Friedrich Kittler, *Optical Media: Berlin Lectures 1999*, trans. Anthony Enns (Cambridge: Polity Press, 2010), 209. On Nipkow and "visions of televisions" in the nineteenth century, see Dieter Daniels, *Kunst als Sendung: Von der Telegrafie zum Internet* (Munich: C.H. Beck, 2002), 76–90.
3 See Albert Abramson, *The History of Television, 1880 to 1941* (Jefferson, NC: McFarland, 1987), 10–50, specifically the chapters "Early Schemes and Inventions: 1880–1899," "The First Devices: 1900–1911," and "Distant Electric Vision: 1911–1920."
4 Orwell finished his manuscript in 1948 and the book was published in June 1949.
5 The BBC started broadcasting regular live TV programs in London in 1936 and developed a nationwide broadcasting network from 1949 onward.
6 "Houston's Jail is Watched . . . by the All-Seeing Eye of TV," reported *BusinessWeek* on November 7, 1953. Quoted in Jonathan Rozenkrantz, *Videographic Cinema: An Archaeology of Electronic Images and Imaginaries* (New York: Bloomsbury, 2020), 96.
7 Dietmar Kammerer, "Police Use of Public Video Surveillance in Germany from 1956: Management of Traffic, Repression of Flows, Persuasion of Offenders," *Surveillance & Society* 6, no. 1 (2009), 43–7.
8 See Inga Kroener, *CCTV: A Technology under the Radar?* (Abingdon: Routledge, 2016).
9 Michel Foucault, *Discipline and Punish: The Birth of the Prison* (New York: Vintage Books, 1978), 201.
10 Ibid., 203.
11 David Lyon, *Electronic Eye: The Rise of Surveillance Society* (Minneapolis: University of Minnesota Press, 1994), 70f.
12 See ibid., 67, 76.
13 Thomas Mathiesen, "The Viewer Society: Michel Foucault's 'Panopticon' Revisited," *Theoretical Criminology* 1, no. 2 (May 1997), 219 [italics in the original]. The author also points out that Foucault does not mention television.
14 Mathiesen, "The Viewer Society," 223. From a media-historical perspective, Bentham's Panopticon could also be compared to the panorama as the first visual mass medium, with the inspectors in the center of the Panopticon taking the role of the viewers in the center of the illusionistic spectacle.
15 Rozenkrantz, *Videographic Cinema*, 108.
16 Dietmar Kammerer, *Bilder der Überwachung* (Frankfurt am Main: Suhrkamp, 2008), 346.
17 For an overview, see *Routledge Handbook of Surveillance Studies*, ed. Kirstie Ball, Kevin D. Haggerty, and David Lyon (Abingdon: Routledge, 2012).
18 Kammerer, *Bilder der Überwachung*, 190. The reference to Peter Geimer can also be found here.
19 On artistic strategies of countersurveillance, see Kammerer, *Bilder der Überwachung*, 323–44, and "Surveillance in Literature, Film and Television," in *Routledge Handbook of Surveillance Studies*, 99–106. See also Winfried Pauleit, "Videosurveillance and Postmodern Subjects," in *CTRL [SPACE]: Rhetorics of Surveillance from Bentham to Big Brother*, ed. Thomas Y. Levin, Ursula Frohne, and Peter Weibel (Cambridge, MA: MIT Press, 2002), 465–79; Nicole Falkenhayner, *Media, Surveillance and Affect: Narrating Feeling-States* (London: Routledge, 2019); and "CCTV beyond

Surveillance: The Cultural Relevance of the Surveillance Camera and Its Images in Contemporary Britain," *Journal for the Study of British Cultures* 23, no. 2 (2016), 157–68.

20 Clive Norris highlights the fact that the development of CCTV in the 1990s was initially encouraged by political decision makers without any evaluation. See Norris, "The Success of Failure: Accounting for the Global Growth of CCTV," in *Routledge Handbook of Surveillance Studies*, 251–8.

21 See Norris, "The Success of Failure" and "'There's No Success like Failure and Failure's No Success at All': Some Critical Reflections on Understanding the Global Growth of CCTV Surveillance," in *Eyes Everywhere: The Global Growth of Camera Surveillance*, ed. Aaron Doyle, Randy Lippert, and David Lyon (Abingdon: Routledge, 2011), 23–45.

22 Kammerer, *Bilder der Überwachung*, 347.

23 Norris, "The Success of Failure," 256.

24 The term "post-Panoptical" was introduced by sociologist Zygmunt Bauman in reference to the concept of postmodernity. Bauman argues that because control and exercise of power have become "exterritorial" thanks to digital data streams, the holders of power—or surveillors or aggressors (he writes in relation to the Gulf War and the conflicts following the dissolution of Yugoslavia)—elude spatial presence: "The end of Panopticon augurs *the end of the era of mutual engagement*: between the supervisors and the supervised, capital and labor, leaders and their followers, armies at war." Bauman, *Liquid Modernity* (Cambridge: Polity Press, 2000), 11. In the context of surveillance studies, the term becomes established from 2005. See, among others, *Theorizing Surveillance: The Panopticon and Beyond*, ed. David Lyon (London and New York: Routledge, 2006), specifically Kevin D. Haggerty, "Tear Down the Walls: On Demolishing the Panopticon," 23–45, and Sean P. Hier, Kevin Walby, and Josh Greenberg, "Supplementing the Panoptic Paradigm: Surveillance, Moral Governance, and CCTV," 228–42.

25 "Broadly speaking, more cameras doesn't necessarily reduce crime rates." Paul Bischoff, "Surveillance Camera Statistics: Which Cities Have the Most CCTV Cameras?" *Comparitech*, July 22, 2020, https://www.comparitech.com/vpn-privacy/the-worlds-most-surveilled-cities/. The not publicly available IHS Markit Technology white paper "Security Technologies Top Trends for 2020" forecast that the number of surveillance cameras worldwide would reach 1 billion by the end of that year; quoted in https://www.telecomtv.com/content/video-technology/ihs-markit-technology-white-paper-reveals-top-trends-impacting-the-video-surveillance-market-in-2020-37354/.

26 "[CCTV] is essentially conservative and focused on the maintenance of the status quo. The status quo always serves dominant interests: the old over the young, the rich over the poor, the indigenous over the immigrant, the commercial over the citizenry." Norris, "The Success of Failure," 258.

27 Kammerer, *Bilder der Überwachung*, 204. See also "Introduction to Chapter II: Surveillance as Sorting," in *Routledge Handbook of Surveillance Studies*, 118–21.

28 See John McGrath, "Performing Surveillance," in *Routledge Handbook of Surveillance Studies*, 83–90. See also *CTRL [SPACE]*, specifically the chapter "Surveillant Pleasures," 206–313.

29 See John McGrath, *Loving Big Brother: Surveillance Culture and Performance Space* (London and New York: Routledge, 2004); and Dieter Daniels, *Vom Readymade zum Cyberspace* (Ostfildern: Hatje Cantz, 2003), specifically the chapter "Big Brother Readymade," 26–57.

30 Wendy Chun writes about the webcam actors she met as part of her research: "Rather than 'owning them,' they own you; rather than merely being caught by surveillance cameras like everyone else, they choose when and how they are caught." Chun, *Control and Freedom: Power and Paranoia in the Age of Fiber Optics* (Cambridge, MA: MIT Press, 2006), 284.

31 Chan, *Control and Freedom*, 284. Also playing with expectations of authenticity was the webcam project *Refresh* (1998) by Diller + Scofidio. The authors write that "liveness may be a last vestige of authenticity—seeing and/or hearing the event at the precise moment of its occurrence. The un-mediated *is* the im-mediate." In *Refresh*, these expectations are deceived through a series of fictional webcam narratives. See https://www.diaart.org/exhibition/exhibitions-projects/diller-scofidio-refresh-web-project.

32 "Jennifer Ringley was the first celebrity formed by the Internet . . . with a multiplicity of fan sites, dedicated chat rooms, and hundreds emailing her every day." Steve Dixon, *Digital Performance* (Cambridge, MA: MIT Press, 2007), 448. "By the time it closed, the JenniCam had established itself as the best known of all personal webcam sites, registering 100 million hits per week at its peak in 1998." Theresa Senft, *Camgirls: Celebrity and Community in the Age of Social Networks* (New York: Peter Lang, 2008), 15.

33 Monthly costs of nearly $3,000 forced Ringley in 1997 to put in place fee-based membership access (one image per minute) in addition to a reduced free version (one image every fifteen minutes). "She immediately attracted 5,500 members. The initial $15 a year subscription increased fourfold to $15 per 90 days by 2003, but always maintained a free point of access." Dixon, *Digital Performance*, 449. On the expenses and income of camgirls, see also Senft, *Camgirls*, 19–21. Similar issues with costs generated by bandwidth also affected video bloggers; see, e.g., on the problems faced by Rupert Howe following the success of his video *Should I Stay or Should I Go* (2005), Trine Bjørkmann Berry, *Videoblogging before YouTube* (Amsterdam: Institute of Network Cultures, 2018), 29f.

34 The statements by Jennifer Ringley are quoted from Wendy Chun and all the other authors named here. They can also be found in numerous other publications on digital culture; for example, the website's mission statement from 2000 is reproduced in full in *Image Ethics in the Digital Age*, ed. Larry Gross, John Stuart Katz, and Jay Ruby (Minneapolis: University of Minnesota Press, 2003), XII. The book also features a good chronology of JenniCam's development.

35 Kristine Blair and Pamela Takayoshi, "Navigating the Image of Woman Online," *Kairos* 2, no. 2 (1997): http://kairos.technorhetoric.net/2.2/coverweb/invited/kb3.html. See also Kristine Blair and Pamela Takayoshi, eds., *Feminist Cyberscapes: Mapping Gendered Academic Spaces* (Norwood, NJ: Ablex Press, 1999).

36 Victor Burgin, "Jenni's Room: Exhibitionism and Solitude," *Critical Inquiry* 27, no. 1 (Autumn 2000), 77–89. Quoted in *CTRL [SPACE]*, 231.

37 *CTRL [SPACE]*, 233. On this topic, Wendy Chun writes: "Burgin's argument that users wait quietly for Jenni to come home from work is insightful and complicates his claim that they are voyeurs. For if Ringley is not an exhibitionist, the viewers are not voyeurs." Chun, *Control and Freedom*, 284.

38 Ibid., 103.

39 Based on the example of videoblogs, whose popularity in the early 2000s coincided with that of webcams, Trine Bjørkmann Berry offers a precise definition of the amateur status in digital media: "Firstly, many of the videobloggers I will go on

to discuss self-identify as amateur. . . . In the digital age, the definition of being an amateur includes being someone who pursues a passion for personal, rather than professional, pleasure . . . being an amateur may not be purely about doing something you love, for free, but is also linked to the access to and knowledge of a practice and is usually contrasted with professional work. It also refers in some sense to the notion of the 'early adopter.'" Bjørkmann Berry, *Videoblogging before YouTube*, 12.

40 Chun, *Control and Freedom*, 50.

41 The camgirls examined by Chun used either their own or commercial platforms. As opposed to Jennifer Ringley, larger bandwidth enables them to stream video, which permits live interaction with the audience.

42 "Because this book is an explicitly feminist one, I feel honor-bound to point out that most of my subjects expressed ambivalence about feminism. 'I hear that word used by many people in so many ways,' camgirl Jennifer Ringley told me, 'I prefer not to call myself anything at all.'" Senft, *Camgirls*, 9.

43 Katharine Wimett, *Camgirl.com: Women Creating Space for Themselves Online*, Bachelor's thesis, ArtEZ hogeschool voor de kunsten, 2019, http://www.mistermotley.nl/sites/default/files/Katharine_Wimett_Thesis_1.pdf. For an interactive online version, see https://katharinewimett.nl/thesis/.

44 "Camgirls have found employment that is oftentimes exploitative and enacted within patriarchal systems, but this work also allows them to subvert antiquated ideas about female sexuality and thus produces empowerment." Angela Jones, "'I Get Paid to Have Orgasms': Adult Webcam Models' Negotiation of Pleasure and Danger," *Signs: Journal of Women in Culture and Society* 42, no. 1 (Autumn 2016), 228. See also Angela Jones, *Camming: Money, Power, and Pleasure in the Sex Work Industry* (New York: New York University Press, 2020).

45 Wikipedia entry, https://en.wikipedia.org/wiki/Zapruder_film.

46 Ron Rosenbaum, "What Does the Zapruder Film Really Tell Us?," *Smithsonian Magazine* (October 2013), https://www.smithsonianmag.com/history/what-does-the-zapruder-film-really-tell-us-14194/. Rosenbaum summarizes the film's complex dissemination history. The extensive literature on Zapruder's film is strongly marked by conspiracy theories.

47 Marc Ries, "Vorletzte Bilder," in *Film und Gesellschaft denken mit Siegfried Kracauer*, ed. Bernhard Groß, Vrääth Öhner, and Drehli Robnik (Vienna and Berlin: Turia + Kant, 2018). An English translation ("Penultimate Pictures") can be found in Chapter 4.

48 "Like students in an anthropology class being lectured about events in another culture, the jury at the Rodney King trial was instructed by an expert about what a police officer (someone who they would never be) could see in the events visible on the tape." Charles Goodwin, "Professional Vision," *American Anthropologist* 96, no. 3 (1994), 627. See also the transcripts of the proceedings as well as the statements by all parties involved in the trial, http://law2.umkc.edu/faculty/projects/ftrials/lapd/lapd.html.

49 Similar racist allegations are repeated to this day in the commentary section under the video on YouTube.

50 See Avital Ronell, "Video/Television/Rodney King: Twelve Steps beyond the Pleasure Principle," in *Culture on the Brink: Ideologies of Technology*, ed. Gretchen Bender and Timothy Druckrey (Seattle: Bay Press, 1994), 277–303; "Television and the Fragility of Testimony," *Public* 9 (Spring 1994), 155–65; and "Finitude's Score," in

Thinking Bodies, ed. Juliet Flower MacCannell and Laura Zakarin (Stanford: Stanford University Press, 1994), 87–108.

51 Goodwin, "Professional Vision," 615.

52 On its symbolic charge, see Robert Gooding-Williams, ed., *Reading Rodney King/Reading Urban Uprising* (New York: Routledge, 1993).

53 See Shoshana Felman, *The Juridical Unconscious: Trials and Traumas in the Twentieth Century* (Cambridge, MA: Harvard University Press, 2002). See also Forrest Stuart, "Constructing Police Abuse after Rodney King: How Skid Row Residents and the Los Angeles Police Department Contest Video Evidence," *Law and Social Inquiry* 36, no. 2 (Spring 2011), 327–53.

54 Among the authors of the eyewitness videos, only seventeen-year-old Darnella Frazier, who was the first to share her video on Facebook, is known by name. She immediately found herself the target of controversies and personal attacks. See Joshua Nevett, "George Floyd: The Personal Cost of Filming Police Brutality," *BBC News*, June 11, 2020, https://www.bbc.com/news/world-us-canada-52942519.

55 Evan Hill, Ainara Tiefenthäler, Christiaan Triebert, Drew Jordan, Haley Willis, and Robin Stein, "8 Minutes and 46 Seconds: How George Floyd Was Killed in Police Custody," *New York Times*, May 31, 2020 (updated November 5, 2020), https://www.nytimes.com/2020/05/31/us/george-floyd-investigation.html.

56 The duration of the assault documented by the videos became a symbol of racist police violence, most notably as the time span chosen for silent remembrance and "die-in" protest actions in several US cities, where demonstrators lay on the ground for eight minutes and forty-six seconds. See Wikipedia entry "Eight minutes 46 seconds (8:46)," https://en.wikipedia.org/wiki/Eight_minutes_46_seconds.

57 Philipp Müller analyzes the dissemination of amateur footage of the murder of a policeman after the terrorist attack on the editorial offices of *Charlie Hebdo* in 2008. See Müller, "Realitätenkollaps? Zum Status von Bild und Betrachter bei Gewaltvideos," in *Images in Conflict / Bilder im Konflikt*, ed. Karen Fromm, Sophia Greiff, and Anna Stemmler (Weimar: Jonas Verlag, 2018).

58 On the dissemination of CCTV footage in the printed press, see also the contribution by Kelly Gates in this chapter.

59 At the same time, the examples analyzed by Peters, Juhasz, and Vaidhyanathan show that the ubiquity of smartphone cameras and their steadily improving recording quality leads to the disappearance of the concept of "film amateur" or "videographer," which was still operative in the case of Abraham Zapruder and George Holliday. (See also the contribution "Penultimate Pictures" by Marc Ries in Chapter 4.)

60 On investigations similar to the George Floyd case, see Forensic Architecture, "The Killing of Mark Duggan" [in London in 2011], https://forensic-architecture.org/investigation/the-killing-of-mark-duggan, and "The Killing of Harith Augustus" [in Chicago in 2018], https://forensic-architecture.org/investigation/the-killing-of-harith-augustus.

61 Müller "Realitätenkollaps?" 99.

62 Ibid., 100.

63 The debate over whether images of violence should be made public or not was already budding in the antecedents described here: Zapruder did not want to publish frame 313 of his film, which shows the moment when JFK's head is hit by a bullet. This did not prevent "Frame 313" from being prominently featured by *Time* magazine as one the "100 Most Influential Images of All Time." See http://100photos.time.com/photos/jfk-assassination-abraham-zapruder-frame-313.

64 See (with reference to Judith Butler and Rabhi Mroué) Kathrin Peters, "The Woman in the Blue Bra—Follow the Video," in *Expanded Senses*, ed. Bernd Kracke and Marc Ries (Bielefeld: transcript, 2015), 175–88. See also Judith Butler, "Bodies in Alliance and the Politics of the Street," *transversal.at*, September 2011, https://transversal.at/transversal/1011/butler/en. An extended version can be found in Judith Butler, *Notes toward a Performative Theory of Assembly* (Cambridge, MA: Harvard University Press, 2015), 66–98.

65 Philipp Müller writes about this phenomenon: "When perpetrators carry out an act of violence in public, images are actively integrated into the context of the violent act. . . . By publishing images of violence, not only the intentions of the audience and the editorial team, but also of the criminals are fulfilled. . . . Public spheres produce and perceive images of events directed at them. Perpetrators, accomplices, and bystanders as well as event, image, and viewer converge." Müller, "Realitätenkollaps?," 87.

66 See Dylan Mulvin, "Game Time: A History of the Managerial Authority of the Instant Replay," in *The NFL: Critical and Cultural Perspectives*, ed. Thomas Oates and Zack Furness (Philadelphia: Temple University Press, 2014).

67 Kammerer, *Bilder der Überwachung*, 188 (italics in the original).

68 Kelly Gates, "The Cultural Labor of Surveillance: Video Forensics, Computational Objectivity, and the Production of Visual Evidence," *Social Semiotics* 23, no. 2 (2013), 7; reprinted in this chapter.

69 Website of the National Technical Investigators' Association (NATIA), https://www.natia.org/.

70 Gates, "The Cultural Labor of Surveillance," 13; reprinted in this chapter.

71 Gates, "The Cultural Labor of Surveillance," 2.

72 See Stuart, "Constructing Police Abuse after Rodney King," 327–53.

73 Gates also cites the previously mentioned critical analysis by Charles Goodwin on the role of police experts in the case of the Rodney King video in "The Cultural Labor of Surveillance," 12.

74 For an overview, see Eyal Weizman, *Forensic Architecture: Violence at the Threshold of Detectability* (New York: Zone Books, 2017), specifically pp. 22–41 on his research on the use of drones.

75 Eyal Weizman, "Matter against Memory," in *2000+: The Urgencies of Architectural Theory*, ed. James Graham and Mark Wigley (New York: GSAPP Books, 2015), 240. He goes on to write that "'Forensic aesthetics' is a field of anarchic mediality: all things are mediated and performed through other things" (241).

76 See the mention by Eyal Weizman in "Violence at the Threshold of Detectability," *e-flux Journal* 64 (April 2015), https://www.e-flux.com/journal/64/60861/violence-at-the-threshold-of-detectability/.

77 On the origins of the term "operational images" in Farocki's work and related concepts in the writings of Sybille Kraemer, Tom Holtert, and Paul Virilio ("machine vision"), see Andreas Broeckmann, *Machine Art in the Twentieth Century* (Cambridge, MA: MIT Press, 2016), 145–51.

78 Even remote-controlled drones act in part autonomously: "Drones possess autonomy by the sheer fact of their technicity, as well as by design. It is their technicity, even more than the logistics within which they are bound, that defines their capacity for perception. As well as the visual in its various forms—high-definition, thermal, zoomed-in—the perception of the drone is of control signals, air pressures, wind movements, fuel or battery reserves, and much more." Michael Richardson, "Drone's-

Eye View: Affective Witnessing and Technicities of Perception," in *Image Testimonies: Witnessing in Times of Social Media*, ed. Kerstin Schankweiler, Verena Straub, and Tobias Wendl (New York: Routledge, 2019), 74.

79 Weizman, "Matter against Memory," 249.

80 Ibid., 248.

81 Ibid., 252.

82 Deepfake techniques are applied to video and audio material alike, as well as to combinations of both. See Supasorn Suwajanakorn, Steven M. Seitz, and Ira Kemelmacher-Shlizerman, "Synthesizing Obama: Learning Lip Sync from Audio," *ACM Transactions on Graphics* 36, no. 4 (July 2017), doi:10.1145/3072959.3073640.

83 Produced by Jordan Peele and Jared Sosa in collaboration with *BuzzFeed*, https://www.buzzfeednews.com/article/davidmack/obama-fake-news-jordan-peele-psa-video-buzzfeed.

84 The authors contrast three "beneficial uses" with eleven "harmful uses." Robert Chesney and Danielle Keats Citron, "Deep Fakes: A Looming Challenge for Privacy, Democracy, and National Security," *California Law Review* 107, no. 6 (2019), 1754, https://www.californialawreview.org/print/deep-fakes-a-looming-challenge-for-privacy-democracy-and-national-security/.

85 For an overview of the developments in deepfake detection, see Thanh Thi Nguyen et al., "Deep Learning for Deepfakes Creation and Detection: A Survey," *arXiv.org*, 2019, https://arxiv.org/abs/1909.11573.

86 Ibid., 9.

Photographesomenon: Video Surveillance as a Paradoxical Image-Making Machine (2005)

Winfried Pauleit

1. Video Surveillance as an Image Machine

Video surveillance differs fundamentally from the human gaze in at least the three following respects: First, there is no longer any need for an individual to sit behind the camera or even at a remote monitor. Modern video surveillance is fully automatic and computer-controlled. In fact, the recorded images are only viewed on rare occasions. An effort will only be made to view the tapes in the case of an unsolved crime. Second, video surveillance is an ongoing measure, a permanent control. Consequently, the special signals associated with recording are no longer present: no "Smile!" from the photographer, no clapperboard like in a film production. Video surveillance means the end of nonrecording. Periods of non-recording were in fact a subject of negotiation for the *Big Brother* television experiment, and the parties finally agreed on one hour of non-recording each day. Third, video surveillance takes place with a network of cameras. Just as there are times of non-recording, cameras always only deliver fragments of an occurrence. The multitude of surveillance cameras in a network strive to minimize "off-space," as it is referred to in film. Video surveillance is designed in such a way that supermarkets, city districts, or entire cities can be covered and captured as thoroughly as possible.

The inhuman aspects of video surveillance are the lack of the figure behind the camera and the controlled, limitless recording of time and space. One can think of video surveillance as a divine and totalitarian omnipotent presence. And one can also think of it as a technological referee, as a third account that can be questioned in case of doubt or dispute. It can ultimately be understood as a place open to everyone, as Foucault considered the Benthamian tower of the Panopticon.

Video surveillance is therefore a specific refinement of visual control, and essentially functions analogously to Bentham's eighteenth-century prison model. Bentham believed in the internalization of the controlling gaze and saw himself as an educator. At the same time, he set an aesthetic educational process in motion that no visual control can function without: it constructs the other. Criminals are not only separated out from the normal population as negative examples, they also become visual attractions, as if in a zoo or circus.[1] Video surveillance is therefore an image machine with which we can differentiate ourselves from others. The paradox of this machine is that we require images of others for our own sense of reassurance. In the paradigm of video surveillance, existing without images would guarantee objective security—but at the same time the loss of our very constitution.

Video surveillance is therefore not only a tool used by the police to combat theft or an extension of the eye of the law through technical means, as George Orwell pointed out with his "Big Brother" as a totalitarian surveillance state. This position on video surveillance already presupposes a clear division into an inner eye (and codified law) on the one hand and a domesticated body on the other. A more complex understanding of video surveillance additionally places this technology among media of self-reflection and self-perception. Unlike a mirror, for example, video allows a person to see themselves as they are seen by others. Video technology hereby reveals itself in the known dual function of the image: on the one hand as a mirror for the self, on the other hand a window to the world. Video surveillance can therefore essentially take effect in two directions, creating separation in the sense of a division of inside and outside, or integration of the other/self into one's own self-image. The potential of the video surveillance image machine can also be traced back to photography.[2] Even in the early days of photography, drawings and caricatures revealed a daguerrotypomania, i.e. delusions of producing photographic records of everything and everyone. In a lithograph from 1839, Théodore Maurisset anticipated all of the essential possibilities for control granted by photography, both in the sense of the self-control and self-assurance that this medium made available to the citizens, but at the same time in the sense of separation from the other, depicted with aerial reconnaissance conducted by the military in hot-air balloons. The systematic use of portrait photography in criminology began around 1860, and it first came to a head during the Paris Commune. During this time, the border posts were each equipped with up to 4000 *carte de visite* photographs in order to be able to identify wanted persons when they crossed the border, as photo IDs were not yet commonplace. This is a tangible example of the repurposing of a medium of photographic self-affirmation—the picture on the *carte de visite*—for the control of others, in this case Communards sought by the police.

The Photographesomenon

The use of video surveillance and its preemptive recording generates a specific type of image. It is one that remains invisible in the present. The aim of the recording is to duplicate a particular spatiotemporal structure, creating footage that can subsequently be made available. A second reality emerges as a bargaining chip against unforeseen events. However, the recorded footage is only kept for a short time in order to conserve storage space. The production of visible segments doesn't take place until later on.

The creation of these images is thereby directed toward the future perfect. It is a form of image that operates in a time loop, the kind we otherwise know only from science fiction.[3] One can describe the subsequently created image as a photographesomenon (Light-will-have-been-written), a transfer of photography (light-writing) into the future perfect. The photographesomenon is already recorded (written), even though it will only constitute an image in the future. In contrast to photography, the photographesomenon involves no photographic act, and the recording of the images therefore involves no particular sequence of events or an encouraging presence behind the camera. Instead, it is a retroactive process that selects individual images from available footage.

Conceiving of an image this way is highly controversial in a social and political context. Such a method of collecting images exerts control over more than just the present, and therefore forms the antithesis to a radical democratic understanding of the image that functions in principle like a void in which collective existence begins to structure itself, as the philosopher Jean-Luc Nancy expresses it.[4] At the same time, it seizes the future and asserts that it is already secured, as it were, with the help of video surveillance as the future perfect—whereas other political decisions or political decisions made by others no longer play a role.

The Bulger incident, which took place in Liverpool in 1993, can be regarded as a noteworthy example of this type of image production. A two-year-old boy was kidnapped from a shopping mall by a 10-year-old and an 11-year-old, abused, and later killed. The kidnapping was caught on tape. A few days after the murder, a news program on British television showed a sequence of seven video stills recorded by various surveillance cameras at the mall. The first three show two-year-old James Bulger alone, the following three show only the two perpetrators, and the seventh image depicts their encounter, which can be considered the deciding, fateful moment. The editing of the images is not only defined by the fact that a spatial and temporal selection was made. In addition, the chronology of the recordings and with it that of the (supposed) events is abandoned in favor of a dramatic structure, a kind of parallel montage, in which two different shots are finally brought together in one. The commentary reinforces this dramatic structure. The tension peaks at the end of the sequence when it is condensed into a single frame. This last picture of the sequence unfolds the rhetoric of the panel painting, in which a critical moment is emphasized and actions are given a context, coalescing in a single image.[5]

There are two lines of discourse that can be linked to the new qualities presented in the photographesomenon. On the one hand, there is the discourse of the "pregnant moment" in art, which Lessing outlines in his description of the Laocoön Group.[6] The sculpture depicts Laocoön and his sons battling the snakes shortly before his death. Lessing is concerned with the reasoning behind the central moment chosen by the artist to depict the event—the artistic consolidation into a single image. Lessing argues that the portrayal only hints at the dramatic events of the mortal battle in order to allow them to first unfold in the mind of the viewer. As Lessing describes it, the story of the death from the myth and the visual capacity of the beholder's imagination become superimposed. On the other hand, there is the discourse surrounding the moment of corporeal mortification in photography. Roland Barthes describes it as an entanglement of the living and the dead.[7] And Siegfried Kracauer speaks of a "ghostly reality" in photography that remains unresolved.[8]

For practical reasons, video surveillance cameras are installed in such a way that they point diagonally downward from above, similar to the divine eye known from the history of painting.[9] This creates supervision that most often lacks any reference to a horizon. James Bulger's photographesomenon similarly presents a dually codifiable situation involving a threshold that brings together moments of life and death. One of the perpetrators takes little James Bulger by the hand. Hand in hand, the future victim and future perpetrator face a horizon beyond the image. Only knowledge of the case transforms this image into a pregnant moment, the terrible perversion of which exists in the fact that the picture was not created by an artist, but by an image machine. The photographic character of the image, a bargaining chip of reality, additionally gives the image a ghostly encoding, as it allows us to see the impending death over and over again as we continue to imagine Bulger's murder, in a way similar to that which Lessing describes.

At this point, the political dimension of the image's process, beyond its promise of security, becomes apparent. First, it becomes clear that surveillance technology cannot prevent a murder. And secondly, the secret purpose of this technology emerges: it safeguards the social status quo, in which the articulation of others and the other is almost inevitably associated with crime. [. . .]

From Winfried Pauleit, "Photographesomenon: Videoüberwachung und bildende Kunst," in *Bild—Raum—Kontrolle: Videoüberwachung als Zeichen gesellschaftlichen Wandels*, ed. Leon Hempel and Jörg Metelmann (Frankfurt am Main: Suhrkamp, 2005), 73–90; translated for the present publication by Chelsea Leventhal.

Notes

1 Aldo Legnaro refers to studies by Norris and Armstrong, according to which 90 percent of those intentionally placed under surveillance in Great Britain are male, 40 percent are teenagers, and an above-average percentage are black. See Aldo Legnaro, "Panoptismus: Fiktionen der Übersichtlichkeit," *Ästhetik & Kommunikation* 111 (2000), 73–8, here p. 77.

2 Heather Cameron, "Private Eyes, Public Eyes: Fotografie und Überwachungsgesellschaft," *Nach dem Film* 3, no. 10 (2001), http://www.nachdemfilm.de/no3/cam01dts.html.

3 A photo-literary (or cinematic) example of this form is Chris Marker's film *La Jetée* (France 1962), or the better known re-make, Terry Gilliam's *Twelve Monkeys* (USA 1995). Marker's film tells the story of a man who encounters his own death (in the future perfect).

4 Jean-Luc Nancy, "Stimme wider das Gebrüll: Was tun gegen den Front National?" in *Frankfurter Allgemeine Zeitung*, May 2, 2002, 50.

5 See Ernst H. Gombrich, *The Image and the Eye: Further Studies in the Psychology of Pictorial Representation* (Oxford: Phaidon, 1982); G.E. Lessing, *Laokoon* (Stuttgart: Reclam, 1994). The image from the news report can be considered the critical moment, as it depicts Bulger's first encounter, and therefore first contact, with one of the perpetrators. It is not—as was often claimed in the press—the last image of James Bulger alive. There are other images from surveillance cameras that follow Bulger and his tormentors through the city of Liverpool.

6 The Laocoön Group is an ancient sculpture from the 1st century B.C. that was at the center of academic art theory after its discovery in Rome in 1506. See Lessing, *Laokoon*, 215.

7 Roland Barthes, *Die helle Kammer* (Frankfurt am Main: Suhrkamp, 1989), 89.

8 Siegfried Kracauer, "Die Photographie" (1927), in *Das Ornament der Masse* (Frankfurt am Main: Suhrkamp, 1977), 21–39, here p. 32.

9 See Astrid Schmidt-Burkhardt, "The All-Seer: God's Eye as Proto-Surveillance," in *CTRL [SPACE]—Rhetorics of Surveillance from Bentham to Big Brother*, ed. Thomas Y. Levin, Ursula Frohne, and Peter Weibel (Boston: MIT Press, 2002), 16–31.

CCTV: The Stealthy Emergence of a Fifth Utility? (2002)

Stephen Graham

One of the most visible interactions of place and high-technology communications systems over the past ten years has been the installation of Closed Circuit Television (CCTV). Designed to improve the economic fortunes of public, commercial street systems, such technologies are so widespread that it has been estimated that the average UK urban resident is now monitored more than 300 times a day, making Britain the most visually surveilled nation on Earth.[1] [. . .]

Given this huge growth in CCTV coverage this article critically explores the development of this trend and the implications such technologies have for the nature and experience of space and place for *all* members of society.

Economies of Scale and Scope in CCTV Expansion

Once CCTV systems are installed, their logic is inevitably expansionary. Economies of scale are very marked—once a system is built and monitoring personnel are employed, it makes sense to cover larger and larger areas. Communities and businesses occupying uncovered spaces clamor to get CCTV cover and so avoid any "overspill" effects, as crime moves away from covered areas. Economies of scope are also important in CCTV expansion. New uses are constantly being found for CCTV beyond its initial purpose: from traffic monitoring, checking the performance of street cleaners, monitoring graffiti, preventing underage smoking, to preventing terrorism (or at least providing evidence for tracking down terrorists after attacks). While CCTV systems covering roads and motorways are usually installed for traffic management, it is easy to extend their function to include supporting road pricing, enforcing speed limits, and tracking for suspects and stolen vehicles.

The current shift from analog to digital, computerized CCTV systems also supports expansion. Digital, algorithmic techniques, like those currently being used in the City of London's "Ring of Steel" system and the system in Newham, East London, allow much larger systems to be automatically monitored because the systems can be programmed to automatically search for "abnormal" or "unexpected" events, behaviors, or even people. In the City of London, cars moving the "wrong" way down a street automatically trigger cameras to monitor the scene. Additionally, by linking digital CCTV with image database technology, "algorithmic" CCTV systems can be programmed to automatically scan for specified faces or car number plates or to ensure that people are where they "belong." Such systems are being widely trialed in airports, sports stadia, and public spaces in the wake of the September 11 terrorist attacks.[2]

Parallels with the Development of Utilities in the Nineteenth-Century City

The most striking thing about the wiring up of Britain with CCTV is how similar the process is to the initial development in nineteenth-century cities of the networked utilities such as gas, electricity, water, and telecommunications that are now taken for granted. While we now assume such networks to be ubiquitous and treat them as invisible supports to every aspect of our lives, this was not always so. In the nineteenth century, water, waste, energy, and telegraph utilities first emerged as small, specialized networks, geared toward a myriad of uses, utilizing wide ranges of technologies and covering only small parts of cities. These networks sprang up through complex patchworks of both public and private entrepreneurship. Industries started their own electricity and water networks; town gas networks were built by ambitious municipalities for lighting their streets; and the first phone and telegraph networks were initially used mainly by large businesses and emergency service providers.[3]

These networks, of course, have long since merged and extended to become technologically standardized, multipurpose, nationally-regulated utilities, with virtually universal coverage. The social and economic modernization of society since the nineteenth century has been inextricably bound up with integrating the many small-scale utilities together as part of the national "roll out" of (relatively) standardized energy, water, waste, and telephone networks. By the 1950s people took it for granted that across the whole country they could make direct dial phone calls, heat, light, and power their homes with electricity at a standard voltage and access clean, running water and (in all but the most remote areas) sewerage networks. The massive utility networks necessary to deliver these services were operated by large public monopolies who exploited economies of scale and scope and were regulated at the national level to ensure consistent quality, standard tariffs, and universal coverage.

The Rush to Ubiquity: Normalization, Regularization, and the Fear of Unwatched Spaces

It can be argued that CCTV looks set to follow a similar pattern of development over the next 20 years, to become a kind of "fifth utility." Coverage seems set to extend toward ubiquity, to become more multi-purpose, to be regulated nationally, and to adopt standardized technologies. Every murder, school break-in, or terrorist act further intensifies the spiral of demands for ubiquitous surveillance. Digital compression techniques, webcams, and the development of the Internet and broadband cable networks are already providing the infrastructure for people and organizations to simply plug in and rent their camera networks, much as we use phones or lease lines today. An emerging culture of private, remote monitoring already offers parents the ability to view their children at nursery throughout the day at some U.S. childcare centers. Microcameras, automated tracking, image database, and facial recognition techniques are already enhancing the cost-effectiveness of CCTV. The more CCTV coverage becomes the norm, the more excluded areas will fight to gain coverage.

As with the extension of gas, electricity, phone, and water networks, toward national coverage earlier this century, the rush to ubiquity is on. [. . .]

CCTV is thus well on the way to becoming our fifth utility. In the near future we can speculate about people worrying when they are *not* under the soothing effect of some "friendly eye in the sky" just as they do when beyond the reach of electricity, power, water, flushing toilets, or fixed or mobile telephony. (In the same way the middle classes of the nineteenth century feared the spaces beyond the initial lit commercial cores of the metropolis.) However, it is unlikely that some single, national CCTV system will develop in the model of the water boards or gas boards of the post-war era in Britain. Since their privatization, UK utilities are now made up of a myriad of competing private companies covering different areas, offering different services, and geared to different niche markets. Street systems, too, are increasingly fragmented and managed by a range of public, public-private and private bodies.[4] The CCTV utility is emerging in the same way. There is likely to be some form of national regulator and a myriad of service providers from the telecoms, cable, media, security, and IT industries, offering many different types of service, from simple "watch your home while away" to mobile, private webcams and videophones, to enormous networks covering all the premises of a multinational or multisite organization with algorithmic systems automatically sensing for what is deemed unusual at any given place.

The Dangers of Systematizing and Automating the Exclusion of "Failed Consumers"

The worry, of course, is that the emergence of a CCTV utility will systematize processes of exclusion and discrimination and embed them within automated, algorithmic, invisible systems of (attempted) social control. What is seen to be "abnormal" or "threatening" within automated CCTV tracking systems will, after all, be defined through the opaque definitions of software code. This will often occur tens of thousands of miles away from the points of surveillance in some distant R&D lab. What is to stop this code being explicitly defined to concentrate the cameras' power on, say, young black men, people selling (homeless) magazines, or, as already happens in some U.S. malls, people who simply sit down or "loiter" for periods deemed by power holders to be too long for the imperative of maximum profitability and commercial throughput?

To back up the wider gentrification and privatization of urban commercial cores, sophisticated systems are likely to emerge which actively scan for the "failed consumers" of the metropolis, utilizing increasingly privatized policing and security practices to ensure their subtle (or not so subtle) removal. Indeed, such practices are already widespread in the use of nondigital CCTV within Town Center Management (TCM). In 1998, for example, the private managers of the Covent Garden market center in London decided to "exclude vagrants" from the piazza.[5] Around the UK, as competition for higher-income consumers intensifies between out-of-town malls and city centers, management strategies are combining street theming, private policing, and CCTV on public streets. Users deemed to be "unaesthetic" or "antisocial" are often managed out or pushed elsewhere: "junkies," "down and outs," or others who, in the words of one Town Center Manager, "make the town degraded" are not welcome.[6]

In practice, TCM schemes have been found to "discriminate actively against [beggars and street people] in order to massage the social space of a town center into something more socially conducive to consumers."[7] Moreover, in the UK, CCTV schemes, which back up such street management programs, have been widely found to target people for "no particular reason" than "belonging to a particular subcultural group."[8] Black people, in particular, "were between one-and-a-half and two-and-a-half times more likely to be surveilled than one would expect from their presence in the population."[9] Through CCTV, people and behaviors seen not to "belong" in the increasingly commercialized and privately-managed consumption spaces of British town and city centers tended to experience especially close scrutiny. Norris, Moran, and Armstrong found CCTV control rooms were ridden with racism and sexism.[10] Certain types of young men were targeted with socially constructed suspicion being labeled ("toerags," "yobs," "scrapheads," "Big Issue scum" [named after the UK's homeless magazine], and "drug-dealing scrotes") and consequently scrutinized, followed, and harassed. Malign intent was equated with appearance, youth, clothing, and posture. Thus, CCTV operators are already imposing a "normative space-time ecology" on the watched parts of the city, stipulating who "belongs" where and when, and treating everything else as a suspicious "other" to be disciplined, scrutinized, controlled.[11]

The diffusion and automation of CCTV, and its linkage to digital image databases, however, means that the normative assumptions about the value and risk associated with particular individuals moves from the discretion of human practice to be embedded within the opaque codes of computer systems. Such a development would mean "a tremendous change in our society's conception of a person."[12] It would have dramatic implications for the nature of places, politics, planning, and democratic practice, as automated, opaque systems start to inscribe complex normative ecologies of "acceptable" people and behavior into the fabric of urban places on a continuous and largely unknowable basis. Whole sections of cities might be continually "red-lined," not through the demarcation of spatial zones for receiving poorer services, but through the automated scrutiny of individuals. Individuals will be excluded when venturing into the premium commercial spaces of their city due to their appearance, habits, or challenge to dominant power holders' normative concepts of who belongs where and when within the city. One thing, above all, is very clear: these trends mean that the politics of the street need to be quickly linked to the politics of code in critical research and practice.

From Stephen Graham, "CCTV: The Stealthy Emergence of a Fifth Utility?" in *Planning Theory & Practice* 3, no. 2 (2002), 237–41.

Notes

1 Clive Norris and Gary Armstrong, *The Maximum Surveillance Society: The Rise of CCTV* (Oxford: Berg, 1999).

2 Philip E. Agre, "Your Face Is Not a Bar Code: Arguments against Automatic Face Recognition in Public Places" (2001), version from 2003 available at https://pages.gseis.ucla.edu/faculty/agre/bar-code.html.

3 See Steve Graham and Simon Marvin, *Splintering Urbanism: Networked Infrastructures, Technological Mobilities and the Urban Condition* (London: Routledge, 2001).

4 Ibid.
5 B. Daly, "Covent Garden to 'Exclude Vagrants,'" *Big Issue*, March 11, 1999.
6 Cited in Alan Reeve, "The Private Realm of the Managed Town Centre," *Urban Design International* 1, no. 1 (1996), 70.
7 Ibid., 78.
8 Norris and Armstrong, *The Maximum Surveillance Society*.
9 Ibid., 3.
10 Clive Norris, Jade Moran, and Gary Armstrong, "Algorithmic Surveillance: The Future of Automated Visual Surveillance," in *Surveillance, Closed Circuit Television and Social Control*, ed. Norris, Moran, and Armstrong (Aldershot: Ashgate, 1998), 255–67.
11 Stephen Graham, John Brooks, and Dan Heery, "Towns on the Television: Closed Circuit TV Systems in British Towns and Cities," *Local Government Studies* 22, no. 3 (1996), 3–27.
12 Agre, "Your Face Is Not a Bar Code," 3.

The Cultural Labor of Surveillance: Video Forensics, Computational Objectivity, and the Production of Visual Evidence (2013)

Kelly Gates

A photo of two of the alleged 9/11 hijackers passing through airport security in Portland, Maine, on the morning of the attacks appeared in the October 1, 2001 issue of *TIME* magazine. Another photograph, allegedly depicting three of the London subway bombers on a trial run before they carried out the attacks on July 7, 2005, was published in *The New York Times* two and a half months after the bombings. The surveillance stills from these high-profile incidents are accompanied by thousands of other more banal examples, often depicting events that make the news not so much because of their world-historical importance but because surveillance cameras fortuitously recorded the "money shot." For example, the abduction and murder of Carlie Brucia by a drug addict named Joseph Smith in Sarasota, Florida, on February 1, 2004 received national attention in no small part because a gas station security camera happened to capture Smith approaching the 11-year-old girl and leading her away. A still shot taken from the video, showing Smith's hand clasped around the child's extended arm, circulated widely in the press. It was the decisive evidence that led to his conviction, both in criminal court and in the court of public opinion.

Images like these are readily recognizable as still shots captured from surveillance video—the perspective, usually shot slightly from above and at an angle, a banal location, a grainy or blurry quality, and often a time-date stamp and a camera number imprinted on the image. When reproduced as press photos, the images typically include an image credit printed in tiny type below the photo. In the London subway photo, it read "Metropolitan Police, via Associated Press,"[1] suggesting both a path of information flow and an institutional relationship. This and other contextualizing metadata (the caption, the headline, and the text of article) assign specific meaning to these images, but the meanings of their visual content alone are often radically indeterminate. Nothing in these photographs themselves can definitively identify the people depicted, for example. Surveillance images can be of fairly poor quality, and it can be difficult to see people's faces. If facial recognition technology had been installed with the surveillance systems that captured these images, it is unlikely that it would have matched the faces with accurate identities since the technology does not work well in uncontrolled settings like the ones shown. [. . .]

The vastly increased use of CCTV for monitoring public and private spaces over the last several decades has spurred efforts to "optimize" these systems—to make them function more effectively as technologies of crime control as well as technologies of *proof*.

In this paper, I consider the emerging field of *video forensics* as one technology of CCTV optimization. The work of video forensics includes the production of images like the ones described above, but it is not limited to the production of press photos.

Video forensics involves the postcrime analysis of surveillance video as part of criminal and other types of investigations. It also involves the archival management of recorded surveillance video, as well as the preparation of video evidence for presentation to an audience, whether in courtrooms or other settings.[2] Although I primarily focus on the United States context, the emerging technologies and practices discussed here are not exclusive to the United States, and the questions raised by the evidentiary uses of surveillance images have broad relevance for other national contexts.

On the surface, the status and usefulness of surveillance video as evidence in criminal and other types of investigations would seem self-evident. However, when considering more closely what happens in the process of locating video of interest and analyzing, organizing, and using that video in criminal investigations, it is clear that a significant amount of work goes into transforming recorded surveillance video into usable evidence. In other words, surveillance video in itself has little or no evidentiary value; video evidence must be *produced* from a chaotic field of raw surveillance footage. The status of video evidence as an index of real events—a sign or representation that offers a direct, empirical connection to material reality—is the result of an intentional process of production, a process that requires new forms of technical expertise and police work, as well as the adaption of new technologies borrowed from the world of creative media production. The emerging field of forensic video analysis is one site where an epistemic virtue of "computational objectivity" is taking shape: the belief that neutral scientific image analysis can be achieved by translating certain forms of professional trained judgment into computational processes or, in this case, through the application of computational techniques by police professionals retrained as video specialists. [. . .]

The Cultural Labor of Surveillance

In Christopher Wilson's cultural history of policing,[3] he examines the narrative authority that police held in the United States throughout the twentieth century—how dominant ideas, values, and assumptions about crime and policing circulated back and forth from police policy and practice to crime reporting and the popular genres of crime fiction and True Crime storytelling. As Wilson argues, police power is derived to a significant extent from their narrative authority or their ability to tell authoritative stories about crime and about their own proper role as agents of the state and as arbiters of law and order. In light of this analysis, it would seem that police authority is negotiated in part through the *cultural* forms of labor that police officers perform not so much "fighting crime" directly but *performing* their roles (sometimes for the cameras) and employing media technologies and tactics in a constant battle of interpretations about crime, social disorder, and the limits and extent of police power. [. . .]

When considering the types of "new media work" that the police perform today, what is clear is that the respective roles of the police as generators of data and producers of culture are not mutually exclusive. To understand the relationship between these two indistinct responsibilities of modern police, it helps to understand the ways in which at least some of the work that police do today can be characterized as cultural or "immaterial labor."[4] The concept of immaterial labor is typically associated with the culture industries and, more recently, with the forms of (often unpaid) labor that armies of Internet users perform in the service of building and maintaining the World Wide Web. [. . .]

What is conceptually understood as immaterial labor pervades police work, especially insofar as "the skills involved . . . are increasingly skills involving cybernetics and computer control."[5] The police engage in forms of cybernetic labor as they perform myriad responsibilities on the job: entering and accessing information, using database interfaces at computer terminals in police cars and in police stations, using handheld digital devices to identify suspects (e.g., mobile biometric devices that attach to iPhones), or searching the Internet to do investigative work (e.g., using Facebook to identify faces of otherwise anonymous people captured in surveillance video). When police video analysts use video forensics systems to analyze and manage surveillance video, they are engaged in producing informational content and developing and enacting skills involving cybernetics and computer control. This type of immaterial labor involves a considerable amount of mental and perceptual work, or work that involves cognitive rather than physical activities.[6] [. . .]

When police and other law enforcement personnel do the work of sifting through surveillance camera footage to find content of interest that in turn becomes commercial media product; they are also performing cultural or "immaterial" labor—doing the work necessary to provide material to feed the voracious media appetite for reality-based content. But even when this media content remains within the domain of police investigations and criminal prosecutions, it shares important affinities with entertainment or infotainment media. An aesthetics of surveillant media circulates back and forth from the official domain of policing to the less-official domains of popular and online social media. We are now accustomed to encountering surveillance-style images whether we are watching the news, YouTube, or fictional crime dramas. [. . .]

Every surveillance image—whether video or still shot, "live" or recorded, staged or unstaged—carries with it an implicit rhetorical claim of temporal indexicality. Even though recorded surveillance video does not depict events as they are happening in real time, it nonetheless invokes a sense of temporal indexicality. Recorded video surveillance makes time searchable, albeit within spatial limitations, enabling a form of reality-rewind or "playback." Photography has always invoked a sense of connectedness to the past, but recorded video surveillance adds another dimension to this connectedness—not a symbolic visual link to lost loved ones or historic events, but a replay that appears to give viewers direct access to specific segments of time.

Cinema's use of surveillant narration as a form of realism has its inverse in the techniques that forensic video analysts are developing to process and analyze surveillance video. Video forensic techniques enable their users to make authoritative claims about the indexicality of surveillance images,[7] helping video analysts transform a chaotic and meaningless field of recorded vision into coherent and direct references to real people, places, objects, and events. But much like with cinema, a significant amount of production labor goes into transforming surveillance video into evidence and ensuring that images maintain a seemingly "unproduced" quality. Concerns about lighting conditions, placement of cameras, camera angles and movement are not alien to users of video surveillance systems. These users are also becoming acquainted with editing and postproduction techniques, adapting them to the needs of visual evidence production.

Video Forensics and the Production of Image Indexicality

[. . .] If make-believe surveillance video poses a challenge for the fictional detectives who populate film and television crime dramas, real-life surveillance video also presents major image quality issues for flesh-and-blood investigators. A considerable amount of production work is required to transform recorded surveillance video into evidence in part because the video itself is typically of very poor quality. It is often unusable and indecipherable in its "raw" state. If magnetic videotapes are used, as they still are in some cases, they are often degraded from repeated use. Digital video can take up considerable memory and often has to be compressed for processing and storage. Compression rates can be set too high, leading to low-quality images, deleted frames, and loss of other important visual information. Other image quality problems derive from the physical context of surveillance systems. For example, lighting can be bad (especially in video taken outdoors at night) making faces, license plates, and other objects difficult to see. System design (or lack thereof) can also introduce problems—e.g., cameras are often stationary or poorly placed, resulting in bad camera angles. Or, if the cameras are being *manned* (either handheld or remotely controlled), there can be *too much movement*, creating unstable images and making details difficult to see. [. . .]

At the very least, forensic analysts must make particular choices about what visual information to focus on and what to ignore, informed by their own professional trained judgment. The software functions are not simply technical processes but, instead, require human perceptual labor and decision-making. [. . .]

Computational Objectivity

[. . .] Here I want to suggest that the use of digital imaging technologies to make visible what is invisible and invest images with indexicality points to a new conceptualization of objectivity. This way of thinking about objectivity holds that neutral, scientific results can be achieved through the application of computational forms of analysis—automated, algorithmic techniques performed by computers. In their historical study of the prevailing "epistemic virtues" that have defined objectivity over time, Daston and Galison use the term "mechanical objectivity" to refer to the type of objectivity associated with photography and other visualizing instruments developed in the nineteenth century.[8] Proponents of "mechanical objectivity" subscribed to the belief that mechanical devices could be used to produce scientific images that were uncontaminated by interpretation, in contrast to the artistically rendered, "true-to-nature" illustrations that populated scientific atlases. Photography promised to remove the individual scientist's judgment, and the biasing hand of the illustrator, from scientific image making. But photography and other mechanical visualization techniques never made good on this promise—the problem of image interpretation persisted—and what emerged in the twentieth century, as an acceptable avenue to objectivity, was the epistemic virtue of "trained judgment." In this view, objectivity could best be achieved through the analytical abilities and interpretive skills of well-trained human beings.

What we see emerging today is another kind of objectivity—a "computational objectivity," or an avenue to objective analytical results that aims to translate certain aspects of trained judgment into computational systems. Along with the effort to achieve "computational objectivity," and to promote it as a new epistemic virtue, there is a renewal of the suspect promise that the biased and imperfect perceptual capacities of human beings can be eliminated or designed out of computational forms of image analysis. [. . .]

Surveillance Video "Asset Management"

"Computational objectivity" can be said to encompass not only the application of algorithmic techniques to specific images, but also the computational organization of large collections of images in order to associate them with other data, identify patterns and relationships, and make images available for later use. The need to address image quality issues and to direct viewer attention to particular details in specific video images are only the most obvious problems the investigators face in attempting to exploit the evidentiary potential of surveillance video. Equally, if not more important is what the media production industries call "media asset management"—the problem of how to manage the *quantity* of video being produced by CCTV systems, as well as the smaller collections of video deemed relevant to particular investigations. In other words, the ability to optimize the evidentiary potential of recorded surveillance video—to produce useable evidence from a field of available imagery—is as much an *archival* or database management problem as it is an image analysis problem. For media producers and organizations, effective management of their "media assets" is vitally important to the work of media production. It is, likewise, important to the work of media evidence production.

As a result of the widespread diffusion of CCTV, surveillance video has become one of the most prolific sources of evidence in criminal investigations. One of the first things the police do now when arriving at the scene of a crime is to look for cameras.[9] According to the director of research for the International Association for Police Chiefs: "It used to be you got to a crime scene and what you had was whatever was left there: a cigarette stub or a tire skid . . . Now it's possible to have between 5 and 10 video clips that [police] can gather from that area."[10]

Jonathan Hak, a crown prosecutor from Alberta, Canada, has noted that it is "routine now for police to seize video from places within a mile of where a crime occurred."[11] This new investigative practice of searching for surveillance cameras after a crime has occurred, points to a challenge that works against the meaningful use of recorded surveillance video as evidence, necessitating the development of new technologies and procedures for the managing of video assets as a fundamental part of evidence production: the highly decentralized and ad hoc process of surveillance system diffusion, especially in the United States. [. . .] Although difficult to measure, private video surveillance systems have far outpaced centralized police systems, introducing challenges for police investigators attempting to gather and make use of the video.

Without new ways of managing this multiplication of dispersed visual information—techniques for gathering, archiving, and retrieving information from this vastly expanding field of imagery—the visual information generated by video surveillance systems becomes virtually meaningless. Police, in partnership with the security industry, are in fact developing new ways to manage the visual record of reality from dispersed CCTV systems and other video sources. [. . .]

In addition, rather than continue to gather video by physically searching the area, some police departments have begun negotiating with private businesses to build camera registries and gain access to their surveillance systems on an as-needed basis. The City of Philadelphia, for example, has an online camera registry called "SafeCam," where local businesses can provide information about the location of their surveillance cameras.[12] This way, when a crime occurs the police can go to the registry to see what CCTV systems in the area may have captured relevant visual information, without having to physically search the area for cameras. Other partnerships of this sort are designed to give police direct, real-time, logical (or log-in) access to private video systems on an as-needed basis, such as San Diego's "Operation Secure San Diego" program launched in 2010. As described at the SDPD website, officers can tap into live video feeds from computer terminals in their police cars on the way to a participating place of business in response to a call for assistance. Although descriptions of the program say nothing about police recording the live video streams, it would not be difficult for the police to do so, and it would be consistent with police tendency to be forward thinking about the need for evidence, should an investigation of an incident become necessary. [. . .]

Video archiving and collaborative work-sharing systems promise to help investigators do much more than analyze or enhance specific images. Work-sharing systems are designed to allow users in different locations to work with the same video material, enabling multiple investigators to work on single cases at the same time and providing a means to link different cases over time and even across departments or agencies.

In their large-scale investigation of the 2011 Vancouver Stanley Cup riots, for example, forensic video analysts have made powerful use of work-sharing systems to pool the labor of trained forensics professionals in the United States and Canada, collectively processing tens of thousands of hours of video generated by CCTV cameras and handheld devices the night of the riots. The video forensics' component of the riot investigation is establishing an important precedent that demonstrates the power of distributive, collaborative work-sharing systems for mass identification in crowd scenarios. (Any number of states might find such systems useful for managing or repressing crowds, including not only sporting event riots but also organized mass demonstrations.) [. . .]

Timelines can be constructed to track a suspect's movements in video gathered from multiple sources, or to show how an event or series of events may have played out, piecing together video with other evidence gathered in one or multiple investigations. The timelines and reports produced in this way provide authoritative documentation for courtroom presentation, lending a form of "documentary verification" to investigators' narratives of events.[13]

These capabilities for using media asset management systems to optimize the evidentiary potential of surveillance video raise the question of how the multimedia database form changes the way narratives are constructed, whether in fictional or nonfictional genres of storytelling. In *The Language of New Media*, Lev Manovich examines the relationship between the database and the narrative forms, conceptualizing them "as two competing imaginations, two basic creative impulses, two essential responses to the world."[14] "Modern media is the new battlefield for the competition between database and narrative," he writes, "competing to make meaning out of the world, the database and narrative produce endless hybrids."[15] The question that then arises, according to Manovich, concerns how "our new abilities to store vast amounts of data, to automatically classify, index, link, search, and instantly retrieve it lead to new kinds of narratives."[16] [. . .]

The very real creative possibilities opened up by new database-narrative assemblages means that the emerging field of video forensics must carefully define the limits of its creative potential. Efforts to distinguish forensic video analysis from the domain of creative media production can be found in the promotional language used to define video forensics systems. They can also be found in the new field's commitment to the emerging epistemic virtue of "computational objectivity."

Conclusion

Just as new imaging, editing, and database technologies are enabling Hollywood editors [. . .] to make films that they could not have created otherwise, video forensic systems designed using some of the same technologies are, likewise, enabling an emerging professional class of law enforcement video analysts to accomplish much more with expanding volumes of recorded surveillance video. The varying levels of skill that forensic video analysts acquire in achieving an "aesthetics of objectivity" in the production of video evidence cannot help but be informed by the cultural prevalence of surveillant forms of narration, regardless of how circumscribed evidence production techniques are by legal requirements. An analysis of the social and cultural implications of surveillance video's evidentiary uses should not be limited to its role in particular investigations. More broadly, we need to make sense of the ways that the field of video forensics and other types of media expertise invest police institutions with renewed narrative authority in the new media landscape, giving the police added ammunition in their constant battle of interpretations over the prevailing *ways of seeing* crime, social disorder, and police power itself.

From Kelly Gates, "The Cultural Labor of Surveillance: Video Forensics, Computational Objectivity, and the Production of Visual Evidence," *Social Semiotics* 23, no. 2 (2013), 242–60.

Notes

1 Sarah Lyall, "London Bombers Visited Earlier, Apparently on Practice Run," *The New York Times*, September 21, 2005, A8.

2 On the history of motion picture evidence in the US courts, see Louis-Georges Schwartz, *Mechanical Witness: A History of Motion Picture Evidence in U.S. Courts* (New York: Oxford University Press, 2009).

3 Christopher Wilson, *Cop Knowledge: Police Power and Cultural Narrative in Twentieth-Century America* (Chicago: University of Chicago Press, 2000).

4 In Maurizio Lazzarato's often-cited definition, "immaterial labor" is defined as "the labor that produces the informational and cultural content of the commodity":
The concept of immaterial labor refers to two different aspects of labor. On the one hand, as regards the "informational content" of the commodity, it refers directly to the changes taking place in workers' labor processes . . . where the skills involved in direct labor are increasingly skills involving cybernetics and computer control . . . On the other hand, as regards the activity that produces the "cultural content" of the commodity, immaterial labor involves a series of activities that are not normally recognized as "work," in other words, the kinds of activities involved in defining and fixing cultural and artistic standards, fashions, tastes, consumer norms, and, more strategically, public opinion. See Maurizio Lazzarato, Maurizio, "Immaterial Labour," in *Radical Thought in Italy*, ed. Paolo Virno and Michael Hardt, trans. Paul Colilli and Ed Emory (Minneapolis: University of Minnesota Press, 1996), 132–46.

5 Ibid.

6 Of course, no matter how much physical or manual labor is involved in policing the streets, arresting criminal suspects, or firing weapons, police work has never involved the type of physical or manual labor associated with a Fordist mode of production. From a Marxist perspective, the police are typically classed as "unproductive" labor: their labor does not directly support capital accumulation but functions more indirectly in the protection of property interests, and in the provision of security and social order that enables a capitalist economy to function. (The professionalization of the modern police more or less coincides historically with the rise of liberal democracies and their capitalist economies.) Of course, police officers and other law enforcement professionals are themselves members of the working classes people who sell their labor as a means of subsistence and police workforces are no strangers to forms of alienation in the Marxist sense, or from labor struggles and battles for collective representation. But as historians of the police have demonstrated, the police historically have performed the capitalist-serving labor of strike-busting and other forms of repressive regulation aimed directly at the urban working classes; see Sidney L. Harring, *Policing a Class Society: The Experience of American Cities, 1865–1915* (New Brunswick: Rutgers University Press, 1983); John Tagg, The *Burden of Representation: Essays on Photographies and Histories* (London: MacMillan, 1988).

As workers and agents of the state, the police occupy a contradictory location in the structure of modern capitalist societies.

7 In his history of motion picture evidence in the US courts, Louis-Georges Schwartz argues that: "In court, the cinema of indexicality is not the same as film theory. In cinema such indexicality is an implicit result of the medium itself and works to give the spectator an impression of reality. In court, film's indexicality is a result of the combination of a particular image and the testimony authenticating it, making the process of creating a particular image explicit. Evidentiary film's indexicality functions to purvey the facts of an event to the jury." Schwartz, *Mechanical Witness*, 9.

8 Lorraine Daston and Peter Galison, *Objectivity* (Cambridge, MA: MIT Press, 2007).

9 Jennifer Lee, "Caught on Tape, Then Just Caught: Private Cameras Transform Police Work," *The New York Times*, May 22, 2005 Metro section, 33.

10 Ibid., A36.

11 Quoted in Avid, *Forensics Video Analysis Handbook: A Blueprint for Selecting a Forensic Video Analysis Workstation*, company brochure (Burbank, CA: Avid, 2004).

12 See https://safecam.phillypolice.com/.

13 On "documentary verification," see Craig Robertson, "A Documentary Regime of Verification: The Emergence of the US Passport and the Archival Problematization of Identity," *Cultural Studies* 23, no. 3 (2009), 329–54.

14 Lev Manovich, *The Language of New Media* (Cambridge, MA: MIT Press, 2001), 233.

15 Ibid., 234.

16 Ibid., 237.

Drone Warfare at the Threshold of Detectability (2015)

Eyal Weizman

[. . .] Both the act of military killing and the practice of investigating those killings are image-based practices, afforded through the combination of proximity and remoteness that is the condition of media itself. Drone strikes themselves are performed in a high-resolution designed to show information, but are monitored (by NGOs or the UN) in the poor resolution of satellite photographs designed to hide information. This fact inverts one of the foundational principles of forensics since the nineteenth century, namely, that to resolve a crime the police should be able to see more—in higher resolution, using better optics—than the perpetrator of the crime is able to. This inversion is nested in another, because in the case of drone strikes it is state agencies that are the perpetrators. The difference in vision between remote perpetrator and remote witness is the space of denial—but of a different kind than the denial presented earlier in this essay.[1] [. . .] This form of denial is not simply rhetorical, but rather is made possible by the production of a frontier that has territorial, juridical, and visual characteristics.

Take for example the Waziristan region of Pakistan, since June 2004 one of the focal points for the drone campaign.[2] Waziristan is part of the Federally Administered Tribal Areas (FATA). During the period of the British Raj, FATA was established as an extraterritorial zone of local autonomy. The Pakistani military established checkpoints that filter movement in and out; it also prevented the bringing-in and taking-out of any electronic equipment, including mobile phones, cameras, and navigation equipment.[3] The consequence is an effective media siege in which very few photographs and eyewitness testimonies were allowed to leave these regions. This media blackout enabled drone warfare in these areas. It also helped Pakistani and US sources to deny this campaign ever existed and helped them to misleadingly claim that the casualties of drone strikes died rather in "bomb-making accidents."[4] In masking all signals within it, the pixel is the human-scale equivalent of the territorial-scale media blockage extended over FATA.

I will briefly describe some possibilities of this counter-forensics through two strategies that we have used to bypass those image politics where we can. In the summer of 2012, 22 seconds of video footage was smuggled out of Waziristan, passing through six hands before landing in the NBC offices in Islamabad.[5] It was a rare piece of footage, and was broadcasted. Disturbingly, there was also a lot of information in those images, and no attempt to see anything in them. For most people, it's simply a confirmation that something has happened—we see destruction, we see a hole in the roof, we see a building destroyed, and that's it.

We spent six months looking at these 22 seconds, frame by frame, and we started seeing things. A first thing to see is not through the window, but the window frame itself. The size of the window frame within the photographic frame meant that the person shooting the footage is not at the window but rather inside the room. This person is feeling danger—whether a second U.S. strike or from the Taliban, we don't know. But we know from the size of the frame that this is precious evidence, delivered under perilous circumstances.

We wanted to find the only confirmed target site in Waziristan that we are able to recognize. So the first task is to figure out where this footage is within North Waziristan. The shadow is cast forward, north by northwest—so we are looking northward. We can see that the building from which the photograph was taken is higher than the building destroyed, so we know we have a higher building behind a lower building. We collage the available images together, and get a fuller view of the ruin. We see a bend in the road on the left, and a certain widening of the road on the right. That is initially the typology we're looking for as we scan through the cities of Waziristan—a building that has a high building behind and that kind of arrangement of streets in front.

We find what seems like a match, and start comparing other details. We see fanning on the left, and a tower. There's a higher building, and we can confirm that we see the higher building on the satellite image as well. It's a very laborious process, but over time we become more certain that we've matched the footage to the satellite image. Now we know where the target is. But the problem of pixelation means that we simply cannot know within which pixel the drone rocket has entered and therefore which room. We want to find the room where it happened.

So we look again at the shadows, comparing the length of the shadow to the length of the building, which eventually lets us build a 3-D model of the building that we suspect is the building that was destroyed. We locate it within the extruded map of the city. Now it becomes important to know what time the video was taken, which is very easy with existing architectural software. That becomes very important, because one piece of evidence is a ray of light entering through the hole in the ceiling, which gives us direction again—meaning that we can use it as a compass by which to locate the room within the building.

Then we begin seeing the finer grain of blast holes—fragments on the roof and on the wall itself. We scan the image and we map all of them to understand what happened with the shrapnel after the missile entered the room. We slowly notice that there are two areas in which there are fewer fragments—which suggests that those areas are where the bodies that absorbed the shrapnel stood. The room's walls thus functioned as something akin to a photograph, exposed to the blast in a similar way to which a negative is exposed to light, just as the remains of bodies created voids in the ash layer over Pompeii, or as a nuclear blast famously etched a "human shadow" onto the steps outside the Sumitomo bank in Hiroshima. Combining pathology and forensic architecture, the traces of dead bodies seem to have become part of the architecture. [. . .]

None of this is hard evidence. The courts, the UN investigations, and the processes that we have developed aren't simply theoretical, but still, these elements are weak signals, faint memories, speculations, probabilities that exist at the threshold of visibility and also at the threshold of the law. We never know if these investigations have an evidentiary value until they are tested in courts—these things cannot be known *a priori*. The fact that these signals operate beneath the threshold of science and law makes the practice of forensics in excess of both—offering a point of intersection between aesthetics and politics through theory and practice.

From Eyal Weizman, "Matter against Memory," in *2000+: The Urgencies of Architectural Theory*, ed. James Graham and Mark Wigley (New York: GSAPP Books, 2015), 238–59, an abridged and altered version of two earlier essays by Weizman: "Matter against Memory," in *Forensis: The Architecture of Public Truth* (Berlin: Sternberg Press, 2014), 361–80, and "Violence at the Threshold of Detectability," *e-flux journal*, no. 64, April 2015, https://www.e-flux.com/journal/64/60861/violence-at-the-threshold-of-detectability/. For additional information see also Eyal Weizman, *Forensic Architecture. Violence at the Threshold of Detectability* (New York: Zone Books, 2017), 22–41.

Notes

1 [Earlier in his text, Weizman refers to the forensic investigation of Holocaust denial in the Pelt-Irving trial at the English High Court in 2000.]

2 [The forensic research presented in Weizman's text was commissioned by the United Nations as part of "one of the largest murder investigations going on in the world—the use of drone warfare in Pakistan, Afghanistan, Somalia, Yemen and Gaza" (page 242).]

3 The Federally Administered Tribal Areas are officially a "Prohibited Area" for which nonresidents require special permission to enter.

4 Jacob Burns, "Persistent Exception: Pakistani Law and the Drone War," in *Forensis: The Architecture of Public Truth*, ed. Forensic Architecture (Berlin: Sternberg Press, 2014).

5 Amna Nawaz, NBC's Islamabad bureau chief, who obtained the video clip, explained how they got the video to their Islamabad offices: "In order to take this piece of video out, we actually had to take a couple of weeks to move the video from place to place until it was safely in the hands of somebody we knew can transmit it back to us." Rachel Maddow, "Victims of Secretive US Drone Strikes Gain Voice in Pakistani Lawyer," *MSNBC*, June 29, 2012, http://video.msnbc.msn.com/rachel-maddow/48022434#48022434. See also Rabih Mroue, *The Pixelated Revolution*, performed at Documenta 13, 2012, https://vimeo.com/119433287 [footnote updated by the author].

Webcams, or Democratizing Publicity (2006)

Wendy Hui Kyong Chun

Webcams: supposedly live cameras, placed in homes and public places as well as on persons that transmit images over the Internet at varying frames per second. [. . .]

Webcams encapsulate perfectly the relationship between delusional control and freedom. Porn sites allow members to "control" the action during their live "shows"; nonpornographic sites, such as jennicam.com, spookycam.com, and anacam.com, do not encourage such "interactivity," but place cameras (which may or may not be on) in key locations within their operator's apartment/workplace.[1] They also usually keep a live journal (Ana Voog offers her paying members anagrams updated several times daily). These "girls" seemingly give up their privacy for a fleeting chance at celebrity. To many, these cam whores are perverse either because their actions are pornographic/erotic or because they are simply online, willingly suspending their human right to/need for privacy—something society only requires from (reluctant) celebrities and public figures. Such a willing suspension undermines the liberty that, according to Isaiah Berlin, grounded the United States and other first world nations during the cold war.[2] If perverse, however, the source is unclear: does one become a cam whore because of some latent tendency toward exhibitionism, or does the camera itself induce perverse displays and desires for exposure? Is such "deviant behavior" the price of surveillance, a "contagion of a surveillance induced voyeurism and exhibitionism"?[3]

Importantly, from the webcam operator's perspective or rhetoric, webcams are all about choice (operators choose to be on camera) and freedom (freedom of expression and the freedom to experiment, although again this freedom, like Daniel Paul Schreber's, does seem "this side of bureaucratization and human dignity"[4]). In their frequently asked questions sections, they invariably state that they are doing this because they can, because they don't mind, or because they—as Jennifer Ringley of jennicam emphasized—and not you, are conducting an experiment. Rather than "owning them," they own you; rather than merely being caught by surveillance cameras like everyone else, they choose when and how they are caught. According to Aiden of spookycam, they control the image we receive: they place the camera (and thus choose its blind spots); they turn it off and on. Through their artifice, users get a "false sense of knowing you."[5] Brought up screened (by television and film), users forget that their view is mediated, and that webcams can be and indeed are faked: some operators on camwhores.com openly recycle their more pornographic images (Figure 11.1). Webcams may thus open operators' homes, but they do not expose them entirely. Operators' sites respond to and reveal the increasing irrelevance of liberal conceptions of privacy, and the move from private/public to open/closed.

Even the paid and ever-changing "girls" featured on voyeurdorm.com, who seem unlikely defenders of control-cum-freedom, insist they are in control. "'What I really hate is that every guy demands that you take your top off, all the time,' says Tamra. 'It's like, I will take my top off *when* and *if* I want to. I used to say: Guys, go look

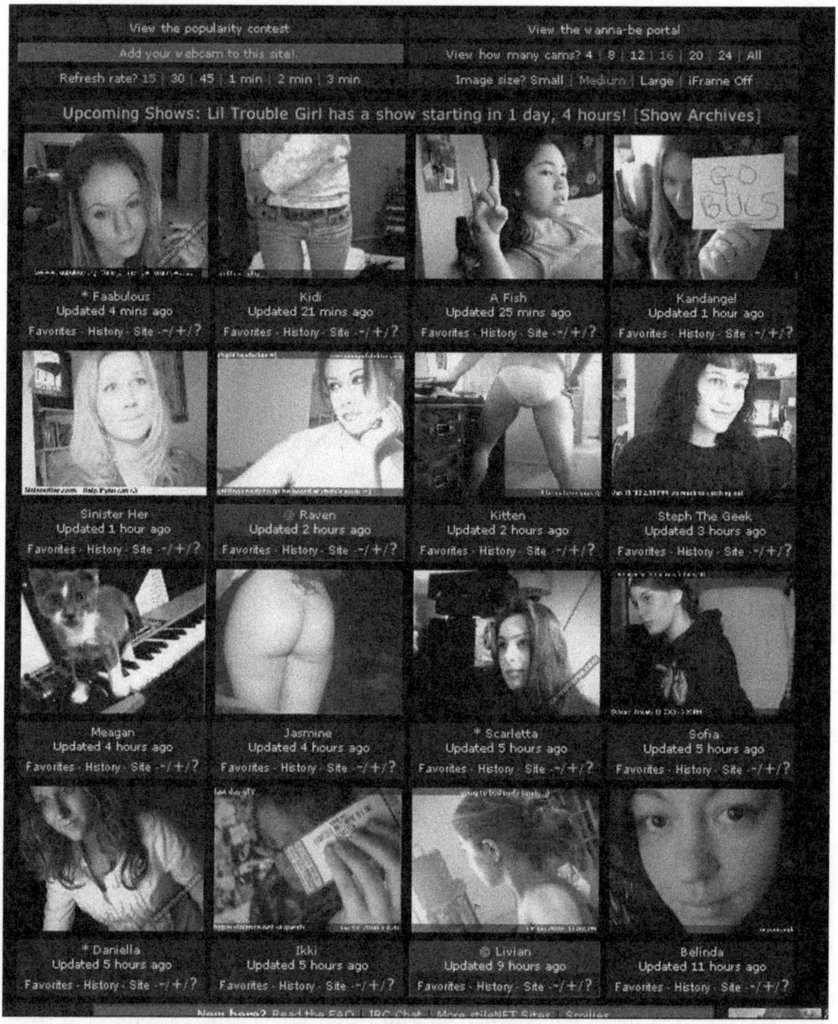

Figure 11.1 Front portal to camwhores.com, screenshot taken on January 19, 2003 at 6:13 p.m. From Wendy Hui Kyong Chun, *Control and Freedom: Power and Paranoia in the Age of Fiber Optics* (Cambridge, MA: MIT Press, 2006), 282.

up the definition of voyeur.'"[6] Interestingly, Tamra views the position of the object of the voyeur to be one of power. Vanessa Grigoriadis, who interviewed the women featured on voyeurdorm.com for nerve.com, sees Tamra's rhetoric as standard webcam ideology:

> If Tamra thinks there's something empowering about deciding when and when not to take her top off on camera, it's because she's been schooled in the Voyeur Dorm party line. The site, Hammill (the owner) maintains earnestly, is not a porn site,

> but a celebration of freedom of expression and sexual pride, a zone that merely records these young women in their natural and unashamed state. Excessive nudity, like lounging around buck-naked, is not encouraged by Hammill and there are no bonuses for it (there are bonuses for studying or other activities that invoke voyeurism and make the site coincide with its name). The girls spend most of their waking hours in baby-Ts and miniskirts, typical mall-going regalia, or maybe the occasional sports bra. That said, they don't shy from exhibitionism: when they swim, it's usually topless, and often on chat they'll strip down at the insistence of the hundreds of rabid men on the other end of the modem, who then duly offer praise about the girls' beauty.[7] Also, whether it speaks to their boredom, their "Gen Y" bi- curiousness, a sense of showmanship, or a genuine desire for female affection, the girls do fool around with each other on camera in ever-shifting pairs.[8]

These "girls," empowered to perform their natural and unashamed state and their mainly newly discovered bisexuality for the camera, are not exhibitionists. According to the Diagnostic and Statistical Manual of Mental Disorders, exhibitionism entails the behavior or urge to expose one's genitals to an unsuspecting stranger: web voyeur members are hardly unsuspecting or strangers (when signing up, they proffer their name and credit card number), and this exposure takes place within one's own house rather than in public.[9] Similarly, webcam members are not voyeurs: the voyeur gets off by watching unsuspecting strangers.[10] The relationship between the cam operator/model and the member can be quite familiar: members chat online with their cam person, send them e-mail, meet at certain public locations, send gifts, or buy things from their eBay site. Almost every cam operator has a "wish list"; Aiden, who describes herself as a mid-level player, received gifts, varying from CDs to laptops, weekly in 2003.

Through these interactions, the viewer feels less "creepy," for the viewer is acknowledged. This acknowledgment alleviates one of guilt, of the guilty pleasure of seeing without being seen, which one receives in excess of the contractual agreement. Geoffrey Batchen, in his analysis of photography as a guilty pleasure, remarks that, "far from being a marginal perversion, seeing without being seen has been a central tenet of the practice of photography throughout its history, a guilty pleasure thought to provide insights into life beyond the reach of the posed picture."[11] This pleasure, manifested in posed photographs shot as if unposed, conflates the unposed with "life." The intimacy between the watcher and his or her window combines this guilty pleasure with the relationship between pet owner and pet: someone or something is there for you—it may not be within view all the time but it is there, willing for you to look at or over it. It is something to love that does not talk or look back, that won't leave: it is a love like Nathaniel's love for Olympia in E.T.A. Hoffmann's *The Sandman*. Those who keep a window onto Ringley or Frank the Cat are looking for someone to look after, and not, as Victor Burgin argues, someone to come home to and have look after them. Webcams can epitomize surveillance as benevolence. When in 2001, "cam girl" Stacy Pershall attempted suicide live on the Internet, her watchers called the ambulance and were able to rescue her.

Many of the interactions between watcher and watchee, however, are hostile, and given the environment of constant competition for adoration, this hostility can be devastating. All cam operators receive threatening e-mails and constant demands to take off one's shirt; many of them collect the strangest of these e-mails in a "freaks" section. [. . .]

As the *Wired* commentator noted, general skepticism directed toward "live" Internet events affected media coverage: no matter how much we want to believe that webcams are indexical, we are skeptical.[12] Commentators who demonize the Internet's duplicity, ignore this skepticism, which infects everything on the Internet. Those who watch webcams and believe, however, are not simply naive, but are lured by the promise of authenticity, reinforced by these sites' "amateur" status.

Through refreshing webcams, computers become live: no longer information-processing machines, their wires appear truly connected elsewhere, their windows truly real-time. The computer screen changes without a mouse click. This surprise—this catching of movement—contrasts starkly to asynchronous Internet applications such as e-mail. Its gripping uneventfulness, its stationary camera, and its jerky refreshing also contrast sharply with television or film. One keeps watching a cam precisely because nothing happens. The plot of these webcams, if there is one, is usually provided by accompanying live journal entries. The window does not need to be in focus: one does not need to watch it all the time. Rather, it is one window among many that one can check for changes—it is an opening. Webcams try to make the system visible, try to make fiber-optic networks transparent, as if there were a simple window, rather than an invisible and noisy system; as if there were such a thing as tele-presence rather than an intricate system of mediation and translation. Webcams promise to make computers prosthetic. As Thomas Campanella puts it, "Webcameras are a set of wired eyes, a digital extension of the human faculty of vision."[13] Yet as Wolfgang Ernst argues, dataveillance is not visual—the age of fiber optics makes the visual metaphoric. Emphasizing images or even a visual crash indicates a fascination with the visual that is surprisingly dissonant with the technology and with technology use, and furthers the intertwining of freedom with control.

From the chapter "Webcams, or Democratizing Publicity" in Wendy Hui Kyong Chun, *Control and Freedom: Power and Paranoia in the Age of Fiber Optics* (Cambridge, MA: MIT Press, 2006), 278–90.

Notes

1 The difference between pornographic and nonpornographic websites arguably depends less on content and more on form, for nonpornographic websites do contain nudity and sexually explicit acts (necessary to prove their "liveness"). Pornographic webcams tend to be on only during fixed periods of the day and feature more chances for "interactivity."

2 [Chun discusses this theory in the other parts of her book with reference to Isaiah Berlin, *Two Concepts of Liberty: An Inaugural Lecture Delivered before the University of Oxford on 31 October 1958* (Oxford: Clarendon Press, 1958).]

3 Brandon W. Joseph, "Nothing Special: Andy Warhol and the Rise of Surveillance," in *CTRL [SPACE]: Rhetorics of Surveillance from Bentham to Big Brother*, ed. Thomas Y. Levin, Ursula Frohne, and Peter Weibel (Cambridge, MA: MIT Press, 2002), 251. [. . .]
4 Friedrich Kittler, *Discourse Networks 1800/1900*, trans. Michael Metteer with Chris Cullens (Stanford, CA: Stanford University Press, 1990), 303.
5 Aiden, Unpublished interview (with Wendy Hui Kyong Chun).
6 Quoted in Vanessa Grigoriadis, "I'm Seen, Therefore I Am," *nerve.com*, www.nerve.com/Dispatches/Grigoriadis/voyeurDorm/ (accessed September 30, 1999) [original link expired].
7 [Modems where used to access the internet via telephone lines.]
8 Grigoriadis, "I'm Seen, Therefore I Am."
9 Victor Burgin, in his analysis of jennicam, argues that Jennifer Ringley is not an exhibitionist because exhibitionism, according to Sigmund Freud, derives from voyeurism: Ringley is not interested in seeing ours, and popular diagnoses of Ringley as exhibitionist simply verify our own voyeurism. In contrast, Burgin, stressing Ringley's age, views jennicam as a substitute for the mother's gaze, which notices and approves of Jennifer: "Jenni is tottering around in her mother's shoes. Under the gaze of her mother she is investigating what it means to be a woman like her mother. That is to say, she is posing the question of female sexuality" ["Jenni's Room: Exhibitionism and Solitude," *Critical Inquiry* 27 (Fall 2000), 85]. [. . .] Burgin notes that we viewers, like lonely adult children, "keep watch through their windows for Jenni to come home from work" ("Jenni's Room," 87). Burgin's argument that users wait quietly for Jenni to come home from work is insightful and complicates his claim that they are voyeurs. For if Ringley is not an exhibitionist, the viewers are not voyeurs.
10 Freud's linking of voyeurism to cruelty, though, in *Three Essays on the Theory of Sexuality*, ed. and trans. James Strachey (London: Hogarth Press, 1962), does seem to explain to some extent the hostility these women face.
11 Geoffrey Batchen, "Guilty Pleasures," in *CTRL [SPACE]*, 459.
12 See Julia Scheeres, "Dying for Attention?" *Wired News*, July 14, 2001, http://www.wired.com/news/culture/0,1284,45247,00.html?tw=wn_story_related (accessed September 3, 2004) [original link expired].
13 Thomas Campanella, "Eden by Wire: Webcameras and the Telepresent Landscape," in *The Robot in the Garden: Telerobotics and Telepistemology in the Age of the Internet*, ed. Ken Goldberg (Cambridge, MA: MIT Press, 2001), 23.

"The Woman in the Blue Bra": Follow the Video (2015/2017)

Kathrin Peters

During the protests in Cairo in December 2011, a woman is beaten up in broad daylight by Egyptian soldiers. Uniformed, helmeted men, about ten of them altogether, beat the woman, who is already lying on the ground, with sticks. In the course of the blows and kicks, while she is pulled and dragged about, her black abaya slides up and falls open. Underneath she is wearing jeans, trainers, and a blue bra. At this point, one of the men kicks her bared chest hard, as if her very nakedness had to be beaten and punished. Her torso flops lifelessly to and fro. Finally, one of the men covers the supine woman with the black fabric and leaves the scene, just as the camera pans upwards to show a crowd running away in the light of the setting sun. At the top of the frame, the recording bears the green logo of the Russian state broadcaster, *Russia Today*. The one and a half minute video quickly went viral under the name "The Woman in the Blue Bra" and can still be viewed on various websites (Figure 11.2).[1]

But what does the video show? Or, put another way, to whom does it show what? Where, in what context, and under what conditions does one see such a video, which does not necessarily remain the same, sometimes not even a video? It has joined the mass of authorless or unauthorized video clips circulating in social media to be linked, copied, and appropriated in blogs, sharing platforms, and news sites. Its diffusion has by no means remained restricted to the digital realm. Stills made their way back to the street, in graffiti and posters, even appearing as cover images on print magazines

Figure 11.2 "Brutal Egypt Security Force Beat Woman Unconscious," video uploaded by Jusef El Abhar, December 18, 2011, https://www.youtube.com/watch?v=oua2y11BMxw.

both Egyptian and European. The established verification processes of editorial commissioning and selection barely function here.

So let us follow the video "The Woman in the Blue Bra," the possible circumstances of its origination and some of the channels by which it has been disseminated and modified. It was published on December 18, 2011, at 10:23 a.m. on *rt.com*, with the recording itself dating from the previous day. Firstly, the video tells us something about the political situation within the Egyptian protest movement at this specific point. In December 2011, parliamentary elections were in full swing, conducted by the Supreme Council of the Armed Forces. Since the uprising had begun in January that year with huge demonstrations, mass detentions, and the occupation of Tahrir Square, the protests had never completely ceased; they flared up again massively that December in response to the electoral rules imposed by the generals. And they were fueled by the circulating images of violent assault.

The scene showing the woman's mistreatment lasts only a few seconds; the video also contains other material, including soldiers storming the tented camp on Tahrir Square. Authorship of the recording is not noted, aside from the station logo denoting ownership. Nor is it discernible whether the recordings originated from a single source or a single recording device, or whether this is a montage of material from different sources. The recordings could have been made by a *Russia Today* reporter, or they could more likely be amateur material, such as mobile phone clips made by bystanders and sent or sold to a news agency.

The style of the footage, characterized by rapid panning and zooming, reflects above all the suddenness of the events; even a professional might not have found the opportunity for aesthetic composition. Today, not only professional reporters use their cameras where the action is; participants and bystanders also have cameras and phones ready to record acts of violence and preserve the recordings as documentary evidence. Nor do today's distribution channels require professional access to editorial structures with staff, equipment, and communications (historically that meant messenger and courier, telegraph, telephone, fax, or computer). Publishing online, on YouTube, Facebook, or on a blog, has become a simple matter—although additional distribution by news agencies is certainly helpful, since no matter how spectacular the video, one can never depend on viral dissemination. This much can be said: in a digital age of social media, camera phones, and smartphones—in other words, since the 2000s—the production and distribution of digital media have become "democratized" or "deprofessionalized," depending on your point of view. Eyewitness reports by those involved (elevated to the rank of "citizen journalists," although if there is one thing they are not, it is journalists) are also highly regarded by commercial agencies. They stand for a sense of "being there" that photojournalism has always aspired to; but reporters often can't fulfill when events occur quickly—ultimately their local knowledge will always be inferior. During the protests in Egypt and other North African countries, Western journalists were content to observe and document the protests from places of safety: living in hotels, photographing from a distance (sometimes from the hotel balcony),[2] and mainly interviewing English-speaking activists.

In the perspective of the English-speaking Egyptian filmmaker Philip Rizk, who has critically analyzed this situation, Western journalists were seeking above all representations that confirmed their concept of a nonviolent liberation movement, in the sense of a democratization according to the Western model. "Only the fixation of certain images seen in daylight through the lens of a camera on Tahrir Square could appease you with that impression," he writes in his "Open Letter to an Onlooker." "Other industries soon followed suit: hard on the heels of the journalists came academics, filmmakers, the world of art, and NGOs, all relying on us as the ideal interpreter of the extraordinary. They all eventually bought into and further fueled the hyper-glorification of the individual, the actor, the youth subject, the revolutionary artist, the woman, the non-violent protester, the Internet user."[3] For Rizk, that ignores both the violence and the heterogeneity of the interests driving the protests. The postcolonial historical discourse perceives only an emancipatory movement pursuing "Western" values, striving against Islamism and dictatorship and for women's emancipation. Protests against capitalism, neo-liberalism, and economic imperatives—in other words, against decidedly "Western" norms—are simply not perceived or in fact not perceptible.

On the very day of publication, various modifications of the "Blue Bra" video appeared on *YouTube*: one of these is backed with mournful singing and written commentary in Arabic ("Brutal Egypt Security Force"), another has a trailer from FIN (Freedom Informant Network) and English-language text ("Disturbing Video"). In both cases the video is given an emotional, but also agitating framing. It is certainly probable that it may have circulated in e-mails and blogs before appearing on *rt.com* and then CNN, which might explain the simultaneous appearance of versions already provided with framing and commentary in diverse contexts. It is the explicit potential of digital images that they can be processed and modified by their users, which is not to say that there is always a fundamental question mark over their veracity. The quality of the technological image as a record of real events remains intact. Added to the image, though, are interpretations of events, reading instructions for an always negotiable truth. One user subjects the "Blue Bra" video to a virtually forensic reading using red frames to pick out details[4]: He shows that the woman was accompanied by at least two male demonstrators. One of the two manages to break free and flee, while the other is kicked and beaten, as are two passers-by who initially walk past the edge of the scene but seconds later are lying helplessly on the ground. One member of the group of military police is identified as particularly brutal; this is a man wearing trainers rather than army boots. He is, it would appear, restrained by the others—not firmly, though, but rather hesitantly and unsuccessfully.

Also on December 18, the *Tahrir Newspaper* published a still from the "Blue Bra" video, freezing the moment when the woman's bare torso is kicked. This is plainly a manipulated frame or screenshot, as the original shows the event from a distance and quite blurred (note that the designation "original" is merely an auxiliary term here, which would better be replaced by "source material" if the first appearance of the footage were not so unclear). The person who made the recording of "The Woman in the Blue Bra" had to seek out the motif through the viewfinder or on the display of the recording device. The camera, whatever kind it was, picks out victim and perpetrators in the crowd, loses sight of them, then finds the scene again. The recordings are notably without sound. I imagine otherwise one would hear shouting and other indications that would help to visually locate the thugs in the crowd. Alongside the acts of violence, the video therefore also documents something else, namely, the difficulty of focusing; it points to both the events and the circumstances of their recording. The movements of the searching camera, and consequently of its images, correspond to the conditions under which the video was made. And precisely this contingency and spontaneity, the rapidity and confusion captured in the images, confirm the authenticity of the events. They remind us that these events were not completely unexpected; in a certain sense *something* was expected to happen. But at the same time neither this concrete moment nor the specific persons were foreseeable.[5]

So while the searching camera movements and the blurring confirm the authenticity of the recording, those indications of origin have little bearing on other registers. The idea that the more grainy or pixelated a photograph, film, or video recording, the more authentic, is nothing but ill-conceived formalism. Also a blurred freeze-frame is unsuited as an iconic image for a front page. As well as enlarging the relevant detail, the still selected for the newspaper must at least have been subjected to later post-focusing, for neither analog nor digital images gain in sharpness when enlarged. Quite the opposite: blow them up far enough and all that remains is grain or pixels, the technical materiality of the image, and certainly no gain in iconicity of the kind required in the text/image context of the newspaper page. The color must have been adjusted too, as the blue bra now contrasts dramatically with the soldiers' camouflage trousers. The iconic front page image fits the "decisive moments" paradigm upon which photojournalism has based its impact in the wake of Henri Cartier-Bresson. So while the low resolution of the digital image—its overall "poor" quality—is the precondition for endless uploading and forwarding, the image must be aesthetically and technically improved as soon as it comes to reproduction in a print medium, in other words, in a "classical" distribution medium.

According to Hito Steyerl, "poor images" are low-resolution digital images that circulate without reproduction rights (or whose copyright is ignored) and whose potential lies in forming political networks, new public spheres, and archives beyond established bodies and companies.[6] Within the chain of "Blue Bra" images, such a "poor" image is certainly a decisive trigger—but one that dovetails into the image strategies of established commercial agencies and their needs for monetization. After diffusing through various networks, the images bear marks and signatures that contradict both the division into public and counter public, and the strict distinction between analog and digital. The chain of reproductions and appropriations of the "Blue Bra" video does not come to a halt even when the "poor" video image is enriched to create a still. Instead it migrates back into the digital networks. Unlike a video, a still can be used on the street: in subsequent demonstrations the front page of the *Tahrir Newspaper* was held aloft for the cameras.[7] Soon enlarged and cropped versions were appearing on protest marches, especially the Women's Protest March on December 21, now in poster quality bearing the byline Reuters/Stringer.[8] "On the streets, before the eyes and cameras of the media, images that were fished out of the flood of digital images now became image objects that were immediately fed back into the stream," argues Tom Holert.[9] "Image objects" can be held up and displayed, not only in local surroundings but also in subsequently circulated images showing the image objects together with the subjects carrying them. Hundreds of photographs of these demonstrations grouped by theme, motif, and event can be found on Flickr, complete with image objects and mobile phones held aloft by the crowd.

The adaptations and appropriations of "The Woman in the Blue Bra" appear in different places in different media with a range of genre references: a graffito on Tahrir Square showed the blue bra as an element of a Superwoman costume. The Brazilian caricaturist Carlos Latuff drew a blue bra scene imagining the woman's revenge. Murals echoed the style of martyr portraits; the blue bra turned up isolated as a graffiti stencil. It has gelled into a symbol capable of encapsulating the entire situation. Whereas such adaptations of the image articulated a concept of female empowerment beyond and outside a supposedly vulnerable femininity and its paternalistic protectors, there were also collages showing the blue bra montaged onto the Egyptian flag, thus containing the women's movement within the nation.[10]

Corporative, artistic, and more or less illegal appropriations of the images produced a mise-en-abyme, a sequence of images each related to the other; and not only a sequence of images, but also of persons who made them and in the process exposed themselves in different ways. The digital cameras and smartphones they carried with them were an essential part of this set of relations, this relationality. For these devices enable easy ad hoc distribution, or at least threaten that in the eyes of the regime. Thus, the protests are not only recorded and documented; the recording changes the protest movement.

These testimonies and the technological means of capturing and recording are not mere tools providing images or recorded voices of a political event that would have been the same without these recordings. Bodies gathering in social movements—what might include social networking in the virtual domain—are enacting by their appearance what they claim and are protesting for. Media technologies make a part of this set of relations through which the protesting and resisting body appears and enacts.[11]

Every reproduction of reality is governed by intentions to show and tell, which subject the recording to a process of selection and framing and place it in a specific context already saturated with (ideally refutable) presuppositions. Accumulated evidence is the outcome of the interaction between a wide range of elements, which cannot be reduced to any variety of determinism, whether technological, social, or political in nature, but instead places all these elements in relation to one another.

With respect to digital media and the technologies for distributing, linking, and reproducing, we find that the possibilities of image manipulation, commentary, and circulation—the chain of images produced by digital retransmission—claim a decisive share in what is evidenced and how certainty is produced. Testimony has been shunted into an always controvertible space of negotiation where credibility is generated, but also remains disputable and is continually disputed (Figure 11.2).

From Kathrin Peters, "Images of Protest: On the 'Woman in the Blu Bra' and Relational Testimony," trans. Meredith Dale, in *Resistance*, ed. Martin Butler, Paul Mecheril, and Lea Brenningmeyer (Bielefeld: transcript, 2017), 135–51; slightly modified for the present publication by the author. Original German text: "Bilder des Protests: 'The

Woman in the Blue Bra' und relationale Zeugenschaft," in *Periphere Visionen: Wissen an den Rändern von Fotografie und Film*, ed. Heide Barrenechea, Marcel Finke, and Moritz Schumm (Munich: Wilhelm Fink Verlag, 2016); text courtesy of Wilhelm Fink Verlag. First version published under the present title in *Expanded Senses*, ed. Bernd Kracke and Marc Ries (Bielefeld: transcript, 2015).

Notes

1 *Russia Today* is an international television news channel founded in 2005. For the video, see *RT*'s "'Blue Bra Girl' Atrocity: Egyptian Military Police More Than Brutal," Isobel Coleman's article "'Blue Bra Girl' Rallies Egypt's Women vs. Oppression" on CNN, and "The Blue Bra Girl: The Shocking Video" on YouTube.

2 See the photo series by Peter von Agtmael of the renowned Magnum agency, in *Cairo, Open City: New Testimonies from an Ongoing Revolution*, ed. Florian Ebner and Constanze Wicke (Leipzig: Spector, 2013), 55, 56, 129.

3 Philip Rizk, "2011 Is Not 1968: An Open Letter to an Onlooker," in Ebner and Wicke, *Cairo, Open City*, 54.

4 A post in a rather obscure, no longer existing blog: willyloman.wordpress.com/2011/12/19/blue-bra-girl-video-a-remarkable-story-of-horror-and-heroism.

5 Cf. Jacques Derrida, "A Certain Impossible Possibility of Saying the Event," trans. Gila Walker, *Critical Inquiry* 33 (2007), 441–61.

6 See Hito Steyerl, "In Defense of the Poor Image," in: id., *The Wretched of the Screen* (Berlin: Sternberg Press, 2012), 32f.

7 See Rowan El Shimi's *Flickr* album "Kasr El Einy Street Street Battle Dec 18 . . ." and the references in Ebner and Wicke, *Cairo. Open City*.

8 See, for example, Kainaz Amaria's photo story "The 'Girl In The Blue Bra'" published by *npr*, https://www.npr.org/sections/pictureshow/2011/12/21/144098384/the-girl-in-the-blue-bra.

9 Tom Holert, *Regieren im Bildraum* (Berlin: b-books, 2008), 61.

10 See Rowan El Shimi, "The Woman in the Blue Bra," in Ebner and Wicke, *Cairo, Open City*, 182.

11 See Judith Butler, *Notes toward a Performative Theory of Assembly* (Cambridge, MA: Harvard University Press), 2015.

Section IV

Dialogues

12

Artistic Practice and Video Theory

Introduction by Dieter Daniels and Jan Thoben

Artistic practice can be regarded as an exemplary arena of reflection on the medium of video. Experimental uses of the medium were often prepared, accompanied, or commented on by texts. This explains why artists are represented with contributions in all chapters and topic areas of this reader.[1] Their particular importance in the video-theoretical context is further evidenced by the cross-disciplinary exchange between theory and practice: media theories as well as artists' own texts often accompany their experimental practice; conversely, artistic works and texts provide key points of reference for theorists. This mutual relationship manifests itself in the media-theoretical analyses throughout this reader in numerous references to both works and texts by artists.[2] These are not limited to art-theoretical approaches but also include media-theoretical and philosophical investigations. Maurizio Lazzarato writes that artists are "the only people who have taught us anything about this technology," explicitly referring to their texts.[3] Art-historical discourses are often centered on key works of video art, as Helen Westgeest has shown in a comparative analysis.[4] Some scholars also incorporate their personal insight from practice-based dialogues with artists into their theoretical writings, as exemplified by the collaboration between Vilém Flusser and Fred Forest or between Maurizio Lazzarato and Angela Melitopoulos (see Chapters 1 and 2). Video can therefore be regarded as the technical image medium in which artistic uses and experiments are key for the discursive development and (self-) reflection of the medium.

In comparison with other topic areas, the literature on video art is quite extensive. Besides exhibition catalogs, it includes numerous anthologies and art-theoretical monographs. Historical surveys in special multimedia formats offer a combination of theory and practice.[5] Collections of writings on video art are often compiled along national narratives. In Europe, in particular, these "minor histories" have been the subject of comprehensive scholarly research.[6] US overviews, on the other hand, while often also having a national focus, nevertheless aspire to the status of international standard works. These widespread publications thereby implicitly tend to canonize the art of one country.[7]

One of the problems with the term "video art" is that it risks being understood as an artform defined and limited by its medium, or even as a historical genre.[8] Ultimately, it is hardly possible to draw such genre boundaries in a meaningful way, as artistic video culture has at all times been characterized by intermedia relations, hybridizations, and transformations.[9] Besides, from the 1990s onward, the term "video art" can no longer be precisely delimited because the medium, both technically and artistically, is no longer the defining characteristic for "video artists." Rather, like photography from the 1970s onward, it has become a common medium of visual art.

Against this background, artistic and scientific theorizations are set in a dialogical relationship in this chapter. In line with the interdisciplinary and pluralistic approach of this reader, connections to, and expansions on, topic areas addressed in previous chapters were decisive for the selection of the texts presented here. These dialogical pairings—other constellations are no doubt conceivable—should be seen as editorial suggestions. The contributions by Erika Balsom and Dieter Daniels look at the works of Peter Campus, Andy Warhol, and Nam June Paik from an art-historical perspective; Jacques Derrida's text was stimulated by a collaboration with Gary Hill that expands into a philosophical reflection on video; and the thematic couplings of Malin Hedlin Hayden and Ulrike Rosenbach, and of Marina Gržinić and Boris Yukhananov, are the result of editorial considerations regarding feminisms and issues of historical identity in Eastern Europe and Russia, respectively.

Beginnings: Andy Warhol, Nam June Paik, Dieter Daniels

The works and texts by Andy Warhol and Nam June Paik presented in this chapter mark the beginning of artistic video practice in 1965. Moreover, they document the two artists' distinctly different degrees of notoriety at the time. The interview with Warhol, published in a stylish magazine, plays with his role as a prominent ambassador for the new medium of video. In contrast, Paik, true to the Fluxus spirit, advertises the screenings of his first videos by means of a self-made leaflet. In the style of a manifesto, he outlines far-reaching perspectives for the medium's artistic and social future from the very start of his career as one of the first "video artists."

As shown by Dieter Daniels, Warhol's and Paik's respective artistic approaches to video anticipate two parallel future tendencies. Warhol's work foreshadows the narcissism debate on video emerging in the 1970s (see Chapter 3). Paik's work, on the other hand, stands at the beginning of equally pervasive discussions on the relationships between video and television (see Chapter 5 on TV and video).

Projections: Peter Campus, Erika Balsom

The text by Peter Campus, who started working with video as a student of experimental psychology, may be considered one of the earliest contributions to the perceptual psychology of video. Without explicitly referring to his own artistic video practice, Campus analyzes the self-reflective potential of the medium, especially with reference to the then new possibility of video projection. Analyzing Campus, Erika Balsom examines the differences between cinema and video projection. In doing so, she refers to the film-theoretical examinations by Stephen Heath and Jean-Louis Baudry on the cinematic apparatus and the spectator, which were published at around the same time as Campus's text. With reference to Campus's video projection works, she emphasizes the artist's "interest in psychodrama," particularly in comparison with his contemporaries in the 1970s.

In the meantime, video projection has become a standard for the presentation of moving images comparable to the cinematic apparatus.[10] In the dialogue between Campus and Balsom it becomes clear that this "cinematic turn" of video projection was not a historic given. Correspondingly, today's standardization of video-as-film may be relativized; a comparative perspective along those lines would also be relevant for current immersive cinematographic systems and virtual reality.

Electronic Linguistics: Gary Hill, Jacques Derrida

Coined by Gary Hill as early as 1977 in the title of an abstract sound-based video, the term "Electronic Linguistics" can be seen as a leitmotif for his entire artistic video work. This early experiment with the signal-based grammar of the electronic image was followed by the "image-text syntax" described in his statement from 1980 reprinted in this chapter. Reflecting on his videotape *Resolution* (1979), Hill explains:

> This was telling me in some way that there was a kind of hidden space that might be an *ingress for language*. This was the opposite of what I might naturally think about an electronic signal and language. In other words, the electronic signal always seemed like a sub-particle in relation to language, which by comparison is rather bulky and time-consuming to think, speak, receive, and comprehend. So the only way to get between the lines and deal with this liminality seemed to be some kind of textuality.[11]

This opens up "another stage of realizing the dialogue with technology as a language site where machines talk back," as George Quasha explains in dialogue with Hill referring to videotapes of the early 1980s.[12]

The combination of spoken language and videographic visualization, which is characteristic of all of Hill's subsequent work, later extended to the integration of philosophical and literary texts. In the case of *Disturbance (among the Jars)* from 1988, it applies to a multilingual adaptation of Gnostic texts found in Nag Hammadi, Egypt, in 1945. Created for Centre Pompidou in Paris, this work features, among other performers, the sound poet Bernard Heidsieck and the philosopher Jacques Derrida, who were asked by the artist to rework the original texts into a personal contribution. The text by Derrida reproduced here relates to this encounter and appeared in 1990 as a reflection on the artist's work in the catalog of the group exhibition *Passages de l'image* at Centre Pompidou.

Derrida's text reaches far beyond the format of a classic catalog essay. Instead, the author uses this opportunity to "take into account, as Gary Hill *does*, what happens to language through the 'video' event."[13] The encounter with Hill's video work thus gives rise to Derrida's reflections on the linguistic and visual concept of "video" on behalf of a leading critic of the "linguistic turn" in philosophy. Derrida borrowed the title of his essay—"Videor"—from Jean-Luc Nancy, who in turn referred to René Descartes's *cogito*. The dialogue between Hill and Derrida can be regarded as a particularly fruitful moment in the reciprocal relationships between artistic and theoretical perspectives.

Feminisms: Ulrike Rosenbach, Malin Hedlin Hayden

Within a time span of some thirty years, the contributions by Ulrike Rosenbach and Malin Hedlin Hayden document the changes in the specific relationship between video art and feminism. Rosenbach is one of the pioneers of feminist artistic video work in performances and videos that offer a critical analysis of stereotypical representations of femininity. Her position complements the contemporaneous text by Anne-Marie Duguet (Chapter 9), which relates to feminist video practices in the wider social field. Joan Jonas's text (Chapter 8) likewise examines the importance of video for the exploration of female identities and in doing so subtly ties in with feminist discourses of the 1970s: "Video as we used it was personal, and the personal was political."[14]

Hayden, on the other hand, critically discusses art-theoretical texts with regard to sweeping categorizations of women artists working with video under the generalizing banner of "feminism." Her analysis applies less to social and artistic practices as described by Rosenbach, Duguet, and Jonas but more to a retrospective categorization of such practices as "feminist." Surveys on video art since the 1990s, Hayden notes, often label video art by women as "feminist" without taking into account the artists' self-understanding and gender identification. In this respect, these texts engage in a complementary dialogue that encompasses practice and theory as much as the historical dynamics of feminist discourses on video (for the sociopolitical context, see the introduction to Chapter 9).

Eastern Europe: Marina Gržinić, Boris Yukhananov

In the 1970s and 1980s, a specific discourse on artistic media practice developed in Eastern Europe. It reflects the paradoxical situation that the artistic avant-gardes, due to state-decreed isolation from contemporaneous electronic media, were not in a position to raise an existing intellectual tradition (embodied, e.g., by the montage theories of Eisenstein, Vertov, Kuleshov, and Pudovkin) to a level comparable to that in the "West." On the other hand, the term "Eastern Europe" in itself remains problematic insofar as it implies a homogeneity that never existed. In the various Eastern European countries, the regulations of artistic media practices and state censorship were handled very differently. Against this backdrop, it makes little sense to speak of a common history of video art in Eastern Europe. Rather, several independent "minor histories" should be accounted for.[15]

This multilayered and still little-explored entanglement of political, ideological, technological, and artistic factors is discussed in this chapter through the example of two historically distant contributions.[16] Boris Yukhananov's text was written shortly before the fall of the Iron Curtain; Marina Gržinić published hers twenty years later. Their perspectives differ accordingly. Yukhananov offers a pointed theoretical reflection on his own practice for the use of video in theater, developed with the simplest of technical means (see also Chapter 7), while Gržinić describes the transformation processes after 1989 and the disappearance of Eastern European identity in the wake of globalization: "Today, the former Eastern European space is nonexistent: it has vanished symbolically, conceptually, politically and socially in the global world."[17] After 1989, in Eastern Europe (as previously in Western Europe), each country developed specific art histories, including in the field of video art, to accentuate newly won national identities in relation to past Soviet hegemony.[18]

Notes

1 See the contributions in Chapters 1–11 by Paul Ryan, Nam June Paik, Dan Graham, Martha Rosler, Douglas Davis, Hollis Frampton, Jean-Luc Godard, Gábor Bódy, Tetsuo Kogawa, Harun Farocki, Dara Birnbaum, Bill Viola, Gary Hill, Joan Jonas, Cory Arcangel, Hito Steyerl, and Juan Downey (listed in the order of their appearance in this reader).

2 This is particularly true for the discussion on the specificity of the video medium. The contributions by Yvonne Spielmann, Ina Blom, Raymond Bellour, Anne-Marie Duguet, Maurizio Lazzarato, and Rosalind Krauss, among others, are referring to works as well as texts by artists.

3 Maurizio Lazzarato, *Videophilosophy: The Perception of Time in Post-Fordism*, ed. and trans. Jay Hetrick (New York: Columbia University Press, 2019), 94. See p. 99 (included in the excerpt reprinted in Chapter 2 of this volume).

4 See Helen Westgeest, *Video Art Theory: A Comparative Approach* (Hoboken: Wiley-Blackwell, 2015), specifically her comparative analysis of texts on Woody Vasulka's *Art of Memory*, "probably one of the most oft-discussed video works in historical overviews of video art" (p. 65).

5 Two examples of multimedia compilations of national video art developments are *Surveying the First Decade: Video Art and Independent Media in the U.S., 1968–1980*, VHS edition with reader, reissued on DVD in 2017, cur. Christine Hill (Chicago: Video Data Bank, 1995), and *40yearsvideoart.de—Part 1*, "Digital Heritage: Video Art in Germany from 1963 to the Present," DVD edition with reader, ed. Rudolf Frieling and Wulf Herzogenrath (Ostfildern: Hatje Cantz, 2006).

6 These "minor histories" are the focus of the research project "Emergence of Video Art in Europe: Historiography, Theory, Sources and Archives (1960–1980)" by Labex Arts-H2H, Laboratoire ESTCA de l'Université Paris 8 Vincennes–Saint-Denis, and École cantonale d'art de Lausanne (ECAL), http://www.estca.univ-paris8.fr/index.php/emergence-de-lart-video-en-europe-1960-1980/. The lecture given by the author in the context of this project dealt with the motives and problems of national narratives based on the developments in Germany. See Dieter Daniels, "VT ≠ TV (Video Tape

Is Not Television)," Institut national d'histoire de l'art (INHA), Paris, December 4, 2019, https://vimeo.com/512863475.

7 Three examples of internationally distributed surveys that contain mainly US contributions without making this bias explicit are Ira Schneider and Beryl Korot, *Video Art: An Anthology* (New York: Harcourt Brace Jovanovich, 1976); Gregory Battcock, ed., *New Artists Video: A Critical Anthology* (New York: E. P. Dutton, 1978); and Doug Hall and Sally Jo Fifer, eds., *Illuminating Video: An Essential Guide to Video Art* (New York: Aperture Press, 1991).

8 The term "video art" gained widespread currency from 1970 and was first mentioned in print by Russell Connor, "Foreword," in *Vision and Television* (Waltham, MA: Rose Art Museum, Brandeis University, 1970) (see Chapter 5). Connor implicitly defines the self-image of the viewer on the monitor as a specificity of the video medium as opposed to television: "The emphasis on participation in much video art and the frequency with which the visitor finds his own image on a monitor has provoked the criticism of catering to fashion and narcissism." His is an early reaction to criticisms of video art's narcissistic tendency (cf. Chapter 3).

9 See, e.g., the contributions by Godard and Farocki on the relation between film and video (Chapter 4), by Paik and Birnbaum on the relation between television and video (Chapter 5), and by Hill and Viola on the relation between sound and video (Chapter 6), as well as hybrid formats of performance and video (Chapter 8). Artists worked with television images even before the availability of video technology and the introduction of the term "video art." For an overview of artworks created between 1960 and 1965 that relate to television through painting, drawing, sculpture, performance, photography, and film, see Dieter Daniels and Stephan Berg, eds., *TeleGen: Kunst und Fernsehen / Art and Television*, exh. cat. Kunstmuseum Bonn and Kunstmuseum Liechtenstein (Munich: Hirmer, 2015).

10 For a critical comparison of cinema and video systems, see the texts by Anne Marie Duguet (Chapter 2) and Hollis Frampton (Chapter 4) in this reader.

11 Quoted in George Quasha and Charles Stein, *An Art of Limina: Gary Hill's Works and Writings* (Barcelona: Ediciones Polígrafa, 2009), 75.

12 George Quasha in dialogue with Gary Hill, "Electronic Linguistics," in *Switching Codes: Thinking through Digital Technology in the Humanities and the Arts*, ed. Thomas Bartscherer and Roderick Coover (Chicago and London: University of Chicago Press, 2011), 254. On Hill's video works in the context of sound and synthesis, see also Chapter 6 in this reader.

13 Jacques Derrida, "Videor" (1990), in *Resolutions: Contemporary Video Practices*, ed. Michael Renov and Erika Suderburg (Minneapolis: University of Minnesota Press, 1996), 75.

14 Joan Jonas, "Transmission," in *Women, Art, and Technology*, ed. Judy Malloy (Cambridge, MA: MIT Press, 2003), 126.

15 On the various developments across Eastern Europe, see Dieter Daniels, "Medien und Kunst zwischen Politik, Ökonomie und Ästhetik in Osteuropa," in *Europa, Europa: Das Jahrhundert der Avantgarde in Mittel- und Osteuropa*, ed. Ryzard Stanislawski and Christoph Brockhaus, exh. cat. Kunst- und Ausstellungshalle der Bundesrepublik Deutschland (Ostfildern: Hatje Cantz, 1994), 472–6.

16 See also the contribution by Gábor Bódy in Chapter 4.

17 Marina Gržinić, "Video in the Time of a Double Political and Technological Transition in the Former Eastern European Context," in *Transitland: Video Art from Central and Eastern Europe 1989–2009*, ed. Edit András (Budapest: Ludwig Museum of Contemporary Art, 2009), 17.

18 These country-specific histories also concern the time before 1989, when these nations (re)gained independence. See, e.g., Tihomir Milovac, ed., *Insert: Retrospective of Croatian Video Art*, exh. cat. MSU Zagreb and MMSU Rijeka (Zagreb: MSU, 2008), as well as the comprehensive multimedia documentation *Video Art in Slovenia, 1969–1998*, which includes two book publications, a CD-ROM, and a website, http://www.videodokument.org/.

Video 1965: Andy Warhol and Nam June Paik: A Specific Moment of Unspecificity (2018/2021)

Dieter Daniels

The beginnings of video art were determined by two factors: one is access to video technology for artists, and the other their fascination with the electronic image, especially with television as a mass medium. As documented in the exhibition catalog *TeleGen*,[1] this fascination preceded the availability of video. The earliest video works by Andy Warhol and Nam June Paik offer a perfect case study for these beginnings. Both artists gained access to video technology almost simultaneously in New York in 1965, albeit under very different conditions and with very different consequences. For Warhol, video would be a mere episode of several weeks, and only one of his experiments is considered a finished work today. Paik, on the other hand, adopted video as his central artistic medium that allowed him to extend the ideas he had earlier developed as "Participation TV." A more thorough analysis of these two early approaches supports the thesis already developed in the introduction to this reader, that video evades an unambiguous specificity, that it instead opens up the possibility of different or even contradictory forms of "differential specificity" (Rosalind Krauss). The art-historical topos of the invention of a new genre is both referred to and relativized in this research: the works by Paik and Warhol discussed here are not "videotapes" in a narrow sense and cannot be classified as the prototypical beginnings of video art. Instead they show two different ways of exploring the characteristics of a medium.

Andy Warhol, *Outer and Inner Space* (1965)

In the mid-1960s, several companies started testing the market for introducing video equipment reduced in size and price—compared to the bulky 2-inch tape VTRs used in television studios—to private consumers or nonbroadcast professionals (e.g. universities, schools, hospitals, psychiatrists). Along with several other companies presenting VTRs for the new 1-inch tape standard, Philips launched the EL-3400 series in 1964.[2] These video recorders came with a price tag of around $5,000, but if you wanted a camera to go along with it, you were set back another $5,000. At this time, Andy Warhol's Factory had become famous for parties attracting the high society with their underground appeal. The Philips marketing department decided that such an environment might convince high-end consumers to invest $10,000 for such a video set. Warhol was, so to say, an early influencer, and Philips loaned him video equipment for some months in the summer of 1965.[3] On July 30, 1965, the EL-3400 VTR with 21 vacuum tubes, weighing 100 lbs, was delivered to his studio while Warhol was capturing his conversation with the actor Ondine on his tape recorder; the audio tapes were later transcribed into a book, the ready-made novel *a*.[4] Richard Ekstract, who organized sponsor contacts and the party at the Factory where the Philips machine and the first videos were presented, conducted an interview with Warhol that made it to the cover of *Tape Recording*, a magazine dedicated to audio tape, which introduced video recording to its readers on the occasion (reprinted in this chapter).

Andy Warhol appeared as the perfect choice to introduce artist's video to the public for two reasons: he loved his audio tape recorder both professionally and personally, even calling it his "wife."[5] And in his underground movies, especially the so-called "screen tests," he exploited the narcissist aspect of exposing people to a camera, which would become important for video later on. The screen-test setting turned out to be the perfect model for Warhol's one and only surviving artwork shot with the Philips video equipment in the summer of 1965.[6] As an ironical appropriation of Hollywood castings, the screen tests posed persons in front of the film camera for the length of a standard 16 mm 100-foot cartridge (about three minutes). Video brought three new components to this procedure: sound, extended running time, and the possibility of feedback. These components are combined in the hybrid film/video piece *Outer and Inner Space* starring the Factory "superstar" Edie Sedgwick talking for 33 minutes in four close-ups of her face (Figure 12.1). Two of her portraits are shot on video, two on film. Presented in a parallel film projection, her two embedded video images gaze up to the right, speaking to someone off-screen, while her two film images show her sitting in front of her own video image, looking directly into the film camera, commenting on the experience of watching herself on television. As Warhol film expert Callie Angel points out, this arrangement "at times creates the illusion that we are watching Sedgwick in conversation with her own image," and the "outer and inner" of the title therefore refers not only to the dichotomy between her outer beauty and inner turmoil, "but also describes the two very different spaces of representation occupied by the video/television medium and by film."[7]

In the interview with Richard Ekstract, Warhol describes his experiments in recording images from a TV screen. As Callie Angel suggests, he was "fascinated by the ability of video playback to double the image of his subject—to place a person in the same frame with his or her own image" so "that the double-screen format was a logical outgrowth of his access to video."[8] Warhol's video experience had a lasting impact on his experimental films, and shortly after Philips took back the video equipment he presented *The Chelsea Girls* (1966), which is probably his best-known film, as a split-screen projection.

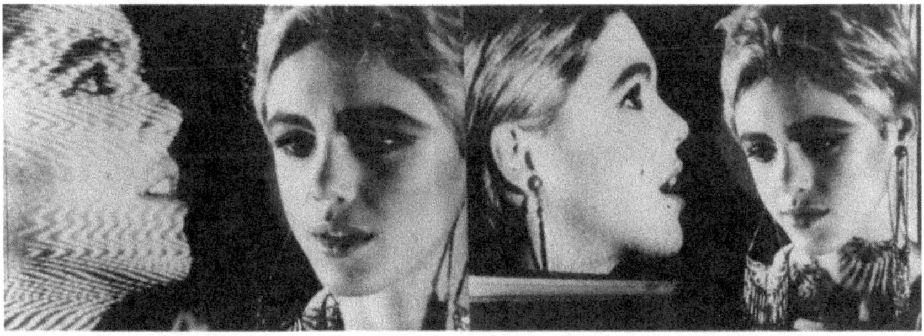

Figure 12.1 Andy Warhol, *Outer and Inner Space*, 1965, 16-mm film, black and white, double screen, 33 min. © 2020 The Andy Warhol Museum, Pittsburgh, PA, a museum of the Carnegie Institute. Film still courtesy The Andy Warhol Museum.

Nam June Paik, *Study I: Mayor Lindsay* (1965)

Shortly after his move to New York, Nam June Paik received a grant from the Rockefeller Foundation thanks to the support of John Cage. This grant enabled him to buy one of the first consumer video recorders on the market, the Sony TCV-2010 from the CV-2000 series. This ½-inch open-reel tape machine sold for $1000 including the camera, so it was significantly smaller and much less expensive than the semi-professional Philips equipment used by Warhol. The TCV-2010 was probably the first successful domestic video recorder. It was not portable like the Sony Portapak introduced three years later, but consumers could record TV broadcasts directly off the air, which was impossible with any other video recorder of the time.[9] In a print ad from 1965, Sony pitched the combination of recorder, camera, and monitor with two different user scenarios: "You can electronically record anything you see or hear and play it back instantly. You can record and keep anything you see on your TV set."[10]

While private customers and most artists would mainly be interested in camera recordings, Paik used the second option for the earliest of his video works surviving to the present day.[11] For *Study I: Mayor Lindsay*, Paik worked with a topical television broadcast from November 1965. With this piece, he becomes the first artist appropriating and manipulating material from television on video, played back on a TV screen without an intermediate step. Bruce Conner and Wolf Vostell had used broadcast footage before, but in default of video equipment had to record it from the TV screen with 16 mm film.[12] Paik's *Study I: Mayor Lindsay* shows U.S. politician John Vliet Lindsay on a photo shoot for newspaper and television immediately after he had been elected mayor of New York on November 2, 1965 (Figure 12.2). He calls out to

Figure 12.2 Nam June Paik, *Study 1: Mayor Lindsay*, November 1965, video, black and white, 4:33 min.

the impatient reporters: "As soon as I'm through I'll pose again." Endlessly repeating that sentence, Paik explores media-specific processes producing a public image: the television footage shows the politician striking a pose for the press photographers, whereas the print press merely presents the finished image.

An interesting but hardly discussed question: How could Paik achieve these effects with a simple consumer device such as the TCV-2010? A single open-reel recorder did not allow any editing or copying of videotapes. The artist had to significantly extend the two scenarios proposed to Sony customers and found similar work-arounds as in his earlier work with audio tape by expanding the linear playback video machine with his own "unique loop device." Thus Paik turned the TCV-2010 into a prototype for what he later conceptualized as "random access information."[13] This early existence of this "unique loop device" was disclosed a decade later in the press release for the presentation of a reworked video tape of *Study I* at the Museum of Modern Art in 1975.[14] The device itself might have been only a temporary solution for looping the open-reel videotape manually. Paik developed a more elaborate interactive video loop for *McLuhan Caged* (see Chapter 1), shown at the Bonino Gallery in his exhibition *Electronic Art II* 1968 with the same TCV-2010 as seen on photos and in film documentation.

The Legacy of Two Early Experiments in Practice and Theory

To conclude I want to point out the ongoing significance of these two early video experiments that took place during the summer/autumn of 1965 in New York. The first aspect concerns video in art exhibitions. At the time of their conception, none of the two works by Warhol and Paik had a larger visibility in the art world. *Study I: Mayor Lindsay* resurfaced after ten years, when Paik had the opportunity to rework the original footage at the WNET TV studio, simulating the effects of his "unique loop device" for a linear videotape, but until the present day there is only one public collection, the Video Forum of the NBK Berlin, which holds a copy of this seminal work. As Callie Angel explains, Warhol's "*Outer and Inner Space* was made at a time when there actually was no such thing as video art, the film was shown only a few times in the 1960s, so it really had no contemporary impact in that context at all, and was probably not seen by anyone who was then identified as or likely to become a video artist."[15]

This said, it may surprise that the staging of both works seems like a premonition of contemporary presentations of video in art exhibitions. Paik's *Study I* appears to be not only the first artwork using television images recorded on video but also the very first loop in video art history. Today the loop is one of the most common ways of editing video in artworks.[16] At the same time, the loop has become the standard dispositive for the presentation of linear video in exhibition settings. These artistic and the curatorial practices of looping seem to correspond to the on/off attention span of exhibition publics for film and video works.

The same applies to the split-screen of *Outer and Inner Space*, which way beyond Warhol's own experimental film work has turned into a typical artistic strategy for video works in an art context, e.g. in the work of Harun Farocki, to name only one out of many examples. Most of these split-screen works develop a specific mode of narration, which has nothing to do with the radical dichotomy of *The Chelsea Girls*. In similar ways the loop has been commodified as a standard dispositive for video and film without the disturbing analytic density of Paik's early works.

The ongoing relevance of these two pioneering works can be seen in the fact that each of them is based on a distinct specificity of the video medium. Warhol used the capacities of the video image's instantaneous doubling; Paik developed the instantaneous repeatability of the looped magnetic tape into an artistic form. In this sense they are exemplary case studies for the "differential specificity" that has haunted any attempt to narrow the criteria of the video medium for any kind of final, concluding, and thereby specific definition.

This brings us to the second aspect of the legacy concerning the theorization of video, or the rather the ongoing history of this theorization. In search for criteria regarding the specificity of video the two seminal texts of the mid-1970s by Rosalind Krauss (reprinted in Chapter 3) and by David Antin (reprinted in Chapter 5) suggested quite complementary concepts. Krauss focused on the inward-bound mirroring capacity, here labeled as narcissism, while Antin warned his contemporaries not to forget the "frightful parent" television while indulging the seductions of video imagination. Since several decades these two tracks of conceptualizing the medium have been continued, with or without referencing Antin or Krauss.

Coming back to *Outer and Inner Space* and *Study I*: no two other artworks seem to be more suitable to illustrate that these seemingly contradictory specificities are both inherent potentials of the video medium, unveiled by Warhol and Paik at the very first moment that artists had a chance to put their hands on video equipment. Their two different strategies in using video seem to be more relevant than chronological arguments, which depend mostly on external factors (Philips's product placement, Sony's product development, and Paik's Rockefeller Grant). These strategies point to two different roots: experimental film for Andy Warhol and electronic sound art for Paik.[17] Both would be equally important for the further development of video art.[18]

Revised version of Dieter Daniels's opening lecture at the symposium *Future Continuous Present(s): Video Art through Time*, curated by Marie-France Rafael and Olaf Stüber, Hamburger Bahnhof, Nationalgalerie Berlin, December 13, 2018. A video of the lecture is available at https://vimeo.com/374128393.

Notes

1 Dieter Daniels and Stephan Berg, eds., *TeleGen: Kunst und Fernsehen / TeleGen: Art and Television* (Munich: Hirmer, 2015). On the precursors of video art also see Christine Mehring, "Television Art's Abstract Starts: Europe circa 1944–1969," *October* no. 125 (Summer 2008), 29–64.

2 On the development of consumer video technology see Christoph Blase, "Welcome to the Labyrinth of Machines: Tapes and Videoformats 1960–1980," in *Record—*

Again! 40yearsofvideoart.de, Part 2, ed. Peter Weibel and Christoph Blase (Ostfildern: Hatje Cantz, 2010), 500–8.

3 For legal reasons Philips sold this VTR under the brand name Norelco in the U.S. Ibid. 503, 506.

4 Andy Warhol, *a, A Novel* (New York: Grove Press, 1968). William Kaizen comments on the passages documenting the delivery and unpacking of the equipment: "Warhol's audio tapes contain one of the first responses to video [. . .]. As such, these tapes record a point of emergence of one medium from another as video began to coalesce from audio, film, and television." Kaizen, "Live on Tape: Video, Liveness and the Immediate," in *Art and the Moving Image: A Critical Reader* (London: Tate Publishing/Afterall, 2008), 258. See also Andy Warhol and Pat Hackett, *POPism: The Warhol Sixties* (New York: Harcourt Brace Jovanovic), 119.

5 Gustavus Stadler, "'My Wife': The Tape Recorder and Warhol's Queer Ways of Listening," *Criticism* 56, no. 3, "Andy Warhol" issue (Summer 2014), 425–56.

6 This video-based work survived because it was not shown as a videotape but within a double film projection, while all remaining videotapes from this period are technically no longer accessible. Callie Angel reports: "During the month that Warhol had this video access, he shot approximately eleven half-hour tapes (at least, that's how many Norelco videotapes have been found in the Warhol Video Collection). [. . .] The Norelco system utilized an unusual video format, called 'slant scan video,' which differed from the helical scan format developed by Sony and other video companies, and which very quickly became obsolete. There are now no working slant scan tape players anywhere in the world, the other videotapes which Warhol shot in 1965 cannot be played back, and the only accessible footage from these early videos exists in this film, which Warhol, in effect, preserved by reshooting them in 16mm." Callie Angel, "Doubling the Screen: Andy Warhol's *Outer and Inner Space*," in *Millennium Film Journal* 38 (Spring 2002), http://mfj-online.org/journalPages/MFJ38/angell.html.

7 Callie Angel, "*Outer and Inner Space*," in *CTRL [SPACE]: Rhetorics of Surveillance from Bentham to Big Brother*, ed. Thomas Y. Levin, Ursula Frohne, and Peter Weibel (Cambridge, MA: MIT Press, 2002), 279, 280.

8 Angel, "Doubling the Screen."

9 The Sony Portapak was a pure camera recorder that did not allow for recording broadcasts off the air, and it required a fixed player from the Sony CV-2000 series to play back the tape. In the literature on Paik's first video works, the TCV-2010 is often confused with the Portapak.

10 https://www.smecc.org/sony_cv_series_video.htm.

11 With his leaflet "Electronic Video Recorder" (reprinted in this chapter), Paik announces the first public presentations of videos for October 4 and 11, 1965. The videos shown there have not survived; they included current footage of Pope Paul VI's visit to New York on October 4. It is unclear if this was a live broadcast or video recordings of a broadcast (as with John Lindsay). The assertion that Paik could not have made live recordings from TV as the battery-operated Sony Portapak only became available later, as Tom Sherman argues, in any case is wrong. See Tom Sherman, "The Premature Birth of Video Art," 2007, http://www.experimentaltvcenter.org/sites/default/files/history/pdf/ShermanThePrematureBirthofVideoArt_2561.pdf. Paik explains his method of powering the TCV-2010 for outdoor use: "Needless to say, for the first day shooting (indeed on October 4) I had to borrow a *zerhacker* (dc-ac converter)." Paik 1984 to Siegfried Zielinski, see footnote 4 in Zielinski's contribution in Chapter 2.

12 Bruce Conner, *Report* (1963–1967), and Wolf Vostell, *Sun in Your Head* (1963). See *TeleGen*, 112–13 and 174–5.

13 Nam June Paik, "Random Access Information," *Artforum* 19, no. 1 (September 1980), 46–9.

14 On Paik's use of a "unique loop device" for *Study I: Mayor Lindsay* and his re-editing of the original footage at WNET TV in 1974, see the Museum of Modern Art' s press release for "Projects: Video III" February 21, 1975, http://www.moma.org/momaorg/shared/pdfs/docs/press_archives/5227/releases/MOMA_1975_0012_10.pdf?2010.

15 Angel, "Doubling the Screen." *Outer and Inner Space* was restored by the Museum of Modern Art in New York in 1998 and premiered as an installation at the Whitney Museum of American Art in October 1998.

16 See Franziska Stöhr, *Endlos: Zur Geschichte des Film- und Videoloops im Zusammenspiel von Technik, Kunst und Ausstellung* (Bielefeld: transcript, 2016).

17 The different strategies are also visible in their works with television images before 1965. Paik used TV to generate and modulate the electronic image in his *Exposition of Music Electronic Television* (1963). In his film *Soap Opera* (1964), Warhol appropriated found footage of TV advertisements, similar to the appropriation strategies of his silkscreen paintings. See *TeleGen*, 114–51 for Paik, 182f for Warhol.

18 Another far-reaching difference: Warhol combined video and film in a cross-media relation but did not interfere with the technological side of these media. Paik modified the electronic image and the television/video apparatus itself. In a contemporary typescript he wrote: "The 80% of my work that is dedicated to purely technological experiment is to explore new effects which normal scientists have not discovered." Nam June Paik, "Outline of Lecture Series on Electronic Television," 1965, unpublished typescript, written as proposal for the New School of Social Research, Archiv Sohm, Staatsgalerie Stuttgart.

Pop Goes the Video Tape: An Underground Interview with Andy Warhol (1965)

Andy Warhol in dialogue with Richard Ekstract

If you think recording sound is fun (and it is), just think of the tremendous possibilities available when you can tape sound and pictures with the same recorder. That day was brought much closer to tape enthusiasts this summer when Ampex, Matsushita, and Sony introduced home video tape recorders in the $1000 price range. The race is now on to produce video tape units for $500 or less. When that happens tape recording will surely be America's number one hobby.

To test the new medium, *Tape Recording* magazine approached tape enthusiast and home moviemaker Andy Warhol to produce some experimental home video tapes. Warhol, for the uninitiated, is an artist who rose to sudden fame a few years ago when the Pop Art movement swept America. His paintings of such common objects as Campbell Soup cans and Brillo boxes became the rage in art circles and now hang in many of the most prominent homes and museums both here and abroad.

About two years ago. Warhol began experimenting with 16mm movies. He was welcomed by the members of the "Underground Movie" camp who make experimental films in the hope of extending the art of motion pictures to new and exciting visual art forms.

Warhol made his reputation in the Underground film movement with films such as *Sleep*, eight hours of film of one person sleeping. Another of his epics was *Empire*, eight hours of film recording the Empire State building. Warhol and his group have now made Underground movies on home video tape to give *Tape Recording*'s readers a preview of the techniques involved in the new medium. Thus we embarked on an adventure which is continuing even as this is being written.

Warhol used a Norelco slant-track video recorder which retails for $3950 and operates in the same manner as its lower priced counterparts. With the recorder, Norelco supplied a remote control television camera with a zoom lens. For special applications, he also used a Concord model MTC 11 hand-held video camera with a Canon zoom lens. Video tape was supplied by Reeves Soundcraft. The rotary head recorder operates at a tape speed of 7½ ips and uses one inch wide video tape.

TAPE RECORDING: How did you get involved in making Underground movies?

WARHOL: I was going to Hollywood. That's how it all happened.

TAPE RECORDING: You mean . . .

WARHOL: Hollywood is the movie capital of the world, so I bought a movie camera to take along. A 16mm Bolex. I was with Taylor Meade, a famous Underground movie star. My first movie was called *Taylor Meade in Hollywood*.

TAPE RECORDING: What did you shoot?

WARHOL: Anything and everything. I was just learning to use the camera.

TAPE RECORDING: How did Underground movies get their start?

WARHOL: I don't know. Lots of people were making these movies and Jonas Mekas organized a co-op, the Cinematheque, to exhibit them.

TAPE RECORDING: What was your next film?

WARHOL: Next came my *Sleep* movie.

TAPE RECORDING: What were you trying to show?

WARHOL: It started with someone sleeping and it just got longer and longer and longer. Actually, I did shoot all the hours for this movie, but I faked the final film to get a better design.

TAPE RECORDING: You mean . . .

WARHOL: Yes, it's the same 100 feet of film spliced together for eight hours. I'd like to do this movie again someday with someone like Brigitte Bardot and just let the camera watch her sleep for eight hours.

TAPE RECORDING: Sounds like fun.

WARHOL: Yes, but frightfully expensive.

TAPE RECORDING: How much do these "longies" cost?

WARHOL: Thousands of dollars.

TAPE RECORDING: Do you get any income from Underground movies?

WARHOL: No.

TAPE RECORDING: Pretty expensive hobby.

WARHOL: All my painting money goes into it.

TAPE RECORDING: Did you make any sound movies?

WARHOL: Yes, I bought an Arricon sound camera with a 1200 foot reel. But the optical sound wasn't very good. The sound on videotape is much better.

TAPE RECORDING: Home videotaping is such a new medium. How does it feel to be pioneering in it?

WARHOL: Like Alice in Wonderland.

TAPE RECORDING: What do you see as the essential difference between film and videotape?

WARHOL: Immediate playback. When you make movies you have to wait and wait and wait.

TAPE RECORDING: How about lighting?

WARHOL: You don't need any for video. Just a light bulb. It's so scary. The tape machine is so easy to use. Anyone can do it.

TAPE RECORDING: Do you prefer tape to film?

WARHOL: Oh, yes.

TAPE RECORDING: How long did it take you to become proficient with the video tape recorder?

WARHOL: A few hours. All you really have to master is the picture rectifier which compensates for the light in the room. Once you know that, it's just a matter of keeping your heads clean. [. . .]

TAPE RECORDING: have you recorded from a television set with the video recorder?

WARHOL: Yes. This is so great. We've done it both direct and from the screen. Even the pictures from the screen are terrific. Someone put his arm in front of the screen to change channels while we were taping and the effect was very dimensional. We found you can position someone in front of a TV set and have it going while you're recording. If you have close-ups on the TV screen, you can cut back and forth and get great effects.

TAPE RECORDING: That's interesting. Have you been trying to do things with tape that you can't do with film?

WARHOL: Yes. We like to take advantage of static. We sometimes stop the tape to get a second image coming through. As you turn off the tape it runs for several seconds and you get this static image. It's weird. So fascinating. [. . .]

TAPE RECORDING: Can you edit video tape?

WARHOL: No.

TAPE RECORDING: Does this bother you?

WARHOL: No. We never edited our films before because we wanted to keep the same look and the same mood. You lose that when you try to re-create a scene days later after you've gotten back the processed film. Therefore, we just accept whatever we got. Now with videotape, we can do instant retakes and maintain our spontaneity and mood. It's terrific. It has been a great help. [. . .]

TAPE RECORDING: Does sound present any particular problems in making videotapes?

WARHOL: Really good, synchronized sound is one of the most exciting things about home videotapes. There is no "double-system" sound or editing needed. It's built right in. The only thing to be careful about is the position of the microphone. A little experimenting before taping is all that's needed.

TAPE RECORDING: How important is sound to your Underground videotapes?

WARHOL: It's important to us because the people we're working with have something to say.

TAPE RECORDING: What's the most fun you've had with your video recorder?

WARHOL: Oh, it's so great at parties. It's just terrific. People love to see themselves on tape and they really behave normally because the equipment is so unobtrusive.

TAPE RECORDING: What kind of comments do you get from people at these parties?

WARHOL: Ooh. Aah. Ooh. Aah.

TAPE RECORDING: Anything else?

WARHOL: Aah. Ooh.

TAPE RECORDING: What else can people do with their home video recorders?

WARHOL: Make the best pornography movies. It's going to be so great.

TAPE RECORDING: You think Mr. and Mrs. America will . . .

WARHOL: Yes. And they'll have their friends in to show them.

TAPE RECORDING: Any other things you like about the video recorder?

WARHOL: Oh, yes. You can spy on people with it, too. I believe in television. It's going to take over from movies.

TAPE RECORDING: Have you any last advice for home movie makers?

WARHOL: Get a video recorder.

From "Pop Goes the Videotape: An Underground Interview with Andy Warhol," *Tape Recording* 12, no. 5 (September–October 1965), 15–19; interview conducted by Richard Ekstract.

Electronic Video Recorder (1965): Facsimile

Nam June Paik

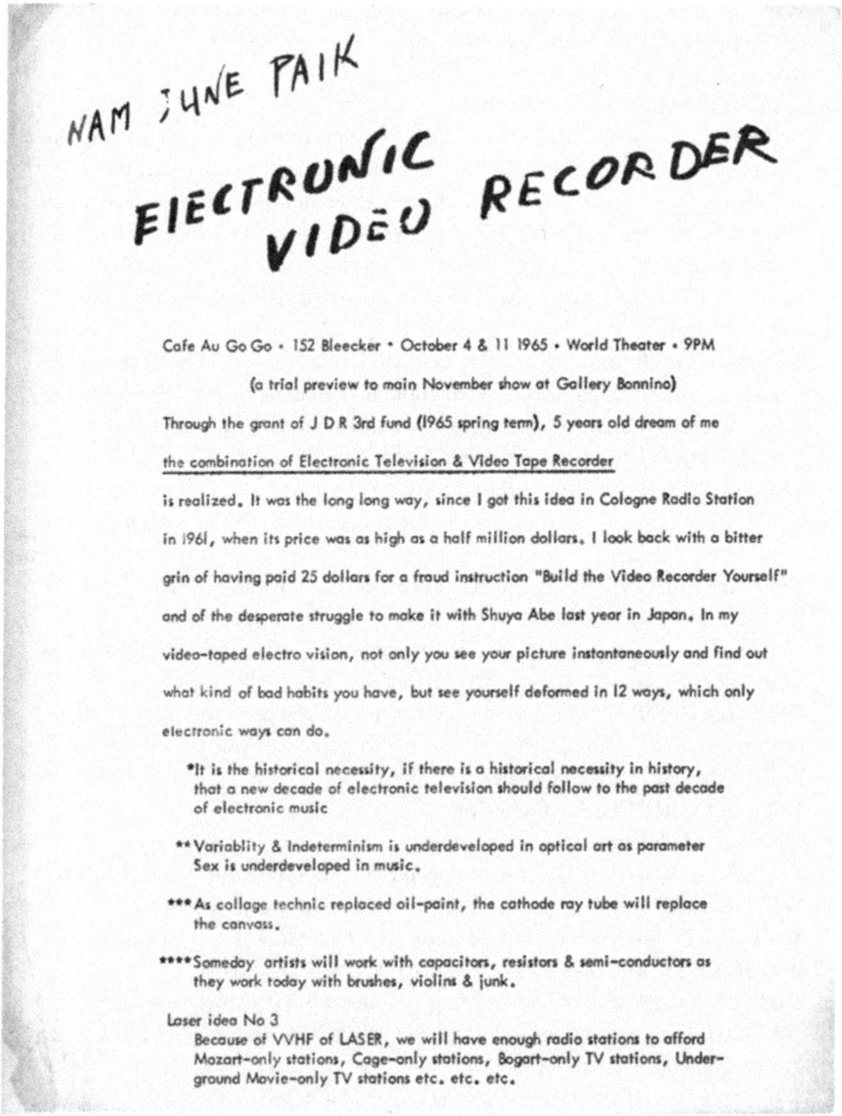

NAM JUNE PAIK

ELECTRONIC VIDEO RECORDER

Cafe Au Go Go • 152 Bleecker • October 4 & 11 1965 • World Theater • 9PM

(a trial preview to main November show at Gallery Bonnino)

Through the grant of J D R 3rd fund (1965 spring term), 5 years old dream of me <u>the combination of Electronic Television & Video Tape Recorder</u> is realized. It was the long long way, since I got this idea in Cologne Radio Station in 1961, when its price was as high as a half million dollars. I look back with a bitter grin of having paid 25 dollars for a fraud instruction "Build the Video Recorder Yourself" and of the desperate struggle to make it with Shuya Abe last year in Japan. In my video-taped electro vision, not only you see your picture instantaneously and find out what kind of bad habits you have, but see yourself deformed in 12 ways, which only electronic ways can do.

*It is the historical necessity, if there is a historical necessity in history, that a new decade of electronic television should follow to the past decade of electronic music

**Variablity & Indeterminism is underdeveloped in optical art as parameter Sex is underdeveloped in music.

***As collage technic replaced oil-paint, the cathode ray tube will replace the canvass.

****Someday artists will work with capacitors, resistors & semi-conductors as they work today with brushes, violins & junk.

Laser idea No 3
Because of VVHF of LASER, we will have enough radio stations to afford Mozart-only stations, Cage-only stations, Bogart-only TV stations, Underground Movie-only TV stations etc. etc. etc.

Figure 12.3 Nam June Paik, *Electronic Video Recorder*, Facsimile of a leaflet distributed by Paik in October 1965, reprinted in *Videa 'n' Videology: Nam June Paik 1959–1973*, ed. Judson Rosebush (Syracuse: Everson Museum of Art, 1974), unpag.

Before the Cinematic Turn: Video Projection in the 1970s (2015)

Erika Balsom

Jacques Aumont has said that the light of projection is often forgotten by film theory because it is always present as an invariable part of the apparatus.[1] With video, however, this is not the case. Unlike the film image, which needs projection for its realization, video confronts projection as but one display option. In video, projection is a choice—a choice that radically reshapes the possibilities of the medium. Its use in contemporary art is now ubiquitous, but this ubiquity is of relatively recent date. In the catalog for his 1996 exhibition, *Being and Time: The Emergence of Video Projection*, Marc Mayer writes that this "new way of experiencing video was developed in earnest during the late 1980s."[2] Originally intended for the business market but quickly taken up by artists, liquid crystal diode (LCD) projectors were introduced in 1990, displacing the three-gun cathode ray tube (CRT) projectors that had preceded them with a more portable and reliable technology that promised higher image quality. A major turning point occurred two years later when Documenta 9 (1992) featured projected video pieces by Stan Douglas, Gary Hill, Bruce Nauman, and Bill Viola. For Liz Kotz, "video projection reached it crucial threshold" with Stan Douglas and Diana Thater's solo exhibitions at David Zwirner Gallery in 1993.[3] As the 1990s went on, large-scale video projection would become an increasingly prominent feature of contemporary art, prompting some to speak of a "cinematic turn" that privileged attributes such as illusionism and spectacle.

The embrace of projection has drastically altered the relationships between image, viewer, and surrounding architecture. It has distanced video from television and is perhaps the single factor most responsible for the massive institutional endorsement of the medium from the early 1990s onwards. In short, unlike theatrical exhibition, in the gallery and museum the adoption of video projection has changed the face of moving image art. At the risk of putting it far too simply, one might say that the widespread employment of video projection is what marks the end of video art and the beginning of artists' cinema.

The massive realignment of the field of practice brought about by this technological innovation necessitates a close look at the place of video projection in the history of art and an examination of its specificity as a mode of display. In particular, it invites a revisitation of employments of video projection that occurred prior to its explosion roughly a quarter-century ago. Though the technique did not reach widespread visibility until the early 1990s, video projection in fact predates video recording technology and has a history of artistic employments going back to the mid-1960s. The appearance of video projection in the early 1990s was, then, its second time around as a new medium of artistic practice. Today, looking back at the technique's first appearances in art and its failure to achieve general adoption at that time can serve to better illuminate the stakes of its contemporary ubiquity.

The first video projection systems were designed to transform television from a petite, domestic entertainment into something spectacular and public. The Eidophor system, which employed an electron beam to diffract light off of a transparent oily surface, was invented in 1939 and prototyped in 1944. Demonstrations of the system, which *Life* magazine dubbed "movie-theater television," commenced in 1947, with sporting events like the 1948 Louis vs Walcott boxing match attracting an audience of three thousand at the Paramount Theatre in Manhattan.[4] Cathode ray tube projectors using the Schmidt optical system of parabolic mirrors and a correction lens were also invented in the late 1930s. CRT projectors were not as bright as those using the Eidophor system and could not produce images as large, but had the advantage of being cheaper and more portable. As Douglas Gomery has noted, the use of such early projection systems in a theatrical context has "fallen between the cracks of traditional film history" because "it never proved profitable in the long-run."[5] And yet, theater television in the immediate postwar era may be seen as an attempt to grapple with the place of cinema in a media environment increasingly dominated by television, one that antedates the more widely-discussed industry responses of CinemaScope and 3-D. It is an early and significant engagement with questions of scale and liveness, attributes that constitute recurring points of interrogation throughout the various uses of projection in an artistic context, as will become clear in the remarks that follow.

While monochrome CRT projectors were used—though often with considerable technical difficulty[6]—during the performances of Alex Hay, Robert Rauschenberg, David Tudor, and Robert Whitman at *9 Evenings: Theater and Engineering* at the Armory in New York City in 1966, a sustained exploration of the technology in an artistic context would not occur until the early 1970s, in the work of Keith Sonnier and Peter Campus. Beginning in 1970, Sonnier used the Kalart Victor Telebeam CRT projector to produce environmental installations, many of which transformed off-air television signals into images that bathed the room in electronic light. In *Channel Mix*, shown at the Castelli Gallery space at 420 West Broadway in February and March of 1972, the artist projected four off-air commercial television channels onto two screens using a special effects generator to create a split-screen effect, thus placing signals that the viewer must normally choose between into spatial coexistence.

Writing about the work in *Artforum*, Robert Pincus-Whitten fastened onto how the artist used projection in such a manner so as to put "into play the accumulated issues of scale inherent in American painting of the last quarter century, issues seemingly absent in the current use of video."[7] To be more precise, scale was not absent as a concern in contemporaneous uses of video; rather, the engagement with scale that existed was one that tended to privilege the small scale of the monitor over the enlarged image of projection. The image on the monitor remains contained and possessable, of a manageable size that neither overwhelms nor dwarfs. While one might find some exploration of video at a larger scale in multi-monitor arrays such as Frank Gillette and Ira Schneider's *Wipe Cycle* (1969), even here individual images remained small. Such a focus on the domestic scale of the image was central to much video art at the time and, for some, constituted a defining feature of the medium. Sonnier's turn to projection placed the video image in a wholly different relationship to its surrounding architecture and ruptured the intimacy of monitor-based viewing. *Channel Mix* envelops the viewer and dissolves interior volumes in a manner that might make one think of cinema. At a time when many films were being shown on television, *Channel Mix* inverted this miniaturization to instead display television under conditions reminiscent of cinema.

Yet in its use of off-air television signals, the installation left behind the pastness of film for the unfolding now proper to broadcast media. Though Jane Feuer has demonstrated the extent to which liveness is constitutive of the ideology, rather than the ontology, of television,[8] there is no denying the extent to which the temporality of television is to be distinguished from that of cinema in its insistence on the category of the "now." In *Channel Mix*, the assertion of the "now" is found both in the temporal address of the off-air broadcast, but also in the way the piece activates the space of reception. In the cinematic situation there is a generalized foreclosure of the cinema space in favor of the illuminated rectangle of the screen (or at least an attempt at such a thing), which results in a strict separation of spaces. Here, quite differently, image and viewer share the room. A body might obstruct a projection or might become a kind of screen. Liveness, then, is emphasized both as the status of the projected image and in the viewer's negotiation of the work.

One discerns similar preoccupations of scale, material actuality, and liveness in Peter Campus's use of CRT projection. In 1972, the artist began to employ a Telebeam projector in his closed-circuit installations. In *Interface* (1972; see Figure 12.4), Campus installed a sheet of glass with a projector on one side and a camera on the other. The viewer standing in front of the glass and facing the camera will be able to see both her reflection and her video image, which emanates from the projector behind her—but the reflection will be in color and mirrored, while the video image will be monochrome and the "right," but less familiar, way around. *Shadow Projection* (1974), the sole video piece to be included in the *Projected Images* exhibition at the Walker Art Center in the fall of that year, played with a similar notion of the uncanny doubling of the self. A screen was placed in the middle of the room with a projector aimed at it from one side and a camera and spotlight from the other. Facing the screen illuminated by rear projection, the spectator would thus see both her own shadow and an image of the back of her head, the latter being visible only within the former because of the strong light coming from straight ahead. As in *Interface*, the piece uses closed-circuit projection to allow the viewer to see herself from a position she cannot occupy.

Campus's use of projection evinces an interest in psychodrama not present in Sonnier's, drawing on tropes of the *Doppelgänger* and the uncanny experience of encountering the self as other. Here, Campus evokes a meaning of the word "projection" that goes beyond its primary use in this context as designating the image's mode of realization. For Jacques Lacan, the psychic operation of projection refers to the process of suture, the imaginary misrecognition by which the gaps and divisions of the symbolic are covered over so that the subject may experience an illusory coherence.[9] In the early 1970s, film theorists such as Stephen Heath and Jean-Louis Baudry conceived of the spectator's relationship to the filmic apparatus as precisely this kind of projection, thus introducing a second meaning of the term into the discourse of cinema studies. These film theoretical accounts of theatrical spectatorship—roughly contemporaneous with Campus's installations—conceive of the viewer of the classical cinematic *dispositif* as occupying an omnipotent, transcendental subject position that allows for the

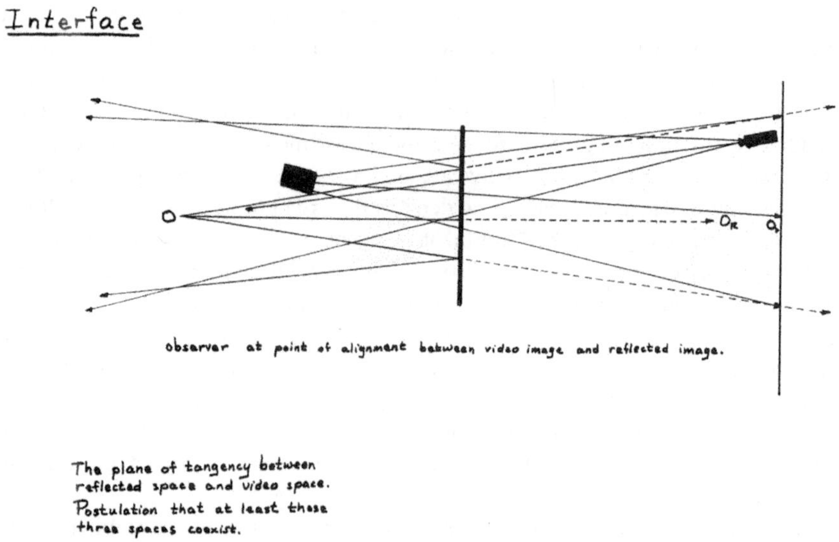

Interface
observer at point of alignment between video image and reflected image.
The plane of tangency between reflected space and video space. Postulation that at least these three spaces coexist.

Figure 12.4 Peter Campus, diagram of *Interface*, 1972. Courtesy of the artist and Cristin Tierney Gallery, New York.

inhabitation of the reassuring fiction that the onscreen world is constituted entirely for him or her.[10] This position is, to be sure, eminently ideological; the political imperative was to trouble it and reveal its falsity. *Interface* and *Shadow Projection* do precisely this by astutely intervening into both these senses of the word "projection": Campus makes use of moving image projection to disrupt the process of psychic projection that typically characterizes its cinematic employments, staging situations in which the subject is denied consistency and decentered. In *Interface* and *Shadow Projection* the illusion of mastery is undone, as the viewer becomes unsettlingly aware of being captured by the apparatus rather than experiencing a fantasy of control. What we find, in short, is a form of anti-cinematic, anti-projective (in the psychic sense) projection.

Both Sonnier and Campus deploy projection to induce a reflection on the relationships formed between bodies and real-time images within the actual space of exhibition. This stands as a marked divergence from typical uses of projection in cinema, which tend to rely on a foreclosure of the space of exhibition so as to create a maximal absorption in the prerecorded image on-screen. These artists thus engage in a disarticulation of the technique of projection from its deep embeddedness in the institution of cinema. They return to the giganticism and liveness of the failed theater television broadcasts, but move outside of the movie theater to instead explore the mobile spectator's embodied relationship with the projected image and the space surrounding it.

Such early deployments of video projection function as the estranged ancestors of the many artists currently working with video projection. In their transportation of the projected video image into the space of the gallery, Sonnier and Campus's relevance to contemporary practice is clear. But these artists figure as estranged, rather than close, ancestors to those working in projection today due to the significant divergences between the character of their experiments with projection and that of the wholehearted embrace of the technique that would occur from the early 1990s onward. While the display of projected images in a gallery tends not to deny the space of reception to the same degree as the movie theater, uses of projection in the art of the 1990s were overwhelmingly allied with a cinematic deployment of projection that privileges the screen-as-window.

Outside of such isolated cases, the use of video projection prior to the late 1980s and early 1990s was quite rare. Key factors discouraging widespread adoption were the bulkiness, high cost, unreliability, and low image quality of the technology. There is also the sense that projection offered a less attractive mode of display for most video artists at this time precisely because it distanced the medium from its grounding in television and also from the work of video pioneers who had engaged with the monitor as a sculptural form. It is significant that those artists who did turn to projection tended to retain attributes of liveness and real-time transmission as integral to their work, thus maintaining the link to television as video's primary point of reference. There is a rhetoric of liberation that surrounds the flight from the monitor in the 1990s—as if video had finally broken free. But it is worth noting that early video art did not necessarily want to "escape" the box; part of what was most intriguing about video was its proximity to television, and engaging with television meant engaging with the television monitor. Artists particularly interested in the technique of projection were most likely to use film, while video artists interested in scale and spatial relations opted for multi-monitor arrays, leaving projected video as a relatively unexplored area.

Today things are rather different. Projection is ubiquitous and tends to be aligned with the illusionism and pictorialism proper to conventional cinema. This ubiquity has attracted criticism: Sean Cubitt, for example, has called video projection "the cliché of biennial art, despised because it is both overused and underexplored," while Dave Beech anticipated in 1999 that it would become known as "a defining embarrassment" of the decade, much as "shoulder pads and big hair" figured for the 1980s.[11] Whether or not such criticism is merited, one thing is certain: in dislodging the necessity of the present, the mostly forgotten past of early projected video opens the possibility that other future projections, very different than those we know today, may be yet to come.

From Erika Balsom, "Before the Cinematic Turn: Video Projection in the 1970s," in *Exhibiting the Moving Image: History Revisited*, ed. François Bovier and Adeena Mey (Dijon: Les Presses du réel; Zürich: JRP/Ringier; Lausanne: University of Art and Design, 2015), 58–73; shortened and edited for the present publication by the author.

Notes

1 Jacques Aumont, *L'Attrait de la lumière* (Crisnée: Éditions Yellow Now, 2010), 19.
2 Marc Mayer, "Digressions toward an Art History of Video," in *Being and Time: The Emergence of Video Projection* (Buffalo: Albright Knox Gallery, 1996), 28.
3 For more on video projection in Documenta 9, see Erika Balsom, *Exhibiting Cinema in Contemporary Art* (Amsterdam: Amsterdam University Press, 2013), 34–6.

4 "Movie-Theater Television," *Life* 24, no. 18 (May 3, 1948), 49f. For more on boxing and theater television, see Anna McCarthy, "'Like an Earthquake!' Theater Television, Boxing, and the Black Public Sphere," *Quarterly Review of Film and Video* 16, no. 3 (1997), 307–23.

5 Douglas Gomery, "Theater Television: The Missing Link of Technological Change in the US Motion Picture Industry," *Velvet Light Trap* 21 (1985), 55.

6 For an account of the malfunctioning of the projector in David Tudor's contribution to the event, see Lowell Cross, "The *9 Evenings*, New York City, 1966," in *Remembering David Tudor: A 75th Anniversary Memoir* (2011), available online at http://www.lowellcross.com/articles/tudor/1966.html [original link expired].

7 Robert Pincus-Witten, "Keith Sonnier: Video and Film as Color-Field," *Artforum* 10, no. 9 (May 1972), 37.

8 See Jane Feuer, "The Concept of Live Television: Ontology as Ideology," in *Regarding Television*, ed. E. Ann Kaplan (Los Angeles: The American Film Institute, 1983), 12–21.

9 See Jacques Lacan, "The Mirror Stage as Formative of the *I* Function as Revealed in Psychoanalytic Experience," in *Écrits: A Selection*, trans. Bruce Fink (New York: W.W. Norton and Company, 2002), 5.

10 See, for example Jean-Louis Baudry, "Ideological Effects of the Basic Cinematographic Apparatus," in *Narrative, Apparatus, Ideology: A Film Theory Reader*, ed. Philip Rosen (New York: Columbia University Press, 1986), 286–98.

11 Sean Cubitt, "Projection," in *Janine Randerson: Peace in Space* (Wellington: New Zealand Film Archive, 2005), n.p.; Dave Beech, "Video After Diderot," *Art Monthly* 225 (April 1999), 7.

Video as a Function of Reality (1974)

Peter Campus

1. If we are to avoid the problem of creating a visual system that will reduce the capacity of the eye, it is necessary to disassociate the video camera from the eye and make it an extension of the room.

Instead of limiting the amount of visual information coming to the eye-brain by replacing the natural field of vision with an abstracted one, it is possible to include the video information in the viewer's field of vision, increasing the potential of the visual situation.

The video camera makes possible an exterior point of view simultaneous with one's own. This advance over the film camera is due to the vidicon tube, similar to the retina of the eye, continuously transposing light (photon) energy to electrical energy.

2. The monitor is an object sitting rigidly in space. This allows the viewer to locate the monitor in space relative to him/her. Compare this to a movie theater where every effort is made to erase one's ability to locate the screen in the viewer's space, containing all possibilities for central (foveal) eye movements. In a video monitor situation, central eye movements tend to move off the surface of the screen, locating the screen and relating the screen to the room.

By locating the monitor in space, the viewer has the option of identifying with the monitor and seeing all image movement as moving through it or identifying with the image movement and thereby losing his/her illusion of stasis.

It is easy to utilize video to clarify perceptual situations because it separates the eye surrogate from the eye-brain experience we are all too familiar with. Scalar clues become obvious. Visual movement separated from eye muscle, head, and body movement information allows us to see things we thought static to move freely past our field of view. A simultaneous comparison makes it even more evident.

If the material on the monitor screen is recorded material (that is emanating from some past moment and of finite duration), it may be considered as subtractive. But this information, negatively located in space-time, is as relevant as any simultaneous situation, and the outer associations are as interesting.

With closed circuit video, duration is reduced to a point (the world point of the Minkowski universe) and the viewer is presented with a simultaneous point of view contained within his/her surrounding space.

3. The reconversion from electrical to light energy that takes place in a video monitor may further be focused on a wall or screen by means of a video projector. This change is quite dramatic, accompanied not only by increased size, but also by a loss of detail and a loss of illusion of depth.

The viewer is generally unable to make scalar distinctions. That is: an enlarged object does not surprise, even though one would perceptually expect the object to be much closer.

Although the image is easy to locate in the context of the room, central eye movements may be contained within the screen sector, allowing the eye-brain to lose its bearings.

4. A further development of the video space–viewer's space situation occurs when the camera is turned on the viewer and the resulting image projected in front of him/her.

Because we are conditioned to a reversed mirror image we are constantly surprised when the direct video image is presented. Any asymmetric movement causes loss of identification with the projected self-image.

The answer to this is only apparent when the viewer becomes aware of the whole mechanism: the camera-projector-screen-viewer. He/she must be aware of the relative position of the camera to understand the image.

Thus this abstraction, presented simultaneously with reality, forms for the viewer a durational perception rooted in observation and leading to a higher order of reality.

5. I have been dealing here with a simultaneous or, more exactly, a nearly simultaneous image. (Nearly simultaneous because there is some time loss but it is of the order of the speed of light, the speed of electrons, or the speed of neural impulses and therefore imperceptible to human consciousness.)

In a closed-circuit video situation one is no longer dealing with images of a temporally finite nature. The duration of the image becomes a property of the room.

Peter Campus, "Video as a Function of Reality," in *Peter Campus*, exhibition brochure (Syracuse, NY: Everson Museum of Art, 1974); reprinted in *Video Writings by Artists (1970–1990)*, ed. Eugeni Bonet (Milan Mousse Publishing, 2017), 182–4.

Peter Campus (born 1938) studied experimental psychology at Ohio State College and film at the City College of New York. His early tapes explore the anatomy of the video signal in relation to human psychology and perception. He was one of a group of artists in the mid-1970s who produced work in the experimental TV labs at WGBH in Boston and WNET in New York. In addition to numerous single-channel works, he has investigated the characteristics of "live" video through closed-circuit video installations and elaborate sculptural works whose structural components include video cameras, projectors, and monitors.

Videor (1990)

Jacques Derrida

— . . . So one would say. It seems to me, at least, that this is the case: quite singular operations, more and more numerous, put to "work" the new "video" power, the possibility that, in an apparently empirical fashion, is called "video." But I say "it seems to me that . . ." since I am not sure I have at my disposal an adequate concept for what today goes by the name video and especially video *art*. It seems to me that we will have to choose from among three rigorously incompatible "specificities." To go quickly by using common names, let us say that these are (1) the specificity of video *in general*; (2) that of video *art*; (3) that of *such works*, or the putting-to-work of a general technique that is called "video." Whether it is shared by these three possibilities, or whether it is proper to each of them, the aforesaid specificity would suppose the determination of an *internal and essential* trait. Now, despite the upheavals in progress, the use of a different technique or of new supports . . .

—But which ones exactly? What is a support for video?

—I am still wondering what these things have in common: for example, video grafted onto the ordinary use of television, surveillance video, and the most daring research, called "video art," which still remains confined in rather narrow circuits, either public or private, and whose "pragmatic" conditions have nothing in common with the other finalizations of video. The possibility of multiple monitors and of a freer play with this multiplicity, the restructuration of the space of production and performance, the new status of what is called an actor, a character, the displacement of the limit between the private and the public, a growing independence with regard to public or political monopolies on the image, a new economy of relations between the direct and the nondirect, between what is carelessly said to be "real" time and "deferred" time, all this constitutes a bundle of considerable transformations and stakes. If, however, video can play such a visible role here, at a new rhythm, it is neither the sole nor the first technique to do so, and this, at least for video art, constitutes an *external* determination. Once again, it seems to me therefore (*mihi videor*) that there is no essential unity among these things that seem to resemble each other or that are assembled together under the name of video.

—But perhaps the video event, among others, reveals precisely the problematic fragility of this distinction between an internal determination and an external determination. That would already be rather disturbing . . .

—So why then do you say, quite rightly, "among others"? In any case, we would agree, I think, that giving up specific identity doesn't hurt anyone, and perhaps it's better that way.

—On the contrary, it always hurts a lot, that's the whole problem . . .

—Why should it still be necessary to try to identify? Especially in this case, why should one have to zero in on the irreducible property of an "art"? Why try to classify, hierarchize, even situate what one still likes to call the "arts"? Neither opposition (major/minor, for example) nor a genealogy ordered with reference to the history of supports or techniques seems pertinent any longer in this regard, supposing that they ever were. And if the very concept of the "beaux arts" were thereby to find itself affected in the dark core of its long life or its nine lives, would that be such a serious loss?

—One could say that my uncertainty in this regard—it has a long history but it keeps growing, it is both uneasy and joyful—has been encouraged by the experience of the "video" simulacrum into which I have seen myself, modestly, swept along for a little while now, ever since I was given the chance to participate, or rather to figure, in *Disturbance* by Gary Hill. Better still, ever since I seemed to see (*videre videor*, as Descartes would say)[1] my simulacrum do no more than *pass by* there, risk a few passing steps that would be led elsewhere by someone else, I didn't know where. Narcissism set adrift. I owe this chance not only the way one owes a chance but the way one is obliged by another to be involved in an experience, without knowing it, without foreseeing it—an experience that combines in such an inventive fashion luck with calculation and *tychē* (chance) with *anankē* (necessity). But, for that very reason, I was in no position to talk and, finally, I had no desire to do so. The blind *passerby* was hardly even an extra; as to what may be said about that, others have done so with better results than I might even attempt, in particular Jean-Paul Fargier in "Magie blanche."[2] On the other hand, concerning that which cannot be said about it and which remains encrypted in the bodily contact with another simulacrum, with a text that, as I was told and as I believed up until the last minute, was "apocryphal" (the more or less improvised choices that I dictated to myself, almost without seeing—only once—in truth, let be dictated to me like the truth of oracular symptoms in the space of my own familial, tattered gnostic, these raveled fragments of the Gospel according to Thomas that Gary Hill put into my hands, the interrupted premeditations and the sheer chance of improvisation, the hasty crossing of repetitions or rehearsals in the course of an irreversible scene, which is to say unrehearsed, live, direct but without direction, in a direct that was to get carried away with itself, from itself in the course of a simulacrum of performance or presentation that would reveal that there is not and never has been a direct, live presentation, not even, as Virilio ventures to put it in a very fine text, a "presentation [of an] electro-optical milieu"),[3] concerning that which, therefore, cannot be said about it and that regards only me and mine, I will say nothing. And for lack of time, I will also reduce to silence a whole possible rhetoric on the subject of, precisely, "video silence," of video "mystique," in the sense that Wittgenstein speaks of "mystique" when he says that concerning that about which one cannot speak, one must remain silent. Here, what one cannot "say" other than by showing it, or rather by putting on a quasi presentation in video on the subject of video, must be silenced. One must put up or shut up, that is, do it or be quiet, take into account, as Gary Hill *does*, what happens to language through the "video" event (parti . . .)

—Ah well, but a moment ago you were saying that you did not see yourself as capable of speaking of an identity—already identifiable, already assured—of the "video" event . . .

—Not yet, one must take into account what happens to language (partitioned or distributed, cut, strung, or tacked together, delinearized, palindromanagrammatized in more than one language and passing like a serpent across seven monitors at the same time) through the "video" event . . .

—But you are sure there is only one monitor, right here, and one line? What do you think you see?

— . . . Anything but mutism, a certain "being silent" of this writing—new but very impure and all the newer for that—which stages discourses or texts that are thought to be of the most "interior" sort. Is it just by chance that Gary Hill solicits, among others, gnostic texts or the writings of Blanchot? One never sees a new art, one thinks one sees it; but a "new art," as people say a little loosely, may be recognized by the fact that it is not recognized; one would say that it cannot be seen because one lacks not only a ready discourse with which to talk about it, but also that implicit discourse that organizes the experience of this art itself and is working even on our optical apparatus, our most elementary vision. And yet, if this "new art" arises, it is because within the vague terrain of the implicit, something is already enveloped—and developing.

—But someone who was neither an actor, nor an extra, just barely a passerby mobilized by a new interplay of the aleatory and the program, couldn't he say something about the way in which "video art" affects the essential status of its interpreters (I do not say its actors, even less its characters; one would say they are just barely its human subjects)? Whoever appears or sees himself appear in a video work of art is neither a "real person" nor a movie or stage actor nor a character in a novel.

—Are you talking about video art or about the art of Gary Hill?

—As this was my first video passion (passion in the sense that, seeing myself passing by reading in front of a camera against an absolutely white studio background that made me think, I don't know why, of the cemetery in Jerusalem seen from the Mount of Olives, I was all the more gravely passive in that I did not know what Gary Hill would do with what I saw myself doing without seeing myself, with me and mine, with my words, the words that I borrowed, selected, recomposed, repeated, nor what he would do with my passing steps whose rhythm was all I could calculate, not the trajectory, and in fact this image was swept along by a well-understood path of necessity, from one aleatory moment to the next, there where I could in no way have foretold or foreseen it would go, but passion also in the sense that right away I *loved* it, that is to say, as always when one loves, I right away wondered *why* I loved *that*, what or whom I loved exactly), I will say only a few words very quickly on the question that, like everyone, I have asked myself and am still asking: if it is an "art," that, and an absolutely new one, especially with regard to the analogues that are painting, photography, cinema, and television, and even the digital image, what would compose this irreducible difference, that very thing? What is going on there? What went on with me? What happened to the passerby that I was using my body, my passing steps, my voice as no art, no other art, so one would say, would have done? It seems to me. Difficult. I tried out all the possible analyses—forgive me if I do not repeat them here—but nothing worked; I could always reduce the set of components of this "art" to some combination of givens older than *that*, video "properly speaking" as art "properly speaking." So one could say that the question is badly put.

—Let us suppose Gary Hill to be exemplary here . . .

—No, not exemplary, otherwise you are going to end up with the same classical problematic that you want to avoid; no, not exemplary, but singular, idiomatic, his work, each of his works is found to be singular and sweeps the general technique called video along in an adventure that renders it irreplaceable, but irreplaceable among other irreplaceables, other unique effects of signature, even if it puts to work many other things, many other "arts" that have nothing to do with video . . .

—All right, but you are still insisting on the "work," on the shape of its unity, on the idiomatic singularity of the signature, as if it were self-protecting and self-legitimating, in an internal fashion, whereas today events called "video" *can* lay bare symptoms that are far more disturbing and provocative: for example, those that lead us to think the singularity of "works" and "signatures" beginning with the very thing that institutes them and threatens them at the same time. Supposing that there is in effect, so it seems, as an effect and as the simulacrum on the basis of which we are speaking, *some* work and *some* signature, let us then start out from this reminder: Gary Hill was to begin with a sculptor, and a sculptor who was first of all tuned into sonority, indeed to the singing of his sculptures, in other words to that unheard-of technical prosthesis that, at the birth of an art, grafts an ear onto an eye or a hand, right away making us doubt the identity, the name, or the classification of the arts. But he is also one of the few, I do not say the only, "video artists" now working, even if he has not always done so, with discourses, many discourses (this is a "new" visual art that—and it is our first enigma—appears to be one of the most discursive), and not only with discourses but also with textual forms that are heterogeneous among themselves, whether literary or not (Blanchot, the Gospels, for example), that seem to be altogether at odds with such a working, with what one thought "video" art had to be, especially if, as seems to be the case, they are anything but the simple pretext assumed by the videogram.

—This obvious fact perhaps calls for the following hypothesis—I indeed say hypothesis, maybe even fiction: The specificity of a "new art"—or, in general, of a new writing—is not in a relation of irreducible dependence (by that I mean without possible substitution or prosthesis) and especially of synchrony with the emergence of a technical generality or a new "support." One would say that the novelty remains to come, still to come with regard to a technical mutation that, by itself, could give rise to the most mechanical repetition of genres or stereotypes, for example narrative, novelistic, theatrical, cinematographic, or televisual . . .

—So it would take time, a kind of latency period, to render the new support, the new technique indispensable, irreducible . . .

—No, not a homogenous period of latency, but the history of an active, vigilant, unpredictable proliferation that will have displaced even the future anterior in its grammar and permitted in return a new experience of the already identifiable "arts," and not only the "arts," another mode of reading the writings one finds in books, for example, but of so many other things as well; this without destroying the aura of new works whose contours are so difficult to delimit and that are delivered over to other social spaces, other modes of production, of "representation," archiving, reproducibility, while giving to a technique of writing in all its several states (shooting, editing, "incrustation," projection, storage, reproduction, archiving, and so on) the chance for a new aura . . .

—But there would have to be another name for that, other names for all these things, it seems to me . . .

—I wouldn't say that that is indispensable; one would have to see. It seems to me that an old name can always name anew: see how Gary Hill makes secret names and dead tongues resonate on his seven monitors . . .

Jacques Derrida, "Videor," trans. Peggy Kamul, in *Resolutions: Contemporary Video Practices*, ed. Michael Renov and Erika Suderburg (Minneapolis: University of Minnesota Press, 1996), 73–7. Originally published in French in the exhibition catalog *Passage de I'mage*, ed. Raymond Bellour, Catherine David, and Christine van Asche (Paris: Editions du Centre Pompidou, 1990), 158–61. The piece was written after Derrida had participated as one of the "readers" in Gary Hill's video installation *Disturbance (among the Jars)* which was featured in the exhibition.

Notes

1 Rene Descartes, second *Méditation*, quoted by Jean-Luc Nancy, who writes in the course of his analysis: "The *videor* is the illusion that, through an extraordinary torsion or perversion, anchors certainty fully in the abyss of illusion. The place of the *videor* is indeed painting, the portrait, at once the most artificial and the most faithful of faces, the most unseeing and the most clairvoyant eye." Nancy, *Ego Sum* (Paris: Flammarion, 1979), 71f.

2 Jean-Paul Fargier, "Magie blanche," in Gary Hill, *Disturbance (among the Jars)* (Villeneuve d'Ascq: Musee d'art moderne, n.d.).

3 Paul Virilio, "La Lumiere indirecte," *Communications* 48, "Video" (1988), 45ff. The point would be to engage a close discussion around the very interesting but very problematic notions of "telepresence," of "present telereality in 'real time' that supplants the reality of the presence of real space." Already problematic with regard to video *in general* (the principal, even unique object of Virilio's analysis), these concepts would be even more so, it seems, with regard to the putting to work of "art" video, as well as the type of simulacrum that structures it.

[Processual Video] (1980)

Gary Hill

My art has steadily moved from a perceptual priority of imaging toward a more conceptual method for developing idea constructs. Remaining throughout my work has been the necessity to dialogue with the technology. The earlier image works, primarily concerned with color and image density, were engaged in the invention of new and more complex images within compositional and rhythmic structures. The current work involves image-text syntax, a kind of electronic linguistic, utilizing the dialogue to manipulate a

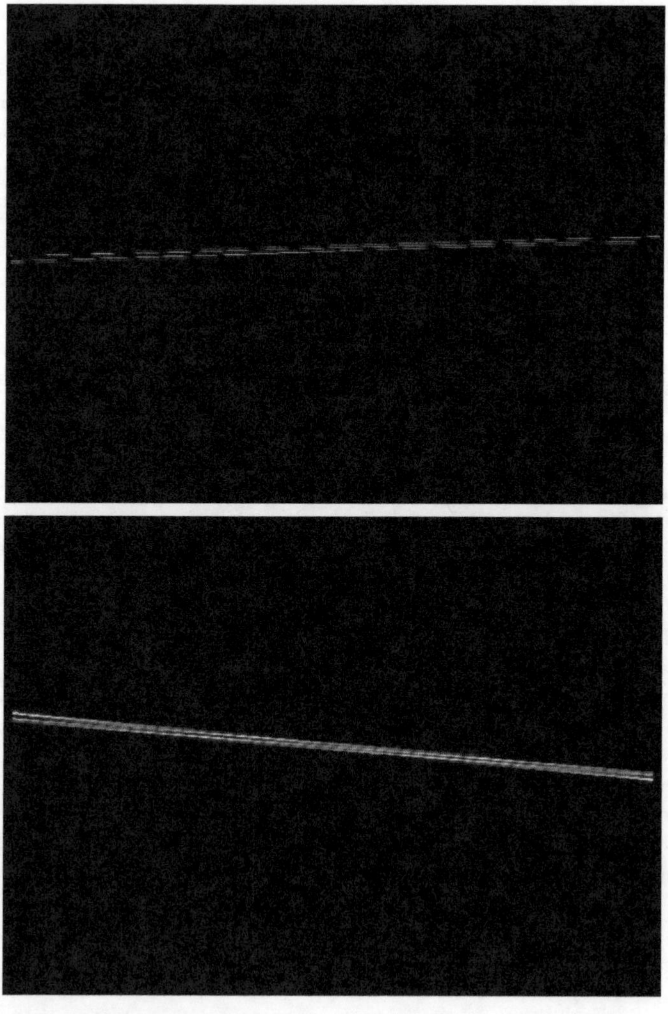

Figure 12.5 Gary Hill, *Processual Video*, 1980, video, black and white, 11:30 min. © VG Bild-Kunst, Bonn 2020.

conceptual space that locates mental points of intersection, where text forms and feeds back into the imaging of those intersects. Processual might be considered a space between the perceptual and conceptual. The processual space serves neither as a composite or balancing of these two modes, it relies on the continual transition or synapse between them. I believe the recent video works presented here are my strongest works to date, and in the matrix of video activity carve out a new space of possibilities (Figure 12.5).

Statement from Gary Hill, *Processual Video*, program notes for the series *Video Viewpoints* (New York: Museum of Modern Art, February 26, 1980), unpag.

Compulsive Categorizations: Gender and Heritage in Video Art (2015)

Malin Hedlin Hayden

In the process of video art becoming an art form, which included the creation of its history, there were several obstacles, not least hesitations toward art history and its adjacent, normative concepts. In the early period of artists employing video as a technique for the production of art, video was understood as a yet uncanonized medium.[1] It was perceived as outside of societal and cultural structures, ideologies, and practices that would tie it to the downside of (art) history: history as limitations and regulations.[2] One of the circulating ideas was that as an entirely new medium, a new artistic material, video was somehow untouched by patriarchal structures. Several writers on the subject note that video art appeared free from a prehistory of male dominance.[3] Sometimes, that it was even without conventions—which seems to be true only to a certain extent, since it drew heavily on both television culture and experimental film.[4] A video art aesthetic, furthermore, appears to have been established rather quickly.[5] Another idea was that video implied a more far-reaching control of both the production process and distribution, or that, as a new artistic medium, it implied a distance to traditional art-historical ideologies and aesthetic values.[6] What these ideas reveal is a neglect, or even amnesia, of acknowledging the impact of *art*. For art, in all its manifestations, was to a rather large extent a male business. If art practice *per se* was manifestly male-dominated and ideologically charged by patriarchal structures and privileges, then how and by what means could a new art form escape this particular structural prerogative? Actually, it did not.

Contrary to these ideas, the historical narrative of video art was immediately invented as precisely dominated by male artists, even during the initial phase of establishing video as fine art and linking it to other events inscribed within art history. The *generality* of most stories is a gendered matter. To this both Martha Rosler and Marita Sturken subscribe, the latter by talking about collectives as "hierarchical and male-dominated," the former by connecting the history of video art to "the myth of Paik."[7]

The 1960s and 1970s became a period of excavating the art-historical archives regarding women artists of the past. Feminist scholars began to intervene and question the status of historical narratives and the discourse of art.[8] Art-historical narratives, generally, proceed from ideas of heritage, of forerunners and descendants. Here two major strategies occur: to position women artists as heirs or followers of important male artists hence opening a spot for inclusion in e.g. general art history surveys; or to create a matrilineal line of historical progressions and changes. The latter implies an exclusive manifestation of women artists by creating a history of "their own." This can be done from an explicitly feminist perspective that investigates various biases. But it can also be performed simply as an unacknowledged manner of creating differences.

Video art came into being as an art form in the mid-1960s—historically juxtaposed with the second wave of the women's movements. Yet it wasn't until the 2000s that feminism/feminist artists started appearing in the historical narratives. There is a strong tendency in historical surveys on video art to use feminism as a frame for understanding and historically, hence narratively, situating video works solely produced by women as a method for thematic, in this context sex-biased, categorizations which operate on many levels of meaning production as well as monetary evaluations.

So the importance of returning to the *written* archive of publications on video art became manifest in the 1990s and 2000s, when "women video artists" emerged on a broad scale, obviously related to the immense breakthrough of video art as a legitimate art form.[9] "Women" artists were increasingly typed by way of gender and often firmly inscribed also as feminist artists. While these two categories have merged rather extensively,[10] the intriguing issue is that they are very different in kind. "Woman" is partly a biological concept, partly a cultural. Whereas a "feminist" indicates an ideological, political position.

This change, however, is in no sense exclusive to video art; feminist perspectives and the broadened field of gender studies within academia have intervened in historical narratives and analysis increasingly. In general art history, "founding mothers" have been acknowledged, answering the question whether there actually had been women artists and, if yes (as of course was the answer), telling about their achievements. Through the production of knowledge about female artists of the past, they were turned into forerunners of today's category of women artists—a genealogy sneaks in precisely through the compartmentalization of "women artists" as not only a specifically gendered categorization, but in the present context as explicitly *feminist* artists. As a suggestion on how to deal with art by women artists without falling completely into the trap of dichotomizing, Marsha Meskimmon writes: "Rather than seeing women's art as a category of objects to be defined, it is more useful to explore the processes by which women's art comes to make meaning. These include the processes by which we, as art historians and critics, make connections and contexts in the present—to paraphrase Rosi Braidotti on the transdisciplinary action of the feminist theorist: 'Creating connections where things were previously disconnected or seemed unrelated, where there seemed to be "nothing to see."'"[11]

When feminism is constructed as a specific topic, it is often recognized in relation to video as the medium which would release those who made use of it from the burdens of patriarchal structures of historical pasts as well as the present.[12] To move beyond traditions as imbued by patriarchal connotations was not only an ambition of video artists, but linked to the women's movement within both the art world(s) and society—as two areas of life and work that were, after all, not justifiably separated from each other. However, this idea of a medium located outside of history, as well as contemporary socio-cultural life, is undercut by the art-historical legacies for video art's prehistory, by the relations established to film, cinema, and television—all dominated by male agents—and through a rather ambiguously developed rationale for gender-biased readings of artists and their work. Thus, to employ video as an artistic means by which to bring forth and communicate issues of inequality and to establish alternative images of femininity and women's situations is one thing, but it is an entirely different argument to claim detachment from history, culture, and society for certain art practices. Still, that feminism emerged as a political and theoretical field to situate one's own practice in should evidently not be underestimated as both a vital source and a position to depart from for a large number of artists.

A recurring situation that is emphasized as newly made possible by the video camera, is turning the camera toward oneself.[13] In relation to feminism, this artistic circumstance is repeatedly, and rightly, argued to have enabled women artists (also) to seriously turn the personal to the political; to audiovisually investigate subjects normally ascribed to the domestic, hence *feminine* spheres, traditionally visualized by men.[14] Video technology was thus regarded as an option particularly apt to alter meaning production of representations of women, womanhood, and femininity, e.g. by artists such as Catherine Elwes, Martha Rosler, Ulrike Rosenbach, Shigeko Kubota, Katherine Maynell, and Marion Urch.[15] Obviously there are other artists who are also often discussed particularly for turning the camera toward themselves (e.g. Bruce Nauman and Vito Acconci), yet not from a distinctly male perspective. Hence, the direction of the camera itself does not automatically imply feminism, as self-portraits are not always foremost about gender, even though everyone is always already gendered.

The point is that the turning of the camera is interpreted from rather different sets of theories, ideologies, and values, depending on the sex of the artist—and it seems a bit too handy to read video works by women as more subjectively charged, hence autobiographically directed, than works by male artists. Likewise, representation as a central issue within feminist art theory is also a concern shared with most art theories, since art is representation aside from its consisting of particular materials. My critique here is about the fact that its (un)thinkable counterpart—the overtly male intervention—is so rarely consciously gendered or interpreted as a domestically situated action.

In the 1960s, it was not easy to take a clear feminist position, there were no established theoretical or ideological frameworks in the art world for meeting the demands—posed critically in terms of both theory and visualizations—of women artists speaking from "a politically charged subject."[16] Appearing then, and working from the position and categorization of being *women* artists, a number of artists were subsequently reinscribed in particular feminist narratives in the 1970s, and this became even more manifest in the 2000s. By this time the question of female authorship had changed radically, from being understood (crudely speaking) as a signature by a gendered agent, to being an issue of how "the female/femininity" is constructed in the first place, and whether womanhood/the feminine can be a site of speech acts at all.[17]

The prevailing idea that video art, by its sheer technology, was unbound from antiquated patriarchal art history, and therefore open in a (more or less) radically new way for women artists to explore, often proved an illusion. The video medium implied a new means of image production and distribution to *everyone* using it. But—with historical hindsight—one was not thereby in a position to avoid the layers of meanings and practical power structures permeating the discourse(s) of art. However, a sense of working outside of power structures and contexts may very well open up new ways of thinking and making art. My conclusion is that the gendered signature, that is, the "woman" video artist, became increasingly elaborated in intimate relation to certain topics of these same artists: that is, read as feminist topics or as explicitly concerning and addressing women. As we have seen, the inclusion of gendered signatures, "women" artists, in the general historical narrative was, by the late 1990s and 2000s, also expected, or occasionally even demanded, to signify feminist practices. Authorship had to be further legitimized as explicitly feminist in order to hold onto its position in these narratives in order to fulfil the demand of the critical position and/or space. The new criterion is thus directed to the practice and the artworks as significant feminist speech acts, and not merely as a representation of a(n already) sexed signature.

In *Compulsive Categorizations*, I argue that with the monographic surveys on video art history since the 1990s there occurs a shift which implies more emphasis on the sex of the artists. In general, female and male artists were treated more equally in the early phase of the establishment of video media works as art, as these were being theorized and historicized by and from various other perspectives. Women video artists were in the minority back then, but they were not addressed as primarily *women* artists, hence not marked as *others* to the same extent—which, however, can be a problem as well. Nevertheless, the fact that a much higher percentage of the represented artists in these written stories are men, who then implicitly come to act from precisely a gendered position, is an issue rarely found in the various texts discussed here. Yet *gender* is never an issue or a conceptual tool employed for deconstructing purposes. This does not mean that gender as a normative and narratological structuring device was or is absent. Particular artists and art works are to a considerable extent addressed from specific gender-informed thinking: namely, women artists and their work as explicitly *feminist* practices. That is, gender is addressed as a *theme* that this particular category of artists almost exclusively is understood to work both from and with.

There are, however, exceptions. In 2000, the Landesmuseum in Vienna organized the show *<Hers>: Video as a Female Terrain.*[18] Despite video art as such often being linked to feminist issues, I was struck by the force of the title's declaration; but perhaps even more so that male artists were also acknowledged as feminist practitioners. My initial hunch was that it was precisely a particularly strong gender-biased premise of so-called feminist (video) art that operated as the grounds for understanding and, consequently, writing critically on video artworks. However, within this field of artistic medium and practices, *<Hers>* still appears as an exception regarding the habit of compartmentalizing artists by way of their sex. In the catalog, curator Stella Rollig states that, despite the leading positions of several women artists in the field of video art, "there is no scholarly or empirical evidence for this."[19] She then asks, rhetorically: "Why are female artists perceived in particular and only (!) in this field in such a strongly disproportionate way?" And no surprise, her conclusion is that this situation is due to the dominance of a patriarchal structure in the field of video, as well as elsewhere in society/culture/the art world. My present investigation of the relations between feminist art theory and video art produced by women artists was triggered by the declaration of this particular exhibition, where video art was exclamatorily stated as a *feminine* practice. "Feminine" is, however, not synonymous with either "female" or "feminist."

Too often the sex of the art producer seems to interfere with interpretations of artworks—if the producer is categorized as a female producer. We have seen that art by women artists is often addressed as feminist art; as if feminist issues were the only political issues relevant in video art made by artists of the female sex. Feminism was quickly assigned as *the* critical perspective by which women artists could make their way into the surveys, hence also the canon of video art. Which artists (names) one chooses to include in a narrative of video art's history may therefore vary to a certain point, but feminist video art cannot—as it seems—be left outside.

From the chapter "Compulsive Categorizations: Gender and Heritage" in Malin Hedlin Hayden, *Video Art Historicized: Traditions and Negotiations* (Aldershot: Ashgate, 2015), 147–54; adapted for the present publication by the author. The book offers a discourse analysis of concepts of art, history, art history, canon, and gender.

Notes

1 Dot Tuer, "Screens of Resistance: Feminism and Video Art," *Canadian Woman Studies/Les cahiers de la femme* 11, no. 1 (1989), 73f.

2 See "Art History or Not: Stories of Reluctance and Crisis" in *Video Art Historicized*, 67–100.

3 Chris Meigh-Andrews, *A History of Video Art: The Development of Form and Function* (Oxford: Berg, 2006), 164 and 236; Michael Rush, *Video Art* (London: Thames & Hudson, 2003), 147.

4 See e.g. Catherine Elwes, *Video Art: A Guided Tour* (London: I.B. Tauris, 2005), 40f.

5 See *Video Art Historicized*, esp. chapters 1 and 2.

6 See e.g. Elwes, *Video Art*, 41; Meigh-Andrews, *A History of Video Art*, 5–9; Yvonne Spielmann, *Video: The Reflexive Medium*, trans. Anja Welle and Stan Jones (London and Cambridge, MA: MIT Press, 2008), passim; Max Liljefors, *Videokonsten: En introduktion* (Lund: Studentlitteratur, 2005), 83f.

7 Martha Rosler, "Video: Shedding the Utopian Moment," in *Illuminating Video: An Essential Guide to Video Art*, ed. Doug Hall and Sally Jo Fifer (New York: Aperture and Bay Area Video Coalition, 1990), 31–50; Marita Sturken, "Paradox in the Evolution of an Art Form: Great Expectations and the Making of a History," in Hall and Fifer, *Illuminating Video*, 101–21.

8 For an early feminist art-historical practice, see e.g., Linda Nochlin and Ann Sutherland, *Women Artists 1550–1950* (Los Angeles: Los Angeles County Museum of Art, 1976). Here the sex-biased strategy as a condition for the exhibition and thus the catalog—also, compulsively—conditions the narrative and the genealogies constructed therein. See also Rozsika Parker and Griselda Pollock, *Old Mistresses: Women, Art and Ideology* (London: Pandora, 1981).

9 See the chapter "Hesitantly Art: Great Expectations of a Medium" in *Video Art Historicized*, 19–65.

10 This with reference to the particular written archives that I focus on in *Video Art Historicized*. None of the essays in Gregory Battcock's *New Artists Video: A Critical Anthology* (New York: E.P. Dutton, 1978) address feminism or women artists separately, nor the early exhibitions, nor any essay in either John G. Hanhardt, ed., *Video Culture: A Critical Investigation* (New York: Visual Studies Workshop Press, 1986), or Ira Schneider and Beryl Korot, eds., *Video Art: An Anthology* (New York and London: The Raindance Foundation, 1976). But in Hall and Fifer,

Illuminating Video, Martha Gever's "The Feminism Factor: Video and Its Relation to Feminism," 226–41, addresses feminism. In Michael Renov and Erika Suderburg, eds., *Resolutions: Contemporary Video Practices*, the essay by David E. James, "Lynn Hershman: The Subject of Autobiography," 124–33, connects feminist ideas to autobiography and the instability of the subject, while Sara Diamond's "Sex Lies with Videotape: Abbreviated Histories of Canadian Video Sex," 189–206, is concerned with censorship and artistic video practices dealing with sex in different contexts.

11 Marsha Meskimmon, "Historiography/Feminisms/Strategies," *n.Paradoxa*, issue 12, March 2000, web.ukonline.co.uk/n.paradoxa/panel3.htm (accessed January 17, 2007).

12 See, for example, JoAnn Hanley, "The First Generation: Women and Video, 1970–1975," in *Feminist Visual Culture*, ed. Fiona Carson and Claire Pajaczkowska (Edinburgh: Edinburgh University Press, 200), 10. See also Martha Gever, "Video Politics: Early Feminist Projects," *Afterimage* 11, no. 1/2 (Summer 1983), 25–7.

13 See e.g. Meigh-Andrews, *A History of Video Art*, 52; Elwes, *Video Art: A Guided Tour*, passim; Rush, *Video Art*, 10; Liljefors, *Videokonsten*, 83ff. For a different perspective on the redirection of the camera, see Rosalind Krauss's essay, "Video: The Aesthetics of Narcissism" (1976), in John Hanhardt, ed., *Video Culture: A Critical Investigation* (New York: Visual Studies Workshop Press [1986], 1990), 179–91.

14 This issue is discussed both by Meigh-Andrews in *A History of Video Art*, and Elwes who, unlike Meigh-Andrews, puts forth her arguments by returning briefly to historical examples of inequalities based on sexual difference in society at large. Elwes, *Video Art: A Guided Tour*, 39–41.

15 Meigh-Andrews, *A History of Video Art*, chapter 13: "The Means of Production: Feminism and 'Otherness'—Race, Gender, Technology and Access," 235–42. The artists are here represented as feminists.

16 Griselda Pollock, "Three Thoughts on Femininity, Creativity and Elapsed Time," *Parkett* 59 (2000), 107–13.

17 On articulations and constructions of gender, feminism, woman, and the feminine, see especially Teresa de Lauretis, *Technologies of Gender: Essays on Theory, Film, and Fiction* (Bloomington: Indiana University Press, 1987); Teresa de Lauretis, "Eccentric Subjects: Feminist Theory and the Historical Consciousness," *Feminist Studies* 16, no. 1 (1990), 115–50; Denise Riley, *Am I That Name? Feminism and the Category of Women in History* (Minneapolis: University of Minnesota Press, 1988); Judith Butler, *Gender Trouble: Feminism and the Subversion of Identity* (London and New York: Routledge, 1999).

18 Stella Rollig, ed., *<Hers>: Video as a Female Terrain* (Vienna: Landesmuseum Wien, 2000).

19 Stella Rollig, "Videos: Who's Got Time for Them?," in Rollig, *<Hers>*, 6.

Video as a Medium of Emancipation (1982)

Ulrike Rosenbach

Why did artists begin to work with video? What fascinated us so much about it?

The first videos that I saw were shown at the *Prospect 71* exhibition at the Kunsthalle Düsseldorf.[1] These were works by American artists and after I had gathered enough technical information, it became clear to me that the possibilities of recording, storing, and reproducing moving images that video provided were exactly what I needed for my work. A system that did not require expensive film processing, which enabled me to produce without having to rely on technical support, and did away with complex developing processes and the time-consuming search for a film editing table—that to me was what video was all about. It was this "amazing thing" that enabled me to stand in front of the camera, monitor myself on the screen, and watch the recorded piece—just like a drawing, a painting; it was the same work process. That was what got me interested in video.

A few months after this encounter I bought my first video equipment through a German mail-order company for 999 Deutsche Marks featuring a very basic video camera.[2] I worked with nothing but black-and-white recordings for years. I started monitoring myself with the camera, my life, my surroundings, my bodily and psychic movements. I was experimenting, working on expanding my camera work in small rooms, and feeling completely at ease. It was fantastic, because it allowed me to gain complete autonomy.

I wasn't interested in television at that time and I wasn't too concerned about the critical aspect of this medium either. Everything was just so new. My social aspirations were linked to the student movement of the late 1960s, which had deeply influenced me.

Walter Benjamin's theory about the reproducibility of the artwork had become fixed in our minds. The notion that not only wealthy citizens or collections and museums were able to own art gave way to an idea of "art for everyone" by means of reproduction and serial production. Graphic editions started popping up like mushrooms. Photo art became popular. The unlimited printability of an image was seen to promote the distribution of art in mass society. The dadaist worker photographer John Heartfield from the 1920s was required reading. But the reproducibility of videotapes wasn't the only important aspect of this new medium. It was all about the catchwords "broadcasting" and "television."

Video technology would finally enable us to broadcast autonomously, in fact, directly, "live." At last, artists were able to distribute their works according to society's perceptual reality. It was our dream to use the TV monitor, the "altar" in the modern family home, in order to reach at least 60 percent of the citizenship with our broadcasts. With our video programs we wanted to achieve a degree of distribution which surpassed that of the museum, gallery, and book market. The awareness of a transformation in the perception process was suddenly everywhere.

The desire to get a handle on these developments grew. Relevant theories came up, such as "visual communication," which started to have an impact on our training, as well as semiotics and linguistics. We took great interest in the writings of Roland Barthes and Umberto Eco. Even museums and galleries were swept along in this need for developing new approaches to art and cultural mediation. The awareness of new reception processes led to a shift in cultural offerings. In an effort to attract younger audiences, cultural programming became more diverse, broader, and focused on multimedia. Galleries changed their names to information centers and studios. Distribution became more important than selling. Art dealers were going through difficult times.

These were the promising beginnings of the new medium video in the cultural field. Meanwhile, we overlooked what video technology had in fact been originally developed for: as a Cold War surveillance technology, for military armament, and, subsequently, spaceflight. We also turned a blind eye to the dominant position held by TV, with its rigidity and social ideology that made our Walter Benjamin theories look naive and ridiculous. In this country television was on its way to becoming an ideological fortress we couldn't conquer with our critical experiments, which were deemed "too poor quality" and not "entertaining enough" to be broadcasted. Even the art market's initial enthusiasm with video ended on a sobering note: "impossible to sell," because nobody owned video players and "boring," because no one could grasp this new aesthetic.

And so, video art remained on the fringe, in the underground, stuck in an alternative position, although it was the most important new medium of the 1970s.

The main focus of our activities shifted toward experimenting and producing. A small group of avant-garde institutions and promoters (like the Oppenheim Studio in Cologne) started presenting video works. The general public hadn't yet grasped the phenomenon of video culture, its magnitude and relevance. Video artists built an insider-outsider community whose interests were only shared by other video makers.

> *Make video, hook yourself up, participate, get together, become emancipated, create independently . . .* (text on the title of a *Video-Magazin* issue from 1978)[3]

But artists weren't the only ones taking on this new medium. Media centers (like Medienladen in Hamburg, Germany) and video libraries (like Video Inn in Vancouver, Canada), which offered a broad rental service, contributed to creating an international communication network. Networks and small cable systems, social district work with video (Kölner Wochenschau), and production groups (Videoheads in Amsterdam, Alternativ Television in Cologne) were emerging in large numbers and building an international community of video makers, who were working inspired by the same motives and dealing with similar limitations.

Almost any video initiative that I got to know at the time was working with small equipment, which not only had the advantage of being cheaper than studio machines, but also easier to handle. There was no need for big production rooms, and it was easy to transport—at least the Portapak 2 systems—which was especially valuable for documentary projects. Production was swift—you brought your Portapak system to the location and were immediately able to broadcast what was happening. Thus, it became the go-to direct system for district work (Channel 13 in New York, Kölner

Wochenschau[4]). With a little know-how and effort, private cabling infrastructure projects came about, connecting shared interests of district or neighborhood residents e.g. in Mill Valley, San Francisco back in 1974, when its music scene (including the Grateful Dead) built a cabling system for the whole village on an old gas station.

The different production groups usually arose from shared interests, but also from shared financial problems. The new video systems were bought and upgraded together. Production groups were then able to work on bigger projects, like recordings with multiple cameras or multimedia events. One of the oldest production groups is Videoheads, whose founder Jack Moore was a very inventive experimentalist—a useful trait for dealing with simple video equipment. All these initiatives had a great impact on video culture, they formed an autonomous group of people who met during video conferences or video events (Erlanger Videotage[5]), debating, exchanging information and video works, etc.

Notably, there was a large proportion of women involved in video art, but also in media production related to social work. I can't really name all the reasons why there were so many women working with video. It was a medium not encumbered with a long cultural tradition based on the quality criteria of men. Video represented a blank canvas, unbiased and free from judgment—a virgin territory for experimentation. The very diverse combinations, which are easier to implement than in film, combinations of sound, documentary, or feature films, the possibilities of including photographs and other moveable pieces in a sort of collage; all this provided a great incentive to finally express the new issues that women were wanting to communicate.

But this initial time of experimentation seems to have come to an end. What we lacked was, in my opinion, a society trusting in autonomous work. We learned that independent media work doesn't comply with the brutal control exerted by the industrial state. We also learned that a critical stance will quickly be interpreted as destructiveness. The trauma that two world wars caused on our parents' generation still seems to have its effect.

The notion of development and growth is now facing problems in the controversy around new social realities that we couldn't possibly foresee at the beginning of the 1970s. Now, at the beginning of a new decade, we realize that we need a shift in perspective in order to be able to address these issues. Video technology, in its infancy in the past decade, has now taken on a new scale. The broad consumption of video enabled by VHS (Video-Home-System) and Betamax systems, which are now accessible to anyone, as well as the all-round use of video surveillance in banks and street traffic, its expansion into telecommunication, and the standardization of digitization that is yet to come—just to name a few—present a wide range of problems and bleak prospects that we have to address if we want to continue working with video within the art field.

The whole sensitive technical apparatus of our age, in its political dimensions, extends to video technology as well. By now, we have learned how vulnerable our system is to the lack of raw materials, and how political ideology manages to make us completely dependent upon the functioning of the industry. Given this development, I almost do not dare to use the word "autonomy" in connection with video as a technology. It's a strange situation in which it's clear that you cannot use the video medium other than in a political context. Video is a modern technology to abuse—a fact already proven by its inception history. In this sense, video is a political medium a priori. It's not biased by its art history, like painting; it is politically biased.

When I'm creating videos I can't help but think of key words like "TV program" or "advertising." Throughout the work process, I'm aware of the compulsive consumerism that can come along with buying a video player and its cheap offer of more entertainment, sports, pornography, or adventure—beyond mere consumerism, these offers represent a new form of using up and lulling away our time. As a video maker I have the opportunity to address or to oppose this by offering an alternative. Working with our society's clichés becomes obvious when working with video—they are part of the medium, so to speak. If I want to work with video, I can't help considering them as subject matter. These are the biases of the medium. To deal with them consciously means to work autonomously; to oppose them critically means to become emancipated. This again means following one's own path. Thoughts and conclusions that do not apply to the video medium only, but to any creative work process in life.

Ulrike Rosenbach, "Video as a Medium of Emancipation," trans. Maike Moncayo (copy-edited for the present publication), in *Video Writings by Artists (1970–1990)*, ed. Eugeni Bonet (Milan: Mousse, 2018), 44–9; original German publication: "Video als Medium der Emanzipation," in *Videokunst in Deutschland, 1963–1982*, ed. Wulf Herzogenrath (Stuttgart: Hatje Cantz, 1982).

Notes

1 [The series of *Prospect* exhibitions at Kunsthalle Düsseldorf, organized between 1968 and 1976, belonged among the pioneering shows through which international artists entered the European art market.]

2 [999.00 DM (Deutsche Marks) equals approximately 1800.00€ today.]

3 [In German: "Video machen, selber verkabeln, mitmachen, sich zusammentun, mündig werden, unabhängig was tun."]

4 [The *Kölner Wochenschau* was a pioneering Cologne-based video magazine that acted as a counter-project to public television, reported on local political and social issues with the medium of video in close proximity to the citizens. Between 1976 and 1981 it was shown at irregular times on monitors in cinemas, on the street, and in bars.]

5 [Erlanger Videotage was a meeting of video groups mostly stemming from German universities. It took place for the first time October 14–16, 1975.]

Video in the Time of a Double, Political and Technological, Transition in the Former Eastern European Context (2009/2020)

Marina Gržinić

The Condition of Possibility of Video(films) in Eastern Europe

[This] essay comprises a conceptual genealogy of contemporary video, film, and performative practices and political spaces in the former Eastern European space, dismantling the singular, established, contemporary Western history of video and media art (conceptual, body and performance) imposed by the Capitalist First World. My endeavor is to develop a theoretical, political, and conceptual framework for a different history of video and experimental film, taking experimental film and video productions from former Eastern Europe as its center. I develop the possibility of establishing a different history of video that comes from the territory once known as Eastern Europe. With this move, I attempt to open up the question of the re-politicization of the field of video in general, questioning the processes of establishing genealogies and histories of practices and interventions termed as video art and experimental video that come from worlds outside the Capitalist First World, implying that Western historiography and Western contemporary theoretical writings are not capable of dealing with such genealogies. The Second World is the former Eastern Europe, which vanished from the processes of interpretation, with only two lines of perception/reworking applied. Prevailing in the West is a particular morality of good taste, bounded by unspoken rules and mores: "do not touch," "no trespassing," etc.—in fact, prejudices and racist views. The point is that the former Eastern European body is seen as less capable, less knowledgeable about using the medium, or too political or too dogmatic. This is a discrimination that I attach to a specific, almost "biological," less capable view of the ex-socialist body and therefore I talk about racism *avant la lettre*, as racism resurfaced fully in the public discourses in the West just in the last decade. It is also significant that the context of video changed radically on the one hand, due to YouTube and its ability to stream online video, and on the other, the World has changed dramatically under the constant surveillance of digital media technology. [. . .]

(Video) film or/and video (film)? What is at stake here could also be formulated as the problem of the status of video as an underground film category and a new—at first electronic, today media—paradigm. The word in brackets gets a precise theoretical positioning; the brackets unmistakably signal the confrontation of the ambiguous positioning of the two practices before and after the 1980s in Eastern Europe. Or, to put it differently and simply contextualize the coinage "video (film)": the video medium was new in the East European mainstream moving image production; therefore in order to contextualize it, a specific reference was needed, and the best was the reference to 8 mm and 16 mm short productions, very present in the ex-socialist European countries. Examples are the powerful Hungarian and Polish experimental films and, of course, the ex-Yugoslavian short films that launched names such as Dušan Makavajev, Želimir Žilnik, Karpo Godina, etc.

Video (films) gained a very special status in the 1980s when the Communist State apparatus (especially the most repressive ones) began to exercise a looser control over artistic and cultural productions. This owed in part to the disintegration processes that started to spurt out in the politically and economically chaotic Eastern European reality of the 1980s. In spite of the differing Communist structures in Hungary, Poland, and especially ex-Yugoslavia, these countries succeeded to develop avant-garde film and art productions throughout the 1970s and connected them to the video medium in the 1980s. Hungary linked its strong avant-garde film tradition to video, or at least developed a conceptual approach to the medium through experimental film research. Poland joined the strong conceptual tradition in the visual arts with body art actions and happenings, performance, and film productions. Ex-Yugoslavia, with its so-called Third Way into Socialism (i.e., "non-aligned self-management Socialism"), had already become a politically specific case (hi)story.

The so-called "first-line" totalitarian Socialist Eastern European countries (i.e., the Soviet Union, Romania, Bulgaria, East Germany, etc.) suffered a delay of a whole decade in developing art connected to the electronic media, including use of the video medium as a social tool, in comparison with Poland, Hungary, and especially ex-Yugoslavia. This delay was due to the repressive nature of the Communist State in these countries, which executed an almost bloodthirsty control of art and cultural productions, not only over the written word but over all instant visual reproductive media and technologies (e.g., copy machines, VHS video technology, and even Polaroid). The severe censorship of literature was quickly extended to cover visual reproductive technology. In this context, the underground film scene, which arose in St. Petersburg (Leningrad) in the mid-1980s, deserves special mention. The city had an active underground scene known as the Necrorealist movement, which produced deconstructivist versions of the official Communist films on Super 8mm and 16mm film. Subsequently, in the late 1980s and '90s, following the collapse of Communism, it proved impossible to stop the transfer of Necrorealist films onto video, facilitating their distribution and presentation at Western European art video, experimental, and media festivals.

On the other hand, the 1980s were an era of the shaping of a new scopic regime of contemporary reality, giving priority to works proceeding from, and intended for, the eye. This oculo-centrism can be applied to political and social events, as well as to cultural and artistic ones. [. . .]

It is possible to detect a similar, if reversed, logic in speaking about the production of video (films) in Eastern Europe. Video, even in its most amateur form, via a nonprofessional home VHS system, allows instantaneous replay of the recorded image. The immediate internal technological production (and postproduction) principle proved crucial for the growth of the medium in Eastern Europe. Through the constant reproducibility of the totalitarian "original" image of power, cracks emerged in this original to the point that the replayed "copy" involved decoding, which was not merely a simple, innocent, internal technological trick of the medium but, moreover, a political stance. The video medium's potential for continuous replay thus brought radical changes to the watchful eye of the Communist totalitarian system of power. These processes of replaying the video image may be perceived as a subversive mediatization of the social and political sphere in Eastern Europe. Therefore, to comprehend the birth of the video medium in Eastern Europe, we must take into consideration this switch from the technologically produced replay to the political one, and recognize that both forms of replay were carried out in Eastern Europe, within the social, political, and cultural underground. Non-professional video equipment (VHS), with its simple handling and speedy production and reproduction, made video one of the most popular and radical forms of media for the 1980s generation. Access to video became a status symbol in itself. The video medium connected itself with marginalized communities of punks, rockers, activists, failed intellectuals, and members of the underground who perceived the video medium as an essential technological tool, which allowed for personal expression and social engagement.

Documentary video (film) projects (realized by amateurs with VHS equipment, and by independent film and video groups with professional video equipment) also enable us to make a comparison with the national television's interpretations of those same events and to relocate the responsibility of national mass media for particular versions of history. Within this context, video (films) offer "authentic" historical, emotional, artistic, and political views on events, conditions, bodies, practices, languages, and topics, narrated through the perspective of their authors. Our knowledge is based not only on what we see but also on what we can render visible. [. . .]

Establishing a new style of visual "writing" with video (films) was a result of the conscious visual reconfiguration of an "original" Socialist alternative cultural structure. This produced innumerable "explosive" contrasts and a series of "technical imperfections" (as I have termed them), which comprehend the outer and inner, sexual and mental order and disorder, conceptual and political, original and recycled space and time. Furthermore, from such a point of view, we can detect and generalize two strategies of visualization in the medium, which reflect two territories: (1) the body in connection with sexuality, and the social and historical corpus of the national official film and (national) television medium; and (2) history in connection with politics. These strategies can also be viewed as two fundamental approaches to video (film) production in Eastern Europe.

(1) The 1980s witnessed the over-sexualization of video (film). This was not only a process of art-political reflexivity of the much-repressed sexuality under Socialism and Communism,[1] but the process of distancing and disassociating the experimental video (film) medium from it sisters: national feature film and television. This process was carried out with the externalization of sexuality, which had been adopted from the underground film tradition.

The externalization of sexuality took the form of overtly staged pornography and the gender confusion ("gender-bending") of gay, lesbian, bisexual, and transgender sexual attitudes. It was a process that can be explained: the sexual and civil rights (!) stereotypes and prototypes were not only consumed in and by the underground but immediately performed. In front of a VHS camera, in private rooms and bedrooms, a status of political positioning of the sexual and social *par excellence* was acquired. In these works, the masquerade of re-appropriation ensured not only the simple question of identity formation for the artists or the underground community, but also the process of negotiation to produce continually ambiguous and unbalanced situations and characters. The acquired hybrid and nonheterosexual positioning of sexuality, in the context of the remarkably impermeable gender boundaries of Communist Eastern Europe, was a way of overtly politicizing the sexual in Socialism and Communism, and fighting for civil rights. These processes of over-sexualization, which can now be perceived as contemporary gender politics, followed the fall of the Berlin Wall, still performed in the former East European countries, spreading from the video (film) medium to performance art, photography, etc. The post-post-Socialist bodies without make-up seem to function as subversive mirror images of the female body in the industrialized, postmodernist West, camouflaged by mass media and constantly redesigned.

We also find video (film) projects that were created by copying, in most cases the political broadcasts of the national television network. These copied sequences were then reedited and reinterpreted, taking into consideration the internal replay logic of the video medium. Selected TV sequences on political events were combined with music and re-edited in vertiginous, rhythmic, repetitive works. This resulted in an almost obscene uncovering of the internal mechanism of the everyday Communist political speeches and doctrine, which itself was based on the ritual of constant repetition. The repetition that is today the primary performative mechanism in the Occident was "invented" in the East; it was a powerful strategy where all was a duplicate or a surrogate of something perceived as a so-called "original" in the West. The copy (the repetition) was central to many artworks—for example, in the 1980s the Slovenian group Laibach excavated the historical German name for the city of Ljubljana used by Nazi Germany during the Second World War, and made from it a political artistic program. Thoroughly replayed and re-edited political speeches began to reveal their internal repetitive logic; the shorter and shorter units of the re-cut political speech started to function as a pornographic act, which put the viewer in a position similar to that of a peep show. The discourse of the orderly politician was transformed through technology into an inarticulate striptease. Thus, a specific syncretism was produced, through which it was possible to detect similarities between different, until then incompatible, levels and expressions. This started to displace differences, not only between these opposite levels and expressions but also within them.

From this, we can formulate a thesis that, in some cases, experimental (video) films functioned as "B-movies" under (post-)Socialism; they function as *kitsch*, grotesque, absurd video (films), impregnated with sex, politics, and rock 'n' roll, in parallel to the B-movies and underground cinema of the West.

(2) The functioning of Socialist societies involved a painful recourse to psychotic discourse, in an attempt to neutralize the side effects of pertinent interpretations and productions through hiding, masking, and renaming history.

Through (video) films, processes of re-appropriation and recycling of different histories and cultures—a condition of the re-politicization of history—have been constructed. The result of such procedures is the development of imagery that refers neither to the past nor the present, but to a time somewhere between certainty and potentiality. The experimental video (film) image presents a persistent searching for the condensed point, simultaneously in the past and the present. It redefines their place inside a contemporary construction of power relations, which also feeds back to the status of the video itself.

From this point, we can derive some significant generalizations about the status of the video in Eastern Europe, regarding the "technological switch of history." In the binary relation that is put forward both for the specificity of the video medium and the sociopolitical context surrounding it, in the case of the Eastern European space it was possible to detect the use of media specificity for the recording of socio-political specificity, and not of one of these poles against the other. The outcome was not—as in the 1980s in the West—works structuring absence (in terms of being preoccupied solely with formal questions of the medium), but a video medium in the East sutured by the social and the political—a crucial difference. The low-tech medium (often in the form of a home technology such as VHS) began to function as a powerful postmodern technology par excellence. It meant the structuring of a wholly political space in the East of Europe, rather than an abstract media space. The thesis may be drawn that with the video medium's internal technological mode of functioning—replay, in particular—video gained a new political context in the East. In the West, replay took on a mass presence in bedrooms and kitchens, where it was used for the repetitive performance of blockbuster films, porn films, and/or personal documentation. With video replay in the East, on the other hand, we are witness to a process of the detailed deconstruction and reconstruction of history. In the so-called post-Socialist countries, video has, at the end of the century, developed into a specific vanishing mediator between history and the spectator in front of the television screen. At the end of the 1990s we have fully embraced the Internet: it took over, video art started to be heavily questioned, and the post-media theories and mobile technologies along with fake news and post-facticity opened a set of different questions. The Internet has assumed the role of the video third eye, or even better reinforced some of its past positions, as video enabled us to read history, to see through the surface of the film image, and, possibly, to perceive the future.

From Marina Gržinić, "Video in the Time of a Double, Political and Technological, Transition in the Former Eastern European Context," in *Transitland: Video Art from Central and Eastern Europe 1989–2009*, ed. Edit András (Budapest: Ludwig Museum of Contemporary Art, 2009), 17–33. This second part of the original essay was abridged by the editors and updated by the author for the present publication.

Note

1 Throughout Eastern Europe, severe measures were introduced against homosexuals, whereby most were punished by law and imprisoned as criminals, or detained in psychiatric institutions. There was a legal penalty for being a homosexual, although in

Slovenia and Croatia, e.g., to note the difference from other Eastern European states, there was no legal ban on homosexuality—yet they were blamed and marginalized in the mass media and public. All the other counter sexual orientations (defined as such in relation and subjugated to the prevalent heterosexual and homophobic reality)—trans*, cross-dressers, transvestites—were invisible in public life, except in a medical context.

[Video Direction Theory] (1989)

Boris Yukhananov (Edited and Annotated by Andreas Schmiedecker)

Hello. My topic today is fairly complex. I suspect this is the first time that a director in the Soviet Union has ever stepped forward to speak publicly about video direction. Let's begin by stating that this is a nonexistent concept. First, the very topic of my talk reveals a certain boundary that must be drawn between video films and films as such. I will try to devote the first (introductory) part of my message to this.

Unlike film, video is a nondiscrete art form. Video thinks in a single continuous line. Different authors, including those who are strictly semiotically minded, have considered the frame, the mid-range shot, or, at least, some kind of picture, to be the measuring unit for film. Unlike cinema, video does not think in pictures. I will now try to speak from the experience that I have practically and (following practice) theoretically acquired over the course of a three-year period of actual interaction with primitive video film, that is, with a VHS or Super 8 camera, mainly of Japanese or European production. Huge cassettes make it possible to interact continuously with the world for three or even four hours, while the very principle of audiovisual equality, located in the space of a video film, completely changes everything on which the author bases his work.

The fact of the matter is, when I speak about directing in video, I must first speak of a video author, because—and this is an essential feature of video production and video creation—the video director basically combines, or seeks to combine, the cameraman and director into a guiding force that determines the layout and development of the process of creating a video. One might also mention that this synthetic act of combining many into one (something you could even define as totalitarian), this act that is inherent in the video process of creating a video film, is also manifested in the desire of the camera to become one with the video author.

I distinguish three levels in this combining of many into one. Let's give the object I will talk about now the name of "video centaur," and let's highlight three variants of this object: a video eye, a video body, and a video hand. In general, they comprise completely different principles of interaction with the world and the camera. When someone holds the camera up to their eye and begins working, never taking their eye from the camera's viewfinder, at that moment they so become one, essentially becoming a living organism, that this camera hears and sees just like a person. The rather cocky phrase, "You have your head in your hands,"[1] is, in fact, true in that moment when the camera is held to my head. This is unlike the kino-eye of Dziga Vertov, which is actually the eye of traditional film and in no way refers to an individual. We speak in our case of the eye of a centaur who possesses a single head plus an attachment in the form of a camera. As such, the video eye is the first principle of our interaction with the world.

A video hand implies a completely different relationship. With my video actors, I play a humorous, perhaps even silly game that is actually essential to my practice of "hatching" a work, if I may put it that way. I call it video karate. I imagine that my hand holds a video camera. (Basically, this is what I have done since the early '70s,[2] for a camera appeared in my hands as a private possession only a few weeks ago.[3] A few years earlier I was able to hold a camera in my hands and periodically feel what it was like to grip it. But in fact the reality of our domestic Russian video output is a kind of video karate, that is, a hand liberated from the video camera . . . [*laughter*]. As such, I could do nothing but imagine holding a camera in my hand). This kind of creative activity is, primarily, deeply and essentially dynamic: I enter into a strange dynamic interaction with the world—in this case, with an audience—and I begin reading it, as if biologically becoming a video camera. This is an extremely useful prime element of my training. In a practical sense it determines all the foundations of the relationship we have discussed, all the diverse, often specific relationships that the video author, video actor, and world enter into. This world is omnipresent, sometimes cutting through, or separating the video actor from, the video author.

The video hand, the camera hand, is completely different from the video eye or the camera eye. The video hand implies an enhanced dynamic reading of the world, a higher energetic trust in the world. Moreover, it is during the shooting, the work of video karate, that the greatest amount of so-called dirt[4] appears. But this is merely so-called dirt, for this notion refers to another manner of thinking and, accordingly, gives rise to completely different evaluative criteria. I could say that video allows the author to become one with the work itself, a process we sometimes observe in Picasso's later drawings done prior to the invention of video film, but which predicted its emergence in the form of mythological characters.

I would now like to speak about the next element, also significant, the third stage of the author's relationship with the camera and, as it were, the third version of that video centaur with which I began my rather shambolic talk. This is that the camera belongs to the body. I participate with my whole body, it's as if I let this machine feed off of me. The camera may lie on my knee engaging in completely static relations with the world. I can put this camera to my forehead on one side and to a window on the other, hoping my head will not shake and that the window will not break; I can attach the camera to my shoulder, my backside, and so on. One way or another, it must belong to the entire body. This is very reminiscent of Grotowski's relationship with the space of the stage, and the space of the place where he holds his training. Precisely at this moment all the elements of human psychophysics converge at a point in the body and, as it were, seek to break through all together, as if through the small door of a large room. This greatly enhances the dynamic energy of video film. The law is very simple: the tape reads and stores even the slightest details of our energetic state. You must trust the video camera, which essentially means you trust yourself, and, by extension, the viewer who will encounter your work on a TV screen, a projection screen, or some other place . . . for the time being there is no other. If you trust all that, then you will agree that the so-called dirt—whether that be a blurry image, noise stored on the tape, or the camera's long wandering that shakes our eyes, in other words, let's call it a drunken camera, or a drunken picture—all this dirt is quite important, for, as I see it (although I don't insist upon it), this is where the material ripens and fills with energy. The material's struggle with the author will later manifest itself as a sufficiently distinct composition—in the form of sufficiently distinct acting, or a brief manifestation of acting, or some concentrated event, or some emphasis that the actor adopts. But in fact the actor is no longer an actor, for an actor never exists independently as an image on tape, just as a video author does not exist independently on tape: they are always a derivative of their interaction. This is a crucial topic that relates directly to an aspect of video directing such as the work of the video author with the video actor. [. . .]

The fact of the matter is that, in principle, video film cannot tell stories. Stories, plots, and narratives are not accessible to it. Only when video film is similar to traditional film and simply changes its technical means, and only when video film does not think of itself as a separate, special, completely different kind of art, does the precise moment arise when, employing the tools of traditional film (i.e., discrete thinking, the work of the cameraman, etc.), video film becomes capable of narrating one or another story. But as soon as we demand from this type of art that which belongs to it, once we ask the dolphin to swim, so to speak, and not to cough or bark on shore, at that moment the dolphin heads into open waters and refuses to send back to us a real, detailed, plot-based and simultaneously discrete world. It wants to swim and inform us how the water runs across its eyes, how the waves slide over its back, and to give us a feel for speed, continuous speed and going deeper—forgive me for this detailed description. [. . .]

And so, the actor and the director. The video actor and the video director outline the proposed space of what is to be playacted. They outline this proposed space of playacting not only as regards behavior, which is something that theater is most often concerned with, but also as regards text, with which theater is not as concerned because most of the time (as is natural for theater) it has access to the text when entering rehearsals. In our case, no text can be presented to the video actor. The video actor's text must be birthed. For only an individual who is birthing text is as sufficiently convincing, natural, and self-adequate as the video camera . . . which, shall we say, anticipates the actor. This is one of the most critical notions, related not only to video film, but also generally in regards to the principles of modern thought and youth culture,[5] and the adequacy and desire of youth culture to correspond in full measure to the times . . . Now, this actor, in the moment that he gives rise to a word, essentially takes on the role of the author. This need for a contemporary feeling begins to be fulfilled in every second of the video playacting of which I speak. As well as every second of the video director's work that defines the performance.

These rules of which I speak are determined by something else that I will call post-structuring. I'll tell you briefly what that is. In principle, post-structuring is a fairly precise phenomenon that is particularly characteristic of video film. This is the method of layering a work, rather like piling up and generating a relatively free matrix (it's not purely spontaneous, but defined in concentrated fragments, as often happens in jazz), from which the structure is further determined. The matrix is the total sum of material that the camera reads during the video author's work. And this matrix, generated by the free, playful spirit of the actor and, as it were, harboring not only the result, but also the process of its creation, this matrix, as it were, goes on a journey. We can call this journey video editing. It is quite variable. Essentially, later on we have the opportunity to make an incredibly wide variety of films from this matrix. We can turn utterly tragic material into a video clip. We can change its sign and right there, inside the video clip, find the contours of some plot. We can compare, etc. But at the same time, the matrix itself will always remain. Variations may be added, and yet we will continue to have the same opportunity to create still another variation, and another, to manage the space and time, the chronotope, to manage everything that, in principle, is decided once and for all by an artist working in another art form. At the same time, in contrast to traditional film, where once we cut the film strip we never again take possession of the whole mass of material we have collected, here we never cut anything, we cut the air, as it were, while new options constantly present themselves, even as we still have access to the old ones.[6] Thus, life seems to be in synch with its variations . . . Let's recall Pasternak, and Andrei Levkin's[7] definition of the whole "fan," that the fan is born of segments and moves in a circle that then produces a ball. In this we recognize the enormous opportunities that subjective video film possesses in reflecting and perceiving the world. In principle, directing must necessarily tune in to this strange, lofty manner of interacting with Being, for this camera was attuned to such lofty interaction from the very beginning.

As such, post-structuring lies at the basis of the very data of the video film. When I create most of my work in film precisely in this way, I do nothing new or special. I simply comply with the natural law that is inherent in this art form.

From Boris Yukhananov, "Teoriya videorezhissury," in the Russian Samzidat publication *Mitin Zhurnal*, no. 25 (1989), reprinted in *Teatral'naja zhizn*, no. 12 (Moscow, 1989); translated for the present publication by John Freedman.

Editor's note: Although Boris Yukhananov is primarily known as an avant-garde theater maker and, since 2013, as the artistic director of Moscow's "Stanislavsky Electrotheatre," his contribution to the theory and practice of video art, unique in its form and content, is worthy of particular consideration.

In Yukhananov's terminology, developed in a series of speeches, articles, and manifests from the second half of the 1980s, video, as a "non-discrete art form," is "a single continuous line," an uninterrupted body of work, rather than the assembly of separate machines (or "departments") of traditional cinema. In contrast to both a constructivist and a post-humanist paradigm, Yukhananov merges technology with the operating video body that can simultaneously create a situation, participate in it, and record it. The interplay of all contributing factors creates a "matrix" (матрица) that will be developed on, expanded, commented, and subverted in the process of both continued taping and later editing.

In that sense, video with its social, political, and communal implications, its quickness and unfinishedness, allows the understanding of an artist's oeuvre that will always favor the process over the result. Oscillating between high-profile theater, theory, and avant-garde art, Yukhananov's video work of the late Soviet era arguably continues a legacy of self-publication or *samizdat* (самиздат)—unofficial copies of mostly literature but also music (on bootleg cassettes) circulating below the radar of official art production and distribution. Born of necessity, the anti-professionalism and a DIY-aesthetic in his video art acts as an identifying, communal vector and a playful subversion of real-life constrictions, such as the impossibility of autonomous work in technically and logistically demanding fields like cinema. Due to the light and easy-to-use equipment of VHS and video-8, the bodily presence of the director and operator enables the development of Yukhananov's intuitive approach to video art, heavily based on the interplay of the creative individual with actors and their environment in the performative situation.

It is precisely this context the present text appeared: while attending a conference on youth culture in Leningrad in October 1988, among some of the main protagonists of avant-garde culture, whom Yukhananov would continue to film and engage with in improvisation games.[8] Along with other texts and speeches from the conference, Yukhananov's contribution was published January 1989 as "Теория видеорежиссуры" (Theory of Video Directing) in issue 25 of the *Mitin Zhurnal* (Митин Журнал), itself an avant-garde literary art magazine that had existed since 1984, publishing texts on contemporary art and theory as well as translations in a small, self-published circulation.

Special thanks to Irina Tokareva.

Notes

1 A reference to Yukhananov's text "У тебя в руках твоя голова" (You have your head in your hands). This "manifesto" from 1986 takes the form of a mock dialogue between a photographer and a director and pre-formulates many ideas of the present text. Yukhananov, "У тебя в руках твоя голова. Диалог о Видео," unpag., no place, 1986, http://borisyukhananov.ru/archive/item.htm?id=1012.

2 In "You have your head in your hands," Yukhananov explicitly emphasizes the lineage of his video technique from his practice of recording the world in his notebook, saying that he was "trying to work with video recording even before I had ever known the word. I would take a piece of paper and try to record everything, recording my impressions and my being in this world, my fantasies in relation to this world." Ibid.

3 Since equipment was difficult to get hold of, the question of where to actually get the cameras from was of some importance in this context. According to Yukahananov's personal recollection, he received his first VHS camera in 1986 as a gift from the photographer Sergei Borisov, one of the most important figures documenting the alternative art scene of Soviet Russia in the 1970s and '80s. After working with VHS for some time, Yukhananov received a Video 8-camera from Hungarian filmmaker Verushka Bódy, whom he met in Moscow, as a token of respect, as he claims. Yukhananov is probably referring to this incident here.

4 "Dirt" (грязь) can be understood as both residue from the filmic process as well as a conscious anti-professionalism to distinguish oneself from the clean establishment. In Yukhananov's own practice this comes to play again as his main video work, the "video novel" *The Mad Prince* (Сумасшедший прин), would only be edited decades later when the material from the 1980s had partially withered away, making noise and "dirt" a factor of the composition.

5 "Youth Culture" (молодая культура) is not only the name of the conference where this text was delivered as a speech, but also an umbrella term and cultural space where more non-conformist ideas were partly allowed to exist in official Soviet culture. Yukhananov both embraces and appropriates the term as he is in fact speaking

with and for a generation of mostly young artists, as well as mocking its patriarchal connotations.

6 Yukhananov will later develop this into an idea of "fatal editing" (Фатальный монтаж). This refers both to the (irreversible) choices made while taping the material as well as the limitations and possibilities of video editing, specifically, the insert cut, that allows the author to "to shoot first some material, then to make inserts into the territory of this material, i.e. to attach the camera to another object at another time. But with the same tape already used. At this second, the insertion replaces the previous one. And this replacement is already fatal, that is, forever." Yukhananov, "Фатальный монтаж," unpag., no place, 1989, http://borisyukhananov.ru/archive/item.htm?id=1011.

7 Andrei Viktorovich Levkin, Russian-Latvian author who participated in the same conference with a text on "Abstract Prose," where he explains the integral mechanism of abstract texts: "Any given word is both a point and a 'fan' of its possible meanings and attributes: intonations, contexts, citations." Yukhananov applies this metaphor to his own video practices.

8 The conference took place on October 17–22, 1988, in the Zubovsky Institute in Leningrad, organized by a group of young academics from the Research Institute for Art Studies (Научно-исследовательскийинститут искусствозанания), among them the artists Sergei Dobrotvorsky, Olga Khrustalyova, and Irina Kuzmina. The proceedings of the conference are partly documented in Yukhananov's film *The Mad Prince: Japanese* (Сумасшедший принц: Японец), 1988–2006.

Index